SO-AHK-051

Dr. Andrea Paschkes
110 East 87 Street
New York, New York 10028

ENCYCLOPEDIA
OF CLINICAL
ASSESSMENT

Volume 2

Robert Henley Woody

General Editor

ENCYCLOPEDIA
OF CLINICAL
ASSESSMENT

Volume 2

Jossey-Bass Publishers

San Francisco • Washington • London • 1980

ENCYCLOPEDIA OF CLINICAL ASSESSMENT
Volume 2
     by Robert Henley Woody, Editor

616.89

E 56

Copyright © 1980 by: Jossey-Bass Inc., Publishers
                             433 California Street
                             San Francisco, California 94104
                             &
                             Jossey-Bass Limited
                             28 Banner Street
                             London EC1Y 8QE

Copyright under International, Pan American, and
Universal Copyright Conventions. All rights
reserved. No part of this book may be reproduced
in any form—except for brief quotation (not to
exceed 1,000 words) in a review or professional
work—without permission in writing from the publishers.

Library of Congress Cataloguing in Publication Data

Main entry under title:

Encyclopedia of clinical assessment.

    Includes bibliographies and indexes.
    1. Personality assessment. 2. Personality.
3. Mental illness—Diagnosis. I. Woody, Robert Henley.
BF698.4.E5   157'.7   80-10463
ISBN 0-87589-446-1 (set)
ISBN 0-87589-460-7 (v. 1)
ISBN 0-87589-461-5 (v. 2)

Manufactured in the United States of America

JACKET DESIGN BY WILLI BAUM

FIRST EDITION

Code 8007

The Jossey-Bass
Social and Behavioral Science Series

Contents

Volume 1

Volume 2

ENCYCLOPEDIA
OF CLINICAL
ASSESSMENT

Volume 2

45

Carolyn Saarni
Victoria Azara

Anxiety (Developmental)

The emotion of anxiety is central to many theories of personality as well as to many assessment techniques derived from or based on these various theories. Several features about the experiential effect of anxiety cut across these differing viewpoints. These have been summarized by Maher (1966) as including (1) a conscious feeling of apprehension or fear without the existence of concrete causes in the environment for such feelings of threat; (2) physiological reactions indicative of bodily distress (for example, respiratory complaints, cardiovascular symptoms, gastrointestinal reactions, sleeplessness, fatigue, and muscle tension); and (3) varying degrees of disorganization in higher-level cognitive processes, which may impair the effectiveness of the individual's coping behavior. These three common features of anxiety characterize the *affect* of anxiety, regardless of age. Obviously, the relative intensity or extent of involvement of these three affective components is variable. What does change in the individual as a function of development are

(1) the coping responses to anxiety as well as to perceived threat, (2) the evaluation of events as threatening, (3) the nature of stressful events that may be called developmental tasks (or milestones), and (4) changes in biological vulnerability to stress and conflict.

Although there are many ways to view the role of anxiety in development, it appears that all development involves change, and for the individual to change (whether in infancy or old age) means to give up some known security for an unknown, uncertain future. This process may be likened to the equilibrium dynamic of Piaget's theory of development (Piaget and Inhelder, 1969) or the dialectical model of development recently advanced by Riegel (1976). The point to be made is that this "unknown-ness" of growth and change precipitates conflict. Anxiety is aroused in this conflict: What unknown threats face us in this uncertain future, and will we be able to cope with or control these unknown threats?

A variety of life-span theorists (among them, Bühler, 1951, 1962; Erikson, 1950; Gould, 1972; Havighurst, 1972) have conceptualized human development as a sequence of stages, loosely tied to chronological age. Havighurst is most closely associated with the theme of developmental tasks, and he believes that his perspective falls in the organismic model of development (which postulates that human beings change or develop as a result of their own constructions, initiations, and biological variables rather than as a function of external circumstances). Essentially, developmental tasks are based on biological development and social expectations, both of which change over the course of the life span. Such developmental tasks may also be viewed as sources of conflict and stress for the individual, resulting in anxiety. As these developmental tasks are achieved (or resolved), conflict and stress subside—as does anxiety. Modifying this ebb-and-flow effect of anxiety over the life span are individual differences in such domains as sensitivity to stress (Lowenthal and Chiriboga, 1973), generalized disposition to threat (for example, because of temperament or trait anxiety), and shifts in motivation (Kuhlen, 1968).

The ebb and flow of developmental anxiety is apparent in the progressive resolution of developmental tasks across the life span. As the individual matures biologically, society's expectations of desirable, appropriate behavior change for that individual. Thus, the individual is faced with the task of acquiring new skills, capacities, and resources and giving up the old ones as he moves from infancy into childhood, from childhood into adolescence, from there into young adulthood, and so forth toward death. In short, the individual is faced with a series of adaptations across the life span as he ages.

Coping patterns within a developmental framework are especially well conceptualized by Murphy and Moriarty (1976) in their longitudinal research on the development of resilience and coping with stress in childhood. They found supportive evidence for the idea that stress may be generated by the environment or from within the individual. Kuhlen's (1968) review of motivational changes during the adult years also sheds light on how individuals develop coping patterns in response to changes in needs, frustrations, arousal cues, environmental stimulations, and expectations. His position is that growth-expansion motives appear to dominate the first half of the adult years, while anxiety and threat are more primary as sources of motivation in the later years. Finally, Neugarten and her colleagues (1964, 1966) have offered a somewhat eclectic view of personality-related coping patterns, which are suggestive of ways in which anxiety and stress are dealt with in old age in American culture.

Anxiety is assessed by means of several types of measures. The most common are self-report questionnaires (such as the Manifest Anxiety Scale developed by Taylor, 1953), physiological measures (indices of autonomic arousal), projective tests (for instance, human figure drawings, the Rorschach, and the Thematic Apperception Test), and actual avoidance behavior. Many researchers and theorists (for example, Breger, 1974; Erikson, 1950; Laing, 1960; Veroff, Feld, and Gurin, 1962) do not actually measure anxiety directly. Rather, they *infer* that anxiety is present when an individual reports many conflicts, stresses, insecurity, or general unhappiness. Still another view is that held by Izard (1977), who contends that the assessment of anxiety is really the assessment of several discrete emotions functioning more or less simultaneously in the individual. Thus, in his view, anxiety is a global term of convenience, and precise affective evaluation should include examination of patterns of discrete emotions that are concurrent in the individual's experience.

For the most part, anxiety assessment techniques presume to measure trait anxiety; that is, the overall level of anxiety is conceptualized as a relatively stable and enduring quality of the individual's personality. State anxiety is temporary or situationally related and varies considerably across time and settings. For the developmental psychologist, the intriguing questions are these: (1) Does *trait* anxiety change over the life span in a systematic fashion or entirely idiosyncratically? (2) Does the frequency and duration of *state* anxiety change systematically over the life span, or are any changes in the patterning of state anxiety random or idiosyncratic to the individual? Plausible answers to these questions will be explored in this chapter.

Background and Current Status

Within psychology the term *developmental anxiety* has not generally been used to designate a particular type of anxious reaction. More frequently researchers and clinicians have inferred that anxiety is present during stressful periods of development (such as adolescence), or they have investigated specific anxiety responses that are characteristic of particular behavioral developments (such as separation anxiety and stranger anxiety in infancy).

The concept of anxiety plays a major role in personality theories (see Hall and Lindzey, 1970; Mischel, 1976). Typically, anxiety is conceptualized within these different theories according to what constitutes serious threat, conflict, or stress for the individual. For example, Freudian theory predicates the experience of anxiety on the internal "danger" of unacceptable impulses breaking through into consciousness. Reinforcement theory emphasizes the association of aversive stimuli with a particular response, whereby eventually the aversive stimulus may become the experience of anxiety itself, and the individual learns to avoid it. Phenomenological-existential theories generally view anxiety as a response generated by the individual's perception of self (or intactness of personality) being threatened. Still other eclectic views postulate anxiety as excessive or unbalanced overarousal (Gellhorn, 1965, 1970; Malmo, 1957) or as a state of helplessness in a no-option distressful situation (Mandler and Watson, 1966; Seligman, 1974).

Critical Discussion

General Areas of Concern

The dynamic for developmental change emerges when asynchrony occurs between at least two "planes of progression" through the life cycle. Riegel (1976) has outlined four such "planes of progression": psychological, sociocultural, biological, and physical-environmental. Typically, individuals experience conflict between or among the first three domains of experience. Such conflict or contradiction may be thought of as having a dialectical structure, which by definition yields to a transformation of thesis and antithesis into synthesis. This last term represents developmental progression. Since anxiety assessment techniques commonly are designed to measure trait anxiety (stable, nonchanging characteristic of the individual), they do not usually address the possibility that the average child-adolescent-adult may face normative life crises which can generate developmental change (Riegel, 1975) but in which anxiety is intensified as a function of the uncertainty and apparent contradiction of new forms of coping. This intensified *state* of anxiety accompanying developmental change might last a considerable period of time. If it lasts more than some specified period of time (for instance, a month or a year), does it then become classified as *trait* anxiety? Developmental psychologists and clinicians specializing in measurement have as yet to coordinate their perspectives on this question. For purposes of clinical evaluation, the psychologist should bear in mind that normal life crises do occur; that such life crises may constitute stressful developmental tasks, resulting in growth as well as anxiety; and that this knowledge provides a *framework* in which the clinician interprets actual anxiety assessment.

Conflict as such does not cause developmental progression, for excessively stressful conflict can negate the potential for growth. Conflict accompanied by mild to moderate stress is more likely to result in adaptive growth. Even with low levels of stress, however, individual differences are significant qualifiers in predicting adaptive growth. That is, what is minimal stress for one person is excessive for another. (For discussions of stress and adaptation, see Lieberman, 1975; Lowenthal and Chiriboga, 1973; Selye, 1973.)

This relationship between degree of felt stress and adaptive resolution of conflict is similar to research findings on the relationship between anxiety, task performance, and task difficulty. Spence and Spence (1964) found that high-anxious individuals learned a simple conditioned response faster than low-anxious subjects did, but this outcome was reversed when the learning task was complex. Similarly, developmental tasks requiring adaptive resolutions of conflict are complex, and high-anxious individuals may experience such tasks with a high degree of felt stress, endure considerable developmental anxiety, and relinquish further growth (through regression, fixation, or denial). In contrast, less anxious individuals may encounter developmental tasks with some degree of developmental anxiety, but they are not debilitated by excessive stress and anxiety as they work through the resolution of contradictory-asynchronous self-structures.

Comparative Philosophies and Theories

In this section consideration will be given to only four theories, specifically focusing on their relevance to developmental anxiety: Freud's ([1926] 1936) conception of anxiety, Lazarus and Averill's (1972) cognitive appraisal view of anxiety, Gellhorn's (1965, 1970) physiological arousal theory, and Erikson's (1950) approach to anxiety.

Freud's ([1926] 1936) conception of anxiety has two parts: reality anxiety (fear upon exposure to danger) and signal or anticipatory anxiety (aroused by perceived threat of danger). Prototypical danger situations involve the separation from or loss of a loved object. These danger situations change with age; that is, as the body zones shift in priority in the course of psychosexual development. Reality anxiety seems to be equivalent to fear in many respects (since there is a specific concrete stimulus), while signal anxiety requires an appraisal process of potential threat. Normal signal anxiety was viewed as adaptive by Freud, for it allows the individual to avoid or prevent the threatening danger through regulating emotional discharge and facilitating the operation of normal defenses. Normal signal anxiety, however, appears to function through avoidance or prevention. This mode of functioning may well block the constructive use of developmental anxiety as a motivational force for trying out new coping forms; that is, for attempting to realign the self within the self.

Lazarus and Averill (1972) and others (for example, Beck, 1976; Ellis, 1962; Mischel, 1973) propose that the individual's cognitive appraisal of a potentially stressful event determines his emotional response. Such a cognitive appraisal includes the individual's beliefs, attitudes, expectations, and sense of control over the aversive event. From a developmental standpoint, the individual's emotional experience is highly contingent on such aspects as level or complexity of cognitive development, access to imitatable models (for social learning of various expectations and attitudes), and perceived sense of vulnerability (or control). It seems appropriate to expect that developmental anxiety will be experienced (coped with) differently as cognitive complexity increases with age (at least into adulthood). Access to complex cognitive appraisal typically expands one's coping resources (for instance, new and different options are seen, and different perspectives of evaluation can be tried out). However, complex cognitive appraisal may also make it difficult to come to a resolution and synchronization, because the complex web of details, options, possible perspectives, and choices encircles one with the "perversity" of multiplicity.

Gellhorn's (1965, 1970) research on the neurophysiology of anxiety reveals the qualitative differences that may occur over the life span in the somatic experience of anxiety. Normally the parasympathetic and sympathetic nervous systems work together reciprocally; that is, an increase in activity in one is accompanied by a decrease in the other. When both systems increase or are not in a balanced reciprocal relation to each other, conflicting demands for arousal and inhibition are made on the organism, and the emotional experience of anxiety results. Gellhorn studied patterns of anxiety (excitatory and inhibitory forms), as well as hereditary predispositions for hypothalamic control in sympathetic and parasympathetic balance and biological individual differences influencing the somatic symptoms of anxiety.

Kuhlen's (1968) review of motivational shifts during the adult years may have some relevance to Gellhorn's research. Kuhlen contends that, in the latter years of adulthood, anxiety and threat become the primary sources of motivation—possibly because of the interaction of negative aging stereotypes in our culture and increasing physiological vulnerability in later years. Without these qualifications, Kuhlen's position suggests an internal breakdown of coping structures in later years.

Erikson's (1950, 1959) psychosocial view of development comes closest to our preferred conceptualization of developmental anxiety. His emphasis on duality and the press for resolution of conflict as a motivating force in development captures the dialectical interweaving of the organism's two antithetical tendencies: (1) to maintain continuity for the sake of organizational coherence and (2) to experience discontinuity in order to develop. It is in the interstices of these two seemingly contradictory dynamics that developmental anxiety emerges. While Erikson does not use this construct, he does refer to the developmental crisis as "a crucial period of increased vulnerability and heightened potential . . . the ontogenetic source of generational strength and, at the same time, a source of maladjustment" (Erikson, 1959, p. 55). For Erikson, crisis is not an imminent catastrophe but a turning point, requiring a radical shift in perspectives. It seems that Erikson's crisis is the crux of growth: developmental anxiety emerges and spurs the organism on afresh and with new adaptiveness to synchronize forms for coping with the inherent conflicts of being alive.

Elaboration on Critical Points

Developmental anxiety as a construct requires a fluid conceptualization of anxiety, which allows for individual consideration of what specifically is experienced as threatening. Thus, an adolescent may experience his most severe anxiety over bodily changes in appearance, while a 65-year-old adult may be most anxious over the prospect of retirement from work. Developmental anxiety lies at the transitional stage between the giving up of old forms of coping and the acquisition of new ones. Therefore, the adolescent "gives up" the child's body to assume more adult-like contours, and the 65-year-old "lets go" of the daily routine of employment to assume more leisurely activities or develop new interests. But such "giving up" or "letting go" and the acquisition of new coping forms are not accomplished overnight. A process of differentiation and experimentation is undertaken and may last for a considerable period of time. This process of transition may be marked by considerable anxiety for a particular individual, or some particular transitions may be more frequently experienced as anxiety laden by many people.

Havighurst (1972) has outlined approximately eight developmental tasks for each chronological age period (infancy and early childhood; middle childhood; adolescence; and early, middle, and late adulthood). Some of these developmental tasks (for example, learning to control elimination of body wastes) may occur only once, whereas many others repeat themselves over the life span. For example, learning to relate well with one's peers begins in earnest in childhood; yet as a developmental task it reappears in adolescence, adulthood, and old age—with new nuances and complexities in each successive age period. These new nuances and complexities present conflicts or contradictions and require resolutions within the self. Van den Daele (1975) has commented on the spiralic nature of these recurrent themes in developmental tasks, and he suggests that they best represent the dialectical nature of development. The ebb-and-flow nature of developmental anxiety is also best illustrated in these recurrent, spiralic tasks; that is, they show that the old coping structures of the self are no longer sufficient for dealing with the newly emerging perspectives of a formerly familiar situation.

Successful negotiations of new coping forms in these recurrent developmental tasks is probably best predicted by the degree to which one achieved adaptive coping forms in the earlier appearance of the developmental task. Thus, a vertical system of coping structures within the individual, as well as within the theme of the task, may be postulated. The intensification of developmental anxiety may occur when the vertical development of coping structures within the individual has been consistently minimally adaptive or when the horizontal system of coping structures is overtaxed at any given point by unusual stress (for instance, when the number of developmental tasks for a given age period all demand resolution within a short period of time, as in adolescence in our culture).

Personal Views and Recommendations

A seemingly sound conceptualization of developmental anxiety has been presented in the preceding discussion. However, of what utility is it to the practitioner? First, the construct is meant to provide a framework in which to evaluate any given individual's anxiety. For example, does the individual show age-related or biological vulnerability to anxiety? Therefore, because new coping forms are still emergent, does the person become unusually stressed and anxious by the uncertainty of these new structures of the self? Second, an objective is to sensitize the clinician to consider whether anxiety is "reactive" (state) anxiety or "characterological" (trait) anxiety in the assessment situation. Certainly, making some effort to establish rapport with the subject/client will minimize the immediate state anxiety response that the individual may have just by being in a psychological testing situation; but the clinician should also consider developmental anxiety as a category of extended state anxiety. Third, the practitioner should not view anxiety or conflict per se as unilaterally negative experiences in a person's life. Rather, the experience of mild to moderate stressful conflict can be a dynamic force for developmental adaptation.

Application to Particular Variables

Consideration will be given here to three techniques of anxiety assessment: the Rorschach, human figure drawings, and self-report questionnaires. Given the construct in question, the focus will be on age differences.

As Rorschach assessment relates to developmental anxiety, one must consider what coping skills can be expected at a particular age and incorporate this understanding into the test analysis process. There are many measures of anxiety on the Rorschach, but for this developmental analysis only two outstanding ones will be considered: (1) shading plus form and (2) content or thematic analysis.

For very young children, shading responses and poor form level are not considered appropriate as indicators of anxiety (Halpern, 1953). Ames and her colleagues (Ames, Metraux, and Walker, 1971; Ames and others, 1973, 1974) have written three volumes discussing age changes in Rorschach responses. Shading responses used as diffusion occurred in only 14 percent of the Ames sample at 2 years of age. There was an overall increase in the number of children using the shading response, with 52 percent giving a shading response at age 7, followed by a gradual drop to 40 percent by age 10. Diffuse shading responses were typical for children under age 5½. By age 7, shading was used more for differentiation of details within the blot. At around 10 years, shading was considered to indicate "bound" anxiety when it was used for textural discrimination in the blot material. If one considers development as progressing toward increasing organization and integration, the notion that shading diffusion diminishes in middle childhood and becomes more organized fits well with developmental theory. Ames and her colleagues found that with increasing age Rorschach responses reflect children's growing cautiousness of approach toward the environment.

By the normally stressful period of adolescence, shading responses were given by 60 percent of Ames' 16-year-old subject population. The shading determinant was found to be the one that increases most strikingly during the adolescent period. Since this age shows so much evidence of stress (by amount of shading responses), it is especially important to determine the form quality of these shading responses in order to infer developmental anxiety.

The adult population has, on the average, two to three shading responses. Current attention to developmental differences within the early and middle adult period has not carried over to analysis of Rorschach responses. Possible differences may be found in the assessment of thematic content of the responses. Schafer (1954) pays particular attention to developmental differences for thematic analysis.

By old age the presence of diffuse shading responses for Ames' sample decreased to 10 percent of the normative population. However, presenile subjects gave 17 percent diffuse shading responses, and senile subjects gave only 1 percent—possibly because anxiety is aroused in presenile subjects through fears of deterioration. Form level of shading responses seems to decrease with deterioration of the subject until it returns to the level of early childhood.

Content or thematic analysis of the Rorschach has high concurrent validity as a measure of anxiety (Goldfried, 1966). When anxiety is assessed through thematic analysis, it is particularly important to consider the age variable. For example, an excessive amount of human detail responses (for instance, hand or foot) in relation to human responses (whole person), beyond the 2 to 1 *Hd:H* ratio, for adults generally indicates anxiety. However, children at the ages of 4 and 9 years often give a high percentage of human detail responses. Frequent anatomy responses (for instance, lung or heart) may be considered as indications of anxiety in adults, whereas children between the ages of 8 and 10 normally give a high percentage of anatomy responses. Sex responses and responses referring to excretory organs occur rarely among children except between the ages of 3 and 5. Developmentally, children of this age period become preoccupied with bodily sex parts as well. For elderly subjects, Schafer (1954) found considerable anxiety-related content; for example, describing the inkblots as worn or torn objects, animals, plants, or ragged garments.

Demographic variables (such as sex, occupation, socioeconomic level, and ethnic-racial background) are pertinent to understanding anxiety indices in thematic analysis; such variables may change the meaning of Rorschach imagery themes. The reader is referred to Schafer (1954) for summary and examples describing the influence of each of these demographic variables on the analysis of thematic content for anxiety indices.

The Rorschach is extensively used in evaluation of psychiatric disorders. While adjustment levels are often inferred from psychiatric subjects' Rorschach responses, the construct *developmental anxiety* is not part of these inferences. The reader is referred to Exner (1974), Exner and Exner (1972), Klopfer (1968, 1976), Rapaport, Gill, and Schafer (1968), and Schafer (1954) for relevant reviews of disorders and Rorschach assessment.

Human figure drawings (HFDs), in conjunction with scaling and observational methods, have been used to investigate normal personality development (see, for instance, Faterson and Witkin, 1970; Laosa, Swartz, and Holtzman, 1973). The content of children's HFDs has also been subjected to a degree of standardization for what is developmentally appropriate at one age and not at another (see Koppitz, 1968). Saarni and Azara (1977) examined HFD anxiety signs in normal adolescents, young adults, and middle-aged adults to determine what, if any, HFD content distinguishes these three age groups from one another. They found that adolescents were significantly more likely to obtain more anxiety signs than the two adult groups. The two adult age groups did not differ from each other in HFD performance. Wolk (1969) examined the HFDs of institutionalized geriatric patients. His results indicated a considerable number of anxiety signs among institutionalized elderly patients. Apparently, there is no recent HFD research on normal elderly people. These investigations, together with Swensen's (1968) review of empirical evaluations of HFDs and Handler and Reyher's (1965) review of anxiety indices in HFDs, suggest that caution be exercised when one is comparing HFD data from children and adults. The form or organization of the drawing is likely to provide more useful information than any one specific anxiety sign (for example, a tiny figure).

Haworth and Normington (1961) once concluded that it is a sign of pathology or sexual inversion for an individual to draw an opposite-sex figure; however, it is now more generally considered flexibly appropriate for girls in particular to draw male figures in response to the request to "draw a person" (Heinrich and Triebe, 1972; Saarni and Azara, 1977). Socialization processes apparently lead girls to equate "person" with a male figure. Other investigations of sex differences have focused on content, anxiety signs, or general organization of the HFD. With reference to anxiety, the HFDs of males are more likely to show conflict over aggression and hostility than those of females are. Sex differences in insecurity or lability as indices of anxiety are inconclusive (Saarni and Azara, 1977). To some extent, boys are less careful and/or less artistic than girls in their HFDs, and this must be taken into account when one is evaluating general form or organization of the drawing.

Demographic variables, such as socioeconomic status, vocation, and ethnicity, have not been widely researched in conjunction with HFDs and evaluation of anxiety. The limited research suggests that a negative milieu in a classroom or school may be associated with increased anxiety signs in the HFDs of children and adolescents (Koppitz, 1960; Saarni and Azara, 1977). However, the most reliable generalization is that insofar as higher education, a comfortable socioeconomic status, satisfaction with one's vocation, and acceptance of one's ethnicity ameliorate conflict within the self and extend one's coping resources, anxiety will also be less.

For disorders in childhood and HFD evaluation, Koppitz (1968) provides an excellent treatment of the effects of brain damage, emotional disturbance, and intellectual deficit on children's HFDs. Wolk's (1969) work with institutionalized elderly patients shows the effects of chronic brain syndrome and decreased motor coordination on HFDs. The use of HFDs with psychiatric populations is extensive; Roback (1968) and Hammer (1958) offer reviews. Notable is Hiler and Nesvig's (1965) research on clinicians' and non-psychologists' inferences of pathology from normal and psychiatric adolescents' HFDs. They found that clinicians and nonpsychologists were virtually equivalent in their accuracy of discrimination (65 percent and 64 percent respectively). The most reliable and valid signs of pathology were HFDs characterized as "bizarre," "distorted," "incomplete," and "transparent." Reliable criteria for normality were "happy expression" and "nothing pathological." Along similarly critical lines is Nichols and Strumpfer's (1962) factor analytic research on HFDs with college students and patients at a Veterans Administration hospital. They found that the overall quality of the drawing accounted for most of the common variance across a variety of HFD scores. In addition, the overall quality of the drawing was *not* related to degree of adjustment in the VA group. In general, it seems that HFDs are most informative when used in conjunction with other scaling material and observations of behavior. With regard to developmental anxiety, it seems inappropriate to generalize from anxiety assessments on the HFD test to the occurrence of anxiety caused by the uncertain and emergent coping structures of the self.

The self-report questionnaires or inventories developed to assess anxiety have reasonably high correlations with one another if they are designed to measure "general anxiety" or "test anxiety." Low to negligible correlations are obtained, however, when anxiety is assessed by different methods using different response modes (such as projective responses or autonomic arousal indices). Conclusive comparisons between children and adults on various anxiety inventories are difficult to make; that is, the more commonly used inventories have different forms for use with children and adults (Castaneda, McCandless, and Palermo, 1956; Spielberger, 1973; Spielberger, Gorsuch, and Lushene, 1970; Taylor, 1953). The reason for this is twofold: the test presentation itself has to be verbally simpler for children, and the evaluation of various specific situations as threatening or anxiety provoking differs in childhood and adulthood. It appears, however, that the primary category of what elicits anxious responses is the same across all age groups: ego- or self-threatening situations. Developmental anxiety would also fall in this category. More prevalent in childhood are anxieties about imagined supernatural events or beings, while at the other end of the age spectrum anxieties about physical deterioration and death become more frequent. In between are the usual anxiety-eliciting situations of loss of self-esteem, loss of love relationships, and, of course, uncertainty over how one will cope with the contradictions of living.

Inventories of anxiety generally indicate that females have greater levels of anxiety than males have (see Ekehammar, 1974). In their study of university students, Janisse and Palys (1976) found a high degree of similarity between males and females in the kinds of situations that made them anxious and in the frequency of occurrence of anxiety-provoking situations. Females did, however, reveal significantly higher intensity of self-reported anxiety, and they viewed more situations as physically threatening than males did. With reference to developmental anxiety, it may be inferred that females are likely to experience the conflict between old and new structures of the self more intensely than males.

Demographic variables have been frequently included in research using anxiety inventories. One general finding is that lower-class minority children frequently show a higher level of anxiety than lower-class majority-status children, and middle-class children generally show lower levels of anxiety than lower-class children (see review by Phillips, Martin, and Meyers, 1972). Furthermore, minority and/or poor children perceive more stress and may also have fewer alternatives for successful coping. The implication of these results for developmental anxiety may be that such youngsters enter normal developmental conflicts overtaxed with other sources of stress and anxiety. As a result, they may react to developmental tasks with greater degrees of disorganization, denial, or fixation.

Anxiety inventories are also frequently used to evaluate various disorders. Spielberger and Sarason (1975) have collected various review papers on the topic of stress and anxiety, many of which include anxiety questionnaires in evaluating psychiatric disorders in particular. One contributor to that volume suggests that as much as "a third of the adult population suffer from nervous complaints, especially anxiety" (Lader, 1975, p. 22). However, Lader also concludes that "anxiety, on balance, is more beneficial than harmful, providing an essential spur to human creativity, invention, and achievement" (p. 24). This view of anxiety is congruent with the positive, growthful aspects of developmental anxiety as described in this chapter.

References

Ames, L., Metraux, R., and Walker, R. *Adolescent Rorschach Responses.* New York: Brunner/Mazel, 1971.

Ames, L., and others. *Rorschach Responses in Old Age.* New York: Brunner/Mazel, 1973.

Ames, L., and others. *Child Rorschach Responses.* New York: Brunner/Mazel, 1974.

Beck, A. *Cognitive Therapy and the Emotional Disorders.* New York: International Universities Press, 1976.

Breger, L. *From Instinct to Identity.* Englewood Cliffs, N.J.: Prentice-Hall, 1974.

Bühler, C. "Maturation and Motivation." *Personality,* 1951, *1,* 184-211.

Bühler, C. "Genetic Aspects of the Self." *Annals of the New York Academy of Sciences,* 1962, *96,* 730-764.

Castaneda, A., McCandless, B. R., and Palermo, D. "The Children's Form of the Manifest Anxiety Scale." *Child Development,* 1956, *27,* 317-326.

Ekehammar, B. "Sex Differences in Self-Reported Anxiety for Different Situations and Modes of Response." *Scandinavian Journal of Psychology,* 1974, *15,* 154-160.

Ellis, A. *Reason and Emotion in Psychotherapy.* New York: Lyle Stuart, 1962.

Erikson, E. *Childhood and Society.* New York: Norton, 1950.

Erikson, E. *Identity and the Life Cycle.* New York: International Universities Press, 1959.

Exner, J. E. *The Rorschach: A Comprehensive System.* New York: Wiley-Interscience, 1974.

Exner, J. E., and Exner, D. E. "How Clinicians Use the Rorschach." *Journal of Personality Assessment,* 1972, *36,* 403-408.

Faterson, H., and Witkin, H. "Longitudinal Study of Development of the Body Concept." *Developmental Psychology,* 1970, *2,* 429-438.

Freud, S. *"Inhibitions, Symptoms, and Anxiety"* [1926]. In J. Strachey (Ed.), *Standard Edition of the Complete Psychological Works of Sigmund Freud.* Vol. 20. London: Hogarth Press, 1936.

Gellhorn, E. "The Neurophysiological Basis of Anxiety: A Hypothesis." *Perspectives in Biology and Medicine,* 1965, *8,* 488-515.

Gellhorn, E. "The Emotions and the Ergotropic and Trophotropic Systems." *Psychologische Forschung,* 1970, *34,* 48-94.

Goldfried, M. R. "The Assessment of Anxiety by Means of the Rorschach." *Journal of Projective Techniques and Personality Assessment,* 1966, *30,* 364-380.

Gould, R. "The Phases of Adult Life: A Study in Developmental Psychology." *American Journal of Psychiatry,* 1972, *129,* 33-43.

Hall, C., and Lindzey, G. *Theories of Personality.* New York: Wiley, 1970.

Halpern, F. *A Clinical Approach to Children's Rorschachs.* New York: Grune and Stratton, 1953.

Hammer, F. *The Clinical Application of Projective Drawings.* Springfield, Ill.: Thomas, 1958.

Handler, L., and Reyher, J. "Figure Drawing Anxiety Indices: A Review of the Literature." *Journal of Projective Techniques and Personality Assessment,* 1965, *29,* 305-313.

Havighurst, R. J. *Developmental Tasks and Education.* New York: McKay, 1972.

Haworth, M., and Normington, C. "A Sexual Differentiation Scale for the DAP Test (for Use with Children)." *Journal of Projective Techniques,* 1961, *25,* 441-449.

Heinrich, P., and Triebe, J. "Sex Preferences in Children's Human Figure Drawings." *Journal of Personality Assessment,* 1972, *36,* 263-267.

Hiler, E., and Nesvig, D. "An Evaluation of Criteria Used by Clinicians to Infer Pathology from Figure Drawings." *Journal of Consulting Psychology,* 1965, *29,* 520-529.

Izard, C. *Human Emotions.* New York: Plenum, 1977.

Janisse, M. P., and Palys, T. S. "Frequency and Intensity of Anxiety in University Students." *Journal of Personality Assessment,* 1976, *40,* 502-515.

Klopfer, W. G. "Current Status of the Rorschach Test." In P. McReynolds (Ed.), *Advances in Psychological Assessment.* Palo Alto, Calif.: Science and Behavior Books, 1968.

Klopfer, W. G., and Taulbee, E. S. "Projective Tests." *Annual Review of Psychology,* 1976, *27,* 543-567.

Koppitz, E. "Teacher's Attitude and Children's Performance on the Bender-Gestalt Test and Human Figure Drawings." *Journal of Clinical Psychology,* 1960, *16,* 204-208.

Koppitz, E. *Psychological Evaluation of Children's Human Figure Drawings.* New York: Grune and Stratton, 1968.

Kuhlen, R. G. "Developmental Changes in Motivation During the Adult Years." In B. Neugarten (Ed.), *Middle Age and Aging.* Chicago: University of Chicago Press, 1968.

Lader, M. "Stress, Clinical Anxiety, and Emotional Disorder." In C. D. Spielberger and I. G. Sarason (Eds.), *Stress and Anxiety.* Vol. 1. New York: Wiley, 1975.

Laing, R. D. *The Divided Self.* London: Tavistock, 1960.

Laosa, L., Swartz, J., and Holtzman, W. "Human Figure Drawings by Normal Children: A Longitudinal Study of Perceptual-Cognitive and Personality Development." *Developmental Psychology,* 1973, *8,* 350-356.

Lazarus, R., and Averill, J. "Emotion and Cognition: With Special Reference to Anxiety." In C. D. Spielberger (Ed.), *Anxiety: Current Trends in Theory and Research.* Vol. 2. New York: Academic Press, 1972.

Lieberman, M. A. "Adaptive Processes in Late Life." In N. Datan and L. Ginsberg (Eds.), *Life-Span Developmental Psychology: Normative Life Crises.* New York: Academic Press, 1975.

Lowenthal, M. F., and Chiriboga, D. "Social Stress and Adaptation: Toward a Life-Course Perspective." In C. Eisdorfer and M. Powell Lawton (Eds.), *The Psychology of Adult Development and Aging.* Washington, D.C.: American Psychological Association, 1973.

Maher, B. A. (Ed.). *Principles of Psychotherapy: An Experimental Approach.* New York: McGraw-Hill, 1966.

Malmo, R. B. "Anxiety and Behavioral Arousal." *Psychological Review,* 1957, *64,* 276-287.

Mandler, G., and Watson, D. L. "Anxiety and the Interruption of Behavior." In C. D. Spielberger (Ed.), *Anxiety and Behavior.* New York: Academic Press, 1966.

Mischel, W. "Toward a Cognitive Social Learning Reconceptualization of Personality." *Psychological Review,* 1973, *80,* 252-283.

Mischel, W. *Introduction to Personality.* New York: Holt, Rinehart and Winston, 1976.

Murphy, L., and Moriarty, A. *Vulnerability, Coping, and Growth.* New Haven, Conn.: Yale University Press, 1976.

Neugarten, B. *Personality in Middle and Late Life.* New York: Atherton, 1964.

Neugarten, B. "Adult Personality: A Developmental View." *Human Development,* 1966, *9,* 61-73.

Nichols, R., and Strumpfer, D. "A Factor Analysis of Draw-a-Person Test Scores." *Journal of Consulting Psychology,* 1962, *26,* 156-161.

Phillips, B. N., Martin, R., and Meyers, J. "Interventions in Relation to Anxiety in School." In C. D. Spielberger (Ed.), *Anxiety: Current Trends in Theory and Research.* Vol. 2. New York: Academic Press, 1972.

Piaget, J., and Inhelder, B. *The Psychology of the Child.* New York: Basic Books, 1969.

Rapaport, D., Gill, M., and Schafer, R. *Diagnostic Psychological Testing.* New York: International Universities Press, 1968.

Riegel, K. "Adult Life Crises: A Dialectic Interpretation of Development." In N. Datan and L. Ginsberg (Eds.), *Life-Span Developmental Psychology: Normative Life Crises.* New York: Academic Press, 1975.

Riegel, K. "The Dialectics of Human Development." *American Psychologist,* 1976, *31,* 689-700.

Roback, H. "Human Figure Drawings: Their Utility in the Clinical Psychologist's Armamentarium for Personality Assessment." *Psychological Bulletin,* 1968, *70,* 1-17.

Saarni, C., and Azara, V. "Developmental Analysis of Human Figure Drawings in Adolescence, Young Adulthood, and Middle Age." *Journal of Personality Assessment,* 1977, *41,* 31-38.

Schafer, R. *Psychoanalytic Interpretation in Rorschach Testing.* New York: Grune and Stratton, 1954.

Seligman, M. "Submissive Death: Giving Up on Life." *Psychology Today,* 1974, *7,* 80-85.

Selye, H. "The Evaluation of the Stress Concept." *American Scientist,* 1973, *61,* 692-699.

Spence, K. W., and Spence, J. T. "Relation of Eyelid Conditioning to Manifest Anxiety, Extroversion, and Rigidity." *Journal of Abnormal and Social Psychology,* 1964, *68,* 144-149.

Spielberger, C. D. (Ed.). *Anxiety: Current Trends in Theory and Research.* Vol. 2. New York: Academic Press, 1972.

Spielberger, C. D. *Manual for the State-Trait Anxiety Inventory for Children.* Palo Alto, Calif.: Consulting Psychologists Press, 1973.

Spielberger, C. D., Gorsuch, R. L., and Lushene, R. E. *State-Trait Anxiety Inventory: Test Manual for Form X.* Palo Alto, Calif.: Consulting Psychologists Press, 1970.

Spielberger, C. D., and Sarason, I. G. (Eds.). *Stress and Anxiety.* Vol. 1. Washington, D.C.: Hemisphere, 1975.

Swensen, C. "Empirical Evaluations of Human Figure Drawings: 1957-1966." *Psychological Bulletin,* 1968, *70,* 20-44.

Taylor, J. "A Personality Scale of Manifest Anxiety." *Journal of Abnormal and Social Psychology,* 1953, *48,* 285-290.

Van Den Daele, L. D. "Ego Development in Dialectical Perspective." *Human Development,* 1975, *18,* 129-142.

Veroff, J., Feld, S., and Gurin, G. "Dimensions of Subjective Adjustment." *Journal of Abnormal and Social Psychology,* 1962, *64,* 192-205.

Wolk, R. L. "Projective Drawings of Aged People." In J. N. Buck and E. F. Hammer (Eds.), *Advances in the House-Tree-Person Technique: Variations and Applications.* Los Angeles: Western Psychological Services, 1969.

46

Julian J. Fabry

Depression

The psychological concept of depression has been variously described as "having the blues"; feeling sad, guilty, hopeless, helpless, and melancholy; or reacting to the grief of losing some love object. It can also be described as a feeling state or symptom, a syndrome or reaction, a character or life style, and/or an illness (Schuyler, 1974). Recently, Depue and Monroe (1978), Spitzer, Sheehy, and Endicott (1977), and Zung (1977) have taken an operational approach to the definition and subsequent classification of depression. Currently it is defined as a dysphoric (chronic) feeling of illness and discontented mood and/or a pervasive loss of interest which is characterized by certain symptoms (Spitzer, Sheehy, and Endicott, 1977).

A number of authors have addressed some of depression's widespread major issues (Beck, 1970; Cammer, 1972; Depue and Monroe, 1978; Fann and others, 1977; Frank, 1975; Freud, 1959; Huesmann, 1978; Kolb, 1977; Lowen, 1972; Rakoff, Stancer, and Kedward, 1977; Schoolar, 1977; Schuyler, 1974; Seligman, 1975; White, 1964; Woody, 1978; Zung, 1977). Specifically, consideration has been given to its mild, moderate, or severe intensity as well as its acute, recurrent, or chronic duration (Cammer, 1972). It has also been viewed as developing in stages (White, 1977). Cammer has also noted that depression "plays no favorites" and can strike anyone. Others (Gaity, 1977; Kane, 1977; Kaplan, 1977; White, 1977) have focused their attention on the various socioeconomic, gender-specific, and age-related groups it encompasses, while others have indicated a strong relationship between depression and suicide.

Background and Current Status

In one of the earliest accounts of depression, the Bible—most notably, in the book of Job—describes the grief and agonized feelings of men and women who seem to have lost faith in themselves and God as well as any hope for the future. In the second century A.D., Plutarch wrote about the helpless feelings of the depressed fighting against the gods. The Greek physician Aretaeus of Cappadocia associated melancholia and mania. He indicated that not everyone has the same form. Some are suspicious of others, some flee to the desert, whereas others hate life. Hippocrates, the father of medicine, proposed four temperaments—among them, the melancholic (depressed), an individual influenced by black bile and phlegm on the brain.

As time progressed, so did the notions regarding the etiology of melancholia. In the Middle Ages, melancholia was regarded as a spell cast on the individual by some wicked or evil spirits. During the eighteenth century, the medical nature of mood disturbances were studied in established institutions and hospitals for mental disorders; and in the early nineteenth century the French physician Philippe Pinel wrote about the gloomy withdrawal of depressed patients. Around the same time, Jean-Pierre Falret described an episodic depression, with remissions and attacks of increasing duration, which seemed to occur more frequently in women than in men. He also indicated that this phenomenon may be associated with a precipitating event.

Around 1896 Emil Kraepelin separated functional psychosis into two groups: dementia praecox and manic-depressive psychosis. He proposed that dementia praecox is chronic and unremitting, indicating a poor prognosis, whereas manic-depression will not end in chronic invalidism. He also maintained that manic-depression covers all abnormalities of mood and is innate rather than the result of social and psychological forces. In contrast, Adolf Meyer, in 1908, indicated that depression is a reaction to life's events. In his work "Mourning and Melancholia," published in 1917, Freud proposed that depression is the process of mourning the loss of a love object: He believed that melancholia is the expression of hostile feelings formerly associated with the lost object and currently directed inward.

With the advent of measurement in the United States, a number of ways were devised for measuring personality. In 1921 Hermann Rorschach developed his inkblot method, a projective technique for measuring a wide range of pathology, including depression. In 1935 Henry Murray developed the Thematic Apperception Test (TAT), another projective technique for measuring a person's drives or needs. The first objective standardized multidimensional personality inventory, the Minnesota Multiphasic Personality Inventory (MMPI), was developed around 1943 by Starke Hathaway and Jovian McKinley. Subsequently (around 1949), Raymond Cattell developed the Sixteen Personality Factors Questionnaire (16 PF), another multidimensional personality assessment, which can indicate depression among other psychological phenomena. This latter instrument has recently (1970) been extended into a Clinical Analysis Questionnaire (CAQ), which measures pathology and is comparable to the MMPI. A forty-item IPAT Depression Scale (1976) has also evolved.

Bibring (1953), in his discussion of the mechanism of depression, examined the relationship between anger or hostility and depression. When anger or hostility is turned inward or remains unexpressed, it appears to retard behavior; when it is outwardly expressed, it appears as agitated behavior. Later, Beck and his colleagues proposed that a negative view of the self, the world, and the future, along with self-blame and criticism, are the primary elements of depression (Beck and others, 1961). Later, Seligman (1975) developed the notion of learned helplessness and proposed its impact on the understanding of depression. Essentially, Seligman postulates that depression occurs as a result of the organism's giving up or not wanting to respond, which is a result of being exposed to previous uncontrollable events. The ensuing fear then gives way to depression.

Critical Discussion

General Areas of Concern

Several physical conditions must be considered prior to the diagnosis of depression, since they have similar symptoms. Commonly, medical diagnostic ideas should augment psychological diagnoses. There are numerous examples of possible physical influences on depression. Hypothyroidism, or the underactivity of the thyroid glands, is manifested as depression. Although somewhat rare, Addison's disease, or the dysfunction of the adrenal glands, also presents depressive signs. In addition, the excessive use of alcohol, sleeping pills, and narcotics may have a depressing effect. Some patients experiencing depression will tend to cope by the abuse of these substances. Conversely, the depression may be a consequence of substance abuse. Some drugs used in the treatment of high blood pressure—for example, reserpine or some of its derivatives—can precipitate depression. Other drugs given as tranquilizers—such as meprobamate (Miltown, Equanil), diazepam (Valium), chlordiazepoxide (Librium), or even phenothiazines (Thorazine, Stelazine)—can precipitate or worsen depression. Amphetamines have also been noted as a contributing agent (Bockar, 1976); once the "up" state wears off, a "down" state usually follows. The degree of depression will depend on the amount or dosage taken and, of course, the psychodynamics and physiology of the person.

Just as with other pathological conditions, depression can be viewed as a disruption in the flow of a person's emotions, thinking, behavior, and physical functioning. In general, the emotions commonly exhibited, in various degrees, during depression are sadness, anxiety, guilt, anger, and a diurnal mood variation (the person feels bad in the morning but gets better as the day progresses). Some of the physical changes that take place during depression are sleep disorders, eating disorders, constipation, menstrual irregularity, impotence in males, frigidity in females, weight loss or gain, physical weakness, fatigue, pain, and diminished sexual drive. Although there are several behavioral changes, they are not specific to depression. For example, patients may cry more than usual or may indicate that it is impossible to achieve emotional release. They may withdraw from social contact. There may be psychomotor retardation. They may walk and talk slowly or have a rigid posture. They may show the opposite tendency. They may become agitated, pace, be restless, and seem driven. In extreme cases, there may be hallucinations. Certain cognitive changes may also take place. Depressed patients may have negative self-concepts, negative views of the world, be pessimistic, and/or blame themselves or even criticize themselves for certain misfortunes. They may be indecisive and believe they are worthless. They may be helpless, which means they are unable to act on the environment or gain satisfaction. They may also think that things are hopeless, that there is nothing anyone can do to augment change in the environment. There may even be delusions.

A heuristic definition of depression with concomitant disturbances of the whole organism has been proposed by Zung (1977). He states that depression is a syndrome of general withdrawal of the functions of life. In the psychic aspect, there is a general disturbance of behavior. The patient's ability to think, feel, experience, and express emotions has been disrupted. In the physiological sphere, disturbances in the patient's growth, metabolism, and reproductive processes have occurred. There is a decrease in appetite and food intake. There may be weight loss, impaired sleep, dysautonomias (familial defect characterized by defective lacrimation, skin blotching, emotional instability, lack of motor coordination, and hyporeflexia), and decreases in energy and libidinal levels. Psychomotor movement is disturbed, as expressed by agitation, restlessness, and aimless wandering or by retardation, inhibitions, and a slowing down of body movements. In the psychological sphere, general disturbances in responsiveness and adaptation take place. There is a loss of a sense of well-being, or there may be confusion, irritability, and indecisiveness. Suicide may become an option or may be viewed as a way out of feeling miserable.

Various attempts have been made to identify specific types of depression. These efforts have led to various dichotomous ways of categorizing this psychological construct. Some depressions are normal. People feel blue on rainy days, or some females may feel this way during their menstrual periods. People also feel grief stricken when a significant other is lost, either through a temporary or permanent separation or through death. Normal depressive reactions become neurotic when the person shifts his attention from the significant other to the self (Schuyler, 1974). These reactive (situational) depressions are usually precipitated by some event. Either some loss (death, job, money), separation (move, divorce, school) or responsibility (new home, mortgage, job) is the precipitating event. The vegetative or physical symptoms typically associated with psychotic depressions, are, however, absent. The reactive can become psychotic if no reality testing occurs and the individual perceives most external references as pertaining only to him.

Psychotic depression (such as manic-depression and recurrent, chronic, involutional psychosis) is characterized by sensory perceptions not founded in reality (hallucinations), false beliefs (delusions), somatic symptoms (sleep disorders, loss of weight), and usually the lack of a precipitating event. Schuyler (1974) has mentioned psychotic depression's association with endogenous (biological or dispositional) depression. Certain metabolic, central nervous system, or brain dysfunctions may be associated with this type of depression. There is usually a family history of endogenous depression. Mendels and Cochrane (1968) have indicated that psychomotor retardation, severe depression, lack of reactivity or response to environmental changes, a loss of interest in life, and visceral changes are some of its symptoms. Others (Cammer, 1972; Kolb, 1977) have noted a loss of weight, early-morning awakening, guilt, and suicidal behavior as characteristics of this type of depression. It appears that younger people suffer from reactive depression, whereas older people are more likely to be associated with endogenous depression. Whether endogenous depression is solely psychotic depends on its symptomotology. This type of depression has also been associated with postpartum depression, aging, toxification, infectious diseases, glandular disorders, severe injuries, surgery, or changes in body structure (Cammer, 1972). However, it has been most closely related to involutional melancholia at menopause. This phenomenon usually occurs with women between the ages of 45 and 55 years and is characterized by frequent crying, the wringing of hands, constant complaining of nerves, and/or a tight band around the head as well as swings in mood. In men, this phenomenon usually occurs between 60 and 65 years and is characterized by agitation, restlessness, loss of sexual interest, and suspicions of the spouse's fidelity. In general, the involutional is characterized by a rigid, perfectionistic life style.

Psychotic depression has also been defined according to manic-depressive psychotic reactions, such as the manic type, the depressive type, or the manic-depressive circular type (Kolb, 1977). Usually there is a family history of these phenomena. The manic type or phase is usually precipitated by a mild depression. This depressive period is then followed by exhilaration or mild excitement. If this lasts, the psychological entity becomes hypomania. During this state the individual appears assertive, buoyantly self-confident, and tirelessly energetic, as well as uninhibited and extremely demanding. If his demands are not met, he becomes openly angry and hostile. These patients seem to go to extremes, exhibiting attention difficulties. Their affective tone is that of eagerness, exaltation, and excitement. There also appears to be an abundance of psychomotor activity.

In some manic-depressives, the episodes are confined to the depressive type. Individuals who are friendly, emotionally sensitive, and timid seem more prone toward this type. Three subtypes for this type of depression exist: mild, acute, and stupor. In the mild depression, there is an absence of striking disturbances. However, there may be a period of fatigue, staleness, and inertia, or there may be physical complaints that have no organic basis. In the acute or severe depressive, many of the previously mentioned characteristics or symptoms are present, and there are more pronounced bodily indications. For example, there may be a depressive "facies"—a sad, dejected face and stooped body posture, with the person looking downward most of the time. There may also be weight loss, constipation, a decrease in sexual desires, and in some males impotence. A diurnal pattern occurs. The person interprets everything as hopeless. The feeling level is decreased, and a feeling of unreality may ensue. In general, there is a loss of interest in life's activities. A sense of fear or anxiety may occur, and/or the person may become confused. Psychomotor activity may appear retarded. The person may find it difficult to initiate action. Delusions centered on self-guilt and self-deprecation may also be present. However, hallucinations do not appear to be a conspicuous symptom. The person may be preoccupied with thoughts that interrupt his attention. In a stupor state, the person is profoundly inhibited, with minimal response to the environment. The person also may be mute and preoccupied with death.

There appears to be no set pattern for the circular type of manic-depressive. There is usually a period of depression of varying length, possibly followed by a period of normality and then a period of mania. The patient is figuratively riding a horse going up and down on a merry-go-round.

Recently, the unipolar and bipolar dimensions of psychotic depression have been emphasized (Depue and Monroe, 1978). The definition of each type, along with its subtypes, is dictated by symptomatic behavior, clinical course, familial and genetic factors, and pharmacological response. In general, unipolar depressives manifest agitated psychomotor activity, hyposomnia, somatic complaining, hypochondriasis, anger directed at themselves and others, and a heightened susceptibility to feelings of anxiety. Bipolars, in the depressed phase, are characterized by psychomotor retardation, hypersomnia, fewer somatic complaints, and mild or no anger and anxiety.

Depue and Monroe have further delineated the classification of bipolar and unipolar into various substrata. The Bipolar I is characterized as a person who has experienced manic and depressive episodes. He has required treatment and hospitalization, but shows intervals of normal mood and function. If the family has a history of this psychological entity, the patient has usually been admitted for a manic episode, whereas if there is no family history, he has been admitted for a depressive episode. The substratum of Bipolar II is typically described as someone having been treated and hospitalized for depressive episodes only. There is also a family history of mania or hypomania. Individuals categorized as Bipolar III have been described as having at least one hospitalization for depression, but they have no personal history of mania or hypomania. These people, however, have a family history of either mania or hypomania. The classification of Bipolar-other describes the person treated on an out-patient basis for depression and hypomania but who has never been hospitalized.

The entity of unipolar has been ascribed to all of the remaining depressions, which have previously been categorized as neurotic, psychotic, and involutional. The Unipolar I classification has been given to those individuals who have been treated and hospitalized for at least one depression, but who have no personal or family history of mania or hypomania. The Unipolar-other category refers to the person who has been treated on an outpatient basis only.

The clinical course for unipolar and bipolar depressives differs in that bipolars are hospitalized earlier (at around 30 years of age), whereas unipolars usually are hospitalized at about 40 years of age. There is usually a poor prognosis for bipolars. There appears to be more marriage instability, alcohol abuse, and suicide among this type. According to Kolb (1977), several studies point to the possibility of different genetic etiologies. Currently there seems to be support for the involvement of an X-linked inheritance in a subgroup of bipolars, whereas unipolars seem to represent a polygenic transmission. Kolb (1977) has also indicated some basic differences between these two major entities in addition to what has been previously mentioned. Specifically, when administered a tricyclic antidepressant or L-dopa, the bipolar will have a manic response. Urinary 17-OHCS decreases in the bipolar and is found to be normal in the unipolar. The growth hormone is found to be normal for the bipolar but decreases for the unipolar. RBC sodium increases for the bipolar but remains normal in the unipolar. RBC COMT is found to be normal in the bipolar, whereas it is lower in the female unipolar type. Platelet MAO decreases in the bipolar and is normal for the unipolar. Plasma tryptophan is found to decrease in the unipolar, whereas no conclusive statement can be made about the bipolar.

Depression can also be considered primary or secondary to other psychopathologies. There seem to be certain overlapping characteristics, especially with anxiety and schizophrenia. Depression and anxiety share the symptoms of suicidal ideation, pessimism, agitation, loss of confidence, intolerance of noise, irritability, and poor concentration. Anxiety manifests itself through panic attacks, emotional lability, attacks of unconsciousness, fears (especially of closed places), depersonalization, derealization, perceptual distortions, and *déjà vu*. These characteristics seem to set it apart from depression. Schizophrenia and psychotic depression share hallucinations, delusions, and motor inactivity. The clinician, however, must be aware that the schizophrenic manifests inappropriate affect, a poverty of ideas, and a decrease in integrated mental processes, whereas the manic-depressive, for example, possesses a greater harmony between mood, ideational content, and behavior (Kolb, 1977).

As previously mentioned, several physical measurements differentiate the bipolar and unipolar depressives; however, the current approaches focus on the substances of norepinephrine and serotonin. These biogenic amines are considered neurotransmitters; that is, naturally occurring substances in the brain cells which are released by the nerve cells naturally or when stimulated. The extent of the presence of these substances has been measured largely through the cerebrospinal fluid and the existence of the norepinephrine metabolite 3-hydroxy-4-methoxy phenyl glycol (MHPG) in renal urine specimens. Davis (1977, p. 2) has indicated that "some of the MHPG originates from the periphery, but a fair amount originates in the brain." What proportion comes from the periphery or the brain is currently unknown. It is not a perfect measure of brain norepinephrine, but it is considered an observable marker. Low MHPG, then, is deductively associated with low brain norepinephrine, and high MHPG is attributed to high brain norepinephrine. Van Praag (1977) has indicated that the cerebrospinal fluid does not yield reliable information regarding another substance deficiency associated with endogenous depression; therefore, he recommends the use of renal MHPG also. Schulyer (1974) has found that cerebrospinal fluid is affected by a number of variables (such as diet, activity level, fear, stress, and illness), which confound the interpretation of the chemical composition of the substance under investigation. Therefore, MHPG as currently measured through a renal urine specimen appears to be the choice method of the physical marker of depression.

There also are a number of psychological approaches to the measurement of depression. The most commonly used projective methods are the Rorschach and the Thematic Apperception Test. The Rorschach protocols of depressed patients show diminished responsiveness, particularly to color and movement. Whether the patient has a psychotic or a neurotic depression can be judged by the degree to which psychoticism (alienation from reality) is reflected in responses of poor form. Depressive neurosis is characterized by a greater percentage of animal responses and a low incidence of originality. Frank (1975, p. 40) states that involutionals "demonstrate contamination of the form quality of the percepts, stereotypy, and a greater tendency to respond with original responses." They also show qualitative differences in the content of responses. On the Thematic Apperception Test, depression is manifested by a lack of responsiveness, gloomy stories, and a number of wishful fantasies about love, kindness, joy, and happiness (Rapaport, Gill, and Schafer, 1968). Stereotyped phrases about morality and sin seem to be expressed, especially as part of the delusional system of the depressive psychotic.

Two scales of the Minnesota Multiphasic Personality Inventory are related to the concept of depression. There is a Depression scale (measuring symptomatic depression) and a Hypomania scale (designed to measure manic excitement, which typically accompanies manic-depression). These scales have been determined through empirical keying, and the procedure has been documented elsewhere (Welsh and Dahlstrom, 1956). Typically, scores that are two standard deviations above the mean are indicative of these psychopathologies. Scores at high levels appear to be associated with retardation (Depression) and agitation (Hypomania) and reflect, to a certain extent, the patient's energy level. These scales also need to be interpreted in light of the other scales present on the inventory. The primary or secondary nature of depression depends on the relationship of the depression and hypomania scales' interactions with other scales on the inventory. Golden (1979) has commented on the notion of chronic versus acute profiles. If one, two, or three scales are approximately fifteen to twenty T-score points above the rest of the scales, an acute profile is indicated. If the average level of an entire valid profile is high, there is an indication not only of pathology but of chronicity. Golden has also suggested that the slope of the profile can help to determine neurotic versus psychotic patients. Since the scale was empirically keyed, a question was raised regarding the dimensionality of the construct being measured. Harris and Lingoes (1977) propose that the Depression scale is representative of subjective depression (general dysphoria), psychomotor retardation, physical malfunctioning, mental dullness (lacks energy to cope, concentrate, remember), and brooding. Subsequently, Calvin (1974) factor-analyzed the inter-item correlations for the five scales and empirically supported Harris's rationally derived scales, thereby adding to the scales' construct validity.

The Institute for Personality and Ability Testing has developed the Sixteen Personality Factors Questionnaire (16 PF) (Cattell, Eber, and Tatsuoka, 1970), the Clinical Analysis Questionnaire (CAQ) (Delhees and Cattell, 1975), the Depression Scale (Krug and Laughlin, 1976), and the Eight State Questionnaire (Institute for Personality and Ability Testing, 1976). All these inventories measure depression to a certain extent. The Eight State Questionnaire measures mainly the state of depression; the others mostly measure the trait of depression. The 16 PF was developed primarily to measure the normal personality. The mean profile for a depressive reaction (Cattell, Eber, and Tatsuoka, 1970) is characterized by apprehension, suspiciousness, tender-mindedness, imagination, soberness, and the extent that feelings are affected. Karson and O'Dell (1976) claim that the O scale, which measures apprehension, is the key scale to be concerned with regarding depression. They also suggest looking at the F scale and the amount of seriousness that seems to contribute to the clinical picture. Krug (1977) has developed a formula for predicting which depressed patients will respond to the four tricyclic antidepressants: desipramine, imipramine, amitriptyline, or nortriptyline. The CAQ presents five scales specifically associated with depression, as well as other contributing scales. Specifically, measures of Suicidal Depression, Agitated Depression, Anxious Depression, Low-Energy Depression, and Bored Depression can be obtained. The Guilt and Resentment scale can also be contributory in understanding the depressed patient. The IPAT Depression Scale, a 40-item inventory, measures a dimension of depression that is highly related to anxiety. Norms are presented for men and women. The higher the sten score, the greater the probability of depression.

Several other short measurements of depression also exist. The Beck Depression Inventory, a 21-item self-report inventory, has been demonstrated to have moderate validity coefficients and appears to discriminate well between anxiety and depression. The Zung (1975) Self Rating Depression Scale is a 20-item inventory with an even amount of positive and negative statements. It has moderate validity. However, it seems age related. Normal subjects below 19 years of age and subjects over 65 years of age have a tendency to score in the depressive range.

A behavioral approach to the assessment of depression has been proposed (Lewinsohn and Libet, 1972). The Pleasant Events Schedule measures pleasure, activity level, and reinforcer potential of varied activities (MacPhillamy and Lewinsohn, 1974). There are three forms measuring some 320 events and activities that the responder is asked to rate in terms of pleasantness. Studies (Lewinsohn and Libet, 1972) have indicated that depressed patients engage in fewer pleasant events than nondepressed psychiatric controls and normals.

Comparative Philosophies and Theories

Essentially, there are two basic positions regarding depression and its effects on the human organism. One is concerned with the soma (the body), and the other is concerned with the psyche (the mind). Each position has numerous theories associated with it. A selected grouping, representing some of the major contributions, will be presented here.

The theories concerned with the soma are linked with biological and genetic hypotheses. As previously mentioned, depressions occur with menstruation, postpartum, structural body changes, and involutional periods. It is well established that certain types of depression respond to particular medication and electroconvulsive therapy. It is also established that certain drugs (such as Reserpine) produce depression as a side effect. These depressions are usually classified as endogenous, bipolar, and sometimes unipolar entities. The basic assumption with the soma focus is that a biochemical imbalance in the central nervous system, probably the brain, is associated with depression. As mentioned previously, the chemical substances associated with the brain and depression are obtained through the cerebrospinal fluid and renal urine. Two biogenic amines, catecholamines (such as epinephrine, norepinephrine, and dopamine) and indoleamines (such as serotonin and histamine) are usually the focus of attention. As previously stated, Davis (1977) has hypothesized that low MHPG found in renal urine is associated with low norepinephrine synthesis in the brain, and this is associated with some depressions. He further states that there are two theories being postulated. One is the permissive theory, which contends that low levels of brain serotonin and norepinephrine are associated with depression, while low serotonin and high norepinephrine are associated with mania. The other theory postulates two diseases and therefore two types of depressions. One results from low norepinephrine while the other results from low serotonin. Davis further states that not all depressed patients have a norepinephrine deficit. Some do not excrete low levels of MHPG. Some patients respond to a particular tricyclic antidepressant (such as imipramine), while others seem to respond to another (such as amitriptyline). All tricyclics inhibit the uptake of biogenic amines to some degree. Imipramine and amitriptyline (for example, Tofravil and Elavil) inhibit serotonin uptake, whereas nortriptyline and desipramine (for example, Pertofrane or Norpramine) inhibit norepinephrine uptake. These concepts are further complicated, however, because imipramine and amitriptyline are metabolized by the body into nortriptyline and desipramine. Therefore, it is contended that imipramine inhibits serotonin and norepinephrine uptake and becomes the drug of first choice.

Tricyclic antidepressants seem to be the choice drug with reactive and certain unipolar depressions. Lithium carbonate, which enhances the reuptake mechanism previously mentioned, seems to be most effective with bipolar depressives and manic-depressives. Electroconvulsive therapy has also been found effective with depressed patients. It seems to be used most effectively with endogenous and involutional depressives. Monoamine oxidase inhibitors (MAOI) seem useful with "atypical" depressed patients but not with endogenous patients. Schoolar (1977) has indicated that MAOIs appear to work with hysterical outpatients with secondary depression. Many contraindications exist for each of these treatments. Therefore, cautions are more than warranted.

Studies of unipolar and bipolar depressives (Winokur, 1977) indicate that mania is seen more frequently in families with bipolar depression and affective illnesses. Winokur presents some supportive evidence for an X linkage in these families, indicating that the gene(s) for mania may be located on the X chromosome near those for color blindness and the Xg blood group. There also seems to be a greater risk of unipolar illness among relatives of the unipolar type. Winkour also determined that patients admitted for mania had a higher incidence of relatives who had mania than the population in general. However, Winokur's sample was small, and the research has not been cross validated.

Two principal approaches—the psychoanalytical and the cognitive—prevail in understanding the psyche position. However, the behavioral approach stemming from learning theory also needs consideration. Freud's view of depression is related to his notion of libido and energy flow. When an individual loses a real or an imagined love object, a decrease or withdrawal of libido occurs. An unconscious anger or rage at the object also occurs, as a result of the object's abandoning the person. The ego introjects the anger, since the superego will not condone such expression. The energy flow is then turned toward the self through self-accusation, a lowering of self-esteem, and self-punishment. Fenichel (1945) emphasized the loss of self-esteem, and the consequent feelings of personal failure and rejection. Spitz's (1946) concept of separation contributed to an understanding of "loss" in the psychoanalytic context. Subsequently, the view of depression in terms of helplessness and powerlessness was fostered, and these notions paved the way for the cognitive approach.

According to the cognitive approach (Beck, 1970), the person experiences himself as a "loser," with prevailing negative thoughts of self, the world, and the future. This belief system sets up levels of expectations that seem insurmountable. Therefore, the patient becomes defeated.

Whereas the psychoanalytic therapeutic approach attempts to help the patient gain insight into his unconscious conflict through interpretations and transference, the cognitive approach focuses on helping the patient identify myths and maladaptive thinking and become objective in considering alternate explanations.

Between the cognitive and the behavioristic theories is the learned helplessness model (Seligman, 1975). Primarily advanced by Bibring (1953), this model views helplessness as a "giving-up" reaction on the part of the individual. Seligman (1975) postulates that this phenomenon is related to reactive depression. He has demonstrated through laboratory research that the organism must be forced to respond in ways that will relieve the depression. In his view, learned helplessness need not cover the whole spectrum of depression but only those types that exhibit symptoms where the person is "slow to initiate responses, believes himself to be powerless and hopeless, and sees his future as bleak" (p. 81). Recently, Abramson, Seligman, and Teasdale (1978) have made some reformations regarding the theory. They have added an internal (personal) and external (universal) attribution notion to helplessness. They have also given consideration to circumstances which are global or specific and chronic or transient. Some research (Costello, 1978; Tabak and Roth, 1978; Willis and Blaney, 1978) has not supported the theory, however, it has raised much interest in the domain of depression (Huesmann, 1978).

Behaviorists are more inclined to look at the antecedents, behavior, and consequences that control the behavior in question (depression). The observable normal activities (walking, talking, and the like) are reduced in frequency. Many of the behaviors of the depressed person are directed toward avoidance and escape. The depressed patient has lost reinforcers; therefore, there is an insufficient response-contingent positive reinforcement. Lewinsohn and Libet (1972) found a lack of social response, since depressed patients report that they are not involved with pleasant activities. The implication is to get the depressed person to become socially active and emit behaviors that are positively reinforced by others.

Elaboration on Critical Points

One of the most critical points concerns the classification of people into depressive categories, such as neurotic, psychotic, or unipolar and bipolar. Invariably, classifications have the pitfall that befalls most systems, and it is the exceptional or unique individual who does not fit the criteria set for inclusion in a category. The classification of this person also presents a problem to the clinician and researcher. However, we may never be able to find the ideal classification system. A description of those key elements included in an individual's depressive period may be of benefit to the clinician and the person's subsequent treatment in addition to the classification utilized. The classification should consider the proportion of the various elements, such as resentment, guilt, and anxiety, which are present and utilize these as part of the decision for inclusion or exclusion in a specific category. Efforts have already begun to consider the family, genetic disposition, drug response, and hospital admission status in the unipolar and bipolar system. Ultimately, we need a universal, commonly accepted definition and subsequent classification of depression.

The measurement of depression is somewhat imprecise, since it is controlled by its definition. However, as the knowledge about depression increases, so too will its measurement. Currently, it appears that depression can best be assessed through obtaining information about the patient from a family history, a knowledge of previous episodes, direct concurrent observations, others' observations of the patient's behaviors (especially symptoms), the patient's own report of his condition, and some possible physiological markers, which were previously mentioned.

Personal Views and Recommendations

The current definitions and classifications of depressions are efforts to incorporate clinical and empirical evidence regarding this psychological entity. Further analysis of the elements of depression and a synthesis of the various empirical studies is needed. Research into the relationship between depression and the various other forms of psychopathology is also needed as are more investigations regarding the course depression takes when it accompanies these other entities.

Furthermore, emphasis should be placed on the interaction of the physical and psychological variables that contribute to depression. Most of the theories regarding the physical and psychological variables have received mixed support and therefore further investigations would help to clarify the most critical issues.

Application to Particular Variables

Depression is found in infants between the ages of 3 and 12 months after a period of separation from the mother. This anaclitic depression (Spitz, 1946) results in listlessness, retardation of movement, and loss of appetite and weight. White (1977) has proposed that children separated from their mothers go through three phases: protest, despair, and detachment; and it is in the third stage that the schizoid and psychopathic personality is conceived. Lesse (1974) indicates that certain sociopathic behavioral tendencies and hypochondriacal and psychosomatic problems mask depression in children. In general, it appears that younger people suffer more from a unipolar or reactive depression, whereas older people are more prone toward bipolar and endogenous depression. Gaity (1977) has proposed that depression is an inevitable consequence of the aging process.

There is some evidence (Kaplan, 1977) that women are more inclined toward depression as a result of socialization experiences, which appear to inhibit adjustment of females through the lack of experience that would help them establish ways of coping with blame and guilt. Women also appear to be more prone to develop involutional and endogenous types of depression. This latter depression in some women may be attributed to hormonal imbalance (Kane, 1977).

Although some depressed individuals commit suicide, not all suicidals are depressed. Research suggests that depression and suicide are related. A primary consideration in this area has recently surfaced. It is the notion of hopelessness, which appears to be one of the paramount symptoms of suicidal depression. Schuyler (1974) suggests that endogenous types over 40 years of age and agitated depressives seem more prone to engage in suicidal behavior. Exner and Wylie (1977) found that approximately eleven Rorschach variables are included in a constellation for suicide protocols. These data, along with other information, can assist in the evaluation of suicide risk. The person's past suicidal thoughts or behaviors and his past contact with suicidal individuals also need to be considered. The person's current suicidal thoughts and suicidal plan need to be determined as well as the availability of significant "others" to help in the moment of crisis.

References

Abramson, L., Seligman, M., and Teasdale, J. "Learned Helplessness in Humans: Critique and Reformulation." *Journal of Abnormal Psychology,* 1978, *87* (1), 49-74.

Beck, A. T. "The Core Problem in Depression: The Cognitive Triad." *Science and Psychoanalysis,* 1970, *17*, 47.

Beck, A. T., and others. "An Inventory for Measuring Depression." *Archives of General Psychiatry,* 1961, *4,* 561.

Bibring, E. "The Mechanism of Depression." In P. Greenacre (Ed.), *Affective Disorders.* New York: International Universities Press, 1953.

Bockar, J. A. *Primer for the Nonmedical Psychotherapist.* Jamaica, N.Y.: Spectrum, 1976.

Calvin, J. "A Replicated Study of the Concurrent Validity of the Harris Subscales for the MMPI." Unpublished doctoral dissertation, Kent State University, 1974.

Calvin, J. "Two Dimensions or Fifty: Factor Analytical Studies with the MMPI." In J. R. Graham, *The MMPI: A Practical Guide.* New York: Oxford University Press, 1977.

Cammer, L. *Up from Depression.* New York: Simon and Schuster, 1972.

Cattell, R. B., Eber, H. W., and Tatsuoka, M. M. *Handbook for the Sixteen Personality Factors Questionnaire.* Champaign, Ill.: Institute for Personality and Ability Testing, 1970.

Cone, J. D., and Hawkins, R. P. *Behavioral Assessment: New Directions in Clinical Psychology.* New York: Brunner/Mazel, 1977.

Costello, C. G. "A Critical Review of Seligman's Laboratory Experiments on Learned Helplessness and Depression in Humans." *Journal of Abnormal Psychology,* 1978, *87* (1), 21-31.

Davis, J. M. "Central Biogenic Amines and Theories of Depression and Mania." In W. E. Fann and others (Eds.), *Phenomenology and Treatment of Depression.* Jamaica, N.Y.: Spectrum, 1977.

Decker, N. "The Wish to Die: Pathological Depression or Rational Decision." In W. E. Fann and others (Eds.), *Phenomenology and Treatment of Depression.* Jamaica, N.Y.: Spectrum, 1977.

Delhees, K. H., and Cattell, R. B. *Manual for the Clinical Analysis Questionnaire.* Champaign, Ill.: Institute for Personality and Ability Testing, 1975.

Depue, R. A., and Monroe, S. M. "The Unipolar-Bipolar Distinction in the Depressive Disorders." *Psychological Bulletin,* 1978, *85* (2), 1001-1029.

Exner, J. E., and Wylie, J. "Some Rorschach Data Concerning Suicide." *Journal of Personality Assessment,* 1977, *41* (4), 339-348.

Fann, W. E., and others (Eds.). *Phenomenology and Treatment of Depression.* Jamaica, N.Y.: Spectrum, 1977.

Fenichel, O. *The Psychoanalytic Theory of Neuroses.* New York: Norton, 1945.

Frank, G. *Psychiatric Diagnosis: A Review of Research.* Oxford: Pergamon Press, 1975.

Freud, S. *Collected Papers.* Vol. 4. New York: Basic Books, 1959.

Gaitz, C. M. "Depression in the Elderly." In W. E. Fann and others (Eds.), *Phenomenology and Treatment of Depression.* Jamaica, N.Y.: Spectrum, 1977.

Golden, C. *Clinical Interpretation of Objective Tests.* New York: Grune & Stratton, 1979.

Graham, J. R. *The MMPI: A Practical Guide.* New York: Oxford University Press, 1977.

Harris, R., and Lingoes, J. "Subscales for the Minnesota Multiphasic Personality Inventory." In J. R. Graham, *The MMPI: A Practical Guide.* New York: Oxford University Press, 1977.

Huesmann, L. R. (Ed.). "Learned Helplessness as a Model of Depression." *Journal of Abnormal Psychology,* 1978, *87* (1, special issue).

Institute for Personality and Ability Testing. *Manual for the Eight State Questionnaire.* Champaign, Ill.: Institute for Personality and Ability Testing, 1976.

Kane, F. J. "Iatrogenic Depression." In W. E. Fann and others (Eds.), *Phenomenology and Treatment of Depression.* Jamaica, N.Y.: Spectrum, 1977.

Kaplan, H. B. "Gender and Depression: A Sociological Analysis of a Conditional Relationship." In W. E. Fann and others (Eds.), *Phenomenology and Treatment of Depression*. Jamaica, N.Y.: Spectrum, 1977.

Karson, S., and O'Dell, J. W. *A Guide to the Clinical Use of the 16 PF*. Champaign, Ill.: Institute for Personality and Ability Testing, 1976.

Kolb, L. C. *Modern Clinical Psychiatry*. Philadelphia: Saunders, 1977.

Krug, S. E. *Psychological Assessment in Medicine*. Champaign, Ill.: Institute for Personality and Ability Testing, 1977.

Krug, S. E., and Laughlin, J. E. *Handbook for the IPAT Depression Scale*. Champaign, Ill.: Institute for Personality and Ability Testing, 1976.

Lachar, D. *The MMPI: Clinical Assessment and Automated Interpretation*. Los Angeles: Western Psychological Services, 1974.

Lesse, S. *Masked Depression*. New York: Aronson, 1974.

Lewinsohn, P. M., and Libet, J. "Pleasant Events, Activity Schedules and Depressions." *Journal of Abnormal Psychiatry*, 1972, *79*, 291-295.

Lowen, A. *Depression and the Body*. New York: Penguin Books, 1972.

MacPhillamy, D. J., and Lewinsohn, P. M. "Depression as a Function of Levels of Desired and Obtained Pleasure." *Journal of Abnormal Psychology*, 1974, *83*, 651-657.

Mendels, J., and Cochrane, C. "The Nosology of Depression: The Endogenous-Reactive Concept." *American Journal of Psychiatry*, 1968, *124* (Supp.), 1-11.

Rakoff, V. M., Stancer, H. C., and Kedward, H. B. *Psychiatric Diagnosis*. New York: Brunner/Mazel, 1977.

Rapaport, D., Gill, M. M., and Schafer, R. *Diagnostic Psychological Testing*. (Rev. ed.) New York: International Universities Press, 1968.

Rumbant, R. D. "Life Events, Change, Migration, and Depression." In W. E. Fann and others (Eds.), *Phenomenology and Treatment of Depression*. Jamaica, N.Y.: Spectrum, 1977.

Schoolar, J. C. "Mood-Active Agents in Depression." In W. E. Fann and others (Eds.), *Phenomenology and Treatment of Depression*. Jamaica, N.Y.: Spectrum, 1977.

Schuyler, D. *The Depressive Spectrum*. New York: Aronson, 1974.

Seligman, M. E. P. *Helplessness: On Depression, Development, and Death*. San Francisco: Freeman, 1975.

Spitz, R. A. "Anaclitic Depression." *Psychoanalytic Study of the Child*, 1946, *2*, 313.

Spitzer, R. L., Sheehy, M., and Endicott, J. "DSM-III: Guiding Principles." In V. M. Rakoff, H. C. Stancer, and H. B. Kedward (Eds.), *Psychiatric Diagnosis*. New York: Brunner/Mazel, 1977.

Tabak, B. K., and Roth, S. "An Attempt to Reverse Performance Deficits Associated with Depression and Experimentally Induced Helplessness." *Journal of Abnormal Psychology*, 1978, *87* (1), 141-154.

Van Praag, H. M. "The Vulnerable Brain: Biological Factors in the Diagnosis and Treatment of Depression." In V. M. Rakoff, H. C. Stancer, and H. B. Kedward (Eds.), *Psychiatric Diagnosis*. New York: Brunner/Mazel, 1977.

Welsh, G. S., and Dahlstrom, W. G. *Basic Readings on the MMPI in Psychology and Medicine*. Minneapolis: University of Minnesota Press, 1956.

White, R. W. *The Abnormal Personality*. (3rd ed.) New York: Ronald Press, 1964.

White, R. W. "Current Psychoanalytic Concepts of Depression." In W. E. Fann and others (Eds.), *Phenomenology and Treatment of Depression*. Jamaica, N.Y.: Spectrum, 1977.

Willis, M. H., and Blaney, P. H. "Three Tests of the Learned Helplessness Model of Depression." *Journal of Abnormal Psychology*, 1978, *87* (1), 131-136.

Winokur, G. "Genetic Patterns as They Affect Psychiatric Diagnosis." In V. M. Rakoff, H. C. Stancer, and H. B. Kedward (Eds.), *Psychiatric Diagnosis.* New York: Brunner/ Mazel, 1977.

Woody, R. H. "Bodymind Depression." *Voices: The Art and Science of Psychotherapy,* 1978, *14* (2), 38-40.

Zung, W. W. K. *The Measurement of Depression.* Columbus, Ohio: Merrill, 1975.

Zung, W. W. K. "Operational Diagnosis and Diagnostic Categories of Depressive Disorders." In W. E. Fann and others (Eds.), *Phenomenology and Treatment of Depression.* Jamaica, N.Y.: Spectrum, 1977.

47

Donald L. Mosher

Guilt

The concept of guilt is used to designate both a personality disposition, motive, or trait and an episodic emotion or state. *Guilt as a personality disposition* is an affective-cognitive structure, resulting from past experiences in guilt-related situations, which mediates individual differences in perception and action in present guilt-related situations. Mosher (1965) defines the personality disposition of guilt as a generalized expectancy for self-mediated punishment for violating, anticipating violating, or failing to attain an internalized moral standard. *Guilt as motive* is used to explain the avoidance of immoral situations, the attenuation of immoral behaviors, the institution of defensive processes, ascetic denial, self-punishment, confession, atonement, obsessional rumination, and depression. *Guilt as emotion* refers to the painful affective experience of regret, remorse, self-blame, and self-punishment when persons believe that they have committed a moral transgression. The phenomenological experience of guilt is predominantly ideational rather than autonomic; the people judge themselves responsible for a moral violation and feel guilty. The *trait-state* distinction was applied to guilt by Otterbacher and Munz (1973) and by Izard (1977). They transformed a state measure (the intensity of guilty emotion experienced at a particular moment) into a trait measure by asking subjects to report how guilty they felt in general or how frequently they experienced guilty emotion.

Personality theorists have made a number of theoretical distinctions involving the concept of guilt. Freud (1927) conceived of the *superego* as a structural component of personality, consisting of conscience and ego ideal, that developed during the resolution of the oedipus complex. He believed that *unconscious guilt* is best considered as an unconsciously motivated need for punishment, as in moral masochism or in repeated failures in life leading to pain and punishment. In *pathological guilt* the wish or intent is equivalent to the deed, and no act of atonement is sufficient; the wish may be unconscious and the guilt displaced.

Alfred Adler, Karen Horney, Erich Fromm, and Andres Angyal have all made distinctions between the *neurotic's use of guilt* to manipulate others and genuine or *real guilt,* which has moral implications and substance. Neurotics use guilt to avoid blame, to lessen their sense of personal responsibility, and as a substitute for change, whereas real guilt motivates the person to make restitution and to heal the breach with significant others.

May (1958), Boss (1963), and Bugental (1965) have discussed *existential guilt,* arising from the human condition, in which people acknowledge their responsibility and fear condemnation for forfeiting potentialities, for the aloneness that separates them from their fellow humans, and for humankind's alienation from nature.

Guilt is differentiated from fear, anxiety, and shame in psychoanalytic theory (Fenichel, 1945; Freud, 1936; Lewis, 1971; Piers and Singer, 1953) and in differential emotions theory (Izard, 1977; Tomkins, 1962).

The emotion of guilt can be measured through self-reports of guilt to affect adjectives (Haefner, 1956; Izard, 1977; Mosher and Abramson, 1977). Sex guilt, hostility guilt, and morality-conscience guilt can be measured by sentence completion, true-false, and forced-choice inventories developed by Mosher (1961, 1966, 1968). Masturbation guilt can be measured by the Negative Attitudes Toward Masturbation inventory (Abramson and Mosher, 1975).

Background and Current Status

The emotion of guilt emerged through evolutionary-biological processes to ensure the preservation of the species. The importance of the knowledge of good and evil in myths of the origin of humankind is represented in the story of Adam and Eve. In the oldest-known written record, the *Egyptian Book of the Dead,* there is an account of moral obligation and confession. The Ten Commandments of Moses are still represented in the consciences of modern humans. The concepts of sin, law, and justice are great ideas that formed the foundation for a psychology of guilt. Theology, law, drama, and literature have repeatedly returned to the themes of knowledge of right and wrong, culpability for transgression, inner control in the face of temptation, and guilty torment, punishment, and atonement.

Sigmund Freud is the preeminent figure in the evolution of a psychology of guilt. Freud viewed human nature as a grand struggle between the individual's biological propensities to seek sexual pleasure and to act aggressively and the efforts of civilization to control, tame, and sublimate these energies into more socially useful channels. In Freud's view, the transition from external controls, through fear of punishment and loss of love, to inner controls, through conscience and guilt, is a vital aspect of socialization; even if the individual experiences neurotic suffering for excessively punitive guilt reactions, that is preferable to the chaos of the untrammeled pursuit of pleasure. Reason will try to find a path through life midway between the moral categories of instinct and culture (Rieff, 1959).

Guilt is a ubiquitous concept in contemporary clinicians' discussions of personality, psychopathology, and psychotherapy. Clients use the concept of guilt in describing their own behaviors and phenomenological experience. In spite of the apparent need for clinicians to assess both the present prominence of the emotion of guilt and the personality disposition of guilt, guilt is frequently discussed but rarely assessed through formal procedures.

Critical Discussion

General Areas of Concern

The general areas of concern can best be delineated by the following questions: (1) What is the status of the theory of guilt? (Is guilt an important theoretical construct? What is the relationship of guilt to psychopathology? How important is the distinction between guilt as personality disposition and as emotion?) (2) What is the status of the assessment of guilt? (What is the preferred method of assessing guilt? Are moral choices situationally specific or a function of general personality dispositions? Should referents for measuring guilt be specific or general? How valid are present measures of guilt?)

Contemporary clinicians are operating with an informal theory of guilt that is derived primarily from the clinical theory of psychoanalysis, with some contributions from neo-Freudian, existential, and behavioral sources. Most psychologists agree that an overstrict conscience produces neurotic misery and that excessive guilt reactions require alleviation. At the other extreme, the failure of conscience results in the acting out of sexual, aggressive, and immoral behaviors. Guilt, then, motivates the inhibition of immoral actions or is a consequent emotional response to moral violation.

There are three contemporary perspectives on guilt: (1) clinical psychoanalytic theory, (2) differential emotions theory, and (3) social learning theory. Each posits that guilt is an important explanatory concept. The hypothesized relations between guilt and specific forms of psychopathology remain somewhat contradictory from theorist to theorist, although all believe that guilt is significant in some way. All the major theorists believe that it is vital to distinguish between guilt as a personality disposition, as an affective-cognitive structure, or as a system of conscience from guilt as an emotion or as an episodic state.

The assessment of intellectual functioning and handicaps during the first part of the twentieth century provided a tradition of empirical measurement that awaited the development of clinical psychology as an outgrowth of World War II. In the 1940s psychologists began to adapt their intelligence tests to measures of personality functioning and pathology and to extend projective testing to farther-reaching clinical concerns. However, neither projective measures (such as the Rorschach or the TAT) nor objective personality tests were explicitly concerned with measuring guilt. Psychoanalytically oriented psychologists undoubtedly looked for themes of guilt in projective stories, but content-scoring systems remained at the level of simple ratings or theme counts. In the 1950s mounting empirical evidence led to some pessimism about the usefulness of projective and objective tests in predicting diagnostic criteria. Psychotherapy became an important professional function of psychologists. In the 1960s several independent lines of development relevant to assessing guilt began. Nowlis and his students began to develop mood and affect adjectives measures that occasionally included guilty emotion (Haefner, 1956; Nowlis, 1965); Kohlberg (1963) began developing cognitive-developmental measures of moral judgment in the Piagetian tradition; Gottschalk and Gleser (1969) developed a measure of guilt anxiety based on content analysis of five-minute samples of free associations in the psychoanalytic tradition; and Mosher (1961, 1966, 1968) developed sentence completion, true-false, and forced-choice measures of the personality disposition of guilt that were indebted to both psychoanalytic and social learning theories.

The Hartshorne and May (1928) study of honesty and recent arguments (Mischel, 1968) about personality measures have emphasized situational specificity in moral and human behavior. Adherents to the position of situational specificity have argued against an extreme trait position, in which a trait is conceived as an inner entity operating independently of the situation in which the person is placed. However, personality is a set of processes that are manifested in situations. Since personality is an abstraction from the person's processes in situations, it is in no meaningful sense operating independently of situations. Burton's (1963) reanalysis of the Hartshorne and May data revealed consistent individual differences along a broad dimension of resistance to temptation. The dispositional approach to guilt views the person as having affective-cognitive structures that are evoked in situations relevant to guilt and that mediate moral behavior or guilty regret.

The generality or specificity of referents in a measure of guilt is ideally a function of the requirement for prediction. If one has a bounded criterion, then a narrow, specific sample of guilt-relevant content, or even empirical keying to the single criterion, will be useful. If assessment of personality functioning or dynamics is required, then a measure of guilt needs to include a sample of a broader spectrum of guilt-relevant content. For example, the content of the Mosher guilt inventories sampled reports of behavior, attitudes, and emotions in past, present, and future situations in the areas of sex, aggression, and general morality. These three aspects of guilt were discriminable by multitrait-multimethod matrices or by factor analytic procedures. These inventories predict to a wide variety of situations, yet sex guilt predicted best in sexual situations and hostility guilt in situations relevant to aggression, and so on. While sex guilt is a good general predictor of sexual behavior, masturbatory experience was better predicted by a measure of masturbation guilt, which included more specific referents in its item content.

The research reviewed in the section headed "Elaboration on Critical Points" provides considerable evidence for the construct validity of some measures of guilt. However, none of the measures have been used widely in clinical settings to predict an individual client's behavior. It is doubtful that the inventories can predict low base-rate behaviors such as suicide in spite of their apparent theoretical relevance. However, they may well provide important information relevant to the planning, conduct, and outcome of psychotherapy.

Comparative Philosophies and Theories

One of the basic assumptions in Freud's psychoanalytic theory, according to Rapaport (1959), is the assumption of unconscious psychological forces and conflicts. Unconscious sexual and aggressive instincts, wishes, or motives are opposed by the moral standards internalized in the superego. The conflict is between instinctual wish and repressive forces motivated by anxiety and guilt. Dreams, parapraxes, neurotic symptoms, and repressive defenses are all symbolic derivatives or consequences of unconscious childhood oedipal and preoedipal conflicts. Consciousness of the meaning of the conflict is altered to protect the ego. In *The Problem of Anxiety,* Freud (1936) presented the clearest account of his later views of the role of anxiety in inhibitions and symptoms. He distinguished objective anxiety (fear) from neurotic anxiety (objectless fear that neurotic impulses will be expressed and reproduce primal traumas) and moral anxiety (guilt). Signal anxiety serves to warn the ego that a primal trauma will recur unless certain behaviors are inhibited or defenses are instigated which remove the conflict from consciousness or distort its nature in consciousness. With the formation of the superego, the experience of the guilt feeling proper becomes a fourth version of primal trauma that is to be avoided. Most psychoanalysts have continued to emphasize the concept of anxiety and regarded guilt as a less important and derivative concept. While Fenichel (1945) continued to view guilt as a specific anxiety, he emphasized the importance of guilt as a motive for defense and argued that transformation *from* anxiety over loss of love *to* conscience as regulating narcissistic supplies is an essential characteristic of mental normality. Fenichel discussed the relation of guilt to such topics as masturbation, compulsion symptoms, return of the repressed, unconscious punishment, kleptomania, criminals out of guilt feelings, oral sadism, aggressiveness, masochism, impulsive running away, gambling, drug addiction, inferiority feelings, and mourning. The clinical theory of psychoanalysis contains excellent descriptions of guilt dynamics in psychopathology and psychotherapy. The metapsychological theory of psychoanalysis has two features which have hindered an appreciation of the potential explanatory usefulness of the construct of guilt. First, guilt is regarded as a subtype of anxiety, rather than as a discrete or fundamental emotion, and most theoretical accounts slight guilt by focusing on anxiety as the preeminent concept. Second, the assumption of psychological energies and their drive origin led Freud away from formulating an affect theory in favor of a drive theory, in which hypothetical cathexes of energy preempted a role that would have been played more usefully by emotions as the primary motivational system.

Shame was even more slighted than guilt in Freud's psychoanalytic theory, and recent psychoanalytic contributors have focused on differences between shame and guilt. Piers and Singer (1953) view guilt as arising from a tension between the ego and the superego when a moral boundary is transgressed and the unconscious irrational threat is mutilation, whereas shame involves a tension between ego and ego ideal whenever a goal is not reached and the unconscious irrational threat is abandonment. Lewis (1971) distinguishes shame from guilt as a function of differences in stimulus, extent of libidinal component, conscious content, position of self in the field, nature and discharge of hostility, and characteristic defenses. Lewis is concerned with a microanalysis of psychotherapy sessions in order to identify the role of unanalyzed shame in exacerbating the patient's symptoms. She links shame with depressed feelings and guilt with obsessional and paranoid thinking, aggression, isolation, rationalization, and reaction formation.

Tomkins' (1962) theory of differential affects considers emotions the primary motivational system in humans, amplifying the more specifically informative drive system. The fundamental emotions are viewed as having evolutionary-biological significance, and the facial expression of discrete emotion as phylogenetically evolved, universal, pancultural, and significant in social communication. Emotion has neurophysiological, motor-expressive, and experiential components. Proprioceptive feedback from the expressive facial musculature, when transformed into consciousness, is the experience of emotion. Tomkins describes a model of innate activators of affect based on the principle of variations in the density of neural stimulation. Shame is innately activated when a slowly increasing gradient of neural stimulation that is producing excitement is interrupted, producing shame. Tomkins describes many learned activators of emotions, including memory and thinking. Tomkins considers guilt an experientially discriminable aspect of shame, but Izard (1977), in his largely derivative differential emotions theory, regards guilt as a fundamental or discrete emotion. Anxiety is not considered a fundamental emotion but is, instead, described as a complex emotional pattern of several discrete emotions. In Tomkins' account of paranoid schizophrenia, the dominant affects in consciousness are terror and humiliation. The humiliation has its source in inferiority (shame) or in immorality (guilt).

Mosher (1961) used referents suggested by psychoanalytic theory to develop a scoring manual for a sentence completion measure of the personality disposition of guilt. For example, completions indicative of the disposition of guilt include admissions of feeling guilty, ashamed, disgusted, sinful, and revulsed by sexual or aggressive actions or fantasies; attitudes that immoral acts are abnormal, insane, self-destructive, or detrimental to society; and self-reports that judge the self to be evil, unworthy of forgiveness, desiring self-punishment, or practicing ascetic denial, confessing, and engaging in acts of contrition, undoing, and restitution. The absence of personality processes prone to guilt is inferred from completions that (1) deny feelings of guilt, (2) indicate that sexual and aggressive needs are fulfilled with pleasure, (3) state that traditionally disapproved acts are normal and desirable, and (4) plan means of avoiding detection or punishment when disapproved acts are contemplated. His initial research used Rotter's (1954) social learning theory distinction between fear (conceived as a situational expectancy for punishment) and guilt (viewed as a generalized expectancy for self-mediated punishment) to predict response inhibition in a perceptual defense task. This research program paid careful attention to the development of psychometrically sound true-false and forced-choice measures of sex guilt, hostility guilt, and morality-conscience guilt from earlier sentence completions. The construct validation of the measures has been supported in over one hundred empirical investigations.

Elaboration on Critical Points

This section presents a discussion of (1) Gottschalk and Gleser's measure of guilt anxiety, (2) Izard's Differential Emotions Scale, (3) Mosher's affect adjective procedure, (4) Otterbacher and Munz's measures of trait and state of guilt, (5) Mosher's guilt inventories, and (6) Abramson and Mosher's Negative Attitudes Toward Masturbation.

The Gottschalk and Gleser (1969) measure of guilt anxiety is based on a content analysis of five minutes of verbalization about an interesting or a dramatic personal life experience. It is assumed that the thematic content of phrases containing adverse criticism, abuse, condemnation, moral disapproval, guilt, or threat of such an experience implies the presence of an underlying affective state of guilt. The scoring manual includes instructions for scoring six subcategories of anxiety, including guilt anxiety, and overt and covert hostility directed outward, against the self, and ambivalently. This method of content analysis is sound psychometrically and has generated several empirical studies supporting its usefulness.

The Differential Emotions Scale (DES) (Izard and others, 1974) is a self-report instrument designed to assess the intensity (state) or frequency (trait) of the experience of ten fundamental or discrete emotions. Three affect adjectives are used to assess each of the emotions of interest, enjoyment, surprise, distress, anger, disgust, contempt, fear, shame, shyness, and guilt. The test factors correspond to fundamental emotions in differential emotions theory (Izard, 1977). The initial studies using the DES suggested that it is a comprehensive and potentially valid assessor of emotional states.

Mosher has used an affect adjective measure of guilt in several studies, with promising results (Mosher and Abramson, 1977). The affect adjective procedure uses six adjectives for each of eight affects: guilt, shame, disgust, depression, anger, anxiety, sexual arousal, and serenity. The selection of affect adjectives was based on factor analytic work of Nowlis (1965) and Lorr, Daston, and Smith (1967), but the sexual arousal, shame, and disgust adjectives were selected rationally. The adjectives for affective guilt are *guilty, sinful, blameworthy, conscience-stricken, repentant,* and *remorseful.* This approach remains an informal measure.

Otterbacher and Munz (1973) developed a state-trait measure of guilt consisting of eleven adjectives scaled from "innocent" to "unforgivable." The state measure asks subjects to check the adjective that applies at a specific moment, and the trait measure asks the subject to check the one adjective that applies generally. This procedure makes little sense conceptually and has little data to support its usefulness. The adjectives reflect culpability rather than an emotional state, and no one experiences a level of guilt in general (trait) that is independent of transgressions in situations.

The more carefully developed and extensively validated measures of guilt as a personality disposition are the Mosher (1961, 1966, 1968) guilt inventories. Sentence completion, true-false, and forced-choice inventories measuring sex guilt, hostility guilt, and morality-conscience guilt are available in male and female forms. The psychometric properties of the inventories are excellent, with high reliabilities, convergent and discriminant validity, and good controls for social desirability. Over one hundred research investigations provide considerable evidence for construct validity.

These measures of guilt, particularly hostility guilt or morality-conscience guilt, have discriminated first offenders from recidivists at the Ohio Penitentiary (Mosher and Mosher, 1966), delinquent boys from matched controls (Ruma, 1967), and incarcerated homosexual inserters from insertees (Oliver and Mosher, 1968). Guilt was negatively correlated in the r = .40s with delinquents' self-reported assault, theft, and vandalism (Heyman, 1969; Ruma, 1967) and in the r = .60s with the self-reports of undetected and unpunished sex crimes, violent crimes, and total crimes in serious and habitual young adult offenders (Persons, 1970). Male and female undergraduates scoring lower on morality-conscience guilt reported the use of significantly more and a greater variety of illegal drugs (Schill and Althoff, 1975). Among drug abusers, high-sex-guilt men and women used more sedatives, and low-guilt polydrug users preferred stimulants (Ungerer and others, 1976).

The level of cumulative sex experience in college students is moderately negatively correlated with sex guilt (Abramson and Mosher, 1975; D'Augelli and Cross, 1975; Kier, 1972; Langston, 1973, 1975; Mosher, 1973; Mosher and Cross, 1971). High-sex-guilt college students reported fewer sexual partners (Mosher, 1973) and less frequent sexual intercourse (Love, Sloan, and Schmidt, 1976; Mosher 1973). Sex guilt was an excellent predictor of women's sexual philosophy and virginal status and of dating couples' conjoint sexual behavior (D'Augelli and Cross, 1975). High-sex-guilt undergraduate males were less likely to attempt sexual behavior with their dates or to use or justify exploitative tactics to gain sexual access. Sex-guilty males report having seen (Mosher, 1973) and purchased (Love, Sloan, and Schmidt, 1976) less pornography. In the laboratory, unobtrusive measures have revealed that high-guilt men read erotic magazines less in a waiting room (Schill and Chapin, 1972) and watched obscene slides more briefly (Love, Sloan, and Schmidt, 1976) than their less guilty counterparts. Females had different patterns of cardiac acceleration and decelerations as a function of sex guilt while viewing sexual slides (Ray and Thompson, 1974). Urinary acid phosphatase levels, a measure of sexual arousal, were lower at base line and following thirty minutes of exposure to erotica in high-sex-guilt males (Pagano and Kirschner, 1978). While sex guilt did not always preclude subjective sexual arousal (Bahm, 1972; Mosher, 1973; Mosher and Greenberg, 1969), it was negatively related to reports of genital sensations arranged in an ordinal scale (Mosher and Abramson, 1977). High-sex-guilt men and women judged pornography less favorably and had more negative affective reactions (Kier, 1972; Mosher, 1973; Mosher and Abramson, 1977). High-sex-guilt subjects retained less birth control information from a lecture (Abramson and others, 1977) and sexually active high-sex-guilt women reported less effective use of contraceptives (Mosher, 1973). Abortion patients at a university problem pregnancy clinic scored higher on sex guilt than sexually active nonpregnant single university women (Gerard, 1977).

Laboratory studies of hostility guilt indicated that high-hostility-guilt delinquents expressed less retaliatory verbal aggression (Mosher, Mortimer, and Grebel, 1968), high-guilt women produced less questionnaire aggression against a frustrating experimenter (Schill, 1972), and high-guilt males administered less intense (Groh, 1976; Schallow, 1972) or shorter (Hayward, 1970) electric shocks. After aggression in the laboratory, high-hostility-guilt males reported more guilty affect (Cogan, 1969; Oliver and Mosher, 1968). Interviews with delinquents over the transgression leading to incarceration revealed more internalization and guilty affect in high-guilt subjects. Diastolic blood pressure rose after attack or frustration and fell after aggression in the laboratory, except in high-hostility-guilt subjects (Gambaro and Rabin, 1969; Schill, 1972) and was chronically elevated in guilty-aggression-expressing inmates of a state prison (Meyer, 1968).

The forced-choice guilt inventory was related to Kohlberg's level of moral judgment in delinquents (Ruma, 1967; Ruma and Mosher, 1967) and in normals (D'Augelli and Cross, 1975). Delinquents scoring lower on guilt were at preconventional levels of moral judgment, while higher-scoring delinquents were at conventional levels. High-guilt students were morally oriented at the traditional law-and-order stage, and less guilty college students were oriented at either the personal concordance or the social contract stages.

Evidence of convergent and discriminant validity of the Mosher guilt inventories was presented in studies correlating the guilt inventories with the Minnesota Multiphasic Personality Inventory (Oliver and Mosher, 1968; Persons, 1970), the Edwards Personal Preference Schedule (Abramson and others, 1977), measures of social desirability (Dubeck, Schuck, and Cymbalisty, 1971; Mosher, 1966, 1968), the Thorne Sex Inventory (Galbraith, 1969), and measures of defensive preference, hostility, and childrearing attitudes (Schill, Evans, and McGovern, 1976; Schill and others, 1976; Schill and Schneider, 1970a, 1970b).

A measure of Negative Attitudes Toward Masturbation was constructed by Abramson and Mosher (1975). The thirty-item scale consists of three factors: (1) positive attitudes toward masturbation, (2) false beliefs about the harmful nature of masturbation, and (3) personally experienced negative affects associated with masturbation. High scorers reported masturbating less frequently each month (Abramson and Mosher, 1975) and reported less subjective sexual arousal and more affective disgust, guilt, shame, and anger after viewing films of masturbation (Mosher and Abramson, 1977).

Personal Views and Recommendations

To assess the current state of guilty feelings, endorsement is given to the Gottschalk and Gleser content analysis procedure on the Differential Emotions Scale (DES). The Gottschalk approach is more time consuming when formally scored, but familiarity with the scoring system will alert the clinician to implied guilty affect during his intake interview or during psychotherapy. The DES has the advantage of providing, in a relatively brief time period, a profile of ten emotions believed to be discrete or fundamental in differential emotions theory. The approach can be flexibly applied to specific situations or time periods. It is believed that the DES II, the trait measure, will prove less useful than the state measure or the Mosher guilt inventories.

The Mosher guilt inventories are the method of choice for measuring the personality disposition or affective-cognitive structure of guilt. The psychometric properties and validity data compare most favorably with those available for more widely known and used personality measures. The sentence completion method has the advantage of providing additional clinical information. The true-false inventory provides rapid and easy assessment of three aspects of guilt. The forced-choice procedure has been most widely used in research contexts. Negative Attitudes Toward Masturbation is a promising measure of masturbation guilt.

Application to Particular Variables

Clinicians frequently want to assess both the personality disposition of guilt and the present prominence of the emotion of guilt in a wide variety of clients. The assessment of guilt is an issue for clinicians dealing with patients with depressive symptoms, obsessional or paranoid thinking, and delinquents and criminals. Clients seeking psychotherapy for help in dealing with the crises of abortion, rape, marital conflict, divorce, parenting, failure, aging, and mourning often experience a heightened sense of guilt. Inhibition of sexual desire and sex dysfunctions as well as sexual acting-out in affairs or promiscuity implicate guilt as a useful dimension for assessment.

References

Abramson, P. R., and Mosher, D. L. "Development of a Measure of Negative Attitudes Toward Masturbation." *Journal of Consulting and Clinical Psychology*, 1975, *43*, 485-490.

Abramson, P. R., and others. "Personality Correlates of the Mosher Guilt Scales." *Journal of Personality Assessment*, 1977, *41*, 375-382.

Bahm, R. M. "The Influence of Non-sexual Cues, Sexual Explicitness and Sex Guilt on Females' Erotic Response to Literature." Unpublished doctoral dissertation, University of Massachusetts, 1972.

Boss, M. *Psychoanalysis and Daseinanalysis.* (Ludwig R. Lefebre, Trans.) New York: Basic Books, 1963.

Bugental, J. F. T. *The Search for Authenticity.* New York: Holt, Rinehart and Winston, 1965.

Burton, R. V. "Generality of Honesty Reconsidered." *Psychological Review,* 1963, *70*, 481-499.

Cogan, T. M. "Internal Versus External Control, the Attributes of Responsibility, and Guilt over Aggression Behavior." Unpublished master's thesis, University of Connecticut, 1969.

D'Augelli, J. F., and Cross, H. J. "Relationship of Sex Guilt and Moral Reasoning to Premarital Sex in College Women and in Couples." *Journal of Consulting and Clinical Psychology*, 1975, *43*, 40-47.

Dubeck, J. A., Schuck, S. Z., and Cymbalisty, B. Y. "Falsification of the Forced-Choice Guilt Inventory." *Journal of Consulting and Clinical Psychology*, 1971, *36*, 296.

Fenichel, O. *The Psychoanalytic Theory of Neurosis.* New York: Norton, 1945.

Freud, S. *The Ego and the Id.* London: Hogarth Press, 1927.

Freud, S. *The Problem of Anxiety.* New York: Norton, 1936.

Galbraith, G. G. "The Mosher Sex-Guilt Scale and the Thorne Sex Inventory: Intercorrelations." *Journal of Clinical Psychology*, 1969, *25*, 292-294.

Gambaro, S., and Rabin, A. I. "Diastolic Blood Pressure Responses Following Direct and Displaced Aggression After Anger Arousal in High and Low Guilt Subjects." *Journal of Personality and Social Psychology*, 1969, *12*, 87-94.

Gerard, M. "Sex Guilt in Abortion Patients." *Journal of Consulting and Clinical Psychology,* 1977, *45,* 708.

Gottschalk, L., and Gleser, G. *The Measurement of Psychological States Through the Content Analysis of Verbal Behavior.* Berkeley: University of California Press, 1969.

Groh, T. R. "Infant Stimuli as Aggression Inhibiting Cues." Unpublished doctoral dissertation, University of Connecticut, 1976.

Haefner, D. P. *Some Effects of Guilt-Arousing and Fear-Arousing Persuasive Communications on Opinion Change.* Washington, D.C.: U.S. Government Printing Office, 1956.

Hartshorne, H., and May, M. *Studies in the Nature of Character.* Vol. 1: *Studies in Deceit.* New York: Macmillan, 1928.

Hayward, G. W. "Expressed Aggression as a Function of Guilt Level Under Varying Conditions of Legitimacy and External Threat." Unpublished doctoral dissertation, University of Texas, 1970.

Heyman, D. S. "The Effect of Film-Mediated Aggression on Subsequent Aggressive Behavior." Unpublished doctoral dissertation, University of Connecticut, 1969.

Izard, C. E. *Human Emotions.* New York: Plenum, 1977.

Izard, C. E., and others. "The Differential Emotions Scale: A Method of Measuring the Subjective Experience of Discrete Emotions." Unpublished manuscript, Department of Psychology, Vanderbilt University, 1974.

Kier, R. G. "Sex, Individual Differences, and Film Effects on Responses to Sexual Films." Unpublished doctoral dissertation, University of Connecticut, 1972.

Kohlberg, L. "The Development of Children's Orientations Toward a Moral Order. I: Sequence in the Development of Human Thought." *Vita Humana,* 1963, *6,* 11-33.

Langston, R. D. "Sex Guilt and Sex Behavior in College Students." *Journal of Personality Assessment,* 1973, *37,* 467-472.

Langston, R. D. "Stereotyped Sex Role Behavior and Sex Guilt." *Journal of Personality Assessment,* 1975, *39,* 77-81.

Lewis, H. *Shame and Guilt in Neurosis.* New York: International Universities Press, 1971.

Lorr, M., Daston, P., and Smith, I. R. "An Analysis of Mood States." *Educational and Psychological Measurement,* 1967, *27,* 89-96.

Love, R. E., Sloan, L. R., and Schmidt, M. J. "Viewing Pornography and Sex Guilt: The Priggish, the Prudent, and the Profligate." *Journal of Consulting and Clinical Psychology,* 1976, *44,* 624-629.

May, R. "The Origins and Significance of the Existential Movement in Psychology." In R. May, E. Angel, and H. F. Ellenberger (Eds.), *Existence: A New Dimension in Psychiatry and Psychology.* New York: Basic Books, 1958.

Meyer, R. G. "Chronic High Blood Pressure, Essential Hypertension, and the Inhibition of Aggression." *Proceedings of the 76th Annual Convention of the American Psychological Association.* Washington, D.C.: American Psychological Association, 1968.

Mischel, W. *Personality and Assessment.* New York: Wiley, 1968.

Mosher, D. L. "The Development and Validation of a Sentence Completion Measure of Guilt." Unpublished doctoral dissertation, Ohio State University, 1961.

Mosher, D. L. "Interaction of Fear and Guilt in Inhibiting Unacceptable Behavior." *Journal of Consulting Psychology,* 1965, *29,* 161-167.

Mosher, D. L. "The Development and Multitrait-Multimethod Matrix Analysis of Three Measures of Three Aspects of Guilt." *Journal of Consulting Psychology,* 1966, *30,* 25-29.

Mosher, D. L. "Measurement of Guilt in Females by Self-Report Inventories." *Journal of Consulting and Clinical Psychology,* 1968, *32,* 690-695.

Mosher, D. L. "Sex Differences, Sex Experience, Sex Guilt, and Explicitly Sexual Films." *Journal of Social Issues,* 1973, *29,* 95-112.

Mosher, D. L., and Abramson, P. R. "Subjective Sexual Arousal to Films of Masturbation." *Journal of Consulting and Clinical Psychology,* 1977, *45,* 796-807.

Mosher, D. L., and Cross, H. J. "Sex Guilt and Premarital Sexual Experiences of College Students." *Journal of Consulting Psychology,* 1971, *36,* 22-32.

Mosher, D. L., and Greenberg, I. "Females' Affective Responses to Reading Erotic Literature." *Journal of Consulting and Clinical Psychology,* 1969, *33,* 472-477.

Mosher, D. L., Mortimer, R. L., and Grebel, M. G. "Verbal Aggressive Behavior in Delinquent Boys." *Journal of Abnormal Psychology,* 1968, *73,* 454-460.

Mosher, D. L., and Mosher, J. B. "Guilt in Prisoners." *Journal of Clinical Psychology,* 1966, *23,* 171-173.

Nowlis, V. "Research with the Mood Adjective Check List." In S. S. Tomkins and C. E. Izard (Eds.), *Affect, Cognition and Personality.* New York: Springer, 1965.

Oliver, W. A., and Mosher, D. L. "Psychopathology and Guilt in Heterosexual and Subgroups of Homosexual Reformatory Inmates." *Journal of Abnormal Psychology,* 1968, *73,* 323-329.

Otterbacher, J. R., and Munz, D. C. "State-Trait Measure of Experiential Guilt." *Journal of Consulting and Clinical Psychology,* 1973, *40,* 115-121.

Pagano, M., and Kirschner, N. M. "Sex Guilt, Sexual Arousal, and Urinary Acid Phosphatase Output." *Journal of Research in Personality,* 1978, *12,* 68-75.

Persons, R. W. "The Mosher Guilt Scale: Theoretical Formulation, Research Review and Normative Data." *Journal of Projective Techniques and Personality Assessment,* 1970, *34,* 266-270.

Piers, G., and Singer, M. S. *Shame and Guilt: A Psychoanalytic and Cultural Study.* Springfield, Ill.: Thomas, 1953.

Rapaport, D. "The Structure of Psychoanalyatic Theory: A Systematizing Attempt." In S. Koch (Ed.), *Psychology: A Study of a Science.* Vol. 3. New York: McGraw-Hill, 1959.

Ray, R. E., and Thompson, W. D. "Autonomic Correlates of Female Guilt Responses to Erotic Visual Stimuli." *Psychological Reports,* 1974, *34,* 1299-1306.

Rieff, P. *Freud: The Mind of a Moralist.* New York: Viking Press, 1959.

Rotter, J. B. *Social Learning and Clinical Psychology.* Englewood Cliffs, N.J.: Prentice-Hall, 1954.

Ruma, E. H. "Conscience Development in Delinquents and Non-delinquents: The Relationship Between Moral Judgment, Guilt, and Behavior." Unpublished doctoral dissertation, Ohio State University, 1967.

Ruma, E. H., and Mosher, D. L. "Relationships Between Moral Judgment and Guilt in Delinquent Boys." *Journal of Abnormal Psychology,* 1967, *72,* 122-127.

Schallow, J. R. "Direct and Displaced Aggression, Transgression Compliance, and Liking for One's Victim in High- and Low-Guilt Subjects." Unpublished doctoral dissertation, University of Texas, 1972.

Schill, T. R. "Aggression and Blood Pressure Responses of High and Low Guilt Subjects Following Frustration." *Journal of Consulting and Clinical Psychology,* 1972, *38,* 461.

Schill, T., and Althoff, M. "Drug Experiences, Knowledge, and Attitudes of High and Low Guilt Individuals." *Journal of Consulting and Clinical Psychology,* 1975, *43,* 106-107.

Schill, T., and Chapin, J. "Sex Guilt and Males' Preference for Reading Erotic Magazines." *Journal of Consulting and Clinical Psychology,* 1972, *39,* 516.

Schill, T., Evans, R., and McGovern, T. "Child-Rearing Attitudes of Subjects Varying in Guilt." *Journal of Clinical Psychology,* 1976, *32,* 282-284.

Schill, T., and others. "Defense Preference of High and Low Hostility Guilt Subjects." *Journal of Consulting and Clinical Psychology,* 1976, *44,* 867.

Schill, T., and Schneider, L. "Guilt and Self-Report of Hostility." *Psychological Reports,* 1970a, *27,* 713-714.

Schill, T., and Schneider, L. "Relationships Between Hostility Guilt and Several Measures of Hostility." *Psychological Reports,* 1970b, *27,* 967-970.

Tomkins, S. S. *Affect, Imagery, and Consciousness.* Vol. 1: *The Positive Affects.* New York: Springer, 1962.

Tomkins, S. S. *Affect, Imagery, and Consciousness.* Vol. 2: *The Negative Affects.* New York: Springer, 1963.

Ungerer, J. C., and others. "Sex Guilt and Preference for Illegal Drugs Among Drug Abusers." *Journal of Clinical Psychology,* 1976, *32,* 891-895.

48

Louis H. Janda

Affective Guilt States

Although emotions have always enjoyed a prominent place in theories of psychopathology, there has been little progress toward developing conceptual and operational definitions of various emotions as discrete phenomena. Thus, any definition of affective guilt states must be tentative. With these limitations in mind, affective guilt states may be thought of as episodic emotional states that are characterized by thoughts of having done something wrong and/or a desire to confess or expiate the perceived transgression.

It may be useful to distinguish between guilt as a personality disposition and guilt as an affective state. As a personality disposition, guilt is likely to influence the way in which a variety of situations are perceived or the behavior of high-guilt individuals in conflict situations. Affective guilt states include the emotional responses that are experienced following perceived transgressions of one's moral code. Although the two forms of guilt seem to be conceptually related, the precise nature of the relationship is not at all clear.

Background and Current Status

Freud ([1926] 1936) laid the base for much of the theorizing that has occurred about guilt feelings. According to psychodynamic theory, guilt is one of three types of anxiety, the other two types being reality anxiety and neurotic anxiety. Reality anxiety is a fear of real dangers in the external world, and neurotic anxiety is a fear that instincts will get out of control and cause one to do something for which he will be punished. Guilt, or moral anxiety, is a fear of the conscience. Individuals will experience guilt if they do something, or even think of doing something, that violates their moral code (that is, they are conscience stricken). The concept of moral anxiety includes both behavioral and emotional components.

For the most part, psychodynamic theorists view affective guilt states, or guilt feelings, as a symptom of an underlying causal factor. Thus, guilt feelings may indicate a dominant superego or some other personality construct, but they have received little attention as a potential causal factor in their own right. Consequently, the psychodynamic theorist is interested primarily in the assessment of the underlying personality structure and has relatively little interest in the assessment of emotional states. This is consistent with the trait-oriented nature of psychodynamic theory.

The concept of affective guilt states has received little refinement over the years. Psychodynamic theorists, with their affinity for traits, continue to discuss guilt states as symptoms of underlying conditions. The expanding influence of behavioral approaches has not helped stimulate interest in affective guilt states. While the phenomenologists stress the importance of subjective feelings, they have shown little interest in refining the measurement and conceptualization of emotional states. Consequently, there is little in the clinical literature beyond restatements of Freud's initial speculations regarding moral anxiety.

One exception is the work of psychodynamic theorist Otto Fenichel (1945). He expanded Freud's notion that guilt has its origins in fear of loss of love. Fenichel defined guilt feelings as "a topically defined anxiety, the anxiety of the ego toward the superego" (p. 134). He distinguished between two types of guilt feelings. The first occurs in response to perceived misdeeds ("I have done something wrong"). The second pertains to future events ("I should do this" or "I should not do that"). The first type of guilt feelings could serve as a motive for employing defense mechanisms, in the same manner that anxiety can elicit defense mechanisms. The second type is closely related to feelings of self-esteem. The closer one comes to living up to his or her ego ideal, the greater the level of self-esteem.

O. H. Mowrer (1960, 1961) has presented a learning theory analysis of guilt. He has suggested that guilt feelings develop in the context of the parent-child relationship. As children are repeatedly rewarded for proper behavior and punished for improper behavior, they gradually develop their own standards of right and wrong. Mowrer agrees with the psychodynamic notion that identification with the parent is crucial in developing a sense of guilt. According to this theory, the child must have a close affectionate relationship with the parents if he or she is to internalize the parents' standards, because punishment will then represent loss of love to the child. The use of punishment with children who do not have a close relationship with their parents is likely to lead to feelings of anxiety rather than guilt.

In the past decade, the experimental personality literature reveals a growing interest in the concept of guilt. This interest has been stimulated primarily by Mosher's (1965,

1966) development of a scale to measure three aspects of guilt. Although Mosher was primarily interested in guilt as a behavioral disposition or trait, his work has obvious implications for affective guilt states. Mosher (1965) conceptualizes guilt as a generalized expectancy for self-punishment for the violation of or the anticipation of violating one's internalized standards of proper behavior. Mosher suggests that individuals who score high on his measure of guilt will inhibit certain behaviors because they anticipate feeling guilty (that is, they would experience affective guilt states). Since the publication of Mosher's original research, several theorists have investigated the relation between the behavioral disposition of guilt and affective guilt states (Janda and Magri, 1975; Janda, Magri, and Barnhart, 1977; Mosher and Greenberg, 1969; Schwartz, 1973). In addition, several other studies have had affective guilt states as their primary focus (Izard and Caplan, 1974; Otterbacher and Munz, 1973). Perhaps this line of research will stimulate the interest of the practicing clinical psychologists.

Two relatively recent attempts have been made to construct instruments to access affective guilt states. The first, called the Perceived Guilt Index, was devised by Otterbacher and Munz (1973). Using the psychometric techniques of Thurstone's method of equal-appearing intervals and Osgood's semantic differential, they identified eleven words that reflect affective guilt states. The words vary in a numerical intensity value from innocent to unforgivable. The directions ask the individual to indicate which word best describes how he or she is feeling at that particular moment. One can use the scale as a measure of affective trait guilt by instructing individuals to indicate the word that best describes how they normally feel. Otterbacher and Munz have provided data indicating that their scale is factorially pure and sensitive to changes in guilt feelings and that changes in affective guilt traits are preceded by changes in affective guilt states. Some potential problems with the scale will be discussed later.

The second instrument intended to measure affective guilt states is the Differential Emotions Scale constructed by Izard and his colleagues in relation to his work on fundamental emotions. Izard (1971, 1972, 1977) is interested primarily in theories of emotion, but nonetheless his work has resulted in a scale that is intended to measure ten fundamental emotional states, of which guilt is one. The scale consists of thirty adjectives (three for each emotion), and individuals are asked to indicate how accurately each word describes their feelings on a five-point scale. The adjectives on the guilt subscale are *repentant, guilty,* and *blameworthy.* Several studies (Bartlett and Izard, 1972; Izard and Caplan, 1974; Marshall and Izard, 1972) have supported the construct validity of the scale.

Perhaps the best way of characterizing the current status of affective guilt states is by stating that there is some limited interest in the construct. Until Mosher constructed his guilt inventory, there was little systematic research in regard to this concept.

Critical Discussion

General Areas of Concern

Concerns regarding affective guilt states can be divided into three categories: (1) the validity of the instruments designed to measure the construct, (2) the relation of affective guilt states to dispositional guilt and affective trait guilt, and (3) the role of emotions in general in determining human behavior. Otterbacher and Munz (1973) and Izard (Bartlett and Izard, 1972; Izard and Caplan, 1974; Marshall and Izard, 1972) have provided evidence that the Perceived Guilt Index and the Differential Emotions Scale, respectively, have construct validity. However, the nature of the evidence tends to be limited, and the validity of the scales is far from established. More work needs to be done before the applied behavioral scientist can use these scales with confidence.

With regard to the relation of affective guilt states to other aspects of guilt, Mosher has suggested that individuals high in dispositional guilt are likely to experience affective guilt states in certain situations (Mosher and Greenberg, 1969). Thus, Mosher seems to be suggesting a distinction very similar to that of state-trait anxiety. However, as will be discussed later, the research is inconsistent regarding this view. The issue is further complicated by the distinction made by Otterbacher and Munz (1973) between affective trait guilt and affective state guilt. They argue that affective trait guilt is something different from Mosher's measure of dispositional guilt and that the relation between affective state guilt and affective trait guilt is analogous to the notion of state-trait anxiety. At present, it is not clear how these three concepts are related to each other—or whether they are related at all.

Finally, the controversy regarding the role of emotions in human behavior remains unsettled. The James-Lange position (James, 1884) suggests that emotional states result from behavior, while other theorists (for example, Tomkins, 1970) have suggested that emotions are the primary motivational system. A thorough discussion of this topic is beyond the scope of this chapter, but the issue is of crucial importance to those who practice clinical assessment. Are affective guilt states simply a by-product of behavior, or do they play a role in determining behavior?

As noted earlier, at least three forms of guilt have been suggested in the literature: (1) dispositional guilt, (2) affective trait guilt, and (3) affective state guilt. Mosher (1968, p. 690) has defined dispositional guilt as a "generalized expectancy for self-mediated punishment for violating or anticipating violating internalized standards of proper conduct." He further states that the behavioral referents include resistance to temptation and the suppression and inhibition of sexual and hostile behaviors. Following the commission of a prohibited behavior, guilty individuals could be expected to experience feelings of self-criticism and self-blame and to engage in confession and restitutional behavior. The implication of this view is that the disposition of guilt should be related to affective guilt states. At least two studies support this contention. Mosher and Greenberg (1969) found that college women high in dispositional guilt experienced increased affective guilt states when asked to read an erotic passage from a novel. Also, Janda and Magri (1975) found that college women high in dispositional guilt who were asked to respond to a word association test that contained numerous sexual double entendres were more likely to experience affective guilt states than counterparts low in dispositional guilt. However, at least three studies have failed to find such a relationship (Janda, Magri, and Barnhart, 1977; Janda and O'Grady, 1976; Schwartz, 1973). One of these studies (Schwartz, 1973) involved a factor analysis of several measures of guilt and found that those scales that were concerned with guilt as (1) a personality trait and (2) an emotional state loaded on separate factors. At the very least, Mosher's contention that dispositional guilt is related to affective guilt states is questionable. Perhaps a more fruitful approach would involve determining those specific situations in which individuals high in dispositional guilt are likely to experience affective guilt states. It seems likely that an "either-or" position is oversimplified with regard to this issue.

Support for the notion that guilt as a disposition (as measured by Mosher's scale) and guilt as an affective reaction are independent concepts can be found in two studies (Janda and Magri, 1975; Janda, Magri, and Barnhart, 1977). In three samples of college students, the correlation between Mosher's forced-choice guilt inventory and the Perceived Guilt Index G-Trait Scale was not significantly different from zero. Furthermore,

Janda, Magri, and Barnhart (1977) found that scores on the Perceived Guilt Index G-Trait Scale were related to scores on the G-State Scale while scores on the forced-choice guilt inventory were not. The implication of these findings is obvious. Clinical assessment procedures should include procedures specifically intended to measure guilt as a behavioral disposition and guilt as an affective reaction.

Comparative Philosophies and Theories

Although both psychodynamic and social learning theorists have discussed the concept of affective guilt states, there are no noteworthy philosophical or theoretical differences. The differences that do exist appear to be primarily differences in terminology. Mosher's definition of guilt is essentially a translation of Freud's concepts into social learning terms. Furthermore, some research conducted by social learning theorists supports psychodynamic theory. For example, Sears, Maccoby, and Levin (1957) reported data that strongly supports Freud's notion that identification of the child with the parent is crucial if guilt feelings are to develop. The primary difference between the psychodynamic and social learning viewpoints concerns the effects of guilt. The social learning theorist suggests that guilt feelings have relatively straightforward and specifiable effects (such as increasing helping behavior). The psychodynamic theorist argues that guilt feelings can be expressed in behaviors that bear little relation to the source of conflict (for instance, agoraphobia as a result of sexual guilt).

Other philosophies and theories of guilt include the existential and the RET approach of Albert Ellis. Existential theorist Rollo May (1958) has defined three forms of guilt. These forms result from (1) a forfeiting of potentialities, (2) one's separation from one's fellow man, and (3) one's separation from nature. Ellis (1973) has suggested that guilt feelings have their origins in irrational self talk ("I am a terrible person because I did that"). According to Ellis, the irrational self talk that may result in guilt feelings is unnecessary and can be eliminated with therapy. This view is of interest because it is one of the few theories that suggests that guilt is a totally undesirable reaction. Most theories hold that at least moderate degrees of guilt feelings are part of the normal developmental process and are crucial in the socialization of the individual. Neither the existential nor the rational-emotive approach has made a clear distinction between dispositional guilt and affective guilt states, and consequently neither system has stimulated attempts to systematically assess affective guilt states.

Elaboration on Critical Points

In this section, potential problems of measures of affective guilt states will be discussed. As mentioned earlier, two such measures are the Differential Emotions Scale and the Perceived Guilt Index. Both scales do have some construct validity; however, the available research probably does not justify their use in clinical situations. The studies were conducted almost exclusively with college populations that were not selected for any specific qualities. The scales were constructed to be of use in research dealing with personality theory, and no one has attempted to extend their applicability to clinical populations. The scales are both self-report inventories and thus are likely to be affected by dissimulation and social desirability, but there are no studies that indicate to what extent this problem may exist. This is a particularly crucial issue because affective guilt states are very subjective and transitory experiences, so that any demand characteristics of the situation in which the test is taken would seem likely to influence responses.

A particular problem with the Perceived Guilt Index is that it measures only affective guilt states. Thus, the scale forces the individual to choose a response indicating guilt, even though he may feel some emotion other than guilt (for instance, fear, anxiety, or shame). The Differential Emotions Scale has the advantage of tapping a variety of emotions and consequently reduces the possibility that misleading results will be obtained.

A problem with the Differential Emotions Scale is that there are apparently no studies that support the construct validity of the individual scales measuring discrete emotions. Izard has provided evidence that the individual scales are factorially pure; however, the general approach to establishing the validity of the scale has been to compare profiles of groups exposed to certain situations or groups asked to imagine themselves in various situations. Thus, it has been shown that a group of individuals asked to imagine an "anger" situation will have different profiles from a group asked to imagine a "depression" situation. However, there is little information about the sensitivity of the affective state guilt scale. In fact, in one study in which a difference in guilt scores was specifically predicted between a group of subjects who read an erotic passage and a second group who read an academic passage, a significant difference was not obtained. The usefulness of the guilt subscale on the Differential Emotions Scale thus remains to be demonstrated.

Personal Views and Recommendations

There seem to be three logical conclusions: (1) Affective guilt states do play a role in determining behavior, and they are not simply a by-product of other behaviors. (2) Dispositional guilt, as measured by the Mosher forced-choice guilt inventory, and affective guilt states are relatively independent concepts. (3) Neither the Differential Emotions Scale nor the Perceived Guilt Index is a completely adequate measure of affective guilt states, although the latter may hold more promise.

With regard to the first point, it seems reasonable to assume that affective guilt states can influence a variety of behaviors. Social-psychological research has found that inducing guilt in individuals increases helping behavior (Rawlings, 1970; Regan, Williams, and Sparling, 1972). Wolpe (1973) has suggested that guilt feelings can serve to inhibit certain forms of assertive behavior. Many theorists have suggested that sexual guilt and anxiety can contribute to sexual dysfunctions (Kaplan, 1974; Masters and Johnson, 1970). Although these theorists do not usually distinguish between dispositional guilt and affective guilt states, the research at least suggests that the affective guilt states may be important. Also, the recent interest in broad-spectrum behavior therapy seems to hold promise for utilizing concepts of emotional states. Lazarus (1976) has suggested that it is necessary to assess a number of aspects of functioning, including affect. From the perspective of a social learning theorist, Staats (1975) has suggested that an emotional-motivational system is one of three major constituents of personality (the other two being language-cognitive and instrumental repertoire). Affective guilt states seem to be important in both conceptual systems. Many behavioral techniques are intended to reduce emotional arousal. Although the behavior therapist generally labels the emotional arousal as anxiety, in many cases guilt may, in fact, be the target. Behaviorists are typically reluctant to make fine distinctions between emotional states, and guilt feelings have been called a special form of anxiety (Maher, 1966). It would not be surprising if behavior therapists have been modifying behavior by reducing affective guilt states for some time now, even though they have not specifically discussed this construct.

The therapy approach selected to modify affective guilt states will of course depend on the theoretical approach of the therapist. Psychodynamic therapists will use insight-oriented techniques in an attempt to modify the underlying conflicts that are causing the guilt feelings. Social learning theorists, who tend to view guilt feelings as a form of learned emotional arousal, will prefer behavioral techniques such as desensitization, role playing, and cognitive restructuring. Rational-emotive therapists will attempt to teach their guilty clients to think in more logical and scientific ways. Because the nature of the relationship between dispositional guilt, affective trait guilt, and affective state guilt is unclear at this time, the most prudent approach might be to utilize a variety of therapeutic techniques aimed at various aspects of the clients' functioning. Thus, attempts to increase clients' insight, modify their cognitions and self-references, reduce their emotional arousal, and produce positive behavior changes may all be necessary if enduring changes in guilt-related problems are expected.

The Perceived Guilt Index may be a better measure than the Differential Emotions Scale, primarily because it is less susceptible to dissimulation and social desirability. (Although there is no evidence to support this contention, the DES is completely transparent and requires that subjects be honest and objective reporters of their feelings.) The PGI, which utilizes words that have been scaled with regard to the degree of guilt they denote, seems somewhat less transparent; its major limitation, however, is that it taps only affective guilt states, so that a person who is feeling highly anxious, for example, will appear to be guilty simply because there are no alternative response options. The scale could be greatly improved if it were integrated with similar measures of other emotional states, such as the Subjective Stress Survey (Berkun and others, 1962). It would then be possible to differentiate between affective guilt states and general emotional arousal.

Application to Particular Variables

Because attempts to assess affective guilt states are still in the early stages of research, no conclusions regarding variables such as age and sex can be made at this time. The available research has been done with college students of both sexes; therefore, any conclusions regarding the construct of affective guilt states must be limited to this population.

Because the measurement of affective guilt states is in the research stages, it is premature to discuss the ethical considerations for the applied behavioral scientist or clinician. The primary ethical consideration would concern the use of human subjects for research.

It is also premature to discuss the issue of training and certification, since clinicians are not currently assessing affective guilt states in a systematic way. However, should they begin to do so, it would probably be within the context of a larger intervention program. The very nature of the construct does not lend itself to a discrete assessment procedure. Therefore, those who would be interested in the clinical assessment of affective guilt states undoubtedly would be fully trained clinical psychologists.

References

Bartlett, E. S., and Izard, C. E. "A Dimensional and Discrete Emotions Investigation of the Subjective Experience of Emotion." In C. E. Izard (Ed.), *Patterns of Emotions.* New York: Academic Press, 1972.

Berkun, M. M., and others. "Experimental Studies of Stress in Man." *Psychological Monographs,* 1962, *76,* Whole No. 534.

Ellis, A. "Rational-Emotive Therapy." In R. Corsini (Ed.), *Current Psychotherapies.* Itasca, Ill.: Peacock, 1973.

Fenichel, O. *The Psychoanalytic Theory of Neurosis.* New York: Norton, 1945.

Freud, S. *Inhibitions, Symptoms, and Anxiety* [1926]. London: Hogarth Press, 1936.

Izard, C. E. *The Face of Emotion.* New York: Appleton-Century-Crofts, 1971.

Izard, C. E. (Ed.). *Patterns of Emotions.* New York: Academic Press, 1972.

Izard, C. E. *Human Emotions.* New York: Plenum, 1977.

Izard, C. E., and Caplan, S. "Sex Differences in Emotional Responses to Erotic Literature." *Journal of Consulting and Clinical Psychology,* 1974, *42,* 468.

James, W. "What Is an Emotion?" *Mind,* 1884, *9,* 188-205.

Janda, L. H., and Magri, M. B. "Relation Between Affective and Dispositional Guilt." *Journal of Consulting and Clinical Psychology,* 1975, *43,* 116.

Janda, L. H., Magri, M. B., and Barnhart, S. A. "Affective Guilt States in Women and the Perceived Guilt Index." *Journal of Personality Assessment,* 1977, *41,* 79-84.

Janda, L. H., and O'Grady, K. E. "Effects of Guilt and Response Modality upon Associative Sexual Responses." *Journal of Research in Personality,* 1976, *10,* 457-462.

Kaplan, H. S. *The New Sex Therapy.* New York: Brunner/Mazel, 1974.

Lazarus, A. A. *Multimodal Behavior Therapy.* New York: Springer, 1976.

Maher, B. A. *Principles of Psychopathology.* New York: McGraw-Hill, 1966.

Marshall, A. G., and Izard, C. E. "Depression as a Pattern of Emotions and Feelings: Factor-Analytic Investigations." In C. E. Izard (Ed.), *Patterns of Emotions.* New York: Academic Press, 1972.

Masters, W. H., and Johnson, V. E. *Human Sexual Inadequacy.* Boston: Little, Brown, 1970.

May, R. "The Origins and Significance of the Existential Movement in Psychology." In R. May, E. Angel, and H. F. Ellenberger (Eds.), *Existence: A New Dimension in Psychiatry and Psychology.* New York: Basic Books, 1958.

Mosher, D. L. "Interaction of Fear and Guilt in Inhibiting Unacceptable Behavior." *Journal of Consulting Psychology,* 1965, *29,* 161-167.

Mosher, D. L. "The Development and Multitrait-Multimethod Matrix Analysis of Three Measures of Three Aspects of Guilt." *Journal of Consulting Psychology,* 1966, *30,* 25-29.

Mosher, D. L. "Measurement of Guilt in Females by Self-Report Inventories." *Journal of Consulting and Clinical Psychology,* 1968, *32,* 690-695.

Mosher, D. L., and Greenberg, I. "Females' Affective Responses to Reading Erotic Literature." *Journal of Consulting and Clinical Psychology,* 1969, *33,* 472-477.

Mowrer, O. H. *Learning Theory and Behavior.* New York: Wiley, 1960.

Mowrer, O. H. *The Crisis in Psychiatry and Religion.* New York: Van Nostrand, 1961.

Otterbacher, J. R., and Munz, D. C. "State-Trait Measure of Experiential Guilt." *Journal of Consulting and Clinical Psychology,* 1973, *40,* 115-121.

Rawlings, E. "Reactive Guilt and Anticipatory Guilt in Altruistic Behavior." In J. Macauley and L. Berkowitz (Eds.), *Altruism and Helping Behavior: Social Psychological Studies of Some Antecedents and Consequences.* New York: Academic Press, 1970.

Regan, D., Williams, M., and Sparling, S. "Voluntary Expiation of Guilt: A Field Experiment." *Journal of Personality and Social Psychology,* 1972, *24,* 42-45.

Schwartz, S. "Multimethod Analysis of Three Measures of Six Common Personality Traits." *Journal of Personality Assessment,* 1973, *37,* 559-567.

Sears, R. R., Maccoby, E. E., and Levin, H. *Patterns of Child Rearing.* New York: Harper & Row, 1957.

Staats, A. W. *Social Behaviorism.* Homewood, Ill.: Dorsey Press, 1975.

Tomkins, S. S. "Affect as the Primary Motivational System." In M. B. Arnold (Ed.), *Feelings and Emotions.* New York: Academic Press, 1970.

Wolpe, J. *The Practice of Behavior Therapy.* Elmsford, N.Y.: Pergamon Press, 1973.

49

Irvin Moelis

Symbiosis

The word *symbiosis* is borrowed from biology, where it refers to a close functional association of two organisms to their mutual advantage. The concept of human symbiosis as applied to the early infant-mother relationship refers to a phase of object relationship in which infant and mother constitute a dual unity.

Mahler (1952, 1963, 1968) has written extensively about human symbiosis as a stage in the infant's development and as a restitutive phenomenon in a subclass of the infantile psychoses. According to Mahler (1968), the symbiotic phase of normal development begins in the second or third month of life and extends to the tenth month, reaching a peak in the fourth or fifth month. The symbiotic phase follows the normal autistic phase and precedes the separation-individuation phase of development. Mahler (1968, p. 8) characterizes the symbiotic phase as one "in which the infant behaves and functions as though he and his mother were an omnipotent system—a dual unity within one common boundary." The infant's identity is merged with and largely inseparable from that of the mother. Thus, from an intrapsychic or cognitive point of view, the essential feature of the symbiotic phase is the undifferentiation, or fusion, of the mental representations of self and mother.

Conceptualization of the normal separation-individuation phase and its various subphases emphasizes the gradual differentiation of the child from the mother (Mahler, Pine, and Bergman, 1975). The gradual development of the child's capacity to differen-

622

tiate representation of self from mother, together with increasing autonomy and independence from her, leads to the development of an appropriate body image and a stable sense of self and identity. The separation-individuation phase consists of four subphases: (1) differentiation, (2) practicing, (3) rapprochement, and (4) consolidation of individuality and the beginnings of emotional object constancy. While the major psychological achievements of this phase span the period from the fourth or fifth month of life to the thirtieth or thirty-sixth month, the last subphase is open ended; and, as Angel (1967) and Mahler, Pine, and Bergman (1975) suggest, the process remains active and continues as an undercurrent throughout childhood and adolescence, if not the entire life cycle.

Background and Current Status

Mahler's work on the symbiotic origin of infantile psychosis preceded her formulations on the symbiotic phase of normal development and the separation-individuation process. She first suggested the importance of symbiosis in child psychosis in 1949: With reference to the onset of psychosis in later infancy (second to fifth year), Mahler states, "In view of the increased challenge by and requirements of outside reality and the psychosexual conflict in these years, emotional separation from symbiosis with mother acted as immediate trigger for psychotic withdrawal from reality" (Mahler, Ross, and De Fries, 1949, p. 295*n*). At about the same time, other investigators began to discuss symbiotic phenomena from the point of view of the parent-child relationship (Benedek, 1949; Reichard and Tillman, 1950). However, it was Mahler (1952) who, in the context of differentiating autistic from symbiotic infantile psychosis, first used the concept of symbiosis to describe a phase of object relationship in the infant involving the fusion of mental representations of self and mother.

By 1955 Mahler had advanced the hypothesis of the universality of the phase of normal symbiosis and the notion of an obligatory separation-individuation process in normal development (Mahler and Gosliner, 1955). A strong and adequate phase of normal symbiosis was posited as a prerequisite for entrance to and successful movement through the separation-individuation phase. The intrapsychic process of separation-individuation was viewed as crucial to development of the ego, object relationships, and a stable image of the self. The subphase theory of the normal separation-individuation process was formulated in the early 1960s (Mahler and Furer, 1963) and was followed by an elaboration of the symbiosis theory of human development and a summary of the symbiosis theory of infantile psychosis (Mahler, 1968).

The core disturbance in infantile psychosis centers on serious distortions or absence of the normal symbiotic phase of development and subsequent individuation. In symbiotic infantile psychosis, the mental representation of the mother is not differentiated from the self. Mahler (1968, p. 72) states: "As soon as ego differentiation and psychosexual development confront the child and thus challenge him with a measure of separation from and independence of the mother, the illusion of symbiotic omnipotence is threatened and severe panic reactions occur." These panic reactions are usually seen in the third or fourth year, or at the height of the oedipal conflict, and are followed by restitutive phenomena which create the varied symptomatology and which are attempts to maintain or restore the delusional parent-child symbiotic unity. The symbiotic psychotic child may experience the additional panic of complete dissolution of the sense of identity, which is associated with fear of reengulfment by the symbiotic parent.

The concept of human symbiosis plays a central role in theories of child development (Freud, 1965; Mahler, 1963, 1968; Stoller, 1974). Symbiosis is also viewed as a key concept to the understanding of various psychopathological disorders in children and adults. In addition to Mahler's conceptualization of infantile psychosis, symbiosis is considered an important phenomenon in school phobias (Coolidge, Hahn, and Peck, 1957; Sperling, 1974); and Sperling (1974) stresses the importance of symbiotic ties in children with psychosomatic disorders. Other writers have implicated symbiosis as an important phenomenon in adult psychoses, particularly schizophrenia (Lidz and Lidz, 1952; Lyketsos, 1959; Shapiro, 1972). Symbiosis has also been described as a major factor in the borderline psychotic states (Grinker, Werble, and Drye, 1968) and in disorders involving issues of gender identity in males (Ehrenwald, 1960; Stoller, 1974).

Critical Discussion

General Areas of Concern

In spite of the central role that human symbiosis plays in conceptualizations of child development and child and adult psychopathology, there have been few systematic attempts to measure the concept objectively. Mahler's formulations are based on psychoanalytically derived observations from clinical work with psychotic children and on longitudinal studies of both symbiotic and normal child-mother pairs. By observing behaviors that occurred regularly during the course of the symbiotic and separation-individuation phases, she made hypotheses concerning intrapsychic states. Mahler's efforts are impressive and have resulted in rich understanding of normal and severe psychopathological development in children. However, there is a strong need for objective assessment techniques, which can provide additional validation of the concept of symbiosis.

Recent emphasis on the variations within the normal separation-individuation phase poses even greater challenges to those who would develop objective assessment techniques. On the basis of this more current work, Mahler, Pine, and Bergman (1975, p. 13) state: "We have since learned that there are innumerable degrees and forms of partial failure of the separation-individuation process." There is some support for the notion that degrees or residues of symbiotic attachment and variations in the separation-individuation process may be involved in a range of psychopathological states—including transient disturbances and neurosis, as well as the more severe psychotic disturbances.

In a first attempt to develop an objective index of human symbiosis, Moelis, Wright, and Fisher (1977) constructed and partially validated a Symbiosis Scale based on children's responses to the Rorschach. The Symbiosis Scale offers promising clinical application, and a description of its development is presented to illustrate an attempt at translation of symbiosis theory into an objective assessment technique. In developing the scale, Moelis, Wright, and Fisher conceptualized human symbiosis as a personality trait, relevant to the self-perception of the individual, with origins in Mahler's symbiotic and separation-individuation phases of development. Highly symbiotic children were viewed as those whose sense of self is not highly individuated or differentiated from cognitive representations of significant others. Nonsymbiotic children were those who had developed a view of themselves as distinctly separate from others.

The first step in developing the Symbiosis Scale was to compare the Rorschach protocols of children judged to be from families fostering symbiosis with the protocols of children judged to be from nonsymbiotically oriented families. The comparison suggested four classes of content that seemed to differentiate the groups and also seemed consistent with the investigators' notion of human symbiosis. The four categories are (1) parts of animate or inanimate objects (reflecting perception of an incomplete and poorly integrated self-concept or sense of individual identity), (2) touch or physical contact (reflecting perception of poor or faulty differentiation from others, and perhaps a sense of dependent unity between self and others), (3) death (reflecting anxiety around the separa-tion-individuation process, possibly related to fear of the loss of others and/or perceived threat to the sense of personal identity), (4) orality (reflecting emotional need and de-pendence in relation to others). A scoring system was developed for each category, and the Symbiosis Scale represents the sum of the responses reflecting one or more of the four content areas.

Three validation studies were then conducted. In each, the Rorschach protocols of children from families clinically judged to be symbiotically oriented were compared with the protocols of children from nonsymbiotically oriented families. The first study, em-ploying children with neurotic and personality disorder diagnoses, revealed predicted Symbiosis Scale differences at the p = .01 level of significance. A second study, involving predominantly borderline and psychotic children from a residential and day treatment center, yielded Symbiosis Scale results in the predicted direction but not at an acceptable level of statistical significance. In a third study, employing children similar to those in the first sample, the Symbiosis Scale again differentiated the groups at the p = .01 level of significance.

Impressions gained at the clinical level seem consistent with the notion that de-grees of symbiosis and variations within the separation-individuation phase may be related to different forms and severity of psychopathology in children. It seems noteworthy that a number of parents view and relate to their child as though the child were a continuation or extension of themselves, rather than as a separate individual. As a result, the child remains poorly differentiated from the parent(s) and experiences marked difficulty in establishing a separate and autonomous sense of self and personal identity. These children present at less than a psychotic level of adjustment and evidence difficulties in autono-mous functioning at home, in school, and with peers.

Comparative Philosophies and Theories

Although Mahler considers the defining characteristic of human symbiosis to be an incomplete differentiation of the representations of self from those of others, other investigators (Pollock, 1964; Stierlin, 1959) use the same term to describe a relationship of heightened mutual interdependence. Pollock uses the term *symbiosis* as a general con-cept to include mutual dependent relationships that normally occur at all developmental levels. He discusses a developmental hierarchy of symbiotic relationships and holds that development progresses normally if the particular type of symbiosis is given up at the optimal time.

Behaviors involved in symbiosis and separation-individuation have been studied from viewpoints other than psychoanalysis, as witnessed by the literature dealing with attachment and dependency behavior in children. Maccoby and Masters (1970) report general agreement for including the following as part of the cluster of behaviors con-sidered "dependent": seeking physical contact, seeking to be near, seeking attention, seeking praise and approval, and resisting separation. Bowlby (1969) prefers the term *attachment* and uses it to refer to proximity maintenance behavior. Along with psycho-analytic theory, the major theoretical formulations concerning the origins of attachment and dependency include ethological theory (Bowlby, 1969), social learning theory (Ban-dura and Walters, 1963; Bijou and Baer, 1965; Sears, 1963) and cognitive-developmental theory (Schaffer and Emerson, 1964).

Elaboration on Critical Points

Angel (1967) takes exception to Pollock's generalized use of the term *symbiosis* to describe human relationships involving excessive dependence. Angel thinks that this use of the term obscures the concept of symbiosis and detracts from its clinical utility. He presents adult cases to illustrate the difference between true fixation on an infantile object relationship (which involves the merging of self and object representations as described by Mahler) and pseudosymbiosis (which involves merging fantasies used for defensive purposes and where self and object representations are distinct). He further suggests that there are patients whose adult symbiosis is based on a fixation to the higher-level separation-individuation phase rather than the infantile symbiotic phase. These patients evidence separation anxiety, rather than the more abruptly overwhelming fear of annihilation of the symbiotic phase, and have better-differentiated self and object representations. Angel's case illustration does represent a borderline psychotic condition. Nonetheless, his suggestion is consonant with the general notion that levels or degrees of symbiotic disturbance, within Mahler's framework, may be related to severity of psychopathology.

At the same time, issues of dependency, attachment, and closeness are clearly related to Mahler's concept of symbiosis; and alternative measures of symbiosis are needed which take these related concepts into account. Along this line, D. M. Wright has developed an unpublished dichotomous-item Symbiosis Questionnaire for use with latency-aged children. The two subscales composing the Symbiosis Questionnaire are the Incomplete Differentiation Scale and the Proximity Maintenance Scale. The rationale for these subscales is derived from Mahler's notion of symbiosis. The items of the Incomplete Differentiation Scale focus on the feelings, thoughts, and values which are perceived as shared between child and parents. This subscale is designed to measure the degree to which the child's perception of self remains merged with or undifferentiated from representation of others. The items of the Proximity Maintenance Scale reflect tendencies of the child to seek physical proximity and contact with and to resist separation from parental figures. In Mahler's theory, the ability to maintain physical distance via locomotion is a developmental force fostering the differentiation of self from others. It is assumed that proximity maintenance is strongly associated with, and symbolically representative of, incomplete differentiation of self from others. However, proximity maintenance can also be viewed as part of the cluster of behaviors that Maccoby and Masters (1970) consider "dependent." Thus, the statistical relationship between the two subscales and each subscale's relationship to the Symbiosis Scale (Moelis, Wright, and Fisher, 1977) could provide information about the construct validity and the dimensionality of symbiosis.

Personal Views and Recommendations

Historically, Mahler's concept of symbiosis is linked closely to the area of infantile psychosis. However, the more recent focus on the separation-individuation phase offers the potential for understanding a broader spectrum of psychopathology. In this connection, there is a most pressing need for the development of objective indices of the concept of symbiosis. For the child, techniques are needed to assess disturbance and distortion of the separation-individuation process. For the parents, techniques are needed to assess the attitudes and behaviors that perpetuate strong symbiotic ties with their children. Alternative measures of the concept would allow for the meaningful assessment of the relationship of symbiosis to (1) psychopathology, (2) developmental and familial antecedents, (3) normative and unique separation-individuation experiences, and (4) related notions of dependency and attachment in childhood.

Application to Particular Variables

The separation-individuation process remains active and continues as a developmental undercurrent throughout childhood and adolescence, and into early adult life.

Infancy and adolescence, however, are the two developmental stages during which issues involving separation-individuation are paramount. During adolescence the central issue of separation-individuation reemerges as a normative issue. In addition, the early latency age period is an important one in relation to assessment, since increasing maturation and societal demands prompt the child toward more independent functioning involving greater physical separation from the parents, school entry, and wider contact with peers.

Moelis, Wright, and Fisher (1977) found no significant sex differences in the total Symbiosis Scale scores of their three samples of children. However, some investigators have suggested that there are important sex differences in the process of separation-individuation. Mahler, Pine, and Bergman (1975) view the fourth subphase (the beginnings of emotional object constancy), which occurs in the third year of life, as involving an integration of previous subphase development (as related to individuation and to sexual identity). Moreover, Stoller (1974) suggests that symbiosis anxiety (the fear of merging again with the mother) plays a crucial role in the development of masculinity. This area seems a highly relevant one for the application of assessment techniques.

No information is available about the relationship of symbiosis to educational, socioeconomic, vocational, and ethnic/racial variables or to intellectual and psychiatric-organic disorders. Some information is available concerning the relationship of symbiosis to physical disorders. Two colleagues have demonstrated the association of high Symbiosis Scale scores with adult neurological patients whose chronic lower back pain was rated unimproved following surgery (Blumetti and Modesti, 1975). Sperling (1974) suggests that unresolved symbiotic preoedipal fixations play a central role in psychosomatic disorders in children and adolescents. In addition, assessment of symbiosis would be particularly relevant to children who, because of physical disorders, have been hospitalized and separated from their parents. It is thought that issues involving symbiosis and separation-individuation would play a crucial role in the child's adjustment to hospitalization.

As previously described, symbiosis is viewed as a key concept in the understanding of various psychopathological disorders, including symbiotic psychosis of childhood, schizophrenia in adults, school phobias, and disorders of gender identity in males. Issues involving symbiosis and separation-individuation also may be involved in a broad range of less severe disturbances. Moreover, individual differences in symbiosis in childhood are hypothesized to be related to reactions to unique separation-individuation experiences involving parental death, separation, and divorce. Assessment of such differences would also contribute to appropriate treatment recommendations for children, as in the case of foster home and residential placement.

The area of parent-child interaction warrants most careful attention in the assessment of psychopathological disorders related to symbiosis. Indeed, the parent-child interaction is the defining context for the course of symbiosis and the separation-individuation process.

References

Angel, K. "On Symbiosis and Pseudosymbiosis." *Journal of the American Psychoanalytic Association*, 1967, *15*, 294-316.

Bandura, A., and Walters, R. H. "Aggression." In H. W. Stevenson (Ed.), *Child Psychology*. National Society for the Study of Education Yearbook, Part 1. Chicago: University of Chicago Press, 1963.

Benedek, T. "The Psychosomatic Implications of the Primary Unit: Mother-Child." *American Journal of Orthopsychiatry*, 1949, *19*, 642-654.

Bijou, S. W., and Baer, D. M. *Child Development.* Vol. 2. New York: Appleton-Century-Crofts, 1965.

Blumetti, A. E., and Modesti, L. M. "Psychological Predictors of Success or Failure of Surgical Intervention for Intractable Back Pain." Paper presented at the First World Congress on Pain, Florence, Italy, Sept. 1975.

Bowlby, J. *Attachment and Loss.* Vol. 1: *Attachment.* New York: Basic Books, 1969.

Coolidge, J. C., Hahn, P. B., and Peck, A. "School Phobia: Neurotic Crisis or Way of Life." *American Journal of Orthopsychiatry,* 1957, *27,* 296-306.

Ehrenwald, J. "The Symbiotic Matrix of Paranoid Delusions and the Homosexual Alternative." *American Journal of Psychoanalysis,* 1960, *20,* 49-65.

Freud, A. *Normality and Pathology in Childhood: Assessments of Development.* New York: International Universities Press, 1965.

Grinker, R. R., Werble, B., and Drye, R. C. *The Borderline Syndrome: A Behavioral Study of Ego Functions.* New York: Basic Books, 1968.

Lidz, R. W., and Lidz, T. "Therapeutic Considerations Arising from the Intense Symbiotic Needs of Schizophrenic Patients." In E. B. Brody and F. C. Redlich (Eds.), *Psychotherapy with Schizophrenics.* New York: International Universities Press, 1952.

Lyketsos, G. C. "On the Formation of Mother-Daughter Symbiotic Relationship Patterns in Schizophrenia." *Psychiatry,* 1959, *22,* 161-166.

Maccoby, E. E., and Masters, J. C. "Attachment and Dependency." In P. H. Mussen (Ed.), *Carmichael's Manual of Child Psychology.* Vol. 2. New York: Wiley, 1970.

Mahler, M. S. "On Child Psychosis and Schizophrenia: Autistic and Symbiotic Infantile Psychosis." *Psychoanalytic Study of the Child,* 1952, *7,* 286-305.

Mahler, M. S. "Thoughts About Development and Individuation." *Psychoanalytic Study of the Child,* 1963, *18,* 307-324.

Mahler, M. S. *On Human Symbiosis and the Vicissitudes of Individuation.* Vol. 1: *Infantile Psychosis.* New York: International Universities Press, 1968.

Mahler, M. S., and Furer, M. "Description of the Subphases: History of the Separation-Individuation Study." Paper presented at meeting of American Psychoanalytic Association, St. Louis, May 1963.

Mahler, M. S., and Gosliner, B. J. "On Symbiotic Child Psychosis: Genetic, Dynamic and Restitutive Aspects." *Psychoanalytic Study of the Child,* 1955, *10,* 195-212.

Mahler, M. S., Pine, F., and Bergman, A. *The Psychological Birth of the Human Infant: Symbiosis and Individuation.* New York: Basic Books, 1975.

Mahler, M. S., Ross, J. R., Jr., and De Fries, Z. "Clinical Studies in Benign and Malignant Cases of Childhood Psychosis (Schizophrenia-Like)." *American Journal of Orthopsychiatry,* 1949, *19,* 295-305.

Moelis, I., Wright, D. M., and Fisher, S. "The Symbiosis Scale: Inkblot Responses of Children from Symbiotically and Nonsymbiotically Oriented Families." *Journal of Personality Assessment,* 1977, *41,* 238-247.

Pollock, G. H. "On Symbiosis and Symbiotic Neurosis." *International Journal of Psychoanalysis,* 1964, *45,* 1-30.

Reichard, S., and Tillman, C. "Patterns of Parent-Child Relationships in Schizophrenia." *Psychiatry,* 1950, *13,* 247-257.

Schaffer, H. R., and Emerson, P. E. "The Development of Social Attachments in Infancy." *Monographs of the Society for Research in Child Development,* 1964, *29* (3), 1-77.

Sears, R. R. "Dependency Motivation." In M. Jones (Ed.), *Nebraska Symposium on Motivation.* Lincoln: University of Nebraska Press, 1963.

Shapiro, D. A. "Symbiosis in Adulthood." *American Journal of Psychiatry*, 1972, *129*, 289-292.

Sperling, M. *The Major Neuroses and Behavior Disorders in Children*. New York: Aronson, 1974.

Stierlin, H. "The Adaptation to the 'Stronger' Person's Reality: Some Aspects of the Symbiotic Relationship of the Schizophrenic." *Psychiatry*, 1959, *22*, 143-152.

Stoller, R. J. "Symbiosis Anxiety and the Development of Masculinity." *Archives of General Psychiatry*, 1974, *30*, 164-172.

50

▦▦▦▦▦▦▦▦▦▦▦▦▦▦▦▦▦▦▦▦▦▦▦▦

George J. Huba

Daydreaming

▦▦▦▦▦▦▦▦▦▦▦▦▦▦▦▦▦▦▦▦▦▦▦▦▦▦

Ongoing thought—or waking consciousness, with its constantly fluctuating content and intensity—is probably best described by William James's phrase *stream of consciousness*. Within the stream of consciousness, it is possible to distinguish among (1) various sensory and perceptual experiences (such as feelings of unease and imagery in the various modalities), (2) emotional reactions to the content of the stream of consciousness, (3) structured sequences of content with some likelihood of occurrence (daydreams), and (4) sequences of content (not necessarily highly structured) that have a very low probability of actually happening (fantasy).

While it is quite possible to distinguish between aspects of the stream of consciousness (and laypeople seem to do so, although perhaps not using very consistent definitions), it appears that it is difficult to assume that any single molar chunk of the stream of consciousness is representative of the experience of imagery to the exclusion of daydreaming and fantasy, or daydreaming to the exclusion of imagery and fantasy, and so on. For instance, Singer's (1966) recurring adolescent daydream (or fantasy) of Poppy

Note: Preparation of this chapter was partially supported by Grant Number DA01070 from the National Institute on Drug Abuse and by Grant Number BN5 7601261 from the National Science Foundation. The final version of the chapter benefited from discussions with Arzelia P. Walker and Seymour Feshbach.

Ott, football hero, illustrates several issues implicit in the study of the stream of consciousness: "Initially [the daydreams] took the form of actual running and jumping and simulating in detail the events of a full game in which I tackled myself, caught my own passes, and generally enjoyed an active motor participation. Soon I found myself making up my own league. . . . He left Tutter to play professional football and, after some well-documented setbacks, emerged as the greatest football player of all time on a Boston professional team of my own creation" (p. 19).

As Singer's daydream shows, any given inner experience will probably include one or more forms of imagery (for instance, the visualization of Poppy Ott in a football uniform throwing the winning touchdown, voices of the crowd cheering the hero, and sensations of speed while running down the field), highly structured components fairly representative of external reality (the rules of football or a successful adolescent football player advancing to the professional league), and elements that are unlikely to occur in external reality (the same character throwing the football, catching the pass, and then tackling himself). Accordingly, the assessment of inner experience must be multidimensional and it seems critical to classify an event in the inner life of one individual using several descriptors, and to classify the typical inner life of the same individual in terms of the same elemental structures.

Background and Current Status

As Singer (1966) notes, the evidence for and recognition of daydreaming has existed since antiquity. Early accounts of daydreaming (for example, Plato's description of Socrates as frequently lost in thought and oblivious to events happening around him) abound. Similarly, in the visual art of man we find fantastic beasts, views of afterlife, and improbable sexual events recorded in many different cultures before their literate stages. Furthermore, much of the great art of our day (in its various forms such as music, visual art, and literature) undoubtedly existed in the mind of the creator before it was committed to a form suitable for sharing.

During the earliest period of academic psychology, both the introspectionists (Galton, 1883; James, 1890) and the psychoanalytic theorists (Freud, 1900) addressed the topic of inner experience. Early attempts to study inner experience focused on such topics as imagery (Betts, 1909), content (Schaffer, 1936), and the symbolism of spontaneous nondirected thought as expressing drive (Green, 1923). Despite various objections that the study of inner experience is not "objective" and "scientific" (Watson, 1913, 1924), progress was made during the period of behaviorism by a variety of workers who studied the imaginary play of children (Isaacs, 1933; Sherman, 1934), as well as the cognitive phenomena of visual and auditory imagery (Perky, 1910).

During the behaviorist period of psychology, several antibehaviorism trends led to the use of fantasy-based percepts (Rorschach, 1949) and fantasy stories (Murray, 1938) to assess motives and thinking styles. Both traditions have continued, and numerous empirical assessment applications of both approaches exist. For example, extensive tabulations of fantasy percept responses to the Rorschach inkblots have been compiled (for example, by Rapaport, Gill, and Schafer, 1968), and Murray's Thematic Apperception Test (TAT) has been used to study such motives as aggression (Feshbach, 1955), achievement (Atkinson, 1957; McClelland and others, 1972), and power (McClelland, 1975).

A major trend in psychology originated with the emergence of the study of cognition and information-processing models (Neisser, 1967; Newell and Simon, 1972). This general trend toward a model of man as an active processor of information was echoed in the study of consciousness by the major theoretical contributions of Tomkins (1962, 1963). Working within this information-processing viewpoint, Singer (1966, 1974a, 1974b, 1974c, 1975a, 1975b) developed an important model of inner experience as forming a general backdrop to the processing of information contained in external stimuli; and he has written extensively on the adaptive, as well as the disruptive, functions of daydreaming and fantasy. Singer's current conception of inner experience relies heavily on the notion of parallel processing of information (see Neisser, 1967). He argues that information from the ongoing stream of consciousness is combined with information about external stimuli as the individual attempts to make adaptive responses to her or his world. Singer's theoretical conceptions have been incorporated into an extensive questionnaire measure of daydreaming and fantasy processes (Singer and Antrobus, 1963, 1970, 1972; Huba, Segal, and Singer, 1977), which has been used in a systematic research program to assess inner experience in conjunction with other psychological processes (Singer, 1974a, 1975a, 1975b; Starker and Singer, 1975).

Critical Discussion

General Areas of Concern

The assessment of inner experience at an organismic level must be exactly that—a total assessment of the typical inner experience of the individual. Since only the products of inner experience can be observed, one must either infer inner experience from behavior or directly question the individual about his or her inner life. Accordingly, all assessments of inner life must be considered highly subject to measurement error. When one is inferring inner experience, error can creep into the assessment through both inferential slippage and rater error while self-reports of inner experience may contain such sources of error as response styles and systematic self-presentation artifacts (see Wiggins, 1973, for a discussion of problems with assessment procedures).

In the assessment of the stream of consciousness, it seems necessary to consider several distinct domains concomitantly. A necessary list to characterize the inner life of an individual would appear to be: (1) predisposing tendencies conducive to a structured inner experience such as visual imagery, imagery in other modes (auditory, olfactory, and so on), control over imagery, and abilities such as spatial manipulation and verbal reproduction; (2) the individual's typical style of thinking be it impulsive or controlled, preanalytical or analytical, simple or elaborate; (3) the content of spontaneous thought, on the average, in the major categories of self-oriented, other-oriented, or inanimate object-oriented; (4) the extent to which the inner life usually has content that is likely or unlikely to happen; and (5) the emotional states manifested in the spontaneous thought, the emotions caused by various thoughts and their strength, the emotional context of the spontaneous thought, and whether or not various inner experiences are generated to cope with various emotional states. Such a multivariate assessment is, of necessity, long and involved, but it seems probable that only through such detailed study can a person be adequately classified.

Comparative Philosophies and Theories

At the present time, the only multidimensional and relatively complete method of assessing daydreaming tendencies is the Imaginal Processes Inventory (IPI) developed by Singer and Antrobus (1963, 1970, 1972). The twenty-eight self-report IPI scales sample broadly from the interlocking domains of style of thinking (for example, tendency to become bored, distractibility, use of visual and auditory imagery), attitudes toward daydreaming (absorption in daydreaming, acceptance of daydreaming as a "normal" adult activity), and the content of spontaneous thought (guilt daydreams, hostile daydreams, curiosity about the lives of other people and the nature of mechanical devices). All but one of the twenty-eight IPI scales consist of twelve items answered in a Likert format; the Absorption in Daydreaming Scale has twenty items. To control for the acquiescence response style (Wiggins, 1973), approximately half of the items within each scale are keyed in one direction. The IPI scales have respectable levels of internal consistency (see Singer and Antrobus, 1972, for item and scale statistics), and Oakland (1968) has demonstrated that the item pool from which the IPI was drawn is relatively free of correlation with a social desirability measure.

Elaboration on Critical Points

Inspection of the three hundred forty-four items in the total Imaginal Processes Inventory indicates that almost all the content scales ask questions about how often the individual thinks about some reality-based situation. For instance, the Sexual Daydreams Scale includes items such as the following (paraphrased because of the copyright): "At work, my mind goes to thoughts about sex." "Whenever I am bored, I daydream about a person of the opposite sex." "In my fantasies, I am highly desired by someone I admire." The Heroic Daydreams Scale includes items such as "I think about myself stopping a plot to kill a politician." "I daydream about saving a loved one who is trapped in a fire." Consequently, the Imaginal Processes Inventory has the necessary face validity for it to be considered a measure of daydreaming rather than of inner experiences with low likelihood of external referents (fantasies).

Several studies (Giambra, 1974, 1977; Huba, Segal, and Singer, 1977; Isaacs, 1975; Singer and Antrobus, 1963, 1972; Starker, 1974; Starker and Singer, 1975) have identified at least three *second-order* factors underlying the twenty-eight IPI scales, and the most complete study of the primary factors of the IPI (Huba, Segal, and Singer, 1977) shows that there are seven interpretable primary factors and one additional (possibly residual) primary factor. The eight primary factors are substantially correlated and consequently necessitate the second-order factoring to yield a complete taxonomy of the aspects of inner experience sampled by the IPI. Following the terminology suggested by Huba, Segal, and Singer, the *second-order factors* may be called Positive-Constructive Daydreaming, Guilt and Fear of Failure Orientation in Daydreaming, and Attentional Control. The six (out of eight) primary factors shown to be stable across sexes (see Huba, Segal, and Singer, 1977) are Guilty-Dysphoric Daydreaming, Vividness of Self-Reported Imagery, Mindwandering-Distractible Style, Planfulness, Intense Positive Mental Involvement, and Success Orientation in Daydreaming. The Planfulness, Vividness, and Intense Mental Involvement primary factors are partially determined by the Positive-Constructive Daydreaming second-order factor; the Success Orientation, Guilty-Dysphoric, and Vividness primaries are partially subsumed by the Guilt and Fear of Failure Orientation secondary factor; the Mindwandering-Distractible Style and Intense Mental Involvement primary factors are partially determined by the Attentional Control second-order factor. Support for the meaning of the factors has come from a series of thought-sampling studies (Isaacs, 1975; Singer, 1974a).

Personal Views and Recommendations

Any instrument that attempts to assess unobservable psychological processes can be validated only indirectly. From a detailed inspection of the items that comprise it, the Imaginal Processes Inventory seems to possess face validity. One source of indirect validation for this means of measuring inner experience is the replication of the inner structure of the instrument, demonstrated in the factor analytic studies cited above. The results show that there is a fairly stable factor pattern across different types of samples, and the study by Huba, Segal, and Singer (1977) shows direct replication, using confirmatory rotations, of the factor pattern in males and females as well as different types of college drug users. Furthermore, the replicated factor pattern seems consistent with the theoretical expectations of Singer (1966, 1975a, 1975b). Indirect validation is also provided by the thought-sampling studies discussed by Isaacs (1975) and Singer (1974a). It has been shown that the IPI scales, with their measurement of *general tendencies*, are correlated with individuals' reports of their thoughts during different laboratory tasks. While additional sources of data are necessary to fully support claims for validity, current data converge to support, at least moderately, the contention that the instrument measures the domain properly.

Because of the total length of the IPI (344 items), it would be helpful to have a shortened form for current research studies. At the present time, a short form is not available (but is under development). Researchers who wish to use relatively pure markers for the three second-order factors (which is a reasonable research strategy given the number of primary factors) should use (1) the Visual Imagery and Auditory Imagery Scales as markers of the Positive-Constructive Daydreaming tendency, (2) the Hostile Daydreams and Guilt Daydreams Scales as markers of the Guilt and Fear of Failure Orientation, and (3) the Mindwandering and Distractibility Scales as markers of the Attentional Control factor (see Huba, Segal, and Singer, 1977, table 1). The use of such standardized markers should allow for the direct comparison of findings if the ensuing results are rotated to some comparable position by means of currently available methodologies (see Browne, 1972; Huba, 1975; Jöreskog, 1969).

While the questionnaire of Singer and Antrobus (1972) remains the primary method of assessing daydreams and structured fantasies, alternate procedures have been developed in both the laboratory and the clinic. Within the context of traditional psychoanalysis, Reyher (1963; Reyher and Smeltzer, 1968) has individuals generate imagery, which is then evaluated for motivation and affect. A second clinical approach, more therapeutic than assessment oriented, is the guided affective imagery procedure of Leuner (1969). Leuner uses ten formal settings for guided imagery; the situations encompass many possible variants of imagery, daydreaming, and fantasy. Various coding systems for rating images in projective techniques (Singer, 1968) or recalled dreams and fantasies (Foulkes, 1966; Hall and Lind, 1970) would certainly be applicable after the guided affective imagery experiences in the Leuner or Reyher procedures were tape-recorded. Such possible assessments will, however, be ipsative rather than normative and may have greater utility than standardized assessment within clinical settings. The potential user of rating systems should, however, be aware of (1) the necessity for standardized reliable (across-judges) codings, (2) the need for simultaneous ratings on many of the dimensions discussed earlier, and (3) the possibility that judges will impose their own naive or implicit theories (see Wiggins, 1973) of inner experience on the recorded material.

The assessment of the most private aspects of one's self—those experiences that cannot be directly observed by others—is probably best done through anonymous questionnaires in large research studies. In those cases where anonymity is precluded by the goals of the assessment, the investigators must be aware that most individuals have no expectations about the frequency with which other individuals daydream of sex or revenge or heroism and may experience great anxiety and embarrassment about disclosing these private aspects of themselves. Further, it should be noted that the Imaginal

Processes Inventory is a research, rather than a diagnostic, instrument and that there are no appropriate validity or normative studies to support its use for screening or for individual classification. While daydreaming tendencies appear to be systematically related to personality (Giambra, 1977; Segal, Huba, and Singer, 1980; Singer and Antrobus, 1972), there are no data to suggest how one can best combine information about daydreaming tendencies with personality information to develop effective taxonomies of individuals.

Application to Particular Variables

Unless specifically noted otherwise, the following applications, warnings, and comments pertain to the Imaginal Processes Inventory.

While the IPI has been applied primarily to young adult and adolescent groups, Giambra (1974, 1977) has used the IPI in male groups ranging in age from adolescence to the late 60s. Inspection of the IPI items indicates that the various scales would be inappropriately worded for individuals younger than high school age. The TAT scoring systems have been applied to children as young as elementary school age. An alternate procedure for assessing the inner experience of children may be found in Singer's (1974b, pp. 59, 86, 138) discussion of make-believe processes in children.

Mean differences are found between the sexes in various daydreaming tendencies (Segal, Huba, and Singer, 1980), but the factor patterns in the groups are the same. Consequently, the instrument may be used with both sexes. It should be noted that the Sexual Daydreams Scale of the IPI is primarily concerned with heterosexual sex daydreams and is probably inappropriate for homosexual groups.

While the IPI items are not oriented at a target population, the level of language used in the various questions seems most appropriate for a college-educated sample. The item content should be inspected carefully by researchers wishing to use one or more scales with samples who have not had some college training. The IPI does not contain any obvious biases toward a particular socioeconomic level; however, the same warning about the language applied to educational level also applies to the use of IPI scales with lower socioeconomic groups.

The IPI item content is not particularly appropriate to any particular vocational groups, although, to the extent that educational and socioeconomic levels are confounded with vocation, the researcher should heed the warning about the level of the language. The developers of the test do not consider the IPI appropriate for vocational testing (see the warning issued by Singer and Antrobus, 1970, on the second page of the test manual).

Test items on the IPI do not appear to be biased toward events that would be disproportionately experienced by members of different ethnic or racial groups, although the items should be carefully inspected before they are used with minority groups. Singer (1966) summarizes the differences obtained between different racial and ethnic groups on an earlier form of the daydreaming questionnaire.

Knowledge about the relationship of the IPI to psychopathology is drawn primarily from the small study conducted by Starker and Singer (1975). The fantasy perceptions given to the Rorschach are well cataloged (Rapaport, Gill, and Schafer, 1968), and a discussion of these relationships is beyond the scope of the discussion here. Within the range of "normal" personality, the commonalities between daydreaming tendencies and Murray needs (Segal and Singer, 1976; Segal, Huba, and Singer, 1980) and Guilford-Zimmerman temperaments (Giambra, 1977; Singer and Antrobus, 1972) have been documented, with the general conclusion drawn that there is not a large amount of correlation between the domains of personality and daydreaming (Singer and Singer, 1972).

No studies have attempted to link the IPI to physical disorders. Individuals with certain physical disorders may compensate by frequent and vivid daydreams of physical activity, but this hypothesis has not been tested. Possible links of daydreaming tendencies to sexual dysfunction may be inferred from studies of the IPI and male masturbation fantasies (Campagna, 1975) and female intercourse fantasies (Hariton and Singer, 1974).

Singer (1966) reports that in fairly well-educated, intelligent groups there is a minimal correlation between daydreaming frequency and objective measures of intelligence. The current version of the IPI, however, requires at least a moderate facility with standard English, and the wording does not seem to be appropriate for use with individuals with limited verbal skills or ability.

In their study of 113 unselected males at a Veterans Administration hospital, Starker and Singer (1975) report that alcoholism and organic syndrome ratings form a separate factor from markers of the IPI second-order factors. Among the other findings reported by Starker and Singer is that individuals high in depressed affect have significantly fewer positive reactions to daydreams than do individuals with low levels of depressed affect. Surprisingly, the dysphoric individuals also had significantly fewer guilt daydreams. There was a small loading for depressed affect on a factor with large positive loadings for the scales measuring distractibility, fear of failure orientation, mind-wandering tendency, guilt daydreams, and visual imagery. Other measures found by Starker and Singer to be essentially unrelated to the six daydreaming scales include obsessionality, delusions, bizarre behaviors, compulsion, anxiety, drug dependency, impulsiveness, relatedness, visual and auditory hallucinations, and a family history of psychosis. While it was possible, then, to establish a tentative link between depressed affect and daydreaming, the investigators conclude that "There is apparently no evidence that patients with different degrees of psychotic tendency within a psychiatric sample differ to any marked degree in the occurrence of the various styles of daydreaming measured in this investigation" (Starker and Singer, 1975, p. 568).

The Starker and Singer study does not indicate that various indicators of collective or interactional problems are strongly related to daydreaming. Within college samples, Segal, Huba, and Singer [in press(a), in press(b)], have shown that daydreaming scales are not strong predictors of student use or abuse of alcohol and other drugs, but there are strong correlations between daydreaming tendencies and the reasons that students use drugs, particularly alcohol. For example, Segal, Huba, and Singer [in press(b), 1980] present results indicating a close link between the use of alcohol to self-medicate negative affective states and more enduring patterns of inner experience. Additional results by the same authors show that marijuana and other drug use are also related to daydreaming variables. This set of analyses then demonstrates that different types of inner experience will differentially predispose individuals toward using substances in order to cope.

References

Atkinson, J. W. "Motivational Determinants of Risk Taking Behavior." *Psychological Review,* 1957, *64,* 359-372.
Betts, G. H. *The Distribution and Functions of Mental Imagery.* New York: Teachers College Press, Columbia University, 1909.
Browne, M. W. "Oblique Rotation to a Partially Specified Target." *British Journal of Mathematical and Statistical Psychology,* 1972, *25,* 207-212.
Campagna, A. "Masturbation Fantasies in Male College Freshmen." Unpublished doctoral dissertation, Yale University, 1975.

Feshbach, S. "The Drive-Reducing Function of Fantasy Behavior." *Journal of Abnormal and Social Psychology,* 1955, *50,* 3-11.

Foulkes, D. *The Psychology of Sleep.* New York: Scribner's, 1966.

Freud, S. *The Interpretation of Dreams.* In *Standard Edition of the Complete Psychological Works of Sigmund Freud.* Vols. 4 and 5. London: Hogarth Press, 1962. (Originally published 1900.)

Galton, F. *Inquiries into the Human Faculty.* London: Macmillan, 1883.

Giambra, L. M. "Daydreaming Across the Life Span: Late Adolescent to Senior Citizen." *Aging and Human Development,* 1974, *5,* 118-235.

Giambra, L. M. "A Factor Analytic Study of Daydreaming, Imaginal Process, and Temperament: A Replication on an Adult Male Life-Span Sample." *Journal of Gerontology,* 1977, *32,* 675-680.

Green, G. H. *The Daydream: A Study in Development.* London: University of London Press, 1923.

Hall, C. S., and Lind, R. E. *Dreams, Life, and Literature: A Study of Franz Kafka.* Chapel Hill: University of North Carolina Press, 1970.

Hariton, E. B., and Singer, J. L. "Women's Fantasies During Sexual Intercourse." *Journal of Consulting and Clinical Psychology,* 1974, *42,* 313-322.

Huba, G. J. "A Computer Program for Restricted Oblique Procrustes Rotation to a Primary Factor Pattern Matrix." *Behavior Research Methods and Instrumentation,* 1975, *7,* 568.

Huba, G. J., Segal, B., and Singer, J. L. "Consistency of Daydreaming Styles Across Samples of College Male and Female Drug and Alcohol Users." *Journal of Abnormal Psychology,* 1977, *86,* 99-102.

Isaacs, D. "Cognitive Style in Daydreaming." Unpublished doctoral dissertation, City University of New York, 1975.

Isaacs, S. *Social Development in Young Children.* New York: Harcourt Brace, 1933.

James, W. *The Principles of Psychology.* New York: Dover, 1950. (Originally published 1890.)

Jöreskog, K. G. "A General Approach to Confirmatory Maximum Likelihood Factor Analysis." *Psychometrika,* 1969, *34,* 183-202.

Leuner, H. "Guided Affective Imagery (GAI): A Method of Intensive Psychotherapy." *American Journal of Psychotherapy,* 1969, *23,* 4-22.

McClelland, D. C. *Power: The Inner Experience.* New York: Irvington, 1975.

McClelland, D. C., and others. *The Drinking Man.* New York: Free Press, 1972.

Murray, H. A. *Explorations in Personality.* New York: Wiley, 1938.

Neisser, U. *Cognitive Psychology.* New York: Appleton-Century-Crofts, 1967.

Newell, A., and Simon, H. A. *Human Problem Solving.* Englewood Cliffs, N.J.: Prentice-Hall, 1972.

Oakland, J. A. "Note on the Social Desirability Response Set in Singer's Daydreaming Questionnaire." *Psychological Reports,* 1968, *23,* 689-690.

Paivio, A. *Imagery and Verbal Processes.* New York: Holt, Rinehart and Winston, 1971.

Perky, C. W. "An Experimental Study of Imagination." *American Journal of Psychology,* 1910, *21,* 422-452.

Rapaport, D., Gill, M. M., and Schafer, R. *Diagnostic Psychological Testing.* (Rev. ed.) New York: International Universities Press, 1968.

Reyher, J. "Free Imagery: An Uncovering Procedure." *Journal of Clinical Psychology,* 1963, *19,* 454-459.

Reyher, J., and Smeltzer, W. "The Uncovering Properties of Visual Imagery and Verbal

Association: A Comparative Study." *Journal of Abnormal Psychology*, 1968, *73*, 218-222.

Rorschach, H. *Psychodiagnostics*. New York: Grune and Stratton, 1949.

Schaffer, L. F. *The Psychology of Adjustment*. Boston: Houghton Mifflin, 1936.

Segal, B., and Singer, J. L. "Daydreaming, Drug and Alcohol Use in College Students: A Factor Analytic Study." *Addictive Behaviors*, 1976, *1*, 227-235.

Segal, B., Huba, G. J., and Singer, J. L. *Drugs, Daydreaming, and Personality: A Study of College Youth*. Potomac, Md.: Erlbaum, 1980.

Segal, B., Huba, G. J., and Singer, J. L. "The Prediction of College Drug and Alcohol Use from Personality and Daydreaming Tendencies." *International Journal of the Addictions*, in press(a).

Segal, B., Huba, G. J., and Singer, J. L. "Reasons for Drug and Alcohol Use by College Students." *International Journal of the Addictions*, in press(b).

Sherman, M. *Mental Hygiene and Education*. New York: Longmans, 1934.

Singer, J. L. *Daydreaming: An Introduction to the Experimental Study of Inner Experience*. New York: Random House, 1966.

Singer, J. L. "Aggression Arousal, Hostile Humor, Catharsis." *Journal of Personality and Social Psychology*, 1968 (Supp.), *8*, 1-4.

Singer, J. L. "Daydreaming and the Stream of Thought." *American Scientist*, 1974a, *2*, 417-425.

Singer, J. L. *The Child's World of Make Believe*. New York: Academic Press, 1974b.

Singer, J. L. *Imagery and Daydream Methods in Psychotherapy and Behavior Modification*. New York: Academic Press, 1974c.

Singer, J. L. *The Inner World of Daydreaming*. New York: Harper & Row, 1975a.

Singer, J. L. "Navigating the Stream of Consciousness: Research in Daydreaming and Related Inner Experience." *American Psychologist*, 1975b, *30*, 727-739.

Singer, J. L., and Antrobus, J. S. "A Factor-Analytic Study of Daydreaming and Conceptually Related Cognitive and Personality Variables." *Perceptual and Motor Skills*, 1963, *17*, 187-209.

Singer, J. L., and Antrobus, J. S. *Manual for the Imaginal Processes Inventory*. Princeton, N.J.: Educational Testing Service, 1970.

Singer, J. L., and Antrobus, J. S. "Daydreaming, Imaginal Processes, and Personality: A Normative Study." In P. Sheehan (Ed.), *The Function and Nature of Imagery*. New York: Academic Press, 1972.

Singer, J. L., and Singer, D. G. "Personality." *Annual Review of Psychology*, 1972, *23*, 375-412.

Starker, S. "Daydreaming Styles and Nocturnal Dreaming." *Journal of Abnormal Psychology*, 1974, *83*, 52-55.

Starker, S., and Singer, J. L. "Daydreaming and Symptom Patterns of Psychiatric Patients." *Journal of Abnormal Psychology*, 1975, *84*, 567-570.

Tomkins, S. S. *Affect, Imagery, and Consciousness*. Vol. 1: *The Positive Affects*. New York: Springer, 1962.

Tomkins, S. S. *Affect, Imagery, and Consciousness*. Vol. 2: *The Negative Affects*. New York: Springer, 1963.

Watson, J. B. "Psychology as the Behaviorist Views It." *Psychological Review*, 1913, *20*, 158-177.

Watson, J. B. *Behaviorism*. Chicago: University of Chicago Press, 1924.

Wiggins, J. W. *Personality and Prediction: Principles of Personality Assessment*. Reading, Mass.: Addison-Wesley, 1973.

51

Jay Kuten

Psychosexual Development

The notion of psychosexual development (an all-encompassing term that describes the simultaneous and interrelated unfolding of human sexuality and the elements of personality) provides a useful theoretical framework for viewing and understanding aberrant sexual and interpersonal behavior and, perhaps more important, expectable, adaptive behavior (often called "normal behavior"). It deals essentially with stages in growth of the ego, the intrapsychic agency responsible for organizing experience and for coping with the inner world of the unconscious and the outer world. This growth takes place around the central core of sexual maturation throughout the life cycle.

Originally, the ego is narcissistic and pleasure bound, derives pleasure from the self, gives pleasure to the self, and is preoccupied with the self. Eventually, the ego becomes the complex constellation of organizing functions of adult experience (the analytic, integrative, and synthetic functions, to name but a few). Originally without limits, it gradually develops boundaries that are ideally flexible enough to absorb experience (directly as perceptions or indirectly in the form of object relations) but strong enough to maintain the integrity of the individual, even in the face of life stresses.

Sexuality forms the central core of this development. The sexuality of infancy is global and diffuse and, by definition, involves the pleasure of all bodily activities. By definition, too, the infantile ego is almost totally involved with this sexuality, at least at the earliest stage of its growth. As growth proceeds, the various stages of ego development are named in accordance with the center of sexual interest and intensity. While the names of the various stages of psychosexual development bear a significant relationship to the neurophysiological organization and the primacy of specific regions at each given time, the names *oral, anal, phallic,* and *genital,* as applied to ego developmental stages, also have a metaphorical importance, describing the total relationship of the child with his universe and body and those who care for him.

Background and Current Status

Critical to a grasp of the insights involved in the notion of psychosexual develop- ment is a comprehension of Freud's (1905) postulation concerning the sexuality of in- fancy. Certainly Freud did not mean to imply that infantile sexuality has either the same intention ("aim") or means of expression as adult sexuality. This is the most common (and seemingly the most serious) misreading of Freud. It implies that children are nothing more than smaller-scale versions of adults; that their sex lives are genitally centered, like those of adults (but displaced and played out at some bizarre symbolic level with the oral or anal apparatus). This rendering reads Freud backward, from the observation of the adult sexual experience to that of the infant. To begin correctly with the infant, one must begin with the infant body and its fledgling physiological system. One must begin with global pleasure, perceived indiscriminately and totally. One must begin with the first moments of life. For Freud, then, infantile sexuality is the pursuit of pleasure obtained through the activities of any and all organs of the human body. Initially, Freud treated the stages of sexuality as simply a biological unfolding without the interdependent refer- ence to ego structural change that was to become a central part of his theory.

While Freud gradually elaborated his initial presentation, some of his followers began to take issue with his propositions regarding infantile sexuality, and others began to extend his notions of the developmental bases in sexuality to the idea of mental health as attainable through adequate sexual functioning. Thus, Horney (1939) and Fromm (1941) took exception to the importance Freud placed on the body and on the sexual and ana- tomical differences, and they sought to avoid these notions in their work. Abraham (1953), Fenichel (1945), and Reich (1948) placed their emphasis on the "genital charac- ter" and regarded the ability to have orgasms as a sign of mental health. Freud would have given short shrift to his critical former students. He retained the fundamental bio- logic basis of his theory in the notion that the ego is first a physically derived entity. The concept of anxiety tied closely to that of ego development allowed for the construc- tion of an ego psychology. In his later work (Freud, 1926), he took into account the influence of anxiety as an expression of instinctual polarity; that is, of ambivalence at each stage of growth. In this view, anxiety is an unavoidable, necessary concomitant of development.

Erikson (1950) extended Freud's notions to include a significant contribution to and by the culture at each stage in growth. Erikson's elaboration of Freud in the ages and stages beyond the phallic or oedipal stage provided a particularly useful understanding. Nowhere was this more clearly brought about than with regard to adolescence. Erikson found useful the notion of the polarities of identity versus role diffusion as a means of understanding the ego's task at this time. With these terms as a shorthand, Erikson encap-

sulated the major ego shifts that result in an establishment of a firm sense of self necessary to adult functioning.

The theory of psychosexual development has received renewed attention as new
students use its basic structure to view adaptive behavior, in an attempt to elucidate the
elements of the life cycle in adulthood (Levinson, 1978), the specific adaptation of minority groups within the culture (Coles, 1967-1977; Miller, 1976), the sexual dysfunc-
tioning of adults (Kaplan, 1974), or the expectable adaptive struggles of the couple in a
committed relationship (Kuten, 1974, 1976).

Critical Discussion

General Areas of Concern

Sexuality has almost inescapable connotations of genital or paragenital activities
familiar to the world of adults. Personal organization, likewise, implies to the clinician a
relatively stable set of attributes, functions, and capacities that may be plumbed and
tested to arrive at a diagnostic formulation. Immediate caution must be advised here, for
it is essential to this consideration that our viewpoint be as broad and as flexible as possible. Psychosexual development refers to a range of behaviors (some observable, others
inferred) that span the life cycle from conception to death. Distinctly it is our thesis that
these are not static events that complete themselves at a certain point labeled *adult sexuality* (nor even that particular milestones can be conveniently demarcated) but rather
that there exists a fluid elaboration that has origin with life itself, that ebbs and flows
throughout that life. In that metaphorical sexual tide, the personality takes shape.

Of fundamental importance is the recognition of the discrepancy between sexuality of adulthood, with its focus on the genital, and the notion of *infantile sexuality.*
Sexuality in infancy is not centered on the genital; it involves the body as a whole, all its
parts, all its organs, external and internal. Infantile sexuality is the pleasure derived from
the *activities* of the entire body. It includes the pleasure of touching and seeing and the
pleasure of exercising all the senses. It includes the pleasure of muscular activity and of all
perceived functioning of internal organs (such as the peristaltic rhythms along the gut, the
pumping and pulsing of the blood along the vascular network); the pleasure from the
urinary tract and from the genitals, capable early in life of congestion, of tumescence; and
the pleasure of the early functioning of the central and peripheral nervous systems—the
crude computer of the brain starting up, the barraging sensory and motor impulses of the
nerves in contact with the world beyond the body's surface.

This continuum of all-inclusive bodily pleasure to the focused genital experience
of adulthood is a process that occurs simultaneously with the growth of the ego. It gives
shape to that growth within the human family and especially within the context of the
child's relationship with the adult nurturant being (usually the mother, and so hereafter
designated, although a father could potentially assume the same role) who is most responsible for the child's care. The relationship is an essentially symbiotic one, in which the
mother attempts to anticipate and satisfy the infant's every need, as the culture defines
that need. Since the infantile ego is without boundaries, the infant is unable, at first, to
recognize that mother is not simply a part of self. To a newborn there is no clear-cut
beginning and ending of self in time or in space. There is *no* time or space. The infant is
the world, and the world is the infant.

This earliest stage of ego development is known as the *oral stage,* after Freud's
original formulation of the primacy of the mouth and of sucking in obtaining gratification. It encompasses the period from birth until approximately 18 months. At this ear-

liest stage, the mother's attempted total nurturance as an expression of *her* love for the child makes possible the development of basic trust. While maternal loving care provides the foundation for basic trust to grow, its very success promotes the symbiotic attachment that prevents the child from recognizing his or her separate existence. On the one hand, the child is powerless and totally dependent on the mother. On the other hand, the failure to comprehend the mother's separate existence promotes an illusory omnipotence, a belief in one's ability to secure total indulgence in pleasure, free from any restraint or limitation. As long as one can deny one's separateness, so long can one hang on to one's infantile narcissism.

The recognition of separateness comes as a result of pain and discontent when mother fails, as she inevitably must, to fulfill the infant's every demand. Eventually, repetition of the mother's failure traps the child in the reality of helplessness. It sets off the body's basic alarm system: the autonomic discharge in reaction to overwhelming stress. To experience that separateness is to know anxiety, for it recreates the physiological crisis of the first separation from mother at birth. Just as at birth, anxiety at separation is an experience within the ego of the threat of annihilation. Anxiety continues to exert an influence at each stage of growth, provoking adaptive mechanisms within the ego in an attempt to reestablish the lost equilibrium of the symbiotic attachment.

The oral stage, then, is not simply the stage at which erotic activity of the mouth, sucking at mother's breasts, represents the advancing sexuality of the infant; it is also the stage that discovers anxiety—the anxiety represented in wanting, but not being able to find, the mother's breasts. In Freud's own terms, it is the stage that discovers the dualism of *subject* and *object,* in which the ego task is the development of trust as opposed to mistrust. Erikson envisions the challenge to the ego at this stage as between the dualism of *basic trust* and the sense of evil implicit in *mistrust.* In either formulation, the separation evokes anxiety, and the anxiety provokes the development of the ego mechanisms to cope with the separation.

The oral stage, with its central issue of differentiation between inside and outside, gives rise to the ego mechanisms of *projection, introjection,* and *denial.* In projection, the person experiences an inner harm as an outer one. In using introjection, the individual feels as if an outer goodness has become an inner certainty. Denial is simply the negation of pain. As Kris (1951, p. 111) has noted, "Comfort promotes object relations; discomfort promotes formation of psychic structure."

As the ego grows to a certain extent and starts to cope with separation, the child develops the use of *fantasy.* In the mother's absence—or, what amounts to the same thing, her failure to satisfy needs—the child first hallucinates her. The image of her in fantasy can sustain and support the child in relative comfort for a limited time. The transition from the real mother as a means of gratification to the use of her image in fantasy is prototypical for later development of more complex fantasy and imagery. Imagination, creativity, the capacity to play, and indeed the development of intellection in all forms of abstraction may be outgrowths of these primary experiences. While fantasy ameliorates the anxiety of separation, it also separates the child from mother and her closeness in loving union. It helps to dampen anxiety, but it also promotes the growth of an inner world of satisfaction. Its elaboration in imagination helps shape the basis of the child's increasingly real separateness and individuality. By helping to develop better tools, abstraction and intellection, with which to "grasp" the external world, fantasy eventually serves the purpose of anchoring the child in external reality and forcing the child to confront his or her individuality and separateness.

The second stage of ego development is the *anal stage,* which lasts approximately until the fourth year of life. By the time of its beginning, the child has developed the ability to stand erect and to walk. This is the stage during which the child develops communicative speech, the major entranceway to civilization. With the new-found tool of language, the child can let the parents know his or her will by saying, "No!" An explicit step away from the total dependence of early infancy is taken with that word. This, then, is the stage of development marked by the first struggle for power, a struggle between the child's beginning *autonomy* and mother's demand for conformity. This collision of wills has its counterpart in the child's internal struggle over polarities of "good" and "bad," of *autonomy* and *doubt* (Erikson), of activity and passivity, of anxiety expressed as anger and anger becoming guilt.

The anal stage has come to be associated with aggressiveness in all its various connotations. Although infantile anger is also important for the earlier oral stage of development, the earlier anger is ill formed and is generally expressed in the passivity that is characteristic of that developmental phase. Now, with the capacity for sphincter control as a biological substrate, the capacity for generalized control of impulses takes shape in the form of the social modalities of *letting go* and *holding on* (Erikson). In the face of renewed anxiety, infantile helplessness and passivity are now converted into activity. Instead of feeling vulnerable and needy and cast off (through separation from the parent), the child turns the passivity of being left to the activity of rejection. When fantasy is only partially successful and anxiety builds again, the child becomes angry. The anger is thus a shield to the pain of loss; but implicitly it recognizes the loss, accepts it partially, and establishes a distance between the child and the mother. For the child's world "good" is at first a feeling that is inside the self, while "bad" is extruded to the outside world. Being angry with mother (or she with him), the child banishes her to the world outside, and so accepts her individuality, and the love he extends to her as separate from himself, at least for the moment. In the next moment, yearning for her, the child brings her back in fantasy, grieving the loss of her. The struggle continues, back and forth, between anger and love, as the child erects more surely the boundaries between himself and her and eventually, in anger's erection of permanent inner margins, restructures the way he looks at and works with the world.

It is during the anal stage (with its beginning mastery over impulses) that the ego defenses of *doing and undoing, reaction formation,* and *isolation* originate. In *doing and undoing,* the modalities of holding on and letting go are given fullest expression; the person controls the impulse, the rage or anxiety, giving it a structured expression, only to topple the entire thing and yield to the temptation in a way that exposes the helplessness that was defended against all along. In *reaction formation,* the rage is let go so completely that the person can take up its opposite and, instead of having to acknowledge the destructive wishes, becomes the conforming "good" child. *Isolation* also allows escape from the rage, but in so sweeping a way that almost all feeling is lost. Each of the ego defenses fosters the progressive socialization of the child. As in the previous stage, so again here, anxiety builds ego defenses, and ego defenses alter the ego boundaries and the child's interactions with the rest of the world.

Beginning somewhere in the third or fourth year is the stage of psychosexual development known as the oedipal stage. It derives its name from the oedipus complex, which served as Freud's model for the ego's task at this time: the beginning of psychosexual gender differentiation in relation to the self and to the chosen object of loving attachment. This stage marks the most important transition from the all-inclusive generalized and amorphous loving of the body to the focused genital striving. Although elements of these profound alterations are present in earlier stages (for instance, in genital play among different-sexed 2-year-olds), they reach their culmination in this stage. It marks and makes significant the differentiation of the sexes, particularly where the parents are concerned, for it is this stage that sees a clear yielding of a symbiotic tie with the mother with its pronounced exclusivity; in the face of failure of the fantasy of total possession, the child must accept the necessity of sharing, and thus must relinquish part of his infantile narcissism. As a result, the child becomes more genuinely socialized, taking on the beginning capacity for judgment. While in earlier stages he may conform behavior to parental demand out of crude fear or experience of disapproval, his conformity is less the measure of internalized conscience than it is the product of the parent's watchful eye. Now with the capacity for integrative body behavior based on a nervous system whose myelinization is nearing completion, the child has a choice. Because of this newly developing socialization and an ability to generalize from the parents to other caretaking adults, the child can take the first real step away from home; he can attend school, where peers and the world outside the home act as new sources for imparting the values of the culture.

How does all this come about? In Freud's terms, it is a continuation of the series of renunciations and restructurings that occur within the infantile ego. The oedipal project is the same for both girls and boys: to transform the passivity of maternal dependence into activity by having a child by the mother; that is to say, by becoming father of oneself. It is not simply an expression of love for the mother but a product of the conflict engendered by ambivalence, a longing to be close and a loathing of the very closeness. The wish to become father of oneself represents an attempt to overcome that ambivalence by narcissistic inflation.

The narcissistic projects of the anal phase (symbolic retention, mastery, possession of the world) and of the oral phase (symbolic incorporation, swallowing of the world) succumb finally to the pressure of reality, the enforced recognition of the child's helplessness in the face of disappointment and the need to cope with resultant anxiety and anger. Here, too, it is a reality that intrudes and forces itself upon the child: the fact of sexual differentiation. For the little girl, the discovery of her genital and its identity with mother's leads to a revulsion in the face of the possibility of mergence in closeness and the disappointment in the child's inability to fulfill the wish. In that revulsion, the girl turns away from mother, first in the wish to be of the opposite sex from mother and then in the wish to possess the opposite-sexed parent, the father. The boy, too, turns from his original attachment to the mother, out of the hostility engendered in his discovery of the genital difference and his own inferiority. He turns in preference to the father, first simply as a loved substitute and then as a wish to be *like* the father. The turning point in both sexes is marked by the fantasy constructed by the child to explain the sexual difference—the belief that the form of the female genitalia is the result of castration.

Freud believed that the oedipal object—the narcissistic wish to become father of oneself—is only partly given up when the child is confronted with sexual differentiation. It is given up in terms of bodily fulfillment of the wish but is retained in fantasy in the unconscious. In the process, the ego develops the defenses of *sublimation* and *repression.* Sublimation is the transformation of aims from bodily derived concerns to nonbodily (symbolic, cultural) activities. Repression refers to the classical "forgetting" that is the hallmark of the psychoanalytic process. Here, the child "forgets" his total-body sexuality, leaving it for later genital expression. In the process, too, the ambivalence of love and hate, first for the mother and then for the father, leads to a split within the ego and the formation of the *superego,* the agency whereby the parents are internalized. Thus, the child, in horror of the "fact" of the mother's mutilated genital, which is seen as a threat of incorporating the child, turns away from her and experiences a preference for masculinity (the father), either for possession (by the girl) or for identification (by the boy).

This solution, too, is ambivalently held in the face of the castration anxiety. The ambivalence is often described as the twofold oedipus complex, positive and negative. The boy, for example, "has not merely an ambivalent attitude toward his father and an affectionate object relation toward his mother, but at the same time he also behaves like a girl and displays an affectionate attitude to his father and a corresponding hostility and jealousy toward his mother" (Freud, 1926, p. 48). The child then backs away from the threat of being internalized and, in his superego, succeeds in becoming the father by internalizing the parents. The cost of this success is the pain of guilt, the sense "that the individual has committed a crime which, after all, was not only not committed but would have been biologically quite impossible" (Erikson, 1950, p. 86). Erikson, defining this stage in terms of the nuclear conflict for the ego of *initiative* versus *guilt,* points out that the solution of this conflict permits the child to turn toward socially desirable goals, toward peers in cooperative play, and toward teachers and other bearers of the culture's messages in the next stage of development, latency.

Latency was originally so named because of the notion that the heightened sexual interest of the oedipal phase is repressed for the next six or seven years and reemerges at puberty. Certainly, repression of overt sexual interest *vis-à-vis* the parents is an important aspect of this next step in growth; but latency is a period of intense sexuality, sometimes overtly expressed, among peers. In any event, the name does suggest the *relative* quiescence in sexual expression characteristic of this time, compared to its centrality in the stages that precede and succeed it. At this stage the ego must cope with the socially imposed separation from parents in attendance at school or, in cultures other than our own, in the child's apprenticeship in craft or vocation. The child is increasingly capable of apprehending the world, with significantly increased capability in cognitive functioning and locomotor skills. Here begins the first serious use of tools to extend the body's capabilities and the first serious involvement with peers to extend the mind through learning from others.

In his neuroanatomically based developmental scheme, Yakovlev (1948) has pointed out that man is a being in constant evolution through progressive intellectualization by means of a living language, through progressive industrialization by means of development of tools, and through progressive socialization by means of a widening circle of attachments. In each of these spheres, according to Yakovlev, its ontogeny is a continuous feedback system. In the most obvious example, the development of the use of a tool changes irrevocably the world in which the tool is used and the person who makes use of it. From this viewpoint, the child in latency is the exemplar of the living evolutionary process.

Erikson sees the ego task of this time as the development of *industry* as opposed to the sense of *inferiority* aroused by fledgling capacity. In an important sense, this stage is crowned by intellectual striving of all kinds, with particular emphasis on exploration and systematization. Of equal importance, however, is the developing socialization of this period. The ability to share with others; the relative calming of the competition with the parents, arising from resolution of oedipal issues; and increased motor skills permit the child to enter into formal play, with its introduction to the "rules of the game." Peers take on a significance for social learning that parallels the influence of parents and other adults. This influence is heightened during the next stage, *adolescence.*

Adolescence and the stages that succeed it (adulthood, middle age, and old age) are far too complex to allow adequate description here. Only a few salient issues will be discussed. With respect to these four stages in the life cycle, Erikson has described the following polarities of nuclear conflict within the ego appropriate to each successive stage: identity versus role diffusion, intimacy versus isolation, generativity versus stagnation, and ego integrity versus despair.

Adolescence has as its principal challenge the transition from dependence on parents and home to the autonomy of adulthood. According to Blos (1962), this stage involves a recapitulation of all that has gone before, with a final renunciation of parents as object choices and the decision as to sexual preference, homosexual or heterosexual, being made with some finality.

Adolescence, as is known from common observation, is a time of great upheaval, of mood swings, and of rapid changes in attachments and ideologies. Because of the corresponding shifts in ego boundaries, the developing youngster often presents a picture of disturbance bordering on clinical insanity, but the disturbance is often more apparent than real. Caution in diagnosis is especially important, for the ego structure of adolescence is fluid. Defensive maneuvers from the past come into play, and regressions in the service of ego growth are the usual case. The fluidity of the ego boundaries and ease of regression are also a part of the basis of creativity frequently displayed at this stage. Although some of the astonishing creative effort is a defense against the anxiety provoked by all the shifting of attachment that characterizes this time, many a great artistic career has had its initial important expression in adolescence.

The remaining stages of psychosexual development are only now receiving the attention due them. The current research interest in adult living patterns is partial evidence that the notion of final and fixed ego structure is being quickly put to rest. Two recent studies are worth noting.

One approach is that of Levinson (1978) and his co-workers at the Yale University School of Medicine. They have done longitudinal biographical studies of forty men (aged 35-45) of varied professional and economic levels. This work seeks to identify more exactly the critical points in adult life and the ego tasks appropriate to each stage. Thus, between the ages of 17 and 33, a young man goes through what Levinson calls the novice phase of adult life. He faces four main tasks: (1) defining his goals, his dreams of accomplishment as an adult; (2) finding a mentor, an older experienced person to guide him; (3) developing a vocation and committing himself to it; and (4) opening himself to new intimate relationships. Levinson is impressed by the actualizing force of fantasy, the power of the "dream accomplishment" to impel a man toward productivity. Another important determinant of achievement, according to Levinson's studies, is the presence of a mentor or a "special woman," who gives animation to the process of actualizing the dream.

Like Levinson, Vaillant (1978) has been engaged in a longitudinal study, a continuation of a project that had its beginning twenty-five years ago. The studied population are the men of several classes at Harvard College who graduated between 1942 and 1944. Of 287 men in the original sample, approximately 95 are still involved. Vaillant examines his data to determine the critical differences between adaptation and failure. Both are measured on several inventory scales and corroborated by independent observers. Vaillant suggests that the critical difference between adaptive success and failure at this stage is the outcome of the interaction of the ego's coping mechanisms and external support systems. The ego mechanisms that enhance successful coping are *suppression, altruism,* and *humor.* Suppression implies the conscious delay or even extinction of impulse gratification. Altruism is an investment, for its own sake, in the well-being and advancement of people and causes beyond the self. By an external support system,

Vaillant refers to the network of relationships implicit in having friendships and kinship ties of long duration.

Both Levinson's and Vaillant's studies are conspicuous by their failure to consider the fate of women during mid-life period, leaving them open to the charge that, like other theorists, their notion of the adult stage of development is primarily a male model and possibly of limited applicability to women and their concerns at this time of life. Certainly the work of these men and others points to a steady decline in egocentric concerns with the advance from adolescence through adulthood; for men this decline is expressed in a shift toward a more nurturant—some might say more feminine—position. At the same time, Mead (1972) and others (for example, Miller, 1976) suggest that, as women leave childbearing and childrearing behind, they tend to become more expressive and assertive of their own personal needs for self-fulfillment, often entering the work force and developing independent careers. These changes in women may, in turn, evoke anxiety within themselves and other family members (a situation frequently described in the catch-all phrase *mid-life crisis*).

These considerations aside, both Vaillant and Levinson look beyond the person to his place within the social matrix for the sources of strength needed to deal with life's stresses: alterations in family structure as children grow and separate from the family, the death or diminution in capabilities of one's own parents, the limitation of opportunities, and the loss of many cherished fantasies. Alternatively, the adult, having achieved a degree of autonomy and mastery, can make intelligent choices and can assume responsibility for himself and for those whom he cares for.

Old age, arbitrarily defined as the period beyond 65 years, is expectedly the time in which the development of the ego might have some end-point. Certainly it is a time of great stress, particularly in American culture. Bodily concerns must become heightened because of processes of deterioration. Personal associations, the support networks mentioned by Vaillant, may diminish with the death of friends and relatives. Economic and social pressures may operate to separate the individual from meaningful work. Stimuli of all kinds may decrease as a multiplicity of factors urge the aged toward institutional life. At the same time, research is showing that the myths and prejudices once held about old people are without foundation. To take but one example, Masters and Johnson (1966) studied involutional changes in vaginal epithelium in postmenopausal women. These changes are felt to be secondary to sex hormone reduction. But while thinning of vaginal epithelia and shrinkage of labia majora were common findings, a majority also failed to expand the vaginal barrel or develop sufficient lubrication to enable them to have effective and pain-free sexual intercourse. The minority who were able to lubricate and to expand their vaginas were those women who continued to have regular sexual intercourse or masturbation once or twice a week. This finding supports the age-old principle in biology that form follows function.

There is much to learn about this period of life. As the work of Busse and Pfeiffer (1977) suggests, the course and outcome of the adaptive struggle in the aged is multidetermined. Many factors are strictly beyond control of the individual. The views of older theorists are coming into question as renewed scientific interest provokes controversy. Erikson remains among those theorists who view this period as the time for stock taking, for coming to terms with approaching death: "Healthy children will not fear life if their parents have integrity enough not to fear death" (Erikson, 1950, p. 233). But others suggest that old people do not fear death so much as the way in which it may come. Further, in the present-day United States, the stress facing the ego may result not from the fear of future death but from the reality of present life.

Comparative Philosophies and Theories

While alternative explanations of behavior are available, the only comprehensive theory comparable to the conception of ego development described in the preceding section is that of Jean Piaget. His developmental model, which is concerned primarily with the cognitive process, deserves recognition here alongside the previously described theory, which is based largely on affective aspects of experience.

For Piaget, human functioning is based primarily on two adaptive processes: assimilation (a person's adaptation of the environment to the self) and accommodation (the impact of objective reality). The two processes are interlocking, complementary, and opposing forces. In this theory, the core of all human activities is made up of intellectual functions, which serve as the basis of personality formation. Dynamic matters—affect, motives, personal-social development—do not have a prominent place in Piaget's thinking. Rather, he treats the affective component of experience as if it were a part of the cognitive mode, with intellectual processes providing direction. Whereas the emotional component appears to have a subordinate position in Piaget's system, he has repeatedly stated that the two functions, intellect and affect, are like two sides of a coin: "Both are always together as one. Both serve the adaptation to the environment" (Piaget, 1959, p. 275). "We do not love without seeking to understand, and we do not even hate without a subtle use of judgment" (Piaget, 1951, p. 207).

The main thrust of adaptive processes is the achievement of a near equilibrium in the face of a constantly changing reality. While equilibrium is only momentarily attainable, the process of struggle implicitly makes for the changing structures that constitute the separate periods of development of Piaget's schema. The stages of intellectual growth are continuous processes of generalization and differentiation. They emerge in an unchanging and constant sequence, but the age at which a given stage appears may vary considerably with factors such as culture and individual experience.

Individuals achieve at different levels within the hierarchy. Piaget has freely conceded that not all "normal" adults within one culture end up at a common level; adults will demonstrate adult thought only in those content areas in which they have been socialized. This means that a given individual cannot be expected to function at the same structural level for all tasks.

Each stage in development is further characterized by an initial period of preparation in which the structures that define the stage are relatively undifferentiated. Hence behavior tends to be unstable insofar as it is directed toward the cognitive problems whose solution requires *that* stage's intellectual structures. Behavior is not disorganized when confined to tasks solvable by earlier structures. The preparatory phase is succeeded by one of achievement in which the new cognitive structures are more organized and stable. Thus, intellectual development proceeds from structural disequilibrium to structural equilibrium, repeating itself at ever higher levels of functioning.

There are three major stages of cognitive growth: the period of sensorimotor intelligence, the period of concrete operations, and the period of formal operations.

During the period of sensorimotor intelligence (0 to 2 years) the infant moves from a purely reflex level of organization, undifferentiated from the object world to a coherent organization of sensorimotor actions in constant interplay with his immediate environment. The organization of intellect involves simple perceptual and motor adjustments to things, rather than symbolic manipulation of them. The most important developments of this period, self-object differentiation and *object permanence,* are paradigmatic of development during succeeding stages.

Piaget uses the concept of *egocentrism* to describe the cognitive state in which the subject sees the world from only his own viewpoint and is unaware of the existence of other viewpoints or perspectives. It is, thus, an egocentrism of which the subject cannot be aware. Flavell (1963), in his exegesis of Piaget, describes the major event in the first two years as follows:

> There is simultaneously a centrifugal process of gradual objectifica-
> tion of external reality and a centripetal process of burgeoning self-aware-
> ness—the self comes to be seen as an object among objects. Initially, as we
> have said, the infant knows neither self nor world as distinct and differen-
> tiated entities; experiences only a melange of feelings and perceptions con-
> comitant with what an adult observer would label as contacts between his
> actions and outside objects. Cognition really begins at the boundary be-
> tween the self and object and with development invades both self and
> object from this initial "zone of undifferentiation." Knowledge of self and
> knowledge of objects are thus the dual resolution of the successive differ-
> entiation and equilibration of the invariant functions which characterize
> sensory-motor development [p. 61].

But this process does not stop with infancy. Rather as Flavell puts it:

> Just as egocentrism reappears in its various forms in post-infantile
> development, so also do its opposite terms get repeatedly reconstituted at
> ever higher levels: objectificiation of external reality and undistorted
> knowledge of self. As in sensory-motor development, this dual progression
> forms an indissoluble whole: it is by conceptualizing the self as a distinct
> and separate center which perceives reality from a particular viewpoint
> that it becomes possible to correct egocentric distortions about reality; it
> is by penetrating deeper into the fabric of reality that self-knowledge be-
> comes possible. Thus, with the various developmental levels of symbolic
> construction as well as with the elemental sensory-motor behavior, cogni-
> tion always begins on the margins of both self and milieu and works its
> way simultaneously into the inner regions of each [pp. 63-64].

The period of preparation for and organization of concrete operation (2 to 11 years) begins with a *preconceptual phase* (2 to 4 years), during which symbols are con-structed and a sense of their ordering and categorization develops. Representational thought begins, and language flourishes. Then comes the *period of intuitive thought* (4 to 7 years), when the concepts of time, space, and causality are acquired and the child mas-ters the principle of conservation of quantity (permanence and continuity in the face of operational transformation). This phase is succeeded by the *period of concrete operations* (7 to 11 years), when the child develops the concept of numbers and of mathematical operations (such as groupings, exclusions, and conclusions). At this time, the child ap-pears to have a stable and orderly conceptual framework, which he can bring to bear on the world of objects around him.

In the final stage of development, the *period of formal operations* (11 to 15 years), the logical structure of purely abstract thought is mastered; that is, the world of propositional statements, of pure possibility without reference to the concrete. More than 60 percent of the people do not reach this stage. Further adult elaboration beyond ado-lescence is just that, an elaboration along logical and mathematical ordering of thought.

Elaboration on Critical Points

Just as Piaget has acknowledged the influence of psychoanalytic ideas on his own ideas, psychoanalytic formulations regarding developmental models are clearly enhanced because of Piaget's work on cognition. Thus, there is a rough correspondence between the stages of development, at least until adolescence. While Freud appears to stop here, Erikson and the others do not; and, in fact, the most excitement is being generated currently in development of clearer concepts of adult psychosexual development. Piaget's outline ends with the stage of formal operations, which implies that adolescence and adulthood are merely one continuum. While this does not mean that Piaget is less optimistic about the possibility of growth and change in adulthood, yet there is some limitation in any theory which implies that a person's range of mature comprehension should be complete and at its highest achievable level when the youth becomes a young adult. To advocate, as the theory of psychosexual development does, that emotional and social development is not completed within any circumscribed period leaves room for continuous unfolding throughout life. It even implies that whatever development cannot be fully accomplished within a given period can be later developed independent of other developmental aspects.

Perhaps the most important aspect of complementarity between the two theories has to do with the notions of duality and conflict central to each of them. For Piaget, this polarity exists at each stage of development in terms of the notions of assimilation and accommodation. The polarities of psychosexual development are represented in the specific challenges presented to the ego at each stage. A central place of agreement is the notion of self-object differentiation, which Piaget posits as a paradigm for cognitive functioning and which the theory of psychosexual development asserts as a central force in personality formation.

Personal Views and Recommendations

The notion of infantile narcissism (egocentrism) provides an interesting way of viewing adult sexuality. As repeatedly noted, the infant's separation from the loved one (originally mother) evokes anxiety, which, in turn, is partially countered by development of ego mechanisms that act to reduce anxiety (or to promote equilibrium). In the process, at each stage of development the individual develops more effective ego boundaries, which promote the internal sense of individuation and permit more complex levels of interaction and adaptation.

In this view, the fundamental process of change is the following sequence of events: The steady-state equilibrium of closeness is threatened by the perception of change when some event occurs from without (birth of a sibling, a move of the family, a new job) or from within (a new skill is acquired, a new lover is found). This new event represents a threat of separation, which is partially experienced as anxiety and partially blocked in consciousness, after initial stages of development, as defensive mechanisms ward off the experience of loss and anxiety. As development proceeds, ego functions are increasingly less successful in totally dampening anxiety, but the attempt creates more efficient defenses (defenses that are flexible and selective in the discrimination of perceptions allowed to come to awareness) and hence fosters development of ego boundaries. Incomplete success at suppression of painful affective components of anxiety means that sadness and anger (which are elaborations of fundamental anxiety) are felt in spite of ego defenses. Sadness implies a relatively passive acceptance of the loss; anger implies an attempt to convert the passivity of the loss to the activity of rejection. The implication for development is an expectation of sadness and anger as concomitants of each milestone in human experience, at each successive achievement in the stages of development. The infant learns to drink from a cup, but he must give up the breast. The toddler walks, to the delight of everyone; but soon he is carried less. He learns to talk, and never again can he expect to be interpreted, to be totally understood, without making an effort to express needs exactly.

This view of development and affect has certain implications for human growth. In the absence of rituals culturally sanctioned for dealing with change throughout the life cycle, it emphasizes the need for therapeutic intervention when the individual is overwhelmed by the polarities of love and hate, sadness and anger, engendered by the vicissitudes of normal human life. It also provides a useful way of understanding the changes implicit in adult sexuality within long-term committed relationships. Briefly, infantile sexuality, the pleasure of the total body, is an ego state in which the sexual pleasure is equivalent to love, which, in turn, rests on a foundation of closeness, sameness, and continuity. The infantile relationship to the source of pleasure tends toward symbiotic fusion. Adult sexuality depends—for its energy, its impetus and drive—on the differences between the lovers; but differences and separateness soon evoke the anxiety of anticipated loss. Desiring and having the lover are two distinguishable realities. The genital sexuality of adulthood is the beginning of the relationship which becomes love; but love acts to efface the differences that separate lovers and to create, instead, a unity. It is not only the momentary unity of sharing of bodies but a unity of the selves—a unity to restore a feeling from infancy, when there was no sense of separation or limitation. Gradually the differences are given up, and the pain of being vulnerable to the loss of love diminishes. However, there is nothing further to explore. Instead, there is a profound quiet, of being at one with the other in totality—a renewal of the lost first love of child and mother. Like that early relationship, it becomes diffused, scattered over the total body. It becomes the pleasure of holding and being held, of touching and being touched; but it is not specifically the genital experience.

Once established, adult sexual relationships drift toward the symbiotic unity implicit in loving, with its further consequence of the yielding of the genital to the infantile sexuality. However, this adaptive tendency has its corollary in the sudden awareness of separateness that comes in the realization that even the lover must fail to meet one's every need. That awareness must come when the loved one expresses personal needs, individual styles, or individual differences. With that awareness comes a new threat of loss, a new defensive shift, a new structuring of ego boundaries. Often it is accompanied by pain and by anger. The anger is the anger of betrayal, of implicit promises implicitly broken. Whenever there is separation or the threat of it, after loving, there is anger. It is the anger which forces awareness of separateness and which helps bring separateness about. Anger augments the structure of the ego boundaries, arming ego defenses. Anger reaffirms and reestablishes the distance between the lovers, reviving the painful sense of aloneness and making possible a renewed quest for closeness in sexuality. Essentially, then, to the adult sexual relationship is the capacity to bear and to express conflict as representative of individual differences. In this way, adult sexual relationships of enduring vitality are seen as continuous restructuring processes of the ego boundaries (Kuten, 1974, 1976).

Application to Particular Variables

Although the individuals whom Freud treated, and who formed the basis of the experience from which he derived his theories, were middle class, European cultured, and well educated, successful understanding of the life cycles of vastly different people is possible within the theoretical framework. Erikson and other psychoanalysts of the Freudian school have extended his ideas and made them useful in work with divergent groups from a wide range of socioeconomic and cultural backgrounds. Anthropologists such as Mead (1928) have tested its applicability in places and cultures far outside the Western European one. Nevertheless, it is important to acknowledge that educational, cultural, ethnic/racial, and socioeconomic factors do influence psychosexual development. While Freud could successfully regard these influences as a given and subsumed under the notion of an external reality, it was largely because his population was relatively homogeneous. Erikson's work clearly pays homage to cultural influences. Coles (1967-1977) has demonstrated the need to take into account the influence of race and of socioeconomic factors in development.

Clearly, today, we cannot afford the luxury of thinking of an immutable external reality, which, if not exactly continuously nurturant, is at least neutral or benign in influence. We are living in far too "interesting times" (as the Chinese say). The most immediate example is the influence of the women's movement on childrearing practices and in turn, on the way children define themselves and their future sex role. This complex development may, in turn, derive from the renewed interest in civil rights, in general, which began with the U.S. Supreme Court decision in 1954 desegregating the schools. It may also have received special impetus from the protests against the Vietnam War and the political upheaval of the 1960s. It has certainly made its own influence felt worldwide through the medium of television. Together with socioeconomic trends, including a worldwide inflationary spiral, it appears to be resulting in American families with two wage earners. This alone may change childrearing practice from its former intrafamilial setting to an institutional one. Such a structure may influence profoundly the struggles of development and the way in which cultural goals and means are imparted at each stage. For example, the developmental theory as elaborated here assumes an individualistic, competitive, work-oriented culture. The incorporation of group ideals through the use of peers as the socializing influence would certainly alter the outcome of the issues of the oedipal stage. Bettelheim (1969) has examined some of these possibilities with respect to children raised communally in Israel. Bronfenbrenner (1970) has made a similar effort with respect to childrearing in the Soviet Union.

Stepping back from such important global concerns, we need to look at the application of these notions in psychological assessment. This was the original approach of Freud, and it was this need to understand psychopathology that gave impetus to the theory in the first place. After Freud it was long believed that personality types could be defined in terms of the three early stages of psychosexual development. This notion assumes that individuals fail to progress beyond the issues of a given stage as a result of some trauma or of deprivation *occurring at that stage.* In this schema, oral personalities are those with basic needs to incorporate the world and to unite with it in primitive symbiosis. Alcoholics, drug addicts, and so-called borderline personalities would all be included. Anal personalities, equally thought to derive their problems from failure at that critical stage, would demonstrate their problems in terms of retention or expulsion and would include the obsessive-compulsive range of disorders. Likewise, failure at the oedipal stage would lead to personality types such as the hysteric or those having difficulty in successfully approaching and concluding any committed task. This outlook had important implications for therapeutic interventions. It also assumed a relatively fixed notion of ego structure.

Today we question these notions in light of clinical data. We are inclined to view the ego as more fluid and capable of using a multitude of defenses at any stage. To take the disorders represented by the abuse of alcohol as an example, we see a wide range of personality types suffering with this disorder, not merely the orally deprived persons described in the older literature. While persons manifesting problems of the oral phase of development are indeed represented, so too are those with problems of the anal, oedipal, and later stages of development. Individuals with narcissistic personalities demanding constant attention (show-business luminaries come immediately to mind) and persons with adaptive histories and clinical presentations consistent with the diagnosis of schizophrenia may indeed present as alcoholics. Overconscientious, orderly bureaucrats and depressed menopausal women with psychotic delusions centered on the polarities of good and evil, clean and dirty, may present at the alcoholism unit. Executives passed over for promotion in spite of years of productive service and people going through divorce also may present as alcoholics.

The value of the theory of psychosexual development as a part of psychological assessment lies in this very multiplicity of possibilities. In the draft for the proposed third edition of the *Diagnostic and Statistical Manual of Mental Disorders* (American Psychiatric Association, 1978), the Task Force on Nomenclature and Statistics of the American Psychiatric Association has attempted to take into account the various ways in which psychosexual development exerts its influence on the individual's status. While it retains the standard nomenclature, with some broadening of the categories, the advance made is the recommendation that four other groupings or axes be developed for each patient besides the description of the syndrome. Each of the four axes deals with some aspect of psychosexual development: personality (Axis II), physical disorders (Axis III), psychosocial stressors (Axis IV), or level of adaptive functioning (Axis V).

This new approach to diagnosis would describe the immediate clinical picture, the possible sources of stress that helped bring it about, and the indicators of adaptive function that may be mobilized in restoring the patient to adequacy. It is this area of predictability that must be regarded as speculative, depending for its usefulness on the research still to be done about the validity of these assumed hierarchies of stressors and of adaptations.

While this laudable effort to make more exact the influence of psychosexual development on the clinical picture goes on, the clinician's task retains its lonely challenge: that of understanding the individual in his or her totality. If the developmental approach no longer permits as easy generating of categories, it does provide a useful viewpoint. With any patient the emphasis can most effectively be placed on coping mechanisms both in the present and in the past. The clinician should seek to establish as complete a picture as possible of the present condition and its antecedents. Beyond the immediate issues of the clinical condition for which treatment is sought, the person's coping in all aspects of his life must be taken into account.

The multiple facets of any individual's functioning make it possible for him to use coping mechanisms successfully and appropriately in one phase of life—for example, the occupational—and to fail utterly in another—say, the interpersonal. Further, a complete longitudinal review of the person's life history may reveal just how developmental tasks were handled at each stage of that life: how the initial separation from parents was handled in latency, how friendships shifted and sexuality was experienced in adolescence, how intimacy and commitment were encountered in young adulthood. The open-eyed clinician may then observe how the individual sought to overcome deficiencies of one phase with accomplishment in a later one, sometimes with degrees of success, sometimes with a dear price.

The student of human behavior cannot fail to be impressed with the wide range of behaviors that may be encompassed in normal adaptations. For this reason all labeling should be seen as tentative in order to maintain a clinical approach to assessment that remains fully open to human possibilities.

The able clinician will also look inward to take into account those personal issues and biases that may distort the assessment process. It is worth mentioning in this connection that the clinician uses the adaptive mechanism of *empathy* in order to arrive at his understanding. He knows that the distinction between himself and the person identified as his patient rests not on qualitative terms but ultimately on matters of degree.

References

Abraham, K. *Selected Papers.* New York: Basic Books, 1953.

American Psychiatric Association. *Diagnostic and Statistical Manual of Mental Disorders.* (Draft of 3rd ed.) Washington, D.C.: American Psychiatric Association, 1978.

Bettelheim, B. *The Children of the Dream.* New York: Macmillan, 1969.

Blos, P. *On Adolescence.* New York: Free Press, 1962.

Bronfenbrenner, U. *Two Worlds of Childhood: U.S. and U.S.S.R.* New York: Russell Sage Foundation, 1970.

Busse, E. W., and Pfeiffer, E. *Behavior and Adaptation in Later Life.* Boston: Little, Brown, 1977.

Coles, R. *Children of Crisis.* Vols. 1-5. Boston: Little, Brown, 1967-1977.

Erikson, E. H. *Childhood and Society.* New York: Norton, 1950.

Fenichel, O. *The Psychoanalytic Theory of Neurosis.* New York: Norton, 1945.

Flavell, J. H. *The Developmental Psychology of Jean Piaget.* New York: Van Nostrand, 1963.

Freud, S. *Three Essays on Sexuality.* In *Standard Edition of the Complete Psychological Works of Sigmund Freud.* Vol. 7. London: Hogarth Press, 1905.

Freud, S. *Inhibitions, Symptoms, and Anxiety.* In *Standard Edition.* Vol. 20. London: Hogarth Press, 1926.

Fromm, E. *Escape from Freedom.* New York: Holt, Rinehart and Winston, 1941.

Horney, K. *New Ways in Psychoanalysis.* New York: Norton, 1939.

Kaplan, H. S. *The New Sex Therapy.* New York: Brunner/Mazel, 1974.

Kris, E. "Some Comments and Observations on Early Autoerotic Activities." *Psychoanalytic Study of the Child,* 1951, *6,* 96-116.

Kuten, J. *Coming Together—Coming Apart.* New York: Macmillan, 1974.

Kuten, J. "Anger, Sexuality, and the Growth of the Ego." *Journal of Sex and Marital Therapy,* 1976, *2* (4), 289-296.

Levinson, D. *The Seasons of a Man's Life.* New York: Knopf, 1978.

Masters, W. H., and Johnson, V. E. *Human Sexual Response.* Boston: Little, Brown, 1966.

Mead, M. *Coming of Age in Samoa.* New York: Morrow, 1928.

Mead, M. *Blackberry Winter: My Earlier Years.* New York: Morrow, 1972.

Miller, J. B. *Toward a New Psychology of Women.* Boston: Beacon Press, 1976.

Piaget, J. *Play, Dreams and Imagination in Childhood.* London: Heinemann, 1951.

Piaget, J. "Psychologie der Fruehen Kindheit." In D. Katz (Ed.), *Handbuch der Psychologie.* (2nd ed.) Basel, Switzerland: Benno Schwabe, 1959.

Reich, W. *The Discovery of the Orgone.* Vol. 1: *The Function of the Orgasm.* New York: Orgone Institute Press, 1948.

Vaillant, G. *Adaptation to Life.* Boston: Little, Brown, 1978.

Yakovlev, P. "Motility, Behavior and the Brain." *Journal of Nervous and Mental Disease,* 1948, *107* (4), 313-335.

Yakovlev, P., Weinberger, M., and Chipman, C. E. "Heller's Syndrome as a Pattern of Schizophrenic Behavior Disturbance in Early Childhood." *American Journal of Mental Deficiency,* 1948, *53* (2), 318-337.

52

Jacob L. Orlofsky

Sex-Role Orientation

Sex-role orientation refers to the behaviors individuals exhibit and feel are appropriate for them by virtue of their being male or female. Although the terms masculinity and femininity encompass personality traits, interests, and social roles, this chapter focuses primarily on the personality traits which typify males and females. While sex role is related to the concept of *gender identity* (sense of oneself as a male or a female), the two terms are not synonymous; individuals can have a secure sense of gender identity without manifesting predominantly sex-typed personality characteristics. Likewise, the concept should not be confused with *sexual preference* for partners of the same or the other sex. Although a preference for members of the same sex may be somewhat more prevalent among individuals manifesting a predominance of traits more commonly associated with the other sex (cross-sex-typed individuals), both sex-typed and cross-sex-typed individuals may exhibit either type of sexual preference.

Background and Current Status

Masculinity and femininity are sociocultural phenomena, reflecting cultural attitudes as to the proper or accepted roles of men and women. Traits and behaviors that are culturally valued for males in that culture comprise its standards of masculinity; traits which are valued for females in that culture comprise its standards of femininity. A number of theorists have described cultural norms of masculinity and femininity in terms of the dominant orientations of these two complementary domains. Parsons and Bales (1955) describe masculinity as an *instrumental orientation,* a cognitive focus on getting the job done or the problem solved. Femininity is associated with an *expressive orientation,* a focus on feelings and relationships with others, an affective concern for the welfare of others and the harmony of the group. In a similar vein, Bakan (1966) has suggested that masculinity is associated with an agentic orientation, a concern with oneself as an individual, whereas femininity refers to a *communal orientation,* a concern with the relationship between oneself and others. These hypothesized cultural stereotypes of masculinity and femininity have been supported in survey research assessing people's attitudes of how men and women typically and ideally differ and have also received some support in empirical research on actual personality and behavioral differences between the sexes (Bem, 1974; Rosenkrantz and others, 1968; Sheriffs and McKee, 1957).

However, research on psychological differences between the sexes suggests that stereotypical beliefs about the sexes tend to exaggerate the number and magnitude of differences actually present (Maccoby and Jacklin, 1974). Regardless of the accuracy of these beliefs, historically masculinity and femininity have been seen as opposite ends of a single dimension differentiating males and females. According to the traditional values of American society, men are supposed to be masculine in their personality characteristics, women are supposed to be feminine, and neither sex is supposed to be much like the other. Therefore, if men are independent, tough, assertive, and instrumental (or task oriented), women should be dependent, sweet, retiring, nurturant, and expressive (that is, oriented toward feelings and relationships with others) (Bem, 1975a).

Underlying this belief in the oppositeness of the sexes has been the assumption that psychological differences between the sexes are biologically given and are due to basic differences in physiology and anatomy. Freudian psychoanalysis, for example, holds that differences in male and female bodily structures and sexual functions predispose males and females toward differing psychological conflicts and anxieties (for instance, castration anxiety in men and penis envy in women) and to differing personality characteristics (for instance, activity, aggressiveness, dominance in males; passivity, masochism, dependence in females). The view that "anatomy is destiny" has been criticized by a number of writers (such as neo-Freudian Karen Horney, 1939), and there is little evidence that biological factors necessarily predispose men and women to develop opposite personality patterns (and considerable evidence from cross-cultural studies to the contrary) (Bernard, 1974; Weitz, 1977; Yorburg, 1974).

Despite these challenges to the biological emphasis, the cultural stereotypes of masculinity and femininity have filtered into psychologists' concepts, so that even psychologists without a strict biological orientation have tended to view masculinity and femininity as opposites. Even psychological tests of sex role reflect this bias. Until very recently, the tests were designed to pit masculine characteristics and interests against feminine qualities; thus, if an individual scored high on one pole, he or she automatically scored low on the other.

All this began to change, however, when Bakan (1966), Block (1973), and Constantinople (1973) challenged the idea that masculinity and femininity are opposite poles of a single continuum and suggested, instead, that people can—and, in fact, *should*—manifest both masculine and feminine attributes. To be sure, this idea was not entirely novel. Jung (1956), for example, had implied it in his anima/animus concepts, and Freud (1940) had posited that human beings are inherently bisexual, manifesting some of the reactions of the other sex. However, these recent writers focused specifically on the advantages of developing both masculine and feminine traits. Furthermore, Constantinople (1973) pointed out the unsubstantiated assumptions underlying existing sex-role measures and called for the development of new measures, which would allow for independent assessment of masculine-instrumental and feminine-expressive qualities. The question of whether masculinity and femininity are opposites or independent dimensions could then be tested empirically rather than accepted as an article of faith.

A number of such measures have appeared in the last few years, the best known of which is the Bem Sex-Role Inventory (Bem, 1974). This inventory consists of twenty selected personality characteristics (for instance, ambitious, self-reliant, independent, assertive) which were judged by a large sample of college males and females to be more desirable for men than for women and twenty characteristics (among them, affectionate, gentle, understanding, sensitive to the needs of others) rated as more desirable in this society for women than for men.

Use of this and other similar scales has shown that the two dimensions are independent of each other (that is, they do not correlate negatively with each other as traditional views would predict) and that approximately 35 percent of college people, when describing themselves on the self-report items, obtain scores on the two scales that are approximately equal.* That is, they manifest a *balance* between so-called masculine and feminine characteristics. For these people, Bem (1974) has used the term *psychological androgyny*.

Critical Discussion

General Areas of Concern

Bem (1975b) suggests that an androgynous sex role is a new standard of mental health for both sexes. According to Bem, traditional sex roles are restrictive, while androgyny is freeing. The androgynous person incorporates both traditionally masculine and feminine characteristics into his or her self-concept. Thus, this person need not avoid certain kinds of adaptive behaviors as inconsistent with the self-concept just because these behaviors are often associated with the other sex. Androgynous individuals are more free to be all that they are and to actualize all their potentialities. Furthermore, they are able to engage in situationally effective behavior regardless of its stereotype as masculine or feminine.

In contrast, the sex-typed person has a narrower self-concept, which excludes characteristics or behaviors traditionally identified with the other sex. Thus, this person is likely to avoid or be uncomfortable with, or just not be adept at, behaviors labeled appropriate for the other sex. As a result, this person often will not be able to act in the most effective manner. A sex-typed woman, for example, may be afraid to express her anger, assert her preferences, trust her own judgment, or take a leadership role; a sex-typed man may be unable to express his feelings or to be nurturant or empathic with another person (Bem, 1976). The point is, of course, that the two domains of masculinity and femininity are both fundamental for all people. Where one or the other of these capacities is absent or poorly developed, there is a narrowing of personality and a restricted behavioral repertoire.

The empirical evidence for the hypothesized advantages of an androgynous sex role is examined in the following sections of this chapter.

*Approximately 50 percent of college students score as sex typed (higher on the sex-typed than on the cross-sex-typed scale), while 15 percent appear cross sex typed.

Comparative Philosophies and Theories

Pleck (1976, has contrasted traditional and more recent conceptualizations of sex roles with respect to several points: (1) The traditional (psychoanalytic) perspective assumes that there are large differences between men and women in their personality traits, attitudes, and interests. In contrast, the new psychology of sex roles accepts sex differences in some traits (such as certain intellectual skills and aggression) but asserts considerable overlap between the sexes. (2) The traditional perspective assumes that differences between the sexes are, to a large degree, biologically based, although they are also partly learned. The new perspective maintains that some psychological sex differences may be rooted in biological sex differences but that most observed differences are a product of socialization practices and learning. (3) With respect to learned sex-role behaviors, the traditionalist believes that, in order to develop secure gender identities, males and females need to develop a preponderance of traits that society defines as appropriate for their sex. The proponent of the new psychology agrees that individuals need to have an accurate sense of their biological gender but contends that this is a very early development and generally proceeds without difficulty and that, for correct self-classification of gender, the individual does not need to acquire only those personality traits that society deems sex appropriate. (4) In the traditional view, the individual who fails to acquire sex-appropriate masculine or feminine traits will be psychologically maladjusted, manifesting gender-identity confusion and an inverted sexual preference. In terms of the newer theories, personality problems may develop in the rare instance where there is inaccurate assignment of gender because of inconsistencies in the individual's genetic, hormonal, or morphological makeup (Money and Ehrhardt, 1972). However, the failure to learn *only* sex-typed personality traits and behaviors does not predispose the individual to gender-identity confusion or other psychological disturbance, as traditional perspectives assume; rather, the individual who learns *only* sex-appropriate (or cross-sex) masculine or feminine traits is likely to be psychologically handicapped. (5) According to the traditionalist, psychological sex differences and individuals' needs for secure gender identity account for and justify the differing social roles, responsibilities, and privileges of men and women. In the view of the new perspective, however, men's and women's different social roles cannot be accounted for on the basis of innate psychological sex differences or needs for gender identity; instead, they are a function of social, political, and economic forces, many of which are becoming obsolete.

With respect to the first point, there is little evidence of profound personality differences between the sexes. In their review of the research literature on psychological sex differences, Maccoby and Jacklin (1974) found consistent sex differences in certain (trainable) intellectual skills (such as verbal, spatial, and mathematical ability) and in aggressiveness. However, in most other areas where men and women were presumed to differ (areas such as analytical ability, motivation to achieve, self-esteem, and suggestibility), there were no consistent sex differences. While the Maccoby and Jacklin review has been criticized for overlooking other possible psychological differences (Block, 1976), their point is well taken that considerably more variability exists within each sex than between the sexes. Regarding the role of biological bases of sex differences, Matteson (1975) finds consistent—perhaps biologically based—differences in motor activity but sees little evidence to suggest that these could play a major role in determining instrumental qualities in males or expressive qualities in females. With respect to the third point, Money and Ehrhardt's (1972) analysis of gender-identity development reveals that socialization factors and the early classification of the child as male or female are much more significant than genetic or hormonal characteristics (in cases where these are discrepant) in the child's gender-identity development. The fourth point, the alternative views regarding the mental health implications of the various sex role outcomes, and the fifth point, having to do with the social roles of men and women, will be discussed in the following sections.

Elaboration on Critical Points

As has been noted, traditional conceptions of sex-role characteristics assumed that masculinity and femininity are opposite ends of a single bipolar dimension differentiating males and females. Constantinople (1973) has identified certain faulty characteristics of the assessment devices which were developed from this conceptualization.

First, the items used in these Masculinity-Femininity (M-F) scales were selected solely on the basis of their ability to discriminate between males and females. Thus, these scales sampled a variety of personality traits, interests, and overt behaviors without regard to their interrelationship or relevance to cultural standards of masculinity or femininity. Second, these scales used one set of test items to measure both masculinity and femininity, with one direction of response indicative of masculinity and the other direction indicative of femininity. These scales operated as if high masculinity implies low femininity, so that the absence of masculine characteristics necessarily implies the presence of feminine ones. Finally, these scales used a single M-F score, based on the algebraic summation of M and F responses, to place the individual somewhere on a single bipolar dimension, with the partial effect of rendering ambiguous the interpretation of scores clustering around the midpoint.

More recent conceptualizations of sex roles have challenged these practices and have led to the development of sex-role measures along different lines.

First, in contrast to the untested unidimensional assumption of traditional approaches, the new measures assume an orthogonal two-dimensional model of masculinity and femininity (which has been supported by recent empirical findings, described below) such that individuals can score high (or low) on both qualities. Second, instead of using items solely because they discriminate between the sexes, as had been done previously, the recent measures use items that reflect the sociocultural stereotypes of masculinity as a cognitive instrumentality and goal directedness and femininity as an expressive, nurturant, interpersonal orientation. Related to this sociocultural definition of sex roles has been the decision (in three of the four major scales) to restrict the item pool of the new measures to functional, socially valued, sex-typed characteristics. Bem (1974, p. 155), for example, suggests that sex typing involves the internalization of "society's sex-typed standards of desirable behavior for men and women"; and Spence, Helmreich, and Stapp (1975) specifically term their scales "male valued" and "female valued," respectively.

Four self-report measures of sex-role orientation, using separate M and F scales, have recently been developed. Brief descriptions of these scales follow, with special focus on method of item selection and scale construction, procedures for sex-role classification, and relationship between M and F dimensions.

The Bem Sex-Role Inventory (BSRI) (Bem, 1974) consists of separate masculinity, femininity, and "neutral" scales, each composed of twenty items on which respondents describe themselves on a seven-point rating scale. The M and F scales were derived from an initial pool of personality characteristics that seemed "positive in value and either masculine or feminine in tone" (Bem, 1974, p. 156). These items were then rated by college students. The final items were those rated significantly more desirable for males than for females (M scale) or more desirable for females than for males (F scale).

Supporting the conception of independent M and F dimensions, Bem (1974) reports correlations between the two ranging from $r = .11$ to $r = -.14$, depending on sexes and sample. Sex-role classification is done on the basis of subjects' androgyny scores, which are derived by computing the t-ratio for the difference between each person's femininity and masculinity scores. Androgyny scores that fall within a ±1.00 range are classified as balanced, or androgynous, while those greater than +1.00 or less than −1.00 are designated as feminine and masculine typed, respectively.

This use of an F-M subtractive index has been challenged by a number of investigators (Berzins, Welling, and Wetter, 1975; Spence, Helmreich, and Stapp, 1975), who claim that androgyny represents high levels of M and F rather than just a balance between the two qualities. These other investigators propose a fourfold classification scheme based on M and F scale median splits, such that high M and F scores are designated as androgynous while low M and F scores represent an undifferentiated (Spence, Helmreich, and Stapp, 1975) or indeterminate (Berzins, Welling, and Wetter, 1975) role orientation. While this latter procedure appears preferable to Bem's procedure (and has been supported by research differences between high-high and low-low scorers), it also has drawbacks. For one thing, it labels many individuals who score near the medians as sex typed, though their M and F scores are nearly identical. To compensate for this problem, Orlofsky, Aslin, and Ginsburg (1977) have proposed a difference/median-split classification procedure that combines both methods. Individuals are classified according to Bem's difference/androgyny scores into sex-typed, cross-sex-typed, and balanced orientations, and then the balanced group is divided into those individuals who score above either or both medians (androgynous) and those who score below both medians (undifferentiated). In addition to retaining the important notion of androgyny as a balance, this procedure appears to be less susceptible to the effects of social desirability responding than the simple median-split procedure (Orlofsky, Aslin, and Ginsburg, 1977).

A second measure, the Personal Attributes Questionnaire (PAQ), was developed by Spence, Helmreich, and Stapp (1975) from items originally contained in the Sex-Role Stereotype Questionnaire of Rosenkrantz and associates (1968). Three scales (male valued, female valued, and sex specific) comprise the PAQ. In the initial item selection process, college students rated characteristics more typically found in members of one gender than the other, yielding 55 items which significantly differentiated *stereotypical* males and females. Other student judges then rated these 55 items for how characteristic they are of the *ideal* male and female. This procedure yielded eighteen characteristics that were judged to be ideally found in both sexes but more typical of females (female-valued scale), twenty-three items ideally found in both sexes but more typical of males (male-valued scale), and fourteen items judged to be typical of one gender but rated as ideal for only one sex (sex-specific scale). Sex-role classification with the PAQ (as with the other two scales described below) is based on the gender-valued scales only, using the simple median-split procedure; and Spence and Helmreich (1978) have recently developed a short form of the PAQ (twenty-four items), which correlates highly with the original scale. In contrast to the BSRI scales, which show considerable independence, the PAQ M and F scales tend to be positively correlated, especially for males ($r = .47$; for females, $r = .14$), although Spence and Helmreich (1978) report near zero correlations with the short form.

A third scale, the PRF ANDRO scale, has been developed by Berzins, Welling, and Wetter (1975). This scale, designed to approximate the BSRI, contains items selected from a standardized personality test, the Personality Research Form (Jackson, 1967). ANDRO scale items (true-false self-descriptive statements) were selected from the total

PRF item pool on a rational-intuitive basis to encompass the dominant orientations judged to characterize Bem's M (social and intellectual ascendancy, autonomy, orientation toward risks) and F (nurturance, affiliative-expressive concerns, and self-subordination) scales. Advantages of the PRF ANDRO scale include its control for acquiescence response bias and the fact that the items are all drawn from a commonly used research scale. A limitation of the scale is the restricted content range of the PRF items, which were not originally developed for sex-role assessment. The ANDRO M and F scales are substantially correlated with the BSRI scales (ranging from $r = .50$ to $r = .65$), although they do not perfectly overlap by any means. In addition, the M and F scales are somewhat negatively correlated for females ($r = -.24$), although essentially independent for males ($r = -.10$).

A fourth assessment device, developed by Heilbrun (1976), contains items from the Adjective Check List (ACL) (Gough and Heilbrun, 1965). This scale differs in construction and item selection from the others that have been described. Items include those ACL adjectives that "discriminated between college males identified with masculine fathers and college females identified with feminine mothers" (Heilbrun, 1976, p. 184). Thus, this instrument resembles more traditional sex-role measures in that both use gender differences as the criterion for item inclusion. In addition, the ACL scales, unlike the other three measures, use socially undesirable as well as desirable sex-typed traits. For example, Heilbrun's M scale includes adjectives like *conceited, cynical,* and *vindictive,* in addition to the more positive characteristics like *assertive, enterprising,* and *strong.* Similarly, the F scale includes negatively valued items like *fickle, worrying,* and *frivolous.* The ACL scales also have larger negative correlations between the M and F scales ($r = -.24$ for females; $r = -.42$ for males) than the other scales do—suggesting a moderate bipolarity (as in traditional measures) rather than independence of the two scales.

In general, the new sex-role measures, which assess masculine and feminine traits independently, represent a significant advance over earlier measures, which utilize a single bipolar scale. In addition to yielding indices of sex typing and cross-sex typing, as do the traditional scales, the new scales permit the assessment of androgynous and undifferentiated sex roles.

A number of studies have examined the performance of androgynous and sex-typed (and cross-sex-typed) individuals on stereotypically masculine and feminine tasks to determine whether androgynous individuals perform well on both tasks relative to the other groups. Except where otherwise noted, the studies have all utilized the BSRI to assess sex role.

Bem (1975b) found that androgynous and masculine-typed college females, like their male counterparts, showed greater independence in their judgments and were more resistant to conformity pressure than feminine-typed females. Similarly, androgynous and feminine-typed males showed higher levels of playful and nurturant behaviors than masculine-typed males did (Bem, Martyna, and Watson, 1976). Thus, androgynous males and females performed well at both masculine and feminine tasks, whereas sex-typed individuals performed well at only sex-typed tasks. Orlofsky and Windle (1978) examined the performance of the sex-role groups on measures of interpersonal assertiveness (masculine task) and emotional expressivity (feminine task) in TAT stories. As in Bem's research, androgynous individuals tended to perform well on both tasks, while sex-typed individuals performed at a high level on only the sex-specific task. Undifferentiated (low masculinity-low femininity) subjects performed at a moderate level on sex-specific tasks, but, like sex-typed subjects, they did poorly on cross-sex tasks. Finally, cross-sex-typed males did well at the feminine task but poorly on the assertiveness measure, while masculine-typed females did well on both measures. These studies support Bem's contention that psychological androgyny is associated with greater behavioral adaptability than sex typing, although they do not necessarily support her interpretation that sex-typed individuals do poorly at cross-sex tasks because they are motivated to preserve an image of themselves as conforming to sex-role stereotypes and, therefore, avoid cross-sex behavior. A simpler explanation for these findings would be that androgynous individuals have a broader set of behavioral competencies than sex-typed people. Hence, while sex-typed individuals are limited in their behavioral repertoire, androgynous individuals are able to perform effectively whether the situational requirements are for masculine or feminine behaviors.

Still, there is some evidence that motivational factors and avoidance tendencies are at least partially responsible for the restricted behavioral repertoire of sex-typed individuals. A study by Bem and Lenney (1976) asked subjects to perform mundane cross-sex behaviors like preparing a baby bottle or nailing boards together and found that sex-typed individuals were more avoidant of cross-sex tasks than androgynous subjects and that they reported more psychological discomfort and challenge to their sense of masculinity or femininity when compelled to perform these behaviors.

Taken together, these studies provide support for the notion that androgynous individuals possess a broader range of competencies and greater flexibility in their behavior than sex-typed, cross-sex-typed, or undifferentiated individuals. Thus, an important criterion of psychological adaptation, an ability to engage in situationally effective behavior regardless of its traditionally masculine or feminine connotations, has been demonstrated for androgynous individuals.

Other criteria of psychological adaptation have been studied in relation to psychological androgyny versus sex typing. One such referent is ego identity or personality integration. Traditionalists (see, for instance, Hacker, 1957) might argue that an individual manifesting high levels of both masculine and feminine characteristics will have difficulties in personal integration and a confused, fragmented self-image. However, it is equally plausible that the strongest identity integration might be achieved by individuals with well-differentiated personalities. Two studies using quite different measures of ego identity support this second hypothesis. Heilbrun (1976, ACL), using a role-consistency measure of identity, and Orlofsky (1977), using Marcia's (1966) interview/identity status procedure, both demonstrated that androgyny is associated with the highest level of identity resolution in college students. Sex typing, in contrast, tended to occur in individuals (particularly women) who had "foreclosed" on an identity; that is, overidentified with parental values and choices to such an extent that they lacked a truly internal frame of reference. Except for masculine-typed women, cross-sex typing and an undifferentiated sex-role orientation were associated with a diffusion of identity (Orlofsky, 1977).

A third referent for psychological health is self-esteem. A number of studies have found that androgynous individuals have high self-esteem, relative to the other sex-role categories, although masculine-typed males and females evidence high levels of self-esteem as well. In contrast, feminine-typed and undifferentiated individuals, regardless of gender, consistently display low self-esteem relative to the other groups, suggesting that well-developed masculine instrumental characteristics, with or without high levels of femininity, are necessary and sufficient for a positive self-concept and self-confidence (Orlofsky, 1977; Spence, Helmreich, and Stapp, 1975, PAQ; Wetter, 1975, PRF ANDRO).

All the research described thus far suggests that psychological androgyny promotes mental health. However, except for some of the research on behavioral adaptability, this research also suggests that masculine typing is just as adaptive as androgyny, leading to equally high levels of self-esteem and identity resolution—and in females as well as in males. (In fact, a recent study by Jones, Chernovetz, and Hansson, 1978, suggests that masculine-typing may be even more adaptive than androgyny in certain respects, particularly for males. However, the authors' use of questionable classification and statistical procedures makes their conclusions suspect.) In contrast, feminine typing—whether for the cross-sex-typed male or the sex-typed female—has generally appeared as considerably less adaptive. To test whether this pattern holds for the social adjustment of the sex-role groups as well, Orlofsky and Windle (1978) administered a commonly used self-report questionnaire that assesses social alienation and feelings of social rejection and hostility, anxiety, and loneliness. As with the other mental health variables reviewed above, androgynous individuals of both sexes showed the best social adjustment. Unlike the results of other research, however, sex-typed individuals of both sexes also exhibited good social adjustment. In contrast, cross-sex-typed persons of both sexes showed poor social adjustment, as did persons with an undifferentiated orientation. Furthermore, multiple regression analyses on these data indicated that the poor social adjustment of cross-sex-typed men and women was not due to their exhibiting excessive levels of cross-sex behaviors; rather, it was related to their displaying insufficient levels of sex-typed behavior. Thus, at least in the area of social relationships, cross-sex typing appears to have disadvantages for women as well as for men, and sex typing has positive consequences, leading to good social adjustment and a sense of personal well-being. This is not surprising, given the powerful stereotypes of socially acceptable behavior for males and females. Conformity to these stereotypes may lead to behavioral rigidity and, in women, to lowered self-esteem, but it does seem to produce a sense of social acceptability and well-being. Nonconformity to these stereotypes, whereby the individual is deficient in "sex-appropriate" behavior, probably results in a lack of social reinforcement, a sense of being different and unacceptable to others, and consequently feelings of alienation and loneliness. Androgynous individuals, finally, appear to have the best of both worlds. These individuals have a wide range of behaviors and social competencies with which to obtain reinforcements and otherwise interact with the environment, and consequently they make good personal and social adjustments.

One final study should be mentioned, since it bears on this issue of social competency. Kelly and associates (1976) have provided evidence that androgynous individuals are more effective than individuals in the other sex-role groups in a variety of social situations. Their androgynous subjects were rated as highly effective (for instance, speaking with appropriate loudness and manifesting lively affect, short speech latencies, and few verbal stutters), whereas undifferentiated subjects were rated as highly inept and socially ineffective. The masculine- and feminine-typed groups did not differ from one another and tended to fall between the androgynous and undifferentiated groups on the behavioral components of social skills. Interpreting these findings, Kelly and Worell (1977, p. 1112) assert that "complex social responses require the modulation or blending of both masculine- and feminine-typed skills" and conclude that "androgyny probably represents the upper range of a general social competency dimension."

Other research relates to the issue of psychological androgyny and sexual preference. Although considerable past research has linked homosexuality and cross-sex typing, only two studies have used the new sex-role measures. Heilbrun and Thompson (1977), using the ACL M and F scales, found a significant relationship between female homosexuality and masculine sex typing, and a nonsignificant trend toward feminine typing in male homosexuals. Ward (1974), using the PAQ M and F scales, found that male homosexuals tended to cluster in the undifferentiated sex-role group (50 percent) and to some extent in the feminine-typed group (23 percent), and female homosexuals clustered less frequently in the sex-typed group and more frequently in the cross-sex-typed group than female heterosexuals. Commenting on Ward's findings, however, Spence (1977) warns against concluding that cross-sex-typed individuals are likely to display an inverted sexual preference. She notes that while homosexuals often fail to manifest conventional sex-role attributes, the opposite conclusion, that those who fail to exhibit sex-typed characteristics have a high probability of being homosexual, is not supported by the data. While homosexuals may be drawn predominantly from such groups, they still constitute only a relatively small fraction of their number; the majority of individuals who are not sex typed are predominantly heterosexual.

Four basic theories have been put forth to account for sex-role learning. The first type, broadly representative of psychoanalytic and observational learning approaches, posits that children imitate same-sex models (particularly the same-sex parent) more than opposite-sex models for patterning their behavior. A second theory postulates that sex-role characteristics are learned through the differential reinforcement of sex-typed and cross-sex-typed behaviors. Thus, parents (and others) reward and praise boys for masculine behavior and discourage them when they engage in activities that seem feminine; similarly, girls receive positive reinforcement for feminine behavior and negative reinforcement for masculine behavior. A third approach (social learning theory) incorporates the first two, while a fourth (cognitive-developmental theory) encompasses the first two and adds a third process, a self-labeling factor. According to this theory, children first develop a concept of what it is to be male or female, and then, once they have a clear understanding of their own gender identity, they attempt to fit personal behavior to the concept of what is sex appropriate (Kohlberg, 1966). Modeling influences and reinforcement, in this theory, help to determine what the child sees as sex appropriate. This last viewpoint seems best to account for the complexities of sex-role learning. (A more complete discussion of these issues may be found in Maccoby and Jacklin, 1974.)

Research on the development of the androgynous orientation has focused primarily on the role of parental modeling and reinforcement practices, although one study does provide support specifically for the cognitive developmental model. McNamara (1979) showed that cognitive development toward increasing cognitive complexity seems to be a partial prerequisite of androgynous development in male adolescents. Kelly and Worell (1976), using the PRF ANDRO scale and the Parent Behavior Form (PBF) (Worell and Worell, 1974), reported the following differences in parental childrearing practices: Masculine-typed and undifferentiated males described cool, unaffectionate relationships with their parents. Feminine-typed males reported warmth and involvement with the mother, and androgynous males reported affection from both parents. In addition, undifferentiated males reported an absence of cognitive and intellectual involvement with their parents relative to the other groups. For the female categories, masculine-typed women described their parents (particularly the father) as encouraging, stimulating, and rewarding achievement-oriented, intellectually competent, and self-reliant qualities in them. Androgynous women, more than any other sex-role group, reported that they received maternal reinforcement for being curious. In addition, androgynous women described greater maternal involvement and less father permissiveness relative to masculine-typed women. Finally, undifferentiated females reported the least intellectual or achievement encouragement of any kind. This study indicates that both parental and maternal warmth and affection are necessary for the development of psychological androgyny in males, while for females an androgynous orientation is most likely where the mother actively encourages cognitive and intellectual achievement.

A study by Orlofsky (1979), using the BSRI and the PBF, confirmed and expanded on these results for androgynous individuals but differed markedly for cross-sex-typed individuals. First, seven of the thirteen father-behavior scales, but only one of the mother-behavior scales, significantly discriminated among the male sex-role groups, suggesting that the influence of the father's behavior far outweighs the mother's influence in determining the sex-role development of males. This pattern was reversed somewhat for females, as eight maternal-behavior variables, compared to four father variables, significantly differentiated the female groups. As in the Kelly and Worell (1976) study, androgynous males reported receiving liberal amounts of affection from their parents, particularly from the father, but so did masculine-typed males. In addition, these high-masculinity groups both described considerable involvement and cognitive encouragement from the father. Feminine-typed men, in contrast, described their relationships with fathers as consistently poor, with little acceptance or emotional or cognitive involvement and considerable rejection; the mother, according to these cross-sex-typed males, was highly rejecting as well. Even the parental relationships described by undifferentiated males were not as poor as those described by feminine males.

Similar complaints were voiced by cross-sex-typed females. These masculine-typed women described considerable rejection and an absence of warmth or cognitive encouragement from either parent. Androgynous and feminine women described affectionate relationships with both parents, but whereas androgynous women reported considerably more encouragement for cognitive and intellectual achievement from mother (an androgynous model?), feminine women experienced particular closeness and affection with father (an oedipal family constellation?). Undifferentiated women tended to describe their parents' behavior in less favorable terms, but not as negatively as masculine-typed women did.

Although the findings of the Orlofsky and Kelly studies differ somewhat regarding the parental behaviors of sex-typed individuals and considerably for cross-sex-typed subjects, they both suggest that parental—especially paternal—acceptance and warmth foster the development of androgyny in males and that parental—especially maternal—encouragement for intellectual/achievement behaviors fosters similar development in females. Because of the correlational nature of these studies and their reliance on retrospective reports of parental behaviors, one cannot draw definitive conclusions of causality. That is, rather than causing different sex-role outcomes, the parents' behaviors reported by subjects may plausibly have been a reaction to the sex-role behavior and related personality characteristics the child was already exhibiting. Most likely, the parents and the children both influence each other's behavior, so that the pattern of results obtained reflects the interaction styles developed by the various family constellations. Furthermore, no doubt other factors, such as relationships with peers and siblings and school experiences, influence a child's sex-role development. While some of these factors have been researched in the past, none of them have been studied with masculinity and femininity assessed as independent dimensions. This will be the task of future research.

Personal Views and Recommendations

The research described herein supports the validity of the androgyny concept and the new measures developed to assess it. However, a number of issues remain. One issue has to do with the assessment of androgyny and how M and F scores should be combined to yield a sex-role classification scheme. While there is general agreement among investigators to abandon Bem's (1974) three-status classification procedure (Bem, 1977), debate continues on use of Spence, Helmreich, and Stapp's (1975) medians classification procedure or Orlofsky's (1977) difference/medians procedure. The medians procedure is simpler and appears to have greater flexibility for most research applications. However, this procedure seems to be more susceptible than the difference/medians procedure to the effects of social desirability response sets, as described above. Furthermore, the difference/medians procedure is more sensitive to the balance between masculinity and femininity and is, therefore, probably more appropriate for clinical applications and in research where M and F may, if unbalanced, exert inhibitory effects on each other (as in research on behavioral flexibility). (See Spence and Helmreich, in press, for a more detailed discussion of these issues).

Also at issue is whether classification systems should be used at all. Kelly and Worell (1977), for example, recommend that some form of graded continuums or interval scales be developed which might permit more precise predictions than the broad typologies. Along these lines, it should be noted that Spence and her colleagues (for example, Prager, 1977) have been experimenting with various subtractive, additive, and multiplicative combinations of M and F scores in an effort to develop such interval scales. Others (for example, Bem, 1977; Strahan, 1975) have used M and F scores in multiple regression analyses. These provide basically the same information that the typologies provide but without the same loss of precision. Still, it is unlikely that such procedures will totally supplant the use of typologies, since the latter lend themselves to easy interpretation (in research) and are obviously more applicable in clinical assessment with individuals.

Additional methodological and conceptual issues have been raised. For example, Kelly and associates (1977) and Spence and Helmreich (1978) suggest that negatively valued as well as positively valued stereotypically sex-typed traits should be used in assessing sex role, since negative traits may be a functional part of some or all sex-role orientations.

Furthermore, there are a number of questions which remain regarding the dimensionality of sex-role behaviors. Research with the new sex-role inventories has shown that many aspects of masculinity and femininity vary independently, forming two separate dimensions; however, masculinity and femininity themselves may be multidimensional qualities. Spence (1977) has argued that distinctions should be drawn among behavioral, attitudinal, and personality aspects of sex roles and has noted that minimal relationships have been found between sex-role measures and assessments of sex-role ideology, interests, and vocational and recreational preferences. Such findings suggest that caution should be exercised before attributing greater generality to the androgyny concept regarding individuals' life styles than it merits (for example, equating it with sex-role transcendence or egalitarianism). They also suggest that separate measures of masculine and feminine interests and role behaviors will need to be developed if we are to fully assess the ways in which sex roles are changing in contemporary society and the implications of these changes.

Other research has suggested that even within the sphere of sex-typed personality traits, masculinity and femininity may not be unitary phenomena. Factor analysis of the BSRI (Waters, Waters, and Pincus, 1977; Whetton and Swindells, 1977) has suggested a number of factors rather than the two broad masculinity and femininity factors suggested by Bem. Similarly, in an extensive factor analysis of the sex-role attributes of American adolescents, Suziedelis (1977) has shown that while the typical list of masculine adjectives clusters in a single factor for boys, for girls two distinct factors emerge (which he labels Activity and Potency). Similarly, while feminine characteristics cluster in a single factor for girls, these appear to form two distinct clusters for boys (Sociability and Expressivity). Comparing the sexes on these factors, Suziedelis found that girls and boys differ considerably on Expressiveness and Potency, but not much on Sociability and Activity. Thus, separate consideration of these factors appears advisable in future clinical or research assessment of masculinity and femininity. This will require the development of more refined measures and a multidimensional approach to assessing sex-role behaviors.

Finally, a thorny set of problems remain regarding an even more basic aspect of the dimensionality issue, that having to do with whether masculinity and femininity form a single bipolar dimension, as traditional perspectives assume, or two independent dimensions, as recent approaches argue. (Recall that the androgyny concept rests on the validity of the latter dualistic position.) As discussed above, the bulk of the evidence (using correlational analyses with the BSRI, PAQ, and PRF ANDRO M and F scales) favors the dualistic conception. However, there is also evidence that some aspects of masculinity/femininity fit a single bipolar dimension. The PAQ sex-specific (MF) scale is a case in point, as are the ACL M and F scales. The PAQ MF scale, it will be recalled, is composed of items which were rated as more typical of one sex than the other and desirable for only one rather than both sexes (for example, dominance and aggressiveness were rated as typical and desirable for males but not for females; cries easily and needs security were rated as typical and desirable for females but not for males). Spence and Helmreich (1978) report that this is a bipolar scale (that is, the masculine and feminine items are negatively correlated). Thus, masculine and feminine traits are not arranged perfectly into either a dualistic or a bipolar, unidimensional pattern. Rather, certain attributes appear to be independent of each other, others correlate positively with each other, and still others appear to be somewhat mutually exclusive. In part, the pattern of relationship seems to be a function of the manner in which the attributes are identified as masculine or feminine (note the item selection procedures described above for the various scales, which range from ratings of sex-based social desirability for the BSRI to gender differences in item endorsement for the ACL). Clearly, further research with a variety of item selection procedures will be necessary to delineate the range of masculine and feminine characteristics and their interrelationships.

These complications, however, should not obscure the fact that a number of personality traits have been identified with substantial regularity across the new sex-role measures which do fit a dualistic pattern. That these stereotypically masculine and feminine traits have been found to be characteristic of and functional for both sexes has done much to shift psychologists' attention from an outmoded conception of sex roles, based on unverified assumptions of innate or necessary psychological differences between the sexes, to a conceptualization which emphasizes the social skills and behavioral competencies which all individuals, regardless of gender, require for effective living in our changing society. This shift has produced some important conclusions regarding the mental health implications of various sex-role positions, which challenge former views. For example, whereas in the past, sex typing was seen as the most adaptive and cross-sex typing as the least adaptive sex-role outcome, current research suggests that androgynous and undifferentiated orientations (outcomes not even conceptualized previously) occupy these polar positions. Sex typing and cross-sex typing appear to occupy an intermediate range of adaptation. Sex-typed individuals appear to be better adjusted socially than cross-sex-typed individuals by virtue of their greater conformity to societal standards, but both are seen as possessing limited social competencies relative to the androgynous individual. Actually, the issue of sex typing versus cross-sex typing appears to be less important, in certain repsects, than the issue of masculine versus feminine typing, because, as the research on self-esteem indicates, masculine qualities appear to have greater utility than feminine qualities, for females as well as males. Such findings call into question the socialization process which encourages girls to suppress or fail to learn the very behaviors (instrumental, agentic) that lead to high self-esteem in males (and in masculine and androgynous females). But again, androgyny seems to be most adaptive. A broad range of competencies and flexibility in behavior is especially important for both sexes in contemporary society, now that changing social, political, and economic conditions not only allow but also require individuals to function in a variety of roles that were once the almost exclusive province of each sex.

Application to Particular Variables

To date, the new sex-role measures have been used primarily for research, mainly with college populations. While they can be expected to have great potential in future clinical assessment, largely supplanting existing objective and projective measures of sex-role characteristics, such applications have not yet occurred with much frequency. They have yet to be adapted for work with children or older adults, and research is only now proceeding to develop norms for different socioeconomic and ethnic groups.

There are limitations in the use of self-report measures for assessing young children's sex roles, since such measures presuppose an adequate vocabulary. At present, the new sex-role measures have not yet been applied to sex-role assessment in children. For the most part, such assessment has continued to use projective and observational methods (for example, toy or activity preferences). These measures generally suffer from the same inherent bias toward bipolar M-F assessment as traditional M-F scales for adults. Thus, if androgyny is to be assessed in children, current measures will require revision or new measures will have to be developed which allow for independent assessment of masculinity and femininity.

References

Bakan, D. *The Duality of Human Existence.* Chicago: Rand McNally, 1966.

Bem, S. L. "The Measurement of Psychological Androgyny." *Journal of Consulting and Clinical Psychology,* 1974, *42,* 155-162.

Bem, S. L. "Androgyny vs. the Tight Little Lives of Fluffy Women and Chesty Men." *Psychology Today,* 1975a, *9* (4), 58-62.

Bem, S. L. "Sex Role Adaptability: One Consequence of Psychological Androgyny." *Journal of Personality and Social Psychology,* 1975b, *31,* 634-643.

Bem, S. L. "Probing the Promise of Androgyny." In A. G. Kaplan and J. P. Bean (Eds.), *Beyond Sex Role Stereotypes: Readings Toward a Psychology of Androgyny.* Boston: Little, Brown, 1976.

Bem, S. L. "On the Utility of Alternative Procedures for Assessing Psychological Androgyny." *Journal of Consulting and Clinical Psychology,* 1977, *45,* 196-205.

Bem, S. L., and Lenney, E. "Sex Typing and the Avoidance of Cross-Sex Behavior." *Journal of Personality and Social Psychology,* 1976, *33,* 48-54.

Bem, S. L., Martyna, W., and Watson, C. "Sex Typing and Androgyny: Further Explorations of the Expressive Domain." *Journal of Personality and Social Psychology,* 1976, *34,* 1016-1023.

Bernard, J. *Sex Differences: An Overview.* New York: MSS Modular Publications, 1974.

Berzins, J. I., Welling, M. A., and Wetter, R. E. "The PRF ANDRO Scale." Unpublished manual, University of Kentucky, 1975.

Block, J. H. "Conceptions of Sex Role: Some Cross-Cultural and Longitudinal Perspectives." *American Psychologist*, 1973, *28*, 512-526.

Block, J. H. "Issues, Problems, and Pitfalls in Assessing Sex Differences: A Critical Review of the Psychology of Sex Differences." *Merrill Palmer Quarterly*, 1976, *22*, 283-308.

Constantinople, A. "Masculinity-Femininity: An Exception to a Famous Dictum." *Psychological Bulletin*, 1973, *80*, 389-407.

Fasteau, M. F. *The Male Machine*. New York: Dell, 1975.

Freud, S. *An Outline of Psychoanalysis*. New York: Norton, 1940.

Gough, H. G., and Heilbrun, A. B. *Manual for the Adjective Check List and the Need Scales for the ACL*. Palo Alto, Calif.: Consulting Psychologists Press, 1965.

Hacker, H. "The New Burdens of Masculinity." *Marriage and Family Living*, 1957, *3*, 227-233.

Heilbrun, A. B. "Measurement of Masculine and Feminine Sex Role Identities as Independent Dimensions." *Journal of Consulting and Clinical Psychology*, 1976, *44*, 183-190.

Heilbrun, A. B., and Thompson, N. L. "Sex Role Identity and Male and Female Homosexuality." *Sex Roles*, 1977, *3*, 65-79.

Horney, K. *New Ways in Psychoanalysis*. New York: Norton, 1939.

Jackson, D. N. *Personality Research Form Manual*. Goshen, N.Y.: Research Psychologists Press, 1967.

Jones, W. H., Chernovitz, M. E., and Hansson, R. O. "The Enigma of Androgyny: Differential Implications for Males and Females?" *Journal of Consulting and Clinical Psychology*, 1978, *46*, 298-313.

Jung, C. G. *Two Essays on Analytical Psychology*. New York: Meridian Books, 1956.

Kelly, J. A., and Worell, J. "New Formulations of Sex Roles and Androgyny: A Critical Review." *Journal of Consulting and Clinical Psychology*, 1977, *45*, 1101-1115.

Kelly, J. A., and Worell, L. "Parent Behaviors Related to Masculine, Feminine, and Androgynous Sex Role Orientations." *Journal of Consulting and Clinical Psychology*, 1976, *44*, 843-851.

Kelly, J. A., and others. "Sex Roles as Social Skills: A Behavioral Analysis of 'Masculinity,' 'Femininity' and 'Psychological Androgyny.' " Paper presented at meeting of Association for the Advancement of Behavior Therapy, New York, Dec. 1976.

Kelly, J. A., and others. "Socially Undesirable Sex-Correlated Characteristics: Implications for Androgyny and Adjustment." *Journal of Consulting and Clinical Psychology*, 1977, *45*, 1186-1187.

Kohlberg, L. "A Cognitive-Developmental Analysis of Children's Sex-Role Concepts and Attitudes." In E. E. Maccoby (Ed.), *The Development of Sex Differences*. Stanford, Calif.: Stanford University Press, 1966.

Maccoby, E. E., and Jacklin, C. N. *The Psychology of Sex Differences*. Stanford, Calif.: Stanford University Press, 1974.

McNamara, J. T. "Cognitive Development and Psychological Androgyny in Adolescent Males." Unpublished doctoral dissertation, University of Missouri, St. Louis, 1979.

Marcia, J. E. "Development and Validation of Ego Identity Status." *Journal of Personality and Social Psychology*, 1966, *3*, 551-558.

Matteson, D. R. *Adolescence Today: Sex Roles and the Search for Identity*. Homewood, Ill.: Dorsey Press, 1975.

Money, J., and Ehrhardt, A. *Man and Woman, Boy and Girl*. Baltimore: Johns Hopkins University Press, 1972.

Mussen, P. H. "Long-Term Consequents of Masculinity of Interests in Adolescence." *Journal of Consulting Psychology*, 1962, *26*, 435-440.

Orlofsky, J. L. "Sex Role Orientation, Identity Formation, and Self-Esteem in College Men and Women." *Sex Roles*, 1977, *3*, 561-575.

Orlofsky, J. L. "Parental Antecedents of Sex Role Orientation in College Men and Women." *Sex Roles*, 1979, *5*, 495-512.

Orlofsky, J. L., Aslin, A. L., and Ginsburg, S. D. "Differential Effectiveness of Two Classification Procedures on the Bem Sex-Role Inventory." *Journal of Personality Assessment*, 1977, *41*, 414-416.

Orlofsky, J. L., and Windle, M. T. "Sex Role Orientation, Behavioral Adaptability, and Personal Adjustment." *Sex Roles*, 1978, *4*, 801-811.

Parsons, T., and Bales, R. F. *Family Socialization and Interaction Process.* New York: Free Press, 1955.

Pleck, J. H. "The Psychology of Sex Roles: Traditional and New Views." In L. A. Carter and A. F. Scott (Eds.), *Women and Men: Changing Roles, Relationships and Perceptions.* New York: Aspen Institute for Humanistic Studies, 1976.

Prager, K. J. "The Relationship Between Identity Status, Intimacy Status, Self-Esteem, and Psychological Androgyny in College Women." Unpublished doctoral dissertation, University of Texas, Austin, 1977.

Rosenkrantz, P. S., and others. "Sex-Role Stereotypes and Self-Concepts in College Students." *Journal of Consulting and Clinical Psychology*, 1968, *32*, 287-295.

Sheriffs, A. C., and McKee, J. P. "Qualitative Aspects of Beliefs About Men and Women." *Journal of Personality*, 1957, *25*, 451-464.

Spence, J. T. "Traits, Roles and the Concept of Androgyny." Paper presented at conference on Perspectives on the Psychology of Women, Michigan State University, 1977.

Spence, J. T., and Helmreich, R. *The Psychological Dimensions of Masculinity and Femininity: Their Correlates and Antecedents.* Austin: University of Texas Press, 1978.

Spence, J. T., and Helmreich, R. "On Assessing Androgyny." *Sex Roles*, in press.

Spence, J. T., Helmreich, R., and Stapp, J. "Ratings of Self and Peers on Sex-Role Attributes and Their Relations to Self-Esteem and Conceptions of Masculinity and Femininity." *Journal of Personality and Social Psychology*, 1975, *32*, 29-39.

Strahan, R. F. "Remarks on Bem's Measurement of Psychological Androgyny: Alternative Methods and a Supplementary Analysis." *Journal of Consulting and Clinical Psychology*, 1975, *43*, 568-571.

Suziedelis, A. "Differentiation of 'Masculine' and 'Feminine' Among Adolescent Girls." Paper presented at 85th meeting of American Psychological Association, San Francisco, 1977.

Ward, S. "Range of Sex-Role Identity and Self-Esteem in a Homosexual Sample." Unpublished honors thesis, University of Texas, Austin, 1974.

Waters, C. W., Waters, L. K., and Pincus, S. "Factor Analysis of Masculine and Feminine Sex-Typed Items from the Bem Sex-Role Inventory." *Psychological Reports*, 1977, *40*, 567-570.

Weitz, S. *Sex Roles: Biological, Psychological, and Social Foundations.* New York: Oxford University Press, 1977.

Wetter, R. E. "Levels of Self-Esteem Associated with Four Sex-Role Categories." Paper presented at symposium on sex roles, at meeting of American Psychological Association, Chicago, Aug. 1975.

Whetton, C., and Swindells, T. "A Factor Analysis of the Bem Sex-Role Inventory." *Journal of Clinical Psychology,* 1977, *33,* 150-153.

Worell, L., and Worell, J. "The Parent Behavior Form." Unpublished manual, University of Kentucky, 1974.

Yorburg, B. *Sexual Identity: Sex Roles and Social Change.* New York: Wiley, 1974.

53

Eugene E. Levitt

Sexual Dysfunction

Sexual dysfunction refers to a disorder in which the individual is chronically unable to obtain expected gratification from sexual acts, usually coitus, in the absence of physical etiology. In addition, the disorder must be severe enough to result in unavoidable unhappiness and to cause the sufferer to seek remedial assistance.

Background and Current Status

The term *sexual dysfunction* has enjoyed a recent sharp increase in national prominence. Since the publication of the vanguard work by Masters and Johnson in 1970, numerous magazine and newspaper articles and professional and scientific reports have been devoted to the topic. Earlier, the term itself was not in common use. Sexual problems were surely known to exist, but the prevailing professional philosophy was that they were merely a secondary facet of a basic emotional disorder. One treated the main neurosis, alleviated it, and the sexual problem disappeared. Focusing on the dysfunction—defining it and developing treatment strategies aimed directly at it—was futile as long as the underlying disorder remained unremedied.

The foregoing was, at least, the prevalent theory. The work of Masters and Johnson, perhaps conjunctively with a relaxation in taboos about candid discussion of sexual problems and the rise of behavior therapy, resulted in a reexamination of the theory. The discovery of note was that it had never worked well. Ignored sexual dysfunctions tended *not* to fade away. They needed to be dealt with in their own right.

The change in treatment strategy brought with it for the first time the need to define the various sexual dysfunctions clearly. A number of classification systems have been proposed, all stemming essentially from the original Masters and Johnson quadripartite classification: orgasmic dysfunction and dyspareunia (painful intercourse) in women; impotence and premature ejaculation in men. More recent classifications (Kaplan, 1974; Levine and Yost, 1976; Mellan, 1971; Sotile, Kilmann, and Scovern, 1977) increase the complexity of the original Masters and Johnson classification system by introducing causal factors and the presence or absence of occasional orgasm into the definitions. Classification systems may thus be either totally descriptive or partly dynamic. No system seems to be clearly based on treatment approaches.

Despite the general agreement among classification systems, some serious problems concerning definition remain unresolved. An important definiendum is duration. A man who cannot, at this moment, obtain a desired erection is, at this moment, impotent. How often must this condition occur in order to warrant a diagnosis of dysfunction as an entity? The same consideration applies to orgasm and painful intercourse in the female. The definition of "premature" in premature ejaculation presents an especially slippery problem; a consensual standard seems impossible to derive.

An original Masters and Johnson solution was to ignore the frequency factor in female orgasmic dysfunction, although they did use the term *primary orgasmic dysfunction* to distinguish the woman who had never had an orgasm by any means. A primary type of impotence was also distinguished, but both impotence and premature ejaculation were defined by arbitrary frequencies. Impotence referred to the penile behavior of a man who is unable to obtain an erection for copulation when desired in as many as 25 percent of attempts. The frequency that defined premature ejaculation was absence of orgasm in the female partner in 50 percent of coital encounters. (Semmens and Semmens, 1976, have formalized the affected-partner standard by including it in their definition of dysfunction: *premature ejaculation causing female dysfunction.*)

The arbitrariness of these definitions is obvious. The Masters and Johnson definition of premature ejaculation, for example, could classify as functional a man with an average orgasm latency of less than a minute, while his fellow, who may be able to maintain an erection for two or three times as long, may be diagnosed as dysfunctional. A sexagenerian couple could be quite satisfied with successful coitus in three of four attempts.

The problem is that the conventional classification systems are composed of idealized definitions. The directly underlying assumptions are that (1) the female should have intercourse invariably without pain and with orgasm and (2) the male should always be able to obtain an erection when it is desired and should invariably be able to maintain that erection until both he and his partner are completely satisfied. In reality, such perfect persons are rarely found. Many individuals who are dysfunctional according to idealized definitions are nevertheless satisfied with their sexual adjustments and see no reason to seek improvement. The individual who is dissatisfied with his or her sexual performance and who becomes a patient, therefore, yields a somewhat different set of definitions. Impotence becomes inability to perform in about three out of every four attempts; premature means ejaculation that occurs either before intromission or, at best, two to three seconds after. Female sexual dysfunctions run the full range suggested by Sotile, Kilmann, and Scovern (1977), from lack of sex drive through "sexual anesthesia" to arousal difficulties. Dyspareunia invariably is sufficiently distracting to cause loss of interest in sexual behavior. These definitions conform to the realities of the clinical assessment situation.

Critical Discussion

General Areas of Concern

The assessment of dysfunction is simultaneously an assessment of function, just as diagnosing disease is at the same time an evaluation of health. It hardly matters whether one talks of function or dysfunction. Clinical assessment is, however, somewhat different from experimental measurement. The bulk of the measuring instruments in the sexual dysfunction area were designed to evaluate function in the research situation. Many can be adapted for clinical use, but some appear impractical. The latter category includes all the physiological measures of sexual arousal, such as the penile plethysmograph (Abel and Blanchard, 1976), the vaginal plethysmograph (Geer, Morokoff, and Greenwood, 1974), and radio telemetric techniques (Fox and Medill, 1973). Direct observation of the patient in sexual behavior remains taboo. The social order still requires that primary information whereby sexual dysfunction is examined be obtained *verbally,* from the patient and/or his or her partner or partners. The Effeminacy Scale (Schatzberg and others, 1975), a list of 67 behaviors, is administered by observing the subjects. However, none of the behaviors are overtly sexual, and the instrument has no evident value in assessing sexual functioning.

Several reviews of measurement procedures in the sexual function area (Bancroft, 1974; Barlow, 1977; Levitt, 1976a) indicate that a number of the measures developed for various experimental interests reach beyond the scope of clinical assessment of dysfunction. Instruments for the assessment of gender identity (Eysenck, 1971a; Freund and others, 1974; Goldberg, 1971), of homosexual inclination (Feldman and others, 1966; Ohlson and Wilson, 1974), of motivation for gender reassignment (Lindgren and Pauly, 1975), and of general attitude toward sexuality (Eysenck, 1971b; Thorne, 1966) usually have no more than indirect relevance for the individual case of dysfunction.

Comparative Philosophies and Theories

Most of the objective instruments described in this chapter are not in common use in clinical assessment of sexual dysfunction. The case history based on clinical interview is probably the usual diagnostic method. There is a sharp difference in viewpoint over the degree of detail that is required in a case history. Doubtlessly there are not many practitioners who closely follow the method of Masters and Johnson (1970), in which two days are devoted to assessment and the outline of the case history covers seventeen printed pages. Diagnostic interviews requiring anywhere from two to four hours, however, are not uncommon. The length of these evaluations is justified on the grounds that the clinician cannot know which facts, especially those antecedent to the current situation, may eventually prove to be important in the therapy process.

Lengthy diagnostic interviews invariably include a heavy emphasis on anamnesis. An opposing point of view is that a really detailed case history is wasteful because anamnestic data are generally not useful in treatment. Since contemporary treatment tends to be either behavioral or a combination of the behavioral and the dynamic, diagnostic evaluation should focus more sharply on the patient's current situation. A few historical facts may turn out to be significant in therapy, but they will almost always be directly related to the presenting problem. They can be elicited simply by obtaining the history of the major symptoms.

Elaboration on Critical Points

There are five types of measures that are either used in clinical assessment or can be adapted for such use: (1) structured interviews; (2) simple scales, usually for the estimation of arousal; (3) sex experiences checklists; (4) instruments that combine the checklist with subjective reaction measures; and (5) the patient diary.

Structured Interviews. The detailed, structured, sex history interview was popularized by Masters and Johnson (1970). Similar assessment techniques have been proposed by Pion and Wagner (1976), Hartman and Fithian (1972), Cooper (1969), and the Group for the Advancement of Psychiatry (1973). Most agencies that deal extensively with sexually dysfunctional patients have developed their own particular interview schedules or patient-administered questionnaires. A published example is the Sexual Performance Evaluation of the Marriage Council of Philadelphia, which appears as an appendix in the GAP report.

The use of entire structured sex history interviews in clinical assessment is probably not common. It is a time-consuming, shotgun tactic that may require three or more hours of the diagnostician's time, with a considerable accumulation of information that is irrelevant to treatment. Elaborate histories are standard in psychodiagnosis in general, simply because it is often not possible to determine beforehand which pieces of information will eventually be useful. In most instances, however, the presenting complaint of the psychiatric patient tends to be more vague and diffuse and less crystallized than the problem of the individual suffering from a sexual dysfunction. Some agencies have developed standard interviews or patient questionnaires for each type of dysfunction. The GAP report suggests that "depending upon the individual clinical situation, one or more lines of inquiry" in its proposed sex history interview "could be sufficient and appropriate" (p. 70). Kolodny (1971) used a short form of the elaborate Masters and Johnson (1970) sex history outline.

Unidimensional Scales. The simplest approach to the assessment of dysfunction is a so-called "scale" that is anchored by at least two points and is treated ordinally. An example is Kohlenberg's (1974) ten-point scale for self-assessment of arousal in masturbation, anchored at zero (not arousing) and ten (extremely arousing). The next-higher development is a scale that features a verbal description of each point. An example of this type was employed by Tennent, Bancroft, and Cass (1974) to obtain patient self-reports about sexual ideation (see Table 1).

Table 1. A Simple Scale for Assessing Sexual Ideation

Score	Behavior
0	No sexual thoughts at all
1	Sexual thoughts very infrequent
2	Sexual thoughts some days but not every day
3	Sexual thoughts at least once or twice a day
4	Sexual thoughts frequent but only sometimes associated with sexual excitement
5	Sexual thoughts frequent and usually associated with feelings of sexual excitement

From Tennent, Bancroft, and Cass (1974).

In principle, an index of this kind can be adapted to provide a quantitative measure of any patient reaction. It is used in various forms in most of the more complex instruments for the measurement of sexual function-dysfunction.

Experiences Checklists. An obvious tactic in the assessment of sexual dysfunction is the identification of sexual areas in which the patient has and has not functioned; that is, a survey of the breadth of the patient's sexual experience. All that is required is a list of possible experiences, calling for a yes-no response.

A number of so-called sex experiences checklists have been developed, beginning with relatively short ones like those of Podel and Perkins (1957) and Brady and Levitt (1965). Recent formulations (Bentler, 1968a, 1968b; Griffitt, 1975; Zuckerman, 1973) are more elaborate, differing in the scope of included behaviors and in specific wording but otherwise similar in structure and intent to the earlier versions.

Experience checklists appear to have been developed largely for research purposes, but they have evident utility in clinical assessment. Their value is limited because they deal only with a single dimension of sexual functioning and ignore other important dimensions, such as experience frequency and effects of the experience.

Subjective Reaction Measures. One of the first attempts to develop an all-purpose assessment instrument that would be superior to the simple checklist was the Sexual Interest Measure (Harbison and others, 1974), for some odd reason abbreviated by its authors as SIN. The SIN borrowed a polar adjective scale proposed earlier by Marks and Sartorius (1967) (see Table 2). It is used to provide seven-point measures of four possible

Table 2. A Segment of the SIN Matrix

Concept	Adjective	1	2	3	4	5	6	7	
Kissing	Seductive								Repulsive
	Sexy								Sexless
	Exciting								Dull
	Erotic								Frigid

From Harbison and others (1974).

reactions to each of five sexual behaviors: kissing, being kissed, touching, being touched, and intercourse. Obviously, the number of behaviors is minimal compared to a sex experiences checklist, but the clinician is, of course, free to add as needed. The dimensions can also be varied to suit clinical requisites. In fact, the four included in the SIN are questionable choices because of potential overlap. "Sexy" and "erotic" are very likely to be perceived as synonymous by the respondent, with "seductive" not far behind. "Interesting" as a substitute for "exciting" might yield a broader response. The SIN is not recommended itself for clinical evaluation, but its construction principles can be employed to create assessment tools according to the demands of the clinical situation.

A more direct attempt to extend the utility of the experiences checklist led to the development of the Sexual Interaction Inventory (SII) by Lopiccolo and Steger (1974). The SII consists of seventeen heterosexual behaviors, each requiring six responses, each on a six-point scale. Two deal with occurrence ("never" through "always"). The other four deal with reactions ("extremely unpleasant" through "extremely pleasant"). An illustrative portion of the SII is reproduced in Table 3.

The SII is a promising tool both in clinical assessment and research. Its limitations are a function of the fact that it was designed for heterosexual, married couples. Also, the use of the pleasant-unpleasant dimension could prove troublesome on occasion because it is not clearly synonymous with arousing-not arousing.

The Sexual Arousal Inventory (Hoon, Hoon, and Wincze, 1976) is an attempt to circumvent the shortcomings of the SII. The expression "loved one" is employed instead of "male and female" as in the SII. The word "ejaculates" does not appear among the

Table 3. Illustrations of Items in the SII

The male caressing the female's breasts with his mouth (lips or tongue).
When you and your mate engage in sexual behavior, does this particular activity usually occur? How often would you like this activity to occur?

1. Currently occurs:
    1. ___ Never
    2. ___ Rarely (10% of the time)
    3. ___ Occasionally (25% of the time)
    4. ___ Fairly often (50% of the time)
    5. ___ Usually (75% of the time)
    6. ___ Always

2. I would like it to occur:
    1. ___ Never
    2. ___ Rarely (10% of the time)
    3. ___ Occasionally (25% of the time)
    4. ___ Fairly often (50% of the time)
    5. ___ Usually (75% of the time)
    6. ___ Always

How pleasant do you currently find this activity to be? How pleasant do you think your mate finds this activity to be?

3. I find this activity:
    1. ___ Extremely unpleasant
    2. ___ Moderately unpleasant
    3. ___ Slightly unpleasant
    4. ___ Slightly pleasant
    5. ___ Moderately pleasant
    6. ___ Extremely pleasant

4. I think my mate finds this activity:
    1. ___ Extremely unpleasant
    2. ___ Moderately unpleasant
    3. ___ Slightly unpleasant
    4. ___ Slightly pleasant
    5. ___ Moderately pleasant
    6. ___ Extremely pleasant

From Lopiccolo and Steger (1974).

behaviors. Where there are five behaviors on the SII dealing with orgasm, there is only one on the SAI, with a complementary increase in attention to foreplay and fantasy stimulation. The response scale of the SAI is worth special note (see Table 4). It represents an unusual attention to explicating scale points. It also introduces the possibility that the behavior may be repulsive or distracting or that the respondent may not be certain whether it is actually sexually arousing. An impressive correlation of $r = .75$ has been reported between SAI scores and vaginal blood volume in a small group of subjects (Wincze, Hoon, and Hoon, 1976).

Table 4. Response Scale of the SAI

−1	adversely affects arousal; unthinkable, repulsive, distracting
0	doesn't affect sexual arousal
1	possibly causes sexual arousal
2	sometimes causes sexual arousal; slightly arousing
3	usually causes sexual arousal; moderately arousing
4	almost always sexually arousing; very arousing
5	always causes sexual arousal; extremely arousing

From Hoon, Hoon, and Wincze (1976).

A problem with the SAI is that it lacks a frequency component. Not only is the respondent not required to indicate whether he or she has actually had a particular sexual experience, but a response is appropriate even if the behavior has never actually been experienced. The response procedure does not separate fantasy from actuality.

The Patient Diary. Patient-administered questionnaires are not at all uncommon in assessing sexual dysfunction, as in psychodiagnosis in general. The questionnaire usually is administered at intake or at the formal beginning of a diagnostic phase, and it calls on the patient for an anamnestic effort. A variable degree of unreliability is inherent in data collected by recall.

An alternative—or at least a collateral adjunct—is the patient diary, an ongoing daily record of sexual behavior, arousal, thoughts, or whatever other data are necessary for assessment as well as for evaluating the course of treatment. The substance of the diary is likely to be determined by the dysfunction. Table 5 presents a segment of the diary used by Cooper and Ismail (1972) to evaluate the outcome of drug treatment of impotence.

Table 5. Items from the Cooper-Ismail Patient Diary for Assessing Impotence

Daily Self-Rating Schedule 9 p.m.-9 a.m.

(1) Occurrence of spontaneous erection   yes/no
No. of times _____   Duration of erection _____ mins.
With/without sexual fantasies _____

Quality of erection:	Strong	Average	Poor
	1	2	3

Presence of sexual desire:	Strong	Average	Poor
	1	2	3

(2) Occurrence of coital attempt   yes/no
No. of times _____   Time of occurrence _____ am/pm
With/without ejaculation _____

Degree of satisfaction:	Satisfied	Unsatisfied
	1	2

Presence of sexual desire:	Strong	Average	Poor
	1	2	3

From Cooper and Ismail (1972).

Patient diaries covering all major sexual dysfunctions have been in use for a number of years at the Institute for Sex Research in Hamburg, West Germany. The *Tagebuch* is regularly employed in assessing dysfunction and outcome of treatment (see Arentewicz and Schmidt, 1976). An item from the Hamburg ISR patient diary is reproduced in Table 6 to illustrate the format.

Table 6. Sample Item from Patient Diary Used at Hamburg Institute for Sex Research

	Mon.	Tues.	Wed.
Did you want to have sexual intercourse with your partner?			
No			
Yes, somewhat			[and so on.]
Yes, strongly			
Don't know			

From Arentewicz and Schmidt (1976).

The diary is likely to be distinctly more accurate as an assessment tool than a past-history technique. It is possible, however, that the focus on behavior that is needed to fill out the diary may itself have some effect on that behavior. This phenomenon has been found with other sorts of self-monitored behaviors (Zimmerman and Levitt, 1975). The influence of self-monitoring is usually benign; the symptom's true intensity becomes visible for the first time, validating the patient's quest for treatment, or it is accurately perceived as exaggerated and not consequential enough to warrant a formal intervention. Thus far, there are no available data on the incidental effects of the diaries of sexually dysfunctional patients.

Personal Views and Recommendations

If a behavioral treatment is to be used—the treatment of choice currently—then the bulk of a detailed case history will be wasted. Of course, it is necessary to know the course of symptomatology—it makes a difference whether the dysfunction is secondary or primary. In general, the significant facts are in the patient's *current situation*: his symptoms, practices, feelings, and knowledge, and those of his partner. History taking should focus on the contemporaneous. It is important to know whether an impotent patient can masturbate to climax, but it is unlikely to matter when he first masturbated or how often he masturbated in the past. A diagnostic interview need not last longer than about an hour.

The argument of traditionalists who insist on elaborate case histories is analogous to the position that a laparotomy should be performed on every patient who complains of lower abdominal pain because surgery will eventually be necessary for a small number of them.

When diagnostic interviews are conducted by a co-sexual therapy team, the cross-sex interviews can often be quite brief. It is not at all necessary to replicate the same-sex interview, which is likely to prove extremely wasteful. The cross-sex interview should be restricted to elucidation of areas where the same-sex interviews produced conflicting results; or potentially significant areas that were opened by one of the therapists but not the other; or areas where it is deemed desirable to attempt to collect information by a person of the opposite sex. With an experienced team, the cross-sex interviews frequently take no more than a half hour.

The neglect of objective instruments in clinical assessment is unfortunate. These measures can improve the view of the case while consuming little of the clinician's time. Furthermore, they constitute an objective basis for the evaluation of therapy. Practitioners in the sex counseling and therapy area should give serious consideration to the use of objective tests in assessment, modifying them when necessary and possible to fit the needs of individual cases.

Application to Particular Variables

The incidence of sexual dysfunction depends, of course, on the classification system. No really reliable estimates can be made if one uses idealized definitions. The oft-quoted view of Masters and Johnson (1970) that half of American marriages are dysfunctional stands on uncertain grounds.

If it is agreed that seeking professional help is an essential aspect of the definition of any sexual dysfunction, professionals can at least estimate *relative* incidence with some confidence from reports by treatment agencies. Levitt (1976b) aggregated a series of such epidemiological studies, which showed that almost two thirds of sexually dysfunctional persons are women. Fifty percent of all cases complained of orgasmic dysfunction, and the remaining 15 percent suffered from dyspareunia. The male segment was composed of 20 percent who sought help for impotence and 15 percent who were premature ejaculators. These comparative estimates square with several large-scale general surveys (Bell and Bell, 1972; Gebhard, 1966) which suggest that somewhere between five and ten million American adult women have never had an orgasm in coitus, and not more than four million adult males under the age of 65 are classifiable as impotent (Kinsey, Pomeroy, and Martin, 1948).

The female dysfunctions tend to be uncorrelated with age; in contrast, impotence is positively related to age, with the bulk of the sufferers in the 55-65 age group. Since younger persons are more likely to seek help for sexual problems, it is possible that a larger proportion of dysfunctional females are seen by professional interventionists, thus emphasizing further the differential incidence of male and female dysfunctions.

References

Abel, G. G., and Blanchard, E. B. "The Measurement and Generation of Sexual Arousal in Male Sexual Deviates." In M. Hersen, R. M. Eisler, and P. M. Miller (Eds.), *Progress in Behavior Modification.* Vol. 2. New York: Academic Press, 1976.

Arentewicz, G., and Schmidt, G. "Treatment of Patients Suffering from Sexual Function Disturbances: Problems and Results." Paper presented at annual meeting of International Academy of Sex Research, Hamburg, Germany, 1976.

Bancroft, J. *Deviant Sexual Behavior: Modification and Change.* Oxford: Clarendon Press, 1974.

Barlow, D. H. "Assessment of Sexual Behavior." In A. R. Ciminero, K. S. Calhoun, and H. E. Adams (Eds.), *Handbook of Behavioral Assessment.* New York: Wiley, 1977.

Bell, P. L., and Bell, R. R. "Sexual Satisfaction Among Married Women." *Medical Aspects of Human Sexuality,* 1972, *6,* 136-144.

Bentler, P. M. "Heterosexual Behavior Assessment. I: Males." *Behavior Research and Therapy,* 1968a, *6,* 21-25.

Bentler, P. M. "Heterosexual Behavior Assessment. II: Females." *Behavior Research and Therapy,* 1968b, *6,* 27-30.

Brady, J. P., and Levitt, E. E. "The Scalability of Sexual Experiences." *Psychological Record,* 1965, *15,* 275-279.

Cooper, A. J. "Disorders of Sexual Potency in the Male: A Clinical and Statistical Study of Some Factors Related to Short-Term Prognosis." *British Journal of Psychiatry,* 1969, *114,* 709-719.

Cooper, A. J., and Ismail, A. A. A. "A Pilot Study of Mesterolone in Impotence." *Psychopharmacologia,* 1972, *26,* 379-386.

Eysenck, H. J. "Masculinity-Femininity, Personality, and Sexual Attitudes." *Journal of Sex Research,* 1971a, *7,* 83-88.

Eysenck, H. J. "Personality and Sexual Adjustment." *British Journal of Psychiatry,* 1971b, *118,* 593-608.

Feldman, M. P., and others. "The Application of Anticipatory Avoidance Learning to the Treatment of Homosexuality. III: The Sexual Orientation Method." *Behavior Research and Therapy,* 1966, *4,* 289-299.

Fox, C. A., and Medill, G. T. "Monitoring Sexual Activity—Methods for Measuring Natural Coitus." In G. Raspé and S. Bernhard (Eds.), *Advances in Biosciences, 10.* Elmsford, N.Y.: Pergamon Press, 1973.

Freund, K., and others. "Measuring Feminine Gender Identity in Homosexual Males." *Archives of Sexual Behavior,* 1974, *3,* 249-261.

Gebhard, P. H. "Factors in Marital Orgasm." *Journal of Social Issues,* 1966, *22,* 88-95.

Geer, J., Morokoff, P., and Greenwood, P. "Sexual Arousal in Women: The Development of a Measurement Device for Vaginal Blood Volume." *Archives of Sexual Behavior,* 1974, *3,* 559-564.

Goldberg, L. R. "A Historical Survey of Personality Scales and Inventories." In P. McReynolds (Ed.), *Advances in Psychological Assessment.* Vol. 2. Palo Alto, Calif.: Science and Behavior Books, 1971.

Griffitt, W. "Sexual Experience and Sexual Responsiveness: Sex Differences." *Archives of Sexual Behavior,* 1975, *4,* 529-540.

Group for the Advancement of Psychiatry. *Assessment of Sexual Function: A Guide to Interviewing.* New York: Aronson, 1973.

Harbison, J. M., and others. "A Questionnaire Method of Sexual Interest." *Archives of Sexual Behavior,* 1974, *3,* 357-366.

Hartman, W. E., and Fithian, M. A. *Treatment of Sexual Dysfunction: A Bio-Psycho-Social Approach.* Long Beach, Calif.: Center for Marital and Sexual Studies, 1972.

Hoon, E. F., Hoon, P. W., and Wincze, J. P. "An Inventory for the Measurement of Female Sexual Arousability: The SAI." *Archives of Sexual Behavior,* 1976, *5,* 291-300.

Kaplan, H. S. *The New Sex Therapy: Active Treatment of Sexual Dysfunctions.* New York: Brunner/Mazel, 1974.

Kinsey, A. C., Pomeroy, W. B., and Martin, C. E. *Sexual Behavior in the Human Male.* Philadelphia: Saunders, 1948.

Kohlenberg, R. J. "Directed Masturbation and the Treatment of Primary Orgasmic Dysfunction." *Archives of Sexual Behavior,* 1974, *3,* 349-356.

Kolodny, R. C. "Sexual Dysfunction in Diabetic Females." *Diabetes,* 1971, *20,* 557-559.

Levine, S. B., and Yost, M. A. "Frequency of Sexual Dysfunction in a General Gynecological Clinic: An Epidemiological Approach." *Archives of Sexual Behavior,* 1976, *5,* 229-238.

Levitt, E. E. "A Hasty Overview of Objective Psychological Measurement of Human Sexuality." Paper presented at annual meeting of International Academy of Sex Research, Hamburg, Germany, 1976a.

Levitt, E. E. "Sexual Dysfunction as a Public Health Problem." Paper presented at annual meeting of Indiana Health Association, 1976b.

Lindgren, T. W., and Pauly, I. B. "A Body Image Scale for Evaluating Transsexuals." *Archives of Sexual Behavior,* 1975, *4,* 639-656.

Lopiccolo, J., and Steger, J. C. "The Sexual Interaction Inventory: A New Instrument for Assessment of Sexual Dysfunction." *Archives of Sexual Behavior,* 1974, *3,* 585-595.

Marks, I. M., and Sartorius, N. H. "A Contribution to the Measurement of Sexual Attitude: The Semantic Differential as a Measure of Sexual Attitude in Sexual Deviations." *Journal of Nervous and Mental Disease,* 1967, *145,* 441-451.

Masters, W. H., and Johnson, V. E. *Human Sexual Inadequacy.* Boston: Little, Brown, 1970.

Mellan, J. "Interpersonal Relationships of Female Patients with Sexual Disorder as Assessed by Leary's Test." *Archives of Sexual Behavior,* 1971, *1,* 263-267.

Ohlson, E. L., and Wilson, M. "Differentiating Female Homosexuals from Female Heterosexuals by Use of the MMPI." *Journal of Sex Research,* 1974, *10,* 308-315.

Pion, R. J., and Wagner, N. W. "Diagnosis and Treatment of Inadequate Sexual Response." In J. J. Sciarra (Ed.), *Davis' Gynecology and Obstetrics.* (Rev. ed.) New York: Harper & Row, 1976.

Podell, L., and Perkins, J. C. "A Guttman Scale for Sexual Experience—A Methodological Note." *Journal of Abnormal and Social Psychology,* 1957, *54,* 420-422.

Quinn, J. T., and others. "The Assessment of Sexual Function." In T. Thompson and W. S. Dockens, III (Eds.), *Applications of Behavior Modification.* New York: Academic Press, 1975.

Schatzberg, A. F., and others. "Effeminacy. I: A Quantitative Rating Scale." *Archives of Sexual Behavior,* 1975, *4,* 31-41.

Semmens, J. P., and Semmens, F. J. H. "The Co-Therapist Approach to the Treatment of Female Sexual Dysfunction." In J. J. Sciarra (Ed.), *Davis' Gynecology and Obstetrics.* (Rev. ed.) New York: Harper & Row, 1976.

Sotile, W. M., Kilmann, P. R., and Scovern, A. W. "Definitions and Classifications of Psychogenic Female Sexual Dysfunction." *Journal of Sex Education and Therapy,* 1977, *3,* 21-27.

Tennent, G., Bancroft, J., and Cass, J. "The Control of Deviant Sexual Behavior by Drugs: A Double-Blind Controlled Study of Benperidol, Chlorpromazine and Placebo." *Archives of Sexual Behavior,* 1974, *3,* 261-271.

Thorne, F. C. "The Sex Inventory." *Journal of Clinical Psychology,* 1966, *22,* 367-374.

Wincze, J. P., Hoon, E. F., and Hoon, P. W. "Physiological Responsivity of Normal and Sexually Dysfunctional Women During Erotic Stimulus Exposure." *Journal of Psychosomatic Research,* 1976, *20,* 445-451.

Zimmerman, J., and Levitt, E. E. "Why Not Give Your Client a Counter: A Survey of What Happened When We Did." *Behavior Research and Therapy,* 1975, *13,* 333-337.

Zuckerman, M. "Scales for Sex Experience for Males and Females." *Journal of Consulting and Clinical Psychology,* 1973, *41,* 27-29.

54

╔══════════════════════════════════════╗

Robert A. Mednick

Sexual Fantasy

╚══════════════════════════════════════╝

Sexual fantasy is a dynamic intrapsychic process which contains imaginal sexual content and is sexually arousing. Various definitions of fantasy and sexual fantasy have been provided by English and English (1958), May (1966, 1969, 1971), Singer (1966, 1975), Mednick (1977a), Shanor (1974), Davidson (1975), and Laplanche and Pontalis (1973). Five central factors which have been used to define or examine sexual fantasy have included: (1) manifest content; (2) nature of the emotional response; (3) activation of the fantasy from an outside stimulus or from inner mental stimulation; (4) dynamics within the action sequences in the fantasy; and (5) the intentionality of the fantasy in the mental life of the fantasist. Some *conditions* under which sexual fantasy has been examined have included daydreaming, masturbation, sexual intercourse, during excretory functions, pregnancy, nursing, in psychotherapeutic treatment or during psychodiagnostic testing, and within states of aggression.

The *content* of sexual fantasy productions includes both manifest material and unconscious symbolic expressions. This topographical approach (Silverman, Bronstein, and Mendelsohn, 1976) conceptually frames sexual fantasy into conscious and unconscious processes. Isaacs (1948) introduced this distinction by labeling conscious processes "fantasy" and unconscious processes "phantasy."

The *developmental* dimension of sexual fantasy has been a crucial consideration in assessment and clinical treatment. The significance of this dimension has recently been focused on by Sarnoff (1974), Moore (1975), and Lachmann and Stolorow (1976). Here sexual fantasy is seen as instrumental in perceptual organization, personality differentiation, and representative of cognitive, creative, and defensive capacities. Studies by Giambra (1974), Cramer and Bryson (1973), and Cramer and Hogan (1975) support the position that fantasy expression varies as a function of personality development.

Background and Current Status

The archaic foundations of "sexual fantasy" are found within etymology and the protoscience of mythology. Regarding the latter, mythologies referenced to sexual fantasy within clinical assessment have included "Icarus" (May, 1966, 1969; Fried, 1971), "Oedipus" and "Danaides" (Neumann, 1956), and the "Trickster" (Mednick, 1975).

The early clinical assessment of sexual fantasy has been traced to a historical account of medieval sexual behavior in the case of the physician Gilbert du Laurens (Taylor, 1954). Two women were reportedly brought to acknowledge that their visitations by an Incubus were, in fact, a "wish-fantasy" related to sexual congress. Even as late as 1904, Ellis cited a case where Pierre Janet used sexual daydreaming to explain demon possession.

Following Freud's ([1897] 1963) classical attention to sexual fantasy rather than actual seduction as stimuli for conflict, and Ellis' (1920, 1928) clinical contributions on autoeroticism, the clinical focus on sexual fantasy proliferated. Pioneers such as Horney (1939), Deutsch (1944), and Isaacs (1948) provided a basis for later quantitative investigations and refinement in conceptual understanding and clinical assessment as related to treatment. Within the developing emergence of psychodiagnostics, the assessment of sexual fantasy advanced between the years 1936 and 1945 when the Rorschach systems of Beck, Hertz, and Klopfer evolved. Special attention was given to the human movement (M) responses as representing fantasy activity (Page, 1957).

The use of the Rorschach to study fantasy, as observed in the investigations by Singer and Sugarman (1955) and Page (1957), was the stepping stone toward advancements in clinical assessment. These advancements were initiated by Singer and Schonbar (1961) and Singer and McCraven (1961) and ushered in the contemporary phase in the clinical assessment of "sexual fantasy."

Psychological scientists have extended their views of sexual fantasy beyond the early mechanistic model, which drew parallels between nocturnal dreaming and fantasy. Clinicians have also advanced beyond seeing sexual fantasy predominantly as a pathological manifestation. The temper of contemporary investigations and clinical utilization of sexual fantasy illuminates its functional aspects in terms of cognitive style, synthetic, creative, adaptive, generative, and therapeutic potentialities (Abel and Blanchard, 1974; Benedek, 1968; Friend, 1974; Hariton, 1972; Hariton and Singer, 1974; Moore, 1975). Sexual fantasy has increasingly been seen as a significant human phenomenon for the understanding of human adaptation and functioning. This perspective is seen in the fields of clinical assessment of psychological defenses (Laughlin, 1970), ego functions assessment (Bellak, Hurvich, and Gediman, 1973), and differential diagnosis (Hoch, 1972). In psychotherapeutic treatment, the clinically appropriate exploration of sexual fantasy has been found revealing of whether personality disturbances are representative of structural conflict or developmental arrest and incapacity (Lachmann and Stolorow, 1976; Stolorow and Lachmann, 1978). This determination has been shown to have crucial diagnostic and treatment implications, especially in working with the narcissistic and borderline conditions.

Recent empirical investigations on fantasy by May (1971), Mednick (1977a), and Davidson (1975) have encompassed assessment considerations of gender identity and fantasy patterns. Pivotal contributions by Hariton and Singer (1974) and Giambra (1974) have provided further understanding of sexual fantasy productions as related to personality configurations and developmental changes along one's life span.

In clinical assessment, various instruments and methods have been used to examine the phenomenon of sexual fantasy. For example, May (1966, 1969, 1971, 1975) has used Thematic Apperception Test-like stimuli and a quantitative scoring system to assess gender-specific fantasy patterns. This approach has also been applied to children, and is observed in the studies by Cramer and Bryson (1973) and Cramer and Hogan (1975).

The questionnaire has increasingly been used to investigate sexual fantasy. The most contemporary fantasy questionnaire, the Imaginal Processes Inventory (IPI) (Singer and Antrobus, 1972), contains 344 items with 28 subscales, scale 19 being "Sexual Daydreams." The IPI has been used to investigate such variables and conditions as sensitization-repression, aggression, adaption to hospitalization, and daydreaming across the life span. Other questionnaires developed by Shanor (1974) and Mednick (1977a, 1977b) have been designed to study the frequency and content of sexual fantasy in various fantasy conditions.

Factor analytic studies on women's sexual fantasies have stressed the adaptive and enhancing aspects of sexual fantasy. Central investigations in this area have been reported by Davidson (1975), Hariton (1972), and Hariton and Singer (1974). In the latter investigations, three distinct factors emerged, including "erotic fantasy," "negative sexuality," and "submissive fantasy." The "submissive fantasy" factor was bipolar and contained "force" and "romantic" fantasies. "Force" fantasies were correlated with "strong orgasm," and this was interpreted as supporting the *drive enhancement* quality of these fantasies.

Critical Discussion

General Areas of Concern

During the past ten years, research on sexual fantasy has progressively focused on some specific areas of concern. Particular dimensions of these concerns often overlap and interrelate. Three primary global concerns include (1) the controversy between the "pathogenic versus creative-synthetic" function of sexual fantasy; (2) the assessment and use of sexual fantasy in psychotherapy and clinical treatment; and (3) the relationships between sexual and aggressive fantasies.

The controversial question as to whether sexual fantasy plays a functional versus dysfunctional role in psychological functioning has been an ongoing concern of theorists, researchers, and clinicians. Investigators (for example, Hariton and Singer, 1974; Singer and McCraven, 1961) who have focused on this controversy typically have referred to Freud's ([1907] 1963) early statement that "A happy person never phantasies, only an unsatisfied one" (p. 146). Lihn's (1971) view that fantasies may be used to preserve masochistic relationships and the position that sexual fantasies are compensations for "unavoidable deprivations in life" (Lample de Groot, 1965, p. 352) contribute to the dysfunctional pole of controversy.

A wider survey of Freud's ([1907] 1963, [1911] 1963) and other more contemporary psychodynamic theorists' views on sexual fantasy emphasizes an adaptive and functional understanding of sexual fantasy. For example, Bach (1972), Moore (1975), and Stolorow and Lachmann (1975, 1978) have drawn attention to crucial adaptive aspects of sexual fantasy processes. These include intrapsychic reparation, and assistance in self-identity formation. In addition, particular sexual fantasy processes in therapeutic treatment have been seen to clinically represent intrapsychic developmental maturation. This emergent view has particular significance to clinical assessment and treatment. It considers sexual fantasy as a creative expression and a potential facilitator of self-adjustment within specific developmental and life contexts.

In the experimental research tradition, a series of investigations over the last decade have also pointed to the adaptive, creative, and self-enhancing functions of sexual fantasy. Data obtained by Streissguth, Wagner, and Wechsler (1969) in their rare study of daydreaming and hospitalization were interpreted as indicating that daydreaming in itself is not pathological. Similar findings have been indicated by Hariton (1972) and Hariton and Singer (1974, pp. 320-321) where sexual fantasy was "not generally related to interpersonal disturbances, adjustment problems, or lack of fulfillment in the sexual area."

There has been increasing fundamental agreement between psychodynamic views and empirical findings with respect to the functional role of masturbatory fantasy. For example, the psychodynamic view that masturbatory fantasy assists in establishing "trial experience" for later healthy adult sexual relationships has been supported by Hariton and Singer (1974). Positive correlations were found between strong orgasm, and fantasy-arousing patterns developed during adolescence.

Sexual fantasy in psychotherapy and clinical treatment has long been a primary area of concern. The production, understanding, and appropriate use of sexual fantasy in the transference relationship plays a significant role in the treatment process. Considerable refinement of theoretical understanding and tactical applications in clinical treatment has evolved since the early work of Ferenczi (1976) and Isaacs (1948). For example, distinctions between "erotic" and "erotized" transference phenomena are shown in discussions by Swartz (1969) and Blum (1973). Discussions by Neu (1973), Berry-Bertrand (1974), and Fine (1976) reflect the pervasive extent to which fantasy processes are instrumental to therapeutic movement.

Within the more global purview of clinical treatment, Abel and Blanchard (1974) have described an integration of behavioral and psychodynamic approaches. The resulting position is that sexual fantasy is regarded as an independent variable subject to direct modification. This position is in line with the learning theory and behavior modification approaches which have directly used imagery in changing behavior. For example, studies by Marquis (1970) and Gershman (1970) have focused directly on sexual fantasy using such behavioral methods as "programming of masturbation fantasies" in orgasmic reconditioning, thought-stopping, and covert sensitization. There has been considerable ethical concern in using these procedures, one aspect of which is that the whole personality and overall functioning of the individual is not, methodologically, taken into consideration fully (see Bieber, 1977).

The question of a linkage between sexuality and aggression in fantasy processes warrants close attention. This formulation has roots in theoretical legacy and has had contemporary prominence in research and clinical treatment. A particularly clear and early account of the sexual-aggressive fantasy linkage is depicted in Ferenczi's (1976) outmoded and incorrect technique of forcing his patients to produce aggressive fantasies.

Studies by Clark (1953), Barclay and Haber (1965), and Barclay (1969) have supported the hypothesis of a "connection" between aggression and sexuality. These studies reported that aggressive activity heightened sexual response, and vice versa. Data from more recent studies by Barclay (1970) and Beit-Hallahmi (1971) have continued to support this hypothesis. Moreover, findings revealed that increases in the *frequency* of sexual fantasy and aggressive fantasy are positively correlated. Later studies by Baron (1974) and Jaffee and others (1974) have continued to investigate the sex-aggression linkage formulation. Baron's (1974) findings, however, have pointed to a variance in this formulation. Indications suggested that heightened sexual arousal from erotic stimuli may inhibit aggression.

Comparative Philosophies and Theories

Historically, various theoretical positions on sexual fantasy have been distinguished by their respective emphasis on specific dimensions of behavior. For example, the four primary dimensions of behavior which have been emphasized include (1) intrapsychic developmental effects attributed to the early mother-child relationship; (2) the nature of constitutional and physiological drive-state factors; (3) cognitive-perceptual and information processing activities; and (4) social learning.

From recent studies of adult sexual fantasy during the past five years, a "personality-cognitive" model has emerged. This theoretical model emphasizes that sexual fantasy is essentially a function of cognitive style, and a creative idiosyncratic expression of the individual. A second central theoretical model of sexual fantasy which has emerged from the clinical treatment sector of research is the "Fusion Hypothesis" model. This model derives from the data of psychoanalytic case studies, and posits that physical autoerotic activity and sexual fantasy become experientially *welded* together. The welding or "fusion" is ultimately expressed in personality development at the maturational point where the "masturbation-fantasy complex" emerges.

Elaboration on Critical Points

The human *predisposition* to experience sexual fantasy has classically been understood from the early interactions between the mother and infant. This theoretical view is identified generally as the "hunger metaphor model," and has been summarized by Rapaport (1960), Cameron (1963), and Singer (1974). The infant is seen as primitively imagining a representation of the mother's breast during the period of delay between need arousal and eventual gratification of need by arrival of the mother. The main theoretical point of the hunger metaphor model is the infant's experiencing a "connection" between its feelings of need and the associated presence of the need-gratifying object, mother. Isaacs (1948) and Neu (1973) have elaborated aspects of this model. They have placed respective emphasis on fantasy as an expression of bodily processes, and connections between idea, wish, and affect.

More contemporary clinical developmental models of fantasy have been delineated by Klein (1975), Jacobson (1964), and Mahler (1968). These developmental models view fantasy respectively as expressions of impulses, phase-specific mental operations which play a role in personality differentiation, and self-identity articulation during separation-individuation.

Investigations by May (1966, 1969, 1971), Cramer and Bryson (1973), and Cramer and Hogan (1975) have examined gender-specific fantasy patterns from specific theoretical positions. Theories examined were those elaborated earlier by Deutsch (1944), Murray (1955), and Erikson (1950, 1951). The emphasis of these studies directed attention to gender variations in fantasy patterns as a function of basic psychological differences between the sexes rather than cultural conditioning.

Theoretical explanations to account for physiological arousals during sexual fantasy can be viewed as stemming from two theoretical traditions. The first is the social learning theory approach. This approach takes the view that an arousal is a response to social cues, gender-role training, and cultural effects. This latter factor has been considered by Maslow (1942) as fostering a stereotypic submissive posture in women's sexual fantasies. A second theoretical tradition which has proposed explanations for linkages between physiological arousal and fantasy is related to dynamics of the masturbation act. An early formulation of this theoretical model (Freud [1907] 1963) described the relationship between evocation of a fantasy and concurrent behavior which served to gratify the fantasy representations. More contemporary elaborations of this model have been made by Moore (1975) and Sarnoff (1974).

Contemporary theoretical models have been proposed by Singer (1973, 1974) and Hariton (1972). Singer's "information-processing" model draws from the work of Werner and Kaplan (1963), and emphasizes Piaget's *assimilation* and *accommodation* processes, cognitive schema, and verbal encoding processes. According to Singer (1974), fantasy emerges from "hierarchical cognitive structures" and "informational processing routines" (p. 214). Hariton's (1972) research has suggested a "personality-cognitive" model to theoretically account for the *creative enrichment* which coital fantasies can bring to sexual experience.

Personal Views and Recommendations

The significance of sexual fantasy to the assessment of personality has its parallel in physiology where the processes within the cell can reveal the overall state of the organism. Sexual fantasy is a complex multidimensional set of processes which often express the deepest strivings of the individual in living and relating. However, a grasp of these expressions generally requires clinical examination beyond the manifest sexual fantasy content.

If studied carefully, especially within the context of clinical treatment, sexual fantasy can point to specific maturational wishes, interpersonal fears both past and present, and strivings for developmental consolidation of self-experience. These latter strivings are particularly illuminating in understanding personality functioning within the narcissistic sector. Whether sexual fantasy is clinically assessed as an expression of pathological or self-enhancing processes, it is nonetheless a creative expression of the whole individual.

The effective utilization of sexual fantasy in clinical assessment requires that it be viewed through the matrix of psychological conditions, like any other primary clinical data. This matrix includes the personality dimensions of the individual's level of self-object differentiation, ego structuralization and defense activity, psychosexual development, and diagnostic position.

Application to Particular Variables

Regarding age and family hierarchy, there is some evidence that first-born children reveal a "greater development of certain fantasy-play characteristics . . . than do children otherwise placed in the family" (Singer and McCraven, 1961, p. 272). Developmental shifts in the character of fantasy in children 4 to 8 years of age have been evidenced (Sutton-Smith, Botvin, and Mahony, 1976). A series of studies (Cramer, 1975; Cramer and Bryson, 1973; Cramer and Hogan, 1975) with children between the ages of 3 years and 7 months to 12 years and 10 months have produced the following findings: (1) sex-related differences appear in play before they appear in fantasy; (2) boys are two years behind girls in manifesting adult sex-related verbal fantasy patterns; (3) at age 9, sexual differentiation in verbal fantasy patterns is clearly evident; and (4) it is the girl who changes fantasy patterns, while the boy maintains the same fantasy pattern at age 9 as at age 5 years. Boys' fantasy patterns, however, do later change toward greater "masculinity" about two years following the girls' changes. Finally, Giambra's (1974) normative study examined daydreaming across the adult life span of males from ages 17 to 91 years. Two primary findings relevant here were that (1) "daydreaming frequency clearly declined with age with the periods of greatest decline after age 23, after age 44, and after age 74" (p. 120); and (2) "the content which showed the greatest decline with age was sexual" (p. 132).

Regarding sex differences in sexual fantasy, findings by Schmidt, Sigusch, and Schäfer (1973) have challenged the findings of Kinsey and his associates (1953). Especially challenged is Kinsey's contention that women are far less responsive than men to nontactile stimulation in the production of sexual fantasy. The controversy of these findings has been reviewed by Gebhard (1973), and has directed attention to the variances in format used to methodologically elicit fantasy reports. Similarly, a study by Griffitt in 1975 produced findings which challenge Kinsey's (1953) statement that "females' fantasies did not generally extend beyond the parameters of [their] actual experience" (p. 165).

The issue of gender-specific differences in the *frequency* of sexual fantasy has been addressed by many clinicians and researchers (Freud, [1907] 1963; Hollender, 1963; Wagman, 1967a, 1967b; Hessellund, 1976; Kinsey and others, 1953; Deutsch, 1944; Demartino, 1969; Hariton and Singer, 1974; Gagnon and Simon, 1973). Most research reports have found that men as a group report a greater frequency of sexual fantasy than women (Hessellund, 1976). In their study with 44 women, Singer and Schonbar (1961) found that daydreaming frequency was correlated with greater identification with the mother than with the father. Hessellund (1976) has found sex differences in sexual fantasy with respect to the situations where fantasy occurs, and that men seem more inclined to have fantasies involving several persons.

As described earlier, a series of studies by May (1966, 1969), Cramer (1975), and Bramante (1970) have revealed fundamental dynamic sex differences in fantasy patterns. Using a different method, Mednick (1977a) has also found gender-specific variances in sexual fantasy. Women were found to generally fantasize themselves as "recipients" of sexual activity significantly more than men. Barclay's (1973) descriptive account has noted that females frequently fantasy "being taken against their will," although "caring for someone" was probably the most common sexual fantasy theme. Barclay's (1973) claim that "visual aspects of fantasies may represent an innate difference between men and women" (p. 209) was challenged by Fisher's (1973) commentary. Barclay's contention is also found to vary from Davidson's (1975) findings in his study with 202 women. Hariton and Singer's (1974) investigation found that women's most frequent coital fantasy involves "thoughts of an imaginary lover," while the "being overpowered" fantasy ranked second in frequency.

Specific social groups which have been studied in research on sexual fantasy have included, among others, housewives (Hariton and Singer, 1974), prostitutes (Greenwald, 1970), servicemen (Windholz, 1969), prisoners (Beit-Hallahmi, 1971), and pregnant women (Pines, 1972).

Some attention has been focused directly on the demographic factor of ethnicity and racial origin in the study of sexual fantasy. Singer and McCraven's (1961) study on "Daydreaming Patterns of American Subcultural Groups" examined daydreaming and sexual fantasy among samples of Anglo-Saxons, Germans, Irish, Italians, Jews, and

Negroes. Findings revealed that "the Italian, Negro, and Jewish [participants reported] a significantly greater frequency of daydreaming than the Irish, Anglo-Saxon, and German groups" (p. 276). While "no group differences in Heterosexual, Genital Drive fantasies emerged" (p. 277), an "Overall Direct Drive (Erotic)" measure which pooled other categories revealed that Jewish, Italian, and Negro groups showed the highest frequencies of fantasy.

Two rare studies which have investigated fantasy in physically disordered populations have been those of Streissguth, Wagner, and Wechsler (1969) and Raft, Spencer, and Toomey (1976). The medical classes of the participants in the former study included cardiology, gastrointestinal, arthritis, chest and infectious diseases, metabolic and endocrine disorders, and other medical conditions. Medical patients reported the lowest frequency of sexual daydreaming, as compared to psychiatric and control groups. Medical patients also appeared to be more distressed by their fantasy experiences.

Sexual fantasy has also been studied using psychiatric populations. In Streissguth, Wagner, and Wechsler's (1969) study which included a psychiatric population, a portion of the investigation examined sexual daydreaming. Psychiatric patients in the study were diagnosed as either schizophrenic, neurotic reaction, character disorder, or affective psychoses. The psychiatric group reported greater frequencies of daydreaming than the "medical" or "control" groups, and their daydreams were "more improbable . . . more conscience-ridden . . . and include more themes of a pregenital and sexual nature" (p. 222). Rychlak (1973) investigated fantasy in a population of 24 males, 12 of which were pooled in a "mildly abnormal," group as operationally determined by any three scale scores on the MMPI clinical scales falling above 70. Findings revealed that "abnormal" boys fantasized greater frequencies of "negative" ideas and images than "normals."

The following survey is confined to research investigations, but does not derive from examinations of populations with functional disorders. Singer and Schonbar (1961) have noted that pathological extremes of fantasy behavior "may involve the excessive resort to fantasy with consequent paralysis of fruitful motor exploration . . . or failure to develop fantasy tendencies" (p. 2). Singer and McCraven (1961) have indicated that "children who . . . identify more closely with mother than father may be expected to develop greater tendencies toward "inner living" fantasy" (p. 272). Hariton (1972) found that high levels of coital fantasy in women were associated with specific personality configurations and not with marital maladjustment or personal sex problems. White (1964) has emphasized that excessive daydreaming or bizarre content of fantasy is not to be considered a cause but rather a consequence of maladjustment.

References

Abel, G. G., and Blanchard, E. B. "The Role of Fantasy in the Treatment of Sexual Deviation." *Archives of General Psychiatry*, 1974, *30*, 467-475.

Bach, S. "Notes on Some Imaginary Companions." *Psychoanalytic Study of the Child*, 1972, *26*, 159-171.

Barclay, A. M. "The Effect of Hostility on Physiological and Fantasy Responses." *Journal of Personality*, 1969, *37*, 651-667.

Barclay, A. M. "The Effect of Female Aggressiveness on Aggressive and Sexual Fantasies." *Journal of Projective Techniques and Personality Assessment*, 1970, *34*, 19-26.

Barclay, A. M. "Sexual Fantasies in Men and Women." *Medical Aspects of Human Sexuality*, 1973, *7*, 205-216.

Barclay, A. M., and Haber, R. N. "The Relation of Aggressive to Sexual Motivation." *Journal of Personality,* 1965, *33,* 462-475.

Baron, R. A. "The Aggression-Inhibiting Influence of Heightened Sexual Arousal." *Journal of Personality and Social Psychology,* 1974, *30,* 318-322.

Beit-Hallahmi, B. "Sexual and Aggressive Fantasies in Violent and Nonviolent Prison Inmates." *Journal of Personality Assessment,* 1971, *35,* 326-330.

Bellak, L., Hurvich, M., and Gediman, H. K. *Ego Functions in Schizophrenics, Neurotics, and Normals.* New York: Wiley, 1973.

Benedek, T. "Discussion of Sherfey's Paper on Female Sexuality." *Journal of the American Psychoanalytic Association,* 1968, *16,* 424-448.

Berry-Bertrand, N. "From Fantasy to Reality in the Transference (or the Double Aspect of the Psychoanalyst)." *International Journal of Psycho-analysis,* 1974, *55,* 471-477.

Bieber, I. "Sexuality: 1956-1976." *Journal of the American Academy of Psychoanalysis,* 1977, *5,* 195-206.

Blum, H. P. "The Concept of Erotized Transference." *Journal of the American Psychoanalytic Association,* 1973, *21,* 61-76.

Bramante, M. R. "Sex Differences in Fantasy Patterns: A Replication and Elaboration." Unpublished doctoral dissertation, City University of New York, 1970.

Cameron, N. *Personality Development and Psychopathology.* Boston: Houghton Mifflin, 1963.

Clark, R. A. "The Effects of Sexual Motivation on Phantasy." *Journal of Experimental Psychology,* 1953, *44,* 3-11.

Cramer, P. "The Development of Play and Fantasy in Boys and Girls: Empirical Studies." *Psychoanalysis and Contemporary Science,* 1975, *4,* 529-567.

Cramer, P., and Bryson, J. "The Development of Sex-Related Fantasy Patterns." *Developmental Psychology,* 1973, *8,* 131-134.

Cramer, P., and Hogan, K. A. "Sex Differences in Verbal and Play Fantasy." *Developmental Psychology,* 1975, *11,* 145-154.

Davidson, A. D. "The Relationship of Reported Sexual Daydreaming to Sexual Attitude, Sexual Knowledge, and Reported Sexual Experience in College Women." Unpublished doctoral dissertation, University of Cincinnati, 1975.

Demartino, M. F. *The New Female Sexuality.* New York: Julian, 1969.

Deutsch, H. *The Psychology of Women.* New York: Grune and Stratton, 1944.

Ellis, H. H. "Auto-Erotism." In *Studies in the Psychology of Sex.* Vol. 1. Philadelphia: Davis, 1904.

Ellis, H. H. "Love and Pain." In *Studies in the Psychology of Sex.* Vol. 3. Philadelphia: Davis, 1920.

Ellis, H. H. "The History of Florrie and the Mechanism of Sexual Deviation." In *Studies in the Psychology of Sex.* Vol. 7. Philadelphia: Davis, 1928.

English, H. B., and English, A. C. *A Comprehensive Dictionary of Psychological and Psychoanalytic Terms.* New York: Longmans, 1958.

Erikson, E. H. *Childhood and Society.* New York: Norton, 1950.

Erikson, E. H. "Sex Differences in the Play Configurations of Preadolescents." *Journal of Orthopsychiatry,* 1951, *21,* 667-692.

Ferenczi, S. "On Forced Fantasies: Activity in the Association Technique." In M. S. Bergmann and F. R. Hartman (Eds.), *The Evolution of Psychoanalytic Technique.* New York: Basic Books, 1976.

Fine, R. "The Uncommunicative Genius." *Psychoanalytic Review,* 1976, *63,* 409-425.

Fisher, S. "Commentary [on 'Sexual Fantasies in Men and Women,' Barclay, 1973]." *Medical Aspects of Human Sexuality,* 1973, *7,* 216.

Freud, S. "Extracts from the Fliess Papers" [letter 69: 1897]. In J. Strachey (Ed.), *Standard Edition of the Complete Psychological Works of Sigmund Freud.* Vol. 1. London: Hogarth Press, 1963.

Freud, S. "Creative Writers and Daydreaming" [1907]. In *Standard Edition.* Vol. 9. London: Hogarth Press, 1963.

Freud, S. "Formulations on the Two Principles of Mental Functioning" [1911]. In *Standard Edition.* Vol. 12. London: Hogarth Press, 1963.

Fried, C. "Icarianism, Masochism, and Sex Differences in Fantasy." *Journal of Personality Assessment,* 1971, *35,* 38-55.

Friend, M. "Discussion [of 'Narcissism, Adolescent Masturbation Fantasies, and the Search for Reality,' Sarnoff, 1974]. *Journal of the Philadelphia Association for Psychoanalysis,* 1974, *1,* 244-245.

Gagnon, S., and Simon, W. *Sexual Conduct.* Chicago: Aldine, 1973.

Galton, F. "Statistics of Mental Imagery." *Mind,* 1880, *5,* 301-318.

Gebhard, P. H. "Sex Differences in Sexual Response." *Archives of Sexual Behavior,* 1973, *2,* 201-203.

Gershman, L. "Case Conference: A Transvestite Fantasy Treated by Thought-Stopping, Covert Sensitization, and Aversive Shock." *Journal of Behavior Therapy and Experimental Psychiatry,* 1970, *1,* 153-161.

Giambra, L. M. "Daydreaming Across the Life Span: Late Adolescent to Senior Citizen." *International Journal of Aging and Human Development,* 1974, *5,* 115-140.

Greenwald, H. *The Elegant Prostitute.* New York: Ballantine, 1970.

Hariton, E. B. "Women's Fantasies During Sexual Intercourse with Their Husbands: A Normative Study with Tests of Personality and Theoretical Models." Unpublished doctoral dissertation, City University of New York, 1972.

Hariton, E. B., and Singer, J. L. "Women's Fantasies During Sexual Intercourse: Normative and Theoretical Implications." *Journal of Consulting and Clinical Psychology,* 1974, *42,* 313-322.

Hessellund, H. "Masturbation and Sexual Fantasies in Married Couples." *Archives of Sexual Behavior,* 1976, *5,* 133-147.

Hoch, P. H. *Differential Diagnosis in Clinical Psychiatry.* New York: Aronson, 1972.

Hollender, M. H. "Women's Fantasies During Sexual Intercourse." *Archives of General Psychiatry,* 1963, *8,* 86-90.

Horney, K. *New Ways in Psychoanalysis.* New York: Norton, 1939.

Isaacs, S. "The Nature and Function of Phantasy." *International Journal of Psycho-analysis,* 1948, *29,* 73-97.

Jacobson, E. *The Self and the Object World.* New York: International Universities Press, 1964.

Jaffee, Y., and others. "Sexual Arousal and Behavioral Aggression." *Journal of Personality and Social Psychology,* 1974, *30,* 759-764.

James, W. *The Principles of Psychology.* Vol. 2. New York: Holt, Rinehart and Winston, 1896.

Khan, M. M. R. *The Privacy of the Self.* New York: International Universities Press, 1974.

Kinsey, A. C., and others. *Sexual Behavior in the Human Female.* Philadelphia: Saunders, 1953.

Klein, E. *A Comprehensive Etymological Dictionary of the English Language.* Amsterdam: Elsevier, 1966.

Klein, M. *The Psychoanalysis of Children.* London: Hogarth Press, 1975.

Lachmann, F. M., and Stolorow, R. D. "Idealization and Grandiosity: Developmental Considerations and Treatment Implications." *Psychoanalytic Quarterly,* 1976, *45,* 565-587.

Lample de Groot, J. *The Development of Mind.* London: Norton, 1965.

Laplanche, J., and Pontalis, J.-B. *The Language of Psychoanalysis.* New York: Norton, 1973.

Laughlin, H. P. *The Ego and Its Defenses.* New York: Appleton-Century-Crofts, 1970.

Lihn, H. "Sexual Masochism: A Case Report." *International Journal of Psycho-analysis,* 1971, *52,* 469-478.

Mahler, M. S. *On Human Symbiosis and the Vicissitudes of Individuation.* New York: International Universities Press, 1968.

Marquis, J. N. "Orgasmic Reconditioning: Changing Sexual Object Choice Through Controlling Masturbation Fantasies." *Journal of Behavior Therapy and Experimental Psychiatry,* 1970, *1,* 263-271.

Maslow, A. H. "Self-Esteem (Dominance Feeling) and Sexuality in Women." *Journal of Social Psychology,* 1942, *16,* 259-264.

May, R. "Sex Differences in Fantasy Patterns." *Journal of Projective Techniques and Personality Assessment,* 1966, *30,* 576-586.

May, R. "Deprivation-Enhancement Fantasy Patterns in Men and Women." *Journal of Projective Techniques and Personality Assessment,* 1969, *33,* 464-469.

May, R. "A Method for Studying the Development of Gender Identity." *Developmental Psychology,* 1971, *5,* 484-487.

May, R. "Further Studies on Deprivation/Enhancement Patterns." *Journal of Personality Assessment,* 1975, *39,* 116-122.

Mednick, R. A. "Content and Frequency of Sexual Fantasy as a Function of the Frequency and Content of Death Fantasy and Death Anxiety." Unpublished doctoral dissertation, United States International University, San Diego, 1975.

Mednick, R. A. "Gender-Specific Variances in Sexual Fantasy." *Journal of Personality Assessment,* 1977a, *41,* 248-254.

Mednick, R. A. "Death Anxiety and Sexual Fantasy." *Omega: Journal of Death and Dying,* 1977b, *8,* 117-127.

Moore, W. T. "Genital Masturbation and Adolescent Development." *Journal of the Philadelphia Association for Psychoanalysis,* 1975, *2,* 20-37.

Murray, H. "American Icarus." In A. Burton and R. E. Harris (Eds.), *Clinical Studies of Personality.* New York: Harper & Row, 1955.

Neu, J. "Fantasy and Memory: The Aetiological Role of Thoughts According to Freud." *International Journal of Psycho-analysis,* 1973, *54,* 383-398.

Neumann, E. *Amor and Psyche: The Psychic Development of the Feminine.* Princeton, N.J.: Princeton University Press, 1956.

Onions, C. T., Friedrichsen, G. W., and Burchfield, R. W. *The Oxford Dictionary of English Etymology.* New York: Oxford University Press, 1966.

Page, H. A. "Studies in Fantasy—Daydreaming Frequency and Rorschach Scoring Categories." *Journal of Consulting Psychology,* 1957, *21,* 111-114.

Partridge, E. *Origins: A Short Etymological Dictionary of Modern English.* New York: Macmillan, 1966.

Phillippe, J. *L'Image Mentale: Evolution et Dissolution.* Paris: Bailliere, 1903.

Pines, D. "Pregnancy and Motherhood: Interaction Between Fantasy and Reality." *British Journal of Medical Psychology,* 1972, *45,* 333-343.

Raft, D., Spencer, R. F., and Toomey, T. C. "Ambiguity of Gender Identity Fantasies and Aspects of Normality and Pathology in Hypopituitary Dwarfism and Turner's Syndrome: Three Cases." *Journal of Sex Research,* 1976, *12,* 161-172.

Rapaport, D. "The Psychoanalytic Theory of Motivation." In *Nebraska Symposium on Motivation.* Lincoln: University of Nebraska Press, 1960.

Rodin, J. "Effects of Distraction on the Performance of Obese and Normal Subjects." *Journal of Comparative and Physiological Psychology,* 1973, *83,* 68-78.

Rychlak, J. F. "Time Orientation in the Positive and Negative Free Phantasies of Mildly Abnormal Versus Normal High School Males." *Journal of Consulting and Clinical Psychology,* 1973, *41,* 175-180.

Sarnoff, C. A. "Narcissism, Adolescent Masturbation Fantasies, and the Search for Reality." *Journal of the Philadelphia Association for Psychoanalysis,* 1974, *1,* 243-245.

Schmidt, G., Sigusch, V., and Schäfer, S. "Responses to Reading Erotic Stories: Male-Female Differences." *Archives of Sexual Behavior,* 1973, *2,* 181-199.

Shanor, K. I. "Social Variables of Women's Sexual Fantasies." Unpublished doctoral dissertation, United States International University, San Diego, 1974.

Silverman, L. H., Bronstein, A., and Mendelsohn, E. "The Further Use of the Subliminal Psychodynamic Activation Method for the Experimental Study of the Clinical Theory of Psychoanalysis: On the Specificity of the Relationship Between Symptoms and Unconscious Conflicts." *Psychotherapy: Theory, Research, and Practice,* 1976, *13,* 2-16.

Singer, J. L. *Daydreaming.* New York: Random House, 1966.

Singer, J. L. *The Child's World of Make-Believe: Experimental Studies in Imaginative Play.* New York: Academic Press, 1973.

Singer, J. L. *Imagery and Daydream Methods in Psychotherapy and Behavior Modification.* New York: Academic Press, 1974.

Singer, J. L. "Navigating the Stream of Consciousness: Research in Daydreaming and Related Inner Experience." *American Psychologist,* 1975, *30,* 727-738.

Singer, J. L., and Antrobus, J. S. "Daydreaming, Imaginal Processes, and Personality: A Normative Study." In P. Sheehan (Ed.), *The Function and Nature of Imagery.* New York: Academic Press, 1972.

Singer, J. L., and McCraven, V. G. "Daydreaming Patterns of American Subcultural Groups." *International Journal of Social Psychiatry,* 1961, *7,* 272-282.

Singer, J. L., and Schonbar, R. A. "Correlates of Daydreaming: A Dimension of Self-Awareness." *Journal of Consulting Psychology,* 1961, *25,* 1-6.

Singer, J. L., and Sugarman, D. "A Note on Some Projected Familial Attitudes Associated with Rorschach Movement Response." *Journal of Consulting Psychology,* 1955, *19,* 117-119.

Skeat, W. W. *A Concise Etymological Dictionary of the English Language.* New York: Putnam's, 1963.

Stolorow, R. D., and Lachmann, F. M. "Early Object Loss and Denial: Developmental Considerations." *Psychoanalytic Quarterly,* 1975, *44,* 596-611.

Stolorow, R. D., and Lachmann, F. M. "The Developmental Prestages of Defenses: Diagnostic and Therapeutic Implications." *Psychoanalytic Quarterly,* 1978, *47,* 73-102.

Streissguth, A. P., Wagner, N. N., and Wechsler, J. C. "Effects of Sex, Illness, and Hospitalization on Daydreaming." *Journal of Consulting and Clinical Psychology,* 1969, *33,* 218-225.

Stricker, S. *Studien über die Sprachvorstellungen.* Vienna: Braumüller, 1880.

Sutton-Smith, B., Botvin, G., and Mahony, D. "Developmental Structures in Fantasy Narratives." *Human Development,* 1976, *19,* 1-13.

Swartz, J. "The Erotized Transference and Other Transference Problems." In J. A. Lindon (Ed.), *The Psychoanalytic Forum.* Vol. 3. New York: Science House, 1969.

Taylor, G. R. *Sex in History.* New York: Vanguard, 1954.

Wagman, M. "Relationship of Sensitization-Repression Dimension to Daydream Behavior Types." *Perceptual and Motor Skills,* 1967a, *24,* 1251-1254.

Wagman, M. "Sex Differences in Types of Daydreams." *Journal of Personality and Social Psychology,* 1967b, *7,* 329-332.

Werner, H., and Kaplan, B. *Symbolic Realization.* New York: Wiley, 1963.

White, R. W. *The Abnormal Personality.* New York: Ronald Press, 1964.

Windholz, G. "Discrepancy of Self and Ideal-Self and Frequency of Hero, Sexual, and Hostile Daydreams Reported by Males." *Psychological Reports,* 1969, *25,* 136-138.

55

Joseph D. Matarazzo
Loren D. Pankratz

Intelligence

The word *intelligence* is used by the laity in a global sense to denote success in school or work or one's community, although sometimes it is used with pejorative connotations, such as "bookish" or "egg-headed." Psychologist-specialists have used the term as a construct to indicate the ability to learn, the amount of knowledge available, the ability to adapt to new situations or mental sets, or merely that which an intelligence test measures. In this chapter the term *intelligence* will, with a few obvious exceptions, be used as a synonym for the IQ score.

Despite the obvious pragmatic utility of IQ tests, American academic psychologists have always disagreed with one another on the nature of the fundamental essence or human quality the tests are attempting to assess. In 1921, matters became so confused that the editor of the *Journal of Educational Psychology* invited a number of leading psychologists to write a paper on "What I conceive intelligence to be, and by what means it can best be measured by group tests." This invitation went out to seventeen leading psychologists, and their answers were published in the same journal. No two psychologists agreed on the conception of intelligence as a global term independent of specific referrents or correlates of the Intelligence Quotient (or IQ score). This state of affairs has continued until the present time, in spite of the important subsequent theoretical and psychometric contributions by current academicians and psychologists.

Today's standardized intelligence tests are small samples of certain measurable mental activities that have been shown through validation studies to require intelligence as scientists define this construct subjectively. However, it is an error to believe that intelligence is *merely* that which an intelligence test measures. Such a narrow view ignores the clear evidence that the IQ score provided by an intelligence test (1) predicts success in academic performance and other measures of success for the top 90 percent of the general population and (2) identifies those individuals in the bottom 10 percent who require different types of medical, behavioral, and educational interventions. Nevertheless, this quantitative measure is far from perfect as a sole measure of adaptive ability; therefore, we state that intelligence tests provide IQ scores, not direct measures of intelligence. The IQ score is what the individual earns when his performance on a specified set of items or tasks is compared to the scores of a particular sample of subjects who took the same test for purposes of providing norms. An IQ score so obtained and intelligence as subjectively understood by the laity are thus not synonymous, although they have much in common.

It is generally agreed that all ability tests (whether called *intelligence, aptitude,* or *achievement*) are measures of current performance. There are no measures of innate capacity, even from those tests called "culture fair." The difference between an intelligence (or aptitude) test and an achievement test is merely the purpose for which it is used. Tests for intelligence, achievement, and aptitude intercorrelate to an extent equal to the test-retest reliability of each of them. A test used for the prediction of future performance is called an aptitude test, while the same test used to evaluate past learning is called an achievement test. The National Merit Scholarship Examination may be categorized as an intelligence test, but precisely the same items were used in the Iowa Tests of Educational Development for assessing achievement (Cleary and others, 1975). Another group of tests, designated as mastery tests, seek to determine how much students know on a topic, but they are not designed to compare or rank subjects against each other.

Background and Current Status

In the city-states of Athens and Sparta, young men were selected for military duty and athletic competition by evidence of high physical prowess. The Greeks also paid attention to differences in quickness of mind, selecting those youngsters who would be given a formal education (Doyle, 1974). In comparably ancient times, China instituted a system of competitive achievement tests similar to today's written Civil Service examinations (DuBois, 1970). The need for better intellectual assessment became pressing when public education became universal during the nineteenth-century industrial revolution in Europe and the United States. School was no longer a privilege for the wealthy and upper class but was a right for everyone.

In 1869 Sir Francis Galton published the "Classification of Men According to Their Natural Gifts." He alluded to the presence of both a general ability and special abilities, later to be called *g* and *s* by theorist-psychologists such as Charles Spearman, Edward Thorndike, and L. L. Thurstone. But mostly Galton measured the anatomical and psychophysical attributes of his subjects. Galton also developed the statistical concept of correlation, which was later refined by Karl Pearson. With correlational statistics it became possible to compare the performance of subjects on their complex classroom activities with their performance on memory functions or their physical and psychophysical measures. The result soon would launch a debate among academic psychologists about whether intelligence consists of one general or many specific factors. Meanwhile, Alfred Binet began to search for mental tasks that would help predict which children were educable in the French public schools.

All these activities took place with no generally accepted definition of intelligence. Indeed, until the twentieth century the concept of intelligence was discussed mainly in the prescientific writings of philosophers. William James's two-volume *Principles of Psychology,* published in 1890, had only two index references to intelligence, and both of these related to its philosophical usages. The chapters on the scope of psychology, habit, memory, mind, stream of thought, and other topics leave little doubt that, in fact, James was interested in the idea of intelligence; however, he could not provide means for the assessment of intellectual qualities. Not until 1905, when Binet and his colleague Theophile Simon published their first intelligence scales, was such assessment undertaken.

Binet formally began working on the global and pragmatic assessment of intelligence about 1891. He had already studied his own two young children and concluded that it should be possible to measure the obvious differences between the intellectual capacities of the child and the adult. By coincidence, there was intense pressure in Paris at that time for the separation of children according to whether they were fully educable, educable with special help in the schools, or retarded to the point of being unable to benefit from public school placement. Through his association in 1899 with both Simon and a civic group consisting of teachers, principals, administrators, judges, general practitioners, sociologists, parents, and others, Binet began to search for quantitative measures that would more accurately reflect the obvious differences in the abilities of normal youngsters, compared with one another, as well as between them and among and between institutionalized retarded children. The result was the 1905 and 1908 Binet-Simon Scales. More than a careful scientist, Binet was a sensitive practitioner. He carefully spelled out the needed objectivity and sensitivity of the examiner in regard to ethical issues in a way that would be helpful for those engaged in assessment today.

The 1905 Binet-Simon Scale was a hastily constructed omnibus test containing thirty items with a poorly described scoring method and no provision for ranking youngsters according to different levels of relative ability. It was not until the 1908 Binet-Simon Scale that the concept of *mental age* was formally introduced. The fifty-eight items of that test were clustered for different age levels from 3 through 13 years. The Binet-Simon permitted an examiner to judge, in units of one year, any given child's mental age relative to all other children of that same chronological age. The 1911 edition was further revised, so that there were five subtests presented at each age level except one, extending the age levels upward to include 15-year-olds, plus five tests for adults. Binet resisted finer gradations of mental age than a whole number. He saw his test as merely a *sample* of the child's current intellectual behavior and not of fixed or innate intelligence.

In 1912 Wilhelm Stern recommended a procedure for determining an individual's IQ—namely, by dividing the mental by the chronological age:

$$IQ = \frac{MA}{CA} \times 100$$

or in less technical language:

$$IQ = \frac{\text{a person's attained or actual test score}}{\text{expected mean test score for that age}} \times 100$$

With the onset of World War I, the United States needed an objective test of intelligence for use with large numbers of newly inducted soldiers. Psychologist Robert Yerkes was asked to produce such an objective test, and he recruited a team of other psychologists (including Lewis Terman from Stanford University) to help. This group put together the Army Alpha (a group test for literates, which was based on the Otis group test produced by one of Terman's students) and the Army Beta (for non-English-speaking recruits and those native-born Americans who were illiterate). In about two years, nearly two million American men were tested. Although the tests were of great benefit to the army, they set the stage in the United States for an era of impersonal mass testing in schools and industry, usually without safeguards of privacy or the benefit of proper counsel about the possible meaning of the scores.

Although mass testing received extensive attention after World War I, many practitioners also attempted to use intellectual assessment for the understanding and aiding of individuals, in the spirit of Binet. One such practitioner was David Wechsler, who began work at New York's Bellevue Hospital in 1932. Another was Lewis Terman, who had revised and completely restandardized the 1911 Binet-Simon Scale in 1916. In 1937 Terman again revised this Stanford-Binet test, with two comparable forms. The third revision, form M-L (for *M*aud Merrill and *L*ewis Terman), was completed in 1960, although Terman died in 1956. There are now 1972 norms available for the test. The Stanford-Binet has retained the same format of presenting a series of age-related tasks to the subjects. However, in the 1960 revision the mental age concept was replaced by a deviation quotient for each age level (akin to the one introduced by Wechsler, described later), so that some of the earlier limitations of the use of the test with adults were overcome. It is still, however, used primarily with children.

Since Wechsler's patients were mostly adults, and emotionally disturbed, and many of them came from New York City's non-English-speaking immigrant population, he found the Stanford-Binet clinically unsuitable for his adult patients, as did other practitioners. In 1939 Wechsler thus introduced his Bellevue Intelligence Scale. Put together by trial and error, the battery consisted of ten subtests, which measured verbal and performance abilities. With his test Wechsler attempted to present a more complete picture of the individual. The resulting psychometric scores were not interpreted in a vacuum. Rather, their clinical interpretation was accomplished within a context utilizing sociocultural variables (such as education and occupation). The better-standardized and equally clinically oriented Wechsler Adult Intelligence Scale (WAIS) was introduced by Wechsler in 1955, and it is currently being updated and restandardized into what will be the WAIS-R. Both the 1939 and 1955 Wechsler scales were found to be highly useful with adults, since the effective age range is considered to be from 16 to 75. In addition, Wechsler introduced two other scales: the 1949 Wechsler Intelligence Scale for Children (WISC), for ages 6 to 16; and the 1967 Wechsler Preschool and Primary Scale of Intelligence (WPPSI), for ages 4 to 6½ years. The WISC was revised in 1974 and was called the WISC-R.

Wechsler saw that age norms would need to be considered in determining test norms for adults, since mean raw scores on most intelligence tests cease to increase significantly beyond the age of 15 or 16. The *deviation intelligence quotient* was his solution to the problem; it was employed in 1939 in the first Wechsler-Bellevue and in the construction of the WISC, the WAIS, and the WPPSI. (As mentioned, Terman and Merrill subsequently adopted a deviation quotient for their 1960 revision of the Stanford-Binet.) The deviation IQ is determined by the relative standing among age peers rather than by dividing mental age by chronological age, as was done in the early days. To compute a deviation IQ, one administers a test to a representative sample of subjects of a specified age. The raw scores on the test distribute themselves normally and yield a mean and a standard deviation for the group. The value for the raw score mean is arbitrarily assigned a scaled score value of an IQ of 100; the IQ equivalent of every other raw score above and below the mean is quickly obtained by the use of probability tables. Thus, the deviation IQ is a measure of the number of standard deviations above or below the raw score mean attained by each person in that age group. IQs so obtained are directly comparable from one age group to another and serially in time for the same person.

All the Wechsler scales consist of two major sections, Verbal and Performance, each with five or six subtests. The Verbal subtests include Information, Comprehension, Similarities (deciding what two things have in common, like a pencil and a typewriter), Arithmetic, Vocabulary, and Digit Span (the ability to repeat a series of numbers). The raw number of correct answers on each subtest is converted into a derived standard score for that subtest; when all five (or six) subtest scores are added together, they yield the person's Verbal IQ. The five Performance subtests require the use of perceptual-manipulative skills more than verbal skills. The subtests include Block Design (reproducing geometric patterns with colored blocks), Picture Completion (identifying the missing part of a picture), Picture Arrangement (putting several pictures in order to convey a story), Object Assembly (placing scattered pieces together to make a face or other object), and Digit Symbol (substituting a different symbol for each of a series of numbers, using a code). The standard scores for each subtest are added to yield a Performance IQ. The Verbal and Performance standard scores are also added and yield a Full Scale IQ. These various Wechsler Scales and the 1972 revision of the Stanford-Binet are, for all practical purposes, the major scales in use in the clinical assessment of individuals.

J. P. Guilford and Raymond Cattell are two contemporary academician-theorists who conceptualize intelligence and the measurement of intelligence in ways very different from these pragmatic approach of Terman and Wechsler. Guilford (1967) created a three-dimensional model of intelligence based on factor analysis. His three-dimensional cube contains 120 different cells, one for each of what are believed to be highly specifiable but separate intellectual abilities. This a priori theoretical model has provided new ways of exploring the concept of intelligence. It has heuristic value, and it has produced some new ways of looking at intelligence. Cattell (1963) has also produced a conceptual model of intelligence which postulates two types of intelligence, *fluid* and *crystallized*. Cattell's vigorous research program over the decades also has resulted in the development of new tests and improved factor analytic methods for sharpening theoretical ideas. However, to date neither the Guilford nor the Cattell tests have had much clinical use or application, and they remain primarily research tools.

Critical Discussion

General Areas of Concern

By far the most important concern in the assessment of intelligence is the failure, to date, of either the academician-theorists or the clinician-practitioners to present a definition of intelligence, or even of IQ score, that is capable of universal acceptance. Most individuals in these two camps acknowledge that the tests widely used in individual clinical assessment (the Stanford-Binet and the Wechsler Scales) and those responsibly used for mass administration are highly useful, effective tools, which—in the context of other data on social-behavioral adaptation—provide information about individual differences and characteristics not available from any other source. Not only is the information yielded of immeasurable aid to the individual patient or client being assessed, but the results of many decades of research to date clearly reveal that the IQ score has numerous research-specifiable correlates and validity indices, which make prediction highly possible in the hands of a compassionate counselor providing aid to an individual in need of such counsel. Thus, beginning with a global concern to assess the "intelligence" of each child in order to provide an education program best suited to enrich that child's education, Binet had to be content to redefine this global concept of intelligence into a more manageable and measurable aspect of it, called "mental age"—later refined further and called "IQ."

At issue for Binet—and subsequently for Terman, Wechsler, and every other test developer—was the gnawing question of what constitutes an adequate measure of IQ. Binet, Terman, and Wechsler used an omnibus test made up of a wide variety of test items which they found worked and which, merely on faith, they believed adequately sampled the universe of intellectual abilities. Nevertheless, other writers, test constructors, and investigators have wondered whether a simple vocabulary test of fifteen items might not be sufficient to measure IQ, especially given the high correlation between total score on such a vocabulary test and IQ as determined by a much larger battery of subtests. Concurrently, and from the opposite pole, Guilford would argue that tests such as the Stanford-Binet and the WAIS are inadequate to sample intelligence, which—in his view—is composed of 120 separate abilities, each of which needs to be evaluated separately. To date, however, practitioners have eschewed the large (research) batteries of Guilford and Cattell, thereby tacitly acknowledging that tests such as the eleven-subtest WAIS sample as much of the universe of a person's intelligence as is clinically necessary.

In fact, the WAIS is regarded as one of the three most popular of all psychological tests (Wade and Baker, 1977). Because of its popularity, there have been many attempts to imitate, replace, and abbreviate it.

Short Forms. Administration of the WAIS (about 60-90 minutes) does consume the time of the clinician or psychometrician. The advantage of shortening it is that an abbreviated form would provide the clinical contact with the subject while reducing the time necessary for administering the test. Various empirical and statistical approaches have been proposed. One method is to eliminate entire subtests; another is to eliminate items within subtests. One of the most successful of these methods appears to be that of Satz and Mogel (1962). In their method, parts of each subtest are dropped and the remainder prorated to yield raw scores, which are then converted to scale scores and IQs in the usual manner. The research on short forms suggests that they are fairly adequate when one is merely looking for a general measure of intelligence. However, short forms may not adequately measure an IQ in certain ranges of scores (Adams, Kobos, and Preston, 1977), and the shortened versions result in reduction of reliability, exposing the clinician to the likelihood of error. But the most serious criticism from some psychodynamically oriented clinicians is that the shortened versions do not permit reliable profile analysis or subscale scatter interpretation. Although Goebel and Satz (1975) deny both types of problems, the best advice for those searching for a usable short form may be that of Luszki and associates (1970): "Stop looking."

Group Forms. Group forms offer the advantage of administration to several or many people at the same time or to one individual without the presence of an examiner. This is particularly attractive where there are large numbers of clients to serve, such as in schools or clinics with limited personnel. Group forms for schools will not be discussed here because the issues there typically are a search for deficits in specific areas of achievement rather than in clinical assessment of intelligence per se. Group forms for use in clinics have been studied extensively by Charles Watson and his associates at the St. Cloud Veterans Administration Hospital. They studied the most popular intelligence tests, applying three criteria: (1) strong overall correlation with the WAIS, (2) correlation with the WAIS in various intelligence ranges, and (3) administration time. In a summary of their research, Watson, Klett, and Kucala (1975) indicate that the most promising tests were the Henmon-Nelson, the California Short Form, and the Science Research Associates (SRA) Tests of Educational Ability (although the VA patients tended to find the SRA emotionally frustrating). The summary makes clear, however, that the group tests should not be considered equivalent to the WAIS IQs.

Nonverbal Tests. Nonverbal tests have been used since World War I to avoid the problems of ethnic differences and cultural disadvantages, such as illiteracy. Unfortunately, individuals who perform poorly on the standard tests of intelligence generally show equally large deficits on nonverbal tests. Similarly, persons with specific disabilities who perform poorly on the WAIS will generally show equally large deficits on nonverbal tests. For example, Watson and Severson (1976) have concluded that the Peabody Picture Vocabulary Test is not a good predictor of WISC scores for children with cleft palates. The conclusion is that the clinician should administer those parts of the standard test that are possible to administer, considering the handicap, because a special test is not likely to lead to a greater estimation of ability.

The Porteus Mazes, D 48 "Domino test," Raven's Progressive Matrices, the Culture-Fair Test, the Revised Beta Examination, and the Quick Test are all designed for examination of general intelligence with a deemphasis on verbal skills. These tests generally correlate poorly with the WAIS (see Watson and Klett, 1974), and they also lack the profile information. Therefore, these tests probably should not be used as substitutes for the WAIS, even for the culturally disadvantaged. They should not be considered worthless, however, because some of them may provide additional dimensions of skills and nonintellectual data about patients. This can readily be seen with the Porteus, which has an objective measure of "rule breaking." Koslowsky, Deren, and Sofer (1976) indicate that the Draw-a-Person is a usable intelligence test for screening purposes in a prison population. Thus, the nonstandard tests do provide clinical information; and, whether justified or not, personal clinical experience and the information provided about personality structure by these nonstandard tests seem to perpetuate their use (Wade and Baker, 1977).

Comparative Philosophies and Theories

The basic question among theorists is whether intelligence is essentially a unitary human characteristic or a composite of many different, specific intellectual subparts. At the beginning of this century, Charles Spearman of the University of London, after analyzing the transcripts of college students and their performance on an achievement test, noted that a given student tended to perform consistently in various subjects and areas. He therefore postulated that a general intelligence factor, *g*, determines how high or how low a student will score on any achievement test, or any subject in the classroom, or on Binet's test. Spearman hypothesized that the individual differences noted in grades or tests are primarily a reflection of the differences in *g* from one individual to another. In contrast, E. L. Thorndike of Columbia University failed to find similarly high intercorrelations between tests. He postulated that, above and beyond a *g* factor, intelligence is made up primarily of a number of independent or noncorrelated specific abilities, which he called *s*, each with its own neural substate in the brain, and each of which is sampled in different combinations by different mental tests.

The controversy between these two notions has raged over the decades until the present time. More and more sophisticated statistical and mathematical approaches have been used to explore this issue. Among today's theorists and writers, Guilford (1967) postulates a theoretical model in which intellect is made up of 120 identifiable and measurable components. Cattell (1963) postulates two major factors or components (fluid intelligence and crystallized intelligence). Jensen (1970) postulates two different components of intelligence (level 1 and level 2). Representing the other side is Wechsler (1939), who feels that intelligence is a unitary and global part of the total person and that it includes personality, drive, motivation, and other nonintellective aspects, as well as those ordinarily considered intellective.

Elaboration on Critical Points

An important psychometric as well as clinical finding is that the performance of most adults on tests of intellectual ability generally shows the tendency for scores of different subtests to converge at about the same level (Lezak, 1976). This appears to reflect the conditions of normal development of the brain, in which all parts share common genetic input, nourishment, diseases, and the same level of stimulation. This tendency for consistency makes assessment a manageable task but makes the description of individual differences difficult, especially for people of similar intellectual ability. That is why the clinician must be familiar with the testing material through reading and extensive direct experience. It is especially important for the clinician to be able to identify individual differences that arise from social limitations, emotional disturbances, physical illness or handicap, and brain dysfunction. Additionally, the clinician should be prepared to identify special abilities, interests, and experiences which the client may utilize, since the assessment challenge is to assess human potential, not deficit (Matarazzo, 1972).

Personal Views and Recommendations

Since professional knowledge regarding the nature of intelligence is still meager and rudimentary, clinicians will do well to continue to focus on each individual and try to ascertain that individual's strengths and potential. Until psychological science has yielded more data, researchers on the nature of intelligence should try to determine how to enhance intellectual potential, no matter at what level of general intelligence that person begins. Professional psychologists who have practiced in a given community long enough to follow the lives of even a few clients quickly learn, as do most parents and teachers of any experience, that an IQ score, when used *in isolation,* is a questionable quantitative datum. However, it is of considerable value when it is considered along with such crucial assessment information as (1) motivation or application or other drive-related psychological resources which the individual has available or which can be brought into play; (2) the individual's personal, physical, and material resources; and (3) the number and types of opportunities (educational, familial, community, and so on) now available or potentially available to this individual.

Recent court decisions have disallowed the use of intellectual and personality tests in private industry and public civil service unless there is first established clear evidence that the tests relate to job performance. In some situations it was established in the resulting litigation that tests had been used for screening purposes; but they had primarily screened out minorities and persons with special handicaps who, later experience demonstrated, could in fact do the job if they were given the opportunity or, in some instances, the minimal training required to do so. There have been class action suits by both psychologists and the consumers of testing to ban the use of tests for culturally disadvantaged students. The psychologist needs to be especially discerning where tests are used for purposes of classification.

An ethical issue that is not immediately apparent is that of labeling (Mercer, 1973). Schools, clinics, and institutions use labels as shorthand ways of processing information. However, the label that may seem innocuous in one setting may prove to be a stigma in another setting or, over time, in the same setting. Labels are narrower (contain less information) than what people actually are, and they may create expectations that are restrictive. Also, the most harmless label can easily become used in a pejorative sense, especially with the passage of time. Today the mentally retarded person is referred to as intellectually or educationally handicapped. Not too many years ago such retarded persons were labeled idiot, imbecile, and moron, with no thought of the pejorative sense in which these words were being used.

To provide perspective in this area, Sundberg and Tyler (1962, p. 131) point out the potential ethical abuses in the use of tests of intelligence but also state: "The solution is not the prohibition of all tests. *Not* using a test when a good one is available is as unethical as misusing one. The truth of the matter is that tests *are tools*. In the hands of a capable and creative person they can be used with remarkable outcomes. In the hands of a fool or an unscrupulous person they become a pseudoscientific perversion."

Application to Particular Variables

Age. Several generations of psychologists were brought up with the idea that intellectual abilities (actually, raw score on an IQ test and, thus, mental age itself) increase with age until late adolescence or early adulthood and then slowly but progressively decline thereafter. This was believed because when children, parents, and grandparents were given tests such as the Army Alpha in a single mass administration (cross-sectional design), the mean scores of these different age groups suggested such a rising and then declining curve. This assumption was later challenged when longitudinal studies of the same individual, tested from birth into the 50s, showed no such decline beyond age 20 for most abilities tapped by IQ tests (Bradway and Thompson, 1962; Jones, 1967; Kangas and Bradway, 1971). As a result, many psychologists dropped the notion that raw scores on an IQ test decline after early adulthood. Nevertheless, the issue is far from clear-cut even today. Horn and Donaldson (1976) have reviewed these issues critically and offer the opinion that the evidence is still not conclusive for either argument. They provide an excellent review of the methodological problems inherent in the earlier cross-sectional and the more recent longitudinal studies.

Sex. Almost without exception, intelligence tests have been constructed so that items do not favor one sex or the other; when items do favor one sex—for example, if girls do better on verbal items and boys on arithmetic items—test constructors include an equal number of such sex-related, differentially sensitive items in the test. Thus, in subsequent studies of other samples of individuals, the mean scores of males and of females (as well as their mental age and IQ) typically are found *not* to differ. Longitudinal research even reveals that items favoring girls or boys at one age cease doing so, or even reverse themselves, at other ages (Matarazzo, 1972, p. 200). Back and Dana (1977) recently reported that, in their third-grade population of subjects, female examinees obtained scores 7.2 points higher than male examinees on the Full Scale WISC. However, studies utilizing other similarly small and unrepresentative samples have reported opposite findings. There clearly is much more research to be done on sexual differences, and the results of one study should not be evaluated in isolation. For now, one may conclude that there are *no* sex differences in IQ.

   Education. In common with the first such study by Yerkes (who correlated years of schooling with score on the Army Alpha), the correlation between years of schooling and IQ has been shown to be approximately $r = .70$ in each succeeding generation of tests of ability. Do years of schooling predict one's IQ, or does one's IQ determine or predict the number of years of schooling one subsequently will complete? The answer to this question awaits more definitive research. Yet, despite this confounding of cause and effect in years of schooling and IQ, there are good research data on the relationship between academic success and IQ. Here it appears that IQ contributes significantly to grade point average, and not the other way around. Thus, numerous studies show that the correlation between measured IQ and academic success in the classroom is about $r = .50$. (The rest of the variance undoubtedly is due to motivation, effort, interest in the subject, and a whole series of other personal, idiosyncratic variables.) This correlation of $r = .50$ appears to hold true for grade school, high school, college, and graduate and professional school (Matarazzo, 1972, 1978). The power of intelligence tests to predict academic success in school was evident in a large-scale longitudinal study reported by Dillon (1949). Dillon started with 2,600 youngsters in the seventh grade and sorted them into five groups based on their intelligence test scores. Thereafter, year by year Dillon tabulated the number of children who dropped out of school at subsequent grade levels. Out of the total 2,600 seventh graders, 400 had IQs below 85. Each year, from the seventh grade on, attrition took its toll in this group, leaving only 14 children (4 percent of the original 400 in this group) to graduate from the twelfth grade. Of the five groups, which ranged in IQ from 85 to 115, each successive group had a better percentage graduating; in the top group (IQ of 115 and above), 86 percent of the students who started together in the seventh grade graduated. Thus, intelligence test scores, when used responsibly, can help identify youngsters at risk in the early school years.

   Socioeconomic Status. The relationship between IQ and socioeconomic status has been of interest since the early days of Binet's work. Extensive work in this area has been reviewed periodically (Loevinger, 1940; Miner, 1957; Neff, 1938; Tyler, 1965). In his review of this voluminous literature, Matarazzo (1972) suggests that socioeconomic status, defined by any of a variety of indices (income, education, type of occupation, social class, and related indices) correlates with IQ in the neighborhood of $r = .40$.

   Canter (1956) found an interesting relationship between IQ scores for various occupations and the *judged social status* of those occupations. Rather than identifying individual scores, he correlated the median IQ scores of groups in twenty-five different occupations with the independently ranked social status of the same occupations. The result was an impressive $r = .96$. This result was subsequently cross-validated, with a correlation of $r = .91$, in a study by Duncan (summarized by Jensen, 1969). Social status rankings are undoubtedly influenced by a person's estimate of the amount of intelligence needed for a given occupation.

   The relationships between race and socioeconomic status have made it extremely difficult to evaluate racial and ethnic differences independent of this confounding with socioeconomic status. Lesser, Fifer, and Clark (1965) studied four different cultural subgroups of first-grade children. Although there were differences among the mean scores of the four ethnic groups, within each ethnic group the children in the lowest socioeconomic subgroup earned substantially lower mean scores than did their higher socioeconomic counterparts.

Many studies have made it clear that extreme environments will profoundly alter the capacity of the presumed hereditary component of IQ to manifest itself. This has been shown in the longitudinal research of Heber and Garber (1975), who for the past decade have been longitudinally studying a group of inner-city newborns whose older siblings and mothers had measured IQ scores of about 70. Massive educational intervention from birth on was provided to the twenty newborns in the experimental group and none to the twenty newborns in the control group. The results seem to indicate that it is possible to retard the progressive drop in IQ which is found in socioeconomically deprived infants; and that by age 16 this sample of ghetto children, otherwise destined to be mentally retarded, quite likely will have a mean IQ of 100 and will be performing satisfactorily in school and in their community.

Vocation. Most of the studies on IQ and occupational attainment have been with military recruits from World Wars I and II. On the average, the higher the IQ, (1) the higher the level of responsibility the person had as a preinducted civilian, (2) the greater the responsibility given in military life, and (3) the higher the occupational attainment found ten to fifteen years after discharge. In a study of some 10,000 air force cadets, Thorndike and Hagen (1959) found a remarkable relationship between the pattern of scores of 18-year-old examinees and their occupations in civilian life twelve years later. For example, those who were working as accountants at age 30 had scored highest twelve years earlier on numerical fluency relative to the other cadets. Similarly, civilian airplane pilots had done best on visual perception, mechanical, and psychomotor tests; and machine mechanics had scored best on mechanical tests and poorly on general intelligence. These results provide striking examples of the predictive validity of such multibattery tests of intelligence relative to subsequent vocational or occupational attainment.

Measures of IQ and occupational attainment are generally considered to be correlated at about $r = .50$. However, studies of the relationship between IQ and occupational success have generally revealed coefficients of only modest values, averaging about $r = .20$ (Ghiselli, 1966). This is far lower than the values of $r = .50$ typically found in studies of IQ and academic success. Although the reasons for these lower correlations are not fully understood, it is easier to define and quantitatively measure success in an academic setting than it is in the world of work. Supervisors' ratings may reflect many nonintellectual factors, such as interpersonal relationships. It is meaningless to measure success at work in terms of production for most occupations, and income is also likely to be a poor criterion of success.

Ethnic/Racial Factors. Almost no scientist or scholar familiar with the research data in this complicated field denies that the evidence as of today is consistent from study to study; that is, on the average, groups of blacks earn lower IQ test scores than do groups of whites. (Studies with yellow and brown races to date are too few to generalize our findings to them.) However, this is merely an empirical finding. It merely relates a test *score,* and only that, to color of pigmentation of the skin. What might this black-white difference in mean IQ suggest if one discusses it as an empirical finding and not in terms of its false and more inflammatory implications? To discover, as has been done, differences in IQ score which correlate with differences in the pigmentation of skin is no different from demonstrating that today's blacks are probably more athletically able than are comparable groups of whites. What is needed is for curious scientists to ask the appropriate questions and to design the appropriate studies to explain further these initial findings of differences between the races. For example, professionals should launch beginning searches for the anatomical, endocrinological, biochemical, and environmental correlates and precursors of these exciting "marker" or "criterion" variables.

As was done for sex differences, a test could be constructed which will eliminate items that discriminate against one group. Thus, items could be thrown out until the mean score of one group no longer was lower than the mean score of the other group. Despite some limited successes, such a usable test has not yet been constructed. Alternatively, a test favoring blacks could be constructed. Williams (1972) accomplished just this aim by his culture-specific test for black children, the Black Intelligence Test of Cultural Homogeneity (BITCH), which measures knowledge of street vocabulary and yields higher scores for black than for white teenagers. Unfortunately, there are no published data to support its use as an intelligence test. In a recent study by Matarazzo and Wiens (1977), it failed to correlate either with IQ on the Full Scale WAIS or with any of that scale's eleven subtests.

The influence of socioeconomic factors on racial differences in IQ can be shown from the often-quoted study of Baughman and Dahlstrom (1968). They studied a large population of black and white children in rural North Carolina and found a thirteen-point difference between the means of the two groups. However, there were difficulties in the interpretation of the differences. First, there was considerable overlap in the two distributions of IQ scores of the two groups. There were also sex differences within both races on a number of individual subtests. Most important, there were marked socioeconomic differences. For example, the parents of white children had two more years of education, the black families had a substantially lower income, and the black children came from larger families. These differences only underscore the problems of reaching conclusions about the intelligence of one race versus another.

Data recently presented by Scarr and Weinberg (1976, 1977) show that black children adopted at birth by white parents attain a mean IQ score slightly *above* average and almost, but not quite, the same mean as that of white children reared in the same families. This study, along with others (for instance, Heber and Garber, 1975), strongly suggests that the IQ can be altered by the environment. The influence of heredity is undeniable, as revealed in decades of research, but an IQ score is also an index of social conditions, not exclusively a biological inevitability. If the distribution of nutrition, home experience, and schooling is changed in the next generation, the heritability index most likely will change (Cronbach, 1975).

Although the data on race and IQ are voluminous and also confusing, some summary statements are possible. After careful reading and review of the world literature on the subject of race and IQ, Loehlin, Lindzey, and Spuhler (1975, pp. 238-239) summarize their conclusions as follows:

[The black-white IQ differences so far reported] probably reflect in part inadequacies and biases in the tests themselves, in part differences in environmental conditions among the groups, and in part genetic differences among the groups.

A rather wide range of positions concerning the relative weight to be given these three factors can reasonably be taken on the basis of current evidence, and a sensible person's position might well differ for different abilities, for different groups, and for different tests.

Regardless of the position taken on the relative importance of these three factors, [differences in IQ *within* the black population itself and *within* the white population itself] greatly exceed in magnitude the average differences between such groups.

On the whole, these are rather limited conclusions. It does not appear to us, however, that the state of scientific evidence at the present time justifies stronger ones.

Physical Disorders. Many prenatal and postnatal influences affect later IQ. Poor maternal diet during pregnancy (as well as smoking, drinking, or drug abuse) is correlated with lower IQ scores; so also are anoxia during travel through the birth canal, low birth weight, and forceps injury. Lower IQ scores also are associated with too many or too few X or Y sex chromosomes, with phenylketonuria (PKU), and with other intrauterine influences or differences. In early childhood the IQ can be adversely affected by lead poisoning, brain injury, high fever, measles, poor postnatal nutrition during the first two years of life, and lack of stimulation during the first two years of life (see Matarazzo, 1972, Chapter Twelve, for a comprehensive review of these variables).

Conversely, Money (1971) at Johns Hopkins and his former associates Baker and Ehrhardt (1974) at the State University of New York at Buffalo have reported suggestive evidence that families with a recessive genetic tendency toward excessive levels of prenatal androgen earn *higher* IQ scores than normal (a mean of about 111 instead of 100), although some researchers have offered an alternative interpretation, suggesting that there is no robust evidence for such hormonal enhancement in these studies. Eldridge and associates (1970) similarly report that children with the recessive disorder of torsion dystonia also earn IQ scores that are higher than average (mean of 120). There is even preliminary evidence that high levels of uric acid (as in gout) are associated with higher than average IQ. More studies on the hormonal and genetic correlates of the IQ are needed.

Cerebral palsy is a neurological disorder that can profoundly alter physical and intellectual performance. Even so, there are wide ranges of individual differences. Greenbaum and Buehler (1960) found IQ scores from 10 to 130 in their study of cerebral palsy in two states, but the mean IQ was about 70. The assessment of persons with cerebral palsy (and others with physical handicaps) is complicated because of speech and motor difficulties. Speech and motor difficulties may accompany an underlying difficulty in comprehension, but they also may merely represent an inability to coordinate ideas into meaningful actions, thus masking the comprehension. Communication difficulties are frequently called aphasia, but the problem may be of a receptive (or learning) nature or of an expressive (or motor response) nature. Agnosia refers to perceptual or receptive deficits, including deficits in awareness, recognition, discrimination patterning, and orientation. Apraxia (literally "no work") refers to disturbances of expressive functions, such as verbal or motor functions. Thus, it may be quite meaningless to give Block Design to someone with a motor disability. A more appropriate test for such a handicapped individual might be the Raven Matrices, which one can answer merely by pointing to the correct response. Similarly, it may be necessary to avoid an oral vocabulary test and to use instead the Peabody Picture Vocabulary Test. Benham (1972a, 1972b) has provided some information on the assessment of children and infants with cerebal palsy. Similarly, the practicing clinician of today has special tests available for assessing intelligence in individuals who are blind, deaf, and otherwise physically impaired.

Intellectual Disorders. Since the introduction of the 1905 Binet-Simon Scale, such tests have been used as one of the two necessary ingredients in the assessment of mental retardation. The second ingredient needed is an index of socioadaptive behavior. A diagnosis of mental retardation is not made on the basis of IQ alone. Information about the assessment of mental retardation is covered in Chapter Fifty-Six of this volume.

Organic Dysfunction. It is probably fair to say that the assessment of organic dysfunction begins with a Wechsler-Bellevue I or WAIS for adults and WISC-R for children in the United States and a few other English-speaking countries (for a brief view of assessment in Russia, see Luria and Majovski, 1977). The WAIS Full Scale IQ and the potential patterning or "scatter" among its eleven subtests will generally identify areas of intellectual deficit. Neuropsychological assessment with the WAIS and Halstead-Reitan or other batteries is basically a search for those areas where the brain no longer performs as it once did. In assessing premorbid intellectual abilities, the clinician must either gather historical data about actual past performance (grammar school achievement test records, army scores, high school or college achievement test scores) or make some assumptions about intellectual level based on actual academic accomplishments or on occupational or avocational achievement. These estimates quite likely will reflect the lowest level, not the highest potential of attainment. A Wechsler subtest scaled score that is five to six points (two standard deviations) lower than the scaled score of one or more other subtests should be considered as a possible indication of organic impairment, especially in the absence of clinical indices of psychosis or other serious psychiatric dysfunction. Further uses of measures of intellectual deficit in neuropsychological assessment can be found in Lezak (1976); Reitan and Davison (1974); Russell, Neuringer, and Goldstein (1970); and Matarazzo (1972).

Functional Disorders. Many of the functional psychiatric disorders as well as other emotional states—from momentary situational distractibility to anxiety and depression through the most serious behavioral disorders, such as schizophrenia—can influence performance on tests that measure intellectual ability. However, the search for intelligence test patterns or profiles that differentiate, by themselves, one emotional or psychiatric state from another has proved totally unsuccessful to date. Although recent research suggests that one or another WAIS subtest (Digit Span, for example) may be a mirror of momentary state anxiety, even these results represent a difference between group *means,* and such a finding does not hold in a large enough number of *individual* cases to permit its universal use in clinical practice.

Collective/Interactional Factors. There is little doubt that the human personal-sensory interaction provided the newborn child can profoundly affect that child's later measured intelligence or IQ. This observation was first made clinically by Rene Spitz, who showed that, compared to a control group of infants who lived with their own mothers, infants in a foundling home (where there was one nurse for each ten infants) progressively deteriorated in their intellectual development over the first twelve months of life until they reached a mean IQ of about 60. When such an infant was returned to a mother or mother substitute before six months of life, this progressive drop in intellectual functioning was reversed. Spitz's findings were corroborated by investigators in other parts of the world, and these findings were given wide dissemination by Bowlby (1965). Provence and Lipton (1962) later confirmed a similar finding of progressive intellectual loss in 75 infants relative to 75 control infants in a well-designed study carried out in the Department of Pediatrics at Yale University.

Other research showing the importance of the family, especially the stimulation provided by members of middle-class families to their offspring relative to the absence of such stimulation for newborns raised in ghetto families, has been reported by Heber and Garber (1975) and by Scarr and Weinberg (1976, 1977).

References

Adams, R. L., Kobos, J. C., and Preston, J. "Effect of Racial-Ethnic Grouping, Age, and IQ Range on the Validity of the Satz-Mogel Short Form of the Wechsler Adult Intelligence Scale." *Journal of Consulting and Clinical Psychology,* 1977, *45,* 489-499.
Back, R., and Dana, R. H. "Examiner Sex Bias and Wechsler Intelligence Scale for Children Scores." *Journal of Consulting and Clinical Psychology,* 1977, *45,* 500.
Baker, S. W., and Ehrhardt, A. A. "Prenatal Androgen, Intelligence, and Cognitive Sex

Difference." In R. C. Friedman, R. M. Richart, and R. L. Vande Wiele (Eds.), *Sex Differences in Behavior*. New York: Wiley, 1974.

Baughman, E. E., and Dahlstrom, W. G. *Negro and White Children: A Psychological Study in the Rural South*. New York: Academic Press, 1968.

Benham, K. M. "Activity Level of Retarded Cerebral Palsied Children." *Exceptional Children*, 1972a, *38*, 641-642.

Benham, K. M. "Progress in Mental Development of Retarded Cerebral Palsied Infants." *Exceptional Children*, 1972b, *39*, 240.

Bowlby, J. *Child Care and the Growth of Love*. New York: Penguin Books, 1965.

Bradway, K. P., and Thompson, C. W. "Intelligence at Adulthood: A Twenty-Five Year Follow-Up." *Journal of Educational Psychology*, 1962, *53*, 1-14.

Canter, R. R. "Intelligence and the Social Status of Occupations." *Personnel Guidance Journal*, 1956, *34*, 258-260.

Cattell, R. B. "Theory of Fluid and Crystallized Intelligence: A Critical Experiment." *Journal of Educational Psychology*, 1963, *54*, 1-22.

Cleary, T. A., and others. "Educational Uses of Tests with Disadvantaged Students." *American Psychologist*, 1975, *30*, 15-41.

Cronbach, L. J. "Five Decades of Public Controversy over Mental Testing." *American Psychologist*, 1975, *30*, 1-14.

Dillon, H. J. *Early School Leavers: A Major Educational Problem*. New York: National Child Labor Committee, 1949.

Doyle, K. O., Jr. "Theory and Practice of Ability Testing in Ancient Greece." *Journal of the History of the Behavioral Sciences*, 1974, *10*, 202-212.

DuBois, P. H. *A History of Psychological Testing*. Boston: Allyn and Bacon, 1970.

Eldridge, R., and others. "Superior Intelligence in Recessively Inherited Torsion Dystonia." *Lancet*, 1970, *1*, 65-67.

Ghiselli, E. E. *The Validity of Occupational Aptitude Tests*. New York: Wiley, 1966.

Goebel, R. A., and Satz, P. "Profile Analysis and the Abbreviated Wechsler Adult Intelligence Scale: A Multivariate Approach." *Journal of Consulting and Clinical Psychology*, 1975, *43*, 780-785.

Green, R. F., and Reimanis, G. "The Age-Intelligence Relationship: Longitudinal Studies Can Mislead." *Industrial Gerontology*, 1970, *6*, 1-16.

Greenbaum, M., and Buehler, J. A. "Further Findings on the Intelligence of Children with Cerebral Palsy." *American Journal of Mental Deficiency*, 1960, *65*, 261-264.

Guilford, J. P. *The Nature of Human Intelligence*. New York: McGraw-Hill, 1967.

Heber, R., and Garber, H. "The Milwaukee Project: A Study of the Use of Family Intervention to Prevent Cultural-Familial Mental Retardation." In B. Z. Friedlander, G. M. Sterritt, and G. E. Kirk (Eds.), *Exceptional Infant*. Vol. 3: *Assessment and Intervention*. New York: Brunner/Mazel, 1975.

Horn, J. L., and Donaldson, G. "On the Myth of Intellectual Decline in Adulthood." *American Psychologist*, 1976, *31*, 701-719.

Jackson, G. D. "On the Report of the Ad Hoc Committee on Educational Uses of Tests with Disadvantaged Students." *American Psychologist*, 1975, *30*, 88-93.

Jarvik, L. F., and Falek, A. "Intellectual Stability and Survival in the Aged." *Journal of Gerontology*, 1963, *18*, 173-176.

Jensen, A. R. "How Much Can We Boost I.Q. and Scholastic Achievement?" *Harvard Educational Review*, 1969, *39*, 1-123.

Jensen, A. R. "A Theory of Primary and Secondary Familial Mental Retardation." In N. R. Ellis (Ed.), *International Review of Research in Mental Retardation*. Vol. 4. New York: Academic Press, 1970.

Jones, M. C. "A Report on Three Growth Studies at the University of California." *Gerontologist,* 1967, *7,* 49-54.

Kangas, J., and Bradway, K. "Intelligence at Middle Age: A Thirty-Eight Year Follow-Up." *Developmental Psychology,* 1971, *5,* 333-337.

Koslowsky, M., Deren, S., and Sofer, S. "Clinical Decision Making: Use of Selection Ratios to Predict Intelligence." *Journal of Consulting and Clinical Psychology,* 1976, *44,* 771-774.

Lesser, G. S., Fifer, G., and Clark, D. H. "Mental Abilities of Children from Different Social-Class and Cultural Groups." *Monographs of the Society for Research in Child Development,* 1965, *30* (4, Serial No. 102).

Lezak, M. D. *Neuropsychological Assessment.* New York: Oxford University Press, 1976.

Loehlin, J. C., Lindzey, G., and Spuhler, J. N. *Race Difference in Intelligence.* San Francisco: Freeman, 1975.

Loevinger, J. "Intelligence as Related to Socioeconomic Factors." In *Intelligence: Its Nature and Nurture.* Part I: *Comparative and Critical Exposition.* Bloomington, Ill.: National Society for the Study of Education, 1940.

Luria, A. R., and Majovski, L. V. "Basic Approaches Used in American and Soviet Clinical Neuropsychology." *American Psychologist,* 1977, *32,* 959-968.

Luszki, M. B., and others. "Long Search for a Short WAIS: Stop Looking." *Journal of Consulting and Clinical Psychology,* 1970, *34,* 425-431.

Matarazzo, J. D. *Wechsler's Measurement and Appraisal of Adult Intelligence.* (5th ed.) Baltimore: Williams & Wilkins, 1972.

Matarazzo, J. D. "Heredity and Environmental Correlates of IQ." *Journal of Continuing Education in Psychiatry,* Jan. 1978, pp. 35-46.

Matarazzo, J. D., and Wiens, A. M. "Black Intelligence Test of Cultural Homogeneity and Wechsler Adult Intelligence Scale Scores of Black and White Police Applicants." *Journal of Applied Psychology,* 1977, *62,* 57-63.

Mercer, J. R. *Labelling the Mentally Retarded.* Los Angeles: University of California Press, 1973.

Miner, J. B. *Intelligence in the United States.* New York: Springer, 1957.

Money, J. "Prenatal Hormones and Intelligence: A Possible Relationship." *Impact of Science on Society,* 1971, *21,* 285-290.

Neff, W. S. "Socioeconomic Status and Intelligence: A Critical Survey." *Psychological Bulletin,* 1938, *35,* 727-757.

Provence, S., and Lipton, R. C. *Infants in Institutions.* New York: International Universities Press, 1962.

Reitan, R. M., and Davison, L. A. *Clinical Neuropsychology: Current Status and Applications.* New York: Wiley, 1974.

Russell, E. W., Neuringer, C., and Goldstein, G. *Assessment of Brain Damage: A Neuropsychological Approach.* New York: Wiley-Interscience, 1970.

Satz, P., and Mogel, S. "An Abbreviation of the WAIS for Clinical Use." *Journal of Clinical Psychology,* 1962, *18,* 77-79.

Scarr, S., and Weinberg, R. A. "IQ Test Performance of Black Children Adopted by White Families." *American Psychologist,* 1976, *31,* 726-739.

Scarr, S., and Weinberg, R. A. "Intellectual Similarities Within Families of Both Adopted and Biological Children." *Intelligence,* 1977, *1,* 170-191.

Sundberg, N. D., and Tyler, L. E. *Clinical Psychology.* New York: Appleton-Century-Crofts, 1962.

Thorndike, R. L., and Hagen, E. *Ten Thousand Careers.* New York: Wiley, 1959.

Tyler, L. E. *The Psychology of Human Differences.* (3rd ed.) New York: Appleton-Century-Crofts, 1965.

Wade, T. C., and Baker, T. B. "Opinions and Use of Psychological Tests." *American Psychologist,* 1977, *32,* 874-882.

Watson, C. G., and Klett, W. G. "Are Nonverbal IQ Tests Adequate Substitutes for the WAIS?" *Journal of Clinical Psychology,* 1974, *30,* 55-57.

Watson, C. G., Klett, W. G., and Kucala, T. "Which Brief IQ Test Is Best for Your Setting?" *Newsletter for Research in Mental Health and Behavioral Science,* 1975, *17* (4), 5-8.

Watson, C. G., and Severson, R. A. "The Peabody Picture Vocabulary Test as a Measure of Intelligence in Children with Palatal Problems." *Cleft Palate Journal,* 1976, *13,* 367-370.

Wechsler, D. *The Measurement of Adult Intelligence.* Baltimore: Williams & Wilkins, 1939.

Williams, R. L. "The Black Intelligence Test of Cultural Homogeneity (BITCH)-100: A Culture-Specific Test." Paper presented at meeting of American Psychological Association, Honolulu, Sept. 1972.

56

Robert L. Anderson

Mental Retardation

The term *mental retardation* is currently used in three classification systems commonly employed in the United States: the *International Classification of Diseases, Adapted for Use in the United States* (U.S. Department of Health, Education, and Welfare, 1967); the American Association on Mental Deficiency's *Manual on Terminology and Classification in Mental Retardation* (Grossman, 1973); and the *Diagnostic and Statistical Manual of Mental Disorders (DSM-II)* (American Psychiatric Association, 1968). The relative uniformity of conceptualization in all three systems makes it possible to discontinue the use of (1) earlier terms (such as idiot, imbecile, or moron) to identify the level of retardation and (2) the concepts of feeblemindedness and mental deficiency to identify the condition. Mental subnormality has been variously conceived, identified, and treated, depending on its geographical location and the professional discipline involved in dealing with the condition. The more uniform terminology facilitates communication across disciplines and national boundaries.

The most commonly accepted definition of mental retardation is found in the AAMD's *Manual on Terminology and Classification in Mental Retardation* (Grossman, 1973, p. 11): "Mental retardation refers to significantly subaverage general intellectual functioning existing concurrently with deficits in adaptive behavior, and manifested in the developmental period."

The primary parameters of mental retardation are level of intelligence, adaptive behavior, and age at which the condition is manifest. The requirement of deficits in behavior existing concurrently with significantly subaverage intelligence makes the nature of mental retardation somewhat more definitive than in the past. Specifically, the condition will originate before age 19 (the developmental period), the level of intellectual functioning (as assessed by one or more standardized tests developed for that purpose) will be two or more standard deviations below the mean, and the adaptive behavior of the individual will fail to meet the standards of personal independence and social responsibility expected of persons of similar age and cultural background.

This conceptualization of mental retardation identifies a condition based entirely on behavioral performance without regard to etiology, either physiological or social. Similarly, no assumptions are made relative to the prognosis of such conditions. A more refined description of the behavior of retarded persons is facilitated by the accepted AAMD classification system, including four levels corresponding to IQ score ranges. Starting with IQ scores of two standard deviations below the mean, performance levels indicative of mild (2-3), moderate (3-4), severe (4-5), and profound (5 or more) are identified with each successive standard deviation. No comparable scaling has been established for the concurrent deficits in adaptive behavior.

A medical classification system identifying known or suspected etiological factors and associated physical, psychological, or environmental conditions is included in both the AAMD and the *DSM-II* systems. The major headings are:

1. Following infection or intoxication
2. Following trauma or physical agent
3. With disorders of metabolism or nutrition
4. Associated with gross brain disease (postnatal)
5. Associated with diseases and conditions due to unknown prenatal influence
6. With chromosomal abnormality
7. Gestational disorders
8. Following psychiatric disorder
9. Environmental influences
10. Other conditions

Known etiologies are commonly identified with the more severely impaired individuals who are distinctly different from other members of their families and are found in all socioeconomic, cultural, and ethnic groups. These are generally presumed to be organically impaired persons whose intellectual potential and adaptive abilities have been depressed by biological abnormalities. In the more mildly impaired persons, including those individuals with so-called cultural-familial mental retardation, the impairment appears to result from an interaction of biological and social factors. The confidence level at which one can identify the etiology of the condition is inversely related to the level of functional intelligence. Identifiable clinical syndromes commonly associated with mental retardation are found with greatest frequency at levels of moderate and severe intellectual impairment.

Background and Current Status

The condition now classified as mental retardation has probably existed from earliest times. In England statutory mention dates back to the reign of Edward I (1272-1307), at which time a distinction was made between the "born fool" and the lunatic (Clarke and Clarke, 1974). Blanton (1975) credits the psychiatrist J. E. D. Esquirol with the first clear definition of mental retardation. In 1845, Esquirol described "idiocy" as "a condition in which the intellectual faculties are never manifested, or have never been developed sufficiently to enable the idiot to acquire such amount of knowledge as persons of his own age and placed in similar circumstances with himself are capable of receiving." Two classes of retardates, idiots and imbeciles, were identified on the basis of speech development. The use of the term *idiot* was perpetuated by Edouard Seguin in 1866 through his book *Idiocy and Its Treatment by Physiological Method.*

Legislation passed in the latter half of the nineteenth century and the beginning of the twentieth century indicated a growing awareness of differences in the nature of the condition, prognostic outcomes, and etiology. The Idiots Act of 1886 distinguished between idiocy and imbecility, with both requiring institutional care. The Education Act of 1870 identified two levels of noninstitutional retardates: the educable imbecile and the feebleminded. The Elementary Education (Defective and Epileptic Children) Act of 1899 added another classificatory term and concept, mentally defective. Persons with this level of retardation were perceived to need special education training but not institutionalization. The Mental Deficiency Act of 1913 and the Education Act of 1921 identified the entire range of intellectual and adaptive functions that are now perceived within the concept of mental retardation. Sarason and Doris (1969), Blanton (1975), and Clarke and Clarke (1974) provide excellent reviews of the evolution of the concept.

Physicians, psychologists, educators, and social scientists introduced a variety of labels for given concepts relating to mental retardation. *Mental deficiency, mental impairment,* and *mental handicap* have been used to identify the condition. *Moron, educable, trainable,* and *borderline* have been used to describe the degree of impairment and the appropriate educational programming.

The medical, psychiatric, psychological, and educational professions now uniformly accept *mental retardation* as the generic term. They agree on the definition and the levels of impairment stated earlier. The Education of All Handicapped Children Act (Public Law 94-142, 1975) includes mental retardation as a major diagnostic category, using a definition essentially the same as the AAMD definition.

The incidence of mental retardation, based on empirical sampling surveys, is estimated to be 6,791,800 people in the United States. Estimates based on the percentage of the population that would function two or more standard deviations below the mean on standardized intelligence tests would predict an incidence of 4,732,000 in a population of 208,000,000. Evidence indicates that a lesser number (approximately 1 percent of the population) would be identified as mentally retarded if such persons were required to function at two or more standard deviations below the mean on *both* measures of intelligence and adaptive behavior (Mercer, 1973). Approximately 10 percent of the mentally retarded, or 200,000 persons, are institutionalized (Tjossem, 1976). Approximately 2,100 infants born each week are either mentally retarded or become mentally retarded during their lifetime (Kauffman and Payne, 1975). It is statistically probable that 89 percent of the mentally retarded are mildly impaired, 6 percent moderately impaired, and 5 percent severely and profoundly impaired. At the present time, the etiology of over 75 percent of the cases of mental retardation remains unknown (Dunn, 1973).

Critical Discussion

General Areas of Concern

The magnitude of the problem of mental retardation is reflected in human misery, plus the social and financial burdens that such conditions place on families, schools, and other social agencies. Beginning in the early 1960s, social and political action was directed toward an all-out attack on mental retardation. During the past two decades, executive, judicial, and legislative branches of federal and state governments became intimately involved in dealing with these problems. In 1961 President John F. Kennedy appointed a panel to prepare a national plan to combat mental retardation. The panel, under the direction of Leonard Mayo, published *A Proposed Program for National Action to Combat Mental Retardation* (Mayo, 1962). The panel, in keeping with a developing philosophy of community mental health, identified the major concerns and made the following recommendations:

1. Research in the causes of retardation and in methods of care, habilitation, and learning.
2. Preventive health measures.
3. Strengthened educational programs generally and extended and enriched programs of special education.
4. More comprehensive and improved clinical services.
5. Improved methods and facilities for care.
6. A new legal, as well as social, concept of the retarded.
7. Helping overcome the serious problems of manpower.
8. Programs of education and information to increase public awareness.

The panel recognized that the primary responsibility for financing and improving services for the mentally retarded would rest with the states and local communities. However, the federal government would assist in attaining the primary goals of prevention, cure, and amelioration of mental retardation.

The President's Committee on Mental Retardation (PCMR) was established in 1966 to promote national planning and mobilize basic programs in the field of mental retardation. The annual reports of this committee have been influential in establishing public policy and directing national efforts. An Executive Order (No. 11776, 1974) continues and expands the work of the committee and establishes three major goals: (1) to reduce the occurrence of mental retardation by half before the end of the century; (2) to return to the community one third of the persons presently in public institutions; and (3) to assure retarded individuals full status as citizens under law.

Judicial rulings relating to the clinical assessment of mental retardation and its subsequent treatment have determined the acceptable practices in the various professions. The requirement of nondiscriminatory assessment was established in a number of cases, such as *Hobson* v. *Hansen* (1967), *Diana* v. *State Board of Education* (1970), and *Larry P.* v. *Riles* (1972). *Merrikan* v. *Cressman* (1973) placed new responsibilities on clinicians and the instruments they use. One part of the decision states, "When a program talks about labeling someone as a particular type and such a label could remain with him for the remainder of his life, the margin of error must be almost nil" (p. 920). Due process rights for parents of suspect children to help ensure appropriate classification and appropriate educational programming for their children were established by *Pennsylvania Association for Retarded Children* v. *Commonwealth* (1972) and *Mills* v. *Board of Education* (1972). The impact of these decisions is being experienced by physicians, psychologists, educators, and all other professional persons involved in the identification, care, and treatment of mentally retarded persons.

The litigation of the late 1960s and early 1970s was supplanted by legislative activity by federal and state governments in the mid 1970s. Influential federal laws include the Rehabilitation Act of 1973 (Public Law 93-112), the Education Amendments of 1974 (Public Law 93-516), and the Education of All Handicapped Children Act of 1975 (Public Law 94-142). Legislative commitment to accomplishing the goals of the President's Committee on Mental Retardation is evidenced by its support of research on problems of mental retardation, including studies of causation, programs of prevention, early identification, and intervention strategies. State legislatures have generally developed mandatory education acts paralleling Public Law 94-142, in some cases even extending the population to be served. For example, the Mandatory Special Education Act in Michigan (Public Act 198, 1973) requires service to all handicapped persons from birth through age 25.

The consequences of the above-noted litigation and legislation relative to mental retardation are significant for clinical psychologists, school psychologists, and others involved in clinical assessment. Clinicians must, henceforth, select and use instruments that are culturally and racially nondiscriminatory. They must include multiple measures in their assessments. They must employ instruments validated for the specific purpose for which they are used. They must ensure that the evaluation materials and techniques are appropriate to the individual's sensory capacities, speaking skills, motor facility, and other such conditions as may unduly interfere with optimal performance by the individual being assessed. They must possess assessment skills appropriate to all levels of mental retardation and to all ages from birth to maturity. In addition, it is expected that the product of the assessment will provide the information that is needed to develop an appropriate diagnosis of the person (without implying etiology) and decide on appropriate intervention strategies.

Severely and profoundly impaired persons, plus a large number of moderately impaired individuals, are identified by medical specialists at an early age. They constitute a population with evidence of central nervous system impairment (Birch and others, 1970) and associated clinical syndromes: Down's syndrome, hydrocephaly, microcephaly, phenylketonuria (PKU), and other genetic or accidental conditions. The role of the psychologist has generally been to provide some assessment of intellect and/or adaptation to specify the specific level of retardation. Recently developed instruments are replacing the traditionally used Vineland Social Maturity Scale. The AAMD Adaptive Behavior Scale (Nihira and others, 1974), the Balthazar Scales of Adaptive Behavior I and II (Balthazar, 1972, 1973), the Cain-Levine Social Competency Scale (Cain, Levine, and Elzey, 1963), and the Progress Assessment Chart (Gunzburg, 1974) provide reliable and systematic indices of adaptive behavior. The intelligence measures required to validate the diagnosis of mental retardation are more suspect at this level. Historically, the Cattell Infant Scale (Cattell, 1940), a downward extension of the Binet test, was commonly used for this purpose. The more recent Bayley Scales of Infant Development (Bayley, 1969) provide developmental measures for ages 2 to 30 months. The McCarthy Scales for ages 2½ to 8½ years have been developed to facilitate psychoeducational decisions (Kauffman and Payne, 1975; McCarthy, 1972). Such traditionally administered instruments as the WISC-R, the WAIS, and the Binet may be used with older persons but are of limited utility with this population. With such instruments, it is often necessary to revert to the ratio IQ concept to identify an appropriate level of mental functioning. Fortunately, questions of nondiscriminatory assessment and predictive validity are seldom of concern with this population because severe and profound retardation are not race or culture specific. The primary challenge to the clinician in this population is to prepare an assessment that is meaningful for programming purposes. Recommendations for effective assessment will be presented later.

The closer the individual approximates normal or average performance, the more

significant become such issues as discriminatory testing (racial or cultural bias), test validity, adaptive social behavior, language facility, limited learning experiences, and potentially damaging effects of labeling. The last of these issues has been a key factor in much
of the litigation and the development of public policy. Mercer's (1973) epidemiological
study of mental retardation is reported in *Labeling the Mental Retarded.* The federally
supported Project on the Classification of Exceptional Children, as summarized by Hobbs
(1975) in *The Futures of Children,* also deals with the problem. Both publications reflect
the need to avoid labeling and, consequently, stigmatizing persons because of situation-
specific retardation. The most common situation in which upper-moderate and mild mental retardates are identified is in the school. The so-called "six-hour retardate" is situationally retarded; that is, retarded only when the individual must play the role of student.
This identification has been traditionally made from evidence of poor performance both
on a test of intelligence and in academic work.

The current definition of mental retardation seeks to eliminate inaccurate diagnosis and misclassification by requiring additional evidence of retardation in the form of
"concurrent deficits in adaptive behavior." Adaptive behavior scale performance must
supplement the academic and intelligence data before one can defend a diagnosis of
mental retardation. The Public School Version of the AAMD Adaptive Behavior Scale
(Lambert and others, 1975) was developed to provide an alternative to the Vineland Social Maturity Scale, the Cain-Levine Social Competency Scale, and the AAMD Adaptive
Behavior Scale—which are applicable only to retarded functioning at the moderate level
and below (MacMillan, 1977). Unfortunately, labeling, stigmatizing, and inappropriate
educational placements continue.

Comparative Philosophies and Theories

The changes in public policy, legislative requirements, clinical practice, and educational programming reflect significant developments in theories relating to mental retardation. While the nature-nurture, heredity-environment, and nativist-sensationist controversies persist, the accumulating evidence concerning the etiology of mental retardation
favors an interactionist position (which attributes mental retardation to the interaction of
hereditary and environmental factors). The legitimacy of each of these positions is best
understood if one recognizes that mental retardation is a condition identified solely from
behavior (cognitive and adaptive) but commonly associated with genetic syndromes (such
as Down's syndrome and PKU) and clinical disorders (such as cerebral palsy and hydro-
cephalus). Robinson and Robinson (1976, pp. 51-52) introduce their discussion of the
etiological factors in mental retardation as follows:

> We intend to make it clear that there is rarely a single cause or a
> simple explanation of any type of intellectual disability. In some cases, the
> retardation seems to be primarily a function of the hereditary endowment;
> in others, it seems to be the result of a complex interaction between
> genetic endowment and a multitude of environmental factors; and in still
> other cases, the retardation seems to be attributable to factors which are
> primarily environmental. An etiologic process may affect the child at any
> stage of the life span. It may occur at the time of conception, at any point
> in utero, during birth, or after birth. One child may suffer the effects of
> something which happened in a single instant, whereas another's handicap
> may be caused by a complicated series of interrelated events occurring
> over several months or years. In one, the defect may be diffused through-
> out the central nervous system; in another, it may be quite circumscribed.

In the first quarter of the twentieth century, such renowned psychologists as Lewis Terman, Henry Goddard, and Robert Yerkes supported the theory of genetically determined mental retardation (Kamin, 1975). A modern theorist who continues to support the genetic position is Jensen (1966, 1969), who insists that genes and prenatal development account for 80 percent of the variance in intelligence while only 20 percent of the variance can be accounted for by the environment. While Jensen recognizes the environment as a threshold variable (a minimal quality of environment for normal development), he believes that beyond this point the environment does not cause significant differences in intellect. His theory of primary and secondary familial mental retardation (Jensen, 1970) posits two levels of learning abilities. Level I, associative abilities, is similar in low and middle socioeconomic classes. Level II, cognitive abilities, is more highly developed in the middle class. Primary familial retardation, evidenced by deficiency in both Level I and Level II, is typical of profoundly and severely retarded. Secondary mental retardation is indicated by a deficiency in Level II and signals the mild level of retardation.

Environmentalists may emphasize either the physical environment (prenatal and postnatal) or the psychosocial environment in their research efforts to determine the etiology of mental retardation. The prenatal hazards of a physical nature include maternal undernutrition during pregnancy, acute maternal infections (such as rubella virus), chronic maternal infections (such as syphilis), maternal sensitization (for example, Rh negative), maternal dysfunction (for example, hypertension and diabetes), radiation, drugs, perinatal asphyxia, and direct injury to the head and brain (Robinson and Robinson, 1976). Postnatal hazards include head injury, brain tumors, infections (such as meningitis and encephalitis), malnutrition, and lead poisoning. These conditions commonly lead to identifiable brain damage and consequent cognitive deficits.

The theorists who emphasize the role of the psychosocial environment in the etiology of mental retardation observe that "in spite of biomedical progress uncovering genetic conditions and toxic agents in the environment that may be linked to retardation, in at least 75 percent of the cases of retardation nothing can be confidently pinpointed as the cause of the condition" (MacMillan, 1977, p. 79).

An early champion of the environmentalist position was Watson (1919), who argued that conditioning and learning, rather than genetics, account for human achievement. Currently, the most influential of the learning theories in the field of mental retardation is operant theory, evolving from the work of E. L. Thorndike and extended by Skinner (1938). The most ambitious extension of this approach applied to mental retardation was undertaken by Bijou (1966). In explaining mental retardation in terms of operant principles, Bijou says, "A retarded individual is one who has a limited repertory of behavior shaped by events that constitute his history" (1966, p. 2). This view reflects notions of mental retardation as a symptom of underlying pathology. The behaviorist considers the person's current behavior as a product of antecedent and consequent stimuli.

The interactionist position is well represented in the cognitive-developmental theory of Piaget (1950). He contends that mental development occurs as a natural interactive process between the child and his environment. Piaget is opposed to theories that regard the child as a passive receptor of environmental stimuli, and he is opposed to maturational theories that ignore the importance of experience.

Inhelder (1968) and Woodward (1963) have advanced the interactionist model by relating Piaget's theory to mental retardation. Recognizing a genotype that will pass through the stages at a slower rate, they emphasize the importance of providing an environment that is stage appropriate. Inhelder (1968) suggested the following scheme for classifying mental retardates according to their ultimate developmental stage: (1) profoundly and severely retarded fixate at the sensorimotor stage, (2) moderately retarded fixate at the preoperational intuitive stage, and (3) mildly retarded fixate at the concrete operations stage. Individuals attaining the formal operations stage should not be considered retarded. These adaptations of Piagetian theory are of consequence for both assessment and intervention strategies.

Elaboration on Critical Points

The changes in public policy relative to the problem of mental retardation and developments within the field of clinical psychology over the past two decades have materially influenced the criteria of effective and appropriate clinical assessment. Psychometric evaluations that assign people to gross categories (such as mildly retarded) and educational programs that treat all individuals so classified with the same program are no longer acceptable. Maloney and Ward (1976, p. 38) view psychometric testing as "primarily concerned with describing and studying groups of people, while psychological assessment focuses on a description and an analysis of a particular individual in a problem situation." Clinical assessment is a process in which all relevant data—historical, demographic, medical, behavioral, sociocultural, and observational—are analyzed and integrated into a meaningful description of a unique individual. That description and the data from which it is developed provide the substantive base for the preparation of an "individualized educational program" or intervention strategy.

The development of an ecological perspective in dealing with mentally retarded persons (Berkson, 1978; Hobbs, 1975; Schoggen, 1978) adds yet another dimension for assessment. This assessment involves the observation of complex events—such as family interactions, peer group interactions, and teacher-student interactions—in the natural life settings of the mental retardate. It is expected that multivariate and interactional designs (employing the data of individual behavior and specific environmental factors) will yield a better understanding of the individual, so that more effective intervention strategies will evolve.

The most inclusive assessment process that has been published to date is the System of Multicultural Pluralistic Assessment (SOMPA) by Mercer (1979). It is a process designed to provide for nondiscriminatory assessment and to facilitate the evaluation of cognitive, perceptual-motor, and adaptive behaviors. Recognizing the multiplicity of factors that are significant in the etiology of mental retardation, the system employs medical data, cognitive data, and social data to assist in reaching a diagnosis.

SOMPA was designed to produce an Estimated Learning Potential (ELP) by using scores related to the appropriate ethnic and sociocultural norms. The system has been standardized on children from Anglo, Hispanic, and black cultural backgrounds. It utilized three different assessment models to provide a different perspective of the child's competencies. In addition, the parent is a significant partner in the assessment process. The medical model assesses physical dexterity, psychomotor functioning via the Bender Visual Motor Gestalt Test, height-weight ratio, visual acuity, auditory acuity, and the child's health history by parental interview. The social system model uses the WISC-R with traditional norms to measure "school functioning level" (SFL) and a newly developed Adaptive Behavior Inventory for Children (ABIC) completed by parent interview to obtain measures of adaptive behavior. This inventory focuses on performance in specific roles in specific social systems. The social systems included are: the family, community, peer group, school and the economy. The pluralistic model develops sociocultural scales in which the individual is scored relative to his own ethnic group and relative to the school culture. The ELP is generated by judging the child's performance on the WISC-R in relation to the performance of other children of the same sociocultural background and thus compensating for differences in experience, expectation, motivation, and similar factors. A complete analysis of the assumptions, rationale, and philosophy for each of the three models is beyond the scope of this chapter. However, four specific assumptions of pluralistic assessment will assure the reader that the data from each model are significant for clinical assessment. These assumptions are enumerated by Mercer (1979, p. 145) as follows:

> 1. The user is assuming that the WISC-R is measuring behavior which is learned and that the behaviors covered are primarily those required for successful performance in academic roles in American schools. Hence, a child's performance compared to the standard norms for the test measures his or her achievement relative to the norms and culture of the school.
>
> 2. The user assumes (a) that the four sociocultural scales are adequate measures of whatever sociocultural factors separate the culture of the school from the culture of the home and (b) that equating children on the four sociocultural scales controls for differences in their opportunity to acquire the skills and knowledge needed to succeed in school, their motivation to acquire the skills and knowledge needed, and their response to the test-taking situation.
>
> 3. The user assumes that the child is free of emotional or adaptive problems which might invalidate scores on the WISC-R. This assumption can be tested using other SOMPA measures, such as the ABIC.
>
> 4. The user assumes that the child is free of sensory or motor disabilities which might invalidate scores on the WISC-R. This assumption can also be tested by using the measures in the medical model—the manual dexterity battery, Bender Gestalt, health history inventory, and measures of vision, hearing, and height-weight ratio.

SOMPA, as a norm-referenced assessment technique, meets both the technical requirements and the standards of effective practice in clinical assessment. The relative utility for educational intervention remains to be established; however, the quantity and quality of the information available in the SOMPA profile should provide numerous clues to effective intervention strategies.

As behaviorists have assumed an active role in dealing with problems of mental retardation, they have rapidly developed methods of behavioral assessment and treatment. Assessment is considered an integral part of treatment, and behavior modification strategy requires careful assessment before, during, and after treatment. Hersen and Bellack (1976, p. ix) state: "And contrary to the thinking of some critics of behavior modification, measurement has meant evaluation of all three response modalities—the motoric, the physiological, and the cognitive."

In developing effective intervention plans, the behaviorists concentrate on behaviors that need to be changed and environmental conditions that can be altered to effect the change. The assessment techniques, although they do not currently meet the criteria for standardized instruments for classification purposes, are nonetheless valuable supplements to descriptive data and program development. The students of behavioral assessment have recently begun to develop clear assessment technology and to apply the psychometric questions of reliability, validity, norms, and utility to their instruments (Sundberg, Snowden, and Reynolds, 1978).

From the standpoint of behavioral assessment and treatment of mental retardates, global categories (such as behavioral deficits or excesses, lack of responsiveness to particular stimuli, problems of stimulus control, and socially unacceptable behaviors) are not sufficiently precise to be useful. Kazdin and Straw (1976, p. 340) state: "The behavior that needs to be altered (that is, the target behavior) must be carefully specified. Thus, the most important feature of the behavioral approach is overt response assessment." Behavioral assessment requires that (1) responses be identified by a careful and precise definition; (2) the definition be objective, clear, and complete; and (3) the definition facilitate reliable recording by observers. Since knowledge of the environment in which responses occur is considered essential to understanding and modifying behavior, assessment of stimulus events—particularly the antecedents and consequents of target behaviors—is essential. The sources of such assessment data with the retarded are direct observation, reports of significant others (such as relatives, teachers, ward staff), and case records. Kazdin and Straw (1976, p. 362) conclude their review of assessment methodology with the mentally retarded as follows: "Behavioral assessment is designed specifically to meet the requirements of a given client and treatment program. There is no single method to assess particular behaviors. There are no inventories of retarded behavior that are routinely used when specific areas such as self-care skills, language acquisition, social interaction, and other areas are focused upon in behavior modification."

The goal of proper assessment is to provide the clinician with the information needed to effect proper treatment. Each treatment strategy is unique to the individual. It is based on the assessment data that reveal specific stimulus conditions (antecedents) and reinforcing events (consequents) that are responsible for undesirable behavior or the absence of the desired behavior. With this knowledge, the educator or the therapist can arrange the circumstances required to effect the change.

Less extensive alternatives to the assessment of competence have been recommended by a number of authors. Budoff and his colleagues (Budoff, 1967; Budoff, Corman, and Gimon, 1976) have developed an approach to clinical assessment designed primarily to measure cognitive competencies in mentally retarded individuals. The learning potential (LP) assessment procedure is conceived as a nondiscriminatory assessment process. It is based on a definition of intelligence as the ability to learn and profit from appropriate experience. The procedure consists of pretesting the children with nonverbal reasoning problems, then instructing the children on principles relevant to the task, and then posttesting. The gain reflected in posttesting is the indicator of learning potential or the child's ability to profit from tutorial experience. Sundberg, Snowden, and Reynolds (1978, p. 198) evaluate the procedure as follows: "Because 'How well will this person learn?' is a specific, intervention-related question, this method applied in a variety of contexts should answer clinician demands for practically useful information."

Jensen (1970), in presenting his theory of primary and secondary familial mental retardation, has suggested that Level I, associative abilities, is tapped by tests such as digit span and serial learning. Level II, cognitive abilities, may be measured by such instruments as Raven's Progressive Matrices and Cattell's Culture-Fair Tests.

Uzgiris and Hunt (1975), following Piaget, have developed six ordinal scales of psychological development intended for assessment of infants. The scales may be used to compare the relative advancement or retardation in infants of the same age. They are also intended to help ascertain the kinds of interactions required to promote succeeding steps in development.

Personal Views and Recommendations

The successful clinician will produce a psychological assessment that captures the very essence of the individual being evaluated—including the cognitive, social, emotional, perceptual, language, motor, academic, and physical characteristics that make each individual unique. The assessment must further include information about the parents, siblings and teachers of the retarded person. Their attitudes, expectations, aspirations, and capabilities significantly influence their interactions with the retarded person. These significant others play a major role in determining the success of any treatment program.

The purpose of such assessment will be to provide an objective and meaningful set of data for decision making. Such data will be obtained from interviews, observations, and recordings of behaviors. However, these data take on meaning only when matched against standards, norms, criteria, or expectations. To that end, each observer must develop a frame of reference from which to operate. Developmental schedules, maturational milestones, and pathological symptoms provide guidelines in the assessment of individuals. Cultural norms, family expectations, socioeconomic potentials, and parental flexibility are significant factors for environmental evaluations. Few of the above have standardized instruments that one might utilize.

The more severe the degree of mental retardation and the younger the child, the less appropriate are the traditionally used measurement devices. For appropriate evaluation of severely and profoundly mentally impaired persons and the provision of appropriate educational programming, professionals generally must reject tests such as the Binet and WISC-R as instruments of evaluation. Since these instruments were developed for the normal and near-normal populations, the inappropriateness of their use with severely mentally impaired individuals becomes evident. Beyond qualifying the individual for service as mentally impaired, these instruments are of little value. They are not appropriate for measuring or even describing the abilities possessed by the severely handicapped, since they assess few abilities or levels of performance that such persons can evidence. Identifying all the things a handicapped person cannot do does little to identify reasonable starting points for learning. Reporting of IQs ranging from 1 to 40 or reporting "untestable" is of little value to the planning of an educational program.

To give meaning to a psychoeducational evaluation, one must make significant shifts in the assessment orientations originally established for the school psychologist and other clinical personnel. No purpose is served by identifying an individual's deficits. No educational program can be developed from information regarding IQ scores or mental ages. This traditional orientation needs to be replaced by one emphasizing an accurate description of *what the individual can do, which sensory modalities can be utilized* for purposes of learning, *what kinds of reinforcements are effective,* and *what communication skills can be employed.* Norm-referenced measures are relatively useless. Diagnostic-prescriptive measures are unavailable for this population. What can be meaningfully employed are criterion-referenced measures that establish the starting points for future learning. Consequently, psychologists and other professional persons must capitalize on their basic knowledge of development, the nature of children, and their own creativity to obtain the best evaluation of the nature of each unique individual.

Judicial decisions proclaiming the "right to treatment" and the "right to education," plus the requirements of Public Law 94-142, have brought a host of new problems to all professional persons dealing with mental retardates. Special educators must now become competent to teach profoundly and severely mentally retarded, in addition to the moderate and mild levels commonly identified with classes for the trainable and educable retardates. Furthermore, they must prepare to teach retarded people of all ages, especially children of preschool age, if early intervention is to become a reality. Psychologists, like-wise, must learn assessment instruments and techniques that are appropriate for the iden-tification, classification, and evaluation of retarded persons from birth through adult-hood. They must become knowledgeable of intervention strategies that might accommo-date the needs of the individual as revealed by the assessment of his unique characteristics. Similar extensions and additions will be required in the training programs of all professionals serving the mentally retarded population.

Application to Particular Variables

Age. Epidemiological studies indicate that school-age persons are overlabeled, while preschool children and adults are underlabeled (compared to their percentages in the general population). Only preschoolers with physical disabilities and very low IQs are appropriately identified (Clarke and Clarke, 1974; Mercer, 1973). For early identification and intervention programs, improved assessment techniques at early ages are much needed.

Sex. The number of males diagnosed as mentally retarded exceeds the number of females—particularly if there are no physical disabilities present (MacMillan, 1977; Mer-cer, 1973). Various theoretical explanations have been suggested to account for these dif-ferences, since assessment instruments are developed without a sex bias.

Education. Limited formal education has generally been a consequence of mental retardation. In psychological assessment, therefore, clinicians must not rely on test results obtained with instruments that assume the client has had any formal education or par-ticular learning experiences.

Socioeconomic Status. Mercer (1973) reports that lower-class persons are over-labeled and persons from higher socioeconomic backgrounds are underlabeled (compared to their percentages in the general population). Lower-class children predominate at the mildly retarded level (the "six-hour retardates"). The issues of nondiscriminatory assess-ment and measures of adaptive behavior are of particular concern when persons from the lower socioeconomic levels are being evaluated. Evidence indicates that members of the lower socioeconomic levels live in nonstimulating conditions and have reduced opportuni-ties for learning (Kaufman and Kaufman, 1977). These factors are of major significance when one is planning assessment and intervention strategies.

Vocation. Epidemiologically, vocational status is significant only as it relates to socioeconomic status.

Ethnic/Racial Factors. Data based on existing prevalence studies indicate that, at every level of socioeconomic status, there is a higher incidence of black people being la-beled retarded than in the white population (MacMillan, 1977; Mercer, 1979). Spanish-surname children whose parents are recent immigrants also are overrepresented in the retarded population. The court decisions cited previously are based largely on such evi-dence. Notice that several assessment strategies have been presented herein to help ensure appropriate identification and classification decisions.

Physical Disorders. Seven of the ten known or suspected etiological factors in-cluded in the medical classification system for mental retardation are physical or biologi-cal in nature. Iivanainen (1974) reports that neurological pathologies can be found in about 90 percent of patients in the below-50 IQ range. Organic disease or pathology is responsible for and/or present in nearly all cases of gross mental defect and for some cases in which the defect is relatively mild (Clarke and Clarke, 1974; Erickson, 1978). The responsible physical agencies may be of genetic or environmental origin. Environmental factors causing physical insult may be either prenatal, perinatal, or postnatal in origin.

Psychiatric Disorders. Organic conditions thought to be responsible for disturbed behavior in mental retardates are generally discussed under brain injury or minimal brain damage. Hyperactivity, distractibility, seizures, perseveration, irritability, and lack of impulse control are common in mental retardates. Such behaviors are of consequence for both assessment and programming.

Functional disorders, autism and childhood psychosis, often accompany mental retardation (Erickson, 1978). Between 70 to 80 percent of children diagnosed as autistic or psychotic have an intelligence rating in the mentally retarded range. The primary symptom is disturbed interpersonal relationships, but repetitive and stereotyped motor behaviors are also common.

References

American Psychiatric Association. *Diagnostic and Statistical Manual of Mental Disorders.* (2nd ed.) Washington, D.C.: American Psychiatric Association, 1968.

Balthazar, E. E. *The Balthazar Scales of Adaptive Behavior.* I: *The Scales of Functional Independence.* Palo Alto, Calif.: Consulting Psychologists Press, 1972.

Balthazar, E. E. *The Balthazar Scales of Adaptive Behavior.* II: *The Scales of Social Adaptation.* Palo Alto, Calif.: Consulting Psychologists Press, 1973.

Bayley, N. *Manual for the Bayley Scales of Infant Development.* New York: Psychological Corporation, 1969.

Berkson, G. "Social Ecology and Ethology of Mental Retardation." In G. P. Sackett (Ed.), *Observing Behavior.* Vol. 1: *Theory and Application in Mental Retardation.* Baltimore: University Park Press, 1978.

Bijou, S. W. "A Functional Analysis of Retarded Development." In N. R. Ellis (Ed.), *International Review of Research in Mental Retardation.* Vol. 1. New York: Academic Press, 1966.

Birch, H. G., and others. *Mental Subnormality in the Community: A Clinical and Epidemiological Study.* Baltimore: Williams and Wilkins, 1970.

Blanton, R. L. "Historical Perspectives on Classification of Mental Retardation." In N. Hobbs (Ed.), *Issues in the Classification of Children.* Vol. 1. San Francisco: Jossey-Bass, 1975.

Budoff, M. "Learning Potential Among Institutionalized Young Adult Retardates." *American Journal of Mental Deficiency,* 1967, *72,* 404-411.

Budoff, M., Corman, L., and Gimon, A. "An Educational Test of Learning Potential Assessment with Spanish-Speaking Youth." *Inter-American Journal of Psychology,* 1976, *10,* 13-24.

Cain, L. F., Levine, S., and Elzey, E. F. *Manual for the Cain-Levine Social Competency Scale.* Palo Alto, Calif.: Consulting Psychologists Press, 1963.

Cattell, P. *The Measurement of Intelligence of Infants and Young Children.* New York: Psychological Corporation, 1940.

Clarke, A. M., and Clarke, A. D. B. *Mental Deficiency: The Changing Outlook.* New York: Free Press, 1974.

Diana v. *State Board of Education.* C-7037 (RFP Dist. N. Calif.), 1970.

Dunn, L. M. *Exceptional Children in the Schools: Special Education in Transition.* (2nd ed.) New York: Holt, Rinehart and Winston, 1973.

Erickson, M. T. *Child Psychopathology: Assessment, Etiology, and Treatment.* Englewood Cliffs, N.J.: Prentice-Hall, 1978.

Grossman, H. J. (Ed.). *Manual on Terminology and Classification in Mental Retardation.* Washington, D.C.: American Association on Mental Deficiency, 1973.

Gunzburg, H. C. *Progress Assessment Chart of Social and Personal Development.* (3rd ed.) Birmingham, England: SEFA Publications, 1974.

Hersen, M., and Bellack, A. S. (Eds.). *Behavioral Assessment: A Practical Handbook.* Elmsford, N.Y.: Pergamon Press, 1976.

Hobbs, N. (Ed.). *Issues in the Classification of Children.* (2 vols.) San Francisco: Jossey-Bass, 1975.

Hobbs, N. *The Futures of Children.* San Francisco: Jossey-Bass, 1975.

Hobson v. *Hansen.* 269 Supp. 401, 1967.

Iivanainen, M. *A Study of the Origins of Mental Retardation.* Philadelphia: Lippincott, 1974.

Inhelder, B. *The Diagnosis of Reasoning in the Mentally Retarded.* New York: John Day, 1968.

Jensen, A. R. "Verbal Mediation and Educational Potential." *Psychology in the Schools,* 1966, *3,* 99-109.

Jensen, A. R. "How Much Can We Boost I.Q. and Scholastic Achievement?" *Harvard Educational Review,* 1969, *39,* 1-119.

Jensen, A. R. "A Theory of Primary and Secondary Familial Retardation." In N. R. Ellis (Ed.), *International Review of Research in Mental Retardation.* Vol. 4. New York: Academic Press, 1970.

Kamin, L. J. "Social and Legal Consequences of I.Q. Tests as Classification Instruments: Some Warnings from Our Past." *Journal of School Psychology,* 1975, *13* (4), 317-322.

Kauffman, J. M., and Payne, J. S. *Mental Retardation: Introduction and Personal Perspectives.* Columbus, Ohio: Merrill, 1975.

Kaufman, A. S., and Kaufman, N. L. *Clinical Evaluation of Young Children with the McCarthy Scales.* New York: Grune and Stratton, 1977.

Kazdin, A. E., and Straw, M. K. "Assessment of Behavior of the Mentally Retarded." In M. Hersen and A. S. Bellack (Eds.), *Behavioral Assessment: A Practical Handbook.* Elmsford, N.Y.: Pergamon Press, 1976.

Lambert, N., and others. *Manual for the AAMD Adaptive Behavior Scale: Public School Version.* Washington, D.C.: American Association on Mental Deficiency, 1975.

Larry P. v. *Riles.* 343 F. Supp. 1306, 1972.

McCarthy, D. *Manual for the McCarthy Scales of Children's Abilities.* New York: Psychological Corporation, 1972.

MacMillan, D. L. *Mental Retardation in School and Society.* Boston: Little, Brown, 1977.

Maloney, M. P., and Ward, M. P. *Psychological Assessment: A Conceptual Approach.* New York: Oxford University Press, 1976.

Mayo, L. W. *A Proposed Program for National Action to Combat Mental Retardation.* Washington, D.C.: U.S. Government Printing Office, 1962.

Mercer, J. R. *Labeling the Mentally Retarded.* Berkeley: University of California Press, 1973.

Mercer, J. R. *SOMPA—System of Multicultural Pluralistic Assessment: Technical Manual.* New York: Psychological Corporation, 1979.

Merrikan v. *Cressman.* 364 F. Supp. 913, 1973.

Mills v. *Board of Education.* 348 F. Supp. 866, 1972.

Nihira, K., and others. *AAMD Adaptive Behavior Scale.* Washington, D.C.: American Association on Mental Deficiency, 1974.

Pennsylvania Association for Retarded Children v. *Commonwealth.* 334 F. Supp. 1257, 1972.

Piaget, J. *The Psychology of Intelligence.* New York: Harcourt Brace Jovanovich, 1950.

Robinson, N. M., and Robinson, H. B. *The Mentally Retarded Child: A Psychological Approach.* New York: McGraw-Hill, 1976.

Sarason, S. B., and Doris, J. *Psychological Problems in Mental Deficiency.* (4th ed.) New York: Harper & Row, 1969.

Schoggen, P. "Ecological Psychology and Mental Retardation." In G. P. Sackett (Ed.), *Observing Behavior.* Vol. 1: *Theory and Applications in Mental Retardation.* Baltimore: University Park Press, 1978.

Skinner, B. F. *The Behavior of Organisms.* New York: Appleton-Century-Crofts, 1938.

Sundberg, N. D., Snowden, L. R., and Reynolds, W. M. "Toward Assessment of Personal Competence and Incompetencies in Life Situations." In M. R. Rosenzweig and L. W. Porter (Eds.), *Annual Review of Psychology.* Palo Alto, Calif.: Annual Reviews, 1978.

Tjossem, T. D. (Ed.). *Intervention Strategies for High Risk Infants and Young Children.* Baltimore: University Park Press, 1976.

U.S. Department of Health, Education, and Welfare. *International Classification of Diseases, Adapted for Use in the United States.* (8th ed.) Washington, D.C.: U.S. Government Printing Office, 1967.

Uzgiris, I. C., and Hunt, J. McV. *Assessment in Infancy: Ordinal Scales of Psychological Development.* Urbana: University of Illinois Press, 1975.

Watson, J. B. *Behaviorism.* Philadelphia: Lippincott, 1919.

Woodward, M. "The Application of Piaget's Theory to Research in Mental Deficiency." In N. R. Ellis (Ed.), *Handbook of Mental Deficiency.* New York: McGraw-Hill, 1963.

57

Robert S. Albert

Genius

Of all the many ideas about exceptional persons and unusual achievement, the oldest active explanation is the concept of *genius*. It is over two thousand years old. Over this long period of time, it has undergone a number of changes in what it connotes, but it has been remarkably stable as to whom it refers. The major change in this history has come during the past one hundred twenty-five years, the period during which persons interested in the subject of genius and geniuses have become much more willing to subject their opinions and hypotheses to critical empirical observation. From this increased scientific vigor has come a greater reliance upon the study of two rather distinct populations: eminent adults (living and dead) and gifted youth. With the introduction of social science methodology into the study of genius, the important questions regarding the connections, if any, between creative abilities and exceptional intellectual development and the role of educational, social, and family factors in such development have become more sharply focused and less open to value-laden judgments and loose speculation. The end product of this important historical change has been the beginning of a compact field of research interest focused upon the study of eminent persons and the factors and the experiences contributing to their eminence. This line of investigation, initiated by Galton (1869), has developed links to a diverse number of important topics. Without an understanding of the origin and early applications of the concept of genius, it is difficult to adequately appreciate the great strides made and the great promise inherent in the increasingly robust state of the contemporary study of genius.

Historically, "genius" has designated persons and/or styles of thinking and performances that clearly break with the past; alter radically the customary means of attack on problems in art, philosophy, politics, science, and welfare; or represent the essence of high performance in these areas. The main emphasis has been on the unexpected, the unpredicted, and the almost unfathomable occurrence and results of "genius." Two key experiential manifestations of genius are (1) the rare but radical *disruption* of preceding manners, attitudes, customs, or cognitive habits; and (2) the performance of complex tasks in manners and styles very rarely observed. Although not always an aspect of these two manifestations, adult-level artistic or scientific works that are extremely precocious are also taken as manifestations. At the same time, persons of genius are often considered extremists or potentially disruptive forces militating against personal and societal tranquility. Genius is also held to be untutored and beyond the influence of conventional education—a product of nature rather than nurture. Such persons have been viewed with much ambivalence and suspicion and are as often stigmatized as praised with the appellation of "genius."

Background and Current Status

The exact origin of the concept of genius is not clear. The concept has been in use for more than two thousand years. During this time, genius has been generally associated with the mystical, as opposed to a more human and mundane process of development or use of abilities. Although there is no exact Greek word parallel to the word *genius,* the Greeks placed great emphasis on an individual's *Daimon,* a guardian spirit. The term *Daimon* thus implied an individual's own natural abilities, as well as motivations and appetites. Over time, it became progressively associated with an individual's character and therefore was an intrinsic moral or social quality of that person. Everybody had some individual genius or *Daimon,* which was honored and worshiped on birthdays. This democratic notion of genius disappeared over the years, to be supplanted by connotations of exceptionality, deviancy, or elitism. Ironically, this second notion came about because, in addition to their idea of an individual *Daimon,* the early Greeks also linked genius with madness. In Aristotle's view, there is "no great genius without madness," madness being frenzied inspiration from the gods. This viewpoint became quite influential during the late eighteenth, nineteenth, and early twentieth centuries.

In Roman history, genius was associated more with households than with individuals. Specifically, it came to designate Roman emperors and their households, palaces, and spheres of influence—and, ultimately, whole civilizations and geographical regions, even continents. Among Romans, genius was also regarded as a male creative force. Each important man brought genius with him, was protected and guided by his own genius, and passed it on through the birth of his children as part of his illustrious family's history. Genius for Romans was not a democratic attribute.

During the Middle Ages, the idea developed that special talent or unusual ability in an individual (almost always a male) is a manifestation of some outside "spirit" using this person as a conduit, acting through him. In the early Renaissance, the *divine* quality of great artists and artisans was emphasized, but later in this period genius became associated more closely with unusual and powerful *human* talent or creativity. In the eighteenth century, the differences between genius and talent, and their respective roles in human affairs, were debated. The central issues of "natural," untutored ability and the purposes and means of education also were widely discussed. Writers in this period tried to find "rational" means for understanding persons referred to as geniuses. They also tried to determine whether the manifestations and the sheer number of persons of genius could be changed, controlled, or deliberately enhanced. This century-long debate, part of the English Enlightenment's championing of scientific methods of inquiry over religious and monarchial dogmas, broke off early in the nineteenth century. However, it was instrumental in raising before the public the issues of educational policy and its impact upon differently endowed children and of the place and goals of education in democratic societies. These issues are still involved in our discussions of gifted children and the necessity of special educational programs versus mainstream educational programs for the gifted.

There was very little interest in or new ideas about genius between the end of the eighteenth century and the middle of the nineteenth century. Sir Francis Galton's *Hereditary Genius* (1869) is a landmark for several reasons. First, it successfully applied statistics and empirical reasoning to a major problem in human affairs: the possibility and extent to which hereditary processes determine human capacity and careers. A second important feature is Galton's effort to measure the allusive and speculative concept "genius." Galton focused his interest not only on living persons but on the observable achievements of their lives. For the first time, genius was treated as an observable, measurable human attribute. Although there was an apparent social-class bias in Galton's selection of persons of genius, and although evidence of racial prejudice appears in the later chapters, Galton did clarify the concept of genius and render it amenable to empirical investigation.

A third important feature of Galton's work is his methodology. It is the psychometric tradition and continues to this day. Its major practitioner in the study of genius, other than Galton, is Lewis Terman, who undertook the monumental study entitled *Genetic Studies of Genius.* In 1925 he published the first of five volumes regarding the prevalence and developmental characteristics of over one thousand intellectually gifted children. Volume 2, authored by Catherine Cox and entitled *The Early Mental Traits of Three Hundred Geniuses* (Cox, 1926), describes the intellectual development and personal characteristics of historically famous persons. One of Cox's major achievements is to show that persons who have achieved great fame in various fields differ in *both* their intellectual development (as represented by IQ) and their salient personality characteristics. This finding has been elaborated in subsequent research (Barron, 1969). Between the 1920s and the 1950s, the psychometric study of genius concentrated primarily on the behavioral, cognitive, and personality concomitants of high IQ scores. Some leaders in this effort were Terman and his co-workers (Terman, 1925; Burks, Jensen, and Terman, 1930; Terman and Oden, 1947, 1959), Hollingworth (1926, 1942; Hollingworth and Cobb, n.d.), Burt (1975), Pressey (1949), and Torrance (1971). More recently, Stanley and his group at Johns Hopkins (Stanley, 1977; Stanley, George, and Solano, 1977; Stanley, Keating, and Fox, 1974) have attempted to identify and understand the mathematically gifted preadolescent, while synthesizing many of the early insights into a pioneering educational research program.

A second major tradition in the study of genius is the linking of genius to madness. This view has survived into the present, although it languished until the nineteenth century (when it became the predominant view of genius). Some famous expositions are those of Kretschmer (1931), Lange-Eichbaum (1932), Lombroso (1895), Moreau de Tours (1885), Morel (1857), and Freud (1913). It should be noted that the one person, Freud, who did more than anyone else to give a rational and empirical basis to this view of genius also produced a book typical of this genre. Although Ellis (1904) published a study showing that only 4 percent of his 1,030 genius-like subjects could be classified clearly as insane or psychologically pathological, many persons, lay and professional, have remained relatively unconvinced. Later, one of Terman's students, White (1930), investigated the incidence of psychopathology among Cox's and Ellis's subjects, again with little evidence for equating genius and psychopathology.

Psychohistory, the major contemporary methodology for the study of famous people, comes directly from Freud's efforts. The best-known practitioner is Erik Erikson, whose books on Luther and Gandhi (Erikson, 1958, 1969) are influential examples of this merging of psychoanalytic theory and historical research. Like Galton, Freud brought new techniques and concepts to the study of genius. Freud's monumental breakthrough is that he was able to show that persons of genius can be "rationalized." That is to say, their earliest development and much of their career can be understood in psychological terms, rather than by invoking highly inflammatory labels or preternatural forces for purposes of explanation. Moreover, both Freud and Galton contributed to our present perspective of eminent persons as being different from other persons in degree rather than in their nature. After Freud, all persons' development was to be understood as lawful and more or less alike. Both men focused on famous men's families as the most critical set of psychological factors involved in high-level achievement. Thus, Freud, like Galton, helped to bring geniuses into alignment with less extraordinary persons, although Freud assumed that they were necessarily neurotic. In his study of genius, Freud focused on the individual's efforts—consciously and unconsciously—to overcome personal and interpersonal obstacles. After Freud, it has been a standard practice in the study of important and/or highly creative persons to investigate their intrapersonal dynamics and interpersonal conflicts for clues to their unusual motivation and careers (see, for example, Lowenfeld, 1941).

Overall, one can say that beginning from the middle of the nineteenth century to this day, most persons deeply interested in the study of genius have worked in the empirical tradition. The study of genius has taken a definite turn toward studying living eminent persons, a major change from speculations and predominantly literary studies of the famous. Quite recently, however, with the application of some very imaginative statistical analysis to archival data, Simonton (1975a, 1975b, 1976, 1977) has developed important information on some of the basic historical and sociological parameters to extraordinary achievement.

As part of the methodological change over the years, most researchers have quietly dropped the term *genius* and replaced it with *eminent person*. In addition, two different traditional orientations have based their research on different populations. Psychoanalysts have mainly studied famous artists, and researchers with a psychometric and more eclectic viewpoint have mainly studied eminent scientists. It is becoming clear that the findings on one population are not necessarily applicable to the other population and that their early family experiences as well as their cognitive talents differ from one another.

This historical review has shown us a number of significant changes in our thinking about and the techniques for studying persons of genius. But it does not indicate what we have learned because of these changes. For this one must look closely at the work of the past thirty years.

Much of the work in this area has been to rectify the early problems of thinking and fact regarding genius. An excellent example of the constructive nature of the changes undergone and the types of information generated from them is Anne Roe's research in the early 1950s. Instead of studying "genius" or geniuses, Roe (1951a, 1951b, 1953) selected a number of unquestionably eminent living scientists for extensive observation and interview regarding their early development and careers. While confirming some of Cox's (1926) earlier work, Roe's research clearly showed for the first time that, while high intelligence is a necessary ingredient to first-rate scientific work, a complex pattern of deep commitment and long work hours is equally essential. She also notes among her samples a preponderance of middle-class professional fathers, 72 percent first borns or only sons, a large percentage of early parental deaths, early social isolation from subjects' peers, and the importance of doing research in high school or college with a sympathetic teacher. Together, these data strongly suggest that a cognitive style of thinking congruent with science; a family that esteems work and success; a family experience, such as early parental death, that requires coming to terms in the early years with strong feelings of loss; estrangement; and the discovery and confirmation of one's talents to do and to enjoy research in an area of interest are critical in getting one in a career position for achieving later eminence. Roe also found that eminent scientists in biology, physics, and the social sciences differ in their early home life (social scientists come from more emo- tionally binding homes), time of career decisions (social scientists decide later and after seriously considering literature), and peer relationships (social scientists are more involved with peers and date much earlier than physical scientists). Eiduson (1962) and Chambers (1964) have elaborated on Roe's research, exploring in more depth and detail the person- ality dimension of scientific eminence. For example, Eiduson found that researchers had few strong positive ties to either parent and enjoyed fantasy and intellectual pursuits at an early age. Chambers (1964) studied scientists in different fields and, like Roe, found differences among them. For example, he found that psychologists are more impulsive and introverted than chemists and tend to come from more involving, affectionate fami- lies—even though these homes, as Roe had reported earlier, were at times emotionally binding.

MacKinnon (1962, 1963, 1965, 1975), in his work with architects, also has elabo- rated on Roe's work, exploring more extensively the personality dimension of their eminence. He found that architects are not asocial but do value their independence and autonomy, their productivity, their commitment to intellectual matters and esthetically enjoyable experiences, and their creativity. Like the research scientists studied by Roe and by Eiduson, they did not all come from tranquil homes; some homes were marked with tension or brutality. They are able to tolerate tension, are emotionally expressive and uninhibited, and came from homes where one or both parents were artistic in interest and skill.

In their research, both Roe and MacKinnon relied on their subjects' retrospection; therefore, their results are prone to the problems in such efforts. Nonetheless, each solidi- fied one important change in the study of genius: a merging of psychometric analysis with a concern for the dynamics of an eminent person's development, career choices, and pro- fessional performances.

There is one important point to keep in mind regarding such research. Although it offers many interesting insights into the lives and careers of eminent persons, it does not inform us about the persons in the same field or vocation who do not achieve eminence. Without sufficient control groups and longitudinal designs in the study of geniuses, we shall always lack substantial information about the factors and experiences that influence one person's successful career and another's lack of success.

Additionally, there is the problem of important lines of investigation being ini- tiated only to be prematurely dropped. One unfortunate example is the possibility of significant cognitive and educational differences operating among children of different levels of giftedness. Such possibilities were suggested in Cox's (1926) research and discussed even earlier by philosophers for centuries. It is true that various writers also have studied what one can term *exceptionally* gifted children (children with IQ of 150 or higher), concentrating on their intellectual differences from usually gifted children and children with average IQs (Davidson, 1931; Hildreth, 1938, 1954; Hollingworth, 1942; Jones, 1923; Lorge and Hollingworth, 1936; Meeker, 1968). Although this research covered some forty-five years, it was never of major interest to many researchers or educators. This is unfortunate because the issues remain important—early identification and training of persons of potential eminence and the careers in which eminence is most likely to be achieved by young persons of different levels of ability, different values and aptitudes, and different personality make-up. The educational (and other) implications in recognizing that gifted children are a very heterogeneous population have yet to be fully dealt with (Gallagher, 1975; Miller and Bialer, 1970; Willerman, 1979).

Overall, the bulk of these studies demonstrate five salient points: (1) children of exceptionally gifted IQ often go through their cognitive development faster than children of "average giftedness"; (2) exceptionally gifted children can be identified by both the accelerated rate and range of abstract academic subjects they can master; (3) exceptionally gifted children usually began to speak and learned to read at very early ages; (4) there appears more heterogeneity among gifted children than is often acknowledged (Albert, 1971; Willerman, 1979); and (5) the exceptionally gifted are no more distinguished by their originality than are the gifted (giftedness being primarily a matter of intelligence and academic ability). In recent years, there has been an unfortunate application of "giftedness" not only to high IQ scores but to creative ability—unfortunate because research has shown that intelligence and creative ability are almost entirely independent of one another when subjects' IQs are in the gifted or higher range and that neither can be measured adequately by the same instruments (Albert, 1969; Guilford, 1959; MacKinnon, 1962; Wallach, 1971).

Another influential line of research has followed from Guilford's (1959, 1966, 1967) distinction between convergent and divergent cognitive styles. Convergent processes are involved mostly in one's search for clear, specific answers, processes probably most clearly instrumental in answering multiple-choice questions. Divergent processes generate more associational, less restricted, more personal responses; these most clearly operate in answering open-ended questions, for which there is no one best answer. A number of researchers into originality or creativity were inspired by Guilford's work; perhaps the most prominent are Getzels and Jackson (1962), Hudson (1967), Wallach and Kogan (1965), and Wallach and Wing (1969). Guilford's work encouraged professionals to rethink definitions of creativity and to consider whether creativity differs from intelligence and how the two concepts are to be measured.

Critical Discussion

General Areas of Concern

The concept of genius is vulnerable to changing philosophies as are the related concepts of creativity and giftedness. Over the years their meanings and their usage have changed, partly as new facts arose and partly as a function of nonscientific concerns and emphases (Albert, 1969; Joncich, 1964). Such change is different from saying that there are important sociological variables at play in the attainment of eminence or in the promotion of important and original products upon which eminence is based, although there are firm research data supporting this statement (Gray, 1966; Kroeber, 1944; Naroll and others, 1971; Simonton, 1975a, 1975b, 1976, 1977, 1978; Zuckerman, 1977).

Interest in creativity goes back to Aristotle, and the modern concerns reach back to Galton, but at no time was this interest as great as in the 1950s and 1960s. Since the early 1950s, creative behavior has been a very popular topic among psychologists and educators alike. Because geniuses are supposedly extraordinarily creative and gifted, let us examine briefly how these two concepts have come together in the past three decades.

Two forces brought "creativity" to the fore: the arrival of psychoanalysis right after World War II as a major theory in child psychology as well as in clinical psychology and the development of measurement techniques during World War II. Psychoanalysis brought an interest in the lives of famous persons through its use of them as examples of the power of the theory to explain many facets of human development and different types of behavior, especially of geniuses. Their creative behavior was the most intriguing aspect under scrutiny. The questions of the source of creative ability and of why only some persons were noticeably creative led to an interest in the antecedents of this ability. Although the topic of genius and geniuses was then of little professional interest, creativity and its nurturance was an area of very high professional interest. Along with this interest occurred an awareness that it was difficult to measure adequately the highest levels of intelligence among groups of eminent persons. Barron, MacKinnon, and Roe soon discovered that eminent persons were creative *and* exceptionally gifted intellectually. (One is tempted to say this was a rediscovery, for Cox, 1926, Jones, 1923, and Rockwell, 1927, had made somewhat the same point earlier but with much less data.) To put the matter simply, it was repeatedly shown that it takes high intellectual abilities and other skills to be unusually creative and to become eminent.

The low, often insignificant, correlations between some measures of creativity and intelligence for homogeneous high-ability groups soon led to the belief that creativity and intelligence were almost completely distinct from one another and, of all things, that intelligence might be less important than creativity in the production of original products and the solution of complex problems. This proposition is difficult to accept when one realizes that the median IQ for eminent persons in a variety of fields appears to be in the range of 145-150, an IQ significantly higher than (1) the 120 IQ accepted as the threshhold above which creativity and intelligence are believed to become separate cognitive domains and (2) the median 145-150 IQ for eminent persons is also significantly above the 130 IQ often used as the measure of giftedness by state educational programs. However, it is well below the time IQs of Cox's 300 historical geniuses; according to her calculations that was 160 IQ, with many of her subjects having IQs above 180 and only a few with an IQ below 140. Some years later, Hollingworth (1942) agreed that 180 IQ was most likely the level for "true genius."

It is important to be clear on one fact here: the IQ is an index, one score representing a subject's performances on a variety of measures of different aptitudes. Increasingly, it is becoming harder to hold that a single IQ test can either measure all of the essential cognitive processes involved in what we commonly think of as intelligent behavior or that its final score can adequately give us all the critical information we hope to ascertain from it. Galton long ago made intelligence—not IQ—an initial feature to the achievement of eminence and every major researcher in eminence since has supported his viewpoint. Unfortunately, what was not being asked in the 1950s or 1960s often enough or forcefully enough was a serious question, namely what facilitates the creative use of intelligence.

Over the years the literature on creativity and intelligence has indicated that generally IQ scores and creativity test scores correlate with one another almost as highly as they do with other test scores within their own domains. The fact that for the higher, more restricted ranges of IQ, the two tests correlate insignificantly, and often near zero, raises the question of what constitutes the relationship, if any, between creativity and intelligence at that level, especially in the light of recurrent separation of creativity scores and IQ at and above 120. One possible conclusion is that at such a point the relationship between the two becomes quite different than it is at lower scores and with more heterogeneous populations. If the relationship does change between creativity and intelligence, then we might miss measuring it by resorting to the same instruments. Clearly, as we use more refined tests and a greater variety of tests, we find results suggesting that some selected aspects of "intelligence" and of "creativity" do correlate highly and others do not. Both Anastasi and Schaefer (1971) and Guilford (1971) have argued, from the results of many studies, that intelligence and creativity are "many-faceted" concepts, each encompassing a variety of abilities, not only one. We agree.

Elaboration on Critical Points

Part of the present difficulty in sorting out what is intelligence and what is creativity originates in some major research by Getzels and Jackson (1962); unfortunately, many read it as supporting the emphasis upon nonintellectual abilities in the production of original responses and a belittlement of intelligence's role in such performance among groups of extremely intelligent adolescents (mean IQ 150) and extremely creative adolescents (mean IQ 127). Getzels and Jackson's measure of convergent processes (which they took to represent intelligence) and divergent processes (representing creativity), as well as their description of their two experimental samples, led initially to the belief that there are substantial differences between those subjects who perform well on divergent tests and those who perform well on convergent tests. When one realizes that *all* of Getzels and Jackson's subjects were intellectually gifted and that the academic achievement of both experimental groups was higher than that of their school controls and equal to one another's, some of their main points become more questionable than enlightening. Without any follow-up of these subjects there is no way of knowing whether any of the reported differences among their subjects have long-term career or personal significance.

We would suggest, along with Hudson (1967), that what has been demonstrated is that there are different sets of interest, personal values, and cognitive styles operating among highly intelligent persons who achieve eminence in a variety of fields. If this is true, a number of research findings fall into place, including those of Getzels and Jackson. There are some important personality factors and differences in the development and careers of creative persons, as opposed to their less creative controls. One long-term project on the empirical correlates of genius (Albert, 1969, 1971, 1975, 1978, in press) has shown that time after time (1) persons who attain outstanding eminence usually are involved in their future careers early in adolescence (recall the previous statement that the higher the IQ, the earlier this foreshadowing); (2) that such persons, as a group, not only begin their careers earlier than their peers, but are more productive in them for longer periods of time; and (3) that this lengthy, continuous, innovative productivity involves such personality attributes as moderately high needs to achieve, to be independent, and to be innovative, as well as high persistence, self-reliance, a sense of responsibility to one's own interests and career, and with a sense of social responsibility. Many of these traits are recognizable as aspects of the high ego strength that Barron (1969) clearly identified among his samples of eminent persons. What we find, when putting these research findings together, is that eminent persons are very intelligent, well-educated and informed, hard-working, and willing to take risks of being wrong and/or different in order to be independent and innovative. These are abilities and characteristics that twenty-five years of research has shown to be characteristic of eminent persons and rarely found in combination.

This complexity of ability and personality also appears to be the result of long development in rather distinctive family environments (Barron, 1969; MacKinnon, 1962, 1963, 1965; McCurdy, 1957; Oden, 1968; Roe, 1951a, 1951b, 1953; Simonton, 1976). When we look closely at these family environments, we notice several recurrent characteristics. Many eminent persons do not have close or stable relationships with their parents, or their parents with one another, a factor more apparent for persons achieving eminence in nonscientific fields than for those eminent in the sciences. A complicated, tense parent-child relationship helps the eminent-to-be person learn how to cope with tensions, complexity, and a sense of being quite special to usually one, but sometimes both, parents (Albert, 1978, in press). In cases where the eminent-to-be person is highly scientific or mathematically gifted, he or she is likely to describe their parent-child relationship as one of distance more than of hostility; where the gifts are more artistic, the child is likely to have been extremely involved with one or both parents, usually at different points in the child's development, and this closeness was in some cases reinforced by the early death of an older sibling, usually a brother (Albert, in press). Because these experiences in a family occur together infrequently, one can appreciate why the combination of high intelligence, abundant talent, and strong personality found among many eminent persons is itself something of a rarity. Among the frequently noted characteristics of geniuses and eminent persons from Galton's original work (1869) to the present has been their extraordinarily high level of "natural ability" or intelligence (Barron, 1969; Cox, 1926; Roe, 1951a, 1952b, 1953; Willerman, 1979). There is no substantial reason for disparaging intelligence's contribution in such productive, creative persons.

Many studies during the 1950s, 1960s, and early 1970s have shown that it is a relatively rare combination of gifted intelligence and cognitive flexibility—coupled with strong, clear interests, moderately high needs for achievement and independence, and long-term family stimulation and support for such development and thinking—that underlies an adolescent's ability to perform well academically and "creatively." What Getzels and Jackson showed within a cross-sectional study of adolescents, Oden (1968) later demonstrated in a major forty-year follow-up of Terman's gifted children. Perhaps the two most striking differences between the most and the least successful of these subjects were (1) their families' stance on education and cultural experience and (2) the different degrees of family stability and cohesion. The more successful subjects came from relatively more stable families, and their parents were better educated and clearly valued education and cultural experience for themselves and their children. It appears that authoritative, career-successful parents with high self-esteem generally have children who also are generally competent and academically successful and show promise of some adult achievement and success. Where parents are themselves noticeably creative, this ability too gets carried into the children's development, so that it is also a mistaken idea that families cannot tolerate more than one creative member. To the contrary, as Galton first showed, many families—for example, the Churchills and Kennedys in politics, the Comptons in science, and the Bachs in music—appear to be fertile environments for developing creative abilities. Since one often observes the presence of similar abilities and talents among members of a family, it is possible that hereditary factors are involved in talents and cognitive aptitudes.

From the earliest research of Terman, then, various characteristics have been consistently identified with intellectually gifted children. In recent years this research, like that describing creative persons, has presented very few surprises (see Stein, 1974). Good summaries of these "standard" findings are by Carroll and Larring (1974) and Torrance (1971). And, as was noted earlier, a composite has begun to be developed for geniuses (Albert, 1971, 1975, 1978; Simonton, 1978).

Intellectually gifted children are healthier physically and psychologically than less gifted children. They walk, speak, and tend to read earlier, often with much less tutorage. Other characteristics that identify gifted children are their variety of interests and long pursuit of them. Another finding of particular note is gifted children's early ability to organize, to structure, and to synthesize complex and abstract ideas. A stable finding, since Barron (1969), among noticeably creative persons of all ages is their pursuit and use of stimulus material that is complex, initially in disorder, and unclear in its meaning. The similarities between the gifted and the creative in this regard should be evident. Research on eminent adults presents some of the above characteristics plus others, usually emphasizing a daring, independent mindedness; a tolerance of differences, and an intuitiveness in selection of problems and methods of solution. Creative persons also are less stereotyped in their sexual identities than less creative men or women, although neither homosexuality nor lesbianism has been strongly associated with creativity or eminence. Theoretical and aesthetic values appear to guide creative behavior; religious, political, and economic values are quite secondary.

Thus, one sees in the behavior of the creative adult that some of the early cognitive traits of the intellectually gifted child have come to fruition, along with the progressive acquisition of a specific set of personality attributes, highly focused motivations, and values that guide and facilitate a fuller employment of gifted cognitive skills (see Welsh, 1977). Such a constellation often puts a strain on creative persons internally and creates cleavage between them and some significant part of their environments. Thus, it is not surprising to find that creative persons *are* tense, irritable, and "pulled in" while engaged in creative operations. Clearly, it is in the *emotional* domain that creative, eminent persons are most distinctive from their equally intelligent but less creative and less eminent controls. Nonetheless, another personality trait shown by creative persons is their unusual ability to withstand long periods of loneliness, tension, and emotional strain while in pursuit of their interests and careers; they rarely become severely psychologically ill. Moreover, creative persons, from late childhood on, often exhibit an explicit sense of responsibility to both their careers (or interests) and to others. They are rarely as irresponsible or impulsive as often described in popular literature. In none of the above descriptions does one find justification for the instability and irresponsible, bizarre behavior that was often attributed as the mark of genius.

Personal Views and Recommendations

What is now most needed are longitudinal studies of exceptionally gifted children and their families, for these are apparently the richest source of future eminent persons. Only such research can reveal what, in the long run, significantly contributes to or impedes such development. Without such research, there will be put piecemeal knowledge of some very important persons and processes. Also, Stanley (1976) has shown that whenever research has asked specific questions of a specific population and used reliable instruments specific to the behaviors in question, scientific progress occurs. Progress in the study of genius has come only through this effort and not through the more dramatic earlier descriptions of putative genius, no matter how entertaining or well written they may be (Sarton, 1921).

Application to Particular Variables

Age. The more precocious the child is in his intellectual development, display of talent, or artistic performance, the earlier one usually finds that these are reliable and valid signs of giftedness (Albert, 1971; Willerman and Fiedler, 1977). In terms of eminent persons, it has been found that they, too, often show these signs of early giftedness *and* also often begin their careers in which they achieved eminence at a younger than usual age (Albert, 1971, 1975; Cox, 1926; Lehman, 1953; Simonton, 1975a). The rule appears to be: "the more gifted the child, the younger the career starts and the higher the attainment."

Sex. Far more men appear to have achieved high eminence and are studied in regard to it. What is known of genius is overwhelmingly male oriented. All major works on genius or eminence have been, until recently, much more concerned with men of eminence than with eminent women.

Education. The idea persists that geniuses need little or no formal education. This notion stems from an unclear idea of what is a genius and from the "unexpected" quality of many important discoveries and artistic creations. Although there is no one standard research to refute this proposition, case studies and empirical observations of eminent persons in many fields invariably show that such persons are usually better educated than the average person of their time and socioeconomic circumstances. What one often finds is the presence of a highly involved parent or other family member starting the eminent-to-be person in his or her field, followed by a significantly involved teacher or tutor who continues the instruction and also encourages the ambitions of the pupil (see Zuckerman, 1977). There is no evidence for believing that ignorance leads to eminence or worthwhile careers; there is evidence for believing that a sound but not binding education will give substance to early interests and direction to giftedness.

Socioeconomic Status. Although one often hears or reads dramatic stories of the poverty-stricken child who becomes a great person, the evidence regarding the socioeconomic backgrounds of eminent persons—evidence from Galton (1869) through Cox (1926) to Roe (1951a, 1951b, 1953), MacKinnon (1963), and Oden (1968), up to more recent research on eminent persons (Simonton, 1975b; Zuckerman, 1977)—shows that most eminent persons come from middle- or higher-placed families. Eminent persons usually come from families that are aware of the opportunities for further advancement and/or service to their communities. This characteristic fits with the theme of prosocial responsibility so often noticed in the careers of eminent persons, although their products may disturb the equanimity of their field or times. When one looks closely into the history of the families of eminent persons, one often finds that there has been a "build-up" of specific talents and interests over several generations. This "build-up" is through the marriage of talented persons and their sharing of interests, ambitions, and values. The child who becomes an eminent person in later life is often the recipient of both this hereditary and family-trained high ability as is the case of Sir Francis Galton himself (Albert, in press; Burt, 1975; Galton, 1869). Once one uses other criteria besides income, one sees that the families from which most eminent persons come are psychologically stimulating *and* relatively stable. These families appear to be well educated and well above the poverty level of subsistence. It is true that some great men and women (mainly in the arts and in sports) have been orphans or from poor families; when one connects what has already been said of education as well as age and sex, it should be clear that the family is not only a genetic pool for intelligence and talents but an educational environment of immense complexity and power.

Vocation. It has been pointed out that eminent persons are not merely lucky but represent the end product of many complicated long-term developmental processes. Such persons, as mentioned, are more than intelligent; they are usually exceptionally involved and educated in their field and well suited psychologically to its requirements and stresses. Intelligence alone will not lead to eminence, nor will an interest in something. Instead, a combination of gifted cognitive abilities, personality traits, and values energizes and sustains eminent careers.

It is evident that different general fields have different cognitive and personality requirements for success in them and draw their more successful recruits from different types of early backgrounds and temperaments. The better the match between the requirements of a particular field and an interested person with high intelligence, the more likely eminence will occur in that career. One confounding factor in making this vocational choice is the fact that gifted persons, children and adults, have a wider range of interests than most of their less gifted contemporaries and usually more than one strong talent. Because of this, one would think it would be difficult for a very gifted person to choose the best vocation. Perhaps so, but one notices in the histories of eminent persons a steady, active search for the vocation that will allow them to integrate their interests and talents. The careers of some very famous persons (for instance, Darwin and Freud) are the outcome of such endeavors over several decades.

In the main, eminent persons in the physical sciences and the performing arts appear to show clear indications of requisite abilities early in life. They also make earlier career decisions and thus earlier career starts than persons who become eminent in other fields. To a large extent this is a function of the clearer, earlier, spontaneous appearance of most mathematical and artistic talents than is the case for general giftedness. Talents other than mathematics or the performing arts appear to reach their more mature levels of development later and to be more "open" to the vicissitudes of experience, education, and opportunity than either mathematical or artistic giftedness in attaining the necessary levels of development for achieving eminence; they appear to require a wider range of experience in their development and for their proper early identification. The attainment of genius, rare as it is, is much more a function of early giftedness being nurtured, well educated, and specifically encouraged than it is a gift of the gods, a product of madness, or a matter of luck, as was commonly believed through the first half of this century.

References

Albert, R. S. "Genius: Present-Day Status of the Concept and Its Implication for the Study of Creativity and Giftedness." *American Psychologist,* 1969, *24,* 743-753.

Albert, R. S. "Cognitive Development and Parental Loss Among the Gifted, the Exceptionally Gifted and the Creative." *Psychological Reports,* 1971, *29,* 19-26.

Albert, R. S. "Toward a Behavioral Definition of Genius." *American Psychologist,* 1975, *30,* 140-151.

Albert, R. S. "Observations and Suggestions Regarding Giftedness, Familial Influence and the Attainment of Eminence." *Gifted Child Quarterly,* 1978, *22,* 201-211.

Albert, R. S. "Family Positions and the Attainment of Eminence: A Study of Special Family Positions and Special Family Experiences." *Gifted Child Quarterly,* in press.

Anastasi, A., and Schaefer, C. E. "Note on the Concepts of Creativity and Intelligence." *Journal of Creative Behavior,* 1971, *5,* 113-116.

Barron, F. *Creative Person and Creative Process.* New York: Holt, Rinehart and Winston, 1969.

Baumrind, D. "Child Care Practices Anteceding Three Patterns of Preschool Behavior." *Genetic Psychology Monographs,* 1967, *75,* 43-88.

Baumrind, D. "Current Patterns of Parental Authority." *Developmental Psychology Monographs,* 1971, *1* (1), 1-103.

Burks, B. S., Jensen, D. W., and Terman, L. M. *Genetic Studies of Genius.* Vol. 3: *The Promise of Youth.* Stanford, Calif.: Stanford University Press, 1930.

Burt, C. *The Gifted Child.* London: Hodder and Stoughton, 1975.

Carroll, J. L., and Larring, L. R. "Giftedness and Creativity: Recent Attempts at Definition: A Literature Review." *Gifted Child Quarterly,* 1974, *18,* 23-29.

Chambers, J. "Relating Personality and Biographical Factors to Scientific Creativity." *Psychological Monographs,* 1964, *78* (7, Whole No. 584).

Cox, C. M. *Genetic Studies of Genius.* Vol. 2: *The Early Mental Traits of Three Hundred Geniuses.* Stanford, Calif.: Stanford University Press, 1926.

Davidson, H. "An Experimental Study of Bright, Average, and Dull Children at the Four Year Mental Level." *Genetic Psychology Monographs,* 1931, *9,* 119-289.

Eiduson, B. T. *Scientists: Their Psychological World.* New York: Basic Books, 1962.

Ellis, H. *A Study of British Genius.* London: Hurst and Blackett, 1904.

Erikson, E. H. *Young Man Luther: A Study in Psychoanalysis and History.* New York: Norton, 1958.

Erikson, E. H. *Gandhi's Truth.* New York: Norton, 1969.

Freud, S. *Leonardo da Vinci: A Study in Sexuality* [1913]. New York: Random House, 1947.

Gallagher, J. J. *Teaching the Gifted Child.* Boston: Allyn & Bacon, 1975.

Galton, F. *Hereditary Genius: An Inquiry into Its Laws and Consequences.* New York: Macmillan, 1869.

Getzels, J. W., and Jackson, P. W. *Creativity and Intelligence: Explorations with Gifted Students.* New York: Wiley, 1962.

Gray, C. E. "A Measurement of Creativity in Western Civilization." *American Anthropologist,* 1966, *68,* 1384-1417.

Guilford, J. P. "Creativity." *American Psychologist,* 1950, *5,* 444-454.

Guilford, J. P. "Traits of Creativity." In H. H. Anderson (Ed.), *Creativity and Its Cultivation.* New York: Harper & Row, 1959.

Guilford, J. P. "Intelligence: 1965 Model." *American Psychologist,* 1966, *21,* 20-26.

Guilford, J. P. "Creativity, Yesterday, Today, and Tomorrow." *Journal of Creative Behavior,* 1967, *1,* 3-14.

Guilford, J. P. "Some Misconceptions Regarding Measurement of Creative Talents." *Journal of Creative Behavior,* 1971, *5,* 77-87.

Hildreth, G. "The Educational Achievement of Gifted Children." *Child Development,* 1938, *9,* 365-371.

Hildreth, G. "Three Gifted Children: A Developmental Study." *Journal of Genetic Psychology,* 1954, *85,* 239-262.

Hollingworth, L. S. *Gifted Children: Their Nature and Nurture.* New York: Macmillan, 1926.

Hollingworth, L. S. *Children Above 180 IQ Stanford-Binet.* New York: World Book, 1942.

Hollingworth, L. S., and Cobb, M. W. "Children Clustering at 165 IQ and Children Clustering at 145 IQ Compared for Three Years in Achievement." In *Twenty-Seventh Yearbook of the National Society for the Study of Education.* Pt. 3. Chicago, Ill.: n.d.

Hudson, L. *Contrary Imaginations.* Middlesex, England: Penguin Books, 1967.

Joncich, G. "A Culture-Bound Concept of Creativity: A Social Historian's Critique, Centering on a Recent American Report." *Educational Report,* 1964, *14,* 133-143.

Jones, A. M. "The Superior Child: A Series of Case Studies." *Psychological Clinic,* 1923, *15,* 1-8, 116-123, 130-137.

Kretschmer, E. *The Psychology of Men of Genius.* New York: Harcourt Brace Jovanovich, 1931.

Kroeber, A. *Configurations of Culture Growth.* Berkeley: University of California Press, 1944.

Lange-Eichbaum, W. *The Problem of Genius.* New York: Macmillan, 1932.

Lehman, H. D. *Age and Achievement.* Princeton, N.J.: Princeton University Press, 1953.

Lombroso, C. *The Man of Genius.* New York: Scribner's, 1895.

Lorge, I., and Hollingworth, L. "Adult Status of Highly Intelligent Children." *Journal of Genetic Psychology,* 1936, *63,* 215-226.

Lowenfeld, H. "Psychic Trauma and Productive Experience in the Artist." *Psychoanalytic Quarterly,* 1941, *10,* 116-130.

McCurdy, H. G. "The Childhood Pattern of Genius." *Journal of Elisha Mitchell Science Society,* 1957, *73,* 448-462.

MacKinnon, D. W. "The Nature and Nurture of Creative Talent." *American Psychologist,* 1962, *17,* 484-495.

MacKinnon, D. W. "Creativity and Images of the Self." In R. W. White (Ed.), *The Study of Lives.* New York: Atherton, 1963.

MacKinnon, D. W. "Personality and the Realization of Creative Potential." *American Psychologist,* 1965, *20,* 273-281.

MacKinnon, D. W. "IPAR's Contribution to the Conceptualization and Study of Creativity." In I. A. Taylor and J. W. Getzels (Eds.), *Perspectives in Creativity.* Chicago: Aldine, 1975.

Meeker, M. "Differential Syndromes of Giftedness and Curriculum Planning: A Four-Year Follow-Up." *Journal of Special Education,* 1968, *2,* 185-194.

Miller, M. B., and Bialer, I. "Intellectual Deviancy." In H. C. Haywood (Ed.), *Psychometric Intelligence.* New York: Appleton-Century-Crofts, 1970.

Moreau de Tours, P. *Fous et Bauffons.* Paris: Baillière, 1885.

Morel, A. *Traité des Dégénérescenses de l'Espèce Humaine.* Paris: Baillière, 1857.

Nahm, M. C. *The Artist as Creator: An Essay of Human Freedom.* Baltimore: Johns Hopkins University Press, 1956.

Naroll, R., and others. "Creativity: A Cross-Historical Pilot Survey." *Journal of Cross-Cultural Psychology,* 1971, *2,* 181-188.

Oden, M. "The Fulfillment of Promise: 40-Year Follow-Up." *Genetic Psychology Monographs,* 1968, *77* (1), 3-93.

Pressey, S. L. *Educational Acceleration: Appraisals and Basic Problems.* Columbus: Ohio University Press, 1949.

Rockwell, J. G. "Genius and the IQ." *Psychological Review,* 1927, *34,* 377-384.

Roe, A. "A Psychological Study of Eminent Biologists." *Psychological Monographs,* 1951a, *65* (14, Whole No. 331).

Roe, A. "A Psychological Study of Physical Scientists." *Genetic Psychology Monographs,* 1951b, *43,* 121-235.

Roe, A. "A Psychological Study of Eminent Psychologists and Anthropologists, and a Comparison with Biological and Physical Scientists." *Psychological Monographs,* 1953, *67* (2, Whole No. 352).

Sarton, G. "Evariste Galois." *Scientific Monthly,* 1921, *13,* 363-375.

Simonton, D. K. "Age and Literary Creativity: A Cross-Cultural and Transhistorical Survey." *Journal of Cross-Cultural Psychology*, 1975a, *6*, 259-277.

Simonton, D. K. "Sociocultural Context of Individual Creativity: A Transhistorical Times-Series Analysis." *Journal of Personality and Social Psychology*, 1975b, *32*, 1119-1133.

Simonton, D. K. "Biographical Determinants of Achieved Eminence: A Multivariate Approach to the Cox Data." *Journal of Personality and Social Psychology*, 1976, *33*, 218-226.

Simonton, D. K. "Creative Productivity, Age, and Stress: A Biographical Time-Series Analysis of 10 Classical Composers." *Journal of Personality and Social Psychology*, 1977, *35*, 791-804.

Simonton, D. K. "The Eminent Genius in History: The Critical Role of Creative Development." *Gifted Child Quarterly*, 1978, *22*, 187-195.

Stanley, J. C. "Test Better Finder of Great Math Talent Than Teachers Are." *American Psychologist*, 1976, *31*, 313-314.

Stanley, J. C., George, W. C., and Solano, C. H. (Eds.). *The Gifted and the Creative: A Fifty-Year Perspective*. Baltimore: Johns Hopkins University Press, 1977.

Stanley, J. C., Keating, D. P., and Fox, L. H. (Eds.). *Mathematical Talent: Discovery, Description, and Development*. Baltimore: Johns Hopkins University Press, 1974.

Stein, M. I. *Stimulating Creativity*. Vol. 1: *Individual Differences*. New York: Academic Press, 1974.

Terman, L. M. *Genetic Studies of Genius*. Vol. 1: *Mental and Physical Traits of a Thousand Gifted Children*. Stanford, Calif.: Stanford University Press, 1925.

Terman, L. M., and Oden, M. *Genetic Studies of Genius*. Vol. 4: *The Gifted Child Grows Up*. Stanford, Calif.: Stanford University Press, 1947.

Terman, L. M., and Oden, M. *Genetic Studies of Genius*. Vol. 5: *The Gifted Child at Mid-Life*. Stanford, Calif.: Stanford University Press, 1959.

Torrance, E. P. "Psychology of Gifted Children and Youth." In W. M. Cruickshank (Ed.), *Psychology of Exceptional Children and Youth*. (3rd ed.) Englewood Cliffs, N.J.: Prentice-Hall, 1971.

Wallach, M. A. *The Intelligence/Creativity Distinction*. Morristown, N.Y.: General Learning Press, 1971.

Wallach, M. A., and Kogan, N. *Modes of Thinking in Young Children: A Study of the Creativity-Intelligence Distinction*. New York: Holt, Rinehart and Winston, 1965.

Wallach, M. A., and Wing, C. W. *The Talented Student: A Validation of the Creativity-Intelligence Distinction*. New York: Holt, Rinehart and Winston, 1969.

Welsh, G. S. "Personality Correlates of Intelligence and Creativity in Gifted Adolescents." In J. C. Stanley, W. C. George, and C. H. Solano (Eds.), *The Gifted and the Creative: A Fifty-Year Perspective*. Baltimore: Johns Hopkins University Press, 1977.

White, R. K. "Note on the Psychopathology of Genius." *Journal of Social Psychology*, 1930, *1*, 311-315.

Willerman, L. *The Psychology of Individual and Group Differences*. San Francisco: Freeman, 1979.

Willerman, L., and Fiedler, M. F. "Intellectually Precocious Preschool Children: Early Development and Later Intellectual Accomplishments." *Journal of Genetic Psychology*, 1977, *131*, 13-20.

Zuckerman, H. *Scientific Elite*. New York: Free Press, 1977.

58

Lloyd D. Noppe

Creative Thinking

Creative thought, the process that contributes to the development of new and valuable ideas or products, is a relatively recent assessment phenomenon. Many research investigations have attempted to clarify the nature of creative thinking; however, multiple perspectives and unreliable assessments have served to fragment conceptual progress. Despite both methodological and theoretical complexities, the significance of understanding creative thought more completely has encouraged researchers to guide the state of assessment out of its infancy.

The identification and promotion of creative thinkers should be considered a critical goal by educators, psychologists, and all informed citizens. Due to the rapid pace of global change (social, economic, political, technological), an individual who can perceive the elements of a problem or interpret the meanings of a situation, resolve difficulties, and discover new approaches is invaluable. Therefore, creative thought remains a vital if elusive process for comprehension and improvement of the human condition.

Perhaps the major obstacle to successful clinical assessment of creative thinking is the variation in definitions that govern methods of measurement. Certain points of view, in fact, suggest that attempts to "capture" the essence of creative thought are fruitless. Although the ultimate evaluation of creative thinking must always refer to final products, many writers and researchers are convinced that reasonably effective indicators can be employed within a clinical setting. The various instruments and theories, however, should be considered cautiously. As Jackson and Messick (1965, p. 328) state: "Theories of creativity are themselves creative products. As such, they must abide by the same laws as those they are designed to unearth. A realization of this fact should temper our zeal in advocating any single prescription for how best to proceed. The day on which we are certain about how to construct a theory of creativity will also be the day on which we are certain about how to construct a poem."

Background and Current Status

Creative thought has been the subject of philosophical speculation for countless centuries. The beginnings of more scientific and empirical study may be traced to the late nineteenth and early twentieth centuries, with the writings of Galton (1869), Lombroso (1895), Freud (1913), Chassell (1916), Terman (1925), and Wallas (1926). Theoretical emphases ranged from genetics to abnormality and were responsible, in part, for the establishment of certain myths regarding creative thought—myths that persist today. For example, both Galton and Terman stressed the role of inheritance; as a result, many people assume that genius begets genius. The role of personality in creative thought was similarly imbued with an unfortunate emphasis. Lombroso attempted to equate genius with insanity, while Freud described Leonardo da Vinci's creativity as the sublimation of libidinal energy. Subsequently, there has been a plethora of "mad scientists," "crazy artists," and sexually repressed writers. Wallas provided a cognitive balance by offering a four-step sequence of creative thought: preparation, incubation, illumination, and verification. These basic ideas influenced the later conceptualizations of Wertheimer (1945), Guilford (1950), and Kris (1952).

Thus, theories of creative thinking were founded on a variety of assumptions that were never thoroughly unified or even adequately tested until much later. Meaningful assessment of creative thought could not rest on the vague, unfinished foundations built by the earliest investigators. The myths perpetuated and procedures suggested gradually became tarnished in the light of more contemporary attitudes and modern research results.

Guilford's laboratory provided the first comprehensive investigation of creative thought. Numerous paper-and-pencil instruments were constructed, based on the structure-of-intellect model (Guilford, 1967). In particular, divergent production ability was regarded as the hallmark of creative thought and was represented by such tests as Plot Titles, Unusual Uses, and Matchstick Problems. The theoretical tradition and associated measurement variations fostered by Guilford were followed up by Torrance (1963), Getzels and Jackson (1962), and others.

Guilford's factor analytic, trait approach to creative thought focused on the construction of normative-referenced and specifically defined tests. It may be sharply contrasted to the type of investigations promoted by theorists concerned with the creative personality. For example, Roe's (1949) reports of temperamental characteristics shared by eminent biologists, artists, or psychologists stimulated researchers to develop personality profiles of creative thinkers. Attributes such as independence, preference for complexity, flexibility, and determination were frequently found in creative individuals (Barron, 1969; Crutchfield, 1961; MacKinnon, 1962). Golann (1963) has suggested that a determination of the personality and stylistic modes related to creative thought holds the most promise for future development.

Another significant source of empirical research has been the associative theory promoted by Mednick (1962). The principal assessment device based on this approach has been the Remote Associates Test, which measures a person's ability to coordinate a set of three unrelated words by thinking of a fourth word that may be associated with each. Maltzman (1960) also has described creative thought in terms of the active process of generating associations. In a fascinating blend of associative theory and instrumentation derived from Guilford's tradition, Wallach and Kogan (1965) extended the approach of Maltzman and Mednick to children.

Dellas and Gaier (1970) have critically reviewed the research and theory on creative thought. They especially note the absence of replication studies to support the psychometric instruments employed. In addition, they point out the following six weaknesses: (1) semantic and conceptual ambiguity, (2) limited sampling, (3) imprecise reporting, (4) powerful statistical analyses at the expense of theoretically grounded hypotheses, (5) little initiation of longitudinal studies, and (6) an overemphasis on intellectual factors. Nevertheless, they state that "despite differences in age, cultural background, area of operation or eminence, a particular constellation of psychological traits emerges consistently in the creative individual, and forms a recognizable schema of the creative personality" (pp. 67-68). Although they do not indicate whether these characteristics are causes or consequences of creative thought, Dellas and Gaier strongly recommended including conceptually refined cognitive style and personality variables.

The increasing acceptance among theorists of the integration of personality and cognitive factors has also contributed positively to recent developments in approaches to creativity. New conceptions have emerged which attempt to consider both intellectual and emotional aspects of the creative process (Gruber and Barrett, 1974; Rothenberg, 1976). In addition, empirical research has focused on the cognitive styles framework of creative thinking. For example, fixity-mobility has been explored and found to be related to certain creativity measures (Gamble and Kellner, 1968; Golden, 1975). Field dependence-independence has been similarly correlated with creative thought (Del Gaudio, 1976; Noppe and Gallagher, 1977). Furthermore, other investigators continue to study the relationships between creativity and personality factors (Maini, 1973; Uhes and Shaver, 1970). In sum, the recommendations of Golann (1963) and Dellas and Gaier (1970) have been seriously considered. Progress toward the assessment of creative thought may shortly begin to accelerate, thereby matching the state of theoretical advance.

Critical Discussion

General Areas of Concern

Methods of assessing creative thinking include self-report measures, projective techniques, personality and cognitive instruments, ratings by others, and tests of other types. In view of the multifaceted approach to creative thought adopted by contemporary writers, a clear taxonomy of assessment procedures would be difficult to construct. Furthermore, unnecessarily strict classification of instruments may tend to encourage their more limited use rather than the employment of combinations of measures to provide multitrait-multimethod validation as suggested by Campbell and Fiske (1959).

Golann (1963) discusses creative thought in terms of four primary emphases: (1) products, (2) personality, (3) process, and (4) measurement. Each emphasis includes some form of assessment, although the literature cited does not, by any means, indicate the exclusive use of particular procedures according to the first three categories Golann established. As mentioned, Dellas and Gaier (1970) organized creative thought research within two general trends—cognitive and personological. While less redundancy is apparent in their system, it is not substantially more effective than Golann's approach.

Perhaps a theoretical models orientation (psychoanalytic versus cognitive versus associative) would best describe procedural differences in the past. However, the contemporary source of difficulty in adopting any of these classification schemes remains the eclectic nature of creative thinking theory as well as the use of multiple types of assessment by individual investigators. In order to resolve the dilemma of assessment classification, Table 1 presents representative examples of available procedures according to general methodology.

Table 1. Classification of Creative-Thinking Assessment

I. *Projective Techniques* A. Rorschach (Hersch, 1962) B. Thematic Apperception Test (Myden, 1959) C. Kent-Rosanoff Word Association (Rothenberg, 1973)	II. *Self-Report Methods* A. Biographical inventory (Taylor and Holland, 1964) B. Self-ratings of creativity (Wright, Fox, and Noppe, 1975) C. Interview/questionnaire (Roe, 1952)
III. *Personality Scales* A. California Psychological Inventory (Gough, 1961) B. Minnesota Multiphasic Personality Inventory (Rees and Goldman, 1961) C. Myers-Briggs Type Indicator (MacKinnon, 1961)	IV. *Cognitive Tests* A. Divergent thinking tests (Guilford, 1967) B. Remote Associates Test (Mednick, Mednick, and Mednick, 1964) C. Torrance Tests of Creative Thinking (Torrance and Dauw, 1965)
V. *Reports of Others* A. Peer/judge nominations (Drevdahl, 1956) B. Product/idea ratings (Harmon, 1958) C. Teacher/supervisor ratings (Rivlin, 1959)	VI. *Miscellaneous Instruments* A. Revised Art Scale (Barron, 1963) B. Preconscious Activities Scale (Holland and Baird, 1968) C. Rokeach Dogmatism Scale (Ohnmacht and McMorris, 1971)

Note: Within each category, the examples are followed by an empirical source employing the procedure.

One of the most perplexing aspects of assessing creative thought is the lack of a concrete referent. In attempting to measure a process, researchers are confronted with having to analyze totally inferential material. The rating of creative products or ideas appears to be the logical solution to this problem. In evaluating the results of the creative process (creative products), however, investigators often fail to examine the process itself and remain inextricably bound to a post hoc analysis. Therefore, inferring process from product is no less hypothetical reasoning than inferring a creative thought process from other assessment procedures. Methods of assessment, including product ratings, all require multivariate validation.

Research on creative thought is plagued by the employment of one unvalidated method after another. Conclusions drawn from such measures are, not surprisingly, often quite contradictory. All the assessment methods classified in Table 1 have been investigated. Each has been severely criticized, yet each has strong supporters, who continue to follow the procedures without regard to substantial validity.

Projective techniques have been a part of research on creative thinking for more than thirty years. Dellas and Gaier (1970, p. 61), commenting on the Rorschach test, point out the weaknesses of such techniques: "Despite a plethora of studies reporting the effectiveness of this instrument in diagnosis, its validity, as well as its reliability, is still recognized as problematic. Furthermore, different scoring systems used in its interpretation raise the question of comparability of results." While any projective technique suffers from potentially subjective analysis, subject faking, and situational factors (and is very time consuming), these instruments are extremely rich and individually revealing. The continued use of projectives is recommended because of their overwhelming popularity and the confidence engendered among reputable clinicians.

Forced-choice personality inventories have some of the same positive and negative qualities as the projective techniques, particularly social desirability responding and richness of data. Personality scales have, commendably, received more psychometric attention. They are less subjective and are easy to administer; however, results are not as individually precise. Research using a personality inventory for creative thought assessment tends to lead to overgeneralization from specific samples to a creative personality type that has yet to be validated with the subscales available. Both projective techniques and personality scales focus on general correlates of creative thought, which do not aid in explaining the creative process.

Self-report methods of creative thinking are clearly the most subjective type of analysis. While standardized personality inventories do not specifically imply the assessment of creative thought, direct self-report procedures cannot avoid the influences of a society in which creativity is highly valued social desirability responding. Since persons probably do know themselves best, however, perhaps self-report provides important insights. Various types of self-report may examine personality and/or process aspects of creative thought. Certainly, more subtle self-report approaches offer highly relevant, although not entirely unbiased, data.

The assessment of creative thought based on reports about people by others has been a popular empirical procedure since the advent of self-report. With the source of subjectivity one step removed from either researcher or subject, a false sense of confidence can be attributed to assessments of creativity by other observers. Bias is shifted to a third party, who may or may not be objective or qualified in ranking the creativity of others. Since thought is ultimately judged for creativity by collective others, the approach is potentially most valid. Reports by others may be encouraged, especially when multiple judges are involved, in spite of the limited data generated regarding the creative process.

Least concerned with personological aspects of creative thought, cognitive tests emphasize the process approach to assessment. These procedures probably compose the majority of creative thinking assessment, although reliability and validity data are quite uncertain. Dellas and Gaier (1970) suggest that cognitive tests do not adequately measure creative thought because they overlap with intelligence factors and because they are too simple (so that they tap only a low level of creativity). The "essence" of creative thought may have eluded cognitive testing; however, research indicates that the creative process is amenable to objective study. Refinement of valid cognitive assessment procedures will permit the consideration of creative thought from a cognitive styles perspective.

The instruments classified as miscellaneous include (1) preference tests, (2) isolated scales from multiple test batteries, (3) newly developed methods of various sorts, and (4) older devices which do not readily fall into one of the other classifications. It is impossible to draw overall conclusions concerning their adequacy in assessing creative thought because of the great diversity among them. There are potentially excellent prospects for assessment from this group for two reasons: (1) a variety of cognitive/personality approaches and (2) the absence of significant theoretical models (which otherwise tends to limit use among variously oriented researchers).

Comparative Philosophies and Theories

According to the psychoanalytic formulations of Kris (1952) and Kubie (1958), creative thinkers are neither schizophrenic nor unusually neurotic. Kris stresses that the process of ego-controlled regression makes preconscious and unconscious intuition available to the creative thinker. Kubie places less emphasis on the ego and id and attributes creative thought to the preconscious alone. These theoretical notions were largely developed from clinical interviews and observations. The use of projective techniques and personality inventories by psychoanalytically oriented researchers has provided only limited support for what are, at best, fairly vague assertions of theory. Nevertheless, many creativity researchers have acknowledged the significance of nonconscious processes (frequently termed *incubation*) for creative thought.

Mednick's (1962) associative theory of creative thinking is widely known; it is, however, often criticized for reliance on a single instrument of dubious validity. At the core of Mednick's approach is an availability, to the creative thinker, of much associative content which may be combined in some novel, useful fashion. The creative individual is assumed to have the capacity to generate unusual combinations of ideas that eventually lead to original principles or products. Critics of the Remote Associates Test argue that, since only one correct answer is allowed for each item, the instrument measures an aspect of intelligence and not original thought. Although it is a popular assessment device and a compelling theoretical approach, Bloomberg (1973) decries associative creativity as too heavily committed to a single, elementary variable.

A striking contrast to Mednick's approach is the cognitive psychometric model of Guilford (1967). If associative theory appears too restrictive and unitary, the factorial components of human intelligence developed by Guilford represent the opposite extreme. Proponents of the structure-of-intellect model emphasize the multidimensionality of thought, while detractors tend to "regard our [trait psychologists'] fractionalization and fragmentation of ability into more and more factors of less and less importance as indicative of scatterbrainedness" (McNemar, 1964, p. 872).

Both Guilford and Mednick have constructed fairly cognitive methods of assessing creative thought, yet the recent surge of interest in cognition by many social scientists has aided the movement toward a newer form of cognitive-developmental theory. Originally stimulated by the work of Werner (1957) and his associates and vigorously pursued by Witkin and his associates (1962), the cognitive styles approach to creative thought has generated empirical research of an integrative nature. Seeking to relate personological and cognitive factors involved in creative thought, cognitive style theorists have employed a variety of assessment procedures in the attempt to build a model congruent with general cognitive-developmental theory.

Bloomberg (1973) has noted that cognitive style researchers evoke an organismic approach to creative thought that is similar to humanistic writings. He states: "On the other hand, psychoanalytically oriented critics point to their [cognitive-developmentalists'] circumscribed interest in cognition and their general neglect of emotionality as well as personality variables" (p. 19). Psychoanalysts might be justly criticized for disregarding intellectual factors in favor of personality variables; however, each position is an exaggeration of theoretical foci. Humanistic theorists, in turn, berate psychoanalysts for implying that the individual's creative conflict with society is inevitably dangerous, rather than healthy and ideal. While the humanists espouse the creative potential of everyone, it remains for conjecture whether creative thinking is a capacity so generously proportioned. Furthermore, there has been little development of assessment procedures or substantive research on creative thought from humanistic theorists.

Elaboration on Critical Points

Three issues related to the assessment of creative thinking merit further consideration.

First, the relationship of creativity and intelligence has been the subject of both controversy and misunderstanding. Part of the problem concerns definitions and measurement methods. The crux of the matter, however, remains theoretical. No clear conception of creativity or intelligence has been universally accepted, and ideas forwarded by various investigators in each domain include overlapping components. A further source of confusion arises when some theorists (such as Guilford) have developed elaborate schemes that describe human intelligence and creativity in similar terms. Getzels and Jackson (1962), in a frequently cited investigation of gifted children, first attempted to distinguish the two constructs. While methodological problems do not permit a resolution of the issue, many later studies by other researchers have also reached the following conclusions. Essentially, at the upper ranges of IQ scores correlations with creativity assessments are low. Positive, moderate relationships are found when a full range of IQ scores are employed in a single study. It appears that somewhat different factors are responsible for high creativity and high intelligence, although, as Guilford (1966, p. 74) suggests, "No one can be very low in intelligence score and also be very creative."

A second issue is the disentanglement of creative thought and problem solving. Solutions to ordinary problems seem to depend on previous learning patterns and rather structured procedures. Wertheimer (1945), however, discussed problem solving with respect to intuition and productive thinking, thereby blurring typically stated distinctions. Bruner (1964, p. 19) characterizes creative problem solving as a solution that has "the quality of obviousness" about it, so that it produces "a shock of recognition, following which there is no longer astonishment." In addition to being elegant and valuable, creative problem solving is also original. Therefore, the use of creative-thinking assessment procedures which require "correct" solutions must be interpreted cautiously; that is, they tap only inferred processes and do not yield genuinely creative responses.

The third and final issue (previously hinted at) concerns the relationship between creative and abnormal thought. Kubie (1958) has been instrumental in altering the implicit notion of bizarreness attributed by early psychoanalysts to the creative thinker. Humanistically oriented analysts (such as Maslow, 1968) maintain that only self-actualized persons can be truly creative. Indeed, creative individuals have indicated an unusual constellation of personality factors when assessed by inventories and projective techniques. A listing of eight examples should be helpful: (1) introverted, (2) sexually ambivalent (classic roles and interests), (3) sensitive, (4) curious, (5) assertive, (6) enthusiastic, (7) self-accepting, and (8) tolerant of ambiguity. Clearly, these qualities are not entirely negative. If the personality profiles of creative thinkers are characterized by wide variations from an average profile, there is still no evidence to suggest that such deviations warrant serious concern.

Personal Views and Recommendations

Previous conceptions of creative thinking have explained part of the complex nature of the creative process yet have failed to penetrate the entire mystery. New models of creative thought are obligated to account for past progress, point out substantial areas of weakness, and create a unified approach. The assessment of individual creative potential will follow increasing theoretical sophistication only if valid procedures are devised.

At present, research methods used in the investigation of creative thinking do not possess the requisite sensitivity for clinical interpretation. Unfortunately, the specific suggestions needed to improve creative thought research are neither simple nor convenient.

To deduce, elaborate, and refine a theoretical model, an expensive and long-term dedication to creativity research is required. Even a significant first step would necessitate years of possibly tedious work. A major criticism of studies on the creative process has been the limitations of sampling. For example, longitudinal research has been virtually ignored. Following the course of development typical of a creative thinker might yield enormous insights. Anecdotal data provided by the parents of creative people tend to be unreliable. The actual use of known creative individuals in most research would be especially desirable; however, obtaining sufficiently adequate samples for such validation studies seems unlikely. Researchers will inevitably face the problem of determining who the creatives might be for their investigations, or at least suggesting selection criteria. Is genuine creative thought recognized during the lifetime of the creator? If so, who are the qualified few able to make the decisions? If not, how is the ordinary creative distinguished from the true creative in a clinical setting?

If cognitive and personological assessments of creative thinking are to be validated, a variety of representative samples (including recognized creatives, children, and controls) must be analyzed according to multivariate designs. All types of assessment procedures should add to an understanding of creative thought; however, statistical analyses, commensurate with conceptual intricacies, must be employed. Use of multiple assessment techniques will be particularly important for the establishment of convergent and divergent validity. Working back and forth between theoretical ideas and methods of assessing creative thought should gradually improve the harmony between them. Although it may never be possible to accurately predict every potential creative thinker, there is a reasonably optimistic hope for achieving high-quality clinical assessment.

Application to Particular Variables

Instruments for the assessment of creative thought have been employed with samples ranging across nearly the entire human life span. Since longitudinal studies are rare, there is little evidence to support the predictive validity of any major instrument for use with children or adults. While creative-thinking measures may be administered at all age levels, the question of when genuine potential can be identified has eluded researchers. In fact, theoretical debate continues regarding the possibility of genuine creativity prior to late adolescence. Process versus product definitions may be fueling the controversy. Therefore, validation of personality assessments for creative thought would offer an attractive approach to age distinctions by avoiding a focus on specific creative acts or on intellectual abilities. Furthermore, such assessment might predict individuals whose creative thought matures slowly or those whose shining hour fades rapidly.

Much creativity research has employed samples of one sex or neglected to analyze the data separately. When sex differences are occasionally found, follow-up investigations are rarely carried out in order to cross-validate conclusions. The focus of sex differences appears to concern variations in developmental patterns or reactions to the sex-role expectations of society (Barron, 1963). For example, males are encouraged to be independent, spatially oriented, and exploratory, whereas females are rewarded for submissive, verbal, and dependent behavior. Creative males tend to exhibit more feminine personality characteristics than other males, and creative females indicate a constellation of more masculine traits than other females do (Dellas and Gaier, 1970). Reports of actual creative individuals, rather than examination of experimental results, confirm the similarity between creative males and their female counterparts (Ghiselin, 1952).

Assessment of creative thought in terms of variations in educational level has one implicit danger. In the same fashion as intelligence testing has proved to be a delicate issue, the early labeling of creative individuals may unnecessarily foster self-fulfilling prophecies and the undue loss of self-esteem among those termed uncreative. Educators must pay careful attention to designing learning environments that do not discriminate against relatively less creative students but provide a challenging atmosphere for all.

Self-education can be seen as an influential aspect of creative thought; however, formal education may play a positive or negative role in fostering creative thought, depending on the nature of that experience. In either case, assessment procedures for less educated persons may have to consider emphasizing personality rather than cognitive aspects of creative thought.

Biographical material, the relationship between creativity and intelligence, and common sense indicate that lower socioeconomic people will be less likely to be assessed as creative thinkers. However, more recent opportunities extended across socioeconomic levels may change assessment procedures and stereotypical attitudes. Farnham-Diggory (1972, pp. 508-509) has suggested that "Creative children from disadvantaged backgrounds may appear to have lower IQs than they would actually have if the IQ test were culturally appropriate. Because of this, their creativity may be a better index of their true intelligence than IQ tests are." Since no research has been conducted to support or refute this claim, assessment of creative thought according to socioeconomic status remains an unresolved issue.

Again, limited research on vocational differences in creative thought exists. Few investigations explore comparative samples; and generalizations among different investigations are risky, particularly in view of the lack of consistent assessment procedures (Dellas and Gaier, 1970). An interesting area for future studies would be the interaction of vocational and age variables. Anecdotal reports have indicated that creative mathematicians and physicists reach their peaks much earlier than writers and poets do (Roe, 1952). Perhaps the creative prime, for whatever reasons, varies according to career specialization.

References

Barron, F. *Creativity and Psychological Health: Origins of Personality and Creative Freedom.* New York: Van Nostrand, 1963.

Barron, F. *Creative Person and Creative Process.* New York: Holt, Rinehart and Winston, 1969.

Bloomberg, M. "Introduction: Approaches to Creativity." In M. Bloomberg (Ed.), *Creativity: Theory and Research.* New Haven, Conn.: Yale University Press, 1973.

Bruner, J. S. *On Knowing: Essays for the Left Hand.* Cambridge, Mass.: Harvard University Press, 1964.

Campbell, D. T., and Fiske, D. W. "Convergent and Discriminant Validation by the Multitrait-Multimethod Matrix." *Psychological Bulletin,* 1959, *56,* 81-105.

Chassell, L. M. "Tests for Originality." *Journal of Educational Psychology,* 1916, *7,* 317-329.

Crutchfield, R. S. "The Creative Process." In D. W. MacKinnon (Ed.), *Conference on the Creative Person.* Berkeley: Institute of Personality Assessment and Research, University of California, 1961.

Del Gaudio, A. C. "Psychological Differentiation and Mobility as Related to Creativity." *Perceptual and Motor Skills,* 1976, *43,* 831-841.

Dellas, M., and Gaier, E. L. "Identification of Creativity: The Individual." *Psychological Bulletin,* 1970, *73,* 55-73.

Drevdahl, J. E. "Factors of Importance for Creativity." *Journal of Clinical Psychology,* 1956, *12,* 21-26.

Farnham-Diggory, S. *Cognitive Processes in Education: A Psychological Preparation for Teaching and Curriculum Development.* New York: Harper & Row, 1972.

Freud, S. *Leonardo da Vinci: A Study in Sexuality* [1913]. New York: Random House, 1947.

Galton, F. *Hereditary Genius: An Inquiry into Its Laws and Consequences* [1869]. New York: Horizon Press, 1952.

Gamble, K. R., and Kellner, H. "Creative Functioning and Cognitive Regression." *Journal of Personality and Social Psychology,* 1968, *9,* 266-271.

Getzels, J. W., and Jackson, P. W. *Creativity and Intelligence: Explorations with Gifted Students.* New York: Wiley, 1962.

Ghiselin, B. *The Creative Process.* Berkeley: University of California Press, 1952.

Golann, S. E. "Psychological Study of Creativity." *Psychological Bulletin,* 1963, *60,* 548-565.

Golden, C. J. "The Measurement of Creativity by the Stroop Color and Word Test." *Journal of Personality Assessment,* 1975, *39,* 502-506.

Gough, H. G. "Techniques for Identifying the Creative Research Scientist." In D. W. MacKinnon (Ed.), *Conference on the Creative Person.* Berkeley: Institute of Personality Assessment and Research, University of California, 1961.

Gruber, H. E., and Barrett, P. H. *Darwin on Man.* New York: Dutton, 1974.

Guilford, J. P. "Creativity." *American Psychologist,* 1950, *5,* 444-454.

Guilford, J. P. "Basic Problems in Teaching for Creativity." In C. W. Taylor and F. E. Williams (Eds.), *Instructional Media and Creativity.* New York: Wiley, 1966.

Guilford, J. P. *The Nature of Human Intelligence.* New York: McGraw-Hill, 1967.

Harmon, L. R. "The Development of a Criterion of Scientific Competence." In C. Taylor (Ed.), *The 1957 University of Utah Research Conference on the Identification of Creative Scientific Talent.* Salt Lake City: University of Utah Press, 1958.

Hersch, C. "The Cognitive Functioning of the Creative Person: A Developmental Analysis." *Journal of Projective Techniques,* 1962, *26,* 193-200.

Holland, J. L., and Baird, L. L. "The Preconscious Activity Scale: The Development and Validation of an Original Measure." *Journal of Creative Behavior,* 1968, *2,* 217-225.

Jackson, P. W., and Messick, S. "The Person, the Product, and the Response: Conceptual Problems in the Assessment of Creativity." *Journal of Personality,* 1965, *33,* 309-329.

Kris, E. *Psychoanalytic Explorations in Art.* New York: International Universities Press, 1952.

Kubie, L. S. *The Neurotic Distortion of the Creative Process.* New York: Noonday Press, 1958.

Lombroso, C. *The Man of Genius.* New York: Scribner's, 1895.

MacKinnon, D. W. "The Study of Creativity and Creativity in Architects." In D. W. MacKinnon (Ed.), *Conference on the Creative Person.* Berkeley: Institute of Personality Assessment and Research, University of California, 1961.

MacKinnon, D. W. "The Nature and Nurture of Creative Talent." *American Psychologist,* 1962, *17,* 484-495.

McNemar, Q. "Lost: Our Intelligence? Why?" *American Psychologist,* 1964, *19,* 871-882.

Maini, S. M. "Personality and Cognitive Differences Between an Original and a Non-original Group." *Perceptual and Motor Skills,* 1973, *37,* 555-563.

Maltzman, I. "On the Training of Originality." *Psychological Review,* 1960, *67,* 229-242.

Maslow, A. "Some Educational Implications of the Humanistic Psychologies." *Harvard Educational Review,* 1968, *38,* 685-696.

Mednick, M. T., Mednick, S. A., and Mednick, E. V. "Incubation of Creative Performance and Specific Associative Priming." *Journal of Abnormal and Social Psychology,* 1964, *69,* 84-88.

Mednick, S. A. "The Associative Basis of the Creative Process." *Psychological Review,* 1962, *69,* 220-232.

Myden, W. "Interpretation and Evaluation of Certain Personality Characteristics Involved in Creative Production." *Perceptual and Motor Skills,* 1959, *9,* 139-158.

Noppe, L. D., and Gallagher, J. M. "A Cognitive Style Approach to Creative Thought." *Journal of Personality Assessment,* 1977, *41,* 85-90.

Ohnmacht, F. W., and McMorris, R. F. "Creativity as a Function of Field Independence and Dogmatism." *Journal of Psychology,* 1971, *79,* 165-168.

Rees, M. E., and Goldman, M. "Some Relationships Between Creativity and Personality." *Journal of General Psychology,* 1961, *65,* 145-161.

Rivlin, L. "Creativity and Self-Attitudes and Sociability of High School Students." *Journal of Educational Psychology,* 1959, *50,* 147-152.

Roe, A. "Psychological Examinations of Eminent Biologists." *Journal of Consulting Psychology,* 1949, *13,* 225-246.

Roe, A. *The Making of a Scientist.* New York: Dodd, Mead, 1952.

Rothenberg, A. "Word Association and Creativity." *Psychological Reports,* 1973, *33,* 3-12.

Rothenberg, A. "Janusian Thinking and Creativity." In W. Muensterberger, A. H. Esman, and L. B. Boyer (Eds.), *The Psychoanalytic Study of Society.* New Haven, Conn.: Yale University Press, 1976.

Taylor, C. W., and Holland, J. "Predictors of Creative Performance." In C. W. Taylor (Ed.), *Creativity: Progress and Potential.* New York: McGraw-Hill, 1964.

Terman, L. M. *Genetic Studies of Genius.* Vol. 1: *Mental and Physical Traits of a Thousand Gifted Children.* Stanford, Calif.: Stanford University Press, 1925.

Torrance, E. P. *Education and the Creative Potential.* Minneapolis: University of Minnesota Press, 1963.

Torrance, E. P., and Dauw, D. C. "Aspirations and Dreams of Three Groups of Creatively Gifted High School Seniors and Comparable Unselected Group." *Gifted Child Quarterly,* 1965, *9,* 177-182.

Uhes, M. J., and Shaver, J. P. "Dogmatism and Divergent-Convergent Abilities." *Journal of Psychology,* 1970, *75,* 3-11.

Wallach, M. A., and Kogan, N. *Modes of Thinking in Young Children: A Study of the Creativity-Intelligence Distinction.* New York: Holt, Rinehart and Winston, 1965.

Wallas, G. *The Art of Thought.* New York: Harcourt Brace Jovanovich, 1926.

Werner, H. "The Concept of Development from a Comparative and Organismic Point of View." In D. B. Harris (Ed.), *The Concept of Development: An Issue in the Study of Human Behavior.* Minneapolis: University of Minnesota Press, 1957.

Wertheimer, M. *Productive Thinking.* New York: Harper & Row, 1945.

Witkin, H. A., and others. *Psychological Differentiation: Studies of Development.* New York: Wiley, 1962.

Wright, R. J., Fox, M., and Noppe, L. "The Interrelationship of Creativity, Self-Esteem, and Creative Self-Concept." *Psychology,* 1975, *12,* 11-15.

59

Thomas M. Stephens

Academic Learning Problems

A basic assumption regarding academic learning problems is that the student is not acquiring academic skills (such as language, reading, writing, and arithmetic) as well as are students of the same age, intelligence, and/or grade placement. When the difficulties are pronounced, students may be diagnosed clinically as, for example, learning disabled or dyslexic. Factors interfering with the acquisition of academic learning may be internal to learners (physical, emotional, and/or mental causes), or they may be environmentally induced (poor home conditions or inadequate teaching). Causation generally is believed to be the result of multiple factors.

Measurements used for identifying academic learning problems may include direct observations (Cooper, 1974), criterion-referenced tests (Stephens, 1977), and norm-referenced tests (Salvia and Ysseldyke, 1978). Usually it is necessary to use all three types of measures for total educational placement and programming.

Academic learning problems rarely can be separated entirely from related social learning difficulties. For example, successful academic learning in classrooms requires attention; withholding of some degree of personal satisfaction; and skill in following directions, organizing, and interpersonal relationships. Social behaviors of this type are often given as prerequisite skills for successful formal academic learning.

Background and Current Status

Differences in the rate and quality of academic learning have existed since the beginning of formal instruction. By the late 1500s, tests were described for identifying both the mentally retarded (Hilliard, 1965) and gifted children (Sumption and Luecking, 1960).

Prior to compulsory education in the United States, students with academic learning problems dropped out of school. With compulsory education, students who could not keep up in their studies were punished, first physically and later in more humane and subtle ways.

Once differences in rate of academic learning were recognized, it was necessary to determine at which points those differences became significant. Measurement in education grew out of the need to identify significant individual differences in learning. As those children who were obviously exceptional were identified and properly placed in school, finer distinctions in learning differences were made. Public school classes for the education of those who were handicapped (deaf, blind, mentally retarded, crippled, and emotionally disturbed) were initiated at the beginning of this century. Later, those with mild learning problems also received special attention.

Remedial and corrective education were early efforts to assist children with academic learning problems. These special programs often grew out of clinical education practices and were intimately related to the clinical testing movement in education and psychology. (These practices are referred to as clinical because they were often conducted in agencies other than public schools; the settings were typically associated with universities and mental health facilities.) The clinical education movement emphasized diagnostic testing. Out of it grew medically related diagnostic terms for classifying and identifying academic learning problems (Thompson, 1966). Such diagnostic labels as *aphasia* and *dyslexia* were used to identify the more severe learning problems.

Prior to the late 1950s, clinical investigations were emphasized instead of practical school applications. Beginning with the study of brain-injured adults, attention then moved to studying similarly handicapped children. By the late 1950s, children of normal intelligence who evidenced learning problems were considered for special assistance in schools.

More recently and immediately prior to the advent of the phrase *learning disabilities,* perceptual-motor classifications emerged. Kephart (1960) pioneered in relating motor functions to learning process problems. He attributed the learning failures of students with low-average or better intelligence to deficits in their neurological systems, thus establishing the belief that the *process* by which they learned must be corrected. Some of the perceptual-motor elements considered were laterality, directionality, body image, form perception, and figure-ground perception. In the early 1960s, language problems were also viewed as process disorders. Bush and Waugh (1976) review language disorders extensively. They discuss categories and classification schemes presented by Bateman (1964), Johnson and Myklebust (1967), and Kirk, McCarthy, and Kirk (1968), among others. These early "process trainers" laid the groundwork for the concept of *diagnostic teaching,* whereby students' learning difficulties were first measured and instruction, or treatment, was prescribed according to measurement results.

Diagnostic teaching became popular in the mid 1960s (Peters, 1965). It was an outcome of more precise measurements and improved instructional technology. In education, diagnosis is typically followed by a prescribed instructional program. Thus, the term *diagnostic-prescriptive teaching* was soon applied to most systems of instruction for students with academic learning difficulties.

Assessment practices rooted in assumptions concerning learning process disorders continued into the 1970s in the United States, but these assumptions came under increasingly heavy criticism during this same period. Critics raised issues concerning the use of standardized measures for identifying handicapped learners, the validity and reliability of these tests, and the assumptions on which they were developed and used. By the early 1970s, criticism of measures used to assess learning disabilities became widespread. The assumptions inherent in process approaches to measurement were critically analyzed by Ysseldyke and Salvia (1974). Intervention strategies based on the process model were attacked by Quay (1973), Mann (1971), Stephens (1970, 1976, 1977), and Hammill and Larsen (1974, 1978).

The tests that claim to measure the learning process of students typically yield diagnostic teaching profiles. These provide a graphic description of students' strengths and weaknesses. However, when divided these tests have poor validity and reliability, thus lacking the precision needed to prescribe instruction. Since these tests are a necessary part of the treatment program, process instruction or ability training is believed to be based on teaching strategies in relation to the diagnostic profile. Among these, the Frostig Program for the Development of Visual Perception (Frostig and Horne, 1964) has been widely used and studied. Jacobs (1967; Jacobs, Wirthlin, and Miller, 1968) found that the Frostig training program did not result in higher reading scores. Wiederholt and Hammill's (1971) findings were similar.

Another test that greatly influenced programs for the learning disabled is the Illinois Test of Psycholinguistic Abilities (Kirk, McCarthy, and Kirk, 1968). This test, referred to as the ITPA, yields a diagnostic profile for use in teaching. A series of research articles has raised serious questions about the ITPA's usefulness (Hammill and Larsen, 1974, 1978; Lund, Foster, and Perez, 1978).

With the approach of the 1980s, measurement and treatment of children with academic learning problems appear to be represented by two schools of thought. The first is represented by the *ability training* advocates, while the second model has been termed *skill training* (Stephens, 1977). Advocates of ability training emphasize remediating the underlying processes, such as visual, auditory, and perceptual difficulties, that in their view contribute to inadequate learning. Among the major proponents of ability training are Barsch (1967), Bateman (1968), Cruickshank (1977), Delacato (1966), Frostig (1970), Johnson and Myklebust (1967), Kephart (1964), and Kirk, McCarthy, and Kirk (1968). Skill training begins by identifying the precise responses that are in error. Correct responses are then taught. Assumptions are not made regarding causes of learning problems. Causality is usually not considered important for remediation. Major advocates of skill training are Bijou (1973), Englemann (1969), Haring and Phillips (1972), Lovitt (1973), Mann (1971), Staats (1963), and Stephens (1977).

Ability and skill trainers' concepts of what constitutes academic learning problems also differ. Identification of students who have learning difficulties may be the same regardless of how the problems are viewed, but the information needed for instruction differs greatly, depending on how the problems will be treated. Thus, the assessment procedures and measurement tools will vary with the type of instructional treatment.

Critical Discussion

General Areas of Concern

All diagnostic-prescriptive teaching rests on certain assumptions about the technology of instruction and the ways in which academic learning occurs. Technology of instruction has advanced considerably in post-World War II America. Much of this technology is useful for correcting academic learning problems.

Foremost among the new teaching techniques is an instructional system in which objectives are specified. Behaviorally defined instructional objectives are central to diagnostic-prescriptive teaching. Prescriptive aspects of teaching are the training variables; these are manipulated in order to relate them to the outcome behavior. Thus, the outcomes or instructional objectives comprise the dependent variables, and the instruction or training represents the independent variable. When instructional objectives are specified in behavioral terms, the behavior can be analyzed and divided into instructional tasks. These tasks often must be subdivided in order to teach students with academic learning problems.

Task analysis, another recent instructional technique, permits teachers to design instruction based on students' prerequisite responses. An underlying assumption of task analysis is that conditions for learning each task differ significantly. Because of the numerous tasks comprising academic learning, categories must be devised for classifying behavior in instructionally relevant formats. For example, in categorizing beginning reading skills, one classification scheme (Stephens, 1973) uses seven major categories and forty-eight subcategories. These categories are shown in Table 1.

Table 1. Categories for Beginning Reading Skills

Auditory Discrimination	*Phonetic Analysis*	*Sight Words*
environmental sounds	blends	first
identifying rhymes	final consonants	preprimer
matching sounds	consonant variants	primer
repeating sounds	digraphs	second
following instruction	diphthongs	third
	phonetic words in context	
Oral Reading	long vowels	*Visual Discrimination*
clarity	short vowels	likenesses/differences
intonation, expression		matching symbols
	Structural Analysis	recognizing letters
Comprehension	contractions	recognizing numbers
classifying, categorizing	compound words	repeating visual patterns
drawing conclusions	punctuation	
identifying speaker	prefix/suffix	
inference	singular/plural	
interpretation	syllabification	
labeling	uppercase/lowercase	
location skills	word building	
main idea		
matching		
opposites		
recall		
sequencing events		
following written word		
meaning		

Source: Stephens (1973).

An academic curriculum of instruction can be assumed to be constant and available for all school-age children. Once a scheme has been designed for describing and classifying academic performances, school personnel can assess students against these objectives. These assessment findings are then used for determining entry points into the academic curriculum.

Curriculum content must be organized and sequenced. Some academic skills, such as in beginning reading and arithmetic, are hierarchical. In other instances, they are organized sequentially, solely for management purposes.

Valid and reliable measurement approaches represent important and critical concerns in diagnostic-prescriptive teaching. As mentioned, ability trainers, representing the process learning view, have been criticized because of their reliance on tests of questionable validity (Black, 1974; Smith and Marx, 1972) and poor reliability (Ysseldyke and Salvia, 1974). Skill trainers tend to use direct observations (Cooper, 1974) and criterion-referenced measures in their student assessment practices. The use of direct observations is both time consuming and limited in usefulness. When direct observations are used, however, careful definitions of responses are essential for valid measurement. For reliable measurement, interobserver agreement should be at least 80 percent. Criterion-referenced testing is most useful in objectives-based instructional programs (Glaser, 1963; Popham and Husek, 1969). But criterion-referenced measures have been criticized because they often fail to meet acceptable standards of validity and reliability (Hambleton and others, 1978).

Comparative Philosophies and Theories

Three types of remedial approaches to the same manifest academic learning problem have been described by Quay (1973). Type 1 approaches involve practices that are expected to change academic performance in an unspecified future, but the precise ways in which change will take place are not rationally understood. An example of type 1 practices is gross-motor training for purposes of improving reading skills. Type 2 activities are logically related to instructional outcomes. These practices too—for example, perceptual discrimination training in reading instruction—are used in expectation of improved future academic learning. In type 3 instruction, the techniques consist of direct instruction of the terminal academic performance. These practices involve teaching a part of the outcome behavior. No attempts are made to correct deficiencies that are not directly related to the required performances.

Ability training usually relies on types 1 and 2, while skill trainers use types 2 and 3. Advocates of these two models of instruction have different philosophies and theories of assessment and instruction. These differences are reflected in their instructional practices and in the tools used for testing.

Assessment tools used in treating academic learning problems are represented by norm-referenced testing, direct observation of performances, and criterion-referenced measures. In addition, checklists and various clinical instruments are used in assessment. The rapid acceptance of diagnostic-prescriptive teaching has resulted in the use of assessment tools that yield diagnostic profiles.

Contemporary academic remedial programs tend to be organized into instructional management systems. These systems are represented by various models of instruction. Three examples of such models are Applied Behavior Analysis, Diagnostic Teaching, and Directive Teaching.

Applied Behavior Analysis (Lovitt, 1975) consists of directly measuring the behavior of concern through the collection of responses. An analysis of responses is made for each student prior to intervention, during what is termed the *base line period,* and during the treatment interventions. Offshoots of Applied Behavior Analysis are Precision Teaching (Kunzelman, 1970) and Responsive Teaching (Hall, 1972).

Diagnostic Teaching is typically represented by approaches that begin with a thorough clinical assessment followed by prescribed instruction. Prescriptive Teaching (Peters, 1965), the work of Donald E. P. Smith and his associates (Smith, 1976a, 1976b, 1976c; Smith, Smith, and Brink, 1976), and the work of Johnson and Myklebust (1967) are examples of Diagnostic Teaching approaches. In Diagnostic Teaching, the basis of instruction is often informational but not necessarily data based.

Directive Teaching (Stephens, 1970, 1976) is an instructional management system for teachers of children with academic learning problems. The Directive Teaching Instructional Management System (Stephens, 1977) consists of four major components: assessment, planning, instruction, and evaluation. Assessment contains criterion-referenced measures and tactics for direct observation of performances. These are derived from the curriculum contained in the system. The planning component is represented by decisions which teachers and other school personnel make in relation to the assessment findings. Instructional procedures and materials consist of strategies containing methods for teaching. Typically, tactics derived from social modeling and operant theories are contained in the instructional strategies (Stephens, Hartman, and Lucas, 1978). The instructional component contains commercially obtained references which are keyed to the skills, so that teachers can extend instruction beyond the materials contained in the system. Evaluation is accomplished in Directive Teaching by comparing students' performances on the assessment measures with their functioning after instruction. The same criterion-referenced measures used in assessment are applied during evaluation.

Elaboration on Critical Points

Traditional approaches for identifying, assessing, and teaching students with academic learning problems failed to specify instructional outcomes in behavioral terms. Because school personnel were forced to deal with hypothetical constructs, such as minimal brain dysfunction, they found it difficult to relate their assessment practices to the instructional program. Often these approaches considered observable characteristics to be symptomatic of academic difficulties but not in themselves representations of learning difficulties. Thus, responses as such were not considered worthy of corrective instruction.

Among learning-disabled children, diagnostic practices typically started with the observed responses as clinical signs that more severe problems existed. Inferences were then derived from academic performances, and clinical tests were administered in hopes of confirming a suspicion or hypothesis of the "real nature" of the disorder. This sequence—from observable through inferential to hypothetical thinking—may be depicted in this way:

Level 1	*Condition*
Observable	Reverses letters when printing
Inferential	Perceptual-motor problem
Hypothetical	Neurological deficit

Traditional practices, following diagnosis, typically focused on correcting those problems that were identified at inferential levels. Thus, the process- or ability-based instruction became a common practice among teachers of the learning disabled. School personnel often encouraged parents to obtain medical services or other specialized assistance to ameliorate those disorders identified at the hypothetical levels.

Contemporary approaches, however, have attempted to match instruction to assessment by using criterion-referenced measures and direct observations. These measures are developed from the instructional content and are used for assessing students' entry-level performances against those behaviors available for teaching. The same measures that are used for entry-level assessment are also useful for evaluating the effects of instruction.

Instructional design assumes certain results from teaching. Those who are ability trainers expect their treatment, such as visual-motor training, to correct academic performance problems. Skill trainers assume that instruction directed at the observed performance deficit will remediate learning problems.

Program design for academic instruction is a key ingredient for correcting learning problems. The type and emphasis of the content and the methods used in teaching represent the academic instructional component. Both ability and skill trainers make use of task analysis, contingency contracting, chaining, social modeling, and other tactics derived from operant and social learning theories. Ability training advocates, however, direct their teaching toward improving aptitudes and processes, whereas skill trainers focus their instruction on academic content. Although both expect gains on the respective outcome variables, ability trainers look for long-term effects; skill trainers expect more immediate gains in academic achievements.

Personal Views and Recommendations

A systems approach to assessing and teaching students with academic learning problems is increasingly possible and most likely to help such students. These programs should incorporate procedures for systematic assessment and instruction. One such system is Directive Teaching (Stephens, 1970, 1976, 1977, 1979).

Directive Teaching follows four basic steps. Each has incorporated into it instructional technology representing tools for the use of school practitioners, as shown below.

The Directive Teaching System

- Step 1—Assessing Student Performance
    Tools: Direct observation, criterion-referenced tasks, skill statements, performance
        criteria
- Step 2—Instructional Planning
    Tools: Behavioral objectives, task analysis, commercial materials
- Step 3—Instructing
    Tools: Stimulus control, cueing, social modeling, chaining, social reinforcement,
        contingency management, worksheets, games
- Step 4—Evaluating Effects of Instruction
    Tools: Direct observation, criterion-referenced tasks, skill statements, performance
        criteria, recording of progress.

A system such as this helps school personnel structure their services for students. The evaluation component feeds into an ongoing system of assessment and instruction. Such a program also facilitates the tracking of students' progress within the instructional system.

A criterion-referenced concept is incorporated into all assessment tasks in Directive Teaching, so that corrective instruction will (1) begin with specific information concerning each student's skill proficiencies and (2) avoid the comparison of an individual student's performances against a standardized norm group.

Another fundamental principle incorporated into the assessment tasks is that they should be identical to the skills to be taught. Task-specific instruction is built into each teaching strategy. All related activities, including practice, focus on each skill. This permits students to progress from teacher directed instruction to independent practice on the same skill.

Once skill lists are established and categorized, other instructional materials can be keyed to those skills. These additional materials can represent commercially available products as well as those produced by teachers. The keying of each to the relevant skills helps teachers to develop instructional strategies in a minimal amount of time and provides teachers with a wider range of activities for students to practice each skill following instruction. For example, if a particular basal textbook series is used in classrooms, teachers can use this series more systematically by relating specific activities to the skill being taught; following mastery of the skill, they can use commercial materials for extended practice beyond their immediate supervision.

Those who are responsible for assessing students with academic learning problems will find it necessary to collaborate with teachers. Through this relationship their clinical testing can feed into an instructional system. They can also assist and advise those teachers who are not yet adept in systematic instruction and the use of positive reinforcement.

Special provisions and policies should be established by schools to provide parents and students with full protection of their rights as consumers of educational services. For example, parents must be informed about the testing and must give their consent before it takes place; parents and, when feasible, students should be involved in planning for special school services and placement; nondiscriminatory tests must be used; regular reports of students' progress should be made available to parents in understandable language; special instruction should be reevaluated on a regular and current basis; and due process and appeal procedures should be provided for parents who wish to challenge the school personnels' recommendations and decisions.

Application to Particular Variables

Age is a central factor for formal instruction. By the primary grades, children who have basic learning problems have demonstrated their difficulties through poor school performance. These problems are corrected or alleviated during the elementary school years. When they are not, the prognosis for normal school achievement is lessened.

Increasingly, "at-risk" children are identified prior to formal schooling. These preschoolers may display developmental lag such as language delay and poor health. However, academic learning problems cannot be definitely established until some exposure to formal schooling has taken place.

Academic learning problems are not restricted to either sex. Typically, more boys display problems than girls do. No differentiation in special instruction is needed on the basis of sex.

All ethnic/racial groups are known to be represented by students with academic learning problems. No distinctive differences in response to special instruction are known on the basis of ethnic or racial backgrounds.

School personnel who provide services for students with academic learning problems do require special training. School psychologists and diagnosticians are essential for providing comprehensive services to such students. School counselors, speech therapists, and remedial teachers are also needed for effective school-based programs. Although such personnel are prepared at preservice levels, in-service training is essential for implementing a systematic program of assessment, planning, instruction, and evaluation. Such training should be implemented in purposeful and functional ways. First, the total program of service should be conceptualized. Second, the components of the program should be described in terms of services to students and personnel needed to provide the services. Third, after qualified personnel have been employed, they should be trained to carry out the functions within the total program. The training should not be idiosyncratic. Instead, all training should be interrelated and totally compatible within the planned system. Finally, an ongoing evaluation and monitoring of the services should be maintained, with changes made as indicated.

References

Barsch, R. *Achieving Perceptual-Motor Efficiency.* Seattle: Special Child, 1967.

Bateman, B. "Learning Disabilities—Yesterday, Today and Tomorrow." *Exceptional Children,* 1964, *31,* 167-177.

Bateman, B. "The Efficiency of an Auditory and a Visual Method of First Grade Reading Instruction with Auditory and Visual Learners." In K. Smith (Ed.), *Perception and Reading.* Newark, Del.: International Reading Association, 1968.

Bijou, S. "Behavior Modification in Teaching the Retarded Child." In C. E. Thoresen (Ed.), *Behavior Modification in Education.* Seventy-Second Yearbook of the National Society for the Study of Education. Chicago: University of Chicago Press, 1973.

Black, F. "Achievement Test Performance of High and Low Perceiving Learning Disabled Children." *Journal of Learning Disabilities,* 1974, *7,* 178-182.

Bush, W., and Waugh, K. *Diagnosing Learning Disabilities.* (2nd ed.) Columbus: Merrill, 1976.

Cooper, J. *Measurement and Analysis of Behavioral Techniques.* Columbus: Merrill, 1974.

Cruickshank, W. "Myths and Realities in Learning Disabilities." *Journal of Learning Disabilities,* 1977, *10,* 57-64.

Delacato, C. *Neurological Organization and Reading.* Springfield, Ill.: Thomas, 1966.

Englemann, S. *Preventing Failure in the Primary Grades.* Chicago: Science Research Associates, 1969.

Frostig, M. *Movement Education: Theory and Practice.* Chicago: Follett, 1970.

Frostig, M., and Horne, D. *The Frostig Program for the Development of Visual Perception: Teacher's Guide.* Chicago: Follett, 1964.

Glaser, R. "Instructional Technology and the Measurement of Learning Outcomes." *American Psychologist,* 1963, *18,* 519-521.

Hall, R. "Responsive Teaching: Focus on Measurement and Research in the Classroom and the Home." In E. Meyen, G. Vergason, and R. Whelan (Eds.), *Strategies for Teaching Exceptional Children.* Denver: Love, 1972.

Hambleton, R., and others. "Criterion-Referenced Testing and Measurement: A Review of Technical Issues and Developments." *Review of Educational Research,* 1978, *48* (1), 1-48.

Hammill, D., and Larsen, S. "The Effectiveness of Psycholinguistic Training." *Exceptional Children,* 1974, *41,* 5-14.

Hammill, D., and Larsen, S. "The Effectiveness of Psycholinguistic Training: A Reaffirmation of Position." *Exceptional Children,* 1978, *44,* 402-417.

Haring, N., and Phillips, E. *Educating Emotionally Disturbed Children.* New York: McGraw-Hill, 1962.

Hilliard, L. *Mental Deficiency.* Boston: Little, Brown, 1965.

Jacobs, J. "A Follow-Up Evaluation of the Frostig Visual-Perceptual Training Program." *Educational Leadership Research Supplement,* 1967, *4,* 8-18.

Jacobs, J., Wirthlin, L., and Miller, C. "A Follow-Up Evaluation of the Frostig Visual-

Perceptual Training Program." *Educational Leadership Research Supplement,* 1968, *4,* 169-175.

Johnson, D., and Myklebust, H. *Learning Disabilities: Educational Principles and Practices.* New York: Grune and Stratton, 1967.

Kephart, N. *The Slow Learner in the Classroom.* Columbus: Merrill, 1960.

Kephart, N. "Perceptual-Motor Aspects of Learning Disabilities." *Exceptional Children,* 1964, *31,* 201-206.

Kirk, S., McCarthy, J., and Kirk, W. *Examiner's Manual, Illinois Test of Psycholinguistic Abilities.* Urbana: University of Illinois Press, 1968.

Kunzelman, H. *Precision Teaching: An Initial Training Sequence.* Seattle: Special Child, 1970.

Lovitt, T. "Self-Management Projects with Children with Behavioral Disabilities." *Journal of Learning Disabilities,* 1973, *6,* 138-147.

Lovitt, T. "Applied Behavior Analysis and Learning Disabilities. Part 1: Characteristics of ABA, General Recommendations and Methodological Limitations." *Journal of Learning Disabilities,* 1975, *8,* 432-443.

Lund, K., Foster, G., and Perez, F. "The Effectiveness of Psycholinguistic Training: A Reevaluation." *Exceptional Children,* 1978, *44,* 310-321.

Mann, L. "Perceptual Training Revisited: The Training of Nothing at All." *Rehabilitation Literature,* 1971, *32,* 322-335.

Peters, L. *Prescriptive Teaching.* New York: McGraw-Hill, 1965.

Popham, W., and Husek, T. "Implications of Criterion-Referenced Measurement." *Journal of Educational Measurement,* 1969, *6,* 1-9.

Quay, H. "Special Education: Assumptions, Techniques, and Evaluative Criteria." *Exceptional Children,* 1973, *40,* 165-170.

Salvia, J., and Ysseldyke, J. *Assessment in Special and Remedial Education.* Boston: Houghton Mifflin, 1978.

Smith, D. *A Technology of Reading and Writing.* Vol. 1: *Learning to Read and Write, a Task Analysis.* New York: Academic Press, 1976a.

Smith, D. *A Technology of Reading and Writing.* Vol. 3: *The Adaptive Classroom.* New York: Academic Press, 1976b.

Smith, D. *A Technology of Reading and Writing.* Vol. 4: *Preparing Instructional Tasks.* New York: Academic Press, 1976c.

Smith, J., Smith, D., and Brink, J. *A Technology of Reading and Writing.* Vol. 2: *Criterion-Referenced Tests for Reading and Writing.* New York: Academic Press, 1976.

Smith, P., and Marx, R. "Some Cautions on the Use of the Frostig Test: A Factor Analytic Study." *Journal of Learning Disabilities,* 1972, *5,* 357-362.

Staats, A. *Complex Human Behavior.* New York: Holt, Rinehart and Winston, 1963.

Stephens, T. *Directive Teaching of Children with Learning and Behavioral Handicaps.* Columbus: Merrill, 1970.

Stephens, T. *The Directive Teaching Instructional Management System: Reading and Arithmetic.* Columbus: Ohio State University Press, 1973.

Stephens, T. *Directive Teaching of Children with Learning and Behavioral Handicaps.* (2nd ed.) Columbus: Merrill, 1976.

Stephens, T. *Teaching Skills to Children with Learning and Behavioral Disorders.* Columbus: Merrill, 1977.

Stephens, T. *Social Skills in the Classroom.* Columbus: Cedars Press, 1979.

Stephens, T., Hartman, A., and Lucas, V. *Teaching Children Basic Skills: A Curriculum Handbook.* Columbus: Merrill, 1978.

Sumption, M., and Luecking, E. *Education of the Gifted.* New York: Ronald Press, 1960.

Thompson, L. *Reading Disability: Developmental Dyslexia.* Springfield, Ill.: Thomas, 1966.

Wiederholt, J., and Hammill, D. "Use of the Frostig-Horne Perception Program in the Urban School." *Psychology in the Schools,* 1971, *8,* 268-274.

Ysseldyke, J., and Salvia, J. "Diagnostic-Prescriptive Teaching: Two Models." *Exceptional Children,* 1974, *41,* 181-186.

60

James R. Barclay

Classroom Motivation

References to the concept of motivation in standard educational research works are notably few. There is only one reference to the concept in the *Second Handbook of Research on Teaching* (Travers, 1973) and a handful of references in the first edition of the same work (Gage, 1963). Motivation as a concept is less referred to in recent years because of the complexity of the concept. It is an older notion that has been refined in many ways by recent research. Today there are at least three descriptions of motivation: (1) *arousal,* defined in terms of drive, habit, and efforts to maintain homeostasis (Hull, 1943); (2) *achievement-motivation,* which relates to internal perception and task-orientation (McClelland and others, 1953; deCharms, 1976); and (3) *expectation,* which constitutes a perceptual bridge between the forces of environmental press and inner needs (Barclay, 1970; Brophy and Good, 1974; Mason, 1972).

The classroom climate has been viewed as a moderating variable that reflects all three motivation concepts. The earliest approaches to the measurement of classroom climate focused basically on *individual differences,* applying some instrument or other to a group of children and then drawing inferences relative to the characteristics of the group. This approach has been typical of studies of self-concept (Wylie, 1961, 1974), sociometric studies (Gronlund, 1959), and studies of achievement and teacher-societal characteristics (Bush, 1954; Coleman, 1966). A second approach has focused on *aggregate compositions,* wherein climates are characterized by environmental "press" circumstances (Astin, 1963; Moos, 1978; Pace and Stern, 1958). A third approach has focused on *temperament-aptitude-treatment* interactions (Barclay, 1972, 1974a, 1974b, 1978; Buss and Plomin, 1975; Cronbach and Snow, 1977; Thomas and Chess, 1977).

Background and Current Status

Early investigations of motivation concentrated on neurological-physical characteristics. Later the perspective of Gestalt psychology brought the focus to the concept of perception. More recently, social learning theory has attempted to bridge both physical and perceptual correlates of motivation (Bandura, 1969) and to relate social perception to expectations (Brophy and Good, 1974).

The concept of classroom climate has undergone similar evolution. First of all, efforts to measure the environment of learning as such have been identified with many early studies of various instruments. In the 1950s and 1960s, the concept of classroom climate was considered nearly isomorphic with other climate variables, such as heat, light, and comfort. A psychological shift occurred when efforts were made to evaluate environments in terms of such personal interaction modes as democratic or authoritarian styles. In the 1970s, researchers became more aware that the classroom is a reflection of a broader ecology and constitutes a microcosm of the outside world. Moreover, the earlier assumption that treatments or interventions can be applied generically to groups of children, like seeds in a field, has given way to a search for ways to enhance individual attributes.

Berlyne (1967) asserts that considerable elaboration has taken place in the concept of arousal, suggesting that, (1) three different modes of arousal are known: autonomic, electrocortical, and behavioral; that (2) the generalized law of effect has been revised to include not only rewards operating through contiguous mechanisms, but also expectancy, incentive, and positive feedback mechanisms; and that (3) the determinants of arousal have both psychophysical and ecological consequences.

The research consequences from the study of arousal have been generalized in social learning theory. Bandura (1972) believes that in the individual modeling occurs which is dependent both on the characteristics of the model and subjective qualities of the viewer, for example, attending, the ability to retain modeled events in memory, the ability to rehearse either actually or vicariously the model characteristics, and, finally, integration of all of these characteristics in what is called the motivational process. Another consequence of the arousal differentiation is related to the voluntary control of imagery (Homme, 1965; Mahoney and Thoresen, 1974; Thoresen and Mahoney, 1974).

The evolution of the concept of achievement motivation has many more threads. The notion of applying the more philosophical Gestaltist ideas to human social behavior must be attributed to Lewin (1935). Lewin took philosophical notions and translated them into a language of physics, utilizing concepts of valence, barrier, and force in a new way. Drawing around himself a group of students and colleagues that included, among others, Jerome Bruner, Fritz Heider, Sigmund Koch, Jack Kounin, Ronald Lippitt, Boyd McCandless, Alfred Marrow, Gardner Murphy, Lois Barclay Murphy, Robert Sears, and

E. C. Tolman, he stimulated a vast interest in charting the relationship of motivation to dynamic influences in the environment. Certainly, Lewin's work and thought are reflected in Murray's (1938) definition of psychological needs and in Maslow's (1954) hierarchy of needs.

Heckhausen (1968), in summarizing research on achievement motivation, emphasizes the important constituent of self-determined behavior. The concept strongly advocated by this approach is that internal motivation is not a by-product of environmental manipulation alone but, rather, the result of a complex interaction between needs of the organism and demands of the environment. Thus, Heckhausen believes that the individual's fear of failure is a crucial factor in the development of internal motivation. This notion is expanded more recently in the work of McClelland and Alschuler (1971) and the intrinsic-extrinsic system of classroom control described by deCharms (1976). Heckhausen concludes that certain parental styles of behavior (especially their encouragement of early independence and their warm emotional reinforcement of accomplishment) tend to promote high achievement motivation in their sons. This finding is consistent with what Baumrind (1971) found relative to parenting styles and the social responsibility of children in schools. She found that the authoritative family structure, rather than the laissez-faire or the authoritarian one, more positively promoted social responsibility in school-age children.

Ausubel (1963) suggested that motivation was related to meaning. Meaning was derived from good teaching order and presentation. The reception of this structure, particularly if considered meaningful by the learner, helped to build intrinsic motivation.

With the expansion of the idea of arousal to include perceptual and situational variables, it has become evident that any real consideration of the concept must take into account both physiological and social determinants; the two interact. For some individuals, motivation is most often extrinsically triggered by environmental pressure of shaping. For others, internal needs shape the very structure of perception and often ignore external consequences.

Though research continues in areas related to arousal and achievement motivation, recent findings have emphasized the construct of expectation. Rosenthal and Jacobson (1966, 1968) built a case for the role of expectations in the classroom by suggesting to some teachers that a portion of their children could be typified as "late bloomers." They then found impressive differences in actual test scores later on. Despite a number of methodological flaws in the 1966 study, it is still considered valid (Snow, 1969).

Brophy and Good (1974), in an extensive review of the concept of expectation and studies related to it, indicate that expectations often serve as "self-fulfilling prophecies." This is particularly so where labels are affixed to individuals and a pattern of behavior is associated with that label. According to Brophy and Good, known sources of expectations are related to socioeconomic status, race, sex, student personality, physical attractiveness, seating arrangements, and achievement-intelligence characteristics, including writing and speech patterns. Though these observations are related specifically to teachers, there is little doubt that they also apply to other people.

The above factors act as a series of screens that professionals use to appraise social behavior. Low socioeconomic status is associated with low intelligence and social skills (Coleman, 1966). Girls are more often favored by teachers than boys (Brophy and Good, 1974). Social popularity and leadership appear to be related to all of the aforementioned factors plus physical attractiveness (Barclay, 1977; Kehle, 1972). Possession of these attributes together with task-order achievement is often associated with motivation. In point of fact, this inferred construct is often the by-product of a complex interaction (deCharms, 1976).

Focus on the measurement of environments has also evolved through the research from general to specific goals. Early work was done by Pace and Stern (1958). Later, Holland (1958, 1959, 1966) expanded the concept of environmental "press" to specific personality types: (1) Realistic, (2) Intellectual, (3) Social, (4) Conventional, (5) Enterprising, and (6) Artistic.

Holland has been interested primarily in the collegiate environment. Barclay, however, applied Holland's theory to the elementary and secondary school environment, with similar results. In one study, Barclay (1967a) developed an elementary school version of Holland's scales and used them along with sociometric indices and teacher ratings to measure the nature of the elementary classroom "press." He later utilized Holland's basic theory in the construction of an inventory to measure the classroom climate, the Barclay Classroom Climate Inventory (Barclay, 1977). In another study, Barclay (1967b) used an array of achievement and psychological variables to measure teachers' expectations of secondary school students. Results indicated that teachers in certain departments (for example, foreign language and science) had definite expectations about effective student behavior. His findings confirmed the existence of Holland-type dimensions within the high school setting (1967b) and definite tendencies for students to prefer certain types of skills, associated with paternal occupations, even in the elementary school (1967a).

More complete applications of the aggregate approach to the measurement of environmental press have been demonstrated by Astin (1963), Walberg (1974), and Moos (1978). All three of these efforts represent long-standing research approaches to the measurement of environments through the use of a series of measures that are aggregated and that result in new measurement distributions based on classroom units or similar entities. Astin's work was applied to the collegiate environment, while Walberg and Moos have concentrated on the high school environment.

Astin (1963) devised an environmental assessment technique which he applied both to students entering colleges and universities and to collegiate faculties. Six major characteristics of entering freshman classes were identified: (1) Intellectualism, (2) Estheticism, (3) Status, (4) Leadership, (5) Pragmatism, and (6) Masculinity. Astin obtained data on entering freshmen at 1,015 colleges and universities to produce standard scores for each institution on the six freshman input factors plus some other institutional data. These results, expressed as T scores, made it possible to compare more than 80 percent of all the colleges and universities in the United States. It was apparent that universities and colleges could be described in terms of Astin's dimensions. Thus, one institution might be very high on Intellectualism and another one high on Pragmatism. In addition, departments and specific colleges within universities could also be described in terms of differentials in environmental press. Astin's work also had value in the sense that an individual could be matched to schools and environments that were congruent with his or her aptitudes and interests.

In studies with high school physics students, Walberg and Algren (1970) and Anderson (1970) attempted to relate personality and cognitive factors in teachers and students to outcomes in learning. In an extension of similar concepts, Spuck (1974) and McIsaac (1974) applied computer technology and graphics to characteristics of populations.

Moos (1978) and his colleagues have attempted to develop a profile of classroom climates. Utilizing a Classroom Environment Scale that measures the social perceptions of students and teachers, Moos applied a cluster analysis technique to 382 junior high and senior high school classrooms. He found that control-oriented classrooms differed from innovative ones on the following dimensions: involvement, affiliation, teacher support, task orientation, competition, order and organization, rule clarity, teacher control, and innovation.

Astin, Walberg, and Moos, then, have attempted to identify student characteristics from self-report data (and in some instances with teacher or environmental inputs), to subject those inputs to a variety of statistical analyses, and to create a typology that char- acterizes classroom climates and environmental presses. These studies are typified by sophisticated methodology and norms based on classroom or collegiate units rather than on individuals.

In the foregoing research trends, there is a noticeable absence of climate studies in the elementary school area. The most systematic effort to develop a measurement of classroom environments on the elementary level has been made by Barclay over a twenty- year period. (An account of this research and reviews of approximately fifty studies relat- ing to the development of this system is contained in Barclay's *Manual of the Barclay Classroom Climate Inventory,* 1977.) Beginning with measures of teacher expectations and the use of sociometrics to determine a psychological support system for individuals, Barclay has extended his system to a measure of individual differences within the class- room setting—a typology based on multitrait, multisource inputs (self-report, teacher judgments, and peer ratings)—and a prevention method for early identification of children who indicate a poor support system or a high degree of risk in self-control, verbal produc- tion, cognitive motivation, and other selected areas (Barclay, 1977). Barclay's system for analyzing individual differences in the classroom setting is machine scanned and presented via a computerized report that summarizes the interest patterns of the individual child, the extent of peer support, and teacher expectations and then presents prescriptions directly to teachers relative to children who appear to have personal and social problems in the environmental context.

Barclay's system is an interactive one that identifies temperament-aptitude clus- ters derived both from personal and environmental characteristics. In a metatheory analy- sis of three different longitudinal studies, he found evidence that different classroom arrangements and learning methods affected children of different temperaments in unique ways. Thus, some children benefited from a behavioral approach, and a very few showed positive gains from an "open classroom," but most showed consistent benefits from tradi- tional structured learning (Barclay, 1978). He concludes, on the basis of the research, that learning environments must be matched to aptitudes of children.

In summary, contemporary developments in classroom motivation include basic research into aspects of motivation, such as arousal and social modeling, further extension of the achievement motivation research into expectations, and development of ap- proaches to the measurement of educational climates. Though continued efforts are still made to administer a test or tests to groups of students and then to generalize about environments, more appropriate and statistically sound methods have been developed in the aggregate approach and the more recent temperament-aptitude-treatment approach to the measurement of environments.

Critical Discussion

General Areas of Concern

Perhaps the greatest problem with research on classroom motivation is the failure to recognize the complexity of motivational phenomena. Though much early research was accomplished through the application of a specific test to a specific group, the con- clusions that could be drawn from these "fishing expeditions" were limited. Much of self- concept research is characterized by such efforts. A perusal of any issue of *Psychological Abstracts* will provide ample evidence of the repetitious and unproductive nature of such research. Moreover, many times individual researchers will generalize to the nature of classroom climates on the basis of one or two such tests, failing to recognize the need for aggregated units as a basis of measurement. Typically, some achievement, personality, intelligence, or interest test is given; but the interrelationships of such measures and their covert as well as manifest meaning is often overlooked. Such variables as socioeconomic class, race, previous reinforcement, and achievement levels are often omitted or not understood.

If there is one fact that emerges from the mass of research that has been done relative to motivation and classroom climates, it is the reality of individual differences. There are no "cookbook" recipes for developing motivation in groups. One of the major concerns for clinical practice is to shift from a crisis orientation to a preventive stance. Where clinicians deal with the classroom situation, computerized assessment techniques can provide them with an indication of the peer-teacher support system that exists, the suspected problems that are emerging, and a set of clues on which to base their inquiries, observations, and testing. Since teacher expectations and peer support provide a major input into the environmental contingencies that support both positive and negative behavior, mental health consultants and clinicians can utilize results from classroom analysis as a base for obtaining much information about the actual conditions of classroom life (Barclay, 1977).

Although aggregate profile analysis of classroom units may provide some overall information relative to descriptive characteristics, individual analysis also is important in such a setting. Individual analysis can enable one to generate strategies of intervention that may be useful to certain segments of the classroom group—for instance, the slow achiever who needs repeated drilling or the deviant but brilliant child who needs more stimulation and self-selection of activities for learning.

In short, clinical skills are needed in addition to group data. Clinical skills can ferret out the actual criteria of performance that teachers exhibit in their set of expectations. Clinical skills, combined with individual-group assessment, can provide some alternative to proposals that will tend to group all children in similar treatments.

Comparative Philosophies and Theories

Though, initially, theories regarding arousal and cognitive motivation stemmed from behavioral and Gestalt approaches, respectively, a review of the trends in research relative to both camps indicates that behavioral approaches are moving toward a cognitive recognition of neuropsychological processes and that Gestalt approaches have been influenced by the social learning model. The two approaches still tend to emphasize the programming effects of the environment (behaviorism) or the determining nature of perception (Gestalt), but today, more than ever, there is a recognition of the interactive effect of both environment and constitutional characteristics.

Elaboration on Critical Points

The interactive nature of temperament-aptitude clusters with treatment outcomes is the paramount issue in current research. The aptitude-treatment interaction has had great promise and poor fulfillment (Cronbach and Snow, 1977) because aptitude has been defined inadequately (most often as a score on an achievement test, rather than a composite configuration of personality-temperament characteristics) and because treatments have also been defined loosely. Rigorous pursuit of multitrait, multisource instrumentations, utilizing aptitude-treatment interactions, should provide a real breakthrough in matching student characteristics to optimum learning situations. Use of this approach may provide another avenue for the development of a metatheory about human behavior similar to the results recently obtained for psychotherapy by Smith and Glass (1977).

Personal Views and Recommendations

School psychology should focus primarily on the prevention of problem behaviors in the schools. Clinical psychologists more often enter the picture after the problem in an individual case has reached crisis status. Although most mental health professionals agree that prevention is important, and that somehow the ecology of the school and the community are involved, there will be little concrete dedication to the psychology of prevention until a methodology and technology of early needs assessment is developed. Such a technology must focus on the understanding of individual differences in a group setting. It is important for us to identify early those children who exhibit a high-risk status and who have a poor psychological support system at home or in the school. Obviously, we cannot be absolutely sure about suspected problems, and we do run the risk of false positives in our identification instruments. But intervention of a positive nature, such as increasing teacher attention and psychological support, can do little harm to any child. Failure to recognize such needed support can result in very negative consequences.

An ecological perspective also requires that certain objectives be emphasized in training programs: (1) a recognition of the consultative nature of the psychologist in the school (the psychologist is not the change agent; parents, peers, and teachers are); (2) a recognition of the potential benefit of such intervention, with the cost-effectiveness of prevention programs and personnel balanced against years of later unproductive dependence for children not reached by such interventions; (3) a recognition of a number of allied strategies for human interventions, including feedback mechanisms, social reinforcement, and environmental change; and (4) a method for evaluating the consequences of needs assessment, consultation, strategy, intervention, and outcomes. Clinical skills remain crucial ones, but the existing information base and knowledge of ecological factors in interaction are such that these skills can be vastly enhanced through the use of appropriate screening procedures.

Application to Particular Variables

The earlier the appraisal or diagnosis of poor task-oriented behavior, the better. Thus, age is crucial to the early recognition and preventive approach to motivation deficits. Again, sex differences are known. The reference here is specifically to the fact that girls and boys are socialized in different ways. Teachers, by and large, expect more of boys and evaluate them more critically. Moreover, in typical classroom settings, race, socioeconomic background, and intelligence are all factors that alter perceptibly the pattern of expectations that teachers have for performance. Achievement itself acts as a mighty reinforcer for children, since success in tasks undertaken appears to be a hefty component in self-esteem and in a variety of personal and social competencies.

Classroom motivation is the by-product of many factors that combine to provide an index of task-oriented behavior. In many critical situations, where gross physical anomalies, mental retardation, or organic problems are present in children, computerized assessments of these children provide few surprises, but with the vast majority of children—who fall within the standard deviation of ability, intelligence, and personality characteristics—classroom climate inventories provide information about psychological support systems, suspected or actual problem areas, and interest patterns that are virtually inaccessible to clinicians in any other way. Where computerized systems have been able to sort out the factors that influence human behavior, both in reference to the specificity of the group situation itself and in reference to normative characteristics of the population, they provide a vast treasury of information helpful to both preventive and crisis intervention.

References

Anderson, G. J. "Effects of Classroom Social Climate on Individual Learning." Paper presented at AERA national meeting, Minneapolis, 1970.

Astin, A. *Who Goes Where to College?* Chicago: Science Research Associates, 1963.

Ausubel, D. P. *The Psychology of Meaningful Verbal Learning.* New York: Grune and Stratton, 1963.

Bandura, A. *Principles of Behavior Modification.* New York: Holt, Rinehart and Winston, 1969.

Bandura, A. "Modeling Theory: Some Traditions, Trends, and Disputes." In R. D. Park (Ed.), *Recent Trends in Social Learning Theory.* New York: Academic Press, 1972.

Barclay, J. R. "Effecting Behavior Change in the Elementary Classroom: An Exploratory Study." *Journal of Counseling Psychology,* 1967a, *14,* 240-247.

Barclay, J. R. "Approach to the Measurement of Teacher "Press" in the Secondary Curriculum." *Journal of Counseling Psychology,* 1967b, *14,* 550-567.

Barclay, J. R. "Expectancy and Social Interaction in Classroom Learning." Paper presented at APA symposium "What Experimental Psychology has to Offer—Donor Learning Theory and Principles: Recipient, the Classroom," APA national convention, Miami, 1970.

Barclay, J. R. *A Research Manual for the Barclay Classroom Climate Inventory.* Lexington, Ky.: Educational Skills Development, 1972.

Barclay, J. R. "System-Wide Analysis of Social Interaction and Affective Problems in Schools." In P. O. Davidson, F. W. Clark, and L. A. Hamerlynck (Eds.), *Evaluation of Behavioral Programs in Community, Residential, and School Settings.* Champaign, Ill.: Research Press, 1974a.

Barclay, J. R. "Needs Assessment in the Elementary School." In H. J. Walberg (Ed.), *Evaluation of Educational Performance: A Sourcebook of Methods, Instruments and Examples.* Berkeley, Calif.: McCutchan, 1974b.

Barclay, J. R. *Appraising Individual Differences in the Classroom: A Manual of the Barclay Classroom Climate Inventory.* (4th ed.) Lexington, Ky.: Educational Skills Development, 1977.

Barclay, J. R. "Temperament Clusters and Individual Differences in the Elementary Classroom." Paper presented at symposium "Temperament Treatment Interaction: A New Key to the Change Process," at AERA national meeting, Toronto, 1978.

Baumrind, D. "Current Patterns of Parental Authority." *Developmental Psychology,* 1971, *4* (1).

Bennett, N. *Teaching Styles and Pupil Progress.* London: Open Books, 1976.

Berlyne, D. E. "Arousal and Reinforcement." In D. Levine (Ed.), *Nebraska Symposium on Motivation.* Lincoln: University of Nebraska Press, 1967.

Brophy, J. E., and Good, T. L. *Teacher-Student Relationships: Causes and Consequences.* New York: Holt, Rinehart and Winston, 1974.

Bush, R. N. *The Teacher-Pupil Relationship.* Englewood Cliffs, N.J.: Prentice-Hall, 1954.

Buss, A. H. "The Emerging Field of the Sociology of Psychological Knowledge." *American Psychologist,* 1975, *30* (10), 988-1002.

Buss, A. H., and Plomin, R. *A Temperament Theory of Personality Development.* New York: Wiley, 1975.

Coleman, J. S. *Equality of Educational Opportunity.* Washington, D.C.: U.S. Dept. of Health, Education, and Welfare, U.S. Office of Education, 1966.

Cronbach, L. J., and Snow, R. E. *Aptitude and Instructional Methods.* New York: Wiley, 1977.

deCharms, R. *Enhancing Motivation.* New York: Wiley, 1976.

Gage, N. L. (Ed.). *Handbook of Research on Teaching.* Chicago: Rand McNally, 1963.

Gronlund, N. B. *Sociometry in the Classroom.* New York: Harper & Row, 1959.

Heckhausen, H. "Achievement Motive Research: Current Problems and Some Contributions Towards a General Theory of Motivation." In W. J. Arnold (Ed.), *Nebraska Symposium on Motivation.* Lincoln; University of Nebraska Press, 1968.

Holland, J. L. "A Personality Inventory Employing Occupational Titles." *Journal of Applied Psychology,* 1958, *42,* 336-342.

Holland, J. L. "A Theory of Vocational Choice." *Journal of Counseling Psychology,* 1959, *6* (1), 35-44.

Holland, J. L. *The Psychology of Vocational Choice.* Lexington, Mass.: Ginn, 1966.

Homme, L. "Control of Coverants, the Operants of the Mind." *Psychological Record,* 1965, *15,* 501-511.

Hull, C. L. *Principles of Behavior.* New York: Appleton-Century-Crofts, 1943.

Kehle, T. J. "Effect of the Student's Physical Attractiveness, Sex, Race, Intelligence, and Socioeconomic Status on Teachers' Expectations for the Student's Personality and Academic Performance." Unpublished doctoral dissertation, University of Kentucky, 1972.

Lewin, K. *A Dynamic Theory of Personality: Selected Papers of Kurt Lewin.* New York: McGraw-Hill, 1935.

McClelland, D. C., and Alschuler, A. S. *Final Report of Achievement Motivation Development Project.* Washington, D.C.: U.S. Office of Education, Bureau of Research, 1971.

McClelland, D. C., and others. *The Achievement Motive.* New York: Appleton-Century-Crofts, 1953.

McIsaac, D. N. "Trend Surface Analysis." In H. J. Walberg (Ed.), *Evaluating Educational Performance.* Berkeley, Calif.: McCutchan, 1974.

Mahoney, M. J., and Thoresen, C. E. *Self-Control: Power to the Person.* Monterey, Calif.: Brooks/Cole, 1974.

Maslow, A. H. *Motivation and Personality.* New York: Harper & Row, 1954.

Mason, E. "Teacher Expectancy: What Does It Mean?" In G. R. Gredler (Ed.), *Ethical and Legal Problems of School Psychology.* Harrisburg, Pa.: State Department of Education, 1972.

Moos, R. H. "A Typology of Junior High and High School Classrooms." *American Educational Research Journal,* 1978, *15* (1), 53-68.

Murray, H. A. *Explorations in Personality.* New York: Oxford University Press, 1938.

Pace, C. R., and Stern, G. G. "An Approach to the Measurement of Psychological Characteristics of College Environments." *Journal of Educational Psychology, 49,* 1958, 269-277.

Rosenthal, R., and Jacobson, L. "Teacher Expectancies: Determinants of Pupils' I.Q. Gains." *Psychological Reports,* 1966, *19,* 115-118.

Rosenthal, R., and Jacobson, L. *Pygmalion in the Classroom: Teacher Expectation and Pupils' Intellectual Development.* New York: Holt, Rinehart and Winston, 1968.

Smith, M. L., and Glass, G. V. "Meta-analysis of Psychotherapy Outcome Studies." *American Psychologist,* 1977, *32* (9), 752-760.

Snow, R. E. "Unfinished Pygmalion." *Contemporary Psychology,* 1969, *14* (4), 197-199.

Spuck, D. W. "Geocode Analysis." In H. J. Walberg (Ed.), *Evaluating Educational Performance.* Berkeley, Calif.: McCutchan, 1974.

Thomas, A., and Chess, S. *Temperament and Development.* New York: Brunner/Mazel, 1977.

Thoresen, C. E., and Mahoney, M. J. *Behavioral Self-Control.* New York: Holt, Rinehart and Winston, 1974.

Travers, R. M. W. (Ed.). *Second Handbook of Research on Teaching.* Chicago: Rand McNally, 1973.

Walberg, H. J. (Ed.). *Evaluating Educational Performance.* Berkeley, Calif.: McCutchan, 1974.

Walberg, H. J., and Algren, A. "Predictors of the Social Environment of Learning." *American Educational Research Journal,* 1970, *7* (2), 153-165.

Walberg, H. J., and Anderson, G. J. "Classroom Climate and Individual Learning." *Journal of Educational Psychology,* 1968, *59,* 414-419.

Wylie, R. C. *The Self-Concept.* Lincoln: University of Nebraska Press, 1961.

Wylie, R. C. *The Self-Concept: A Review of Methodological Considerations and Measuring Instruments.* Lincoln: University of Nebraska Press, 1974.

61

David A. Sabatino

Special Education Needs

Special education differs from the other curricular divisions in education by the fact that it is population sensitive, not subject matter sensitive. All the other educations (higher education, regular education, or vocational education) divide themselves into programmatic aggregates or curricular substructures. Special education is defined by the characteristics associated with subpopulations of persons in the preschool to early adult age range (3 to 21 years, generally) who have identified handicapping conditions. Therefore, the identifiable handicapping conditions not only earmark the specific type of special education but also define the type of reimbursement to be provided—the educational assumption being that a handicapping condition requires protective educational settings (smaller class size, resource room assistance, supportive and extraordinary services, adaptive teaching techniques, and adopted instructional materials), all of which cost more money than basic educational programs. Since legislative bodies reimburse school districts or states for the number and/or type of handicapped students served in special education programs, local educational agencies must comply with state and federal regulations of identifying and placing handicapped children into appropriate categories.

The common nine special education handicapping classifications designated by the Bureau of Education for the Handicapped are shown in Table 1, with the served (projected) and unserved status in number estimates and percents. The importance in studying the estimated percentage of served and unserved for each group of handicapped is that an interesting parallel exists between the amount of service a specific handicapped group is receiving and the agreement on assessment techniques and definition used to describe that specified population of handicapped children. The higher the agreement on operationalizing a definition diagnostically, the greater the availability of services.

Table 1. Estimated Number of Handicapped Children Served and Unserved
By Type of Handicap

	1975-76 Served (Projected)	1975-76 Unserved	Total Served and Unserved	Percent Served	Percent Unserved
Speech Impaired	2,020,000	273,000	2,293,000	88	12
Mentally Retarded	1,350,000	157,000	1,507,000	90	10
Learning Disabilities	260,000	1,706,000	1,966,000	13	87
Emotionally Disturbed	255,000	1,055,000	1,310,000	19	81
Crippled and Other Health Impaired	255,000	73,000	328,000	78	22
Deaf	45,000	4,000	49,000	92	8
Hard of Hearing	66,000	262,000	328,000	20	80
Visually Handicapped	43,000	23,000	66,000	65	35
Deaf-Blind and Other	(not readable)		40,000	40	60

Source: Federal Register, 1977.

Obviously, when speech production interferes in communication, when a person's function on an operationally defined intelligence test places his performance in the mentally retarded range, or where obvious sensory-physical impairments (such as deafness, blindness, or orthopedic disabilities) occur, a high degree of diagnostic stability results. Conversely, when sixty definitions exist for learning disabilities (Hammill, 1971), none of which have been operationalized nationwide, and when the social relativity of human adjustment must be played against the backdrop of a given culture or subculture in a given space of time (as in behavioral disorders), then diagnostic classification fails to achieve agreement in definition or by practice. An example is persons who are hard of hearing. Unlike their deaf counterparts, the obviousness of their disability is not evident. The degree of hearing loss can easily be defined in decibels at specified frequencies, but the relationship of hearing loss and individual performance in school varies for each person so affected.

The classification of handicapped persons probably had its beginning in the Hippocratic search for organization, which has greatly influenced all medical and, therefore, historically medically dependent diagnostic systems, such as special education. Traditionally, diagnosis leading to classification required that four questions be answered:

1. Does the person *differ from that group known as normal* in some trait, behavior, or characteristic?

2. What is the *degree of difference*?

3. What are *the common symtomologies, etiologies, or characteristics* of the person in comparison to those in classified groups?

4. Can the *origin of the difference* be traced to its ultimate beginning?

The responses to these questions have resulted in a major misunderstanding between what is meant by diagnosis, classification, and labeling. Currently, the so-called special education classification structures ignore etiology and pathology; they generalize about a particular symptomology.

Two faults have resulted from developing and using special education classifications based on sorting out the most common characteristics. First, any given individual may have characteristics that can be associated with one diagnostic classification but are actually attributes of quite a different etiology. For example, a child who fails to focus attention on and understand speech sounds may be classified as hearing impaired; however, the inability to receive meaningful speech sounds may also result from brain damage or several other causative factors. The second problem is that handicapped children are generally placed into special education structures on the basis of a medical, behavioral, or measurement diagnostic classification, and not on the basis of their instructional programmatic needs. To assume that all persons with common symptoms possess a similar educational problem is erroneous. Test results from commonly administered intelligence measures are frequently used to classify children as mentally retarded. Yet, it is highly inconceivable that any two students classified as educably mentally retarded with the same IQ on the same test would, in fact, learn in a similar manner. IQ scores are not directly translatable into educational objectives for children *labeled* under similar classifications. To alleviate somewhat the diagnostic-labeling-classification dilemma, the Bureau for the Education of the Handicapped (Federal Register, 1977) has established educationally related classifications for eight categories of handicapping conditions.

Glossary of Educational Classifications

- *Mental Retardation.* The general cognitive capacity of these individuals is so limited that they cannot meet the educational demands of the regular classroom.
- *Emotional Disturbance.* The individual possesses severe and frequent maladaptive behavior which seriously reduces attention level and learning. For educational purposes, these children are grouped according to the following degrees of severity and/or frequency of maladaptive behavior—mild, moderate, and severe.
- *Hearing Impairment.* A deviation in hearing sufficient to impair normal communication.
    Hard of hearing. A loss of hearing that is educationally significant, but residual hearing is sufficient to interpret language with or without a hearing aid.
    Deaf. The sense of hearing, with or without a hearing aid, is not sufficient to interpret language.
- *Visual Impairment*
    Low vision. The individual's vision is limited, but sufficient residual vision is available that it can be used as a primary avenue of learning. Print can be used as the primary mode of reading with the aid of special facilities, materials, and/or media. (Included are legally blind children who are able to read large type.)
    Blind. The individual's vision is so defective that sight cannot be used as a primary avenue of learning and print cannot be used as the primary mode of reading. (Excluded from this group are legally blind children who are able to read large type.)
- *Physical Handicap.* In this condition, neuromuscular disabilities, characterized by disturbances of the voluntary motor functions and accompanied by weakened physical condition, reduce [the individual's] activity and efficiency in school work or require special educational management. The condition usually results from some insult to the central nervous system.
- *Communication Disorder.* Communication-disordered individuals possess speech devia-

tions which draw unfavorable attention as a result of the production of unpleasant and/ or unintelligible speech or speech that is inappropriate to age.
• *Learning Disabilities.* [Specific learning disabilities may be considered] disorders in one or more of the so-called "basic psychological processes" involved in understanding or in using spoken or written language. These may appear as disorders of listening, thinking, talking, reading, writing, spelling, or arithmetic. They include conditions which have been referred to as perceptual handicaps, brain injury, minimal brain dysfunction, dyslexia, developmental aphasia, etc. They do not include learning problems which are due primarily to visual, hearing, sensory problems, physical (motor) handicaps, mental retardation, emotional disturbance, or environmental disadvantage.
• *Multiple Handicaps.* The multiply handicapped possess more than one disabling condition, each of which requires a special educational program.

Diagnostic classification in special education should simply provide some basic information by which an educational program can be structured. An educational program for the handicapped should have an instructional objective and an appropriate environment in which to deliver the necessary instruction. Unfortunately, however, diagnostic classification resulting from formal tests is often not directly linked to educational interventions. Instead, in many instances "diagnosis has become synonymous with testing" (Engel, 1969, p. 231). As a result, psychoeducational diagnostic tests are studied for their own sake, and the tests themselves often determine *what* is being sought.

Background and Current Status

In the early nineteenth century a young doctor, Jean-Marc Gaspard Itard, began work with a preadolescent boy who had roamed the forests around Aveyron in southern France. The "wild boy," as he was known, had sought human interaction, finally accepting residence with a local farm family. Itard soon undertook the boy's training in the National Institute for Deaf-Mutes, even though others contended that the boy had been left in the wild because he was an idiot and that his case was hopeless. The importance of the environment became apparent as the boy's behavior changed. Itard's student, Edouard Seguin, later used similar teaching methods to prove at the Hospital for Incurables that even the most desperate cases can be changed by education. Simultaneously, in 1838 J. E. D. Esquirol, a leading psychiatrist, defined idiocy and imbecility not as chronic diseases, which they had generally been considered, but as conditions resulting from underdeveloped "intellectual faculties." This work was supported by French neurologist Jean Charcot, who developed sophisticated examination techniques and a systematic classification of central nervous system pathology. The combined work of these French pioneers resulted in diagnostic procedures, classification systems, and treatment methods, based largely on sensory (physiological) stimulation, to "cure" the mentally retarded. Special education had received its beginning, for at the Hospital for Incurables George Sumner and Maria Montessori witnessed Itard's techniques for judging the degree of educability in a population of low-functioning children and youth. The need for ascertaining the "type" and "amount" of "special education" had been recognized.

Among the nineteenth-century scholars concerned with measuring interpersonal trait differences was an Englishman who would alter the course of human measurement. Francis Galton used anthropometric measures—among them height, weight, and visual and hearing acuity—to classify individuals. By 1889 the famed German psychologist Emil Kraepelin had developed complex measures of perceptual-motor function. The appeal and longevity of his work can be appreciated when one realizes that the geometric designs originally drawn by Wertheimer (1923) were redeveloped by Bender (1938) as the Visual Motor Gestalt Test, one of the most frequently administered psychological tests with children suspected of educational handicaps.

At the turn of the twentieth century, the French Minister of Public Instruction was still wrestling with an age-old problem: how to consistently identify the handicapped. Having agreed on the terminology to be used (idiot, the lowest level; imbecile, the intermediate level; and moron, or mildly mentally retarded), a psychologist, Alfred Binet, and a physician, Theophile Simon, were commissioned to develop a consistent means of classifying children. Binet and Simon produced, through a standardized procedure of observation, a psychological classification of quantifiable differences in children's intellectual facilities (traits). By 1905 Binet and Simon had developed twenty-nine such tests designed to measure specific traits. By 1908 they had developed a classification of tests beginning at age 3 and continuing through age 13. Thus, the work preceding 1905 established human intelligence as a comprehensive integration of several traits, including memory, attention, comprehension, muscular coordination, relations, judgment, initiative, and ability to adapt. Further, the criteria for measurement of these traits were standardized at various chronological age levels.

Henry Goddard, director of research at the Vineland Training School, uncovered the Binet tests in 1908 and subsequently translated and developed an American standardized version of the 1908 scales (completed in 1910). Using the 1910 scales, he prepared a classification of feeblemindedness for the American Association on Mental Deficiency. Doll (1917) added the term *social adequacy* to Goddard's classification of idiot, imbecile, and moron.

In 1916 Louis Terman, not content with previous advances, released a new version of the original Binet scales, based on his definition of intelligence—which, for the concise Terman, was simply the ability to "think abstractly." This scale, known as the Stanford-Binet, was subsequently revised in 1937 and again in 1960. Almost immediately, the Stanford-Binet showed an ability to produce a high positive relationship with reading comprehension, other academic achievement measures, and general school success. In fact, early special class placements for exceptional children, particularly the mentally retarded, were so dependent on a single criterion (the Binet tests) that they were called "Binet classes."

In the rapid expansion of special classes in the public school, two parallel forces were at work: (1) the work in psychology, which attempted to determine traits and classify people according to their ability to function (one person in comparison to another); and (2) remedial approaches for the education of handicapped students, employing physiological stimulation, controlled socialization experiences, and other functional skills emphasizing preparation for life.

Critical Discussion

General Areas of Concern

Standardized assessment procedures, the mainstream of clinical work with children for nearly one hundred years, are under heavy attack by special educators. The adversaries of the classification systems in special education have advanced several strong arguments:

1. The classification of children into handicapping categories creates labels that activate self-fulfilling prophecies among the adults that work with them, which probably carry over to the child's own self-concept.

2. A categorical label is a lifetime phenomenon, which comes attached to all records, when the implications may be all educational and not related to adult life.

3. A label is the result of a one-time brief observation, which frequently compares one person to others. It may, therefore, be based on a behavioral sample that is irrelevant, unreliable, invalid, or prejudicial.

4. A label rendered by diagnosis, at some point in time, refutes the belief that behavior and performance are influenced by development and change.

5. Most of the diagnostic procedures used to define the classification structures are not educationally related. In short, most formal appraisal instruments do not describe school-type learning, and the score which results does not indicate what treatment should be given, how it should begin, in what setting it should proceed, or what the major objectives of that treatment should be. They are, in fact, not samples of educationally related traits.

6. The major criticism of the diagnostic process, particularly those aspects necessary to classify persons as handicapped, is that formal tests compare a person's performance to a mythical group on an interpersonal basis. Currently, most special educators believe that the emphasis on classification should be reduced and that the focus on intrapersonal comparisons of traits and behaviors should be increased.

Hammill (1971) and Reese (1976) have suggested that formal and informal assessment should occur simultaneously. Haring and Bateman (1977) organized diagnostic schemes into (1) diagnostic-remedial (the use of formal tests) and (2) task-analytic (the functional analysis of behavioral approaches). They carefully differentiated both of these from the diagnostic search for etiologies, and both approaches were deemed useful when used educationally.

One of the major concerns of the modern special educator is to devise a continuous educational plan that will provide an *instructional objective,* which delineates what will be accomplished, and an *instructional strategy,* which delineates how and where it will be accomplished. There is an interdependency between these two aspects. If an instructional objective is too demanding, it is unlikely that a strategy will result; if it is too easy, any strategy may accomplish the goal. A sequence of strategies could fail to address the objective because the wrong instructional method or material is selected; or the strategies could be improperly sequenced, with too large a step between each strategy.

Most authorities in the field (for example, Gorth and Hambleton, 1972) now believe that, in the absence of norm-referenced tests designed to ascertain the specific skills designated in instructional objectives, criterion-referenced measures should be used. Criterion-referenced measures are "deliberately constructed to yield measurements that are directly interpretable in terms of specific performance standards" (Glaser and Nitko, 1971, p. 653). In short, to paraphrase Gorth and Hambleton (1972), continued assessment will determine what the child has learned, what is to be taught, how much is remembered, and what remains to follow the next instructional objective. Continuous monitoring through the use of a criterion-referenced system permits an evaluation of a child's performance against the task. In some combinations, especially with academic achievement, a norm-referenced pretest-posttest structure (instructional objectives) and a criterion-referenced system may be used together.

Comparative Philosophies and Theories

There is general agreement that educational diagnosis should consider three areas of input: the person, the person's ability to form relationships, and the person-learning environment. The information collected in these three areas must be systematically organized around a useful framework; otherwise, three problems will result: (1) the observer will be *viewing only the apparent,* failing to examine less conspicuous behaviors; (2) the observer will not have a consistent basis for observing different people, under varying conditions, or in different relationships; and (3) there will not be a common format for viewing individual behaviors against various classroom environments. Clearly, the same tests or the same observation procedures cannot be administered to every person being described. However, a diagnostic format that systematically identifies and isolates cultural, academic, and nonacademic behaviors will overlook fewer essentials than a haphazard response to a problem. Moreover, such a systematic study of learner characteristics leads to a step-by-step procedure for ascertaining and describing behaviors. In view of this need, a number of prominent special educators have approached this problem.

Dunn (1968, pp. 12-13) includes several step-by-step diagnostic procedures in developing a sound diagnostic procedure: "The first step would be to make a study of the child to find what behaviors he has acquired along the dimension being considered. Next, samples of a sequential program would be designed to move him forward from that point. In presenting the program, the utility of different reinforcers, administered under various conditions, would be investigated. Also, the method by which he can best be taught the material should be determined. Different modalities for reaching the child would also be tried. Thus, since the instructional program itself becomes the diagnostic device, this procedure can be called diagnostic teaching. Failures are program and instructor failures, not pupil failures. . . . This diagnostic procedure is viewed as the best available, since it enables us to assess continuously the problem points of the instructional program against the assets of the child."

Quay (1968) has suggested a conceptual framework (an input, response, and reinforcement model) that permits the assessment of exceptional children on educationally relevant variables. According to Quay, an educationally relevant variable is one that can be manipulated as a learning process in the classroom. As an example of input considerations, he notes that acuity in all senses—visual, hearing, and tactile—might be observed or measured. The response counterpart might be dexterity or the ability to respond accurately and appropriately. The third component, reinforcement, also contains an attentional step which Quay refers to as orientation toward the stimulus. Orientation is itself a reinforcer, but it also helps the child organize future unlearned stimulus inputs by recognizing those aspects which are familiar. Following acuity as an input is perception, which is the ability to differentiate relevant dimensions of a stimulus. Organization is the required response to incoming perceptual information, and storage refers to the ability to retain stimulus data. Effect is the capacity of a reinforcer to actually reinforce; delay of reinforcement and the amount of a reinforcer denote when and how much reinforcement was applied. Ratio is the frequency with which the correct response is reinforced.

Iscoe (1962) has developed a simplified scale for the functional classification of exceptional children. He specifies three domains, each having three functional and/or performance-based considerations within them:

I. Physical Domain
    A. Visibility—the child's appearance.
    B. Locomotion—the ability to move around.
    C. Communication—oral language or other communication skill.
II. Perceived Adjustment Domain
    A. Peer acceptance—how well does child get along with peers.
    B. Family interaction—consistent dynamics of relationships among family members.
    C. Self-esteem—self-concept, feeling toward self.

III. Educational Domain
  A. Motivation—to work at the suggestion of the teacher.
  B. Academic level—actual school performance.
  C. Educational potential—projected school performance based on intelligence tests or other measures.

Elaboration on Critical Points

Public Law 94-142, the Education of All Handicapped Children Act of 1975, requires that an individualized education program (IEP) be prepared as the first step in educating all handicapped children. The importance of an IEP cannot be overemphasized, since it delineates the specific educational objectives and strategies for each handicapped child. It represents the beginning of instructional accountability in special education. The National Association of State Directors of Special Education (1976) has prepared a concise statement explaining the IEP:

> [The IEP is a] written statement describing the educational objectives for and the services to be provided to each handicapped child. Educational objectives and services include both instruction and those related services required to meet the unique needs of the handicapped child and are derived from a careful evaluation of the child and his environment. The elements included in the plan are statements of present educational performance, annual goals, short-term instructional objectives and services to be provided to meet these objectives, conditions under which services will be delivered (where, when, and by whom), and evaluation criteria.

In addition, the plan must proceed on at least two levels. *The total service plan* describes long-term goals and strategies for instructional and related services, and the *individual implementation plan* states short-term objectives and specific strategies for intervention.

Personal Views and Recommendations

The research to date (Ryckman and Wiegerink, 1969; Sabatino, 1968; Sabatino and Hayden, 1970a, 1970b) indicates that at least four major areas must be described in ascertaining the learner characteristics of the handicapped: motor (nonacademic behavior), perceptual (nonacademic behavior), language (directly related to nonacademic and academic behaviors), and academics (academic remediation).

Figure 1 provides a graphic display of Sabatino's (1968) information-processing model. Table 2 provides a description of those behaviors to be ascertained. If such a systematic learner characteristic and instructional material system were to be utilized, each learner characteristic could become a curricular area, and special education would appear more consistent as a teaching content area with the vocational and basic education.

If the major areas identified by Sabatino (1968) are combined with the guidelines for developing an IEP (National Association of State Directors of Special Education, 1976), a comprehensive diagnostic process can be constructed:

1. Educational Functioning
  a. Achievement in subject area
  b. Learning style
  c. Strengths and weaknesses

Figure 1. The Model Used to Describe the Information-Processing Behaviors

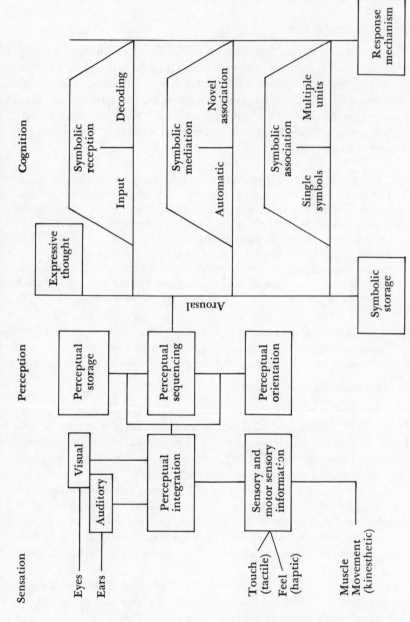

Source: Sabatino, 1968.

Table 2. Descriptor System for Classifying Learner Characteristics

1.0		*Motor*
1.1		Gross
	1.11	Coordination-Balance
	1.12	Strength-Endurance
1.2		Perceptual-Motor
	1.21	Eye-Hand Coordination
	1.22	Directionality
1.3		Body Awareness
2.0		*Perception*
2.1		Visual
	2.11	Discrimination
	2.12	Memory
	2.13	Integration/primary visual input
2.2		Auditory
	2.21	Discrimination
	2.22	Memory
	2.23	Integration/primary auditory input
2.3		Tactile
3.0		*Language*
3.1		Conceptual
	3.11	Concrete
	3.12	Functional
	3.13	Abstract
3.2		Expressive
	3.21	Vocabulary
	3.22	Syntex
3.3		Receptive
4.0		*Academics*
4.1		Reading
	4.11	Letter Recognition
	4.12	Word Attack
	4.121	Phonics
	4.122	Structural Analysis
	4.13	Word Recognition
	4.14	Vocabulary
	4.15	Comprehension
4.2		Spelling
4.3		Writing
	4.31	Manuscript
	4.32	Cursive
4.4		Arithmetic
	4.41	Numeration
	4.42	Computation
	4.43	Measurement

Source: Sabatino, 1968.

2. Social-emotional Functioning
   a. Social/psychological development
      attending/receiving
      responding
      valuing
      organizing
      characterizing

      b. Self-help skills
3. Physical Functioning
      a. Visual
      b. Hearing
      c. Speech
      d. Motor/psychomotor
          gross motor
          fine motor
      e. Medical health
4. Cognitive Functioning
      a. Intelligence
      b. Adaptive behavior
      c. Thinking processes
          knowledge
          comprehension
          application
          analysis
          synthesis
          evaluation
5. Language Functioning
      a. Receptive
      b. Expressive—to what kind of input
      c. Nonverbal
      d. Speech
6. Family
      a. Dominant language
      b. Parent-child interactions
      c. Social service needs
7. Environment
      a. Home
      b. School
      c. Interpersonal
      d. Material

     In summary, those persons who are responsible for the education of handicapped children are now mandated to do so under the law (Public Law 94-142). That mandate requires an Individual Educational Plan, which, in reality, is a monitoring system to provide data on the progress, education setting, and type of instruction handicapped children are achieving. The law requires (1) a statement of the child's present level of educational performance; (2) a statement of annual goals; (3) description of participation in regular or least restrictive environment; (4) justification of recommended placement; (5) statement of services to be provided, including related services beyond the regular or special class teacher; (6) beginning and ending dates; (7) annual reevaluation; (8) overall evaluation criteria.

     A systematic evaluation requires consistently derived input data to initiate and drive the process. In the case of handicapped children, the diagnostic considerations which attempt to ascertain those learner characteristics contributing to special education placement and instructional considerations are required by PL 94-142. Therefore, if a systematic diagnostic structure can be developed nationwide, or at least the same learner characteristics defined similarly from school system to school system, a national effort could be focused on needed instruments and assessment procedures, the relationship of selected learner characteristics to academic achievement, and a movement toward the validation of specified interventions defined as selected learner problems.

Applications to Particular Variables

There are four diagnostic variables directly related to the improvement of educational services for the handicapped:

1. Diagnostic techniques to describe specific learner characteristics that will permit the preparation of social, personal, academic, and vocational objectives.
2. Reliable measures designed to systematically ascertain the information processing behaviors (learner characteristics) of handicapped youth ages 18 to 21.
3. Observational and task analysis procedures to be used with severely handicapped children and youth, in particular the severely mentally retarded and seriously emotionally disturbed (behavioral disordered).
4. Diagnostic procedures sensitive to cultural-linguistic differences, for example, Latinos, Blacks, and Native Americans, which overlay and cloud the identification of handicapping conditions.

In summary, formal (standardized) assessment procedures were designed to differentiate handicapped children on a consistent basis. The purpose of the differentiation was to isolate the handicapped learner from those who would or could benefit from instruction. The derived data from formal assessment augment interindividual comparisons of handicapped and normal students in contrast to intraindividual comparisons based on the learner characteristics for one person.

Binet's original task was to develop test items, which distinguished between those children who needed an adaptive environment from those who could function in a regularized environment, with nonadapted teaching materials and behavioral controls. The influence of Binet dominated the early diagnostic identification of handicapped learners. It became increasingly evident that handicapped children, needing special education services, could be identified by using formal (standardized) tests, but the resulting scores or diagnostic labels did not provide sufficient information for specific instructional remediation. In fact, there are simply no procedures, rules, or operational mechanics yet validated that permit formalized test scores to be used in establishing instructional objectives. This statement challenges the traditional clinical model wherein diagnostically derived labels are used to make dichotomous decisions to place children into either a regular or special education class. Diagnostic procedures are needed to promote the construction of tests that describe specific learner characteristics. Few standardized tests have been developed from models on how information is processed by the central nervous system. The result is an overdependence on archaic diagnostic procedures designed to differentiate handicapped from nonhandicapped groups according to assessment procedures not validated against learner characteristics but rather another global function, academic achievement in the case of Binet-type instruments.

This overdependence is particularly obvious with older students, especially those in the 18-21 year-old range whose education is now mandated by Public Law 94-142. Career educational planning requires the coordination of at least four specific objectives, which should guide the social, personal, vocational, and academic development of handicapped youth into a career orientation that ensures the maximum degree of independent adult living. A traditional dependence on standardized assessment procedures does not provide the data necessary to write the four independent objectives required in an individualized educational plan (IEP), as specified by law.

A major change in the role model of psychologists working with the handicapped learner is needed. There should be an interdisciplinary relationship of behavioral scientists and special educators working together in place of the traditional clinical (assessment-placement) model. Continual scientific investigation in the psychological laboratory on information processing variables that relate to learning in children is also critical to such efforts in response to the four variables identified. The translation of the findings from the applied educational laboratory, as reliable measures of traits, would open a new era in the preparation of specific instructional prescriptions.

It is now apparent that severely handicapped children, those with cultural-linguistics differences, and those in the older age levels (18-21) are suffering the most from outmoded diagnostic procedures. The well-worn assumption that global test scores are sufficient to diagnose handicapped children and youth and prepare plans for independent adult living has come under serious question. The psychologist's earnest search for behavioral descriptive devices that permit a thorough study of the developmental skills necessary to learn specific activities important to daily living is now a major task instrumental to special education service delivery in the 1980s.

References

Bender, L. "A Visual Motor Gestalt Test and Its Clinical Use." *American Orthopsychiatric Association Research Monthly,* 1938, No. 3.

Doll, E. A. "A Brief Binet-Simon Scale." *Psychological Monographs,* 1917, *11.*

Dunn, L. M. "Minimal Brain Dysfunction: A Dilemma for Educators." In H. C. Haywood (Ed.), *Brain Damage in School Aged Children.* Arlington, Va.: Council for Exceptional Children, 1968.

Engel, M. "Dilemmas of Classification and Diagnosis." *Journal of Special Education,* 1969, *3,* 231-239.

Federal Register, Vol. 42, No. 163, 1977. Implementation of Part B of Education of All Handicapped Children Act, August 23, pp. 42478-42480.

Glaser, R., and Nitko, A. "Measurement in Learning and Instruction." In R. Thorndike (Ed.), *Educational Measurement.* Washington, D.C.: American Council on Education, 1971.

Gorth, W., and Hambleton, R. "Measurement Considerations for Criterion-Referenced Testing and Special Education." *Journal of Special Education,* 1972, 6, 303-314.

Hammill, D. "Evaluating Children for Instructional Purposes." *Academic Therapy,* 1971, *4,* 343-344.

Haring, N. G., and Bateman, B. *Teaching the Learning Disabled Child.* Englewood Cliffs, N.J.: Prentice-Hall, 1977.

Iscoe, I. "Functional Classification of Exceptional Children." In E. P. Trapp and P. Himelstein (Eds.), *Readings on the Exceptional Child.* New York: Appleton-Century-Crofts, 1962.

National Association of State Directors of Special Education. *Implementing PL 94-142.* Washington, D.C.: NASDSE, 1976.

Quay, H. C. "The Facets of Educational Exceptionality: A Conceptual Framework for Assessment, Grouping Instruction." *Exceptional Children,* 1968, *35,* 25-32.

Reese, J. H. "An Instructional System for Teachers of Learning Disabled Children." In D. A. Sabatino (Ed.), *Learning Disabilities Handbook: A Technical Guide to Program Development*. DeKalb: Northern Illinois University Press, 1976.

Ryckman, D. B., and Wiegerink, R. "The Factors of the Illinois Test of Psycholinguistic Abilities: A Comparison of 18 Factor Analyses." *Exceptional Children*, 1969, *36*, 107, 113.

Sabatino, D. A. "Information Processing Behaviors Associated with Learning Disabilities." *Journal of Learning Disabilities*, 1968, *1*, 6-16.

Sabatino, D. A., and Hayden, D. L. "Information Processing Behaviors Related to Learning Disabilities and Educable Mental Retardation." *Exceptional Children*, 1970a, *37*, 21-30.

Sabatino, D. A., and Hayden, D. L. "Prescriptive Teaching in a Summer Learning Disabilities Program." *Journal of Learning Disabilities*, 1970b, *3*, 41-48.

Wertheimer, M. "Studies in the Theory of Gestalt Psychology." *Psychologische Forschung*, 1923, *4*, 300-313.

62

Roger R. Harvey

Learning Ability/ Achievement Discrepancy

The basic assumption underlying learning ability/achievement discrepancy is that the child who presently is not achieving well academically does have the ability to learn. It is difficult to define the term precisely, because each component of the term represents broad boundaries of information rather than firm lines of precise knowledge. For the purpose of this discussion, *learning ability* is defined as the efficiency with which individuals (within a set of innate factors) receive and comprehend information, mentally process information previously learned or to be learned, and overtly express that information. Learning ability includes (but is not limited to) cognition, convergent production, evaluation, memory, conceptualization, and adaptation. *Achievement* describes the present grade or age level of attainment of academic skills in reading, spelling, arithmetic, language (oral and written), writing, physical activities, and interpersonal relations. The degree of correspondence between a child's present level of achievement and his or her efficiency of learning abilities is measured in terms of any difference that exists between these two variables.

The presence of such a discrepancy may be determined by three procedures: (1) observation; (2) assessment; and (3) diagnosis. *Observation,* a cooperative effort of the classroom teacher, psychologist, resource teacher, and others, identifies and quantifies overt classroom behavior of children as they interact in various socioacademic situations (teacher-pupil or pupil-pupil activities). *Assessment* measures the child's present acacemic performance and learning behavior as described quantitatively in terms of scores on tests where applicable and qualitatively as descriptions of overt behaviors. Assessment devices consist of normative evaluative measures, criteria referenced measures, informal assessment probes, and routine independent and group tasks. *Diagnosis* is based on estimates of functioning in terms of such variables as learning abilities, academic achievement, ecological factors, personality, and physical/physiological characteristics. The analysis of all available assessment data provides an individual diagnosis that describes the child's characteristic learning behavior within his or her present environment. In addition, the diagnosis identifies possible etiological factors and sets forth hypothetical predictions based on both proposed intervention strategies and consequences that may result from a lack of intervention. For example, reading achievement and spelling achievement are compared by means of an in-depth analysis of deficient as well as efficient performance of skills common to both subjects, such as phonetic attack. In addition, various learning ability factors identified as being significant to the development of phonetic skills are compared, such as the ability to recall distinctive visual and auditory features of letters and words. After the data are collated, the degree of correspondence between the academic skills and the learning ability factors is then determined. Thus, a child may demonstrate no significant deficits in reading and reading comprehension but may be relatively weak in spelling. Assessment of the child's learning abilities, however, may reveal that he or she shows good recall of distinct auditory sounds but has difficulty recalling visual stimuli.

Determining the significance of disparity between learning ability and achievement does not lend itself entirely to a quantitative statement. By means of empathic observation and comparison with other individuals of the same age or grade, a qualitative description detailing learning abilities and academic skills, as well as deficiencies in these areas, is written in the form of a descriptive profile of the child's learning characteristics. The eventual significance of this diagnostic description will depend on information in possible etiological factors and predictive hypotheses about proposed interventions.

Achievement is assessed as the grade level or age level at which a child performs in reading, spelling, arithmetic, oral and written language, writing (penmanship), physical activities, and interpersonal relations. Subject matter achievement, as in science, history, English, is assessed in terms of the distinctive knowledge that the subject matter intended to impart. Poor achievement in either area would necessitate a more detailed assessment of specific skills. For example, reading would include an analysis of letter and word recognition, word meaning, word attack, comprehension, phonics, reading behavior, and other reading skills. A pupil who continuously does poorly in social studies, science, or other subjects where reading is essential would also have his or her reading skills assessed.

Learning ability has been conceived in terms of various theories of intelligence, learning, and cognitive development. Identified learning factors include (but are not limited to) the following:

1. *Cognition*—the reception, recognition, and understanding of information in various forms (Meeker, 1969). It is analyzed in terms of the ability to use the sensory modes (visual, auditory, tactile-kinesthetic) relative to perceptual organization and attending.
2. *Convergent Production*—a process of the systematic and ordered arranging of rules or principles (known or remembered) to converge on the best solution to a problem (Meeker, 1969). Since most classroom activities reflect convergent thinking, assessment should reveal a child's ability to organize information into strategies for the purpose of coming to the solution of given problems.
3. *Evaluation*—the ability to make a judgment or decision as to the adequacy or correctness of information (Meeker, 1969); for example, a decision on a well-defined principle or algorithm, a working rule, or an esthetic standard.
4. *Memory*—universally recognized as a primary mental function, it is the storage and availability of information (Meeker, 1969; Piaget, Inhelder, and Sinclair, 1968; Goulet, 1968; Bruner, 1964). Assessment data should demonstrate a child's abilities with both "episodic memory" (recall of a single event, such as a name, a date, or an object) and "semantic memory" (recall of information systems, such as oral and written language, math equations, or how to ride a bicycle). Also, modes of input (auditory, visual, tactile, and so on) and lapsed time to retrieval should be assessed and evaluated as an integral part of the child's memory process.
5. *Conceptualization*—the ability to evoke a figurative and/or cognitive response to dissimilar or discriminating stimuli (Engelmann, 1969; Piaget, 1952; Martin and Blum, 1961). Assessment information should demonstrate the child's ability to discriminate and comprehend distinctive features that apply to the development of a given concept. A multifaceted response system (drawing, gestures, verbalisms, writing, and any combinations of these) should be used to elicit these discriminations.
6. *Adaptation*—the state of equilibrium attained while interacting with the environment (Piaget, 1950, 1952). Assessment data should include information from the child's past and present environmental ecosystems (classroom, school, home, neighborhood). An interpretation of the child's ability to adapt would be based upon his or her internal equilibrium as inferred from positive and negative reactions to those ecosystems.

Etiological factors that may influence learning ability/achievement discrepancy are assessed by information relating to the child's social and physical interaction with his or her environment currently and in the past. Three areas of etiological influence are relevant.

1. *Personality characteristics*—which are themselves influenced by sociophysical factors—describe (a) overt emotional behaviors toward socioacademic situations; (b) motivation in terms of expectations, aspirations, frustrations, conflicts, and anxieties; (c) attitudes inferred from overt reactions toward socioacademic stimuli; (d) interests concerning a wide variety of specific activities, objects, or types of persons that the child commonly encounters in daily living; and (e) socialization in terms of culture and value systems presently in operation.
2. *Environment*—the interaction of the child with changing and static situational variables. The various ecosystems in which he or she is required to interact with are analyzed.
3. *Physical and physiological status*—in which cooperation between medical and educational personnel is essential in developing a diagnostic description and intervention

program to determine if causes of a physical or physiological nature are influencing the child's ability to learn.

By patterning essential data, inferences pertaining to etiology are made that describe the child's major areas of strengths and weaknesses. If specific skills and behaviors can be identified within major areas of strengths and weaknesses, "secondary inferences" of a more specific nature are made and used to plan intervention strategies or follow-up referrals.

Background and Current Status

Learning ability/achievement discrepancy assessment, while relatively new, is a concept of measuring inter- and intra-individual variance whose roots, for the most part, are not known. Since this model of discrepancy assessment is theoretically tied to most historical aspects of educational and psychological testing, the reader is referred to such authors as Anastasi (1968), Freeman (1962), and Wisland (1974) for a more in-depth review of the history and evolution of testing and diagnosis.

In a study of the history of learning disabilities, Wiederholt (1974) suggests that theories relating to discrepancy functioning were formulated during the nineteenth century and the early part of the twentieth century as they pertained to individuals with brain damage (acquired through accident or injury) who, as a consequence, lost certain learning skills. Although tests were being employed early in the 1800s for the purpose of differentiating mentally normal and subnormal behavior, it was not until the 1920s that marked variations of performance on intelligence test items became apparent. With this revelation, assessment procedures were formulated that compared the child's level of intellectual functioning with his or her academic achievements. According to Chalfant and King (1976), one of the first formulas designed to assess the discrepancy between achievement and intellectual potential was developed in 1932 by Marion Monroe, who used a reading index in which age was divided by the average of mental age, chronological age, and arithmetic computation age. Harris (1970) describes additional formulas of discrepancy assessment that utilize measures of verbal and nonverbal intelligence, age, amount and quality of schooling, familiarity with standard English, and adequacy of sociocultural background.

It was from these early efforts of comparing intelligence to scholastic achievement that the concept of learning ability/achievement discrepancy was formed and adopted as an assessment process. Literally hundreds of assessment strategies are being used today that attempt to measure differences between academic performance and learning potential in children who demonstrate difficulty in acquiring academic skills (Harris, 1970; and Bond and Tinker, 1967). Efforts to conform to one particular formula or standard assessment procedure have been unsuccessful because of problems surrounding the use and interpretation of measures of intellectual functioning, quantification of a child's discrepancy performance, and the failure of most diagnosticians to include environmental characteristics in assessment procedures. In the United States, basic procedures for evaluating all handicapped children have been mandated just recently. These mandates require that assessment measures be administered in the child's native language (or communication system such as sign language); that no more than one assessment procedure be used; and that the evaluation be made by a multidisciplinary team. In addition, the procedures for evaluating specific learning disabilities require that the child's teacher be a part of the multidisciplinary team and that assessment criteria be developed that would guide decisions on possible discrepancies (Federal Register, 1977).

Critical Discussion

General Areas of Concern

Assessing the discrepancy between learning abilities and achievement is a concept that most educators and school psychologists find tenable. By means of astute observation and the accumulation of quantitative and qualitative evidence of the child's academic performance, most experienced teachers can verbalize a fairly accurate description of a child's functioning in academic skills. Teachers do, however, find it difficult to ascertain *why* a child is not achieving in one or more of the expected academic skills. Thus, the teacher refers the child for assessment and diagnosis and expects to receive both a definitive and functional description of the child's learning abilities and a plan of activities for intervention. These teacher expectations give rise to two major concerns pertaining to discrepancy assessment: (1) operationally defining the parameters of learning abilities and disabilities in terms of educational usefulness; and (2) relating the proposed etiological facts to the child's observed learning abilities.

Evaluation of assessment results have traditionally used the IQ as the primary referent for classifying children and placing them in special educational programs. While the IQ has provided a criterion for categorizing children, it has not offered a functional explanation of a child's specific learning disability, neither has it provided a description of a child's specific learning style. Some research supports the notion that children scoring within various IQ ranges of intelligence tend to remain at that IQ level throughout their school years (Goldstein, Moss, and Jordan, 1965; Dunn, 1968). However, Talkington (1967) found that many children once categorized as mentally retarded have been reevaluated as having normal intelligence after a period of specialized training. Arguments pertaining to cultural and experiential bias have had an impact on the use of the IQ as the sole criterion for categorizing children. For children whose language, education, and overall experiences are not similar to those demonstrated in intelligence test items, the interpretation and ensuing prediction of academic achievement become questionable (Clark and Clark, 1967; Babad and Budoff, 1971). These concerns give rise to questions of reliability and the assumed invariability of test scores (Barrett, 1965). While intelligence tests have been used for a number of practical purposes, including predicting success in scholastic and vocational endeavors (Goodenough, 1954), many special educators still have misgivings about using standardized IQ tests with children who lack the test specific experiences and cultural background (Lerner, 1976).

Another concern pertains to the identification of etiological factors from assessment results. Within most educational diagnoses etiology is either absent, or it is expressed in technical neurological terms or vague environmental descriptions.

A diagnosis of neurological dysfunction based solely on observable learning behavior and with no positive clinical findings offers no functional information that can be translated into intervention activities. Thus, the frustration in diagnosing neurological causes for children with a seeming inability to learn stems from the observation that although many of these children display most or all of the behavioral symptoms of minimal brain dysfunction (MBD) findings on traditional neurological exams are normal (Vuckovich, 1968). Also, children who are learning satisfactorily demonstrate many of the subtle signs of minimal neurological dysfunction (Lerner, 1976). It is the unidentifiable neurological cause that offers a vague and sometimes confused correlation with learning ability/achievement discrepancy.

Environmental factors as causes of learning problems is another area that poses difficulties in developing an etiological description of discrepant functioning. While it has long been known that malnutrition can result in limited physical development, only recently have questions pertaining to sociocultural factors been scrutinized for their potential relationship to learning disorders.

In an extensive review of available research, Hallahan and Cruickshank (1973) offer substantial evidence of underachievement due to severe environmental deprivation over a prolonged period of time. Refined procedures for measuring both social and physical environmental factors that influence cognitive growth tend to be missing in most of these studies. Thus, while a diagnostic description may point to a generalized influence of environmental deprivation, there is little definitive information with which to develop an intervention program or implement preventive measures.

Since language development has become the most important skill for academic success, most assessment tools in use today are weighted heavily with tests requiring what is considered to be standard English. The use of such tests, of course, creates a bias against certain cultural groups whose language is considered nonstandard English, such as Chicanos or blacks. While the use of nonstandard English may determine discrepant functioning between learning ability and achievement, it cannot necessarily be inferred that it is the cause.

How children from environmentally deprived settings are able to adapt to or cope with powerful social situations on their own terms becomes essential in making a diagnostic decision. Through the works of such investigators as Bernstein (1961) and Silberman (1964), cross-cultural characteristics of children and how well each child functions within his or her own milieu are beginning to be understood. There is still, however, a great need for research of a multidisciplinary nature that is essential to the development of procedures for diagnosing environmental causes of learning ability/achievement functioning.

Comparative Philosophies and Theories

Evaluation procedures currently employed in the schools and clinics are undergoing dramatic changes. Several models of discrepancy assessment currently are being developed, based on both adjustments to traditional psychoeducation theories and a more refined theoretical stance pertaining to the child's environment. Budoff (1972) has developed a procedure of measuring "learning potential" by using a task-oriented approach in which the child's ability to learn is observed directly. The theory behind this process is that factors of intelligence, such as cognition, can be measured by utilizing a pretest-teaching-posttest approach, thereby measuring a child's facility to benefit from training. Initially the basic cognitive skills of the child are assessed; then the child is "coached" through various problem-solving activities that are similar to posttest activities; the results, as indicated by posttests, can reveal potential abilities that can be used to predict academic success.

Another concept of assessment, which is being given considerable attention, is the clinical and diagnostic approach to discrepant functioning used by the Soviets. Their procedures are based on a dialectical, sociocultural theory that emphasizes the developmental nature of intelligence and its growth through productive social activity. Wozniak (1975) analyzes Soviet dialectics and its comparison to American psychometrics. Generally, the Soviet dialectic method requires the child to perform the task independently. Next, he or she performs a similar task under the tutorship of the examiner. Finally, the child is again required to perform the task independently. This procedure is similar to Budoff's pretest-teaching-posttest approach in that both use a multistep process with a teaching phase. However, there are two apparent differences. First, Budoff's model utilizes psychometric measures for both pre- and postactivities (Ravens Progressive Matrices and Kohs Block Design Test), while at no time does the Soviet procedure employ normative evaluative measures. Second, the tests used in Budoff's learning potential model were selected because test items did not demonstrate a bias in language or sociocultural experiences. However, the procedure does not address itself to a clinical analysis of social interaction between the child and examiner, which, according to dialectic theory, is an important aspect of this process. The learning potential concept does, on the other hand, suggest transfer of problem-solving abilities to subsequent activities requiring similar skills.

A clinical evaluation model described by Thomas and Marshall (1977) centers around the interrelationship of a handicapped child with his or her physical and social environment. The model consists of four phases designed to produce strategies to help facilitate successful adaptation for the child and his family: (1) procedures for gathering information (educational, psychological, and developmental assessments); (2) staffing and initial program recommendations; (3) implementation of initial programming; and (4) periodic reassessment for program modification. By assessing the discrepancies that may exist in the child's physical/physiological, developmental, and family status, the model proposes a plan of habilitation that brings child and family into equilibrium with various identified ecosystems. According to Thomas and Marshall, a handicapped child's ecosystem "includes his family and his education, recreational, health, and vocational milieus" (1977, p. 17). One concept important to this model emphasizes the flexibility, in terms of availability, of the service agency to the adaptive needs of the child and his or her family. The concept of adaptation as viewed by this model is an important consideration in any educational assessment, yet procedures for putting this concept into operation are missing from most school programs.

Laten and Katz (1975) also focus on the child's interaction with various environmental systems in terms of expectancy outcomes. Their procedure first calls for gathering information that describes the different environmental systems in which the child is required to function. Second, the child's self-expectations and the expectations of others who interact with the child are gathered from situations where the child has been both successful and unsuccessful. The third level provides behavioral descriptions developed from information collated from these situational environs. An analysis of these interaction descriptions and expectations is then used to establish reasonable expectations designed to help the child relate better to his or her total environment.

A technique of determining factors that influence the way a child manages the academic demands of the classroom is Applied Behavior Analysis (ABA). Lovitt (1975) describes the ABA procedure as a multifaceted process where the teacher-observer can analyze the classroom variables that have an impact on a child's academic and social skills. Initially, a baseline of on-task performance is developed by means of daily observation and recording over a given period of time. In conjunction with this, descriptions of teaching procedures used in the presentation of tasks are recorded. Relationships between teaching methods and rate of skill acceleration are then assessed. The advantage of the ABA system for use in discrepancy assessment lies in its systematic procedure for analyzing learning style and academic level at which a child can perform. Although it is nonpsychometric, the ABA technique does permit the analysis of specific academic and social skills while employing only one teaching technique at a time. Thus, with astute observation, language or mnemonic activities of cognition, for example, can be informally assessed as the child interacts with the teacher and his or her scholastic environment.

Student-teacher interaction analysis, while not a new concept, is being given renewed attention as a discrepancy assessment strategy. Several observational procedures are available that permit fairly reliable data collection. One such procedure, which codes over 150 distinct teacher-student verbal interactions, is the Dyadic Interaction System (Good and Brophy, 1973). Observed verbal interactions between student and teacher permit the observer to record the types of responses made by both teacher and student within five situational categories, including: (1) response opportunities of the child in attempts to answer the teacher's question; (2) recitation by the child in the presentation of a classroom task; (3) classroom procedural contacts in which child and teacher interact on matters concerning the child's individual needs and classroom management; (4) work-related contacts concerning child-teacher interaction relative to classroom tasks; and (5) behavioral contacts in situations pertaining to conduct. Types of verbal interactions made by both teacher and student are recorded and coded according to quantity and quality of questions, responses, and recitations.

By interpreting Guilford's Structure of Intellect for use within the school curriculum, Meeker (1969) has constructed a psychometric approach to analyzing learning abilities. It is Meeker's contention that "knowledge should be expanded beyond the concept of an IQ score and should include knowledge of the range of individual abilities which make up intelligence" (p. 4). With Guilford's factor analytic model as a foundation, Meeker has developed a test of Structure of Intellect abilities primarily scaled for young children and designed for teacher administration. The purpose of the test is to develop a learning abilities profile of strengths and weaknesses for each child, based on the three-dimensional classification of 120 predicted categories of intellectual abilities postulated by Guilford, and then to relate this profile to a prescription for intervention. Although research is still needed to investigate the relationship of factor analytic models to information processing, Meeker's test (and the present theory and research behind it) offers considerable promise for measuring and analyzing the application of learning abilities.

One major aspect of learning ability/achievement discrepancy assessment needing critical discussion is the exclusive reliance on psychometric measures for quantifying discrepant functioning. Many psychometric tests reduce the opportunity for scientific inquiry. Such observations as variations in children's methods of performance and their attitudes toward the test and the tester are not normally taken into account when computing psychometric scores. A child's poor performance on given test items is analyzed more in terms of his or her score rather than a qualitative description of performance style. Most psychometric measures all but eliminate the opportunity for a child to demonstrate areas of strength that compensate for weak learning abilities. It is this compensatory mechanism of the child that demonstrates what Adelman (1971) describes as the child's "interaction between his strengths, weaknesses, and limitations and the specific classroom situational factors he encounters, including individual differences among teachers and differing approaches to instruction" (p. 528). How a child organizes and reorganizes his or her learning abilities in the process of solving a problem, and how a child internalizes objects and events for the purpose of adaptation become crucial considerations in the assessment process. These aspects of the developmental nature of learning abilities are difficult to assess with psychometric tests alone. Therefore, the use of observational procedures, such as those used in the dialectic process, are proposed as means of assessing the child's present learning abilities and his or her ability to regulate and control the environment.

Personal Views and Recommendations

School curriculums, for the most part, have been constructed on a foundation of knowledge gained through sociocultural experiences and have been implemented for the purpose of perpetuating the society, according to its present and future needs. However, the components of any academic curriculum are also rooted in a theory or theories of intelligence. It is this characteristic of the curriculum that is used to analyze students' learning abilities and to place those with deficient abilities into special education programs that provide an adjusted curriculum designed to correspond to the intellectual capabilities of the child. Traditionally, any differential between the ability to learn and the level of achievement within a curriculum has been based on the presumably unchanging nature of the IQ. Although such differences suggest a factor of discrepant functioning, the arguments surrounding this issue are well known and need not be expounded here. An alternative view of the learning ability/achievement discrepancy concept is briefly discussed subsequently, a view that points to the need for extended investigation of classroom environmental behavior, controlled research in the construction and use of nonpsychometric assessment measures, and an upgrading of pre-service and in-service training programs.

Clearly, there are intra- and inter-individual learning differences among children. Determining the nature of these differences and the reasons for their existence forms the basic concept of learning ability/achievement discrepancy. The process for determining this discrepancy assumes a multifaceted procedure that involves coordinating the disciplines of education, psychology, sociology, medicine, and others. Therefore, the concept is primarily eclectic in that it does not conform to one specific theory or philosophy, and it does not mandate the use of specific assessment measures. This flexibility, however, does require an in-depth understanding of child development and how the child functions in his or her sociophysical environment.

Although the discrepancy assessment model is a flexible concept, it should not be implemented as an instant analysis of learning characteristics. If not carefully controlled, this flexibility could bring about two conditions for questionable practice. First, there is a danger of indiscriminate use of psychometric measures and other informal procedures. Although the process does not call for specifically defined assessment measures, tasks or test items for assessment must be selected on the basis of their usefulness and their ability to meet the theoretical and/or empirical criteria defined in the discrepancy assessment model. Second, the process calls for the cooperative efforts of several disciplines. The qualifications and roles of those who participate in the procedure must be defined, otherwise diagnostic descriptions may not contain precise verifications for placement or programming.

The learning ability/achievement discrepancy assessment model does propose a systematic procedure of inquiry as to how a child interacts with his or her environment. Attitudinally, this pattern of inquiry should be treated as a well-disciplined scientific endeavor but not as a rigid series of absolute certainties. This approach will provide the diagnostician or teacher with the mechanisms for probing into the complexities of learning abilities and disabilities, while at the same time offering him or her an opportunity to challenge and revise conclusions.

The discrepancy assessment process proposes the use of both psychometric measures and dialectic procedures. This is based on the notion that the development of learning abilities and their application to academic skills is both quantitative and qualitative. Strict adherence to psychometric norms representing quantitative relationships among a set of independently measured abilities is avoided. Instead, inferences are drawn from psychometric results, which delimit common variables, and from the qualitative structure of learning performance, which recognizes all existing variables. These inferences and their alterations over a given period of time develop a personal characterization of discrepant functioning. Thus, in the assessment of both learning abilities and academic skills, the role of ecological factors is highly significant in (1) describing how a child's learning abilities are brought to bear on the organization of his or her actions in given academic skills; and (2) determining the etiological factors that may influence the interactions between the child and the ecosystems within which he or she functions.

This view of learning ability/achievement discrepancy is still, to a great extent, grounded in theory. However, given the requisite time and resources, it can be implemented in both school and clinical situations. Thus, policy makers should look closely at present laws that, for funding purposes, tend to force schools to rapidly identify children with learning problems. In many instances these children are placed without a thorough analysis of their identified discrepancy or of how they function within various socio-academic situations. Using quick screening devices or a standard battery of psychometric measures for categorizing and for funding purposes is of little benefit to the child or the teacher who must create an adjusted learning environment. Under the present federal law governing the education for all handicapped children (P.L. 94-142), sufficient time for a proper investigation into discrepant functioning is not only allowed but required. Paradoxically, however, the reporting system to both state and federal agencies has created such an attitude of immediacy and trepidation in the minds of local school officials and teachers that time lines for reporting information have tended to overshadow a concentrated and coordinated effort of discrepancy analysis.

Quality pre-service and in-service training is, of course, essential if the discrepancy model concept is to be implemented on a refined basis. Not only should the competencies and skills pertaining to the mechanics of assessment be upgraded, but a functional, as well as theoretical, knowledge of child development and academic skill development should also be expanded and closely coordinated. Through pre-service and especially in-service training, communication should be established among the various disciplines by sharing knowledge from both cooperative and independent training and research. Only by working together in the service of children who have learning problems can those variables influencing scholastic performance be specifically identified and clarified.

Application to Particular Variables

The assessment of a discrepancy between learning ability and academic achievement applies to *any* individual who is experiencing learning problems in an educational program. Its application is primarily directed toward those children whose sensory mechanisms are intact, and who do not have marked general intellectual deficits, but who demonstrate deviations in learning behavior and psychological development to such an extent that they have difficulty in adjusting to ordinary teaching methods in school. These children may have observable disorders in development of language, speech, and other associated communication skills needed for social interaction. They may show marked deficits in one or more of the academic skills of reading, spelling, arithmetic, and written language. Therefore, the primary purpose of this assessment procedure is to gather information to be used in planning an instructional program for children whose learning behavior is observed to be significantly different from their peers and who may have different learning needs.

References

Adelman, H. S. "The Not So Specific Learning Disability Population." *Exceptional Children*, 1971, *37*, 528-533.

Anastasi, A. *Psychological Testing*. (3rd ed.) London: Macmillan, 1968.

Babad, E., and Budoff, M. "Sensitivity of Learning Potential Measurement in Three Levels of Ability." *Studies in Learning Potential,* 1971, *2,* 22.

Barrett, B. H. "Acquisition of Operant Differentiation and Discrimination in Institutionalized Retarded Children." *American Journal of Orthopsychiatry,* 1965, *35,* 862-885.

Bernstein, B. "Social Class and Linguistic Development: A Theory of Social Learning." In A. H. Halsey, J. Floud, and C. A. Anderson (Eds.), *Education and Society.* New York: Free Press, 1961.

Bond, G. L., and Tinker, M. A. *Reading Difficulties: Their Diagnosis and Correction.* (2nd ed.) New York: Appleton-Century-Crofts, 1967.

Bruner, J. S. "The Course of Cognitive Growth." *American Psychologist,* 1964, *19,* 1-15.

Budoff, M. "Measuring Learning Potential: An Alternative to the Traditional Intelligence Test." *Studies in Learning Potential,* 1972, *3,* 39.

Cattell, J. M. "Mental Tests and Measurements." *Mind,* 1890, *15,* 373-380.

Chalfant, J. C., and King, F. S. "An Approach to Operationalizing the Definition of Learning Disabilities." *Journal of Learning Disabilities,* 1976, *9,* 34-38.

Clark, A. M., and Clark, A. D. B. "Learning Transfer and Cognitive Development." In J. Zubin and C. A. Jervis (Eds.), *Psychopathology of Mental Development.* New York: Grune & Stratton, 1967.

Cole, M., Sharp, D. W., Glick, J., and Dessen, W. "Conceptual and Mnemonic Factors in Paired-Associate Learning." *Journal of Experimental Child Psychology,* 1968, *6,* 125-130.

Cratty, B. "Motor Activities and Learning Disabilities: A Look Ahead." In M. Krasnoff (Ed.), *Learning Disabilities: A Decade Ahead.* Ann Arbor, Mich.: Institute for the Study of Mental Retardation and Related Disabilities, 1974.

Cruickshank, W. M. *The Brain Injured Child in Home, School, and Community.* Syracuse, N.Y.: Syracuse University Press, 1967.

Dunn, L. M. "Special Education for the Mildly Retarded—Is Much of it Justifiable?" *Exceptional Children,* 1968, *35,* 5-22.

Engelmann, S. *Conceptual Learning.* San Rafael, Calif.: Dimensions Publishing, 1969.

Federal Register. "Assistance to States for Education of Handicapped Children." Washington, D.C.: Office of Education, U.S. Department of Health, Education, and Welfare, Part III. Dec. 29, 1977.

Ferguson, G. A. "On Learning and Human Ability." *Canadian Journal of Psychology,* 1954, *8,* 95-112.

Freeman, F. S. *Theory and Practice of Psychological Testing.* New York: Holt, Rinehart and Winston, 1962.

Frostig, M., and Maslow, P. *Learning Problems in the Classroom.* New York: Grune & Stratton, 1973.

Goldstein, H., Moss, J. W., and Jordan, L. J. *The Efficacy of Special Class Training on the Development of Mentally Retarded Children.* Cooperative Research Project No. 619. Washington, D.C.: Office of Education, U.S. Department of Health, Education, and Welfare, 1965.

Good, T., and Brophy, J. *Looking in Classrooms.* New York: Harper & Row, 1973.

Goodenough, F. L. "The Measurement of Mental Growth in Childhood." In L. Carmichael (Ed.), *Manual of Child Psychology.* (2nd ed.) New York: Wiley, 1954.

Goulet, L. R. "Verbal Learning in Children: Implications for Developmental Research." *Psychological Bulletin,* 1968, *69,* 359-376.

Hallahan, D. P., and Cruickshank, W. M. *Psychoeducational Foundations of Learning Disabilities.* Englewood Cliffs, N.J.: Prentice-Hall, 1973.

Harris, A. J. *How to Increase Reading Ability*. (5th ed.) New York: McKay, 1970.

Kirk, S. A., and Elkins, J. "Identifying Developmental Discrepancies at the Preschool Level." *Journal of Learning Disabilities*, 1975, *8*, 417-419.

Kirk, S. A., McCarthy, J. J., and Kirk, W. K. *Illinois Test of Psycholinguistic Abilities*. (Rev. ed.) Urbana: University of Illinois Press, 1968.

Labov, W. *The Study of Nonstandard English*. Champaign, Ill.: National Council of Teachers of English, 1970.

Laten, S., and Katz, G. "A Theoretical Model for Assessment of Adolescents: The Ecological/Behavioral Approach." *Occasional Papers*. Madison: Wisconsin Public Schools, 1975.

Lerner, J. W. *Children with Learning Disabilities*. (2nd ed.) Boston: Houghton Mifflin, 1976.

Lovitt, T. "Characteristics of ABA, General Recommendations, and Methodological Limitations." *Journal of Learning Disabilities*, 1975, *8*, 432-443.

Martin, W. E., and Blum, A. "Inter-test Generalizations and Learning in Mentally Normal and Subnormal Children." *Journal of Comparative and Physiological Psychology*, 1961, *54*, 28-32.

Meeker, M. N. *The Structure of Intellect: Its Interpretation and Uses*. Columbus, Ohio: Merrill, 1969.

Myklebust, H. R. "Learning Disabilities: Definition and Overview." In H. R. Myklebust (Ed.), *Progress in Learning Disabilities*. Vol. 1. New York: Grune & Stratton, 1968.

Paivio, A., and Yarmey, A. D. "Pictures Versus Words as Stimuli and Responses in Paired-Associate Learning." *Psychonomic Science*, 1966, *5*, 235-236.

Piaget, J. *The Psychology of Intelligence*. London: Routledge & Kegan Paul, 1950.

Piaget, J. *The Origins of Intelligence in Children*. New York: International Universities Press, 1952.

Piaget, J., Inhelder, B., and Sinclair, H. *Memoire et Intelligence*. Paris: Presses Universitaries de France, 1968.

Reese, H. W., and Lipsitt, L. P. *Experimental Child Psychology*. New York: Academic Press, 1970.

Shields, D. T. "Brain Responses to Stimuli in Disorders of Information Processing." *Journal of Learning Disabilities*, 1973, *6*, 501-505.

Silberman, C. *Crisis in Black and White*. New York: Random House, 1964.

Strauss, A. A., and Lehtinen, L. E. *Psychopathological Education of the Brain Injured Child*. New York: Grune & Stratton, 1947.

Talkington, L. W. "Over-Achievement of Stimulation? A Case Study." *Digest of the Mentally Retarded*, 1967, *4*, 21-23.

Terman, L. M. *The Measurement of Intelligence*. Boston: Houghton Mifflin, 1916.

Thomas, E. D., and Marshall, M. J. "Clinical Evaluation and Coordination of Services: An Ecological Model." *Exceptional Children*, 1977, *44*, 16-22.

Thurstone, L. L. *Vectors of Mind: Multiple Factor Analysis for the Isolation of Primary Traits*. Chicago: University of Chicago Press, 1935.

Thurstone, L. L. *Primary Mental Abilities*. Chicago: University of Chicago Press, 1938.

Thurstone, L. L. *Multiple-Factor Analysis*. Chicago: University of Chicago Press, 1947.

Vuckovich, D. M. "Pediatric Neurology and Learning Disabilities." In H. Myklebust (Ed.), *Progress in Learning Disabilities*. Vol. 1. New York: Grune & Stratton, 1968.

Wiederholt, J. L. "Historical Perspectives in the Education of the Learning Disabled." In L. Mann and D. Sabatine (Eds.), *The Second Review of Special Education*. Philadelphia: Journal of Special Education Press, 1974.

Wisland, M. V. *Psychoeducational Diagnosis of Exceptional Children.* Springfield, Ill.: Thomas, 1974.

Wozniak, R. H. "Dialecticism and Structuralism: The Philosophical Foundations of Soviet Psychology and Piagetian Cognitive Development Theory." In K. F. Riegal and G. C. Rosenwald (Eds.), *Structure and Transformation: Developmental and Historical Aspects.* New York: Wiley, 1975.

63

David J. McDowell

Integration of Perceptual and Conceptual Processes

Integration theory has been developed by Magaro (1974, in press) and his colleagues (McDowell, Reynolds, and Magaro, 1975; Magaro, Miller, and McDowell, 1976; Magaro and McDowell, 1979) as an explanation of the schizophrenic deficit which predicts differential performance by paranoids and nonparanoids due to distinct cognitive styles of these groups. The theory has more general relevance, however, which this chapter will develop before considering its original domain.

Information processing occurs in a continuum from sensory activation through cognitive interpretation. A traditional division of this continuum is between perceptual and conceptual processes, the former referring roughly to sensory or peripheral processes, the latter to cognitive or central processes. The distinction is useful in considering how persons with nearly identical and intact sensory systems can regularly arrive at quite different, often unique, interpretations of the same data. A full appreciation of an individual's characteristic style in interpreting events requires, of course, the sort of intensive and extensive understanding usually available only in close, prolonged relationships. Nonetheless, some useful generalizations regarding the structure of typical processing may be possible if one considers how certain groups or individuals reliably integrate perceptual and conceptual processes. Integration refers both to the characteristic quantitative emphasis placed on perceptual versus conceptual processes and to the characteristic qualitative aspects of their mediation. The integration concept is process oriented in its focus on stages of information flow and transformation in the human system, but structural in its goal of describing characteristic relations among subsystems. The balance of this section will first consider the importance of integration in cognitive development, then illustrate the operation of several forms of integration in a classic perceptual experiment, and finally suggest how integration theory can be applied to a variety of clinical phenomena.

Carini (1969, 1973) holds that the ratio of sensory to symbolic processes decreases with development. That is, with increasing experience, persons rely increasingly on conceptual structures or operations in the form of sets, expectations, hypotheses, representations, or schemas to organize and give meaning to perceptual data. This progression is clear in the development of perceptual constancies. Size constancy, for example, is achieved when the child no longer bases size judgments solely on retinal image size but learns to consider the retinal image in relation to an estimate of the object's distance. Distance judgments, in turn, are based on a complex interplay of cues, including relative clarity of the object's perimeter and texture, and parallax movement relative to other objects of known size. Such sophisticated, habitual processing strategies are called schemas by Piaget, whose theory of intellectual development relies extensively on the distinction between perception and cognition (Flavell, 1963). Piaget distinguishes these processes both in his specific theory of perception and in his metatheory of intelligence.

In Piaget's theory of perception, perceptual acts or centrations inevitably distort their object because they are *samplings* of the object. Perception does not provide a coherent, organized representation of the whole object, field, or context. Centrations produce a sequence of only partial, and therefore distorting, impressions. This is precisely what occurs in the story of the blind men who examine an elephant for the first time. Schemas are internal representations that develop slowly as a result of repeated interactions between the organism and the environment. Schemas organize incoming data by relating them to a representation (or, in more complex and later stages, to an abstract, logical pattern or sequence of transformations) which effectively supplies a perspective correcting for the distorting effects of perception. Common examples of schemas are those for object permanence (Harris, 1975; Kagan, 1972) and the various conservations (Flavell, 1963; Piaget, 1954). Like Carini, Piaget holds that cognitive development implies increasing reliance on central operations.

Piaget has also developed terms that describe integration at different "locations" on the perceptual-conceptual continuum. In Piagetian theory, intelligence comprises two dialectic forms, assimilation and accommodation. Assimilation involves referring perceptual data to an existing schema, even if the data must be distorted to fit the schema. Accommodation involves the modification or creation of a schema to represent the data more accurately. For example, infants initially assimilate many objects to the sensori-motor sucking schema, then slowly accommodate to those different objects by generating new schemas based on the unique properties of each.

The operation of assimilation and accommodation in adults is classically illustrated in an experiment by Bruner and Postman (1949). These investigators presented normal and anomalous playing cards (red spades and clubs, black hearts and diamonds) tachistoscopically to undergraduates in a series of exposures increasing from .01 to 1 second. Subjects were asked to report everything they saw on each presentation. Each subject viewed a total of five cards (one to four were anomalous and the others normal), with up to fifty-one exposures on each, until the stimulus was reported accurately or the subject reached a criterion of three exposures at a full second. The mean recognition threshold for anomalous cards was four times greater (28 versus 114 milliseconds) than for normal cards. Moreover, twenty-seven of the twenty-eight subjects misreported at least once that a red spade or club was a heart or diamond, or that a black heart or diamond was a spade or club. The researchers identified four types of subject reaction, which can be ordered on a dimension from inaccurate schematization to accurate perception of an anomalous event. *Dominance reactions* involved inaccurate perception based on assimilation of form or color to expectation of a normal card. Thus, a red six of spades was called a six of spades (form dominance) or a six of hearts (color dominance) with no indication that the stimulus was unusual. *Compromise* reactions showed more accommodation to the percept but still produced inaccurate perception as a result of a conflict between schema and stimulus. For example, the card above was reported to be a purple six of spades. *Disruptions* tended to occur at longer stimulus exposures, following "a period in which the subject . . . failed to resolve the stimulus in terms of his available perceptual expectations" (p. 75). The most extreme example of disruption was this response to a red spade exposed for .3 seconds: "I can't make the suit out, whatever it is. It didn't even look like a card that time. I don't know what color it is now or whether it's a spade or a heart. I'm not even sure now what a spade looks like! My God!" (p. 79). Finally, *recognition* of the incongruity, the only reaction involving accurate perception, occurred suddenly, slowly, or not at all. Sudden recognition was shown by a subject who abruptly exclaimed "Good Lord, what have I been saying? That's a *red* six of spades!" (p. 82). Slow recognition was achieved by four of six subjects who were responding with color dominance when they first noticed that the points of what they were calling the spade or heart pips were inverted (a perfectly correlated but intuitively less salient anomaly than the opposite colors). Four subjects went on to recognize the full extent of the anomaly. Six other subjects viewed at least one anomalous card for fifty-one exposures, with three exposures at a full second, without perceiving the card accurately.

Under the conditions of Bruner and Postman's experiment, subjects could achieve accurate perception only by disregarding or overcoming conceptual processes. Accurate perception of unexpected stimuli required more data (longer exposures) than accurate perception of expected events. The normal integration of perceptual and conceptual processes impaired accurate perception. In Piaget's terms, dominance reactions clearly constituted assimilation of perceptual data to schemas developed for normal cards; compromise, disruption, and recognition reactions represented increasing degrees of accommodation, since they involved increasingly accurate interpretation of perceptual data.

The facilitating effects of frequency or expectancy are documented in a wide range of recognition situations. Frequent words are recognized visually at shorter exposure times (Claxton, 1975) and aurally under higher levels of masking noise (Pollack, 1964) than infrequently used words. Words that are predictable from preceding context are recognized under higher levels of noise than words that are unpredictable (Kalikow, Stevens, and Elliott, 1977; McDowell, Reynolds, and Magaro, 1975). Facilitation of recognition by frequency or predictability can be explained as the result of increasing schema strength. Conversely, increasing schema strength interferes with accurate perception of stimuli or events that are *not* predicted, expected, or frequent.

Assimilation is a form of integration involving a major conceptual component and a relatively minor perceptual component. Perceptual data are referred to an existing schema, even if the percept is distorted or its recognition as a unique entity impeded. Similarly, accommodation is a form of integration involving a major perceptual component and a relatively minor conceptual component. In this case, perceptual data are accurately reflected in a modified or novel schema which preserves the unique aspects of those data. As Piaget points out, there can be varying emphases on assimilation versus accommodation. In the present terms, integration may involve varying ratios of perceptual and conceptual processes.

Clinically, the integration formulation can be applied to several interpersonal and behavioral phenomena. For example, many transference and countertransference distortions occur because the patient assimilates the therapist, or the therapist assimilates the patient, to affective object schemas developed in interactions with earlier, often parental, figures. Uncovering and exploring such schemas, and liberating current relationships from their distorting effects, is the explicit task of analytic psychotherapy. Resistance to specific interpretations, which are often attempts to clarify or restructure schemas, may be both defensively motivated and the result of functional autonomy of integrative style and schemas. A later section will develop integration theory's thesis that the integration styles of paranoid and nonparanoid schizophrenia represent extremes by overemphasizing conceptual and perceptual processes, respectively. Nonpsychotic forms of maladaptive integration can be viewed as points within this continuum, with normal cognition occupying a central, well-integrated midpoint.

The two approaches to personality that are most consonant with the cognitive orientation of integration theory are probably those of Kelly (1963) and Lewin (1935), because both emphasize qualitative and quantitative aspects of basic cognitive categories and their control over interpersonal and affective styles. Defenses may be particularly susceptible to an integration analysis. Isolation, for example, requires schemas that are impermeable. In repression, schemas are too selective to include significant affective experience. Some behavioral clinicians may also find integration theory useful, especially its emphasis on mediational processes. Meichenbaum's (1974) cognitive behavior modification, for example, stresses the importance of "covert sentences" in maintaining maladaptive affects and behaviors. Such hypothetical constructs proliferate easily in the literature, but there is no apparent advantage in moving beyond the earlier and more general term *schema* to refer to these constructs. Meichenbaum's phrase points to a specific treatment technique (covert repetition of sentences opposed to the inferred maladaptive schemas), not to a more specific knowledge of cognitive structures or processes.

Background and Current Status

Magaro's (1974) initial formulation of integration was developed in a review that translated several theories of schizophrenia, each using different hypothetical constructs and operational definitions, into a common language, permitting comparisons among theories. To accomplish this goal, Magaro needed a developed theoretical system with an extensive lexicon of psychological processes and a postulate system relating these terms.

He selected Hullian theory as such a framework. The resulting discussion emphasized the interaction of multiple psychological processes in even the simplest performance. Size estimation—a widely used experimental procedure—is an excellent example of a task that appears to be simple, but that, on analysis, requires the coordination of multiple processes.

In schizophrenia research, the regular finding of a schizophrenic performance deficit on a wide variety of procedures may reflect a deficit not in any one psychological process or complex of processes but in the coordination of several types of operations. In a series of experiments in Magaro's laboratory, the effects of paranoid versus nonparanoid status, premorbid adjustment, and chronicity of schizophrenics were assessed (McDowell, Reynolds, and Magaro, 1975; Magaro, 1969, 1972a, 1972b, 1973; Magaro and Vojtisek, 1971; Ross and Magaro, 1976). These experiments, along with a review of empirical and theoretical distinctions between paranoid and nonparanoid schizophrenics (Magaro and McDowell, 1979) resulted in a refined theory that focuses on perceptual versus conceptual processes and the paranoid-nonparanoid distinction in explaining two forms of the schizophrenic performance deficit (Magaro, in press).

The view that schizophrenia involves a disintegration of psychic processes is traceable directly to Bleuler (1911), who coined the term *schizophrenia* to embody his theory that the underlying disorder is a basic associative disturbance produced by a dissociation between affective and cognitive functions. Shakow's (1962, 1977) theory of segmental set also emphasized the failure to maintain intentional or planful strategies due to a separation of processes. Instead of organizing mental activity via a major set or goal, schizophrenics maintain unintegrated and competing minor sets, which are expressions of drive-dominated thought.

Other theorists have used the integration term in different but related ways. Werner (1948) viewed development as a cyclical process of differentiation and integration at increasing levels of complexity. In the dynamic tradition, ego psychology has emphasized the importance of differentiation and integration. As in Piaget's theory, where assimilation and accommodation must first separate in the earliest period of life before they can establish the dialectic producing intellectual growth (Flavell, 1963), so too in ego psychology "the first and most fundamental of the steps in the child's growth which lead to the formation of the ego concerns the ability of the infant to distinguish between his self and the world around him" (Hartmann, Kris, and Loewenstein, 1947, pp. 20-21). The distinction between self and not-self requires a rudimentary schema which Schilder (1950) has called the body image. Theoretically, the self/not-self distinction is important in ego theory because it establishes basic oppositional elements (for example, self and not-self are the psychological loci of the conflict between pleasure and reality principles) whose integration has important implications for reality testing and identity. Freeman, Cameron, and McGhie (1958) postulated that the basic disturbance in schizophrenia is the inability to differentiate self from not-self. The notion of a boundary defect has analogs in the work of Sullivan (1953), Searles (1967), and White (1963, 1965). McDowell (1974), using the boundary notion as the etiological and therapeutic focus, described a case of schizophrenia and its treatment and suggested a social learning mechanism that could be responsible for such a defect. Most recently, Blatt and Wild (1976) have developed an ego-analytic, developmental account of schizophrenia, emphasizing the boundary disturbance as the causative factor.

The common core in each of these conceptualizations is an emphasis on the integration of opposed processes or structures. While the analytic and developmental views are structural and therefore focus on entities like self, not-self, and boundary, Piagetian and integration theories are more often process oriented.

Integration theory is currently being tested in a series of experiments in Magaro's laboratory and by this investigator. Probably the most exciting aspect of this work is the attempt to relate integration theory to the neuropsychology of hemispheric specialization. A variety of experimental and clinical evidence has shown that the right cerebral hemisphere is specialized for holistic, intuitive, imagistic, and simultaneous processing, while the left is more suited for analytic, logical, verbal, and sequential processing (Galin, 1974; Ornstein, 1972, 1973; Semmes, 1968; Stone, 1977). These two systems complement one another in a variety of ways and situations. For example, while the right hemisphere processes facial, gestural, and tonal components of speech communication, the left is the site for lexical comprehension and verbal production (Goodglass and Calderon, 1977; Safer and Leventhal, 1977). This asymmetrical but complementary organization is intriguing for its formal similarity to the distinction between perceptual and conceptual processes in integration theory. In fact, integration theory's dichotomy between conceptual and perceptual processes and Bleuler's opposition between cognitive and affective processes may be resolved into a single distinction within a neuropsychological framework. In a variety of studies (reviewed in Bakan, 1975, and Shimkunas, 1978), the right hemisphere has been shown to be the more active hemisphere in affective or emotional mentation. These findings—together with the right hemisphere's superiority for certain types of perceptual processing (spatial visualization and localization, musical and aesthetic processing; see Kimura, 1973)—suggest that "schizophrenia, classically conceptualized . . . as a splitting of thought from affect, appears to be developing an empirical basis in neuropsychology" (Shimkunas, 1978, p. 215).

Unfortunately, most theorists relating schizophrenia to disorders of hemispheric relations have not yet adequately conceptualized the clinical and empirical differences observed among schizophrenic subgroups. Integration theory directly confronts this issue, as noted below.

Critical Discussion

General Areas of Concern

With the early empiricism of the Enlightenment, psychopathology emerged from the era of demonology to enter the descriptive stage of scientific inquiry. During most of the nineteenth century, physicians and philosophers sought to describe as carefully as possible the bewildering variety of mental aberrations. By late in that century, many psychotic conditions had been reliably distinguished. Immanuel Kant (in Sullivan, 1964) had provided a classic description of paranoia, and Karl Kahlbaum had identified catatonia and hebephrenia (Arieti, 1955). On the basis of hypothetical common deteriorative outcomes and organic etiology, Emil Kraepelin first grouped these three previously unrelated syndromes under the name *dementia praecox,* a term that Benedict Morel had used to distinguish psychoses of early and late life (Arieti, 1955). Kraepelin's detailed clinical descriptions emphasized the multiplicity of signs and symptoms possible in the syndrome. Eugen Bleuler sought to justify this grouping, which he renamed *schizophrenia,* by identifying an underlying disorder present to some degree in all cases: associative disturbance. While Kraepelin and Bleuler established a nosology that would influence psychiatric practice and theory for many decades, the uncritical acceptance of their grouping established a paradigm that impeded the recognition of major empirical differences among the subgroups. Both theorists stated explicitly that the new syndrome was a group of disorders, but their single-label theories resulted in research that often ignored or explained away subgroup differences. The clearest example of the power of implicit theory over explicit observation is given by Shakow (1962), whose comments also provide a representative summary of research findings comparing paranoid and nonparanoid performance.

Shakow's studies at Worcester State Hospital in the 1940s and 1950s constituted the largest sustained investigation of schizophrenia ever conducted. His major statement of the theoretical position that emerged from this work was his article on segmental set (Shakow, 1962), wherein he contrasted "the differing personality patterns of the two major subtypes of schizophrenia, the paranoid and the hebephrenic. These groups consistently seem to deal with situations in distinctive ways. . . . of 58 measurements which we made of a wide range of psychological functions on groups of normal, paranoid, and hebephrenic subjects, we found the paranoid to be nearer the normal in 31 instances and the hebephrenic nearer in only seven instances. These were measurements on which the normal was at one or the other extreme of the distribution. In 20 instances, however, the paranoid and hebephrenic fell on *either* side of the normal" (p. 24).

Shakow continues by describing the "striking differences" between the two types, but concludes this section of his discussion with an abrupt concession to the Kraepelinian paradigm: "The distinctive behavior of each of these subtypes appears to be a different way of responding to the same basic difficulty. The paranoid pattern seems to represent an overreaction to the underlying trend toward disorganization which exists in the psychosis. The hebephrenic gives way to the trend, whereas the paranoid organizes his resources to fight the disruption" (p. 24). The teleological concept of "overreaction," the unobserved "underlying trend," and the singular term *psychosis* in a context of reliable empirical differences all attest to the strength of the traditional view. Naturally, this paradigm discouraged research strategies that might produce data bearing on differences between paranoid and nonparanoid subtypes. That Shakow regularly separated these groups in design and analysis is a credit to his empirical sophistication and commitment. Much contemporary research, however, did not distinguish subgroups. Unfortunately, this is a problem that continues to plague schizophrenia research, although investigators and editors show a slowly increasing awareness of the problem.

Integration theory states that the common defect in schizophrenia is the inability to integrate perceptual and conceptual processes adaptively. Paranoids and nonparanoids, however, express this defect in opposite ways. While paranoids rely on conceptual processes to the relative exclusion of perceptual data, nonparanoids rely on perceptual processes without adequate organization and stability from conceptual processes.

Magaro, Miller, and McDowell (1976) have developed the relationship between integration and Piagetian theory. From previous discussion, it should be clear that the paranoid style emphasizes assimilation in relating a variety of data to a few central (delusional) schemas. The nonparanoid style may be said to emphasize accommodation, since perceptual and affective data generate only fleeting cognitive interpretations that are not anchored in reliable, stable schemas. Hallucinations are examples of perception that is inadequately (and incorrectly) schematized; delusions are schemas that assimilate and distort much perceptual and affective experience. Both paranoid and nonparanoid styles deviate importantly from the normal integrated operation of assimilation and accommodation. Piaget is clear that disequilibrium between these two processes produces poor adaptation. The impermanent accommodations made by very young infants are described by Bower (1971, p. 37): "An object becomes a different object as soon as it moves to a new location. In this world every object is unique. The infant must cope with a large number of objects when only one is really there." Compare Searles' (1967) account of therapy with a hebephrenic woman for whom every change in Searles' mood or position produced "another" Searles, until by the end of a session as many as "two hundred guys" would crowd the room. Both descriptions are examples of accommodations that do not function adaptively because the schemas generated do not endure as assimilative, stable structures.

Although assimilation and accommodation are normally both integrated and balanced, there are three transitional periods in which normative disequilibria precede major steps in cognitive growth. These transitional stages may also be critical for the development of pathological disintegration (Magaro, Miller, and McDowell, 1976). For example, late in the period of concrete operations (approximately ages 10-12), a normative disequilibrium favoring assimilation develops. The child has become quite competent in the concrete world but is unable to coordinate various schemas abstractly in order to think logically about the purely hypothetical. Assimilation has become dominant. This imbalance is resolved by the early adolescent, who adopts a radically more abstract mental attitude in which the real comes to be seen as only a subset of the possible (hence the spectacular idealism of the next few years!). This constitutes the transition from concrete to formal operations, the beginning of truly adult thought. When this resolution does not occur, a residual emphasis on assimilation may predispose to clinical paranoid schizophrenia in later periods of stress. The few available clinical reports of childhood paranoid schizophrenia nearly unanimously report onsets in the period at the end of the first decade of life (Magaro and McDowell, 1979). For more detailed analyses and examples of the types of cognitive pathology that may arise in each transitional period, see Magaro, Miller, and McDowell (1976).

Finally, there is growing empirical evidence for an integration theory of schizophrenia. McDowell, Reynolds, and Magaro (1975), in the first explicit test of the theory, compared the performance of acute paranoid and nonparanoid schizophrenics and normals on a speech detection task that manipulated expectancy of stimuli. Five basic sentence stems were developed which had a high probability of being completed by one word. For example, 95 percent of an undergraduate sample completed the stem "Please pour me some orange _____" with the word *juice*. Each of the five stems was completed once with a probable word like *juice,* and once with a much less probable word that still made sense in context, like *drink* for the stem above. The resulting ten sentences were presented five times each, with only the last word masked by one of five intensities of white noise, yielding a gradient of perceptual difficulty in identifying the final word. Predictions were that paranoids would identify probable words more accurately than normals, who in turn would perform better than nonparanoids. Conversely, it was predicted that nonparanoids would identify improbable words better than normals, who in turn would be superior to paranoids. It was reasoned that (1) the conceptual paranoid style should facilitate recognition of probable words but hinder identification of improbable words and (2) the perceptual nonparanoid style should enable recognition of improbable words but lead to poor recognition of probable words. Predictions were partially but not fully confirmed. Paranoids performed as well as, but no better than, normals on identification of probable words, and both groups performed better than nonparanoids. However, both paranoids and nonparanoids performed more poorly than normals on improbable words. These results suggest an interpretation of the typical findings that paranoids perform better than nonparanoids on most, but not all, laboratory tasks, and have better premorbid adjustments and spend less time in hospital than nonparanoids. In this study, nonparanoids consistently performed more poorly than normals, whereas paranoids performed as well as normals in a predictable environment but as poorly as nonparanoids when the environment was less predictable. Since, by definition, predictable environments are more frequent than unpredictable ones, the paranoid conceptual style may account for the generally more favorable clinical and experimental performance of this subgroup.

While the data did not reflect the predicted pattern of reversed schizophrenic subgroup performance on improbable versus probable words, with normals intermediate in both conditions, signal detection analysis did yield such a pattern. Paranoid responses were biased toward probable words, and nonparanoid responses were biased toward improbable words relative to normals, who were intermediate.

Ross and Magaro (1976), using a different procedure, also found support for integration theory. Ambiguous (blurred) pictures of common objects were preceded by a sentence stem designed to induce an accurate or a misleading expectation about the picture. For example, in the misleading condition, the stem "Jim is going to eat this _____" preceded a blurred picture of a watch. In the accurate condition, a stem like "John listened to the news on the _____" preceded an ambiguous picture of a radio. Paranoids and normals responded correctly in the accurate condition more frequently than nonparanoids. Paranoids inaccurately followed the misleading cues twice as often as controls and three times more often than nonparanoids.

Comparative Philosophies and Theories

Integration theory's identification of two distinct cognitive styles in schizophrenia is similar to dichotomies offered by other theorists. For example, in a review of neurophysiological studies, Ornitz (1969) suggests that "the breakdown in perceptual modulation proceeds in the direction of excessive inhibition in one type of schizophrenia and deficient inhibition in another" (p. 263). Since conceptual structures function to modulate perception, excessive inhibition of perception implies paranoid overreliance on conceptual processes, and deficient inhibition implies nonparanoid emphasis on perceptual processes. Clinically, Bowers (1974) contrasts the phenomenology of paranoid and nonparanoid schizophrenia, describing the former as characterized by "irrefutable cognitive experience" and the latter by "the destructuring of perception and affect" (pp. 179-181). In the language of integration theory, destructuring occurs when nonparanoid perception is too weakly organized by central processes, and irrefutable cognitive experience occurs when the paranoid emphasis on conceptual processes ignores perceptual data (McDowell, Reynolds, and Magaro, 1975).

Experiments by other investigators also support integration theory, although some of these studies are flawed in failing to compare paranoid and nonparanoid performance or, worse, in failing to control for subtype in their schizophrenic samples. Sarbin, Juhasz, and Todd (1971) instructed nonparanoid schizophrenics and normals to identify an odor where there was none. Nonparanoids were more accurate than normals in reporting no odor present, suggesting that they were less influenced by expectations of an odor. Snyder, Rosenthal, and Taylor (1961) found that schizophrenics were more accurate than normals in reproducing unclosed circles, whereas normals made the usual closure response more frequently. In a sense, the schizophrenics' responses were more accurate than the normals' in this task. Studies assessing absolute sensory thresholds of nonparanoids have suggested that this group may actually have greater sensitivity than normals (in Maher, 1966). On a pure signal detection task, paranoids tended to be hyposensitive and nonparanoids hypersensitive compared to normals, with phenothiazine medication acting oppositely in the two groups to move performance of both closer to normals (Rappaport and others, 1972). Soviet studies reviewed by Polyakov (1969), apparently using primarily nonparanoid subjects, are also suggestive of an integration theory formulation. In these studies, schizophrenics identified improbable sentence endings and common objects in anomalous contexts more accurately than normals, but group performance reversed on probable endings and objects in normal contexts.

Other evidence supports the conceptual or assimilative style of the paranoid. McReynolds, Collins, and Acker (1964) found that delusional schizophrenics attempted to identify more pictures, and identified more pictures correctly, than nondelusional schizophrenics on the McGill Closure Test. They concluded that paranoids "have a stronger tendency to organize ambiguous stimuli in a meaningful way" (pp. 211-212). Payne (1966) reported a correlation of .90 between early incorrect identifications of tachistoscopic stimuli and overinclusion scores. An earlier factor analysis had shown that overinclusion is primarily a paranoid symptom (Payne and Hewlett, 1960). Young and Jerome (1972) devised a task requiring the solution of a series of conceptual problems in which relevant cues varied. Paranoids consistently performed less efficiently than non-paranoids following a change of cue. The investigators concluded that "there was some-thing wrong with the paranoid subjects' conceptualization of the task. . . . Rigidity of internal representation is . . . suggested by the paranoid subjects' loss of efficiency when the problem class was changed" (p. 444). In a study using the Street Gestalt Completion figures, Abroms, Taintor, and Lhamon (1966) concluded that "the paranoid operates with the metahypothesis that, to process his experience, it is preferable to form an incor-rect hypothesis than none at all. Furthermore, the greater the degree of paranoid severity, the stronger this metahypothesis" (p. 495). Most recently, Asarnow and Mann (1978) have concluded that paranoid-nonparanoid differences, observed in a careful and inde-pendent investigation of size estimation in schizophrenia, are best explained by integra-tion theory.

It is possible that nonclinical perceptual and conceptual styles can be distin-guished. For example, Binder (1958) instructed normal college students to report when they recognized a form presented in increasing degrees of completeness as one of several highly similar forms learned previously. Subjects with high Paranoid scores on the MMPI tended to delay their reports until the form was no longer ambiguous. While the same intolerance for ambiguity is found in this normal sample as in clinical paranoids, these conceptual-style students were able to wait for more complete information before form-ing judgments. Whether this ability to delay judgment was a function of Binder's proce-dure or is a true distinction between subclinical and pathological expressions of the same conceptual style cannot be determined. However, Bleuler speculated that a large propor-tion of cases of schizophrenia remain subclinical and are therefore never identified (Arieti, 1955). One avenue of research growing out of integration theory would be a search for evidence of nonpathological expressions of the integration styles associated with schizophrenic subgroups.

Elaboration on Critical Points

As noted previously, recent theorizing by Magaro (in press) and studies currently in progress seek to link integration theory to the neuropsychology of hemispheric special-ization. Several independent sources have suggested within the last few years that schizo-phrenic symptoms, particularly disorders of thought and language, may be related to unusual patterns of hemispheric relations. Recent theoretical approaches by Bakan (1975), Blau (1977), Horowitz (1975), and Shimkunas (1978) have suggested that an im-balance between left and right hemisphere processing may produce symptoms including hallucinations, altered perceptions of self and reality, and vague, confusing speech. These approaches have generally focused on nonparanoid schizophrenia and have postulated either a pathological separation of lexical and imagal systems, a relative overactivation of the right hemisphere, or left hemisphere brain damage with consequent right hemisphere compensatory emphasis.

Empirically, schizophrenics are reported to have greater right than left hemisphere EEG voltages, a pattern opposite that of controls. Degree of relative right hemisphere dominance was correlated with symptom severity and tended to reverse with symptomatic improvement both on and off phenothiazines (Serafetinides, 1972, 1973). Schizophrenics also showed unusual lateral asymmetries on peripheral GSR measures, pure-tone threshold, and auditory discrimination, all consistent with relative right hemisphere arousal. In the same study, schizophrenics performed relatively better on WAIS subtests thought to tap right hemisphere processes than on subtests tapping left hemisphere skills (Gruzelier and Hammond, 1976). Boklage (1977) has shown that the case-wise concordance rate for schizophrenia among monozygotic twins rises from 67 percent to 96 percent when twins are also concordant for handedness, suggesting that hemispheric dominance may be related to phenotypic expression of the disorder. Beaumont and Dimond (1973) found that schizophrenics match stimuli as accurately as normals within hemispheres, but are deficient at comparing input arriving in different hemispheres, suggesting that transmission between the hemispheres via the corpus callosum is somehow impaired. Also implicating the corpus callosum is a report that schizophrenics' callosa are reliably thicker at autopsy than those of controls (Rosenthal and Bigelow, 1972). Several reviewers have noted the symptomatic similarities between schizophrenia and syndromes of the corpus callosum (Bakan, 1975; Rosenthal and Bigelow, 1972; Shimkunas, 1978).

Two recent studies of handedness in schizophrenia reported opposite results. Wahl (1976) found no more left-handedness among schizophrenics than normals; but Gur (1977), using samples eight times larger, found significantly higher scores on a questionnaire assessing left hand preference among schizophrenics, indicating a shift away from right motor dominance in this group. However, Gur's statistical strategy of normalizing these quite similar, highly skewed, and bimodal distributions in order to apply parametric tests of mean differences is questionable.

Gur (1978) also conducted a more extensive study of hemispheric function in schizophrenia. In one experiment, normals followed the usual pattern of left hemisphere superiority for language and right hemisphere superiority for spatial tasks, but schizophrenics performed both kinds of tasks more efficiently in the right hemisphere. Unfortunately, paranoids and nonparanoids were not separated for analysis. In another experiment, schizophrenics produced more right eye movements than controls in response to questions of both a verbal and spatial nature. Paranoids and nonparanoids did not differ. Since all groups looked right more often following verbal than spatial questions, the regular finding that direction of eye movement represents activation of the contralateral hemisphere was confirmed. Gur concluded from these experiments that schizophrenia is characterized by both left hemisphere dysfunction *and* overactivation.

Clooney and Murray (1977) compared reaction times of paranoids, nonparanoids, and normals on a task requiring subjects to process letter arrays presented in the right, left, or central visual fields. While reaction times of paranoids and nonparanoids did not differ reliably when all letters were the same, paranoids responded most slowly to arrays in the left field and nonparanoids responded most slowly to arrays in the right field. Statistical analyses conducted by Clooney and Murray produced no evidence of hemispheric dysfunction in either subgroup, but the pattern above indicates impaired paranoid right hemisphere processing and impaired nonparanoid left hemisphere processing. Such a pattern would be predicted by integration theory.

Finally, Alpert, Rubinstein, and Kesselman (1976) have shown that hallucinating and nonhallucinating acute schizophrenics differ both from normals and from one another in their patterns of hemispheric specialization for language reception. This result is particularly interesting in light of integration theory, because it is the first clear evidence that paranoids and nonparanoids differ in pattern of hemispheric specialization. Moreover, studies implicating the corpus callosum in schizophrenia provide a possible neuroanatomical structure responsible for impaired integration. Thus, the theory may be recast in terms of hemispheric specialization. One approach would be to hypothesize that a corpus callosum defect occurs in all types of schizophrenia and that paranoids subsequently emphasize left hemisphere processes, while nonparanoids emphasize right hemisphere processes. Neither group receives adequate input from the contralateral, disintegrated hemisphere. Since the left hemisphere is the site of speech production centers, this formulation may explain the usually better cognitive and clinical performance of paranoids and the disordered language characteristic of the nonparanoid groups. This approach also identifies a single defect that is expressed through either of two formally similar mechanisms (emphasis of a single hemisphere) producing two intuitively related but empirically distinct disorders, and could thus preserve the grouping established by Kraepelin and Bleuler.

Personal Views and Recommendations

The preceding speculations are offered because they are a particularly elegant neuropsychological translation of a purely psychological theory and because a number of independent scientists have advanced related views. The reader is encouraged to consult Bakan (1975), Blau (1977), Boklage (1977), Gur (1978), Horowitz (1975), and Shimkunas (1978) for their contributions to the notion that hemispheric relations may be disordered in schizophrenia.

Considerable caution is required, however, in such speculations. Many hypotheses could account for the limited data available. While it is possible that an organic defect or defects are responsible for unusual patterns of integration in schizophrenia, specifying these defects is another matter. A callosal defect might predispose toward the disorder, with an inherited dimension of laterality determining whether paranoid or nonparanoid symptoms develop. Alternately, there might be no callosal defect, but brain damage contralateral to the preferred hemisphere could produce compensatory emphasis of that hemisphere and primary deficiencies in the damaged hemisphere. An equally plausible general hypothesis is that unusual patterns of hemispheric relations, including unusual forms of integration or use of the corpus callosum, may be learned or purely psychological in nature. For instance, Lidz's (1973) theory of learned irrationality could be extended to the present area. Differential social reinforcement of right versus left hemisphere mentation by families of developing schizophrenics could account for learned patterns of hemispheric processing. Levy and Trevarthen (1976) have shown that hemispheric locus of processing can be determined by expectations of task requirements rather than task material itself. Even an enlarged corpus callosum, if a reliable phenomenon, could result from experiential factors. It is known from other contexts that experience can modify brain structures in animals (Rosenzweig, Bennett, and Diamond, 1972). Therefore, investigators must not foreclose prematurely on any of the possibilities that may account for unusual integration in schizophrenic subgroups. Research and theory in this area have generally ignored subgroup distinctions, and attempts to find a common defect shared by paranoids and nonparanoids may be motivated by the same paradigm that has impeded research for years.

Application to Particular Variables

While increasing cognitive competence generally presumes a transition from perceptual to conceptual styles, there have been no developmental studies assessing integration in different age groups. This is a major area for future research.

There is no theoretical reason to expect sex differences in integration, although reliable sex differences on several cognitive dimensions (see Maccoby, 1966) suggest that such differences in integration might exist. Moreover, some data (Bradshaw, Gates, and Nettleton, 1977; Ketterer and Smith, 1977) suggest sex differences in hemispheric specialization and relations. Research is currently in progress in this investigator's laboratory to assess hemispheric differences by sex in semantic prediction.

The established relation between risk for schizophrenia and low socioeconomic status is the subject of competing explanations (Kohn, 1973, 1976). While integration theory does not specify socioeconomic status as an important variable, this dimension, like sex, is related to many psychological and social constructs and should be explored.

Vocational choices and adjustment depend on certain cognitive skills; a musician must accommodate to many melodies, rhythms, forms, and interpretations (and music is primarily processed in the right hemisphere), while an attorney must be able to assimilate the details of a particular case to the relevant precedents. As those examples are intended to suggest, different integrative styles may be associated with different occupational choices and success within various occupations. Similarly, choice of college major may be used in part on integrative styles that predispose toward enjoyment or success in specific fields. Some empirical work has already related hemispheric-processing preference to occupation (Doktor and Bloom, 1977; Peterson and Lansky, 1977) and college major (Bakan, 1969; Combs and others, 1977), and a study in this investigator's laboratory on this issue is in progress.

Persons with certain forms of mental subnormality show unusually developed abilities in a few areas. For example, idiots savants present a clinical picture of a few over-developed skills, often in computative areas, against a general background of moderate to severe retardation. This pattern is suggestive of a few repetitively exercised schemas functioning quite efficiently without the overgeneralization of the paranoid style. The study of such cases with instruments designed to test integration processes may provide useful data.

Studies of a variety of organic conditions—such as aphasia (Jackson, 1864, in Taylor, 1958), lateralized brain injury (Hécaen, 1962), commissurotomy and hemispherectomy (Zaidel, 1977), and congenital callosal agenesis (Dennis, 1976)—have provided much information on the specialization of cerebral hemispheres and fascinating insights into disorders of neuropsychological lateralization. Medical techniques like direct brain stimulation and the Wada test likewise provide valuable information, although obvious limitations of expense and safety preclude their use with large numbers of subjects. In short, organic conditions and invasive procedures have been a major source of clinical data and have thereby fostered experimental research on hemispheric specialization.

Since integration refers to a balance of psychological processes, it is trivial to observe that integration will be impaired by lateralized or central lesions or lateralized drug effects. The uncertain generalizability from pathological conditions to nonclinical cases is especially relevant in this area. While organic conditions will continue to provide vital information, integration theory requires techniques that do not depend on injury, malformation, drugs, or surgery to produce the state or process under study. For this reason, integration theory is appropriately tested with information-processing strategies. Similarly, the uncertain extent and correlates of any natural lesion diminish the utility of conceptualizing organic conditions via integration theory.

Integration theory focuses on the integration defect in paranoid and nonparanoid schizophrenia. The practical effects of the theory may ultimately be most evident in treatment that it generates. If, as now seems possible, hemispheric relations are disordered in schizophrenia, biofeedback procedures designed to train new patterns of integration may be possible. There is every reason to expect that relative activation of hemispheres can be brought under voluntary control via EEG biofeedback. This notion clearly requires testing. If it is validated, integration theory may point to a major breakthrough in treatment of schizophrenia.

References

Abroms, G. M., Taintor, Z. C., and Lhamon, W. T. "Percept Assimilation and Paranoid Severity." *Archives of General Psychiatry,* 1966, *14,* 491-496.

Alpert, M., Rubinstein, H., and Kesselman, M. "Asymmetry of Information Processing in Hallucinators and Nonhallucinators." *Journal of Nervous and Mental Disease,* 1976, *162,* 258-265.

Arieti, S. *Interpretation of Schizophrenia.* New York: Brunner/Mazel, 1955.

Asarnow, R. F., and Mann, R. "Size Estimation in Paranoid and Nonparanoid Schizophrenics." *Journal of Nervous and Mental Disease,* 1978, *166,* 96-103.

Bakan, P. "Hypnotizability, Laterality of Eye-Movements and Functional Brain Asymmetry." *Perceptual and Motor Skills,* 1969, *28,* 927-932.

Bakan, P. "Dreaming, REM Sleep, and the Right Hemisphere: A Theoretical Integration." Paper presented at Second Interational Congress of Sleep Research, Edinburgh, Scotland, June 30, 1975. (Available from P. Bakan, Department of Psychology, Simon Fraser University, Burnaby, British Columbia, Canada.)

Beaumont, J. G., and Dimond, S. J. "Brain Disconnection and Schizophrenia." *British Journal of Psychiatry,* 1973, *123,* 661-662.

Binder, A. "Personality Variables and Recognition Response Level." *Journal of Abnormal and Social Psychology,* 1958, *57,* 136-142.

Blatt, S. J., and Wild, C. M. *Schizophrenia: A Developmental Analysis.* New York: Academic Press, 1976.

Blau, T. H. "Torque and Schizophrenic Vulnerability: As the World Turns." *American Psychologist,* 1977, *32,* 997-1005.

Bleuler, E. *Dementia Praecox or the Group of Schizophrenias* [1911]. New York: International Universities Press, 1950.

Boklage, C. E. "Schizophrenia, Brain Asymmetry Development, and Twinning: Cellular Relationship with Etiological and Possibly Prognostic Implications." *Biological Psychiatry,* 1977, *12,* 19-35.

Bower, T. G. R. "The Object in the World of the Infant." *Scientific American,* 1971, *225,* 30-38.

Bowers, M. B. *Retreat from Sanity.* New York: Penguin Books, 1974.

Bradshaw, J. L., Gates, A., and Nettleton, N. C. "Bihemispheric Involvement in Lexical Decisions: Handedness and a Possible Sex Difference." *Neuropsychologia,* 1977, *15,* 277-286.

Bruner, J. S., and Postman, L. J. "On the Perception of Incongruity: A Paradigm" [1949]. In J. S. Bruner, *Beyond the Information Given.* New York: Norton, 1973.

Carini, L. "The Theory of Symbolic Transformations." *Acta Psychologica,* 1969, *31,* 1-44.

Carini, L. "Explanations of Percepts and Concepts in Schizophrenia." *Psychiatria Neurologia Neurochirurgia,* 1973, *76,* 129-138.

Claxton, G. L. "Sources of Information in Word Perception." *Canadian Journal of Psychology,* 1975, *29,* 292-301.

Clooney, J. L., and Murray, D. J. "Same-Different Judgments in Paranoid and Schizophrenic Patients: A Laterality Study." *Journal of Abnormal Psychology,* 1977, *86,* 655-658.

Combs, A. L., and others. "Relationship of Lateral Eye-Movement to Cognitive Mode, Hemispheric Interaction, and Choice of College Major." *Perceptual and Motor Skills,* 1977, *45,* 983-990.

Dennis, M. "Impaired Sensory and Motor Differentiation with Corpus Callosum Agenesis: A Lack of Callosal Inhibition During Ontogeny?" *Neuropsychologia,* 1976, *14,* 455-469.

Doktor, R., and Bloom, D. M. "Selective Lateralization of Cognitive Style Related to Occupation as Determined by EEG Alpha Asymmetry." *Psychophysiology,* 1977, *14,* 385-387.

Flavell, J. H. *The Developmental Psychology of Jean Piaget.* New York: Van Nostrand, 1963.

Freeman, T., Cameron, J. L., and McGhie, A. *Chronic Schizophrenia.* New York: International Universities Press, 1958.

Galin, D. "Implications for Psychiatry of Left and Right Cerebral Specialization." *Archives of General Psychiatry,* 1974, *31,* 572-583.

Goodglass, H., and Calderon, M. "Parallel Processing of Verbal and Musical Stimuli in Right and Left Hemispheres." *Neuropsychologia,* 1977, *15,* 397-407.

Gruzelier, J., and Hammond, N. "Schizophrenia: A Dominant Hemisphere Temporal-Limbic Disorder?" *Research Communications in Psychology, Psychiatry, and Behavior,* 1976, *1,* 33-72.

Gur, R. E. "Motoric Laterality Imbalance in Schizophrenia." *Archives of General Psychiatry,* 1977, *34,* 33-37.

Gur, R. E. "Left Hemisphere Dysfunction and Left Hemisphere Overactivation in Schizophrenia." *Journal of Abnormal Psychology,* 1978, *87,* 226-238.

Harris, P. L. "Development of Search and Object Permanence During Infancy." *Psychological Bulletin,* 1975, *82,* 332-344.

Hartmann, H., Kris, E., and Loewenstein, R. M. "Comments on the Formation of Psychic Structure." *Psychoanalytic Study of the Child,* 1947, *2,* 11-38.

Hécaen, H. "Clinical Symptomatology in Right and Left Hemispheric Lesions." In V. B. Mountcastle (Ed.), *Interhemispheric Relations and Cerebral Dominance.* Baltimore: Johns Hopkins University Press, 1962.

Horowitz, M. J. "A Cognitive Model of Hallucinations." *American Journal of Psychiatry,* 1975, *132,* 789-795.

Kagan, J. "Do Infants Think?" *Scientific American,* 1972, *226,* 74-82.

Kalikow, D. N., Stevens, K. N., and Elliott, L. L. "Development of a Test of Speech Intelligibility in Noise Using Sentence Materials with Controlled Word Predictability." *Journal of the Acoustical Society of America,* 1977, *61,* 1337-1351.

Kelly, G. A. *A Theory of Personality.* New York: Norton, 1963.

Ketterer, M. W., and Smith, B. D. "Bilateral Electrodermal Activity, Lateralized Cerebral Processing and Sex." *Psychophysiology,* 1977, *14,* 513-516.

Kimura, D. "The Asymmetry of the Human Brain." *Scientific American,* 1973, *228,* 70-78.

Kohn, M. L. "Social Class and Schizophrenia: A Critical Review and a Reformulation." *Schizophrenia Bulletin,* 1973, No. 7, 60-79.

Kohn, M. L. "The Interaction of Social Class and Other Factors in the Etiology of Schizophrenia." *American Journal of Psychiatry,* 1976, *133,* 177-180.

Levy, J., and Trevarthen, C. "Metacontrol of Hemispheric Function in Human Split-Brain Patients." *Journal of Experimental Psychology: Human Perception and Performance,* 1976, *2,* 299-312.

Lewin, K. *A Dynamic Theory of Personality.* New York: McGraw-Hill, 1935.

Lidz, T. *The Origin and Treatment of Schizophrenic Disorders.* New York: Basic Books, 1973.

Maccoby, E. E. (Ed.). *The Development of Sex Differences.* Palo Alto, Calif.: Stanford University Press, 1966.

McDowell, D. J. "Ego-Building in Schizophrenia: Activity Treatment of an Acute Psychotic Patient." *Bulletin of the Menninger Clinic,* 1974, *38,* 257-262.

McDowell, D. J., Reynolds, B., and Magaro, P. A. "The Integration Defect in Paranoid and Nonparanoid Schizophrenia." *Journal of Abnormal Psychology,* 1975, *84,* 629-636.

McReynolds, P., Collins, B., and Acker, M. "Delusional Thinking and Cognitive Organization in Schizophrenia." *Journal of Abnormal and Social Psychology,* 1964, *69,* 210-212.

Magaro, P. A. "Size Estimation in Schizophrenia as a Function of Censure, Diagnosis, Premorbid Adjustment, and Chronicity." *Journal of Abnormal Psychology,* 1969, *74,* 306-313.

Magaro, P. A. "Basal Level and Reactivity in Schizophrenia as a Function of Premorbid Adjustment, Chronicity, and Diagnosis." *Journal of Genetic Psychology,* 1972a, *120,* 61-73.

Magaro, P. A. "Form Discrimination Performance of Schizophrenics as a Function of Social Censure, Premorbid Adjustment, Chronicity, and Diagnosis." *Journal of Abnormal Psychology,* 1972b, *80,* 58-66.

Magaro, P. A. "Skin Conductance Level and Reactivity in Schizophrenia as a Function of Chronicity, Premorbid Adjustment, Diagnosis, and Medication." *Journal of Abnormal Psychology,* 1973, *81,* 270-281.

Magaro, P. A. "Theories of the Schizophrenic Performance Deficit: An Integration Theory Synthesis." In B. A. Maher (Ed.), *Progress in Experimental Personality Research.* Vol. 7. New York: Academic Press, 1974.

Magaro, P. A. *Cognition in Schizophrenia and Paranoia: The Integration of Cognitive Processes.* Hillsdale, N.J.: Erlbaum, in press.

Magaro, P. A., and McDowell, D. J. "Distinguishing the Paranoid Process: Research and Theory." Unpublished manuscript, 1979. (Available from P. A. Magaro, Department of Psychology, Little Hall, University of Maine, Orono, Maine 04473.)

Magaro, P. A., Miller, I. W., and McDowell, D. J. "Autism, Childhood Schizophrenia, and Paranoid and Nonparanoid Adult Schizophrenia: An Integration Theory Synthesis." In D. V. Siva Sankar (Ed.), *Mental Health in Children.* Vol. 2. Westbury, N.Y.: PJD Publications, 1976.

Magaro, P. A., and Vojtisek, J. E. "Embedded Figures Performance of Schizophrenics as a Function of Chronicity, Premorbid Adjustment, Diagnosis, and Medication." *Journal of Abnormal Psychology,* 1971, *77,* 184-191.

Maher, B. A. *Principles of Psychopathology.* New York: McGraw-Hill, 1966.

Meichenbaum, D. *Cognitive Behavior Modification.* Morristown, N.J.: General Learning Press, 1974.

Ornitz, E. M. "Disorders of Perception Common to Early Infantile Autism and Schizophrenia." *Comprehensive Psychiatry,* 1969, *10,* 259-274.

Ornstein, R. E. *The Psychology of Consciousness.* New York: Viking Press, 1972.

Ornstein, R. E. (Ed.). *The Nature of Human Consciousness.* San Francisco: Freeman, 1973.

Payne, R. W. "The Measurement and Significance of Overinclusive Thinking and Retardation in Schizophrenic Patients." In P. Hoch and J. Zubin (Eds.), *Psychopathology of Schizophrenia.* New York: Grune and Stratton, 1966.

Payne, R. W., and Hewlett, J. H. G. "Thought Disorder in Psychotic Patients." In H. J. Eysenck (Ed.), *Experiments in Personality.* Vol. 2. London: Routledge and Kegan Paul, 1960.

Peterson, J. M., and Lansky, L. M. "Left-Handedness Among Architects: Partial Replication and Some New Data." *Perceptual and Motor Skills,* 1977, *45,* 1216-1218.

Piaget, J. *The Construction of Reality in the Child.* New York: Basic Books, 1954.

Pollack, I. "Message Probability and Message Reception." *Journal of the Acoustic Society of America,* 1964, *36,* 937-945.

Polyakov, U. F. "The Experimental Investigation of Cognitive Functioning in Schizophrenia." In M. Cole and I. Maltzman (Eds.), *Contemporary Soviet Psychology.* New York: Basic Books, 1969.

Rappaport, M., and others. "Auditory Signal Detection in Schizophrenics." *Psychopharmacologia,* 1972, *24,* 6-28.

Rosenthal, R., and Bigelow, C. B. "Quantitative Brain Measurements in Chronic Schizophrenics." *British Journal of Psychiatry,* 1972, *121,* 259-264.

Rosenzweig, M. R., Bennett, E. L., and Diamond, M. C. "Brain Changes in Response to Experience." *Scientific American,* 1972, *226,* 22-29.

Ross, M. B., and Magaro, P. A. "Cognitive Differentiation Between Paranoid and Nonparanoid Schizophrenics." *Psychological Reports,* 1976, *38,* 991-994.

Safer, M. A., and Leventhal, H. "Ear Differences in Evaluating Emotional Tones of Voice and Verbal Content." *Journal of Experimental Psychology: Human Perception and Performance,* 1977, *3,* 75-82.

Sarbin, T. R., Juhasz, J. B., and Todd, P. "The Social Psychology of 'Hallucinations.'" *Psychological Record,* 1971, *21,* 87-93.

Schilder, P. *The Image and Appearance of the Human Body.* New York: International Universities Press, 1950.

Searles, H. F. "The Schizophrenic Individual's Experience of His World." *Psychiatry,* 1967, *30,* 119-131.

Semmes, J. "Hemispheric Specialization: A Possible Clue to Mechanism." *Neuropsychologia,* 1968, *6,* 11-26.

Serafetinides, E. A. "Laterality and Voltage in the EEG of Psychiatric Patients." *Diseases of the Nervous System,* 1972, *33,* 622-623.

Serafetinides, E. A. "Voltage Laterality in the EEG of Psychiatric Patients." *Diseases of the Nervous System,* 1973, *34,* 190-191.

Shakow, D. "Segmental Set." *Archives of General Psychiatry,* 1962, *6,* 17-33.

Shakow, D. "Segmental Set: The Adaptive Process in Schizophrenia." *American Psychologist,* 1977, *32,* 129-139.

Shimkunas, A. "Hemispheric Asymmetry and Schizophrenic Thought Disorder." In S. Schwartz (Ed.), *Language and Cognition in Schizophrenia.* Hillsdale, N.J.: Lawrence Erlbaum Associates, 1978.

Snyder, S., Rosenthal, D., and Taylor, I. A. "Perceptual Closure in Schizophrenia." *Journal of Abnormal and Social Psychology,* 1961, *63,* 131-136.

Stone, M. H. "Dreams, Free Association, and the Non-Dominant Hemisphere: An Integration of Psychoanalytical, Neurophysiological, and Historical Data." *Journal of the
American Academy of Psychoanalysis,* 1977, *5,* 255-284.

Sullivan, C. T. (Ed. and trans.). *Kant's The Classification of Mental Disorders.* Doylestown, Pa.: Doylestown Foundation, 1964.

Sullivan, H. S. *The Interpersonal Theory of Psychiatry.* New York: Norton, 1953.

Taylor, J. (Ed.). *Selected Writings of John Hughlings Jackson.* New York: Basic Books,
1958.

Wahl, O. F. "Handedness in Schizophrenia." *Preceptual and Motor Skills,* 1976, *42,*
944-946.

Werner, H. *Comparative Psychology of Mental Development.* Chicago: Follett, 1948.

White, R. W. "Ego and Reality in Psychoanalytic Theory." *Psychological Issues,* 1963, *3*
(Whole No. 11).

White, R. W. "The Experience of Efficacy in Schizophrenia." *Psychiatry,* 1965, *28,*
199-211.

Young, M. L., and Jerome, E. A. "Problem-Solving Performance of Paranoid and Nonparanoid Schizophrenics." *Archives of General Psychiatry,* 1972, *26,* 442-444.

Zaidel, E. "Unilateral Auditory Language Comprehension on the Token Test Following
Cerebral Commissurotomy and Hemispherectomy." *Neuropsychologia,* 1977, *15,*
1-18.

64

Jeffrey Urist

Object Relations

The clinical assessment of object relations focuses on the internal basis for an individual's capacity to experience human relatedness. The assessment of object relations rests fundamentally on the understanding that past relations between self and others give rise to the development of internal psychic structure. The concept of structure is an abstract one; yet, as will be seen, it manifests itself in observable and assessable ways.

Relationships in the external world have internal representation in the form of conscious and unconscious ideas and other mental content. In the experiencing of "real" relationships between self and others in the external world, the individual processes and registers present experience in the context of the ways in which past experience has been organized. In attempting to "make sense" out of interpersonal experience, the individual brings to bear psychological processes whose function it is to register and organize mental representations of the self and of others. These processes act not only on "real" perceptions of "real" relationships but, especially early in life, must take on the task of organizing an affectively charged interweaving of psychic content, deriving more from fantasy than from any veridical perception of the external world.

Assessing object relations refers, then, to an evaluation of intrapsychic functioning, not to social behaviors per se. In such an assessment, we are interested in observing the ways in which feelings and conscious and unconscious ideas about the self, about other people, and about the relations between self and others are organized in an individual's mind. The capacities necessary to perform the task of successfully organizing that aspect of human experience are based on the development of mental structures which are thought, under average expectable circumstances, to mature over an individual's lifespan according to a developmental timetable. The assessment of psychopathology—particularly in the areas of depression, borderline conditions, psychosis, and character disorder—has become crucially tied to theories of the development of an individual's capacity to experience self and other within relationships. Various qualities of a patient's repertoire of mental representations are seen as representing definable points along a developmental continuum. This developmental perspective has been incorporated into assessment procedures, so that the developmental level of the patient's capacity for object relationships is often seen as the focal diagnostic and therapeutic issue (Kernberg, 1966).

Assessing the effects of past relationships on the development of the structural capacity for object relations is intimately tied to the idea of a normal maturational sequence for structural development in this area. The shifting relationship between mother and infant typically forms the basis for a model of conceptualizing changes in the developmental level of object relations. Such developmental shifts in childhood create new ways for the child to experience relatedness between self and others. These shifts in the child require empathic responses from the environment. Winnicott (1960, p. 588) describes this situation as follows: "One half of the theory of the parent-infant relationship concerns the infant, and is the theory of the infant's journey from absolute dependence, through relative dependence, to independence. . . . The other half of the theory . . . concerns changes in the mother that meet the specific and developing needs of the infant." This view of development emphasizes the degree of fit between the child's shifting needs on the one hand and the responding environment on the other. The relative success of this fit will affect the formation of structure. A relatively successful degree of fit will allow for greater internalization, where—with the help of "in-tune" parenting—the child gradually acquires the internal capacity to handle functions that had previously been performed by the parent. For example, in learning to soothe oneself, the individual takes over a function that resided originally in the parent.

Background and Current Status

The underlying structural emphasis of much of the work reviewed herein grows out of the more general body of ego psychology. As will be seen in the discussion of assessment, the question of where to look in order to assess object relations revolves around structural concepts—specifically, that of mental representation. Related structural concepts (such as self representation and object representation) emerge from the work of Hartmann (1950) and the attempts of ego psychology to understand the development of the self and of the formation of identity. Following Hartmann's clarification of the distinction between ego and self, Jacobson (1964) extended the scope of ego psychology into the area of the structural development of the self and its relation to objects. Her aim was an integration of a theory of structural development with Freud's economic theory of libido.

The term *object* originated in Freud's early thinking about instinct theory; he saw the mother, or more specifically the breast, as the first object of the child's instincts. Throughout his work, particularly on narcissism (1914) and on processes of internalization (1917), Freud made reference to structural events in the development of the individual that in today's terminology would refer to the self and to the object world.

Tracing the development of concepts related to object relations through Freud's work is difficult because he often used the same term to connote subtly different processes and phenomena. Freud's use of the word *ego* is typical of this problem. While at times in his later work he seems to be describing what today would clearly be considered the "self," Freud used "ego" to refer also to a set of executive functions, to the id-super-ego mediator, and sometimes to a combination of these meanings. In his later work, however, he did concern himself with the question of the development of the individual's sense of self and the sense of the "otherness" of objects.

In his concern with relationship between the pleasure principle and the reality principle, Freud (1925) pointed to the infant's tendency to experience pleasure as "inside" (self) and unpleasure as "outside" (not-self). He called this the stage of "the purified pleasure ego" and saw it not only as an early stage in the organization of defensive processes but also as an archaic phase in the organization of images of self and other.

Following his elucidation of the earliest foundations of the distinction between self and not-self, Freud traced the development of the individual's ability to invest emotionally in others independently of their potential for pleasure or frustration. He described a stage where the infant experiences any object with a potential to provide pleasure as if this object were part of the infant's own body. This investment is a narcissistic one; that is, the object is related to as if it belongs to the subject's own body. In Freud's view, this narcissistic investment gradually gives way to an object relationship. This shift involves a transformation of energies; that is, narcissistic libido is turned into object libido. Object libido represents the fuel for an individual's capacity to love another, as opposed to a love of the self. Freud saw this transformation of energy as being reversible and emphasized that in large part the basis for all object attachment is the child's narcissistic love for what he experiences as his own body: "To begin with, the child does not distinguish between the breast and its own body. When the breast has to be separated from the body and shifted to the outside, because the child so often finds it absent, it carries with it, as an object, a part of the original narcissistic libidinal cathexis" (Freud, [1940], 1961, p. 188).

Whereas Freud regarded the ability to love another person as a necessity for health and ultimately for life itself, he regarded object seeking as subject to the dictates of the pleasure principle. He did not ascribe to object seeking itself the status of a primary motivating force. Fairbairne (1952), however, regarded object seeking itself as a major force in the life of the organism. Both Fairbairne and Klein (1948) placed great emphasis on very early object relationships. They stressed the effects of primitive aggression on the child's struggle to maintain a positive tie to the internal images of the mother. Klein's work in particular has been criticized for a failure to take into account the primitive level of ego development of the very young children to whom she attributed a highly developed capacity for organizing experience. At the same time, however, such criticism (see Zetzel, 1953) points to Klein's major contribution. That is, she noted that the child's earliest, powerfully ambivalent, attitude toward objects influences the eventual adult organization of self and object representation. Whereas Klein equated the process of internalization with the infantile fantasy of oral incorporation, Fairbairne attempted to determine how the structure of the self is formed out of the chaos of infantile ambivalence. In particular, he pursued Klein's emphasis on the mechanism of splitting, suggesting that it represents the immature ego's attempt to deal with archaic, incorporative, devouring, and destructive wishes that threaten the infant's tie to its internal object representations.

Kernberg's (1967, 1976) work on the structural derivatives of object relations brings together Fairbairne's and Klein's emphasis on internal dynamic structures with a more refined analysis of ego development. He, too, attributes particular importance to the role of aggression in the formation of early psychic structure. Whereas Fairbairne and Klein assumed that there is an ego present from birth and that inner and outer reality are distinguishable from early life, Kernberg emphasizes the primary role played by early, powerful, drive-related affects in the development of the ability to differentiate between inner and outer phenomena. His crucial contribution is in pointing out the impact of ambivalence in early ego development and how the ego's task of managing ambivalence becomes linked with the formation and organization of mental representation. He presents a three stage developmental model for the structural shifts that occur in the organization process in early childhood of self and object representation. He presents a three-stage process in the development in the relationship between self and object representation.

The first stage is that of *introjection*. It corresponds generally to Freud's concept of the purified pleasure ego, described above. There is minimal differentiation between self and object at this point. Mental images are organized as either self or not-self according to their potential for comfort or pleasure. In a manner consistent with the overall fragmented state of the ego at this stage, images of the self or of not-self are fragmented according to their "affective valence." In other words, when the mother is experienced as gratifying the infant's needs, the images, affects, and sensations associated with the "good" mother-child dyad are split off from those images, affects, and sensations related to experiences with the mother that were frustrating or "bad." The images of the "good," satisfying mother-child dyad are organized together and distinguished separately from the negatively charged images. There is little distinction between self and not-self here; the distinction is rather between good versus bad, satisfaction versus frustration, loving admiration and idealization versus hatred, depreciation, and envy.

In Kernberg's second stage, that of *identification,* these early split-off, affectively opposite self fragments and object fragments begin to achieve some degree of cohesiveness. Here, self and object are better differentiated from each other. However, this distinction is not yet definitely established. The experience of the object is determined less by highly charged, drive-dominated affect states and more by a sense of the role or function of the object. No longer is a "good" part object taken in globally and fused with part images of the self. In the stage of identification, the internalization process reflects increased structuralization, where specific functions, which hitherto had been performed by the external object, now become part of the repertoire of the self.

Kernberg (1966, p. 242) refers to the third stage as one of *ego identity*:

> (1) a consolidation of ego structures connected with a sense of continuity of the self, the self being the organization of the self-image components of introjections and identifications, to which the child's perception of its functioning in all areas of its life and its progressive sense of mastering the basic adaptational tasks contribute significantly ... ; (2) a consistent overall conception of the "world of objects" derived from the organization of the object-image components of introjections and identifications and a sense of consistency of one's interpersonal interactions; the behavioral aspects, that is, general consistency in the behavior patterns, being even more important aspects of ego identity than those of identifications; (3) a recognition of this consistency in interactions as characteristic of the individual by his interpersonal environment and the perception by the individual of this recognition by the environment ("confirmation").

The internal format of Kernberg's model has its parallels in the work of other investigators (Brody, 1965; Jacobson, 1964; Mahler, 1971; Spitz, 1965) who have written about the early developmental stages of object relationships. Although they disagree about the timing of these developmental shifts and about the relative emphasis to be placed on cognitive, affective, or instinctual considerations, most of these investigators tend to portray these early structural processes in terms of a maturational schema roughly similar to that of Kernberg. Most of them recognize an "objectless" or autistic period at the beginning of life, which then gives way to the development of object relations. In the opinion of most theorists, object relations begin with an early "symbiotic" or "primary narcissistic" phase, involving a lack of differentiation between images of self and images of not-self. They then posit a second phase of "separation-individuation," "secondary narcissism," or "need satisfaction," where there is clearly a psychological distinction between self and other but where the young child's interest in others is essentially narcissistic. Here, others are experienced predominantly in terms of the needs of the self, in the sense that others are defined as though they were still an extension of the self. In the third stage, definitions of both self and other achieve a sense of wholeness and continuity; others are interesting in their own right, no longer exclusively as potential providers of pleasure or frustration. Terms such as *object love, object constancy, ego identity,* and *self constancy* have been used to delimit and describe this third stage.

This developmental progression has been portrayed in numerous ways. For example, Brody (1965) suggests a three-stage model where he distinguishes between the infant's interest in food, a feeder, and, finally, a mother. Regardless of the particular terminology, Brody and others emphasize the idea of a gradual shift from an undifferentiated fused state of mother-infant symbiosis to an ultimate capacity for experiencing self and other as separate, as whole, as continuous, and as existing in their own right independently of the affective context or a prevailing need state.

Kohut (1971) uses the term *self-object* to refer to the situation where self and other are no longer fused but are not yet experienced as separate, whole, continuous entities. Kohut emphasizes that a narcissistic attachment refers not to the object of one's love (that is, it is not necessarily a cathexis of the self) but to the nature of the attachment (narcissistic versus object libido), so that others can be chosen as narcissistic objects (selfobjects). Narcissism and object love, according to Kohut, run independent developmental courses. Narcissism in this view is not a more primitive form of object relationship. The capacity for the regulation of self-esteem runs its own course alongside the individual's growing capacity to love others. Kohut's contribution lies in his offering a more refined understanding of the regulation of self-esteem as an ongoing but separate developmental process.

Kohut (1971) emphasizes the effect of early narcissistic injury and elucidates two narcissistic positions that, in his view, have major developmental significance. The first he calls "the idealized transference," where "after the disturbance of the equilibrium of primary narcissism, the psyche saves a part of the lost experience of global narcissistic perfection by assigning it to an archaic (transitional) self-object, the idealized part image. Since all bliss and power now reside in the idealized object, the child feels empty and powerless when he is separated from it" (p. 27). The second position is that of "the mirror transference," where others are experienced only as audience to provide approval and validation of the grandiose self.

Normal development in this area, according to Kohut, requires an empathic mother, who, by modulating a sequence of gradual frustrations, encourages the child to experience psychic separateness from her. Gradual, too, is the process by which the child is slowly disillusioned about the assumed perfection of the idealized parent. When provided in small doses, this disillusionment leads to the internalization and structuralization of mental functions that were previously performed by external figures. This capacity for

internal modulation of such disappointments provides the basis for the child's own regulation of self-esteem, which is "transmuted" from other to self. Traumatic narcissistic injury or particular failures in the mother's capacity to exercise such regulating and modulating functions may interfere with the child's developing a capacity for the regulation of
self-esteem. Kohut would understand such an interference as a developmental failure in
the transmuting of the function of self-esteem regulation, so that the child does not internalize this function. Others, such as Kernberg (1966, 1967, 1968, 1976), would emphasize not the failure to acquire the function but the failure to make free unconflicted use
of the function. Regardless of the relative emphasis on conflict versus deficit, most theorists attribute various clinical conditions—including certain types of depression, as well
as borderline and narcissistic pathology—to developmental failures in the area of self-
esteem regulation.

Mahler (1968, 1976) offers a developmental theory of separation and individuation based on direct observational studies of the development of children during the first
three years of life. Her schematic view of the first years of life consists of an autistic
phase, followed by a symbiotic phase, and then by a phase of separation-individuation.
This phase of separation-individuation is broken down into four subphases. "Differentiation" is followed by "practicing," then by the "rapprochement" subphase, and finally by
the fourth subphase, which Mahler calls "on the way to object constancy." In the third
year, the toddler comes to recognize and relinquish the unrealistically inflated, grandiose
aspects of his early sense of self. The validating presence of the mother during this time
facilitates the toddler's resolution of this narcissistic crisis and ensures the continued development of an interest in others and a capacity for object constancy.

Critical Discussion

General Areas of Concern

Diagnostic assessment of the individual's world of mental representations has been
an area of concern for more than fifty years. A review of the Rorschach literature (Urist,
1977) reveals that the assessment of an individual's internal repertoire of self and object
representations can be dated back to Rorschach's (1923) earliest blind test analyses.
Hertzman and Pearce (1947) emphasize that the content of human percepts on the Rorschach reflects self and object representations. Blatt and Ritzler (1974) address the diagnostic significance of distortions of human percepts on the Rorschach from the point of
view of ego boundary disturbance. Specific aspects of mature object relations (for example, empathy) have long been the focus of well-accepted diagnostic teaching techniques,
as in Klopfer's work on the human movement response on the Rorschach (Klopfer and
others, 1954); Mayman (1967) highlights the use of the Rorschach for the elucidation of
qualities of self and object representations. The work of Schachtel (1966) also deals with
the assessment of various themes involving the experiencing of self and other as evidenced
on the Rorschach. A test such as the Rorschach offers the diagnostician-researcher a
simultaneous picture of the individual's object relations, impulse life, defenses, affects,
and perceptual-cognitive functioning (Urist, 1977), so that these areas can be studied not
only in and of themselves but in interaction with each other.

The Early Memories Test (Mayman, 1968) was developed to help the diagnostician assess current aspects of the individual's experience of self and other. According to
Mayman, the depiction of relationships within memories conveys aspects of the subject's
characteristic ways of organizing self and object representations. Mayman's approach has
been applied to autobiographical data, as well as to more traditional projective tests, such

as the TAT and the Rorschach (Urist, 1973, 1976). Krohn (1972) has used a similar technique in assessing self and object representations appearing in the manifest content of dreams. Phillipson (1955) has devised a specific object relations test in order to focus on and assess the subject's repertoire of mental representations.

Comparative Philosophies and Theories

A theory regarding the development of object relations enables one to differentiate, for example, between (1) the defensive use of splitting in a borderline patient's struggle with conflicting aggressive and sexual wishes and (2) the isolation used by an obsessional patient in dealing with similar wishes. In other words, the theory of psychosexual development in childhood (oral, anal, phallic-oedipal, and genital stages) has been augmented by a theory that focuses on the developmental level of organization of self and object representation. Questions about the cohesiveness of the self, the intactness of the boundary between self representation and object representation, and the intactness of object representations in the face of frustration often turn to be crucial clinical questions.

The problem for the theory, then, becomes one of integrating knowledge about the development of the child's impulse life with knowledge about the development of object relations. In fact, this integrative task can be expanded to include such areas as cognitive development, motor development, development of affects, and defenses. As increasing attention is drawn toward the area of object relations, critics (for example, Brenner, 1976) have pointed to a one-sided emphasis on structure and the failure of object relations theory to integrate the idea of structural development with the concept of conflict. Such critics often raise questions about the nature of psychotherapy in a system where pathology is defined in terms of structural deficits independent of conflict. The model of psychopathology as a "deficiency disease" has been contrasted with the model of psychopathology as unresolved conflict. When, for example, a patient complains of an inability to perform function X, is that to be understood clinically as a structural deficit, a function which the patient never acquired and which the therapist must provide? Or is it to be understood as an inhibition attributable to a conflict, which, once resolved, will result in the patient's regaining that particular function? (For further discussion of this controversy, see Brenner, 1976; Kernberg, 1976.)

Elaboration on Critical Points

As one moves back and forth between the theoretical literature on object relations and the diagnostic assessment literature, the major problems seem to involve the following questions: What is one trying to measure when one tries to assess object relations? How does one observe psychic structure? How can one confidently link observable behavior back to a theoretical construct, especially to one which relates to complex and often preverbal subjective states? How do projective test data (or any behavior for that matter) reveal anything about an individual's object relations?

To the extent that the theory provides a normal developmental schedule for the unfolding of object relations, there is a framework for assessment. While the theory has not yet provided as clear and precise a timetable as would be preferred, and even though the key junction points have not been sufficiently delineated with regard to intersection with other developmental lines, there are some valuable guidelines for assessment. Certain developmental achievements (for example, the ability to differentiate between one's mental representations of self and of the other, the ability to maintain an internal attachment to the representation of a frustrating object, and the capacity to be interested in another person) represent signposts along a developmental continuum. In the assessment of object relations, these signposts can be used for the purpose of locating individuals with regard to their structural development.

Personal Views and Recommendations

A developmental assessment of object relations involves learning not so much *what* the individual's ideas and feelings about people are but, rather, *how* the individual experiences and organizes these ideas and feelings. One principal source of confusion in assessment results from the use of object relations concepts outside of a structural model. The confusion represents a failure to distinguish conceptually between external relationships in the real world and the internal images or mental representations of those relationships. Assessment becomes clearer when it is understood that the attempt is to assess internal structure rather than external relationships.

A second major area of conceptual confusion stems from the idea that the assessment of object relations involves assessing one thing. The task of assessment, however, becomes focused as one evaluates object relations in terms of various discrete *qualities* of the individual's experience of self and of others. For example, the richness and complexity of mental representations, the quality of aliveness, and the stability or enduring quality of self and object representations are qualitative dimensions that have important diagnostic significance. Such qualities of mental representations can provide the focus for a structural assessment of an individual's repertoire of mental representations. Qualitative dimensions, such as those presented below in scale form, can be understood to reflect the ordering of developmental stages in the unfolding of object relations. The scales can be read as if they were to be applied to any test or interview data that involve a description of people and/or the self. The dimensions are not to be regarded as independent of one another but, rather, as representing overlapping perspectives for the assessment of object relations.

The *Richness and Complexity Scale* consists of the following seven points:

1. Individuals are portrayed as richly complex figures in their own right. Not only are people experienced with a vividness and humanity, but the grasp of personal nuance gives a sense of a richly drawn portrait. The ability to experience people in a complex way (with an appreciation of the various, often conflicting, facets of their personalities) implies a sense of comfort with both ambiguity and ambivalence.
2. An appreciation of the complexity of others and of the self is restricted by a recurrence of neurotic themes, which skew a potentially richer, broader range of experience. Even though they might be quite subtle, the presence of overriding neurotic concerns leads to a sense of repetitiveness and restriction in the interpersonal sphere. While people are experienced as rich and complex figures, the free access to the richness and complexity of others and of the sense of self is, to some extent, constricted.
3. A sense of people is well elaborated; yet a certain simplistic, childish naiveté about people restricts the depth and breadth of interpersonal experience. Even though individuals here may experience intense relationships with others, there is a sense of narrowness and shallowness based on a tendency toward global idealization or devaluation. The feeling about people is very much like that of a "bad" movie, where there are heroes and villains and few shades of grey.
4. People are experienced autocentrically, in terms of how they affect one's own self. Those facets of people's personalities that do not bear directly on one's own situation are ignored or depreciated. The result is a narrowed capacity for experiencing others. The individual recognizes that people have "personalities," but the potential range of

personal traits, values, interests, and character quirks is neither seen nor appreciated.
5. The individual is unable to maintain a cohesive sense of people as having an enduring or stable identity. As opposed to a narrowness characterized by naiveté or clichéd simplicity, the narrowness of the sense of people reflects an underlying disorganization and fluidity. People are not seen as having a continuous organized personality. Relationships may be experienced as deep and intense, yet individuals involved in such relationships are not perceived as whole people.
6. There is a flat, unidimensional quality to the experience of people. There is no sense of people having a personality. People are experienced only as a flat background, whereas the foreground consists of the function they perform. The emphasis is on "food" rather than on "feeder." As opposed to higher-level narcissistic positions (where there is an investment in people as providers of a function), the emphasis is on the function itself, so that the human interactive aspects of a relationship are regarded as virtually irrelevant.
7. People are regarded as flat, empty creatures. There is a cold, almost chilling quality to this sense of people as vacuous and insubstantial. This quality may be characterized as bizarre, ghost-like tenuousness or as an inanimate mechanical starkness. People are experienced not only in a flat, hollow, or brittle way but actually as "things," as "humanoid" rather than human.

The second dimension to be presented is that of *Differentiation and Individuation.* This scale describes the experience of the individuality of self and of other, ranging from a sense of uniqueness and individuality to a sense of humanity as an undifferentiated mass made up of interchangeable parts.

1. There is a refined awareness of subtle distinctions between people's personalities. In addition to this ability to observe distinctions, there is an appreciation of individual uniqueness and an enjoyment in experiencing diversity among people. This capacity to appreciate diversity conveys more than an intellectual interest; it carries a sense of emotional enrichment.
2. The capacity to make subtle and sensitive distinctions between people seems to be limited under certain circumstances of stress by the emergence of neurotic transference issues. Specific neurotic themes override the individual's capacity to experience people as individuals. For example, a proclivity to relate to women in a depreciating way or to experience men in authority in a particular way may blur real differences between individuals. Outside the scope of neurotic conflict, however, relationships are experienced in such a way as to acknowledge a differentiated sense of people's individuality.
3. There is a tendency to gloss over those personal qualities that make people truly unique individuals, due to a proclivity to group together "good, nice" people versus "bad, mean" people. There is a naïve or childlike quality to this type of grouping. The person probably is able to bring together positive and negative traits of people, but he prefers not to do so. If he were somehow pushed to adopt more differentiating or more subtly discriminating attitudes, he probably would be able to do so. The true uniqueness or individuality of people, however, becomes submerged in this more global preference to see people in terms of "good" versus "bad."
4. Differentiation between figures is drawn here in terms of the function performed by people. Qualities or character traits that do not relate to issues of function are less

relevant and do not contribute to the sense of an individual's being truly unique. The functional emphasis has an autocentric ring as well; people seem to be differentiated more by "what they do for me" rather than in terms of who they are. People can be experienced as "special" only insofar as they provide in some exceptional way toward the satisfaction of a need.

5. The capacity to experience others is impeded by a difficulty in differentiating self representation from object representation. Qualities of uniqueness are lost, since others are experienced basically in terms of the degree to which they mirror the self. An individual here may feel "I know what he feels because he's just like me." Conversely, the individual may feel "He will not like me because I am not just like him." Attributes of the self or of the other that do not contribute to such a mirroring process are experienced either as irrelevant or as threatening to relationships. Individuality and uniqueness are experienced as negating the relationship between people. Not only are these qualities of uniqueness not valued, but they are seen as threatening and dangerous.

6. The world of relationships is experienced as a blur, so that no one person is a unique entity and all figures seem interchangeable. The attitude toward people is much like the joke about the man who did not want a book for Christmas because he already had a book. Social relationships are experienced globally as a confusing, undifferentiated mass.

7. There is a basic disturbance in the ability to distinguish between the self and not-self. People lack any defined boundaries, and the integrity of individuals as separate beings is massively compromised. The identity of person A becomes fused with that of person B, just as the identity of the self becomes merged with the identity of the other. The absence of boundaries results in a situation where there is no individuality among people.

The third scale concerns a dimension that will be referred to as *Mutuality of Autonomy*. It encompasses a major part, but not all, of the question of the capacity for object constancy (see Fraiberg, 1969) and the extent to which other people are experienced as having an autonomous existence and stable definition and identity in their own right. The same question can be raised with regard to the self; that is, to what extent is the self experienced as stable, enduring, and autonomous vis-à-vis others. Are relationships experienced in terms of mutually interacting autonomous participants, or does the experience of relationships convey the sense of a comprising autonomy? The *Mutuality of Autonomy Scale* is presented as follows:

1. Relationships are characterized by a clear sense of the autonomy of each of the partners, where the overall tone is one of mutual respect rather than neurotic compromise. Relationships can be deep, meaningful, and satisfying with no risk to the integrity of the participants. Such interactions are portrayed as mutually enhancing rather than draining or depleting. Within the relationship, the autonomy of one's partner is not only tolerated but is appreciated and valued.

2. Relationships here clearly reflect a sense of individuals mutually interacting. The capacity to come together for purposes of collaboration, cooperation, or competition is present. While the autonomy of the individual in such relationships is maintained, the emphasis is not on the relationship itself but, rather, on the particular goal or context. People are clearly separate; however, the mutual give and take between them is in the service of, or defined in terms of, some other purpose.

3. There is no serious disparagement of mutuality or of the autonomy of individuals and relationships, but there is also no consistent, enduring sense of engagement. Relationships may suddenly become conflictual and lose importance, then be reinvested with intensity of interest. Commitment to relationships appears to be secondary to some sense of shifting internal recognition or to internal neurotic conflicts. When engaged, individuals experience meaningful object relationships; however, this level of relatedness fluctuates back and forth with a more functionally defined, need-satisfying level of relatedness.

4. Relationships reflect an underlying "functional" orientation; the emphasis is clearly on the *function* rather than on the *person*. Such relationships may convey a false sense of mutuality, as in "You scratch my back and I'll scratch yours." The underlying assumption, however, is that one helps others in order to earn the right to expect help unquestioningly from others in return. Helping others is seen then as a justification for regarding them as providers of a function.

5. People are portrayed as getting along with each other only insofar as they are alike. The importance of "likeness" here goes well beyond an appreciation for shared interests and tastes; the tone is more of people's needing to act as reflections of each other. The underlying assumption is that people *must* be alike in order to maintain an interest in or concern for one another.

6. Relationships here are characterized by an overriding absence of any real sense of people as active autonomous agents in their relations with each other. A predominant theme is one of coercion, manipulation, or control. Helping others here, for example, is experienced as a justification for controlling them. Interactions are portrayed as intrusive or parasitic. In order for one person to gain, another must lose. There is a quality of omnipotent control here that pervades relationships, even to the point of physical intrusiveness or in the mode of the very young child's perception of the mother's control over the child's bodily functions.

7. Relations between people are portrayed in terms of malevolent, overpowering envelopment. The extreme absence of autonomy is conveyed in any number of metaphors and themes, where the threat of engulfment within relationships is seen in terms of primitive, oral envelopment: "gobbling up," "sweeping up," "swooping down." Autonomy is deteriorated to the level of an experience or fear of incorporation.

Application to Particular Variables

The assessment of object relations (as described above) must take into account other variables as one attempts to apply assessment techniques across a wide range of populations. Factors such as verbal intelligence, education, or organic impairment may all figure significantly. For example, a consistently flat or hollow description of people would obviously mean something different coming from an individual with an IQ of 70 than from someone with an IQ of 100 or 130. Such variables as intelligence or organic impairment may require more refined assessment techniques in order to determine, for example, whether one is observing an interference in the capacity to experience other people or an interference in the capacity to describe that experience. The focus, however, has not been on particular tests or on technique per se. An assessment of object relations is, by definition, relevant across all human populations. As both formal and informal conceptions of mental health and illness become more centered around the capacity to form, enjoy, and maintain relationships, the ability to assess and to understand the development of these capacities becomes more and more crucial in addressing the control problems, both of individuals and of the societies they constitute.

References

Blatt, S., and Ritzler, B. "Thought Disorder and Boundary Disturbance in Psychosis." *Journal of Consulting and Clinical Psychology,* 1974, *42,* 370-381.

Brenner, C. *Psychoanalytic Technique and Psychic Conflict.* New York: International Universities Press, 1976.

Brody, W. "On the Dynamics of Narcissism: Externalization and Early Ego Development." *Psychoanalytic Study of the Child,* 1965, *20,* 165-193.

Fairbairne, W. R. *An Object Relations Theory of Personality.* New York: Basic Books, 1952.

Fraiberg, S. "Libidinal Object Constancy and Mental Representation." *Psychoanalytic Study of the Child,* 1969, *24,* 9-47.

Freud, S. *On Narcissism: An Introduction* [1914]. In *Standard Edition of the Complete Psychological Works of Sigmund Freud.* Vol. 14. London: Hogarth Press, 1957.

Freud, S. "Mourning and Melancholia" [1917]. In *Standard Edition.* Vol. 14. London: Hogarth Press, 1957.

Freud, S. "Negation" [1925]. In *Standard Edition.* Vol. 19. London: Hogarth Press, 1961.

Freud, S. "An Outline of Psychoanalysis." [1940]. In *Standard Edition.* Vol. 23. London: Hogarth Press, 1961.

Guntrip, H. *Schizoid Phenomena, Object Relations and the Self.* New York: International Universities Press, 1968.

Hartmann, H. "Comments on the Psychoanalytic Theory of the Ego" [1950]. In *Essays on Ego Psychology.* New York: International Universities Press, 1964.

Hertzman, M., and Pearce, J. "The Personal Meaning of the Human Figure in the Rorschach." *Psychiatry,* 1947, *10,* 413-422.

Jacobson, E. *The Self and the Object World.* New York: International Universities Press, 1964.

Kernberg, O. "Structural Derivatives of Object Relationships." *International Journal of Psychoanalysis,* 1966, *47,* 236-253.

Kernberg, O. "Borderline Personality Organization." *International Journal of Psychoanalysis,* 1967, *48,* 3-47.

Kernberg, O. "The Treatment of Patients with Borderline Personality Organization." *International Journal of Psychoanalysis,* 1968, *49,* 600-619.

Kernberg, O. *Object Relations Theory and Clinical Psychoanalysis.* New York: Aronson, 1976.

Klein, M. *Contributions to Psychoanalysis.* London: Hogarth Press, 1948.

Klein, M. *Analysis of the Self.* New York: International Universities Press, 1970.

Klopfer, B., and others (Eds.). *Developments in the Rorschach Technique.* New York: Harcourt Brace Jovanovich, 1954.

Kohut, H. *The Analysis of the Self.* New York: International Universities Press, 1971.

Krohn, A. "Level of Object Representation in the Manifest Dream and Projective Tests—A Construct Validation Study." Unpublished doctoral dissertation, University of Michigan, 1972.

Krohn, A., and Mayman, M. "Object Relations in Dreams and Projective Tests." *Bulletin of the Menninger Clinic,* 1974, *38,* 445-466.

Mahler, M. *On Human Symbiosis and the Vicissitudes of Individuation.* Vol. I. New York: International Universities Press, 1968.

Mahler, M. "A Study of the Separation-Individuation Process and Its Possible Application to Borderline Phenomena in the Psychoanalytic Situation." *Psychoanalytic Study of the Child,* 1971, *26,* 403-424.

Mahler, M., Pine, F., and Bergmann, A. *The Psychological Birth of the Human Infant.* New York: Basic Books, 1976.

Mayman, M. "Object-Representations and Object Relationships in Rorschach Responses." *Journal of Projective Techniques and Personality Assessment,* 1967, *31,* 17-24.

Mayman, M. "Early Memories and Character Structure." *Journal of Projective Techniques and Personality Assessment,* 1968, *32,* 303-316.

Phillipson, H. *The Object Relations Technique.* London: Tavistock, 1955.

Reich, A. "Pathological Forms of Self-Esteem Regulation." *Psychoanalytic Study of the Child,* 1960, *15,* 215-232.

Rorschach, H. "The Application of the Form Interpretation Test." *Zeitschrift für die gesamte Neurologie und Psychiatrie,* 1923, *82.*

Sandler, J., and Rosenblatt, B. "The Concept of the Representational World." *Psychoanalytic Study of the Child,* 1962, *17,* 128-145.

Schachtel, E. *Experiential Foundations of the Rorschach.* New York: Basic Books, 1966.

Spitz, R. *The First Year of Life.* New York: International Universities Press, 1965.

Urist, J. "The Rorschach Test as a Multidimensional Measure of Object Relations." Unpublished doctoral dissertation, University of Michigan, 1973.

Urist, J. "Some Structural Considerations in the Relationship Between M and Empathy." *Journal of Personality Assessment,* 1976, *41,* 573-578.

Urist, J. "The Rorschach Test and the Assessment of Object Relations." *Journal of Personality Assessment,* 1977, *41,* 3-9.

Wexler, M. "The Structural Problem in Schizophrenia: Therapeutic Implications." *International Journal of Psychoanalysis,* 1951, *32,* 157-166.

Wexler, M. "The Structural Problem in Schizophrenia: The Role of the Internal Object." In E. Brody and F. Redlich (Eds.), *Psychotherapy with Schizophrenics.* New York: International Universities Press, 1952.

Winnicott, D. W. "Transitional Objects and Transitional Phenomena." In *Collected Papers.* New York: Basic Books, 1960.

Zetzel, E. R. "The Depressive Position." In P. Greenacre (Ed.), *Affective Disorders.* New York: International Universities Press, 1953.

65

Lee J. Loshak

Body Image
Creativity

From a theoretical viewpoint, creativity may be taken as an adaptive activity to order and shape the environment (Gutman, 1961). As such, the most basic of creative productions were sparked by man's* frustrations and the realization of the limitations of his innate capacities. These creative productions, at first primitive instruments (such as the hammer), served to extend man's bodily equipment. "With the handle of the hammer, he prolonged his arm; with the head of the hammer, he gave himself a heavier and harder fist" (Gutman, 1961, pp. 434-435). The hammer, then, like other early primitive tools, was modeled after man's own body. Later, instruments became more sophisticated, and man also invented (or created) machines; their basic design still sprang from an adaptive striving and the model of the body (that is, the body image). Still later, sensing his limitations in processing, assessing, and transmitting information, man built computers and other sophisticated equipment, still utilizing the same basic model: "The photographic

*In this chapter, the word *man,* as well as the masculine pronouns, is used generically and is intended to cover both females and males.

834

camera makes use of principles incorporated in the structure of the eye. The telephone network combined with switchboard resembles the network of neurones with their synaptic connections; cables are structured similar to nerves; flexible tubing makes use of a structural feature embodied in the windpipe; valves are found in the heart and veins; ball-and-socket as well as hinge joints are employed in the appendicular skeleton; dovetail joints are found in the skull" (Gutman, 1961, p. 439).

Similarly, in an effort to overcome limitations in communications, man has created musical instruments, which go beyond the human voice and the clapping of hands. Language, painting, and indeed all the arts may be interpreted as creative productions stemming from the urge to order and adapt but based on man's image of his own body.

An alternate theoretical explanation for creativity is that it represents a uniquely personal or private experience of regression in the service of the ego, an opportunity to engage in controlled primary process thinking rather than be encumbered by the rigid rules of order and logic imposed by secondary process thinking. Such a view supplants the earlier Freudian (1910, 1927) notion of artistic and creative production as the result of sublimated libidinal and aggressive energies (Kris, 1952). Creativity, when defined by the ego psychologists, is the healthy production of a strong and flexible ego. The creative individual, as hypothesized by Schafer (1958) and empirically identified by MacKinnon (1964), appears well integrated, self-sufficient, yet often outgoing, communicative, and able to experience a full range of sensations and emotions without neurotic anxiety. If not explicitly, such a theory then implicitly assumes that the creative individual has a clear and realistic understanding of his body. Freud ([1927] 1960, p. 31) remarked: "The ego is first and foremost a body ego; it is not merely a surface entity but it is itself the projection of the surface."*

The two "body image creativity" theories presented seem to be disparate (since the first one regards creativity as an effort to order the environment, whereas the second theory regards creativity as an effort to cast off the rigidity of order, cause-and-effect relationships, and so on); however, both stress the need for a clear understanding of the body image. Gutman (1961), philosophizing, notes that a complete understanding or appreciation of the body requires a deep understanding of the principles of life and even of the cosmos; that is, an appreciation of the periodic nature of the processes of the body and of the cosmos. In this context, since even physicists are now questioning the validity of cause-effect relationships, perhaps the kind of body awareness Gutman speaks of is not so different from the adaptive regression experience; the two theories converge, differing in emphasis rather than in substance.

From an empirical viewpoint, there are many methods of assessing body image and an equally great number of means for assessing creativity. As regards body image creativity, the body image measure of Barrier, developed by Fisher and Cleveland (1968), appears most promising. Barrier has been related to various physical and psychological or personality measures. Bachelis (1965) found that creativity is related to several direct measures of body participation (for example, tactile tests) but is unrelated to more abstract or symbolic representations of a body awareness concept. However, in a factor analytic study, Holtzman and his associates (1961, p. 171) found that Barrier has a high

*Joan Riviere, the authorized translator of *The Ego and the Id*, appended this statement as follows: "That is, the ego is ultimately derived from bodily sensations, chiefly springing from the surface of the body. It may thus be regarded as a mental projection of the surface of the body."

loading on a factor "indicative of well-organized ideational activity, good imaginative capacity, well-differentiated ego boundaries, and awareness of conventional concepts." In a study by Loshak and Reznikoff (1976), which included a variety of creativity measures, a relationship was found between Barrier and only certain measures of creativity; namely, those associated with artistic expression and human interaction. This finding suggests that creativity is probably not a functional unity and that body image (Barrier) may be related to artistic-expressive creativity but unrelated to scientific creativity.

Background and Current Status

Although the concept of body image is of great importance to personality theory, psychiatry, neurology, and psychosomatic medicine, the historical roots of the concept are somewhat difficult to trace, because the concept was at first only implicitly recognized. Early interest in the concept of how one regards one's body was prompted by reports by psychiatric and neurological patients of various distortions in their body perception and sensation. The puzzling reports of phantom limb experiences by amputees, as well as changes in bodily sensations and perceptions resulting from hypnosis and drug ingestion, also prompted a greater focus on the *psychological* aspects of the physical self.

Even before 1900, neurologists were attempting to explain such distortions. The first attempt to assess body image by means other than clinical observation and interview was through a questionnaire developed by Hall (1898). Head (1926) proposed a schema of the body whereby bodily movement was compared, via a feedback process, to the immediately prior bodily movement. He felt that this movement was accomplished, at least in part, on an unconscious level and that, "Every new posture of movement is recorded on this plastic schema, and the activity of the cortex brings every fresh group of sensations evoked by altered posture into relation with it. Immediate postural recognition follows as soon as the relationship is complete" (p. 605). Each movement had to be evaluated relative to an on-going standard of some kind that permitted integration of current movement activity to the immediately prior movement activity in order to guide and coordinate posture and body orientation.

Others (for example, Bollea, 1948; Critchley, 1950; Freed and Paster, 1951) sought to locate a brain site for such an integrating system. Schilder (1935) emphasized the changing nature of the body image with postural changes, clothing, and on different occasions and in different activities. Schneider (1954) posited that the heart is the organ most related to the body image concept, referring to it as the "root of the ego" and drawing a parallel between heart regularity and ego integration. In a similar vein, Fisher and Cleveland (1968) noted that such concepts as ego and self, for example, overlap in meaning with body image, which itself is not limited in significance merely to attitudes toward the body.

Again, if only implicitly, the body image concept is inherent to Freud's libido theory, with fixations at various body zones and the corresponding concern one may invest in these areas. Similarly, as Fisher and Cleveland (1968) have noted, a concern with body image, or offshoots of this concept, can be found in Jung's (1926, 1931, 1944) idea of the mandala, a protective barrier or container; in Reich's (1949) concept of character armor or body armor; in Rank's (1929) emphasis on birth trauma and the individual's later struggles to attain the security of the womb, also a protective body container; and in Adler's (1930) emphasis on inferiority and the compensations that follow because of feelings of perceived organ inferiority.

Perhaps because of the obscure origins of the concept of body image, "body image creativity," as a concept itself, is of rather recent origin, although the importance of body awareness is implicit in several early notions regarding the dynamics of creative production. These views, however, ran counter to the prevailing psychoanalytic view, which regarded creativity as a sublimation process. Stern (1918), for example, saw the processes of self-maintenance and self-development at work in all biological organisms, with self-development reaching its zenith in the creative activity of humankind. Similar to Stern's concept is Bergson's (1906) concept of "élan vital." More recently, Gutman (1961, p. 423) has posited "that all organized and purposive protoplasmic activity deserves to be classified as 'behavior' and that constructive or creative activity simply continues where growth leaves off," continuing to grow, metaphorically, but following as a blueprint the biological design of the human being.

Numerous mystics (for example, Krishna, 1974), speaking of evolution, see further spiritual development as the only satisfactory development or evolution possible for humankind. For such development, the importance of prayer and meditation is emphasized. In the origins of the occult, it is interesting to note belief in the benefits of celibacy. The notion exists that, through celibacy, the greater life force or energy is retained; rather than given out as a seed for new life to be created, it is instead converted into a force for further personal development. Stern (1918), though not speculating on arcane mystical teaching, viewed human creativity as the highest manifestation of the self-expansion principle, a principle which, on the biological level, he saw expressed in growth and reproduction. Given such a view, the observation by Somerset Maugham (1946, p. 185) seems appropriate: "It is not for nothing that artists have called their works the children of their brains and likened the pains of production to the pains of childbirth. It is something like an organic thing that develops, not merely in their brains but in their heart, their nerves, and their viscera, something that their creativity instinct evolves out of the experiences of their soul and their body."

The concept of regression in the service of the ego, first expressed by Kris (1952), appears to be very similar to the mystical-emotional or meditation experience. Kris (1952), Rapaport (1951), and Schafer (1958) have all described the creative process as a brief partial suspension of ego controls, with a willingness to submit secondary process material to primary process influence. Attempts have since been made to validate the relationship between creativity and ego strength. For example, Maslow (1962) sees the creative individual as one who has sufficient emotional health to regress voluntarily. MacKinnon (1964) describes the creative person as one who is capable of relinquishing conscious controls over unconscious images and drives, thereby enabling this material to emerge. Barron (1958), noting that creative people are strong and healthy, asserts that the strong self knows that it can allow regression because it is confident that it can correct itself. The creative individual is thus more open to his inner experiences because he has a stronger, more flexible ego which he can disengage partially, enabling him to experience primary process material without feeling anxious. It should again be emphasized that body image and ego strength are overlapping concepts, interdependent rather than independent, when considered theoretically.

One promising method for assessing body image is that of Barrier and Penetration, developed by Fisher and Cleveland (1968). Barrier refers to assigning "definite structure, definite substance, and definite surface qualities to the bounding peripheries of things" (p. 58). It takes such diverse forms as noting the texture of an animal's skin or decorative pattern of a surface, or elaborating on a person's clothing. It emphasizes the positiveness and definiteness of boundaries. Penetration refers to boundary peripheries "only in the negative sense of emphasizing their weakness, lack of substance and penetrability" (p.

58). It refers to surfaces that are broken, missing, or destroyed. While the Penetration score generally appears to have relevance for psychiatric populations, the Barrier score has been related to achievement motivation (Appleby, 1956; Rust and Ryan, 1953), small-group behavior (Blake and Mouton, 1956; Cleveland and Morton, 1962; Ramer, 1961), hypnotizability (Fisher, 1963), reaction to stress and adjustment to body disablement (Landau, 1960; McConnell and Daston, 1961), occupational interests (Appleby, 1956), and sensory receptivity (A. D. Davis, 1957, 1960; R. C. Davis, 1957; Fisher and Cleveland, 1968). This list, by no means complete, is indeed impressive, and the nature of the various relationships tends to furnish construct validation for the body image-Barrier dimension.

Fisher and Cleveland's work followed the realization that arthritics gave an unusual number of "rather unique" responses to inkblots; they speculated whether these responses were in some way related to the arthritics' perceptions of their bodies. Specifically, the responses—numerous references to hard, protective, or insulative boundaries or peripheries—seemed to parallel the hard exterior and immense containment of rage often observed in arthritics and manifested in their severe muscular rigidity and constriction. Further study indicated that patients with *exterior* symptoms (such as eczema) often responded with similar percepts, while patients with *interior* symptoms (such as gastrointestinal disorders) tended to give few such responses. Fisher and Cleveland determined that these response patterns had *not* emerged as an adjustment to the illness; rather, they had played a role in the etiology of the disorder. When a composite picture of the high-Barrier individual and the developmental pattern of such an individual eventually emerged, it appeared to parallel that of the creative individual or one who is able to regress in the service of the ego.

Any study dealing with creativity, however, is fraught with great difficulty for a number of reasons. Prime among these is the fact that creativity does not appear to be a functional unity, so that it is very difficult to draw conclusions about "creativity" per se. In the study by Loshak and Reznikoff (1976), involving a group of male college undergraduates attending a large private metropolitan university, the performances of high-Barrier and low-Barrier subjects were compared on a variety of creativity measures. High Barrier was found to be related to artistic and expressive creativity, associated with an interest in interpersonal relations or human interaction, but it was not related to scientific creativity or to the Experience Inquiry (Fitzgerald, 1966), which is a measure of openness to experience or pure regression in the service of the ego. Similarly, the study revealed marked variability in the intercorrelations of the creativity measures; only three of ten such correlations attained statistical significance.

Critical Discussion

General Areas of Concern

As noted earlier, the first assessments of body image were tacit and informal and Hall developed the first formal body image questionnaire in 1898. Since that time, numerous formal measures aimed specifically at the assessment of body image, as well as a number of measures that tap body image, have been developed. However, it is questionable whether the various measures for assessing body image are tapping the same theoretical construct. For example, Fisher and Cleveland (1968) developed two body image measures with different meanings yet both are presumed to tap different aspects of the same construct.

Following a study by Jaskar and Reed (1963), in which no significant correlations were found between a self-report measure of body image and three affective measures of body image for both normal and hospitalized populations, Cardone and Olson (1973) compared selected measures of body image at three levels. At the *perceptual* level, they used the Adjustable Body Distorting Mirror (Traub and Orbach, 1964). At the *self-report* level, they used the Body Cathexis-Self Cathexis Scale (Secord and Jourard, 1953) and the Body Experience and Body Focus Questionnaires (Fisher, 1964a). At the *affective* level, they used Barrier and Penetration responses to the Rorschach (Fisher and Cleveland, 1968). While some significant correlations were obtained, the results indicated a general lack of correlation between the various body image measures for a chronic schizophrenic male population. Cardone and Olson (1973) concluded that further study of the body image parameters is needed, so that a more meaningful body image concept can be formulated.

Perhaps the extensive research currently being conducted in biofeedback and visceral perception will assist in such an endeavor. The validity of verbal labeling tests of visceral perception has not yet been adequately established. Various objective measures of visceral perception are also available; such measures, however, often fail to identify the sensory source of the perception (Brener, 1977). This information is necessary if we are to have a fuller understanding of the psychophysical basis of anxiety and a fuller understanding of what is actually happening during the biofeedback process. These questions may be compounded by actual physiological and psychological differences between individuals, which mediate the net result. In this context, studies by Petrie are worth noting. Petrie (1960) has classified individuals who differ in pain tolerance as "augmenters" and "reducers." Noting that augmenters could be pushed in the reducing direction when bombarded with continuous loud noise (Petrie, Holland, and Wolk, 1963), Petrie concluded that some central nervous system mechanism is involved in the regulation of levels of sensory input. Buchsbaum (1976, pp. 110-111), summarizing recent studies comparing average evoked responses (AER) to various modalities at various intensities, notes:

> The plethora of recording and stimulating techniques in the . . . [relevant studies] and the absence of cross-modal studies within the same individual make a comprehensive summary very difficult. Nevertheless, in a general way for visual, auditory, and somatosensory stimuli, AER amplitudes initially increase with increasing intensity; further increases in intensity often bring about a decrease in amplitude in many individuals. These decreases seem not to reflect poor stimulus control, peripheral adjustments, or transducer response, but rather result from underlying CNS mechanisms. . . . Three types of neural pathways may be involved: descending inhibitory, nonspecific arousal, and cortical-cortical. [These pathways] may work together to modulate sensory input levels depending on the vigilance, arousal, and other needs of the organism.

Borkovec (1976) has compared the response patterns of normals and the patients at a university psychological clinic, as reflected on the Autonomic Perception Questionnaire (APQ) (Mandler, Mandler, and Uviller, 1958). The APQ consists of twenty-one items concerning subjective experiences during states of anxiety. By means of a Q-factor analysis (Stephenson, 1953), Borkovec determined that normal female and male subjects differ not only in total APQ scores but also in their patterns of autonomic-cue perception, with three distinct groups or types of perception emerging for females and three separate and distinct groups or types of perception emerging for males. Additionally, analysis of the data suggested that the patterns of subjective autonomic perception of psychiatric patients do not match those of normal subjects. Borkovec interpreted the data as partial confirmation of his view that there are three separate but interacting components to anxiety—physiological, cognitive, and overt behavioral—and that each of these components needs to be dealt with by appropriate (not necessarily the same) techniques.

How biofeedback, meditation, autogenic training, and relaxation—all of which involve physiological processes and, to varying degrees, cognitive functioning—influence the psychologically perceived body image is an intriguing question. Further, assuming that there is a relationship between body image and creativity, one may ask how any one of these techniques, when applied in an effort to increase creativity (for example, theta training via biofeedback; Budzinski, 1976), may also influence the body image.

It should, however, again be emphasized that body image is a theoretical construct, and that the various operational definitions may have markedly different meanings, so that in any study utilizing body image or a related construct, one should probably stick to the operational definition employed and be hesitant to make broader interpretations of the findings. Similarly, the questions of definition and measurement are of utmost importance to the study of creativity; though operational definitions are frequently utilized, there is still the tendency to assume that a given measure of creativity is all encompassing and then to generalize from this measure. It is here that confusion arises. One must not lose sight of the fact that creativity, like body image, is a theoretical construct. Because of this, several questions emerge. Is creativity a functional unity or are there many, or at least several, different kinds of creativity? If so, are they orthogonal, or do they share some common attributes? Must all creativity be viewed as regression in the service of the ego, or are some creative achievements the outward products or sublimation of inner conflict and turmoil? If so, do the creative productions governed by these differing dynamics also differ in any overt fashion? Similarly, what is the net influence of psychotherapy or psychoanalysis on creative production? This final question, of course, has long been debated, although the answer remains in dispute.

Is an independent (noncreative) motive or process at work in truly creative achievers, as contrasted to those whose creativity is limited merely to contrived tests? Conversely, does creative achievement, when assessed by means of a contrived test, bring quasi-extraneous attributes into play? Regardless, should creativity be viewed as a process or product? If it is a process, can it indeed even be observed? If it is a product, is it something that a creative individual can always be expected to produce in a contrived situation (such as a paper-and-pencil test)? Does creativity correlate in any way with intelligence, and what part do other personality variables (such as motivation) play in its overt manifestation?

The findings of numerous studies conflict on the personality attributes associated with the creative individual and on the question of whether there is a relationship between creativity and intelligence, both because of the different subject samples and the differing nature of the tests employed in these studies. As Thorndike (1963, p. 423) notes: "If tests of different 'creativity' subabilities show very low correlations, then which children will be identified as creative will depend very heavily upon the particular collection of subtests that is used. ... That is, one group of 'creative' children, identified by one set of tests, may score high on tests of academic achievement, whereas another, chosen by a different battery, may not." Thorndike could just as readily have noted that the extent of correlation between creativity and intelligence measures is a function of the extent of creativity tapped by the intelligence test, rather than the extent of intelligence tapped by the creativity measure.

Expanding on Thorndike, one may also add to his remarks as follows: One group of "creatives" (adult or children), as identified by one set of tests, will score high on tests of a given personality trait, attitudinal trait, or interest variable, whereas another group of "creatives," chosen by a different battery, very likely may not. This fact was brought out most clearly in the study by Loshak and Reznikoff (1976), in which body-field perceptual differentiation (high Barrier) was found to be associated with only two of five creativity measures (those reflecting an orientation toward expressive and artistic material, communication, and human interaction) and in which only three of the ten intercorrelations between creativity measures attained statistical significance.

Just what is "creative"? Regardless of the means of assessment, the judgment must be subjective (unless it is objectified to the point of the ridiculous when assessed by certain highly contrived tasks). Further, that which is deemed creative is so deemed within the confines of the society. Today, Galileo is revered as a creative genius; in his own time, he was severely censured and threatened with death for interpreting the movement of the moons of Jupiter as rotation around the planet (an interpretation consonant with the heliocentric theory of our solar system, a theory that Galileo strongly endorsed). If a contemporary of Galileo appreciated Galileo's genius, was that person, then, also creative, although to a lesser degree?

In considering creativity in any context, though especially with respect to body image, how does one explain the flash of inspiration experienced by the greatest of artists and the philosophical and spiritual giants through the ages—the idea that seems to have come from someone or something external to themselves (Bucke, 1974)? Is creativity, then, *in its highest manifestation,* a thing apart, a different phenomenon, unlike lesser creative achievements—coming, instead, as a gift from a higher source of order and consciousness? Regardless of one's personal tenets, in assessing creativity one must embrace neither an egocentric nor a sociocentric view at the expense of something far greater.

Comparative Philosophies and Theories

Much confusion in the area of creativity has been clarified by Guilford's (1959a, 1959b) division of thinking into two separate and antithetical spheres: convergent thinking (general intelligence) and divergent thinking (creativity). Noting the frequent lack of relationship between traditional intelligence tests and creative achievement, Guilford examined the historical basis for intelligence tests. He concluded that the Stanford-Binet rewards rapid, precise, consensually accurate responses, thereby penalizing the unconventional, contemplative thinker. According to Guilford, there are five operational, four content, and six product aspects of any ability, producing 120 (5 X 4 X 6) ways of being talented. The model further breaks down so that, for example, one can be a divergent thinker in one of four categories: figural, symbolic, semantic, or behavioral. The need for an elaboration or division is also stressed by other researchers; for example, Burt (1962) believes that creativity may be specific to a field of interest.

Whereas Guilford's work focuses on the intellectual aspect of creativity, others (for example, Barron, 1959; Taylor, 1960) have focused on personality factors, and their findings also indicate that creativity is not a unitary trait but a conglomeration of any of several patterns that are reflected as creativity in a specific area. Hudson (1966) finds even more diversity than does Guilford, noting that (1) while divergent thinkers are inclined toward the arts, some divergent thinkers are not creative; and (2) while convergent thinkers are inclined toward the sciences, some are truly creative and do not plod the accustomed and conventional path.

Kohut (1971), in a discussion of the therapeutic transformations brought about in the analysis of narcissistic personalities, notes that both scientific and artistic creative activities may appear at times in the analysis of such personalities as the result of the freeing of formerly frozen narcissistic cathexis. Kohut therefore considers the question of whether not only artistic but also scientific pursuits should be considered creative activities. He notes that the strict differentiation between arts and science rests on the assertion that the aim of science is the discovery of *preexisting* formations, while through art *new* configurations are introduced to the world (Eissler, 1961), although the distinction is only superficially clear:

> Great scientific discoveries do not simply describe preexisting phe-nomena, but they give the world a novel mode either of seeing their signifi-cance or of seeing their relationship to each other; and a great scientist who makes a pioneering discovery may channel scientific development into a specific direction, just as an artistic genius who creates a new style may thus determine the direction in which his field of art will develop. It may be an overestimation of the actual state of our scientific world view to believe that science could only have gone in the direction in which its development happened to have led. On the other hand, we also must not forget that some of the greatest works of art are not new creations but the reflection of something preexisting, rendered immortal through the artist's (creatively selective) application of pigment on his canvas or as language on the printed page [Kohut, 1971, pp. 308-309].

Despite these remarks, Kohut goes on to differentiate between the artist and the scientist: "Broadly speaking, the narcissistic cathexes of the artist tend to be less neutralized than those of the creative man of science, and his exhibitionistic libido in particular appears to shift frequently with greater fluidity between himself and his narcissistically invested product than is the case with the scientist" (p. 309).

Implicit to Kohut's thinking is the concept of self, or body, distinct from the environment; and creativity as a process involving a blurring of the distinction between the self and the environment. In a slightly different context, Loshak and Reznikoff (1976) assessed the relationship between body-field perceptual differentiation and cre-ativity. Their study is discussed more fully below.

Elaboration on Critical Points

Loshak and Reznikoff (1976) hypothesized that (1) high-Barrier individuals would exhibit (1) the type of creativity associated with communication and human inter-action and (2) the tendency to creative receptivity, or regression in the service of the ego. Fisher and Cleveland (1968) had previously concluded that high-Barrier individuals tend to show an interest in interpersonal relations because a secure body image enables them to clearly differentiate the self from the external world, so that they can engage in social contacts without feeling anxious. The hypotheses put forth by Loshak and Reznikoff were based on the assumption that a secure base of operations, or adequate body image, enables the high-Barrier individual to branch out into unusual and anxiety-laden experi-ences—not only in the external world but also intrapsychically, in controlled primary process thinking. No hypotheses were made concerning scientific creativity.

In order to sample various kinds or aspects of creativity, five measures of creativ-ity were included in the study. First was Human Movement (M), as defined by Kalsched (1972). In order to qualify for M, a response to the Holtzman Inkblots has to meet three criteria (Human Content, Form Appropriateness, and Movement). The Human Movement response has long been associated with a receptivity to *artistic* inspiration (Anderson and Munroe, 1948; Hersch, 1962; Rawls and Slack, 1968) but unrelated to scientific creativity (Bonifacio and Schaefer, 1969; Roe, 1951, 1953). Piotrowski (1957, 1960) sees Ms as indicative of a strong self-steering mechanism and interest in interpersonal relations. He notes: "Psychologists, psychiatrists, social workers, novelists, artists, and other individuals intensely interested in psychosocial relations produce, on the average, many more M than those whose interest in this area is weak or not genuine. Among the latter are engineers, financiers, physicists, anatomists, and many other scientists. . . . They are interested primarily in inanimate matter and abstract formulas, their preoccupations and creative efforts being associated with nonhuman phenomena" (1960, pp. 143-144). Klopfer and his associates (1954) note a relationship between M and creativity or fantasy thought, but they caution that failures to verify this relationship may, at times, reflect an improper specification of the type of creativity involved.

The second measure of creativity, the Experience Inquiry developed by Fitzgerald (1966), is a self-report inventory that operationalizes Schachtel's (1959) concept of "openness to experience." This concept is a modification of Kris's (1952) concept of regression in the service of the ego.

Third and fourth, the Biographical Inventory of Creativity (BIC), is an empirically keyed multiple-choice measure developed by Schaefer and Anastasi (1968) for identifying creative adolescents on the basis of their experiences in the formative years and the pattern of important choices made by these individuals. This measure has two scales, an artist and writer scale (BIC-CrAW) and a math-science scale (BIC-CrMS); there is some overlapping of items on the two scales.

Fifth was the Remote Associates Test (RAT), based on Mednick's (1963, p. 590) definition of creative thinking: "The test items are intended to require the testee to perform creatively. That is, he is asked to form associative elements into new combinations by providing mediating connective links. Since the test situation is contrived, the combination must meet specific criteria that are experimenter imposed." Numerous researchers (for example, Karp, 1960; Kowalski, 1960; Mednick and Halpern, 1962) have found the RAT a valid instrument for differentiating creatives from noncreatives.

Pearson product-moment correlations were calculated for the five creativity measures. The Experience Inquiry correlated significantly with the BIC-CrAW ($r = .48, p < .01$) and with the BIC-CrMS ($r = .33, p < .05$). The two BIC scales significantly correlated ($r = .66, p < .01$) with each other (as anticipated), because of the overlapping of items on the two BIC scales. No other significant correlations were obtained. The creativity scores of subjects falling in the upper and lower quartiles on the Barrier dimension were compared by means of T tests. Barrier was found to be significantly related only to M ($T = 2.42, p < .02$) and the BIC-CrAW ($T = 2.08, p < .05$).

The significant relationships between Barrier and M and between Barrier and the BIC-CrAW had been anticipated, since these creativity scales are related to expression and human interaction. Similarly, the lack of relationship between Barrier and the BIC-CrMS had been anticipated, since high-Barrier individuals tend to become involved with people and expression rather than with objects and scientific endeavors. The lack of a significant relationship between Barrier and the RAT was, at first, surprising. However, most validity studies of the RAT cite creative productions of architects and research scientists and say little about socially oriented creative achievers, such as artists and writers; this could explain why no relationship was found between the RAT and the socially oriented high-Barrier individual. At the same time, the lack of a significant relationship between the RAT and the BIC-CrMS may be indicative of a limited range of subjects in the study or of a genuine diversity in the kinds of scientifically creative individual each measure specifies or selects.

The lack of a significant relationship between Barrier and the Experience Inquiry was especially surprising in light of the highly significant relationship between the BIC-CrAW and each of these measures. The significant correlations therefore probably reflect common method variance more than common trait variance, since the three creativity measures involved are all self-report inventories. Nonetheless, two questions remain: Why did Barrier fail to show a relationship to the Experience Inquiry? Why did the BIC-CrAW and M fail to correlate significantly, since both of these measures are presumed to reflect interest in communication and human interaction? This question is especially puzzling in view of the fact that each of these measures was significantly related to Barrier. Perhaps the potential for "openness to experience" tapped by the Experience Inquiry reflects a very personal or idiosyncratic experience, which may be too difficult to share immediately with others because of the limitations of language; the highly achievement-oriented, socially gregarious high-Barrier individual would be more likely to channel creative interests into areas where one stands a greater chance of obtaining recognition for achievement.

The lack of relationship between the BIC-CrAW and M requires a closer examination of what each of these is likely to be tapping. The BIC-CrAW may well be tapping largely "creative" output stemming from intellectual efforts rather than from inner experience. It should be noted that teachers' nominations supported by specific productions were the criteria used in the initial development of the BIC. Further, the subjects involved in the development of the keys all attended New York City schools that offered special courses to promote creative behavior; perhaps the students applying to and ultimately attending these "special" schools were excessively achievement oriented. Klopfer and his associates (1954) similarly suggest that intellectual efforts were the basis for "false negatives" in a study by Roe (1946), in which some painters deemed creative on the basis of success gave few M responses to the Rorschach. They also regard "individuals who produce good Ms but are so locked in themselves that there is nothing resembling creative output" (p. 260) as "false negatives." Clearly, all the determinants, rather than only M in isolation, must be considered, and the responses must be looked at clinically—and projectively. Holtzman and associates (1961), in a factor analytic study, found that M has high loadings on a factor "indicative of well-organized ideational activity, good imaginative capacity, well-differentiated ego boundaries, and awareness of conventional concepts" (p. 171) and also on a factor "indicative of disordered thought processes coupled with an active, though disturbed, phantasy life" (p. 171). Despite the qualifications placed on human movement responses in the study by Loshak and Reznikoff (1976), evidence suggests that there, too, M reflected both factors extracted by Holtzman, thereby further pointing up the need to assess M clinically. It may also indicate that, in terms of dynamics, creativity at times reflects ego-adaptive or maladaptive activity.

Personal Views and Recommendations

The concept of body image is both theoretically and empirically based. Different meanings often are used interchangeably or treated as equivalents. That something exists in the abstract mind of man, far greater than the homunculus in the physical brain to signify such a concept, has been made clear by many researchers of various disciplines, even though this is something bordering on the intangible.

In a sense, creativity is even more intangible. Something can be deemed creative, yet from whence does it spring? Where is the source of the inspiration? Is one creative, for example, if the product comes through an experience of automatic writing? If one, indeed, receives the gift of creativity from a higher source, where then are the limits of one's personal consciousness? The body, or the greater perception? What, then, is the distinction between the creative spark and such abilities as clairvoyance, telemetry, psychometry? Is creativity in its purest form a glimpse of a higher consciousness, a higher awareness, with a clearer understanding of one's body similarly an awareness of the unity of the cosmos, with all serving as elements in a higher design? Body image, when defined as deep awareness and control of the body, and creativity are then complementary, representing the individual's interface with a higher order of nature. Advances in biofeedback, meditation, parapsychology, and studies of consciousness may bring light and clarity to as yet very obscure domains.

Application to Particular Variables

Studies involving age factors and body image creativity have not yet appeared, since creativity has only recently been studied in terms of the body image dimension. Fisher and Cleveland (1968) found that the mothers of low-Barrier children obtained higher scores on the Fisher Maladjustment ($p < .01$) and Fisher Rigidity ($p < .05$-$.02$) scores (Fisher, 1950). In assessing Rorschach data, Fisher and Cleveland (1968) note that "High- and low-Barrier individuals are distinguished from each other with respect to characteristics of at least one of their parental figures. . . . The low-Barrier person is more likely than the high-Barrier person to grow up in a family atmosphere characterized by instability, overtones of anxiety, insecurity about dealing with reality problems, and chronic tension. . . . The low-Barrier person grows up in a setting which is less secure and more frustrating than that in which the high-Barrier person develops" (p. 257).

These findings appear particularly interesting in the light of numerous studies assessing the personalities and the rearing patterns of the parents of creative and non-creative children. Weisberg and Springer (1961, p. 563), in such a comparative study, note: "The characteristic pattern found in families of creative children is an openness of exchange and active interaction between two well-defined adult personalities. . . . The parents express emotionally laden material, both toward each other and toward the children. It is as if these parents have in large part settled the question of who and what *they* are, and although the knowledge is painful and anxiety-provoking at times, they do not turn aside from it. Instead, they may overreact to it, and thus there is likely to be considerable open hostility from time to time in the homes of the high-ranking children. Along with a less marked dependency of each marital partner on the other, these parents depend less on the parent-child relationship as a means of reinforcing their own security as individuals than do the parents of low-ranking children." Such findings seem to correspond to Fisher and Cleveland's (1968) findings concerning the parents of high-Barrier and low-Barrier individuals.

Sex differences in body image (Barrier) have been observed by numerous researchers (for example, Fisher, 1964b), with females generally obtaining higher scores than males in both adult and child populations—possibly because, in Fisher's view, the female in Western culture is in more direct communication with her body and has a greater sense of security about it than the male. Somewhat similarly, Borkovec (1976) found that females tend to obtain higher total scores than males on the Autonomic Perception Questionnaire.

Within Western culture, the measurement of body image (Barrier) and body image creativity appears to apply to people of various levels of education and in various socioeconomic strata. As noted earlier, vocational choice appears to be intimately related to how one views his body (provided, of course, the individual is in a socioeconomic position that enables him to exert a choice in career).

Definite cultural differences exist in body image, as assessed by the Barrier dimension (Fisher and Cleveland, 1968), although the question of cross-cultural differences in body image creativity is very difficult to assess, since the definition of what is "creative" may differ in each of the cultures studied. Within a Western culture, questions involving racial distinctions in ability have long been, and no doubt will continue to be, heatedly debated.

The concept of body image is implicit, if not explicit, to any form of therapy. The physical and psychological status of the individual and his physical and psychological self-perception are the main points of focus in biofeedback and behavior therapy. Again, if only metaphorically, the body image and related concepts are present in all psychoanalytic thinking. The distortions in the (physical) self-perception of many psychiatric patients often convey dynamic information for which the therapist should always be looking. Similarly, the distortions in body image and the actual physical limitations of the neurologically impaired should be used, whenever possible, in a therapeutic manner. For example, Goldstein used finger movement around the letters to teach those suffering from alexia to read (Goldstein and Steinfeld, 1942). The recognition of specific movements for specific letters is, of course, a reflection of body image (kinesthetic) signals where the visual-cognitive system has failed.

Body image creativity, as conceptualized in this chapter, is associated with a healthy ego. Whether creativity is a healthy process of adaptive regression or a defensive effort through sublimation is a question that will probably be debated for some time. A related question concerns the possible influence of psychotherapy or psychoanalysis on creativity. Adequate resolution of major areas of conflict may enhance creativity, with the creative productions then charted or directed by the residual areas of intrapsychic conflict not completely resolved in therapy. Loshak (1973) hypothesized that common elements in the concepts of high Barrier and ego strength would result in a statistically significant positive correlation between Barrier and Barron's (1953) Ego Strength Scale. Although no relationship was found, it was not conclusively determined whether this was due to limitations of the Ego Strength Scale, a specific defensive style associated with high Barrier, or limitations in the subject pool involved in the study. However, Fisher and Cleveland (1968) found a general trend for greater definiteness of body image boundaries in a heterogeneous group of patients at the conclusion of extensive psychotherapy. Such a finding is consonant with Kohut's (1971) discussion of the processes involved in the successful treatment of the narcissistic personality.

Stein's conceptualization of creativity, though arising from different roots, in many ways parallels Kohut's view. Stein's view, which includes the concepts of body body-field boundaries and intrapsychic boundaries, may help to resolve the question of whether creativity is an adaptive or a maladaptive process. According to Stein (1967, p. 111): "The creative individual is characterized by permeable boundaries that separate the self from the environment and that separate some or all of the regions within the self. . . . The character of the inner personal region obviously varies with the nature of the work that is undertaken. For persons in one area (physics, for example), it may mean greater flexibility in the intellectual sphere, while for others (the artist), it appears as a greater flexibility in the emotional or affective sphere. To be sure, there is an interaction between the two spheres.

References

Adler, A. *Problems of Neurosis.* New York: Cosmopolitan Books, 1930.
Anderson, I., and Munroe, R. "Personality Factors Involved in Student Concentration on

Creative Painting and Commercial Art." *Rorschach Research Exchange,* 1948, *12,* 141-154.

Appleby, L. "The Relationship of a Rorschach Barrier Typology to other Behavioral Measures." Unpublished doctoral dissertation, University of Houston, 1956.

Bachelis, L. A. "Body-Field Perceptual Differentiation as a Variable in Creative Thinking." Unpublished doctoral dissertation, Yeshiva University, 1965.

Barron, F. "An Ego Strength Scale Which Predicts Response to Psychotherapy." *Journal of Consulting Psychology,* 1953, *17,* 327-333.

Barron, F. "The Psychology of Imagination." *Scientific American,* 1958, *199* (3), 150-166.

Barron, F. "Current Work at the Institute of Personality Assessment Research." In C. W. Taylor (Ed.), *The Third University of Utah Research Conference on the Identification of Creative Scientific Talent.* Salt Lake City: University of Utah Press, 1959.

Bergson, H. *Creative Evolution* [1906]. New York: Holt, Rinehart and Winston, 1911.

Blake, R. R., and Mouton, J. S. *Personality Factors Associated with Individual Conduct in a Training Group Situation.* Human Research Training Laboratory Monograph No. 1. Austin: University of Texas Press, 1956.

Bollea, G. "Contributo Sperimentale alla Fisiopatologia del Cosidetto Schema Corporeo." *Rivista Neurologia,* 1948, *18,* 336-342.

Bonifacio, P., and Schaefer, C. "Creativity and the Projection of Movement Responses." *Journal of Projective Techniques and Personality Assessment,* 1969, *33,* 380-384.

Borkovec, T. D. "Physiological and Cognitive Processes in the Regulation of Anxiety." In G. E. Schwartz and D. Shapiro (Eds.), *Consciousness and Self-Regulation: Advances in Research.* Vol. 1. New York: Plenum, 1976.

Brener, J. "Visceral Perception." In J. Beatty and H. Legewie (Eds.), *Biofeedback and Behavior.* New York: Plenum, 1977.

Buchsbaum, M. "Self-Regulation of Stimulus Intensity: Augmenting/Reducing and the Average Evoked Response." In G. E. Schwartz and D. Shapiro (Eds.), *Consciousness and Self-Regulation: Advances in Research.* Vol. 1. New York: Plenum, 1976.

Bucke, M. *Cosmic Consciousness.* New York: Causeway, 1974.

Budzinski, T. H. "Biofeedback and the Twilight States of Consciousness." In G. E. Schwartz and D. Shapiro (Eds.), *Consciousness and Self-Regulation: Advances in Research.* Vol. 1. New York: Plenum, 1976.

Burt, C. "Critical Notice: 'Creativity and Intelligence' by J. W. Getzels and P. W. Jackson." *British Journal of Educational Psychology,* 1962, *32,* 292-298.

Cardone, S., and Olson, R. E. "Intercorrelations Between Some Body Image Measures." *Journal of Personality Assessment,* 1973, *37,* 122-129.

Cleveland, S. E., and Morton, R. B. "Group Behavior and Body Image: A Follow-Up Study." *Human Relations,* 1962, *15,* 77-85.

Critchley, M. "The Body Image in Neurology." *Lancet,* 1950, *1,* 335-340.

Davis, A. D. "Tests of a Body Exterior vs. Body Interior Theory of Physiological Reactivity." Unpublished doctoral dissertation, University of Texas, 1957.

Davis, A. D. "Some Physiological Correlates of Rorschach Body-Image Production." *Journal of Abnormal and Social Psychology,* 1960, *60,* 432-436.

Davis, R. C. "Response Patterns." *Transactions of the New York Academy of Science,* 1957, *19,* 731-739.

Eissler, K. R. *Leonardo da Vinci: Psychoanalytic Notes on the Enigma.* New York: International Universities Press, 1961.

Fisher, S. "Patterns of Personality Rigidity and Some of Their Determinants." *Psychological Monographs,* 1950, *64* (Whole No. 307).

Fisher, S. "Body Image and Hypnotic Response." *International Journal of Clinical and Experimental Hypnosis,* 1963, *11,* 152-157.

Fisher, S. "Body Image and Psychopathology." *Archives of General Psychiatry,* 1964a, *10,* 519-529.

Fisher, S. "Sex Differences in Body Perception." *Psychological Monographs,* 1964b, *78,* 1-22.

Fisher, S., and Cleveland, S. E. *Body Image and Personality.* (Rev. ed.) New York: Dover, 1968.

Fitzgerald, E. T. "Measurement of Openness to Experience: A Study of Regression in the Service of the Ego." *Journal of Personality and Social Psychology,* 1966, *4,* 644-663.

Freed, H., and Paster, J. R. "Evaluation of the "Draw-a-Person" Test (Modified) in Thalamotomy with Particular Reference to the Body-Image." *Journal of Nervous and Mental Disease,* 1951, *114,* 106-120.

Freud, S. *Leonardo da Vinci and a Memory of His Childhood* [1910]. (Trans. by A. Tyson.) New York: Norton, 1964.

Freud, S. *The Ego and the Id* [1927]. (Trans. by J. Riviere.) New York: Norton, 1960.

Goldstein, K., and Steinfeld, J. J. "The Conditioning of Sexual Behavior by Central Agnosia." *Bulletin of the Forest Sanitarium,* 1942, *1.*

Guilford, J. P. "The Dimensions of Aptitude." In *Personality.* New York: McGraw-Hill, 1959a.

Guilford, J. P. "Three Faces of Intellect." *American Psychologist,* 1959b, *14,* 469-479.

Gutman, H. "The Biological Roots of Creativity." *Genetic Psychology Monographs,* 1961, *64,* 419-458.

Hall, G. S. "Some Aspects of the Early Sense of Self." *American Journal of Psychology,* 1898, *9,* 351-395.

Head, H. *Aphasia and Kindred Disorders of Speech.* Cambridge, England: Cambridge University Press, 1926.

Hersch, C. "The Cognitive Functioning of the Creative Person: A Developmental Analysis." *Journal of Projective Techniques,* 1962, *26,* 193-200.

Holtzman, W. H., and others. *Inkblot Perception and Personality.* Austin: University of Texas Press, 1961.

Hudson, L. *Contrary Imaginations.* New York: Schocken Books, 1966.

Jaskar, R. O., and Reed, M. R. "Assessment of Body Image Organization of Hospitalized and Non-hospitalized Subjects." *Journal of Projective Techniques and Personality Assessment,* 1963, *27,* 185-190.

Jung, C. G. *Psychological Types.* London: Routledge & Kegan Paul, 1926.

Jung, C. G. *Psychology of the Unconscious.* New York: Dodd, Mead, 1931.

Jung, C. G. *Psychology and Alchemy.* New York: Pantheon Books, 1944.

Kalsched, D. "Adaptive Regression and Primary Process in Dream Reports." Unpublished doctoral dissertation, Fordham University, 1972.

Karp, S. "A Validity Study of a Measure of Creativity." Unpublished senior honors thesis, University of Michigan, 1960.

Klopfer, B., and others (Eds.). *Developments in the Rorschach Technique.* Vol. 1: *Technique and Theory.* New York: Harcourt Brace Jovanovich, 1954.

Kohut, H. *The Analysis of the Self.* New York: International Universities Press, 1971.

Kowalski, J. "Attitudes and Occupational Interests of Creative Individuals." Unpublished senior honors thesis, University of Michigan, 1960.

Kris, E. *Psychoanalytic Explorations in Art.* New York: International Universities Press, 1952.

Krishna, G. *Higher Consciousness.* New York: Julian Press, 1974.

Landau, M. F. "Body Image in Paraplegia as a Variable in Adjustment to Physical Handicap." Unpublished doctoral dissertation, Columbia University, 1960.

Loshak, L. J. "Creativity, Ego Integration, and Body Image Boundaries." Unpublished doctoral dissertation, Fordham University, 1973.

Loshak, L. J., and Reznikoff, M. "Creativity and Body Image Boundaries." *Journal of Personality Assessment,* 1976, *40,* 81-90.

McConnell, C. L., and Daston, P. G. "Body Image Changes in Pregnancy." *Journal of Projective Techniques,* 1961, *25,* 451-456.

MacKinnon, D. W. "Creativity and Transliminal Experience." Address sponsored by Division 8 of the American Psychological Association at its 72nd annual convention, Los Angeles, Sept. 1964.

Mandler, G., Mandler, J. M., and Uviller, E. T. "Autonomic Feedback: The Perception of Autonomic Activity." *Journal of Abnormal and Social Psychology,* 1958, *56,* 367-373.

Maslow, A. H. "Emotional Blocks to Creativity." In S. Parnes and H. F. Harding (Eds.), *A Source Book for Creative Thinking.* New York: Scribner's, 1962.

Maugham, W. S. *The Summing Up.* New York: Doubleday, 1946.

Mednick, S. A. "The Associative Basis of the Creative Process." In M. T. Mednick and S. A. Mednick (Eds.), *Research in Personality.* New York: Holt, Rinehart and Winston, 1963.

Mednick, S. A., and Halpern, S. "Ease of Concept Attainment as a Function of Associative Rank." *Journal of Experimental Psychology,* 1962, *6,* 628-630.

Petrie, A. "Some Psychological Aspects of Pain and the Relief of the Suffering." *Annals of the New York Academy of Science,* 1960, *86,* 13-27.

Petrie, A., Holland, T., and Wolk, I. "Sensory Stimulation Causing Subdued Experience: Audio-analgesia and Perceptual Augmentation and Reduction." *Journal of Nervous and Mental Disease,* 1963, *137,* 312-321.

Piotrowski, Z. A. *Perceptanalysis.* New York: Macmillan, 1957.

Piotrowski, Z. A. "The Movement Score." In M. A. Rickers-Ovsiankina (Ed.), *Rorschach Psychology.* New York: Wiley, 1960.

Ramer, J. C. "The Rorschach Barrier Score and Social Behavior." Unpublished doctoral dissertation, University of Washington, 1961.

Rank, O. *The Trauma of Birth.* New York: Harcourt Brace Jovanovich, 1929.

Rapaport, D. "Toward a Theory of Thinking." In D. Rapaport (Ed.), *Organization and Pathology of Thought.* New York: Columbia University Press, 1951.

Rawls, J. R., and Slack, G. K. "Artists Versus Non-artists: Rorschach Determinants and Artistic Creativity." *Journal of Projective Techniques and Personality Assessment,* 1968, *32,* 233-237.

Reich, W. *Character Analysis.* New York: Orgone Institute Press, 1949.

Roe, A. "Painting and Personality." *Rorschach Research Exchange,* 1946, *10,* 86-100.

Roe, A. "A Study of the Imagery in Research Scientists." *Journal of Personality,* 1951, *19,* 459-470.

Roe, A. "A Psychological Study of Eminent Psychologists and Anthropologists and a Comparison with Biological and Physical Scientists." *Psychological Monographs,* 1953, *67* (Whole No. 352).

Rust, R. M., and Ryan, F. G. "The Relationship of Some Rorschach Variables to Academic Behavior." *Journal of Personality,* 1953, *21,* 441-456.

Schachtel, E. *Metamorphosis.* New York: Basic Books, 1959.

Schaefer, C. E., and Anastasi, A. "A Biographical Inventory for Identifying Creativity in Adolescent Boys." *Journal of Applied Psychology,* 1968, *52,* 142-148.

Schafer, R. "Regression in the Service of the Ego: The Relevance of a Psychoanalytic Concept for Personality Assessment." In G. Lindzey (Ed.), *Assessment of Human Motives.* New York: Grove Press, 1958.

Schilder, P. *The Image and Appearance of the Human Body* [1935]. New York: International Universities Press, 1950.

Schneider, D. E. "The Image of the Heart and the Synergic Principle in Psychoanalysis (Psychosynergy)." *Psychoanalytic Review,* 1954, *41,* 197-215.

Secord, P. F., and Jourard, S. M. "The Appraisal of Body Cathexis: Body Cathexis and Self." *Journal of Consulting Psychology,* 1953, *17,* 343-347.

Stein, M. I. "Creativity and Culture." In R. Mooney and T. Razik (Eds.), *Explorations in Creativity.* New York: Harper & Row, 1967.

Stephenson, W. *The Study of Behavior.* Chicago: University of Chicago Press, 1953.

Stern, W. *Person und Sache.* Vol. 2: *Die menschliche Persönlichkeit.* Leipzig: Barth, 1918.

Taylor, C. W. "The Creative Individual: A New Portrait in Giftedness." *Educational Leadership,* 1960, *8,* 7-12.

Thorndike, R. L. "The Measurement of Creativity." *Teachers College Record,* 1963, *64,* 422-424.

Traub, A. C., and Orbach, J. "Psychophysical Studies of Body Image." *Archives of General Psychiatry,* 1964, *11,* 53-66.

Weisberg, P. S., and Springer, K. J. "Environmental Factors in Creative Function." *Archives of General Psychiatry,* 1961, *5,* 554-564.

66

David W. Barnett
Karl B. Zucker

Assessment of the Others-Concept

The others-concept is defined as a person's general expectancies or perceptions about other people along a positive-negative continuum. It is viewed as an interactive, complex construct with components at relatively deep levels of personality and with important behavioral expressions. The others-concept has been empirically related to the social behaviors of children interacting in a play situation, to other developmental aspects of psychological growth (for example, moral development and age and sex differences), and to total personality adjustment.

The others-concept has been assessed in children and adults through the use of the Paired Hands Test (PHT) (Zucker and Barnett, 1977). Although the concept is considered of sufficient importance to be independent of a specific assessment technique, the PHT has been exclusively used for the primary research in this area to date, because of several unique features. The PHT, as a personality assessment instrument, combines projective and objective features. Twenty slides (or photographs), each consisting of one black and one white hand in a relationship that implies an interaction between them, are presented one at a time. The child (or adult) is asked to respond by selecting the one statement, out of five presented for each slide, that comes closest to his or her own idea about what the hands are doing. The statements were edited from a collection of verbatim statements and scaled along a friendliness-hostility dimension using a Thurstone-type technique. The subject's numerical score on the test is thought to be an indication of his or her others-concept.

Background and Current Status

Constructs similar to the others-concept have been suggested in the literature, but they have a different emphasis. For example, Mead's (1934) "generalized other" refers to an organization of the roles of others. Mead thought of the "generalized other" as a conception derived from an individual's experiences of the related roles of other participants in a given situation (Lindesmith and Strauss, 1968). Another similar-sounding concept, Jourard's (1958) "other-concept" (the "beliefs one holds concerning someone else's personality"), refers to one other person, rather than to people in general. The life position of "You're OK" described in the literature dealing with transactional analysis most closely approximates the meaning implied in the others-concept (Berne, 1961; Harris, 1969). The term *others-concept* was selected because it was considered to provide meaning for research findings relating children's perceptions of others to social interaction (Barnett and Zucker, 1973, 1975, 1977). Additionally, the others-concept has evolved to be conceptually parallel to the self-concept.

Earlier research leading to the development of the others-concept used the Paired Hands Test for evaluating possible increases in friendliness among highly selected children already presumed to be fairly friendly. Zucker and Jordan (1968) designed the original PHT, but at that time they did not use the term *others-concept.* They used the test in 1966 to study possible changes in friendliness among children attending a Children's International Summer Village; the major purpose of the organization is to provide opportunities for developing friendships across national boundaries (Allen and Mathews, 1961). Friendliness was operationally defined as the frequency of "spontaneous judgments" that the two hands are interacting in a "friendly way." Barnett and Zucker then launched the series of studies mentioned above, in which PHT scores were studied in relation to actual behaviors of children in small groups. The PHT has been found empirically to provide an indication of the extent to which children might interact with others in a warm, nonthreatening, nonabrasive, cooperative, and helpful manner, although many other factors must be taken into consideration before any predictions about specific individuals can be made (Barnett and Zucker, 1973, 1975, 1977). The PHT has correspondingly gone through several revisions; the modifications have been reported in detail in the test manual (Zucker and Barnett, 1977).

Critical Discussion

General Areas of Concern

The others-concept is thought of as complex and interactive in nature because, as could be expected, there have been consistent and significant behavioral expressions of this personological variable, but also significant situational constraints. In three separate studies (Barnett and Zucker, 1973, 1975, 1977), group trends have demonstrated statistically significant findings in the expected direction. That is, persons with higher PHT scores, indicating a more positive others-concept, have been found to interact in a small-group situation in a more task-related and facilitative manner than persons with lower PHT scores. There were, however, some differences in each of the three studies. These are reported in detail in the references cited and have also been presented in summary form (Zucker, 1976).

To date, the behaviors of about 300 children have been studied while they worked on group tasks. The groups were composed of three or four children in the same school and grade. They worked for about a fifteen-minute period. Unidirectional microphones for each child in the group made available individual children's comments, so that each child's verbal participation in the group could be statistically analyzed. The children's comments were judged on the following dimensions in the 1975 and 1977 studies:

1. *Task related (T):* responses (instructions, questions, suggestions, or comments) that had to do directly with the task.
2. *Non-task related (N):* responses that were irrelevant to the task.
3. *Positive (+):* a helpful suggestion or a response that merited compliance, such as agreement or support.
4. *Negative (−):* a response that would typically evoke anger or be generally abrasive or hostile in an actual or implied way.

All the statements were then coded on two of the dimensions. Some examples of actual statements and the way that they were categorized are as follows:

> You're getting it, but it's on there wrong. (T+)
> Man, this is dumb. (N−)
> I've got it, I got it. (T+)
> What part are you making? (T+)
> This bugs me, it really does, it bugs me. (N−)
> I'm for destroying it very nicely and delicately by going crash. (T−)
> No, you should have left it in there, stupid. (T−)
> They aren't going to tell much from us, are they? (N+)
> You should have seen him kiss her. (N+)
> Now you hold this, and I'll hold this. (T+)

A very high level of agreement was found between two expert judges (blindly rating the comments) on the four categories of behaviors. The correlations ranged from $r = .99$ for the T+ ($N = 5,570$) to $r = .93$ for the T− ($N = 1,607$).

The tasks were originally intended to be somewhat similar; however, they did seem to elicit differences in the children's interest and enthusiasm, although this was not specifically studied. The tasks included making things with tinkertoys, arranging dominoes in a specific fashion, assembling jigsaw puzzles, and arriving at a group decision about the topic of a poster and cooperatively executing the group decision with a large blank posterboard and magic markers.

The results have consistently shown a statistically significant trend for children with a high others-concept to interact more positively in the small-group situation than children with a low others-concept. For example, in the 1977 study, including the largest number of children to date ($N = 211$), there was a significant difference on the T+ dimension in the expected direction at the .001 level (F [1,416] $= 28.94, p < .001$). The children scoring higher on the PHT tended to be cooperative, goal-directed, and pleasant, whereas the children with lower scores were, in addition to being less cooperative and goal-directed, more abrasive and sometimes rude to the other members of their group.

These differences represent group trends and not individual results. The differences between subjects with a high and low others-concept were not always readily apparent. On many occasions individuals with a high others-concept made negative, irrelevant comments, whereas children with a low others-concept made rather positive comments. The data have demonstrated the statistically significant trends when a total of over 12,000 separate behaviors of nearly 300 subjects were coded blindly and analyzed in these studies.

The overt expression of the above behavioral dimensions seemed to be either enhanced or constrained by situational variables that were not always predictable. Some situations—as in the more enjoyable task of making the poster, versus the relatively uninteresting task of ordering dominoes by similar faces—seemed to bring out differences between groups of children. In the situations not eliciting significant, and at times dramatic, differences in behaviors, the group trends revealed that the high- and low-scoring children were behaving similarly on the coded dimensions. The situation did not exist in which, overall, children with a positive others-concept behaved more negatively than children with a negative others-concept. The statistically significant behavioral differences, wherever they existed, were always in the expected direction.

Comparative Philosophies and Theories

The self-concept and the others-concept are both related to total personality adjustment, and the advantage of considering both self-concept and others-concept, rather than either one or the other, has been demonstrated (Galluzzi and Zucker, 1977). Other parallels in construct development, assessment, and the personal and social significance of the construct seem evident and need to be explored further. A brief review of the theoretical state of the self-concept, as provided by Shavelson, Hubner, and Stanton (1976) will demonstrate the interrelatedness of the theoretical orientations of both concepts.

Shavelson, Hubner, and Stanton (1976, p. 411) present the following working definition of the self-concept: "a person's perceptions of himself . . . formed through his experience with his environment . . . influenced especially by environmental reinforcements and significant others." They point out the problems associated with a trait conceptualization of the self-concept and emphasize the importance of an interactive approach.

According to Shavelson and his fellow researchers, there are seven critical and necessary features in defining the self-concept as a construct: (1) The self-concept is formed when an indefinite number of experiences contributing to perceptions of one's self are categorized and organized. (2) The self-concept is idiosyncratic and "multifaceted," since significant categories—such as school ability, physical characteristics, and social milieu—typically vary for individuals. (3) The self-concept is hierarchical, ranging from a "general self-concept" to "individual experiences" in "specific situations." (4) The "general self-concept is stable," but considerable variability may relate to specific situations. (5) The self-concept is learned through developmental experiences. (6) The self-concept is "evaluative"; people "describe" and "evaluate" their own performance in personally relevant situations against "ideal" standards or in comparison with the performance of "peers" or perceived evaluations of "significant others." (7) The self-concept has discriminant validity, in that it is "differentiable from other constructs with which it is theoretically related" (Shavelson, Hubner, and Stanton, 1976, pp. 411-415).

Galluzzi and associates (1978) have outlined the developmental considerations involved with the others-concept. The factors which they have considered are general in scope and relate to the psychological principles involved in the issues of parental handling and early childhood social experiences. Basic principles of learning, especially social learning, personality theory, and social psychology, are discussed.

The specific features of the others-concept as an emerging construct need to be explored in more detail, not only in respect to the self-concept but also in the area of interpersonal behaviors that focus more on the concerns suggested by the others-concept. However, the need for a parallel to the self-concept, emphasizing a person's concepts of other people, has been substantiated to a large degree through research.

Elaboration on Critical Points

Four areas of critical importance emerge from the above discussion. The first has been discussed in sufficient detail for the purposes of this chapter and relates to the definition of an emerging construct, the others-concept. The other three areas that warrant further discussion relate to (1) the social significance of the construct, (2) factors and techniques surrounding the clinical assessment of the others-concept, and (3) the methodological concerns of the research.

The social significance of studies of the quality of human interactions seems self-evident. Within the rubric of the others-concept, friendly and cooperative interpersonal behaviors have been studied, as well as other significant personality dimensions, such as personality adjustment, moral development, and the needs of exceptional children (Zucker, 1976). For example, Whiteman, Zucker, and Grimley (1978), using Kohlberg's theoretical framework, found that higher PHT scores were associated with higher levels of moral development. Burzynski (1980) found in group comparisons that children living in Northern Ireland, where tensions are rampant, have a lower others-concept than children in the Republic of Ireland. Hart (1975) reported that children enrolled in regular classes who were judged by their teachers to exhibit behaviors typically associated with learning disabilities or emotional disturbance have a lower others-concept than the other children in their classrooms. Houser (1977) found a low, but significant, positive correlation ($r =$ .40) between internal locus of control and others-concept in secondary-level students. Kirchhoff (1977) found that secondary-level students with a high others-concept were more accommodating, sensitive, conscientious, forthright, spontaneous, and self-disciplined, as measured by the Children's Personality Questionnaire (Porter and Cattell, 1975), than children with a low others-concept.

Historically, much of the research involving interpersonal behaviors has been examined within the context of violence and aggression, an essentially negative focus. In contrast, the area of friendly, prosocial behaviors provides a logical and necessary step in substituting acceptable behaviors for maladaptive behaviors. Other psychological dimensions stressing interactions between persons, such as the psychology of loneliness and depression, might also be eventually considered within the positive, prosocial framework.

As briefly alluded to earlier, traditional psychodynamic concepts may provide one way of understanding some of the factors that influence people's others-concept and their reaction to the PHT stimuli. The projection of one's own hostility can be used as an explanation of why some people may perceive others in a negative light (Galluzzi and others, 1978). In identifying children with either a positive or a negative others-concept, the PHT provides projective stimuli to which the subject assigns meaning. The responses have been scaled along a friendliness-hostility dimension, and a total score is obtained. Other assessment techniques should also be explored in an attempt to identify the others-concept of children, especially those who may be suggested for an intervention group program. Galluzzi and associates (1978) suggest situations to observe (teacher-student interactions, peer interactions, a child's reactions to social situation, and defensive behaviors) that may be significant sources of information about a person's others-concept, in addition to the use of the PHT.

In many ways, the methodological problems encountered in the research described in this chapter are representative of broader concerns in personality research. Mischel (1968, 1973, 1977) has been a critical spokesman of the theoretical and practical problems in personality assessment. A basic question raised has been whether or not a trait or trait-like personality organization exists which is predictive of highly complex social behaviors. Mischel (1968) points to the typically low validity coefficients and questions the incremental validity and utility of "test-derived personality descriptions" (p. 104). The "phenomenological impact" of the environment (Mischel, 1973, p. 279) becomes a powerful moderating variable that increases the difficulty in interpreting personality research. Other writers have suggested that situational influences may not contribute more than traditional (but reliable) psychometric procedures (Hogan, DeSoto, and Solano, 1977).

A balanced approach, emphasizing the need to explore person variables as well as situational variables, is taken by many psychologists and also represents the findings of research reported in this chapter. Theoretically predictable and consistent findings have been found to be associated with the PHT scores; but in a series of behavioral studies concerning the expression of relevant and socially significant behaviors, the results have sometimes been seemingly influenced by situational variables in a somewhat unpredictable fashion. The interactive nature of the person variables and the situational variables is one that needs to be explored. Perhaps this could be done most productively from the point of view of the principle of reciprocal determinism (Bandura, 1978).

Personal Views and Recommendations

The information available to date is based primarily on group research, and most of the studies have focused on subjects identified as having either a high or a low others-concept. There is a need for more clinical studies, information about people who are relatively average with respect to others-concept, and exploration into the interactive influences of situational and person variables. More normative, demographic, and correlational research is also needed. For example, in most studies conducted to date, females have been found to have a higher others-concept than males, but these studies took place in the midwestern area of the United States. In the one large cross-national study that was carried out, no sex difference with respect to others-concept was found in Ireland. Normative data are presented in the PHT Manual in terms of age, grade, sex, ethnic identification, and estimates of socioeconomic status and intelligence, but more information regarding the relationship of all these variables and many others to the others-concept is needed. Longitudinal studies should also be carried out.

The possible areas where the others-concept construct may make practical, as well as theoretical, contributions are manifold. Wherever interpersonal relationships take place, such as in schools, institutions, and industry, the others-concept may help to predict the quality of the interaction to be expected, provided that the roles of the many other influential and interacting factors are properly taken into account, as noted above. The prosocial emphasis on improving a person's others-concept, as opposed to focusing almost exclusively on his or her assumed negative qualities, such as hostility, appears to be promising.

Application to Particular Variables

Demographic data gathered to date have opened up some interesting and significant areas for future exploration. Present findings suggest that there is a general tendency for the others-concept to become more positive with increasing age (Zucker and Barnett, 1977). Although this tentative statement is based mainly on the finding that PHT scores have increased with age and grade in most studies conducted in the midwestern United States, the same trend was also noted in one large study that was carried out in Ireland (Burzynski, 1980).

Socioeconomic status also appears to be related to others-concept. Among children in grades 4 through 6, those judged by their teacher to have come from higher socioeconomic backgrounds have obtained higher PHT scores (Barnett and Zucker, 1977). This trend was seen in Ireland as well as in the various samples studied in the United States (Burzynski, 1980). There are no cross-national studies of socioeconomic status and others-concept among older children (grade 7 and above) and adults, but data from American samples suggest that the relationship between others-concept and socioeconomic status diminishes with age, so that among entering college freshmen there is no significant difference (Burzynski, 1972; Zucker, 1976).

The findings with respect to sex differences have already been noted. Females in midwestern United States samples generally have scored higher than males, but this sex difference was not found among the large sample of children tested in Ireland, suggesting the importance of cultural and other environmental factors in influencing sex differences (Barnett and Zucker, 1977; Burzynski, 1978).

Although the relationship between others-concept and intelligence has been explored, it has not been adequately clarified up to now, due to the confounding factor of socioeconomic background. The others-concept of mentally retarded children in relation to influential factors, such as whether or not they have experienced special class placement, is currently under investigation. Hart (1975) studied the others-concept of a group of children enrolled in regular classes who, according to items checked by their teachers on a screening instrument, were quite likely slow learners or mentally retarded; Hart found that, as a group, these children did not have an others-concept significantly different from that of their classmates.

(For a more complete discussion of demographic variables as they relate to the others-concept, and the possible implications of these relationships, see Barnett and Zucker, in press.)

References

Allen, D. T., and Mathews, W. P. *A Handbook for Children's Summer Villages.* Lausanne, Switzerland: Imprimeries Réunies, 1961.

Bandura, A. "The Self-System in Reciprocal Determinism." *American Psychologist,* 1978, *33,* 344-358.

Barnett, D., and Zucker, K. "An Exploration into Children's Interpersonal Behavior as Related to Their Perceptions of Social Interactions." *Psychology in the Schools,* 1973, *10,* 61-66.

Barnett, D., and Zucker, K. "The Other-Concept and Friendly and Cooperative Behavior in Children." *Psychology in the Schools,* 1975, *12,* 495-501.

Barnett, D., and Zucker, K. "Validating a Measure of Children's Other-Concept Through

Population and Behavior Variables." *Journal of Personality Assessment,* 1977, *41,* 131-143.

Barnett, D., and Zucker, K. "The Others-Concept: Explorations into the Quality of Children's Interpersonal Relationships." In H. Foot, T. Chapman, and J. Smith (Eds.), *Friendship and Childhood Relationships.* Chichester, England: Wiley, in press.

Berne, E. *Transactional Analysis in Psychotherapy.* New York: Grove Press, 1961.

Burzynski, P. "Perception of Social Interaction and Social Behavior Among Adults: An Adult Form of the Paired Hands Test." Unpublished educational specialist thesis, Indiana State University, 1972.

Burzynski, P. "A Cross-National Investigation of the Others-Concept Using the Paired Hands Test." Unpublished doctoral dissertation, Indiana State University, 1980.

Galluzzi, E., and others. *The Teacher's Role in Others-Concept Development.* Terre Haute: Indiana State University Curriculum and Development Center, 1978.

Galluzzi, E., and Zucker, K. "Level of Adjustment and the Self- and Others-Concept." *Psychology in the Schools,* 1977, *14,* 104-108.

Harris, T. A. *I'm OK, You're OK.* New York: Harper & Row, 1969.

Hart, S. "The Others-Concept and Children with Special Needs." Paper presented at meeting of American Psychological Association, Chicago, Aug. 1975.

Hogan, R., DeSoto, C., and Solano, C. "Traits, Tests, and Personality Research." *American Psychologist,* 1977, *32,* 255-264.

Houser, D. "Relationship of Locus of Control and Others-Concept in Children." Paper presented at annual meeting of American Psychological Association, San Francisco, 1977.

Jourard, S. *Personal Adjustment.* New York: Macmillan, 1958.

Kirchhoff, L. "Personality Trait Comparisons Between High and Low Others-Concept Children." Paper presented at annual meeting of American Psychological Association, San Francisco, 1977.

Lindesmith, A., and Strauss, A. *Social Psychology.* (3rd ed.) New York: Holt, Rinehart and Winston, 1968.

Mead, G. *Mind, Self, and Society.* Chicago: University of Chicago Press, 1934.

Mischel, W. *Personality and Assessment.* New York: Wiley, 1968.

Mischel, W. "Toward a Cognitive Social Learning Reconceptualization of Personality." *Psychological Review,* 1973, *80,* 252-283.

Mischel, W. "On the Future of Personality Measurement." *American Psychologist,* 1977, *32,* 246-254.

Porter, R., and Cattell, R. *Children's Personality Questionnaire.* Champaign, Ill.: Institute for Personality and Ability Testing, 1975.

Shavelson, R., Hubner, J., and Stanton, G. "Self-Concept: Validation of Construct Interpretations." *Review of Educational Research,* 1976, *46,* 407-441.

Whiteman, J., Zucker, K., and Grimley, L. "Moral Judgment and the Others-Concept." *Psychological Reports,* 1978, *42,* 283-289.

Zucker, K. "The Others-Concept: Its Place in the Schools." *School Psychology Digest,* 1976, *5,* 4-12.

Zucker, K., and Barnett, D. *The Paired Hands Test Manual.* Dallas: McCarron-Dial Systems, 1977.

Zucker, K., and Jordan, D. "The Paired Hands Test: A Technique for Measuring Friendliness." *Journal of Projective Techniques and Personality Assessment,* 1968, *32,* 522-529.

67

Gary Thomas Long

Interpersonal Distance Preference

Interpersonal distance preference—operationally defined as the physical distance one chooses to establish between one's self and another person—is not now measured by one broadly accepted specific scale or process. Instead, various measuring techniques have been used. Linder (1976), for example, counted the floor tiles between one person's chair and another's. Long, Calhoun, and Selby (1977) scored the responses on a questionnaire that indicates one's choice of chair around a rectangular table (the chairs are scored for distance from an indicated other person, and the description of the characteristics of the situation and/or the other person may be varied). These two examples of measures of interpersonal distance preference represent two distinct types of measure. The first example, counting floor tiles, is an unobtrusive measure taken without the awareness of the subject. The second type of measure is taken with the full awareness of the subject.

There are two major interpretations of the behavioral dimension represented by the measures. One is that the distance preferred represents the positive or negative feeling one has for the person from whom the distance is measured. That is, one prefers closer proximity to persons to whom one is attracted. The relationship between interpersonal distance preference and attraction is well documented (Berscheid and Walster, 1978; Linder, 1976). The other major interpretation is that interpersonal distance preference indicates the level of stress or tension that one is experiencing at the time the preference is expressed. As one's experienced stress level increases, the amount of interpersonal distance one prefers increases (Evans and Howard, 1973).

Background and Current Status

As far back as the seventeenth century, naturalists observed and noted aspects of animal spatial behavior which later were included in the concept of territoriality, as first described by English ornithologist H. E. Howard in 1920 (Hall, 1966). Research into the manner and function of animals' use of space is one of the lines of development leading to interpersonal distance preference. This line of primarily animal research was furthered by the notion of a series of zones surrounding an individual. The approach of another species would trigger certain specific behavior, depending on the zone entered. Other zones were related to the behavior exhibited when members of the same species approached.

A related notion, the notion of individual distance, refers to the characteristic spacing between members of the same species. This spacing varies with the animal's activities (such as feeding or sleeping) and in accordance with the relationship between species members (for example, in the baboon troop, the relative status and age of a member determine how closely another may be approached).

Edward Hall, an anthropologist, gave the research a decided human twist (Hall, 1959, 1963, 1966) when he coined the term *proemics* to refer to the scientific study of spatial behavior in man. He proposed several schemes of zones to describe and explain human spatial behavior. He finally settled on four zones of distance that people employ, depending on their relationship and the activity. These zones, although not described as such, represent the interpersonal distance preference of the actors. Hall was interested in cross-cultural differences in the use of space. He viewed the use of space, one aspect of which is referred to as interpersonal distance preference, as a culturally determined means of communicating. He proposed that one's use of space is a way of expressing one's feeling and that the manner of expression varies from one culture to the next.

The study of nonverbal behavior is the other major contributor to the evolution of the concept of interpersonal distance preference. Nonverbal behavior refers to the nonspoken communication that takes place during social interaction between people or between animals. One type of behavior within this broad category of silent language was described by David Katz in 1937 as "personal space" (Linder, 1976)—a combination of territoriality, density, and individual distance. Another type, *kinesics,* is of most significance in the study of humans. Kinesics refers to the movements and gestures that are emitted by an individual during social interaction. These include body movements across space, postures, gestures, facial expressions, and eye contact. Birdwhistell (1952) made a major contribution with his elaborate system of symbols for recording nonverbal behavior. Although the concept of interpersonal distance does not evolve directly from this line of investigation, it is significant because one recent interpretation of interpersonal distance preference is as a communication of one's internal state or attitude.

Interpersonal distance preference is related to several specific concepts—such as crowding, privacy, personal space, and individual distance—which have been studied under the major headings of territoriality and nonverbal communication. The concept of interpersonal distance preference is related to several of these concepts in important ways, but it did not really evolve from them in any direct or systematic way.

In the course of research on territoriality, nonverbal communication, and related concepts, interpersonal distance preference was often conceptualized as part of something else or a way of measuring something else. For example, in Sommer's (1969) study of personal space, the measure taken was very often that of the interpersonal distance preference of the subject. This measure was interpreted as an indication of "personal space," which is defined as "an area surrounding a person's body into which others may not come" (p. 26). Linder (1976) notes that personal space no longer has a precise meaning in scientific discourse. The recent evolution of the concept of interpersonal distance preference has been largely due to the desire of researchers to achieve a precise definition and measure of some aspect of spatial behavior (such as personal space or crowding).

The concept and the measure of interpersonal distance preference are now being used by investigators interested in a number of different topics. Some of these topic areas are personal space, interpersonal attraction, territoriality, crowding, personality, situational stress, and privacy—in addition to studies of interpersonal distance preference as an area of interest in itself.

Interpersonal distance preference has shown promise as an indicator of individual differences and of momentary states of the individual (states such as affect or tension level). One of Sommer's earliest studies of personal space (Felipe and Sommer, 1966) observed the response of schizophrenics to a close approach by another. Several other studies on psychopathology and interpersonal distance have followed (see, for example, Tolar, 1970). There is an interest in diagnosing and understanding personality abnormalities by observing the use of space. The interest in the use of interpersonal distance preference has developed too recently for investigators to have agreed on a common measure or even to have adopted the same terminology. Even very recent studies measuring the subject's reported distance preference may use a term other than interpersonal distance preferable to describe the phenomena measured. For example, the term *social distance*, as used by Heckel and Hiers (1977), refers to operations very similar to those of Long, Calhoun, and Selby (1977), who use the term *interpersonal distance preference*. Linder (1976) refers to the same behavior as *interaction distance*. At present the concept shows promise of usefulness in a number of areas in which recent interest is high. It is too early in the development and use of the concept to make a definite evaluation of its significance.

Critical Discussion

General Areas of Concern

The concerns about the concept of interpersonal distance preference are of three types: (1) concerns about the method of measurement, (2) concerns about what it means to prefer more or less distance, and (3) concerns about explaining the cause of interpersonal distance preference.

Concerns About Method. Determining a valid, reliable, and practical method for measuring interpersonal distance preference is a major concern. The methods used have been numerous and varied. Although the number of studies dealing with interpersonal distance preference is fairly large, there are insufficient data for any particular method to establish its validity and reliability. This diversity of method leads to problems of noncomparability of research and increases the difficulty in determining the meaning of interpersonal distance preference.

There are three types of measures of interpersonal distance preference; simulation, laboratory, and field (Altman, 1975). In simulation studies, subjects are asked to manipulate representations of people (for instance, felt figures or dolls) in a model setting to indicate the distances they would prefer. Simulations may employ drawings or charts on which the subject responds in writing. This type of measure is relatively easy to construct and to administer. Pencil-and-paper measures may be given to large numbers of people simultaneously, and characteristics of the situations may easily be manipulated by altering the drawings or adding written descriptions to the drawings. The ease of manipulating variables and the ability to handle large numbers of subjects simultaneously are advantages of this approach. The possibility that the behavior measured by this method is artifactual and not generalizable to other settings must be of concern.

Laboratory measures of interpersonal distance preference usually employ a real situation in which the subject expresses a preference about the distance from another person. For example, another person may approach the subject until the subject asks him to stop, or the subject may do the approaching. The characteristics of the subjects, the approachers, or the instructions may be varied in this type of measure. Here the researcher controls the situation in a way to test hypotheses, with people responding to experienced distance rather than the symbolic or imagined distances in the simulation studies. This increased realism may yield a more generalizable measure of the subjects' spatial behavior, but of course only situations that the researcher can create can be studied. Many situations of interest may be very difficult to create.

Laboratory measures, although they offer more realism than the simulation approach, are still not completely natural. The subjects usually know that their spatial preference is being measured. The artificial nature of the situation and the subject's knowledge that he is being observed may affect the behavior of interest. This problem can apply to all laboratory research, so its particular relevance here is dependent on the sensitivity of interpersonal distance to being examined. If the behavior has a particular social meaning and the subjects are motivated to alter the message they are perceived as sending, they may intentionally conceal their true spatial preference. If, however, the distance preference is a cue that communicates something about the feeling or state of the subjects without their awareness, then their behavior might not be affected.

Whether or not the subject is aware of what is communicated by the use of interpersonal distance, the field measures of spatial behavior would be unaffected. Field measures are taken by observing subjects in natural settings without their awareness that they are being observed. People have been observed in cafeterias, on playgrounds and park benches, and/or simply standing in hallways. The distance they establish from another person is the measure of their interpersonal distance preference. This method is easily generalized because it is taken in the kind of setting in which it would be applied.

The subject, being unaware that the measure is being taken, would not intentionally distort or conceal anything. Of course, the lack of control of the situation by the researcher leads to difficulty in measuring many of the types of situations that may be of interest. The question of the appropriateness of measuring people's behavior without their knowledge must be considered by the researcher using this approach. The problem is not unique to measuring interpersonal distance and has been discussed at length elsewhere.

Field measures are not well suited for assessing the interpersonal distance preference of an individual. Field settings do not often lend themselves to repeated measures of the same individual's spatial preference. A series of responses by a subject would be desirable for reliability and validity in a measure used to scale an individual along a dimension. The simulation measures are most adaptable to this application.

Concerns About Meaning. What it means to prefer more or less interpersonal distance has not been determined. The preference for greater interpersonal distance may not always indicate either a positive or negative state in the individual or in his attitude toward another. The identification of the dimension(s) of behavior revealed by interpersonal distance preference is an important concern.

The diversity of methods employed to measure the concept of interpersonal distance preference contributes to the difficulty in identifying the correlates of distance preference. A great many individual and situational characteristics have been observed to vary with interpersonal distance preference. When the variations in these other things are understood, inferences may be made about the meaning of interpersonal distance preference.

Observations have been made in numerous settings and measured in various ways. This variety makes it more difficult to determine the meaning of interpersonal distance preference because the different measures sometimes yield different results. It is difficult to determine whether the different results are caused by different relationships between variables and distance preference or simply appear to be different because the relationships are measured in a different way. Even though the various measures used make exact comparison of research more difficult, there is the advantage of generality when the same concept is measured in different ways and yields similar results. The following studies of the relationship between attraction and interpersonal distance illustrate both these points: (1) the lack of precision resulting from measurement of distance in different settings and in different ways; and (2) the increased generality when the same concept is measured in various ways with a similar relationship resulting.

The general conclusion that "people choose to be physically closer to others they like" has been observed to be true (1) for couples standing at a desk talking to a psychologist (Byrne, Ervin, and Lamberth, 1970); (2) for female pairs in various settings on the streets of London (Heshka and Nelson, 1972); and (3) when people are asked to place miniature figures representing friends in a simulated setting (reviewed by Sundstrom and Altman, 1976). These studies illustrate the advantage of conceptual replication. The lack of precision related to using various measures of the same concept becomes evident when, for example, an explanation is attempted for the fact that males on London streets do not choose to be physically closer to friends than to strangers. Further studies have indicated that, as the setting and the sex of the subject vary, the pattern of interpersonal distance preference does not correspond perfectly with pencil-and-paper measures of interpersonal attraction. It is difficult to determine whether this lack of precision is due to real differences in distance preference as these characteristics vary or to variations resulting from differences in the measurement method. This problem is best solved through further research.

Concerns About Cause. Concerns about explaining the cause of interpersonal distance preference are related to the concerns about the underlying dimension(s). The two types of concerns are separable, however. Questions such as the following are related to explaining the cause of the phenomenon: Is interpersonal distance preference determined by an instinctive need for territory? Is it a language learned during socialization which reflects culturally defined norms of space use? If it is language, is the person aware of his communications? Does interpersonal distance preference reflect one's attempt to adapt to the tension level one is presently experiencing? These questions of concern call for a comprehensive theory of interpersonal distance preference that will make sense of the data now available. There are several theories that attempt to deal with spatial behavior or with concepts related to the use of space. Although most of these do not directly deal with the specific concept of interpersonal distance preference, they have considered some of the questions that a theory of interpersonal distance would consider. The concerns about theory will be discussed in the next section.

Comparative Philosophies and Theories

Theories that deal with interpersonal distance are affected by the same lack of agreement on terms that complicates the study of measures of interpersonal distance. There are a number of theoretical statements about spatial behavior. While they do not all refer directly to interpersonal distance, several of them deal with spatial behavior that is relevant to explaining interpersonal distance. In the discussion of theoretical positions in this section, major implications of the theoretical positions for assessment will be pointed out. The individual theories will not be described in detail.

Hall's proposed interpersonal distance zones illustrate two major aspects of theorizing about spatial behavior. Hall's (1966) theory describes a pattern of concentric circles or zones that surround people. The behaviors that may occur vary as the zone another enters varies. Since the size of these zones varies from culture to culture, they are said to be learned and culturally defined. Further, Hall proposed that the zone used serves to communicate something about the state or feeling of the individual. The notions that spatial behavior is learned and that it is a means of communicating represent major aspects of theoretical positions about interpersonal distance.

Another theoretical approach, that of Duke and Nowicki (1972), is an application of Rotter's (1954) social learning theory to spatial behavior. Duke and Nowicki stress the importance of the role of reinforcement and expectancies about reinforcement in the learning of interpersonal distance preferences. They recognize the potential influence of individual differences in expectancies on the final spatial behavior. The individual difference that they researched directly was locus of control, but the notion that differences in spatial preference can be indicative of other individual differences is a general one and has important implications for the use of interpersonal distance preference in assessment.

Altman (1975) believes that spatial behavior should be explained as a whole and not in fragments such as personal space and crowding. He therefore has proposed a general theory to explain three major aspects of spatial behavior: personal space, territorial behavior, and crowding. Briefly stated, the proposed function of spatial behavior is the establishment of the desired level of privacy. An evaluation of the usefulness of this approach at this time would be premature. The notion that spatial behavior serves an equilibrium function is common to two other theoretical statements about interpersonal distance.

Argyle and Dean (1965) propose that interpersonal distance is one of several regulating mechanisms that individuals use to achieve a desired level of intimacy in social interaction. Distance interacts with other behaviors, such as eye contact and personal disclosures, to determine the intimacy of the interaction. Other things being equal, an increase in interpersonal distance would reduce the intimacy level of the interaction. Of particular interest here is the notion that distance interacts with other aspects of the situation, so that the observation of distance alone would not always indicate the level of intimacy. As mentioned earlier, many aspects of spatial behavior may be related in an interactive way, so that the observation of interpersonal distance alone would not accurately assess behavior. This is a potential difficulty, however, and not a demonstrated problem.

Another theoretical statement relevant to explaining interpersonal distance is one made about personal space by Evans and Howard (1973). They say that personal space is a means for achieving acceptable stress levels and for controlling intraspecies aggression. They refer to certain adaptive features of personal space and note that people who are stressed seem to prefer more space. Their theory about the relationship between stress and interpersonal distance is an interesting one, both as an indication that distance use does reflect internal states and as a reference to the evolutionary value of personal space as a human vestige of territoriality.

Overall, the theories about spatial behavior are preliminary in nature. The statements they make are mostly descriptive. Theory-oriented explanation and prediction of interpersonal distance preference is not far advanced at this point. The positions of Altman and of Duke and Nowicki are too recently developed to fairly evaluate   at this time. The vast majority of research in the field has been atheoretical. The prediction of characteristics of individuals based on their spatial preference has almost entirely been empirically developed.

Elaboration on Critical Points

The theories described above do not offer elaborate or detailed explanations of the cause of interpersonal distance preference. With the exception of Duke and Nowicki, the theories are more descriptive than explanatory. Certain commonalities in some of these approaches, however, have important implications for the application of interpersonal distance to assessment. The view that spatial behavior is a means of communication is common to most of the theories. Hall states directly that the use of space is a way of communicating. The communication need not be intentional, and the communicator may not even be aware of what he is communicating. This approach encourages attempts to read the spatial behavior of individuals as indicative of internal feelings or states. Evans and Howard also view the use of personal space as an indication of the tension state the individual is experiencing. Argyle and Dean, as well as Altman, see spatial behavior as related to feelings or needs of the individual. Argyle and Dean regard spatial behavior as a mechanism for regulating intimacy in a relationship. If this is so, then the observation of spatial behavior will allow the assessment of the intimacy of a relationship. Altman's view that space regulates the privacy of an individual is supportive of the same theme: that spatial behavior reflects the internal states of needs of the individual. These theories are consistent in the general position that the use of space by people can indicate the internal state they are experiencing.

Duke and Nowicki, while not in conflict with the view of the other theories, have shown that interpersonal distance preference can be used as a measure of another individual difference variable—namely, locus of control. In short, they have tied the relationship to a theory. This is noteworthy because the theories have not, at this point, provided significant direction for the research on interpersonal distance. Most of the work in the field has been of the "I wonder what would happen if . . ." variety.

Personal Views and Recommendations

The common theme of spatial behavior as an indicator of an individual's internal state, as well as the growing list of findings of relationships between one's use of space and other personality variables, supports the idea that interpersonal distance preference may be useful in clinical assessment. The concept of interpersonal distance preference shows promise as a measure that can indicate characteristics of individuals. More work is required before the promise can become reality. One of the most important steps will be to develop a body of data on one type of measure of interpersonal distance. The Duke and Nowicki Comfortable Interpersonal Distance Scale or the Long, Calhoun, and Selby measure or some combination of the two pencil-and-paper measures should be thoroughly examined and psychometrically developed. These two measures show the greatest promise for usefulness across a broad range of settings and potential applications. The developers of each of these measures have also focused their attention precisely on interpersonal distance rather than some broader and less clearly defined aspect of spatial behavior. It is time to explore thoroughly the nature of clearly defined aspects of spatial behavior, such as interpersonal distance, and to move away from the broad and nebulous concepts, like territoriality and personal space. A concentration on the specific concept of interpersonal distance while employing one or a small number of measures to operationalize it will allow determination of whether interpersonal distance can or cannot be a useful indicator of individual characteristics. The argument that spatial behavior is interactive to the extent that observing interpersonal distance alone will be uninformative should be answered empirically. If the argument is supported, then another concept and measure of spatial behavior can be developed and tested. The answer with respect to interpersonal distance preference will not likely be found unless there is considerable research using the same measure of the concept.

At the present time, one strategy that seems likely to be successful in using interpersonal distance preference for assessment is to make unobtrusive measures of distance preference and interpret the preference for greater distance as an indication of tension in the relationship. A preference for greater distance could also mean that the individual is less attracted to the other person. One must rely on other indicators to determine which interpretation is better. Of course, the two interpretations are not mutually exclusive and could both be correct.

An alternative strategy would be to use a paper-and-pencil measure and vary the person from whom distance is preferred. This may be a way of identifying relationships that are tension provoking for a client. Observations of the interpersonal distance preference from a parent, spouse, sibling, co-worker, or any other person of interest may reveal information about the client's feelings toward significant others in his or her life. Distance preference could be an indirect and nonthreatening way of expressing tensions in relationships.

Application to Particular Variables

In recent reviews of the literature on spatial behavior, Altman (1975), Baron and Byrne (1977), Evans and Howard (1973), and Linder (1976) have noted that the use of space varies as certain characteristics of the person vary. Some of these variations will be described below in general terms. It should be noted that the measures used, as well as the actual spatial preferences of people, are probably very sensitive to variations in setting. Therefore, the relationships to be indicated below may not be found in all settings.

Children begin to develop or learn stable interpersonal distance preferences when they begin to have social relationships with one another. Initially, they do not seem to be sensitive to interpersonal boundaries, but by adolescence they have established patterns of spatial preference like that of adults. Children younger than 6-8 years require less interpersonal distance than older children in most situations.

Several variables interact with sex to affect interpersonal distance preference, but it is generally observed that females prefer less distance from others than males. Males prefer less distance from a female than from a male. Males do not seem to vary their distance preference with the intimacy of the relationship as much as females do. Findings of sex differences in distance preference seem particularly affected by other aspects of the situation, such as the characteristics of the other person.

Numerous cross-cultural and subcultural studies indicate that people of different cultural groups prefer different interpersonal distances. Typical findings in this area are that Latin Americans, French people, and Arabs prefer less interpersonal distance than Americans, while Germans prefer more. It has been observed that Chicanos stand closer together than whites, who stand closer than blacks. Further, when blacks and whites interact with each other, they prefer greater distances than when either interact with the same race.

People prefer greater distances when interacting with the physically handicapped, the obese, or drug users. There are no data on the preferences of these groups when they interact with "normals."

Several studies indicate that people with various personality abnormalities have different interpersonal distance preferences. The exact pattern of the differences is elusive. Schizophrenics have been observed to prefer more interpersonal distance in some settings, less in others, and to have more variable preference in others. At this point it appears that distance preference does vary in those with personality disorders, but the exact form of the variation is not known.

References

Altman, I. *The Environment and Social Behavior.* Monterey, Calif.: Brooks/Cole, 1975.

Argyle, M., and Dean, J. "Eye-Contact, Distance and Affiliation." *Sociometry,* 1965, *28,* 289-304.

Baron, R., and Byrne, D. *Social Psychology: Understanding Human Interaction.* Boston: Allyn and Bacon, 1977.

Berscheid, E., and Walster, E. *Interpersonal Attraction.* Reading, Mass.: Addison-Wesley, 1978.

Birdwhistell, R. L. *Introduction to Kinesics.* Louisville: University of Louisville Press, 1952.

Byrne, D., Ervin, C. R., and Lamberth, J. "Continuity Between the Experimental Study of Attraction and 'Real Life' Computer Dating." *Journal of Personality and Social Psychology,* 1970, *16,* 157-165.

Duke, M. P., and Nowicki, S., Jr. "A New Measure and Social Learning Model for Interpersonal Distance." *Journal of Experimental Research in Personality,* 1972, *6,* 119-132.

Evans, G., and Howard, R. "Personal Space." *Psychological Bulletin,* 1973, *80,* 334-344.

Felipe, N., and Sommer, R. "Invasions of Personal Space." *Social Problems,* 1966, *14,* 206-214.

Hall, E. T. *The Silent Language.* New York: Doubleday, 1959.

Hall, E. T. "A System for the Notation of Proxemic Behavior." *American Anthropologist,* 1963, *65,* 1003-1026.

Hall, E. T. *The Hidden Dimension.* New York: Doubleday, 1966.

Heckel, R. V., and Hiers, J. M. "Social Distance and Locus of Control." *Journal of Clinical Psychology,* 1977, *33,* 469-471.

Heshka, S., and Nelson, Y. "Interpersonal Speaking Distance as a Function of Age, Sex, and Relationship." *Sociometry,* 1972, *35,* 491-498.

Linder, D. E. "Personal Space." In J. Thibaut, J. Spence, and R. Carson (Eds.), *Contemporary Topics in Social Psychology.* Morristown, N.J.: General Learning Press, 1976.

Long, G. T., Calhoun, L. G., and Selby, J. W. "Personality Characteristics Related to Cross-Situational Consistency of Interpersonal Distance." *Journal of Personality Assessment,* 1977, *41,* 274-278.

Rotter, J. B. *Social Learning and Clinical Psychology.* Englewood Cliffs, N.J.: Prentice-Hall, 1954.

Sommer, R. *Personal Space: The Behavioral Basis for Design.* Englewood Cliffs, N.J.: Prentice-Hall, 1969.

Sundstrom, E., and Altman, I. "Personal Space and Interpersonal Relationships: Research Review and Theoretical Model." *Human Ecology,* 1976, *4,* 47-67.

Tolar, A. "Psychological Distance in Disturbed and Normal Adults." *Journal of Clinical Psychology,* 1970, *26,* 160-162.

68

Alan Gray Slemon

Associative Elaboration

Associative elaboration refers to the ability of a person in a problem or learning situation to produce images, relations, interpretations, inferences, or other associations appropriate to the demands of the situation. Related terms would include transcendence, embellishment, fluency, responsivity, flexibility, complexity, and diligence. The primary characteristic of elaboration is frequency. However, responses must also be appropriate to the stimulus situation. The elaboration score, based on the amount of appropriate embellishment, is supposed to indicate how freely a person can develop detailed or thorough plans or adorn ideas to make them fancy and attractive.

A variety of stimuli have been used to elicit associative elaboration. People may be asked to make up stories about characters in pictures, to suggest solutions to social problems, to state how a toy or some other physical object might be improved, or to add details to abstract drawings. The stimulus dimensions may therefore be verbal or nonverbal, and the responses requested may also be verbal or nonverbal.

Elaboration appears to have considerable utility as a descriptive term, and so it has been adopted by a number of researchers. The underlying assumption in its use appears to be that easy responsivity in learning and problem situations is probably adaptive and that people who are capable of fluent elaboration are more likely to produce functional responses than people who are relatively restricted. Elaboration has been used in the areas of both personality and ability testing.

Background and Current Status

The concept of elaboration appeared in Wallas's (1926) discussion of creative production. In his view, creative thinking includes four stages: preparation, incubation, illumination, and verification. The verification stage consists of both elaboration and evaluation. Elaboration involves development of ideas produced in the illumination stage, and evaluation refers to the critical testing of each of these elaborations against reality. The ability to elaborate, therefore, has a very important place in this theory of creative production.

Another early concept of elaboration is secondary elaboration, a term used by psychoanalysts to describe one of the mechanisms in dream work. Secondary elaboration, according to Freud (1910), is the process by which fragments of latent content are combined into a relatively coherent manifest content without regard for logical inconsistencies among the original elements. This usage is quite different from that in creativity research, where critical evaluation is assumed to be a very important associate of elaboration.

Guilford and Torrance have both had an important influence on the evolution of the concept of elaboration as a component of creative ability. Guilford (1956) emphasizes four important components in creativity: fluency, flexibility, originality, and elaboration. Elaboration involves an individual's ability to develop the details of a plan when given only a bare outline or to add lines to create an object when only a simple, abstract figure is given. Torrance (1962, 1965) emphasizes these same four components of creative thinking, and his definition of elaboration is similar to Guilford's.

Bernstein (1961) uses the term *code elaboration* to refer to a concept of formal speech code. He argues that members of the middle class possess an elaborated linguistic code that is absent in lower-class speech. The degree of code elaboration is measured by such linguistic indices of speech fluency and precision as the number of verbal qualifiers, complex sentences, and variety of verbal categories.

Rohwer (1973) has identified elaboration as an important strategy used in paired-associate learning. He maintains that people facilitate the formation of associations between stimulus-response pairs by adopting an elaboration strategy. The learner produces some referent common to both the stimulus and response terms, and this referent serves as a connection between the two terms or their conceptual representations. This event connecting the two terms may be either a visual image (for example, a visual image of a spoon holding a candle to connect the stimulus "spoon" with the response "candle") or a verbal statement ("The spoon is holding the candle").

Walter and Hellebusch (1974) use *associative elaboration* to refer to a process variable that occurs during word recognition memory tasks. They postulated that word recognition tasks involve a two-stage elaboration process in which words are encoded into representational responses which then activate implicit associative responses. A word is incorrectly identified as having appeared earlier in a list if its representational response is identical to the implicit associative response to an earlier word.

In the area of personality testing, Slemon and associates (1976) developed an Associative Elaboration Scale to measure the extent to which people give TAT stories that are embellished with details beyond those given by the stimulus picture. The scale consists of ten categories, ranging from a zero category for no elaboration to a category for stories with twenty-two or more interpretive comments. Interpretive comments include (1) inferences about events, (2) expressions of affective reactions, and (3) inferences about environmental reinforcing variables.

Normally, TAT story content is used to make inferences about subjects' needs and about the environmental presses that influence them. However, the variety, richness, and quantity of the story elements should give valuable insight into the person's freedom of imaginative response. Slemon and his associates inferred that people who obtain a high score on this scale are not constricted or inhibited imaginatively and can willingly and easily give rich and expressive verbal responses. This use of the quality of responses in order to infer personality characteristics is analogous to practices in other forms of projective techniques. For example, in the Rorschach it is assumed that integrative responses where human movement is attributed to stimuli or where color is appropriately combined with form are indicative of people who have a rich, differentiated, and imaginative reaction to the environment.

The scoring system used in the Associative Elaboration Scale resembles that of Weisskopf's (1950) Transcendence Index; however, the purpose of the two scales differs. Weisskopf reasoned that task stimuli eliciting elaborated story content would probably be valuable for the clinician, because there would be a large amount of interpretable material. She therefore developed the Transcendence Index as a measure of the extent to which TAT stimuli evoke stories that transcend both the instructions and the physical stimuli. Since the Transcendence Index was designed to measure the extent to which stimuli elicit material transcending the instructions, people taking the test are asked to describe the pictures. These instructions contrast with the Associative Elaboration Scale, where the standard TAT instructions to make up a story are used. Weisskopf also had a much more detailed scoring system (with fifteen categories of response). In spite of these differences, the similarity in scoring categories makes it likely that the two scoring systems would give similar overall results—provided the standard TAT instructions to make up a story were used.

In the area of ability testing, elaboration has been used by both Guilford (Guilford and Hoepfner, 1971) and Torrance (1965) to refer to an important component of creative thinking. Both Guilford and Torrance distinguish among elaboration, fluency, flexibility, and originality—which are all thought to be important components of creativity. They restrict the use of the term *elaboration* to systematic and careful development of the details of some plan, idea, or object. Gifted elaborators, therefore, are expected to be people who, when given a project, can diligently work out detailed and complete plans. They can undertake a task or start with some idea or drawing and work out additional details in an attractive and coherent form. A high score on elaboration implies discipline, system, and organization in developing inferences and implications. Torrance and Dauw compared students scoring high on elaboration with those scoring high on originality, in areas such as aspirations, life experiences, scholastic aptitudes, and mental health problems (Dauw, 1966a, 1966b; Torrance and Dauw, 1965a, 1965b). As compared to students scoring high on originality, the elaborators (1) were more likely to aspire to traditional occupations such as medicine and law; (2) were concerned with conscientiously repeating academic tasks until they were satisfied with their performance; (3) were much more concerned about failing and not meeting expectations; and (4) tried to counter stress by withdrawal, avoidance, seclusion, and prayer.

Bernstein (1961) used speech samples rather than responses to personality tests in order to study elaboration of linguistic code. His studies focus on differences in the educational achievement of lower-class and middle-class children, and he maintains that social-class differences in academic performance can be explained by the more precise and functional formal or elaborated linguistic code used in middle-class families. Middle-class children's speech shows more complex sentence structure, more adjectives, and generally more efficiency and objectivity in describing environmental events. Children coming from homes that have not developed elaborated speech will, in Bernstein's opinion, be handicapped in school, since instruction is primarily based on the medium of formal language.

Critical Discussion

General Areas of Concern

The utility of the term *elaboration* as broadly descriptive of ability to produce a variety of responses may create problems because, as noted, a number of investigators have applied it to an array of assessment and learning behaviors. The application of the same term to such a broad range of behaviors may mask or obscure the presence of conceptually different processes. There are additional difficulties in using some of the elaboration scales or indices for clinical assessment. For example, serious questions can be raised about sampling, reliability, validity, and the degree of relationship among various measures of elaboration.

Confusion may arise in the use of the terms *elaboration* and *associative elaboration* because they are sometimes used to refer to qualities of behavior and sometimes to processes underlying behavior. The stimuli used to elicit elaborative behavior and the responses scored include a wide variety of verbal and nonverbal forms.

As a description of behavior, associative elaboration has been defined by Slemon and associates (1976) as the number of interpretive comments that are given by people responding to TAT cards. Elaboration has also been based on the number of responses to such different stimuli as incomplete plans (Guilford and Hoepfner, 1971) and abstract designs (Torrance, 1965). The types of responses studied also vary widely, ranging from interpretive comments through details of plans, additions to drawings, and Bernstein's (1961) speech samples. The limited generality of results among such varying tasks was demonstrated in a factor analytic study by Yamamoto and Frengel (1966), who found that elaboration in the Minnesota Tests of Creative Thinking was highly task specific.

The term *elaboration* has also been applied in some very different fields of psychology. Slemon and associates (1976) use it to describe responses on a personality test, whereas Guilford (1956) and Torrance (1965) have used it in the area of ability testing. Bernstein (1961) refers to code elaboration in the field of sociocultural comparisons of speech patterns. In the area of learning research, Rohwer (1973) has postulated that elaboration strategies are used in order to facilitate learning of paired associates. Walter and Hellebusch (1974) use the same term to refer to a hypothetical two-stage process involved in word recognition tasks. This process is described as an automatic, internal, associative reaction rather than a conscious learning strategy.

Clinical assessment in this area would be aided if norms based on systematic sampling procedures were available. Information about reliability, although available in some cases, is mainly based on incidental samples. With the exception of the Torrance Tests of Creative Thinking—where considerable effort has been made to collect validity data—interpretation is, for the most part, based more on a scoring rationale than on external validity. Therefore, the results should be used in assessment only when they are well supported by information from other sources.

Comparative Philosophies and Theories

There appear to be basic differences in the underlying theoretical orientations of the various approaches to elaboration and its measurement. One group of investigators use the term primarily for its utility in describing observable behavior that, in their view, has adaptive significance. Bernstein (1961) and Torrance (1962, 1965) are clearly interested in the social utility of elaborative behavior and in the way that elaborative behavior is developed by the social environment. Torrance has developed numerous materials and procedures designed to aid in the development of a number of creative abilities, including elaboration. In his work with young children, Torrance (1975) reports considerable success in developing elaborative behavior. Rohwer (1973) describes elaboration in paired-associate learning as a behavioral strategy rather than a process.

Other researchers appear to use the term *elaboration* to refer to more stable and innate structural components. Walter and Hellebusch (1974) clearly conceive of elaboration as an underlying mental process. Similarly, in his structure-of-intellect model, Guilford (1959) portrays intellect as being composed of three intersecting dimensions. In exploring the implications of this model, he identified an ability that he calls *elaboration,* which involves the production of a coordinated series of details in order to complete some bare outline (Guilford and Hoepfner, 1971). The model predicts that there will be four elaboration abilities depending on whether the content of the task presented is figural, symbolic, semantic, or behavioral.

Elaboration on Critical Points

This section briefly reviews selected findings on reliability and validity.

A variety of researchers indicate that elaboration can be scored reliably. Slemon and associates (1976), in a study of clinic children between 7 and 15 years old, report that the interscorer reliability among three independent scorers exceeded $r = .90$ at all ages except year 7 (where there was a very restricted range of elaboration scores). In a review of the Transcendence Index, Prola (1972) reports generally satisfactory interscorer reliabilities with a variety of normal and clinical groups, story and description instructions, and both Children's Apperception Test (CAT) and TAT stimuli. The interscorer reliability of the Torrance Tests of Creative Thinking has generally been found to be satisfactory.

Less information is available about test-retest reliability. Prola (1972) reports a study where there was a one-year test-retest reliability of $r = .95$ on the Transcendence Index. A note of caution is sounded by Crockenberg (1972), who found in a review of creativity tests that reliabilities have varied considerably in different studies, probably due to the marked influence of test conditions.

As with many other psychological tests, the validity measures are not high; however, there are enough positive results to indicate some degree of generality. Several studies (Dudek, 1968; Prola, 1972) found a positive relation between transcendence and Rorschach human movement scores. In various studies of short-term and long-term validity involving follow-ups of adults who were first tested in high school, the correlations reported are not high, but they are encouraging when the many moderating factors of unequal environmental opportunity and complex criterion measures are considered (Torrance, 1972). Ashton (1974) and Kaltsounis (1976) found that high and low elaborators, selected by the nonverbal form of the Torrance Tests of Creative Thinking, differed on a number of items in self-report questionnaires. Carroll (1972) found that sensitizers, who tend to approach and confront threatening stimuli, obtained higher verbal elaboration scores than repressors, who tend to deny and avoid such stimuli. Differences in elaboration were found when groups described how they felt while viewing slides that had previously been scaled as unpleasant or boring; the measure of elaboration was the number of words checked off on a fifty-item list of "feeling" words. Rushton and Young (1974) point out that a consistent relationship has not been found between class structure and Bernstein's measure of code elaboration. Their study showed a task effect, since working-class males did use elaborated code but primarily when writing about familiar technical topics. When this task effect is added to ambiguities in the definition of social class, it is not surprising that research results in this area have been inconsistent.

Personal Views and Recommendations

It would be extremely useful in this area, as in other areas of personality assessment, to have normative data based on a group selected by some systematic sampling procedure. Since information about reliability, developmental norms, and other important psychometric criteria is mainly based on incidental samples, the clinical use of elaboration measures is seriously limited.

Another major problem is the lack of systematic information about relations among these various measures of elaboration. As noted before, a wide range of verbal and nonverbal stimuli are used to evoke elaborative responses, and a wide range of responses are measured. Yamamoto and Frengel (1966) found that elaboration, as measured on the Minnesota Test of Creative Thinking, is relatively task specific; and Guilford and Hoepfner (1971) refer to four elaboration abilities within the structure-of-intellect model.

The question of whether elaboration scores are task specific points to the problem of validity and test improvement. Critics of creativity tests have correctly noted that their performance in validity studies has been modest. A serious problem in validity studies has been that of identifying adequate criterion measures. For example, it is probable that different types of ability are required for creative elaboration in painting and creative elaboration in writing novels. This problem of diversity in criterion measures also presents a problem for test development. Test stimuli (such as TAT cards) were not selected originally in order to distinguish among groups that differ in creativity. Improvement in the validity of elaboration measures probably awaits the development of item selection procedures based on more precise task analyses. This latter approach may be compared to the field of intelligence testing, where Binet's successful test was produced when he began to select items that were related to success in the traditional school program.

An important question for assessment instruments is how their results might aid in education and therapy. If elaborative ability is valuable and if certain people lack it, can it be developed? This question is of particular importance if, as Bernstein argues, deficiencies in elaborated language code can be a very serious handicap in school. More studies, such as those carried out by Torrance (1975), are required to investigate how elaboration and other creative abilities can be enhanced.

Application to Particular Variables

There has been some interest in developmental trends in ability to elaborate. Slemon and associates (1976) report a general increase in associative elaboration from ages 7 to 11, but little or no increase from ages 11 to 15. Rohwer (1973) found developmental trends in children's ability to adopt elaboration strategies during paired-associate learning. In early childhood, elaborations that would function as connectors between stimulus-response pairs usually had to be provided; however, as children moved into adolescence, they became less dependent on prompting and spontaneously adopted elaboration strategies.

The relation between creativity tests and intelligence tests has received some study. Although relations between IQ and various creativity scores have been found on the Torrance Tests of Creative Thinking, Crockenberg (1972), after reviewing the literature in this area, concluded that there is little relation between scores on this test and IQ when groups of above-normal intelligence are used. Slemon and associates (1976) found no relation between associative elaboration and IQ when correlations were calculated within separate age groups of their clinic sample.

With regard to racial and socioeconomic factors, Torrance (1971, 1975) reports that his creativity tests, unlike intelligence tests, show no racial or socioeconomic bias. Bernstein's measure of code elaboration does not distinguish consistently between members of the middle class and those of the lower class. Nash, Thomas, and Weigert (1973) found no evidence of socioeconomic differences in speech samples taken from self-descriptions, and Rushton and Young (1974) report that there were no differences when language samples were taken from essays on technical topics.

Little has been reported on sex differences. Yamamoto and Frengel (1966) studied a group of fifth graders with the Minnesota Tests of Creative Thinking, and they found that boys scored higher on elaboration than girls on two of the three nonverbal tests.

References

Ashton, P. "Personality Characteristics Associated with Originality and Elaboration." *Psychological Reports,* 1974, *34,* 647-650.

Bernstein, B. "Social Structure, Language and Learning." *Educational Research,* 1961, *3,* 163-176.

Carroll, D. "Repression-Sensitization and the Verbal Elaboration of Experience." *Journal of Consulting and Clinical Psychology,* 1972, *38,* 147.

Crockenberg, S. B. "Creativity Tests: A Boon or a Boondoggle for Education?" *Review of Educational Research,* 1972, *42,* 27-45.

Dauw, D. C. "Life Experiences of Original Thinkers and Good Elaborators." *Exceptional Children,* 1966a, *32,* 433-440.

Dauw, D. C. "Scholastic Aptitudes and Vocational Needs of Original Thinkers and Good Elaborators." *Personnel and Guidance Journal,* 1966b, *45,* 171-175.

Dudek, S. Z. "M An Active Energy System Correlating Rorschach M with Ease of Creative Expression." *Journal of Projective Techniques and Personality Assessment,* 1968, *32,* 453-461.

Freud, S. *A General Introduction to Psychoanalysis* [1910]. New York: Liveright, 1935.

Guilford, J. P. "The Structure of Intellect." *Psychological Bulletin,* 1956, *53,* 269-293.

Guilford, J. P. "Three Faces of Intellect." *American Psychologist,* 1959, *14,* 469-479.

Guilford, J. P., and Hoepfner, R. *The Analysis of Intelligence.* New York: McGraw-Hill, 1971.

Kaltsounis, B. "Personality Traits Associated with Originality and Elaboration." *Psychological Reports,* 1976, *38,* 1079-1082.

Nash, J. E., Thomas, D. L., and Weigert, A. J. "Code Elaboration and Self-Concept States." *Journal of Social Psychology,* 1973, *90,* 45-51.

Prola, M. "A Review of the Transcendence Index." *Journal of Personality Assessment,* 1972, *36,* 8-12.

Rohwer, W. D., Jr. "Elaboration and Learning in Childhood and Adolescence." In H. W. Reese (Ed.), *Advances in Child Development and Behavior.* Vol. 8. New York: Academic Press, 1973.

Rushton, J., and Young, G. "Elements of Elaboration in Working Class Writing." *Educational Research,* 1974, *16,* 181-188.

Slemon, A. G., and others. "Associative Elaboration and Integration Scales for Evaluating TAT Protocols." *Journal of Personality Assessment,* 1976, *40,* 365-369.

Torrance, E. P. *Guiding Creative Talent.* Englewood Cliffs, N.J.: Prentice-Hall, 1962.

Torrance, E. P. *Rewarding Creative Behavior: Experiments in Classroom Creativity.* Englewood Cliffs, N.J.: Prentice-Hall, 1965.

Torrance, E. P. "Are the Torrance Tests of Creative Thinking Biased Against or in Favor of Disadvantaged Groups?" *Gifted Child Quarterly,* 1971, *15,* 75-80.

Torrance, E. P. "Predictive Validity of the Torrance Tests of Creative Thinking." *Journal of Creative Behavior,* 1972, *6,* 236-252.

Torrance, E. P. "Creativity Research in Education: Still Alive." In I. A. Taylor and J. W. Getzels (Eds.), *Perspectives in Creativity.* Chicago: Aldine, 1975.

Torrance, E. P., and Dauw, D. C. "Mental Health Problems of Three Groups of Highly Creative High School Seniors." *Gifted Child Quarterly,* 1965a, *9,* 123-127, 130.

Torrance, E. P., and Dauw, D. C. "Aspirations and Dreams of Three Groups of Creatively Gifted High School Seniors and a Comparable Unselected Group." *Gifted Child Quarterly,* 1965b, *9,* 177-182.

Wallas, G. *The Art of Thought.* London: Cape, 1926.

Walter, D. A., and Hellebusch, S. "The Role of Associative Elaboration in Word Recognition: Evidence for a Two-Stage Test Elaboration Sequence." *Journal of Experimental Psychology,* 1974, *103,* 78-84.

Weisskopf, E. A. "A Transcendence Index as a Proposed Measure in the TAT." *Journal of Psychology,* 1950, *29,* 379-390.

Yamamoto, K., and Frengel, B. A. "An Exploratory Component Analysis of the Minnesota Tests of Creative Thinking." *California Journal of Educational Research,* 1966, *17,* 220-229.

69

Paul N. Russell

Visual Search Ability

Visual search or scanning should be viewed as a subtopic within the broader fields of visual pattern recognition, selective attention in vision, and information processing in general. Visual search refers to the search or scan of a larger field for a smaller region, called the target area, which happens to be relevant at the time. Experimental psychologists working within a general information-processing theoretical framework are particularly interested in determining how humans recognize patterns (for instance, letters) and how they select one part of the visual field for focused attention. Those adopting an information-processing theoretical perspective view the human as a complex information-handling device that codes, stores, retrieves, and variously manipulates information in a series of mental operations or stages that intervene between sensory input and response output.

This broad and extensive line of research and theory, which has evolved over the last two decades, has largely been ignored by clinicians, although it has relevance and implication in a clinical context: (1) It provides a richer set of theoretical constructs than has hitherto been available for describing and expressing an understanding of thinking and thought disorder, memory and memory pathology, and attention and attentional disturbances. (2) It is potentially capable of indicating new and different theoretical accounts of abnormal and pathological behavior (for example, theories of cognitive deficit in schizophrenia). (3) It offers a wide variety of well-researched tasks with which to evaluate such theoretical accounts. (4) These tasks could ultimately form the basis of diagnostic and assessment procedures.

This chapter deals with visual search, a single branch of this broad research enterprise, and with a single family of tasks. It is more concerned with attention and pattern recognition than with thought, language, and remembering.

Background and Current Status

Experimental studies of search interpreted in information-processing terms derive from the publications by Neisser (1963; Neisser, Novick, and Lazar, 1963) of experiments in which subjects searched columns of letters for a predesignated target. Of importance for subsequent research was his interpretation of results in terms of an account of how a computing device might recognize patterns. Factors influential in creating a general information-processing cognitive theoretical milieu are traced by Segal and Lachman (1972).

During the 1960s and until the present time, there has been a continuing rapid expansion of interest in human cognitive processes, including visual information processing. A variety of search tasks have evolved, and there has been a development of many mini-theories in addition to the generation of a smaller number of more general accounts.

Critical Discussion

General Areas of Concern

Concerns are most readily defined within the context of Neisser's search experiments, findings, and theoretical interpretation. His stimuli consisted of matrices of randomly selected letters, hereafter called distractors, in which a single target was embedded in an unpredictable position. The matrices had fifty rows, each row containing not more than six letters. Subjects began their search at the top and continued row by row downward until they located the target. The time taken to find the target increased linearly with the number of rows scanned. From the slope of this function, Neisser derived a measure of the time taken to search each row and decide whether or not a target was present. Subjects typically reported that the target letter appeared to leap out at them from the indistinct blur of the unidentified background of distractor characters. When searching through words, subjects certainly had no knowledge of what they had scanned (Neisser and Beller, 1965). Search was slower when target and distractor were more similar: search for the straight-line angular target Z was slower in the context of straight-line distractors (such as E, I, V) than in a context of rounded letters (such as D, O, U), while the reverse was true of the rounded target Q. Search rate generally increased with practice. Although only a single target ever appeared in a matrix, in some conditions it was selected from a pool of up to ten characters, so that subjects searched for any one of up to ten targets. Initially search was slower with larger target sets, but after prolonged practice with a particular set subjects could search for any of ten as quickly as for a single target.

Neisser (1967) interpreted these findings in terms of a theory of how a computing device might recognize patterns. He conceptualized letters as consisting of elemental subparts (vertical, oblique, or curved lines and intersections) called features. According to Neisser's account, analysis of the stimulus input proceeds through a series of levels. The lowest level involves a set of feature analyzers. Each analyzer responds maximally to a specific feature. For example, the letter R might be considered to involve the features of a vertical straight line, an oblique straight line, a curve, and various intersections. Presentation of R would lead to a high level of activation or output from the vertical, oblique, curve, and intersection feature analyzers. In this way the stimulus input R is coded or represented at the first level of analysis in the form of a list of those features found present. Neisser envisaged that the various feature analyzers operate simultaneously and independently of one another. The next level of analysis involves a set of letter analyzers, there being a separate analyzer for each letter of the alphabet. Each letter analyzer has stored within it a description of a particular letter in the form of the features that comprise that particular letter. The function of the letter analyzer is to compare the output from feature analyzers and to respond in proportion to the degree of agreement between stored and extracted feature lists. Since several letters share one or more features, several letter analyzers may respond in varying degrees in the presence of a single letter. For example, P and R share many features, and both P and R letter analyzers would become activated in the presence of either letter. Consequently, a subsequent level or decision stage is needed to assess the level of activation in the various letter analyzers and make a decision as to which letter analyzer is most active. That judged most active corresponds to the letter perceived or identified as present. This system is capable of explaining why letters that look alike (for example, E and F, P and R) are confused. It also copes with the fact that humans experience relatively little difficulty in recognizing letters despite variations in retinal size and orientation and in style of print.

In the context of search tasks, Neisser suggested that letter analyzers other than those for the target (or target set, where more than one target is involved) are in effect turned off, although the complete range of lower-level feature extraction activities continues. Thus, activity is restricted to the feature extraction level until the target appears, and hence distractors are not seen or identified as such. In this way, Neisser explained the paradox that letters can be examined and found not relevant but, although examined, are not perceived, identified, or remembered. Practice becomes effective when the subject learns to optimize feature tests in favor of those features distinctive of the target, and search is more rapid when target and distractor are perceptually distinct, because a smaller sampling or lesser accumulation of featural information is needed for target identification. With a larger target set, fewer features will be distinctive of the target set, but because nontarget letter analyzers are inoperative while feature analyzers continue to function, search for any one of a set of targets can proceed as rapidly as search for a single target.

From the foregoing, the following three concerns are identified: (1) feature extraction processes and the role of practice at this level, (2) the role of practice when the individual is searching for more than one target; and, not previously mentioned, (3) the role of such nonperceptual factors as conceptual semantic attributes and word structure.

Various types of search tasks have evolved since Neisser's studies. Multielement displays—in which a small number of elements are placed within the limits of a small, clearly defined field, often in a single row or two—have frequently been used. These tasks divide into two classes: first, detection studies where displays are presented tachistoscopically for intervals briefer than the duration of an eye fixation and where detection accuracy is of prime interest; second, search time studies where stimuli are presented for longer periods permitting high levels of accuracy and where search time or response latency has been measured. In multielement displays, display size refers to the number of characters displayed and is not to be confused with display area. Also, memory set size refers to the number of elements in the item pool from which the target is selected for any display. The term *memory set* is used because the pool of possible targets has to be remembered if subjects are to know what they are looking for.

Experiments with multielement displays generally confirm Neisser's finding that search is more difficult when target and distractor are perceptually similar. The measures of interest are the rate of increase in response time or rate of decrease in detection accuracy with display size. The results of several studies suggest that the magnitude of this search impairment is proportional to the degree of confusability or featural similarity between target and distractor elements (Egeth, Jonides, and Wall, 1972; Estes, 1972; Estes and Taylor, 1966; McIntyre, Fox, and Neale, 1970; Nickerson, 1966; Rabbitt, 1964). With respect to practice, Neisser suggested that over trials the person learns to base target-present decisions on a small number of distinctive features. If Neisser is correct, changing the distractor set while a subject is searching for a particular target should impede search because the previously established critical features would most likely not be distinctive of the target in a new context. In accord with this, Rabbitt (1967) found that search times increased when a straight-line distractor set was replaced by a curved set, but not when the change was from one straight-line set to another. Further, the degree of disruptions to search with the change of distractor sets reflected the extent of practice with one set prior to changeover.

Where the subject searches for one of several targets, search time tends to increase linearly with the number of targets searched for; that is, with the number of items in the memory set (Nickerson, 1966; Sternberg, 1970). Neisser, Novick, and Lazar (1963) found that this memory set size effect disappeared after prolonged practice, but others have failed to replicate. It turns out that practice is effective in removing memory set effects only when there is a consistent mapping of characters to memory and distractor sets, so that over trials a character that once served as a target never appears as a distractor, and vice versa. Prolonged practice with varied mappings, where the same character may appear as a target on some trials and as a distractor on another, speeds search but does not eliminate memory set size effects (Graboi, 1971; Metlay, Sokoloff, and Kaplan, 1968; Schneider and Shiffrin, 1977; Shiffrin and Schneider, 1977).

Perhaps most interesting of the search findings are the word and category effects. A target letter is found more quickly when one is searching through words rather than through nonword letter strings (Krueger, 1970), although a silent nonpronounced letter is difficult to find (Corcoran, 1966), and search for a common sound phoneme that may be variously spelled is also difficult (Cohen, 1970). Several studies have revealed a category effect. Search for a digit is faster in a context of letters than in a context of digits. The reverse is true of letter search (Brand, 1971). Using multielement search, Jonides and Gleitman (1972) found that search time increased with display size when target and distractor were both letters or both digits, but search time was independent of display size when target and distractors were drawn from different categories. This was also true of the symbol *O*. It was difficult to locate in digits when called zero but not when given its letter name; and the reverse was true in a letter context. Further, search is impeded when target and distractors are associated in some way (Graboi, cited in Rumelhart, 1977) and where upper- and lower-case forms of the same letter appear as target and distractor (Henderson, 1973), but search for any animal name in a context of words drawn from a single different category is no faster than in a context of words drawn from various categories but not including animals (Gibson and Levin, 1975, p. 467). The category results indicate that search is impeded when target and distractor are conceptually related; that is, when they are members of a single category (Brand, 1971; Jonides and Gleitman, 1972), when they are associatively related (Graboi, cited in Rumelhart, 1977), or when they share a common name (Henderson, 1973).

Comparative Philosophies and Theories

Theories or models have generally been problem or topic specific. Some have sought explicitly to explain results from detection accuracy experiments. These have all assumed (1) that there is some mechanism of feature extraction, (2) that a letter is represented in memory store as a feature list, (3) that a comparison process between stored and extracted features is involved, and (4) that a decision is involved. Theories to explain the display size and confusability effects in detection accuracy experiments differ in the emphasis placed on feature extraction and decision or interpretation processes. Most do not accommodate the recent findings that confusability and display size effects on letter detection are modified by the spatial proximity of target and distractor and their retinal location. As Wolford (1975) has pointed out, they generally overlook the requirement that features must be grouped so that those extracted from one letter are not confused with those detected in another location. Smith and Spoehr (1974) provide a good summary. Bjork and Murray (1977) provide a more recent review and data that are problematic for all, although they do not mention Wolford's (1975) review.

Additionally, some have assumed that briefly displayed information exists in the form of a more or less veridical image, called the icon by Neisser (1967), which persists for a brief period after stimulus offset and from which features can be extracted in the same way as if the stimulus were still physically present. The first stage in many information-processing accounts is often the icon, which is also referred to as the sensory information store, sensory register, or sensory buffer store (Atkinson and Shiffrin, 1968). Reviews of literature pertaining to this stage of processing are given by Coltheart (1976) and Dick (1974).

Neisser (1967), as already outlined, offered an explanation of memory set size effects in terms of feature extraction and decision mechanism. An alternative explanation derives from Sternberg (1970). The search task can be viewed as one in which each displayed item is compared in turn with each target item stored in memory. Thus, search time increases with memory set size because more comparisons between displayed and stored items are involved. Since Sternberg was more concerned with memory retrieval and comparison processes, in his experiments memory set size was varied and display size held constant, at one. He then measured the time taken by subjects to report whether or not the single displayed item was a member of the target set. Response times increased linearly with memory set size. Sternberg concluded that display and memory items were compared one after the other in what has been termed *serial processing*. This paradigm has spawned a large literature (Sternberg, 1975). In contrast, Neisser, Novick, and Lazar (1963) found that, after prolonged practice, search was as rapid for any one of up to ten targets as for a single target, implying that stored and displayed items were compared simultaneously in what has been called *parallel processing*. During the period from about 1966 to 1973, numerous researchers became embroiled in what could be called the serial-parallel issue. In this context the Neisser studies provide evidence of parallel processing, while the Sternberg studies provide evidence of serial processing. However, experiments performed within the Sternberg tradition did not include prolonged practice with a consistent mapping of elements into memory and distractor sets. It has now been shown that prolonged practice with a consistent mapping leads to an automatic detection of the target where search time does not increase or accuracy decrease with memory set size or (within the limits probed) with display size (Schneider and Shiffrin, 1977; Shiffrin and Schneider, 1977).

The recognition of a pattern (for example, a letter) has been presented as a process in which an extracted feature list is compared with a list stored somewhere in long-term store. When input happens to match the stored representation, the location in store is said to be activated. Thus, input is represented or encoded by activation in various locations in long-term store. A single input, such as a word, may be represented by activation in several locations. For example, a word may activate regions corresponding to various feature detectors, specific letter names, the word name, its semantic meaning, and a superordinate category. It has generally been assumed that the activations occur in much that order, so that (1) analysis of input proceeds in a series of stages from extraction of specific physical attributes through various degrees of abstraction and generalization; and (2) activation of a prior level is needed before activation may occur at a higher level. Norman and Bobrow (1976) refer to theories of this type as linear stage models.

Such theories have also assumed that more time and processing effort, attention, or processing resource (Kahneman, 1973; Norman and Bobrow, 1975) are required to establish activation at higher levels. According to linear stage theories, then, a search task in which target and distractor can be readily discriminated on the basis of lower-level featural and item name information without recourse to category identification should show no category facilitation or semantic interference effects. Thus, the results of Brand (1971) and Jonides and Gleitman (1972) and others demonstrating category and conceptual effects came as a surprise.

The position has now been modified. Posner and Snyder (1975), for example, review results consistent with the view that activation at all levels arises automatically as a consequence of presentation of a familiar pattern, and that these automatic processes are largely beyond conscious control even when it may be advantageous to suppress them. As they see it, processing resource or effort is needed not to establish the activation or to analyze input but to coordinate activated memory pathways so that appropriate response is made. In addition, they envisage a spreading of activation to other regions of memory where a habitual association or link has been established between the items concerned. For example, presentation of "elm" produces activation in the "elm" region of memory, which also spreads to "green." Current conceptions of long-term store describe it as a complex net of interconnected and interrelated locations called nodes (Collins and Loftus, 1975; Shiffrin and Schneider, 1977). Thus, category, semantic, and associational information is readily available and in all probability cannot be ignored in search tasks. Where target and distractors are drawn from different categories, examination of the level of activation in the memory location corresponding to the target category provides sufficient information for target identification.

Search tasks are not alone in demonstrating that aspects of letter strings are more readily processed when they happen to form words (Gibson and Levin, 1975; Krueger, 1975; Smith and Spoehr, 1974). One problem for theory is to account for the finding that an individual letter is better perceived in the context provided by a word. This is particularly problematic for strictly bottom-up linear stage theories (Norman and Bobrow, 1976), which, as already outlined, assume that analysis proceeds through stages arranged in levels, with output from an immediately lower stage serving as input to the next level. Some following this general approach have suggested that context aids a decision mechanism or interpretation processes; others, that feed-down from higher levels facilitates feature extraction. Smith and Spoehr (1974) organized their review around these concerns, and a major purpose of Krueger's (1975) review was to establish evidence for more efficient feature extraction in the case of familiar items (such as words). Norman and Bobrow (1976) suggest that the linear stage theories, even when modified to include top-down whole-to-part influences, might better be replaced by a system largely without levels and in which specialist analyzers are in constant interactive interplay as they seek interim results directly from one another and from a central data pool to which they all report. A clear exposition at an elementary level is given by Lindsay and Norman (1977, chap. 7).

Elaboration on Critical Points

A recurrent theme of information-processing theories has been the idea that there is a finite limit in human capacity for processing analysis or mental work. This limit in information-processing capability has variously been referred to as a limited capacity channel (Broadbent, 1958), a limit in available capacity, attention, or effort (Kahneman, 1973), or a limit of resource (Norman and Bobrow, 1975). The notion of limit in capacity arises because attempts to perform multiple tasks frequently lead to interference or failure, interference effects being in proportion to their total demands for processing resource.

It has been argued (Schneider and Shiffrin, 1977; Shiffrin and Schneider, 1977) that a limitation in processing resource is involved in at least two ways in search tasks. First, in detection accuracy experiments, available processing resource is said to be divided among the elements presented. According to this view, it is more difficult to detect a target in a display containing a greater number of elements, because less resource is available for each letter; analysis is therefore incomplete; and target decisions are based on incomplete information, which results in detection errors. In search time studies, the sharing of resource among multiple display items results in a slower search, because more time is needed to accumulate sufficient information on which to base an accurate target detection response. Second, if the search process is viewed as one of comparing displayed and memorized items, then with a larger memory set the total processing resource available is divided among a greater number of comparisons, and hence the resource available for each is reduced. This results in longer comparison times per element with larger memory sets. The dual effects of dividing resource among display and memory set items are compounded where search is for one of several targets in a display of several elements.

Earlier amounts of search (Neisser, 1967) imply that the nonrelevant distractor items receive less analysis or consume less of the available resource, because they are not identified or remembered but are merely seen as a blur of background. However, more recent findings demonstrating category and semantic effects, together with the research reviewed by Posner and Snyder (1975), indicate that all items in a display of familiar symbols (such as alphanumeric characters or words) are analyzed to a level where their category and semantic content is available. The findings also imply that this analysis occurs automatically; that is, without intention or awareness and without interfering with other temporally concurrent processing activity.

Automatic analyzing and processing activities, which do not interfere with one another or with other concurrent activity, must be distinguished from controlled processes, which compete for the limited resources of a pool of readily allocatable resource. Schneider and Shiffrin have demonstrated automatic and controlled processes in search tasks (Schneider and Shiffrin, 1977; Shiffrin and Schneider, 1977). In a variety of experiments, their subjects searched rapid sequences of several briefly presented displays. Controlled search, rather like serial processing referred to previously, occurred with low levels of practice where target and distractor sets were consistently mapped, and at all levels of practice with a varied mapping. Schneider and Shiffrin characterize controlled search as load dependent; that is, search speed and accuracy decrease with increases in memory and display sizes (with increased demands on resource). Also, on trials where more than one target element was displayed, subjects experienced difficulty in detecting target repetitions when these occurred on immediately following displays in the rapid sequence. By contrast, automatic detection, which occurred only after prolonged practice with a consistent mapping of target and distractor items, was characterized by rapid accurate response, which was independent of display and memory set sizes. That is, after prolonged practice with a consistent mapping, subjects were able to search for any one of four targets (memory set of four) that might appear in any one of twenty rapidly presented displays containing four elements (display size four), as accurately as they could search for a single target (memory set of one) in a rapid sequence of displays containing a single item (display size one). Further, there was virtually no impairment to search when two different targets had to be detected on the same or immediately following displays in the sequence. That is, simultaneous automatic detections were virtually noninterfering. Subsequently, the automatically detected target items appeared as distractors in a new search task and with consequent disruption to the present controlled search. The disruption arose because subjects realized that the automatic response they had begun to initiate was inappropriate. The present search's disruption, brought about by having a previously automatically detected target serve in a distractor role, demonstrates that the detection of such targets is indeed an automatic process, which once established cannot be controlled or suppressed.

Automatic detection results from prolonged practice where the same response is always required to a given stimulus. Such stimulus-to-response consistency, which occurs with a consistent mapping, is needed for the establishment of automatic detection. According to Schneider and Shiffrin, an assemblage of nodes in long-term store becomes interrelated as a result of prolonged repetition in a consistent mapping and acquires the capability for performing the detection and response routine independently of controlled action. The function of such routines is to relieve the limited resources for controlled processes, and in particular short-term store, of the burdens of an often repeated task. Automatic analysis of letters, digits, and words to a category and semantic level no doubt reflects prolonged and consistent educational experiences.

Thus, some tasks may involve a great deal of analysis or processing, but, because automatic operations are performed, they will make few demands on the supply of resource that is available for controlled processing.

Personal Views and Recommendations

The foregoing demonstrates that the ostensibly visual task of locating a target in a display is in many cases far from being a purely visual task at all. Consequently, many theoretical constructs, in the form of cognitive processing stages, have been introduced to account for the way in which a normal human cognitive system might perform the various search (and other) tasks. This body of research and theory is relevant for clinical assessment because it identifies a number of theoretically interrelated processes that might malfunction or be deficient in one or more pathological conditions. Further, it suggests tasks that can be used to selectively measure particular processes and functioning at a specific stage. Also, because the processes and the tasks used to measure them are interrelated theoretically, some predictions can be made as to how malfunction of one process or at one stage might affect others and over all cognitive capability.

For example, information-processing accounts frequently assert that processes of feature extraction and iconic storage precede other stages. If so, a deficiency in processing at this level should have widespread ramifications, because later stages, even if functioning normally, would be supplied with incomplete input. Functioning at the feature extraction and iconic level can be measured by detection accuracy tasks in which the subject reports which of two targets is present in a briefly presented display containing varying numbers of distractors. With this task, memory and response requirements can be held constant (always one of two targets and hence a simple two-choice response), while processing demands can be manipulated by increasing the number of distractors and target distractor similarity. This technique has been used with schizophrenic subjects (Davidson and Neale, 1974; Neale, 1971). Schizophrenic and control subjects were equally able to identify the target when a single letter was present, but schizophrenic performance was significantly poorer when distractors were present and when processing resource or attention had to be divided among a greater number of items (Neale, 1971), although schizophrenics were not disproportionately affected by high target distractor confusability (Davidson and Neale, 1974). Saccuzzo and associates (Saccuzzo, Hirt, and Spencer, 1974; Saccuzzo and Miller, 1977), using a postexposure mask so that the effective stimulus duration is controlled (Haber, 1970), have shown that schizophrenics are less able than controls to report which target is present, even in a display containing a single item. Saccuzzo and Miller (1977) suggest that detection accuracy tasks might be explored for use in diagnosis. Expense and technical competence associated with using the necessary tachistoscope and perhaps lengthy periods of data collection may militate against it.

Neisser search tasks and search time tasks using multielement displays might also be considered. Again, memory and response requirements can be held constant while the nature of the display is manipulated. This enables a partitioning of total response time into search time and time consumed by other operations. Neisser search and search time tasks were used by Russell and Knight (1977) in a study comparing schizophrenic and control subjects. They found that the search rates of their groups were similar, although schizophrenics required more time to implement a search and produce a response. Card-sorting tasks of the type used by Rabbitt (1967) could also be used unless motor control difficulties are manifest. However, search time, Neisser search, and card-sorting tasks afford less rigorous control over additional factors (such as eye movements) and are likely to be less sensitive than measures based on detection accuracy. In normal persons, the fastest rate at which items can be searched, in the Neisser task at least, is known to be determined by limitations in the rate with which successive eye fixations can be made (Sperling and others, 1971). That is why Schneider and Shiffrin (1977) used a computer-driven visual display unit and a rapid sequence of briefly presented displays. Since these facilities are unlikely to be available to the clinician, in the foreseeable future at least, the technically simpler Neisser search, search time, and card-sorting tasks are perhaps worthy of exploration.

Because the detection accuracy and search time tasks referred to in the preceding paragraphs measure functioning of iconic storage and feature extraction mechanisms, which are likely to be well practiced, automatic, probably innate, and thought to involve the earliest stages of processing operations, impaired performance by a person at this level is indicative of widespread and severe cognitive malfunction. That is perhaps why it has been difficult to find such impairment in schizophrenics. Impairment at this level would more likely be found in persons with general brain damage, the senile, and those surviving extreme anoxia.

Another aspect of processing detailed in previous sections is that of memory comparison (Sternberg, 1970), which is involved in tasks requiring search for any of a number of possible targets. The two-choice response requirement is preserved if a target-present, target-absent response mode is used. Where a single display item is used, and memory set size manipulated, total response time can be partitioned into (1) time involved in comparing memorized items with the displayed item and (2) response production and display item encoding times. Sternberg (1970) demonstrated that comparison time increases linearly with the number of items in the target set; that is, with the number of comparisons involved. Subsequent research has revealed that the rate of comparison is surprisingly similar among schizophrenics, alcoholics, children, and young adults. Rate of comparison is slower in the very old, mental retardates, and Korsakoff patients (Naus, Cermak, and DeLuca, 1977; Sternberg, 1975), perhaps suggesting that memory comparison tasks may be used to identify severe and generalized brain damage.

As noted in previous sections, search performance is affected by semantic and associational relationships between target and distractor items. The full conceptual meaning of a presented verbal item was said to occur automatically as a pattern of activation spread through various locations in long-term store (Posner and Snyder, 1975). In many theories, a person's conceptual knowledge is represented in long-term store as a vast net of interconnected nodes. What is the nature of this memory structure in persons with delusional systems and other manifestations of thought disorder? Has the structure changed in some way? While tasks involving search through words might be used to reveal this memory structure, the types of tasks reviewed by Posner and Snyder (1975) and Collins and Loftus (1975) seem more appropriate. Such tasks may have potential application in disclosing delusional material in paranoids. One study has shown that schizophrenics cannot ignore material relating to their own delusional system when this is presented from a source that they have been instructed to ignore in a selective listening task, although they ignored nondelusional material (Schneider, 1976).

A distinction has been made between automatic processes and pathway activation, on the one hand, and controlled and conscious processes, on the other (Posner and Snyder, 1975; Shiffrin and Schneider, 1977). Controlled and conscious processes draw on a pool of allocatable resource, which, among other things, is used in coordinating internal codes or activated regions of long-term store (Posner and Snyder, 1975) and in establishing automatic routines for frequently repeated operations. In addition, this resource is thought to be involved in the rehearsal and retention of information in a short-term store or active working memory (Shiffrin and Schneider, 1977). It may be useful to regard abnormalities in cognitive function as arising not from malfunction at one or more of a small number of specific stages but from a decrease in the amount of allocatable resource (Knight and Russell, 1978). A general reduction in resource would manifest itself in impaired performance on a wide variety of tasks. Shared-capacity tasks of the type outlined by Kahneman (1973, chap. 10) would be more suitable than search tasks for assessing resource limitations. Such tasks might be used to assess general cognitive capability, the level of which no doubt has bearing on the likelihood of a person's successful rehabilitation and ability to cope with everyday life.

Finally, since the spread of activation in long-term store arising from presentation of verbal material is thought to be an automatic, unconscious process that does not draw on resource, persons with reduced resource should be able to extract complete conceptual and semantic meaning, and the structure of their long-term store should be essentially normal. However, such persons probably lack the resource to coordinate and consciously control and to implement effective strategies.

Pathological cognitive function can be comprehended only to the extent that the workings of the normal system are understood. In the field of cognitive assessment, the traditionally pragmatic but atheoretical test and test battery approach has contributed nothing toward an understanding of the system and of what it seeks to measure. It is hoped that this brief excursion, detailing as it does some recent attempts to etch out the workings of a human cognitive system, will serve to awaken those involved in clinical assessment to the necessity for such a theoretical account and for assessment procedures to be based on theory grounded in fundamental research.

Application to Particular Variables

The research and theory outlined here has not been concerned with relationships between search performance and intelligence as measured by standardized tests (but see Hunt, 1978; Sternberg, 1977), sex, education, socioeconomic status, vocation, and ethnic/racial factors. Gerontological studies have reported a decrement in search performance in the elderly (Rabbitt, 1968; Schaie and Gribbin, 1975). Since search tasks involve words and alphanumeric characters, subjects require adequate vision and some reading skills. Second-grade children can perform a Neisser search task; and, although search rate increases during the school years, it is not predictive of reading attainment (Gibson and Levin, 1975). In the context of the clinical assessment of pathological cognitive function, search tasks appear, potentially at least, to have application with all adults (except the very elderly), provided they possess adequate vision and educational background.

References

Atkinson, R. C., and Shiffrin, R. M. "Human Memory: A Proposed System and Its Control Processes." In K. W. Spence and J. T. Spence (Eds.), *The Psychology of Learning and Motivation.* Vol. 2. New York: Academic Press, 1968.

Bjork, E. L., and Murray, J. T. "On the Nature of Input Channels in Visual Processing." *Psychological Review,* 1977, *84,* 472-484.

Brand, J. "Classification Without Identification in Visual Search." *Quarterly Journal of Experimental Psychology,* 1971, *23,* 178-186.

Broadbent, D. E. *Perception and Communication.* London: Pergamon Press, 1958.

Cohen, G. "Search Times for Combinations of Visual, Phonemic, and Semantic Targets in Reading Prose." *Perception and Psychophysics,* 1970, *8,* 370-372.

Collins, A. M., and Loftus, E. F. "A Spreading-Activation Theory of Semantic Processing." *Psychological Review,* 1975, *82,* 407-428.

Coltheart, M. "Contemporary Models of the Cognitive Processes. I: Iconic Storage and Visual Masking." In V. Hamilton and M. D. Vernon (Eds.), *The Development of Cognitive Processes.* London: Academic Press, 1976.

Corcoran, D. W. J. "An Acoustic Factor in Letter Cancellation." *Nature,* 1966, *210,* 658.

Davidson, G. S., and Neale, J. M. "The Effects of Signal-Noise Similarity on Visual Information Processing of Schizophrenics." *Journal of Abnormal Psychology,* 1974, *83,* 683-686.

Dick, A. O. "Iconic Memory and Its Relation to Perceptual Processing and Other Memory Mechanisms." *Perception and Psychophysics,* 1974, *16,* 575-596.

Egeth, H., Jonides, J., and Wall, S. "Parallel Processing of Multi-element Displays." *Cognitive Psychology,* 1972, *3,* 674-698.

Estes, W. K. "Interactions of Signal and Background Variables in Visual Processing." *Perception and Psychophysics,* 1972, *12,* 278-286.

Estes, W. K., and Taylor, H. A. "Visual Detection in Relation to Display Size and Redundancy of Critical Elements." *Perception and Psychophysics,* 1966, *1,* 9-16.

Gibson, E. J., and Levin, H. *The Psychology of Reading.* Cambridge, Mass.: M.I.T. Press, 1975.

Graboi, D. "Searching for Targets: The Effects of Specific Practice." *Perception and Psychophysics,* 1971, *10,* 300-304.

Haber, R. N. "How to Choose a Mask." *Psychological Bulletin,* 1970, *74,* 373-376.

Henderson, L. "Effects of Letter Names on Visual Search." *Cognitive Psychology,* 1973, *5,* 90-96.

Hunt, E. "Mechanics of Verbal Ability." *Psychological Review,* 1978, *85,* 109-130.

Jonides, J., and Gleitman, H. "A Conceptual Category Effect in Visual Search: O as a Letter or Digit." *Perception and Psychophysics,* 1972, *12,* 457-460.

Kahneman, D. *Attention and Effort.* Englewood Cliffs, N.J.: Prentice-Hall, 1973.

Knight, R. G., and Russell, P. N. "Global Capacity Reduction and Schizophrenia." *British Journal of Social and Clinical Psychology,* 1978, *17,* 275-280.

Krueger, L. E. "Search Time in a Redundant Visual Display." *Journal of Experimental Psychology,* 1970, *83,* 391-399.

Krueger, L. E. "Familiarity Effects in Visual Information Processing." *Psychological Bulletin,* 1975, *82,* 949-974.

Lindsay, P. H., and Norman, D. A. *Human Information Processing: An Introduction to Psychology.* (2nd ed.) New York: Academic Press, 1977.

McIntyre, D., Fox, R., and Neale, J. "Effects of Noise Similarity and Redundancy on Information Processed from Brief Visual Displays." *Perception and Psychophysics,* 1970, *7,* 328-332.

Metlay, W., Sokoloff, M., and Kaplan, I. T. "Visual Search for Multiple Targets." *Journal of Experimental Psychology,* 1968, *85,* 148-150.

Naus, M. J., Cermak, L. S., and DeLuca, D. "Retrieval Processes in Alcoholic Korsakoff Patients." *Neuropsychologia,* 1977, *15,* 737-742.

Neale, J. M. "Perceptual Span in Schizophrenia." *Journal of Abnormal Psychology,* 1971, *77,* 196-204.

Neisser, U. "Decision Time Without Reaction Time." *American Journal of Psychology,* 1963, *76,* 376-385.

Neisser, U. *Cognitive Psychology.* New York: Appleton-Century-Crofts, 1967.

Neisser, U., and Beller, H. K. "Searching Through Word Lists." *British Journal of Psychology,* 1965, *56,* 349-358.

Neisser, U., Novick, R., and Lazar, R. "Searching for Ten Targets Simultaneously." *Perceptual and Motor Skills,* 1963, *17,* 955-961.

Nickerson, R. S. "Response Times with a Memory Dependent Decision Task." *Journal of Experimental Psychology,* 1966, *72,* 761-769.

Norman, D. A., and Bobrow, D. G. "On Data-Limited and Resource-Limited Processes." *Cognitive Psychology,* 1975, *7,* 44-64.

Norman, D. A., and Bobrow, D. G. "On the Role of Active Memory Processes in Perception and Cognition." In C. N. Cofer (Ed.), *The Structure of Human Memory.* San Francisco: Freeman, 1976.

Posner, M. I., and Snyder, C. R. R. "Attention and Cognitive Control." In R. L. Solso (Ed.), *Information Processing and Cognition: The Loyola Symposium.* Hillsdale, N.J.: Erlbaum, 1975.

Rabbitt, P. M. A. "Ignoring Irrelevant Information." *British Journal of Psychology,* 1964, *55,* 403-414.

Rabbitt, P. M. A. "Learning to Ignore Irrelevant Information." *American Journal of Psychology,* 1967, *80,* 1-13.

Rabbitt, P. M. A. "Age and the Use of Structure in Transmitted Information." In G. Talland (Ed.), *Human Aging and Behavior.* New York: Academic Press, 1968.

Rumelhart, D. E. *Human Information Processing.* New York: Wiley, 1977.

Russell, P. N., and Knight, R. G. "Performance of Process Schizophrenics on Tasks Involving Visual Search." *Journal of Abnormal Psychology,* 1977, *86,* 16-26.

Saccuzzo, D. P., Hirt, M., and Spencer, T. J. "Backward Masking as a Measure of Attention in Schizophrenia." *Journal of Abnormal Psychology,* 1974, *83,* 512-522.

Saccuzzo, D. P., and Miller, S. "Critical Interstimulus Interval in Delusional Schizophrenics and Normals." *Journal of Abnormal Psychology,* 1977, *86,* 261-266.

Schaie, K. W., and Gribbin, K. "Adult Development and Aging." *Annual Review of Psychology,* 1975, *26,* 65-96.

Schneider, S. J. "Selective Attention in Schizophrenia." *Journal of Abnormal Psychology,* 1976, *85,* 167-173.

Schneider, W., and Shiffrin, R. M. "Controlled and Automatic Human Information Processing. I: Detection, Search, Attention." *Psychological Review,* 1977, *84,* 1-66.

Segal, E. M., and Lachman, R. "Complex Behavior or Higher Mental Process: Is There a Paradigm Shift?" *American Psychologist,* 1972, *27,* 46-55.

Shiffrin, R. M., and Schneider, W. "Controlled and Automatic Human Information Processing. II: Perceptual Learning, Automatic Attending, and a General Theory." *Psychological Review,* 1977, *84,* 127-190.

Smith, E. E., and Spoehr, K. T. "The Perception of Printed English: A Theoretical Perspective." In B. H. Kantowitz (Ed.), *Human Information Processing: Tutorials in Performance and Cognition.* Hillsdale, N.J.: Erlbaum, 1974.

Sperling, G., and others. "Extremely Rapid Visual Search: The Maximum Rate of Scanning Letters for the Presence of a Numeral." *Science,* 1971, *174,* 307-311.

Sternberg, R. J. *Intelligence, Information Processing and Analogical Reasoning: The Componential Analysis of Human Abilities.* Hillsdale, N.J.: Erlbaum, 1977.

Sternberg, S. "Memory Scanning: Mental Processes Revealed by Reaction-Time Experiments." In J. S. Antrobus (Ed.), *Cognition and Affect.* Boston: Little, Brown, 1970.

Sternberg, S. "Memory Scanning: New Findings and Current Controversies." In D. Deutsch and J. A. Deutsch (Eds.), *Short-Term Memory.* New York: Academic Press, 1975.

Wolford, G. "Perturbation Model for Letter Identification." *Psychological Review,* 1975, *82,* 184-199.

70

Steen F. Larsen

Mnemonic Organization

Mnemonic organization, a central concept in cognitive or information-processing theories of learning and memory, denotes any kind of structure that a person discovers or creates in experienced material in order to be able to remember it later. Therefore, mnemonic organizing may be considered a special case of the general structuring of perception and thinking.

In cognitive theories, organization has a role comparable to the concept of *association* in stimulus-response or associationist theory. But, unlike associations, organization is not assumed to arise automatically. Rather, it is a product of the *control processes* or strategies that the subject applies to the task. Mnemonic organizing should, therefore, be understood in relation to other important types of memory control processes (such as rehearsal, coding, and retrieval) and to cognitive processes in general.

In a more narrow sense, mnemonic organization is used descriptively to refer to relations between the elements (items) of to-be-remembered material which are established and used by the subject, especially when the procedure of *free recall* is employed.

From antiquity—when memory could not be assisted by such tools as today's note pads and computers—knowledgeable people have realized the superiority of mnemonic organization over sheer drilling. It was once called the art of memory (Yates, 1966), but it is now better known as "mnemonic devices" or "memory tricks"—perhaps reflecting a feeling that only the hard work of rote learning is really respectable.

Background and Current Status

Mandler (1967a) and Baddeley (1976) have provided good accounts of the antecedents of modern organizational memory theory. The following summary draws on these sources.

Beginning with the pioneering studies of Ebbinghaus (1885) and during the first half of this century, the psychology of memory was dominated by associative interference theory. Although the nonsense syllables of Ebbinghaus gradually gave way to words as experimental materials, the theory still explained learning and memory in terms of the automatic production of associations and their strengthening through repetitions.

Oppositions to interference theory were rare, perhaps because most experimental psychologists of the period did not care much for theorizing anyway. But some important foreshadowings of an alternative view are worth noting. Around 1920 Otto Selz showed that associative strength may easily be overridden by instructions to the subject, a point which was developed further by Narziss Ach and Kurt Lewin in the concept of "determining tendencies" (see Kintsch, 1977)—or, in current terminology, control processes. In 1932 Bartlett's book *Remembering* forcefully asserted that learning is a process of discovering and creating organization and meaning in the material—an "effort after meaning"—and that remembering is an active process of reconstructing a plausible imitation of the original on scant evidence. Finally, for many years Gestalt psychology attacked associationism with the claim that "insight" created by perceptual reorganization of the situation is of prime importance for learning and memory. This effort culminated in Katona's (1940) demonstration of the power of discovering and using generative rules rather than remembering isolated responses or facts.

These approaches influenced the later development of cognitive theories of memory, including organizational theory. But for nearly two more decades, interference theory remained virtually unaffected. The study of mnemonic organization did not make real progress until methods became available that allowed it to be observed and measured with care and precision. Around 1950 Ebbinghaus's "method of retained members" was revived under the name of *free recall,* and the turning point came when Bousfield (1953) adapted this method to investigate a phenomenon that he termed *clustering.*

In the method of free recall, a subject is given a list of items to be remembered (the input list) and is told that he is free to recall the items in any order that he prefers. Compared with the strict recall conditions of the paired-associate and serial learning methods that once dominated memory research, this method leaves far more room for the subject to develop his own strategies. For the examiner, it permits the *amount* recalled and the *order* in which items are recalled to be observed independently.

Bousfield's (1953) innovation was to select the items on the input list according to well-defined criteria, typically semantic categories, and to observe how this grouping was reflected in the subject's order of recall. For example, an input list of sixty words comprised fifteen animals, fifteen professions, fifteen names, and fifteen vegetables. Though the words were presented in random order, subjects tended to recall them in *clusters*; that is, words from the same category were likely to be put together in recall.

The extent to which recall order agreed with the predetermined organization of the input list was used as a quantitative measure of clustering.

Since then, clustering has been studied extensively with a wide variety of pre-organized materials (see Herriot, Green, and McConkey, 1973; Kintsch, 1977). Investigators have found that practically any kind of preorganization of the input list (for instance, by conceptual categories, interitem associations, word frequency, or orthographic structures) may produce clustering in free recall. In addition, repeated presentations and recalls (multitrial free recall) increase clustering. Finally, degree of clustering nearly always correlates positively with amount recalled—that is, the more perfectly the recall order agrees with the experimenter's organization of the items, the more items are recalled.

Tulving (1962) devised a method applicable to materials that the experimenter had not attempted to organize in advance. He simply proposed to measure organization by the degree of correspondence between the order of items in successive recall trials when input order varied randomly from trial to trial. The method thus required at least two recall trials on the input list. In return it offered important advantages. The subject could now get credit for clustering that did not respect the experimenter's definition of how the list was organized; the method thus recognized that the nominal organization (the experimenter's view) and the functional organization (the one actually used by the subject) do not necessarily agree. Therefore, even totally idiosyncratic ways of organization were allowed and could be observed; the scope of individual strategies was thus extended.

Tulving's experiments and innumerable later studies of the free recall of "unrelated" items have shown that subjects do in fact organize such materials, as judged from the regularity of successive recall orders. Since this organization must have been imposed by the subject alone, Tulving designated it *subjective organization*. Like clustering, subjective organization increases with practice and correlates with amount recalled. The main problem with both methods is that organization is measured retrospectively from the subject's recall performance. Therefore, the functions of organization during the learning phase and the recall phase cannot be distinguished. Two types of modifications have been invented to solve this difficulty.

Mandler (1967b; Mandler and Pearlstone, 1966) separated learning and recall by requiring the subjects to attain a criterion of organizational stability before recall was attempted. Subjects were instructed to sort a set of "unrelated" words into a number of categories of their own choice on the basis of how the words appeared to "belong together." Sorting was repeated until they could do it in almost the same way twice in a row. Then they were asked to recall as many words as possible in any order that they preferred. This *sorting-and-recall method* permits the development and characteristics of organization to be studied and controlled independently of recall. Because the subject-defined category system is known, measures of category clustering may then be applied to study the recall process. The main drawback is that the sorting procedure excludes noncategorical types of organization.

Tulving and Pearlstone (1966) introduced *cuing* as a method for investigating the subjects' use of specific characteristics of the material, either in learning or in recall. Cues are items provided by the experimenter (in addition to the items to be recalled) in order to direct the subject's processing to certain aspects of the material. Cues are usually related to the items in some way—for example, by being category names or close associates to them. The cues may be given either at learning (*presentation cues*) or at recall (*recall cues*) or at both times. Thus, the subject's attention during learning and/or recall may be directed to features that the experimenter wants to study.

These and other methodological advances gave rise to a tremendous increase in research on mnemonic organization, mainly because they opened the way for important theoretical developments. It became possible to make more precise inferences about hypothetical cognitive processes which could be assumed to operate behind the subject's observable performance. These processes may conveniently be divided into storage and retrieval processes, coinciding partly with the presentation and recall phases of the experimental procedure; however, the processes should be kept strictly apart from the procedures because they belong to a different theoretical level.

Consideration was first given to the *retrieval processes*. In a long series of experiments with the sorting-and-recall method, Mandler (1967b, 1977) found that the amount recalled after sorting did not correlate with the number of sorting trials (that is, repetitions) the subject had used but rather with the number of categories the words were sorted into. This result contradicts an associative theory, and it suggests that mnemonic organization functions as a retrieval plan, directing retrieval to proceed category by category. Along the same line, Cohen (1966) showed that from any given category either several items were recalled or none at all. Further, Tulving and Pearlstone (1966) found that retrieval cues in the form of category labels resulted in recall of more categories, but not more items from each category. Tulving and Pearlstone's study is also important because it demonstrates beyond doubt that subjects may have learned a good deal more than they can recall; to use Mandler's (1967a) distinction, items may be *available* (that is, stored) but not *accessible* for retrieval. Even more important, the Tulving and Pearlstone study indicates that retrieval may be improved by cues which direct the subject to material in memory that would otherwise be inaccessible.

Another way to make categories more accessible might be to organize them hierarchically. Mandler (1967b) argued for a hierarchical conception of memory organization in general, and Bower and associates (1969) proved that hierarchical organization of long lists of items does improve recall dramatically. But so do strategies that integrate all the single items in one overall structure—for example, using the list of words as elements in a narrative story (Bower and Clark, 1969). So it seems that the categoriality of mnemonic organization should not be overstated. What matters is only that every detail to be remembered is somehow integrated into a comprehensive organizational scheme (Bower, 1970).

But recall involves more than retrieval of items. People make very few recall errors, and in most instances they are able to reject wrong candidates for recall which are suggested to them. Therefore, it appears that retrieved items are put out only after a check of their correctness has been made, similar to a recognition decision. This view, known as the *two-process theory of recall* (Kintsch, 1970), assumes that the recognition check which is executed after retrieval does not depend on organization because the items have already been located in memory by the retrieval process. In fact, organization does not appreciably affect recognition memory (for exceptions see Mandler, 1977).

At the same time, more attention was attracted to the *storage processes,* or, in other words, to how organization is formed. Tulving and Osler (1968) proposed an *encoding specificity hypothesis* to explain the finding that retrieval cues are effective only if they are presented at the time of storage. The hypothesis contends that both the retrieval cues themselves and their relations to the list items must be stored simultaneously with the list—they have to be coded and stored as part of the same event. This hypothesis is supplemented by the *encoding variability principle* (Martin, 1971), which states that items become easier to recall when they are coded in various ways. The reason is assumed to be that each aspect or context of coding provides additional potential retrieval cues and thus increases the possibility of successful recall. Encoding variability may explain why recall is improved by a number of factors, such as spaced repetitions (which provide a number of different encoding contexts), multimodality presentation of items, and intention to remember (which leads the subject to process the items more extensively).

Both hypotheses are compatible with the *level-of-processing theory* proposed by Craik and Lockhart (1972). They maintained that items may be encoded on several levels, from superficial coding of physical characteristics to deep coding of semantic features. The deeper levels of processing entail a richer and more elaborate coding of items and thus result in better recall. An important aspect of the theory is that the level-of-processing concept provides a bridge between the memorization strategies used by the subject and the resulting coding of the items. Craik and Lockhart (1972) distinguished two main types of memorization strategies: *repetitive rehearsal* (where items are repeated mechanically without any attempt to consider variations of their form and context, thus leading only to superficial coding) and *elaborative rehearsal* (where items are viewed from several different angles and different features are noted, resulting in a richer and deeper coding and, consequently, superior recall). Elaborative rehearsal often goes beyond the elaboration of single items to involve the establishment of relations between two or more items, what might be called *integrative rehearsal.* When subjects are instructed to rehearse items aloud, these three kinds of rehearsal may be observed directly. It has been found that such rehearsal strategies are indeed reflected both in the degree of organization and in the amount recalled; similarly, conditions favorable to integration, such as blocked presentation of related items or instructions to rehearse items in blocks, facilitate both organization and recall (see Herriot, Green, and McConkey, 1973).

Finally, Tulving (1972) introduced the important distinction between *episodic memory* and *semantic memory.* Remembering concrete events located in time and space—such as what happened in an experimental situation—belongs to episodic memory, whereas semantic memory concerns knowledge of general rules, word meanings, and the like. Tulving noted that the coding of word items for episodic memory depends decisively on how the subject conceives of the meaning of the words; that is, on semantic memory. The words themselves need not be learned in an experiment. They are known in advance, and their meaning is stored in the subject's vocabulary, or *subjective lexicon,* from which the features used for elaborating and organizing the words must be available. Therefore, the richness of the subjective lexicon presumably sets the limits for organization of words to be learned, both singly and in relation. Conversely, it may be assumed that the structure that is apparent in the subject's rehearsal, sorting, and recall indicates the nature of organization and content in his subjective lexicon (Miller, 1971).

In recent years researchers have begun to investigate individual differences in mnemonic organization (for reviews see Eysenck, 1977; Johnson, 1974). The normal development of organizational strategies is by now fairly well understood (Flavell, 1977), some studies of schizophrenics have appeared (Larsen and Fromholt, 1976), and systematic research on the relation between memory and intelligence is under way (Guthke, 1977; Hunt, Frost, and Lunneborg, 1973).

The scarcity of such specific research is one reason why these theoretical and methodological advances have had small impact on clinical assessment. The procedures used in assessment are still mostly concerned with quantitative aspects of memory, and the interpretations are dominated by associationist concepts. However, assessment of mnemonic organization offers promising possibilities for observing the interaction of clients' semantic systems and their ability to create and use adaptive cognitive strategies for the important everyday purpose of remembering. In addition, the organizational view of memory leads to more specific suggestions for training and rehabilitation than those which may be derived from the associationist theory.

Critical Discussion

General Areas of Concern

A number of issues must be decided if one intends to assess mnemonic organization in the clinic. First of all, is it relevant to the particular clinical case? At present this
decision must to a considerable extent depend on the clinician's experience; the evidence
on intellectual and psychiatric disorders is briefly treated in a later section. In general it
will be argued, however, that not only problems of memory in the narrow sense but also
the client's conceptual system, cognitive style, and dynamic aspects of thinking and
memory are amenable to investigation by such methods.

Second, how should the assessment be carried out? Because no standardized methods are available for clinical use, decisions must be made on every detail of the test procedure. However, this gives the opportunity of adapting the method to each client and
clinical problem. The main points to consider in devising an appropriate method are the
materials, the procedure, and the registration of organization and recall. The choices
should be governed throughout by the purpose of the testing, particularly whether a cognitive or a projective emphasis is desired. Finally, some of the actuarial characteristics of
the client must be taken into account.

Materials. The items to be learned may be represented as words, pictures, or both.
It is usually most convenient to use words because with pictures recall must be verbal
anyway to avoid difficulties in drawing. Concrete and familiar nouns are preferable in
order to keep task difficulty at an intermediate level, so that floor and ceiling effects are
avoided. The items may be unrelated or related, either categorically, thematically, associatively, or formally (for instance, in spelling).

The number of items (and, with preorganized items, the number of categories)
will depend partly on their organization and on the procedure. As a rule, twenty to forty
items are suitable for people of normal ability, with preorganized materials in the higher
end. With children and retardates down to a mental age of about 5-6 years, sixteen items
in four categories have given no problems.

Preorganized items should be employed if the main purpose is to assess mnemonic
skills as such. The selection of such items may be aided by word frequency counts
(Thorndike and Lorge, 1944), associative norms (Palermo and Jenkins, 1964), and category norms (Battig and Montague, 1969; Toglia and Battig, 1978).

With unorganized lists the client's task resembles that of a projective test to some
extent; that is, a personal system of organization must be constructed and projected onto
the material. This system will then indicate the structure of the individual's semantic
memory. If this aspect is of interest to the examiner, the content of the items should be
carefully considered. Two approaches to item selection are open. One approach is to
choose words from content areas of general importance to everybody; for example, both
affectively loaded and nonaffective words could be represented (Kayton and Koh, 1975).
A suitable set of words might be found in a free-association test, as long as no standard
set has been developed. The other approach consists in selecting words that point to concepts of specific relevance to the client, such as important persons in his or her life, traumatic experiences, and current preoccupations. This must be based totally on clinical
judgment.

Procedure. The examiner's purpose should be the prime determinant in selecting
the procedure. In an initial assessment of a client's mnemonic skills, the procedure should
leave maximal room for the client's own choice of strategies. But if the purpose is to
diagnose particular deficits or potentials for development, a more tightly controlled procedure is appropriate.

Presentation of word items may be visual, auditory, or both; successive or simultaneous; random or with related items presented in blocks. The items may be accompanied by presentation cues, and different rates of presentation may be employed. The important thing in presenting the items is to ensure that they are perceived correctly and unequivocally. With printed words and particularly with pictures, the subject should read or name the items aloud as they are seen. Simultaneous presentation of the whole set of items facilitates organization, but some kind of successive task must still be used to make sure that every item is perceived by the client.

In many cases the best solution appears to be a sorting task, which also allows the examiner to observe directly the structure and content of organization at encoding. If such a task is used, the client must be told what the criterion of sorting is; for instance, two identical sortings in a row. It appears to make no difference, however, whether the client is instructed to recall the words later. Only what the client actually does—namely, the sorting itself—will matter (Kintsch, 1977).

Presentation cues, blocked presentation, or specific instructions may be given to assist the subject in storing the items. Examples of such instructions are to read or name the items during presentation, to sort them actively according to some given system, or to employ a specific rehearsal strategy (for instance, repetition, association, image formation, category blocking). The effects of these instructions on the client's behavior and performance may reveal whether he is able to follow a strategy that is not in his spontaneous repertoire and whether he can take advantage of relations in the material which are not personally discovered but pointed out by a "teacher."

Usually a recall test is employed, so that data on recall organization are obtained. Recall cues or a recognition test may be useful to locate and circumvent specific retrieval difficulties. The whole procedure or any part of it may be run only once or several times in succession. Recall is most often tested a few minutes after presentation or sorting is completed, the short delay serving to counteract recall from short-term memory. Longer delays do not seem to affect recall of sorted items, but with less complete acquisition—for example, only one passive presentation trial—delays may decrease recall significantly.

In other respects, similar considerations apply to this part of the procedure as to presentation: Control may be left to the client's choice so as to reveal his spontaneous strategies, or the examiner may employ more or less specific recall cues—the most specific being a recognition test—to discover details of the client's organization at coding and retrieval.

When presentation is serial, the whole procedure of presentation and recall is usually repeated several times, so that the development of organization can be observed and so that a stable organizational structure is obtained. Even repeated recalls without renewed presentation may be used to assess the stability of the retrieval process as such. In the sorting-and-recall procedure, it is most common to require that sorting is repeated until a criterion of two identical sortings is attained, after which the client is unexpectedly asked to recall the items.

Registration of Organization and Recall. Organization at encoding is difficult to assess unless a sorting task is employed. It may then be characterized quantitatively in terms of the number and size of the categories the subject has formed. To follow the development of organization, the agreement between successive pairs of sorting trials may be calculated, and the particular items and categories involved in changes and misplacements may also be noted.

Standard methods for characterizing organization qualitatively are not available. Normative studies with a fixed set of items, which would make it possible to identify and describe both reasonable and devious sortings, are lacking. At present this qualitative evaluation must be left to clinical judgment. To that end it is worthwhile to obtain a verbal report from the client afterward about his reasons for sorting the items.

The basic measure of recall is the number of correct words. If the list was organized in categories in advance, either by the examiner or by the client's sorting, the number of words recalled from each category may be determined straightforwardly. Then several measures of recall organization which have been used in experimental work are available (for a review, see Herriot, Green, and McConkey, 1973, Appendix 1). The most satisfactory method is Puff's (1970) *percentage of maximum possible clustering,* which may be written as

$$C\% = \frac{N(CR+1) - \Sigma(n_j)^2}{N(\Sigma(n_j-1)+1) - \Sigma(n_j)^2} \times 100$$

where N = total number of words recalled ($= \Sigma n_j$), n_j = number of words recalled from the j'th category, and CR = observed number of category repetitions (that is, the number of times a word from a given category is followed immediately by another word from the same category in the recall protocol). The obtained measure cannot at present be evaluated against empirical norms; but it indicates how systematically the subject is performing the retrieval process, independently of the amount that is recalled.

In the case of unrelated list items, organization must be calculated as the agreement between two successive recall orders. This is more cumbersome, but again Puff's (1970) method may be recommended. It starts by counting intertrial repetitions (ITR); that is, the number of times two items are recalled adjacently in the same order on the two recall trials. Then the words common to the two trials (C) are counted. The measure of subjective organization (SO) is then given as

$$SO\% = \frac{ITR}{C-1} \times 100$$

This measure is also independent of amount recalled.

In qualitative terms, it will be useful to note which words are *omitted* from a category, as well as which categories are omitted altogether. Such observations may have a diagnostic significance similar to long latencies in a free-association test. Also, *intrusions* of nonlist words in recall should be noted because they show that the recognition check has not been able to keep out errors committed by the retrieval process. This may be indicative of general difficulties in keeping unrealistic thoughts and fantasies in control.

Comparative Philosophies and Theories

The assessment of mnemonic organization can be compared with cognitive tests and projective tests. The cognitive view tends to ignore the contents of memory and to concentrate on processes. A test of mnemonic organization is well suited to reveal the control processes that a client spontaneously or habitually applies to the task of remembering. But unlike most cognitive tests, it also offers opportunities for giving assistance to the client—either cues to structural features of the material or directions for choosing a viable strategy. Thus, so-called *production deficiencies* (Flavell, 1977) may be uncovered; that is, failures to apply skills that are actually within the capabilities of the person. This feature may be highly relevant to training and rehabilitation.

The indifference to content is an advantage for the study of cognitive processes where the client's performance should not be hampered by emotional blockings. However, content becomes of prime importance when mnemonic organization is viewed from the projective angle. In the sorting-and-recall procedure, the client's sortings immediately invite projective interpretation. But because content has not generally been of much concern in memory research, the recall test may appear unnecessary in the projective context. The task of remembering, however, yields two definite advantages over most projective tests. First, it is not merely a strange disguise for the real purpose, but a realistic and well-known everyday activity (although of course somewhat artificial in the shape oᶠ a test). Second, it ensures that the ideas brought to bear on the task are not just temporary, fleeting fancies—they must be stable enough to support further sorting or memory in the future. In this way, the cognitive and projective approaches are complementary rather than in contrast.

Elaboration on Critical Points

A large body of research has shown that *age* affects mnemonic organization profoundly. Developmental studies from childhood to young adulthood have been reviewed by Herriot, Green, and McConkey (1973) and by Flavell (1977). Generally speaking, results indicate that amount recalled grows steadily from a chronological age of 5 to 20 years (hereafter abbreviated CA 5-20), whereas organization of recall does not exceed a chance level until about CA 9-10, from where it increases at least until CA 20. Studies of memorization strategies suggest that children below CA 9-10 simply do not spontaneously engage in organizing but rather try to learn by more restricted repetitive processing. With proper assistance—for example, cues in a sorting task—many younger children are able to apply organization at storage. This results in better recall, but the recall order remains unsystematic; thus, the organization appears ineffective at retrieval, presumably because it then has to be applied without external support.

Investigations of memory in *old age* (above CA 55-60) have been reviewed most recently by Eysenck (1977). He concludes that age-related deficits are prevalent only in episodic long-term memory, possibly because "old subjects are inferior to younger subjects at the more complex forms of information processing, including imaginal, semantic, and conceptual levels of processing" (p. 272). This conclusion must be qualified, however, since Eysenck himself cites several studies indicating "that the old do have the ability to use more efficient processes [of organizing] if suitably instructed" (p. 259). The organizational deficit in old age thus seems to be a genuine production deficiency, perhaps due to adherence to habitual strategies.

Sex differences in organization have been investigated as a secondary variable in two studies, which both reported negative results (Cuvo, 1975; Grimmett, 1975). Thus, there is no basis for suspecting that sex is a relevant factor. *Racial differences* were also studied by Grimmett (1975), who found equal recall and organization performance by black and white children when socioeconomic status was controlled. Apparently, *socioeconomic status* must therefore be held responsible for the results discussed by Eysenck (1977), showing that upper-middle-class white children recalled both categorized and unrelated lists better than lower-class blacks; organization was not studied, however.

Socioeconomic status is largely determined by *educational level,* but studies of the importance of this factor for mnemonic organization have been absent. High overall intelligence scores, however, seem to be favorable to performance involving deep levels of mnemonic processing (Eysenck, 1977, p. 292). Because intelligence scores and educational level are highly correlated, educational differences in mnemonic organization might be expected and should therefore be regarded as a potentially confounding variable in clinical applications.

Personal Views and Recommendations

The sorting-and-recall method is regarded here as particularly promising for clinical use; but much work still has to be done before its full potentials may be evaluated. The need for standard materials and normative studies has been noted repeatedly. Another important problem concerns the qualitative assessment of mnemonic organization. A fruitful approach might be to explore the similarities between the sorting task and the Object Sorting Test devised by Rapaport (see Kaplan and others, 1970). Interpretations along parallel lines may be warranted despite obvious differences between the two tasks— that instead of real objects the sorting-and-recall method uses symbolic stimuli, which may even be quite abstract; that it presents a task which requires more than just classification; and so on.

Not the least, to provide a more firm theoretical basis, a rapprochement between contemporary cognitive theory and personality theory will be necessary. This should be encouraged in any case, however.

At this early stage, it would be premature to propose that experience in evaluating mnemonic organization and strategies should be included in professional training or required for certification of psychologists. But as an example of a growing trend in psychology—both in general and clinical psychology—this area emphasizes that a broad, fundamental knowledge of scientific psychology is necessary if the clinical psychologist is to keep abreast of and contribute to new developments in the profession.

Application to Particular Variables

O'Connor and Hermelin (1971) have summarized work on *mental retardation* in childhood and concluded that the coding processes of these children are probably impaired because of an insufficient vocabulary and category system; they do, however, seem to employ mnemonic organization within the limits of their mental age, and they are apparently able to benefit from external assistance. Herriot, Green, and McConkey (1973), in an extensive review that also included adults, arrived at similar conclusions. Further, they did a series of twelve experiments with young adult retardates (CA about 25) whose vocabulary age was 5-8 years. Although the subjects' spontaneous performance was poor in respect to both organization and recall, it could be improved by several kinds of help: presentation cues, grouped presentation, recall cues, and general instruction to organize. The improvement was consistent only in subjects of higher vocabulary age (7-8 years).

These results indicate that the processes and strategies necessary for mnemonic organization are all available to mental retardates at about 7 years of mental age. The problem is to elicit them and get the client to apply them adequately without assistance from others.

Defects of memory are perhaps the most common symptoms of *cerebral disease,* and it is impossible to give an adequate survey of these conditions here. Only brief mention of the work on the amnesic syndrome discussed by Warrington (1971) shall be made. Her findings strongly suggest that amnesic patients are able to classify and organize material normally, but they experience trouble in retrieving it. This interpretation contrasts with the usual physiological consolidation-deficit theory.

Patients with functional disorders apparently suffer from storage rather than retrieval problems. According to O'Connor and Hermelin (1971), *autistic children* have shown deficient encoding organization; for example, they did not perform better with preorganized material than with unrelated. A number of experiments on memory in *schizophrenia* have reported similar results (see Larsen and Fromholt, 1976). Briefly stated, studies of recognition, free recall, sorting, and sorting and recall have given strong evidence that the schizophrenic's major memory problem is to create and maintain a stable mnemonic organization. The subjective lexicon and the processes of retrieval and recognition check appear unaffected in these patients. Indeed, given sufficient time and opportunity, many schizophrenics are able to overcome the problems of organization on their own.

References

Baddeley, A. D. *The Psychology of Memory*. New York: Basic Books, 1976.

Bartlett, F. C. *Remembering*. Cambridge, England: Cambridge University Press, 1932.

Battig, W. F., and Montague, W. E. "Category Norms for Verbal Items in 56 Categories." *Journal of Experimental Psychology*, 1969, *80*, 1-46.

Bousfield, W. A. "The Occurrence of Clustering in the Recall of Randomly Arranged Associates." *Journal of General Psychology*, 1953, *49*, 229-240.

Bower, G. H. "Organizational Factors in Memory." *Cognitive Psychology*, 1970, *1*, 18-46.

Bower, G. H., and Clark, M. C. "Narrative Stories as Mediators for Serial Learning." *Psychonomic Science*, 1969, *14*, 181-182.

Bower, G. H., and others. "Hierarchical Retrieval Schemes in Recall of Categorized Word Lists." *Journal of Verbal Learning and Verbal Behavior*, 1969, *8*, 323-343.

Cohen, B. H. "Some-or-None Characteristics of Coding Behavior." *Journal of Verbal Learning and Verbal Behavior*, 1966, *5*, 182-187.

Craik, F. I. M., and Lockhart, R. S. "Levels of Processing: A Framework for Memory Research." *Journal of Verbal Learning and Verbal Behavior*, 1972, *11*, 671-684.

Cuvo, A. J. "Developmental Differences in Rehearsal and Free Recall." *Journal of Experimental Child Psychology*, 1975, *19*, 265-278.

Ebbinghaus, H. *Über das Gedächtnis*. Berlin, German Federal Republic: Duncker & Humblot, 1885.

Eysenck, M. W. *Human Memory: Theory, Research and Individual Differences*. Oxford, England: Pergamon Press, 1977.

Flavell, J. H. *Cognitive Development*. Englewood Cliffs, N.J.: Prentice-Hall, 1977.

Grimmett, S. A. "Black and White Children's Free Recall of Unorganized and Organized Lists: Jensen's Level I and Level II." *Journal of Negro Education*, 1975, *44*, 24-33.

Guthke, J. "Gedächtnis und Intelligenz." In F. Klix and H. Sydow (Eds.), *Zur Psychologie des Gedächtnisses*. Berlin, German Democratic Republic: Deutscher Verlag der Wissenschaften, 1977.

Herriot, P., Green, J., and McConkey, R. *Organization and Memory: A Review and a Project in Subnormality*. London: Methuen, 1973.

Hunt, E., Frost, N., and Lunneborg, C. "Individual Differences in Cognition: A New Approach to Intelligence." In G. H. Bower (Ed.), *Advances in Learning and Motivation*. Vol. 7. New York: Academic Press, 1973.

Johnson, J. H. "Memory and Personality: An Information Processing Approach." *Journal of Research in Personality*, 1974, *8*, 1-32.

Kaplan, M. L., and others. *The Structural Approach in Psychological Testing*. Elmsford, N.Y.: Pergamon Press, 1970.

Katona, G. *Organizing and Memorizing*. New York: Columbia University Press, 1940.

Kayton, L., and Koh, S. D. "Hypohedonia in Schizophrenia." *Journal of Nervous and Mental Disease*, 1975, *161*, 412-420.

Kintsch, W. *Learning, Memory, and Conceptual Processes*. New York: Wiley, 1970.

Kintsch, W. *Memory and Cognition.* New York: Wiley, 1977.

Larsen, S. F., and Fromholt, P. "Mnemonic Organization and Free Recall in Schizo-phrenia." *Journal of Abnormal Psychology,* 1976, *85,* 61-65.

Mandler, G. "Verbal Learning." In G. Mandler and others (Eds.), *New Directions in Psychology.* Vol. 3. New York: Holt, Rinehart and Winston, 1967a.

Mandler, G. "Organization and Memory." In K. W. Spence and J. T. Spence (Eds.), *The Psychology of Learning and Motivation.* Vol. 1. New York: Academic Press, 1967b.

Mandler, G. "Commentary on 'Organization and Memory.' " In G. Bower (Ed.), *Human Memory: Basic Processes.* New York: Academic Press, 1977.

Mandler, G., and Pearlstone, Z. "Free and Constrained Concept Learning and Subsequent Recall." *Journal of Verbal Learning and Verbal Behavior,* 1966, *5,* 126-131.

Martin, E. "Verbal Learning Theory and Independent Retrieval Phenomena." *Psychological Review,* 1971, *78,* 314-332.

Miller, G. A. "Empirical Methods in the Study of Semantics." In D. D. Steinberg and L. A. Jakobovits (Eds.), *Semantics.* Cambridge, England: Cambridge University Press, 1971.

O'Connor, N., and Hermelin, B. "Cognitive Deficits in Children." *British Medical Bulletin,* 1971, *27,* 227-231.

Palermo, D. S., and Jenkins, J. J. *Word Association Norms: Grade School Through College.* Minneapolis: University of Minnesota Press, 1964.

Puff, C. R. "An Investigation of Two Forms of Organization in Free Recall." *Journal of Verbal Learning and Verbal Behavior,* 1970, *9,* 720-724.

Thorndike, E. L., and Lorge, I. *The Teacher's Word Book of 30,000 Words.* New York: Columbia University Press, 1944.

Toglia, M. P., and Battig, W. F. *Handbook of Semantic Word Norms.* Hillsdale, N.J.: Erl-baum, 1978.

Tulving, E. "Subjective Organization in Free Recall of 'Unrelated' Words." *Psychological Review,* 1962, *69,* 344-354.

Tulving, E. "Episodic and Semantic Memory." In E. Tulving and W. Donaldson (Eds.), *Organization and Memory.* New York: Academic Press, 1972.

Tulving, E., and Osler, S. "Effectiveness of Retrieval Cues in Memory for Words." *Journal of Experimental Psychology,* 1968, *77,* 593-601.

Tulving, E., and Pearlstone, Z. "Availability Versus Accessibility of Information in Memory for Words." *Journal of Verbal Learning and Verbal Behavior,* 1966, *5,* 381-391.

Warrington, E. K. "Neurological Disorders of Memory." *British Medical Bulletin,* 1971, *27,* 243-247.

Yates, F. A. *The Art of Memory.* London: Routledge & Kegan Paul, 1966.

71

Max L. Hutt

Adience-Abience

Adience-abience, as used in this presentation, refers to the degree to which the individual is relatively "open" or closed to visual stimulation and input. Conceptually, it can be defined as a primary defensive orientation whereby the person becomes aware of and attempts to cope with the continuing flood of ever present visual-perceptual stimuli.

An individual who is highly abient is far less likely than one who is high on adience to be able to (1) incorporate and integrate new experiences, (2) adapt constructively to new experiences, or (3) profit easily from learning experiences. Persons high on abience are resistant to therapeutic experiences and are highly rigid in persistent and maladaptive behavior. Although position on the adience-abience dimension is not perfectly related to degree of psychopathology (since the two scales measure somewhat different personality operations), those who show *severe* degrees of psychopathology are presumed to have fairly high degrees of perceptual abience (and empirical evidence corroborates this), whereas those who show little psychopathology are presumed to have fairly high degrees of adience (and empirical evidence corroborates this, too).

The type of adience-abience style that the individual develops emerges from the earliest visual-motoric experiences in infancy and early childhood. Thus, it is presumed to be the basic mode of filtering experience at the perceptual level. Although adience-abience does not correlate extensively with other aspects of approach-avoidance behavior, clinical and experimental evidence suggests that some degree of correlation between these differing modes is present. Therefore, disturbances in this mode may profoundly influence other learning and adaptive experiences. If the individual is unable to receive and then integrate experience, his capacity for developing alternative strategies of adaptation is thereby limited. Alternatively, if he is open to such experiences, he is more easily able to develop appropriate coping and defensive methods for dealing with his world of internal and external events.

Perceptual adience-abience is presumed to underlie other defensive operations and is more basic than certain other defenses (such as repression, introjection, projection, and denial). Of course, later defenses (such as rationalization, reaction formation, and sublimation) are even more profoundly affected by a highly abient perceptual mode.

Background and Current Status

The concept of adience-abience was first developed on the basis of clinical observations of the perceptual-motoric behavior of differing cases of clinical psychopathology, and more particularly on the basis of observations of such behavior on the Hutt Adaptation of the Bender-Gestalt Test (Hutt and Briskin, 1960). These individuals showed characteristic differences in their perceptual-motoric behavior on such test factors as (1) size of reproduction (for example, abient persons tended to reduce the size of figures), (2) change in angulation of the geometric figure, (3) rotation of the figure, and (4) fragmentation of the figure. Based on these empirical observations, a preliminary scale of adience-abience was developed and tested with a group of deaf retardates (Hutt and Fuerefile, 1963). The predictions were confirmed on both a pilot group and on a cross-validation group, thus lending support to clinical observations. Subsequently, as will be presented, the investigation focused on the construct, concurrent, and predictive validities of the scale and evaluated the interjudge and test-retest reliabilities. Finally, a revised edition of the scale was developed and has been undergoing extensive evaluation (Hutt, 1977a).

It may be helpful, at this point, to compare the conceptual dimensions of adience-abience with related concepts of defensive behavior. It has been known for some time—ever since systematic attention was given to the effects of early favorable and early traumatic experience on the personality and cognitive development of infants and very young children—that deprivation of adequate mothering experiences, inconsistent infant-parent interactions, and traumatic emotional experiences can severely damage ego formation, retard intellectual development, and cause the development of psychopathological distortion of the personality (Bettelheim, 1967; Brody and Axelrad, 1971; Freud, 1946; Hoffman and Hoffman, 1964; Hunt, 1961; Hutt and Gibby, 1957; Murphy, 1962). Conversely, favorable and rehabilitative experiences in infancy and very early childhood can improve such functions and can compensate for other unfavorable experiences (Bronfenbrenner, 1974; Garber and Heber, 1977; Welmann, 1940).

Present evidence supports the view that the adience-abience characteristics of an individual are based, first, on his or her degree of *vulnerability to stress* (Hutt, 1977b; Hutt and Gibby, 1979), and then on experiences in infancy that predispose the individual toward an adient or an abient perceptual approach.

Critical Discussion

General Areas of Concern

Since the visual-perceptual mode is one of the most important methods of mediating external and internal stimulation, it is highly modifiable in infancy as a result of ongoing stresses and stimulation. A responsive infant, supported by a protective and moderately stimulating environment, quickly learns to *look toward* anticipated sources of pleasure, thus reinforcing adient perceptual behavior. The child can learn to move his head toward the source of stimulation with open eyes and scan the visual field. The child learns to "take in" information; at the same time, he learns to become perceptive of inner sources of stimulation, since "wants" are quickly accommodated. In time he learns to integrate such adient behaviors and builds the foundation for effective perceptually oriented behaviors. An infant who experiences deprivation of stimulation, excessive stress, or inconstant stimulation quickly learns to turn his head away, close his eyes, and become passive in scanning the perceptual field; he thereby loses effectiveness in responding to visual and related fields. Vulnerability to stress may compound these aberrant trends. As has been demonstrated (Dick, 1968; Ornitz and Ritvo, 1968), perceptual impairment may lead to cognitive retardation and contribute to autistic behavior.

These primary adaptive modes are believed to underlie the tendencies toward the development of supportive defensive mechanisms. For example, *perceptual vigilance* (Postman, 1953) may become excessive and overdetermined as a consequence of earlier traumatic perceptual experiences. Vigilance requires that the subject react after the stimulus has been registered and is therefore a less efficient defense, and a later stage in development, than not perceiving what is out there. In vigilance, the organism learns to defend itself against certain classes of stimuli (those that have previously proved to be threatening), whereas abience is a general defense that reduces the input of all perceptual stimuli. Similarly, adience-abience is presumed to differ from the phenomena of *augmentation-reduction,* in which (pain) stimulation is either enhanced or reduced once it has been perceived (Petrie, 1967). Other mechanisms of defense are similarly thought to operate after the stimulus has been perceived. The mechanism of *selective attention* (Sullivan, 1953) enables the individual to defend against obnoxious stimuli by shifting attention or focus. *Leveling-sharpening* (Gardner and Long, 1960) is a related secondary mechanism. The phenomena of *field-dependence* and *field-independence* seem to be developed in childhood and are clearly similar secondary defense strategies (Witkin and others, 1962).

Closer in ontogeny to the mechanisms of adience-abience than the foregoing are such phenomena as *autocentrism-allocentrism* (Schachtel, 1959), *introversion-extraversion* (Jung, 1939), and biological mechanisms involved in *approach-avoidance behavior* (Schneirla, 1959). Schneirla's concepts are perhaps closest to Hutt's, in that he conceives of basic biphasic, functionally opposed mechanisms which "are the only empirical, objective terms applicable to all motivated behavior of all animals" (p. 2). However, Schneirla focuses on the *total behavioral style of approach-withdrawal,* whereas adience-abience is concerned with perceptual intake versus perceptual rejection. Adience-abience phenomena rest on the foundation of evidence that alteration in the organism's perceptual attention to stimuli can reduce the neural affective response along some other neural pathways (Von Békésy, 1967).

Comparative Philosophies and Theories

Thus far, the discussion has focused on the conceptual basis of adience-abience and its relationships to and differences from other theories of perception. There are other relationships to more general approaches to the nature of perception, and indeed to the nature of man, that merit examination.

For a long time, at least since the formal considerations of perception by Wundt, Müller, and Titchener, perception was considered a primary determiner of behavior; as those theorists viewed the problem, the individual's knowledge of the world is derived from his sensations and perceptions. Titchener (1910) demonstrated that perception is dependent on three qualities of the stimulus: quality (such as degree of pain), intensity (duration of the stimulus), and attensity (clarity of the stimulus). This theory of perception reduced the act of perception to its "atomistic" elements. The Gestaltists, in contrast, emphasized the configurational qualities of the stimulus, that is, they believed that the complex stimulus was always a unique, composite and integral unit and not simply a number of disparate elements. Wertheimer (1912) and other Gestaltists recognized that a complex stimulus (a "whole") is not perceived by the individual as consisting of separate elements, but is perceived as a total pattern. It was not, however, until Krech (1949) and others emphasized the role of the person in the act of perception, the so-called New Look in psychology, that not only the stimulus, but the characteristics of the person doing the perceiving, received adequate emphasis. The unit of behavior was now the *hypothesis,* meaning that perception depends, in part, not on the stimulus but on the "purpose" of the perceiver. There followed many experimental demonstrations that defensive qualities of the perceiver—qualities such as selectivity, vigilance, set, and needs—influence perception.

Surprisingly, it was not until the advent of information theory, with its focus on the means by which perceptions are processed, that the complexities of a great many factors within the individual began to be recognized. Information-processing theory permitted the consideration of a greater variety of skills and processes than had been considered. Hunt (1962), for example, was able to demonstrate experimentally the richness of perception in general and of cognitive functioning in particular.

All these and other approaches to perception do not consider the possibility that both structural properties of the stimulus and the "hypothesis" variables of the individual are basically qualified by the adient-abient style of the person. They deal, instead, with *what* is received and *how* it is processed, rather than with *how much* is received before it can be processed. Despite set, motivation, and need, and despite intensity, attensity, and quality of the stimulus, how much is received (perceived) by the person depends, in the first place, on how "open" or closed" he is; that is, how much is perceived depends on the individual's ability to "accept" the stimulus. It is in this sense that an abient style in perception precludes subsequent selectivity and processing. It is also in this sense that such defensive and processing operations are also dependent on the basic perceptual style.

Elaboration on Critical Points

In its present form, the Adience-Abience Scale is derived from the subject's reproductions of nine Gestalt figures adapted by Hutt (1977a) from those originally experimented with by Wertheimer (1923). The subject is asked to "copy" each of these figures, in turn, as each is presented to him on 3" x 5" cards. The subject is presented with a stack of 8½" x 11" unlined, white sheets of paper; is given no indication of how many sheets of paper can be used or any indication of how he is to proceed; but is simply told "to copy the drawing on the paper, as well as you can." More explicit directions for administration are provided in the publication by Hutt (1977a).

These drawings of the subject are then scored on twelve test factors (Hutt, 1977a). (A scoring template is provided to ensure completely accurate and objective scoring.) Three factors are based on the size of the reproductions and the *amount of space* used to draw the figures. Two factors deal with the *sequence* with which the figures are drawn on the page and the *placement* of the first figure on the page. Three factors deal with *changes in the form* of the Gestalt (closure difficulty, crossing difficulty, and change in degree of angulation). Four factors are related to basic *distortions* of the Gestalt (rotation, fragmentation, simplification, and elaboration). The final corrected scores can range from 1 to 38.

Norms are provided for (1) adult groups (normals, outpatient neurotics, inpatient neurotics, chronic schizophrenics, and brain-damaged patients), (2) the total normative adult population (consisting of 573 cases), and (3) children's groups (ranging in age from 10 to 16 years and including normals, disturbed, and delinquents; N = 331). Suggested norms are also indicated for younger groups.

Various studies have explored the test-retest reliability of the scale and the interscorer reliability of the scale. Test-retest reliability over a two-week period with schizophrenic patients was .84 for both males and females (Hutt and Miller, 1975), and ranged from .85 to .92 for three groups of children (13 to 16 years of age) over a forty-week interval (Hutt and Dates, 1977). Moreover, the major components of the scale revealed similar stability over time, and the relative positions on the adience-abience continuum remained fairly constant. Thus, test-retest reliability is fairly high. Interscorer reliability is even higher, correlations between pairs of independent scorers being .912 (Spearman rho) in the Hutt and Miller study (1975) and .89 and .90 (Kendall's coefficient of concordance) in the Hutt and Dates study (1977).

The problem of validation is a tricky one, since independent criteria of adience-abience are lacking. Validation research has provided empirical support in terms of construct and predictive powers of the scale. In an original test of the scale, deaf-retarded individuals were first dichotomized into high-adience and high-abience subpopulations (Hutt and Fuerefile, 1963) and then compared on six measures of behavioral functioning dealing with interpersonal and intellectual effectiveness. The findings indicated that the scale is effective in discriminating between these populations on the a priori criteria (p values being .01 or better for five of the six criteria). In a cross-validation with 185 additional deaf-retarded subjects in this study, seven criteria were used to test the effectiveness of the Adience-Abience Scale. The scale was found to be effective in predicting (1) higher intellectual performance, (2) less psychopathology, and (3) later age of admission to institutions (the higher the degree of adience, the better functioning in these areas was found). Moreover, separate analyses by age and sex indicated that these factors were not related to degree of adience-abience. Again, most of the tests of significance were at the .01 level or better.

Subsequent validation studies were also encouraging. A test was made of the effectiveness of the scale in differentiating patients who responded well to individual psychotherapy from those who did not (Hutt, 1977a). Those who were high in therapeutic improvement, as compared with those who were low in therapeutic improvement, were differentiated by the adience-abience measure at a p level of .01 (N = 28). The scale also significantly differentiated between schizophrenic patients who had been hospitalized for less than six months and those who had been hospitalized for more than five years (Hutt, 1977a).

A critical study was undertaken to determine whether schizophrenic patients with "inner resources" could be differentiated from schizophrenic patients who did not possess such resources (Hutt, 1969). Two groups of such patients (forty in each group) were matched on the basis of age, sex, and length of hospitalization. They were significantly different, however, on adience-abience scores. Two measures of creativity were applied. The Adience-Abience Scale significantly differentiated these patients on degree of creativity. Another study (Credidio, 1975) tested the measure of adience-abience on college students with respect to their performance on the Gottschaldt Figures Test. This test measures perception of novel stimuli and was thought to be related to "openness" in perceiving. Therefore, as predicted, those who were high in adience performed significantly better on the Gottschaldt Figures Test than those who were high in abience.

Finally, the predictive capacity of the scale was evaluated with a group of male, delinquent adolescents (N = 120) (Hutt, Dates, and Reid, 1977). As expected, a significant degree of correlation was found between adience-abience and recidivism.

Finally, other characteristics of the scale were explored to determine other paramaters that seemed relevant. It had been hypothesized that high degrees of psychopathology would be associated with high degrees of abience, but it was also expected that lesser degrees of psychopathology would not be as closely related to position on the adience-abience continuum. Two studies demonstrated that this formulation was correct. Hutt and Miller (1976) demonstrated that a measure of degree of psychopathology was much more highly correlated with a measure of adience-abience in a schizophrenic population (the r's being, respectively, .67 and .77 for males and females) than in an outpatient (mainly neurotic) population, (the r's being, respectively, .39 and .42 for males and females). In the study with delinquents, Hutt and Dates (1977) found that psychopathology and adience-abience were more closely related *before* treatment (.64 for a population assigned to group treatment and .62 for a population assigned to individual treatment) than *after* treatment lasting some forty weeks (the r's being reduced to .40 and .48, respectively). In contrast, a control group showed greater significance (r's of .66 and .67 respectively) between the two measures during comparable periods of testing. In all the studies that have been reported, it has been found that, above the age level of 10 years, age, sex, and intelligence are not significantly related to scores on the Adience-Abience Scale.

Although further evaluation is needed, these findings suggest that the scale has significant concurrent, construct, and predictive validities.

Personal Views and Recommendations

The adience-abience measure taps a fundamental dimension of the personality, a dimension that previously had not been explicitly defined, measured, or evaluated. Although admittedly crude in some respects, the measure appears to have significant potential value for both research and practical application.

Research evidence clearly indicates that perceptual experience (or, more accurately, perceptual-motoric experience, since all perception involves motoric behavior as well) is the cornerstone of later cognitive development. Piaget (1970) has provided empirical observations and theoretical formulations in which the earliest schemata of intellectual development are based on sensorimotor development. Although cutaneous contact with the world may be an even more primitive means of learning to experience the world (Harlow, 1971) and may furnish the beginnings of basic trust, that kind of experience has neither the range nor the versatility of perceptual experience. It is through the visual world, primarily, that the infant begins to experience "what is out there" and later to distinguish between what is "inside" and what is "outside." Moreover, perceptual experience is readily conditioned—for better or for worse. Thus, the earliest perceptual experiences not only determine, to a large extent, how much is learned but also lay the foundation for a basic parameter of personality style. That style can be generally approach oriented or generally avoidance oriented.

Once a tendency toward a particular perceptual style of adience or abience is conditioned (and, as previously indicated, genetic factors presumably play some role in such dispositions), that particular style tends to persist and become reinforced by self-fulfilling maneuvers. Evidence indicates that the style of adience-abience is highly stable in childhood and later years and is resistant to change. Since perceptual abience limits the input of information, it thereby further limits the individual's capacity for flexible and adaptive behavior. One cannot deal with what is "unknown." Hence, even when intelligence or degree of psychopathology is held constant, the abient individual (other personality factors being held constant) tends to be far less effective in dealing with novel situations, growth experiences, and creative functions. Moreover, unlike other defenses of the personality, which mediate the response to stimulation, abience prevents appropriate mediation, since the input is grossly limited.

Application to Particular Variables

As suggested elsewhere (Hutt, 1976b), the early detection and treatment of individuals who are high in abience can help to prevent further reinforcement of such tendencies. Although current knowledge about how to modify the adience-abience style is quite limited, it seems appropriate to attempt rigorous treatment and education and carry out research to find ever more effective treatment-intervention methods. Short of this, special programs for such individuals (so as to minimize their limitation or to accentuate positive attributes that they may possess) can also be provided. On the positive side, those who are high in adience can be provided with appropriate programs to maximize their capacity for growth and development. Further, as suggested by Hutt (1976a), some mentally retarded individuals may have an inadequate genetic endowment rather than a high degree of abience; others, those whose retardation is the result of such factors as social-cultural deprivation or inadequate (but not traumatic) perceptual-motor experience, can profit considerably from appropriate intervention programs if they have good adient tendencies. Other uses of a measure of adience-abience, such as those suggested in work with delinquents (Hutt, Dates, and Reid, 1977), can involve more adequate selection of those who can most readily profit from psychotherapy.

On the research side, there are many questions to be answered. Fundamental to such questions is the more incisive exploration of the nature of adience-abience and its precise antecedents. Related to such issues are questions having to do with the relationships between adience-abience and many other personality variables and other aspects of perception. A rich lode for investigation is present. There are also questions of (1) how best to measure adience-abience, (2) how to improve the present measure, and (3) how to extend the scale to the earlier years of development. If this measure is to have its most meaningful application, early detection of highly abient individuals and rehabilitative programs are most important.

In clinical use, a measure of adience-abience can have considerable value. As already indicated, some persons with fairly high degrees of psychopathology are, nevertheless, quite adient. It is believed that prognosis is much more favorable in such cases and therapeutic treatment more effective. The scale can have value in offering some degree of "correction" for the more conventional measures of intelligence, since it has been shown that persons who are high in adience tend to have greater inner resources and creativity. The adience-abience measure can also be viewed as having something in common with what is currently termed "learning potential" and, as such, can have important classroom applications. In addition, cross-cultural studies should help to determine whether differences in cultural conditioning affect adience-abience phenomena.

References

Bettelheim, B. *The Empty Fortress.* New York: Free Press, 1967.
Brody, S., and Axelrad, S. *Anxiety and Ego Formation in Infancy.* New York: International Universities Press, 1971.

Bronfenbrenner, U. *Is Early Intervention Effective?* Vol. 2. Ithaca, New York: Cornell University Children's Bureau, 1974.

Credidio, S. G. "A Construct Validity Study of a Measure of Perceptual Approach-Avoidance." Unpublished doctoral dissertation, University of Detroit, 1975.

Dick, R. "Reproduction and Recognition as Indices of Perceptual Impairment." *American Journal of Mental Deficiency,* 1968, *73,* 9-12.

Freud, A. *The Ego and the Mechanisms of Defense.* New York: International Universities Press, 1946.

Garber, H., and Heber, F. R. "The Milwaukee Project: Indications of the Effectiveness of Early Intervention in the Prevention of Mental Retardation." In P. Mittler (Ed.), *Research to Practice in Mental Retardation.* Vol. 1. Baltimore: University Park Press, 1977.

Gardner, R. W., and Long, R. I. "Cognitive Controls as Determinants of Learning and Remembering." *Psychologia,* 1960, *3,* 165-171.

Harlow, H. F. *Learning to Love.* San Francisco: Albion, 1971.

Hoffman, M. L., and Hoffman, L. W. *Review of Child Development.* Vol. 1. New York: Russell Sage Foundation, 1964.

Hunt, E. B. *Concept Learning: An Information Processing Problem.* New York: Wiley, 1962.

Hunt, J. McV. *Intelligence and Experience.* New York: Ronald Press, 1961.

Hutt, M. L. *The Hutt Adaptation of the Bender Gestalt Test.* (2nd ed.) New York: Grune & Stratton, 1969.

Hutt, M. L. "Perceptual Adience-Abience and Cognitive Functioning." Paper presented at Gatlinburg Conference on Research in Mental Retardation, Gatlinburg, Tennessee, March 1976a.

Hutt, M. L. "The Significance of Perceptual Adience-Abience in Child Development." In D. V. Siva Sankar (Ed.), *Mental Health in Children.* Vol. 2. Westbury, N.Y.: PJD Publications, 1976b.

Hutt, M. L. *The Hutt Adaptation of the Bender Gestalt Test.* (3rd ed.) New York: Grune & Stratton, 1977a.

Hutt, M. L. *Psychosynthesis: Vital Therapy.* Oceanside, N.Y.: Dabor Science, 1977b.

Hutt, M. L., and Briskin, G. J. *The Hutt Adaptation of the Bender Gestalt Test.* New York: Grune & Stratton, 1960.

Hutt, M. L., and Dates, B. G. "Reliabilities and Interrelationships of Two HABGT Scales in a Male Delinquent Population." *Journal of Personality Assessment,* 1977, *41,* 353-357.

Hutt, M. L., Dates, B. G., and Reid, D. M. "The Predictive Ability of HABGT Scales for a Male Delinquent Population." *Journal of Personality Assessment,* 1977, *41,* 492-496.

Hutt, M. L., and Fuerefile, D. "The Clinical Meanings and Predictions of a Measure of Perceptual Adience-Abience." Paper presented at annual meeting of American Psychological Association, Philadelphia, 1963.

Hutt, M. L., and Gibby, R. G. *Patterns of Abnormal Behavior.* Boston: Allyn & Bacon, 1957.

Hutt, M. L., and Gibby, R. G. *The Mentally Retarded Child.* (4th ed.) Boston: Allyn & Bacon, 1979.

Hutt, M. L., and Miller, L. J. "Further Studies of a Measure of Adience-Abience: Reliability." *Journal of Personality Assessment,* 1975, *39,* 123-128.

Hutt, M. L., and Miller, L. J. "Interrelationships of Psychopathology and Adience-Abience on the HABGT." *Journal of Personality Assessment,* 1976, *40,* 135-139.

Jung, C. G. *The Integration of the Personality.* New York: Holt, Rinehart and Winston, 1939.

Krech, D. "Notes Toward a Psychological Theory." *Journal of Personality,* 1949, *18,* 66-87.

Murphy, L. B. *The Widening World of Childhood.* New York: Basic Books, 1962.

Ornitz, E., and Ritvo, E. R. "Perceptual Inconstancy in Early Infantile Autism." *Archives of General Psychiatry,* 1968, *18,* 76-98.

Petrie, A. *Individuality in Pain and Suffering.* Chicago: University of Chicago Press, 1967.

Piaget, J. *Main Trends in Psychology.* New York: Harper & Row, 1970.

Postman, L. "On the Problem of Perceptual Defense." *Psychological Review,* 1953, *6,* 198-206.

Schachtel, E. G. *Metamorphosis: On the Development of Affect, Perception, Attention, and Memory.* New York: Basic Books, 1959.

Schneirla, T. C. "An Evolutionary and Developmental Theory of Biphasic Processes Underlying Approach and Withdrawal." In M. R. Jones (Ed.), *Nebraska Symposium on Motivation.* Lincoln: University of Nebraska Press, 1959.

Sullivan, H. S. *The Interpersonal Theory of Psychiatry.* New York: Norton, 1953.

Titchener, E. B. *A Textbook of Psychology.* New York: Macmillan, 1910.

Von Békésy, B. *Sensory Inhibition.* Princeton, N.J.: Princeton University Press, 1967.

Welmann, B. L. "Iowa Studies on the Effects of Schooling." In *39th Yearbook of the National Society for the Study of Education.* Vol. 2. Chicago: University of Chicago, 1940.

Wertheimer, M. "Experimentelle Studien über das Sehen von Bewegung." *Zeitschrift für Psychologie,* 1912, *61,* 161-265.

Wertheimer, M. "Studies in the Theory of Gestalt Psychology." *Psychologische Forschung,* 1923, *4,* 301-350.

Witkin, H. A., and others. *Psychological Differentiation.* Princeton, N.J.: Princeton University Press, 1962.

72

Ray A. Craddick

Behavioral Levels

The levels hypothesis defined by Coleman (1969, pp. 120-121) expresses "an inverse relation between the stimulus structure of the projective test and the depth of unconsciousness of the fantasy elicited." This hypothesis is dependent in turn on the projective hypothesis coined and defined by Rapaport ([1942] 1967, p. 921): "All behavior manifestations of the human being, including the least and most significant, are revealing and expressive of his personality, by which we mean that individual principle of which he is the carrier." The degree of awareness of the meaning of a stimulus or the fantasy elicited by it varies from complete awareness (consciousness), to lack of awareness and expression of the personal unconscious (things once experienced but no longer available to consciousness), through to the level of the collective unconscious (elements inherent in the personality with which the individual might never have had prior direct contact or experience).

Background and Current Status

Jung ([1910] 1971, p. 35) stated, "Every human mind contains much that is unacknowledged and hence unconscious as such." Although early theorists (Frank, 1939;

911

Murray, 1938; Rapaport, 1942) were concerned with conscious and unconscious levels in personality functioning and assessment, it was not cast into a clearly defined theoretical model until Rosenzweig (1950) described three types of methods in personality assessment: subjective, objective, and projective. The subjective mode (Level I) is expressed with opinion behavior; the objective mode (Level II) is expressed with overt behavior; and the projective mode (Level III) is expressed with implicit behavior. Rosenzweig noted that projectives might be used to investigate Levels I and II. Little new theorizing has been done since Rosenzweig's work of 1950, although a recent approach to the study of deeper levels of unconsciousness has been suggested by McCully (1971).

In addition to the studies mentioned above, the current status of behavioral level is reflected in the following series of studies: Hanfmann (1947) has noted that the Sentence Completion Test (SCT) elicits material closer to the level of manifest attitude and behavior than does either the Rorschach or the Thematic Apperception Test (TAT). Carr (1954, 1956, 1958), Fisher and Hinds (1951), Hanfmann and Getzels (1953), Meltzoff (1951), Murstein (1963), Schafer (1954), Shneidman (1956), and Stone (1955) have postulated that different tests may tap different levels of personality. Carr (1954, 1956, 1958) suggests that different levels of personality functioning may become manifest under different conditions. Stone (1955) indicates that different personality tests may measure hostility at different levels of the personality. Shneidman (1956) uses a metaphoric schematic presentation to suggest that the SCT taps the most conscious level of personality; the TAT, preconscious; and the Rorschach, the most unconscious level. Leary (1957) suggests five levels of personality: (1) public communication, (2) conscious description, (3) private symbolization, (4) unexpressed unconsciousness, and (5) values. Thorne (1959) advocates that operational definitions should be used in the diagnosis of levels of personality integration. Eysenck (1960) suggests a scheme for conceptualizing the different levels of personality functions.

In their experimental investigation of the levels hypothesis, Stone and Dellis (1960) used a group of pseudoneurotic schizophrenics who they presumed would express a wide range of impulse control. Their findings suggest that more structured tests like the Wechsler Adult Intelligence Scale (WAIS) and the SCT tap the most conscious level (in which good impulse control is maintained) and that tests like the Rorschach and the Draw-a-Person Test (DAP) tap more of the unconscious (poor impulse control) level. Theiner (1962), examining the levels hypothesis from the viewpoint of expression of socially accepted behavior versus socially unacceptable behavior, found that more acceptable needs are manifested on the more structured tests (SCT), whereas the unacceptable needs are more often expressed on the less structured tests (TAT).

L'Abate (1964) suggests that the interpretation of personality assessment can be achieved through four levels: (1) self-presentation, (2) phenotype, (3) genotype, and (4) history. These four levels represent the subject as presented, the subject's description of himself, reasons for the subject's behavior, and how such genotype was acquired. L'Abate stresses that one must distinguish between the level of organization of the personality, the level of functioning, and the level of interpretation of data. Murstein and Wolf (1968) suggest that the levels hypothesis may hold true only for normal subjects. Coleman (1969) asserts that research should investigate the subjects' awareness of the purpose of the various projective tests and the personal relevance of the test stimuli and their responses. Blatt (1975) points to a need to differentiate levels of predication and notes that inferences from projective tests deal with psychological constructs more than with overt behavior.

In their review of the Picture-Frustration Study (P-F), Rosenzweig and Adelman

(1977) indicate that the research supports an earlier idea that this test reflects behavior primarily at the overt level. However, they state, "an inquiry should, wherever possible, be included at the end of the administration to provide not only scoring aids but also clues as to the level at which the subject deliberately or naively participated in the task" (p. 582). They further suggest that "motivational factors, including social desirability, may affect level of behavior and should always be considered in arriving at interpretations" (p. 584).

Critical Discussion

General Areas of Concern

Until fairly recently, the levels hypothesis has dealt with a confusion of ideas and suppositions. Fantasy as elicited through projective materials has been confused with fantasy evoked during psychoanalysis. Further confusion stems from a lack of specificity of the levels of consciousness and unconsciousness within the personality. Also, more meaningfulness is attributed to the various stimuli in assessment materials than the research supports. In his thoughtful review, Coleman (1969) pessimistically suggests that, in its present form, the levels hypothesis is untestable. The levels hypothesis is based on the idea of a gradient between the levels of consciousness and unconsciousness, and Coleman finds no research evidence to support this assumption. He believes that the subject is either aware or unaware of the personal relevance of a stimulus and his response.

Another assumption that must be investigated more fully is that the more unconscious the level of personality tapped, the more likely it is that primary process material will be evoked. This assumption stems directly from psychoanalytic theory. Early work with the Rorschach assumed that primary process materials are present when the form level of the response is very poor, or nearly nonexistent. The major assumption of equivalence of psychotic responses and poor form level was that secondary processing of responses and fantasy do not dominate the response. As Coleman points out, research has not considered that the stimuli of the Rorschach, and the directions for taking it, encourage more primary than secondary process material. Furthermore, the fantasy elicited from the Rorschach cannot be equated with free associative fantasy given in psychoanalysis.

Much of the early work on levels has been a bootstrap operation wherein the assumption was made that an unstructured test (the Rorschach, for example) taps into more unconscious levels of personality than does a more structured test such as the SCT, with tests like the TAT falling somewhere between. Research conducted with these three tests estimated whether they were in fact measuring the same things. Later research paired tests considered to measure the same or similar personality levels (the WAIS and the SCT, the DAP and the Rorschach) (Stone and Dellis, 1960). Positive intercorrelations between the two tests comprising each pair were interpreted as supporting the hypothesis that the Rorschach and the DAP measure more unconscious levels of the personality than the SCT and the WAIS do.

To date, only one study (Craddick and others, 1976) has directly addressed Coleman's suggestion of measuring the different levels of personality in terms of their structuredness as related to three concepts: self, mother, and father. The test stimuli represented a continuum of structuredness, ranging from highly structured (the stems of the SCT were "I . . . ," "My mother . . . ," and "My father . . .") to TAT cards selected as being relevant to the self (card 8FC, female; 13B, male), the mother (7GF), and the father (7BM). Subjects responded as usual to the stimuli and then were asked to rate each test stimulus and their responses according to the amount of personal meaning each had for the concept under consideration. Subjects used a scale ranging from 0 (the stimulus or response had no personal meaning to the subject for that particular concept) to 100 (total personal meaning). The results supported Coleman's levels hypothesis; that is, the more structured test stimuli (SCT) had more personal meaning for the subjects and permitted them to say more personally relevant statements about the self, mother, and father concepts than did less structured test stimuli (Rorschach). The TAT stood between the SCT and the Rorschach on these ratings.

Another approach for investigating the levels hypothesis used subjects presumed to have varying degrees of impulse control. For example, Stone and Dellis (1960) used pseudoneurotic schizophrenics who were rated on a measure of impulse control. Responses to the WAIS, SCT, TAT, Rorschach, and DAP were scored for degrees of pathology. Results of intercorrelations between the various tests and the degree of impulse control indicated that subjects exhibiting the least impulse control gave the most responses to the unstructured tests (DAP and Rorschach), whereas subjects with the most impulse control gave the most responses to the structured tests (SCT and WAIS). A serious shortcoming of the Stone and Dellis study is that projective tests (such as the Rorschach) are by their very structure more likely to elicit pathological responses than will the WAIS, for example, regardless of the degree of impulse control exhibited by the subject.

Theiner (1962) approached the levels problem by measuring the expression of socially accepted and unaccepted needs on a structured (SCT) and less structured test (TAT). His findings confirmed his hypothesis that the more unacceptable needs would be expressed through the less structured test (TAT) and that the socially acceptable needs would be expressed on the SCT. It is apparent that much more focused research must be directed to this problem.

Comparative Philosophies and Theories

Many theoretical positions assume a level of personality below consciousness, which must be investigated in an indirect manner. There appear to be several reasons for this kind of approach. One is that the subject is unable to express the unconscious in other than an indirect manner. Another is that the subject may consciously try to conceal the unconscious personality because of its private nature. Proponents of these theoretical approaches draw heavily from psychoanalysis (Frank, 1939; Murray, 1938; Rapaport, 1942). In contrast, although drawing somewhat on analytic theory, Rosenzweig's (1950) three-level theory is based on empirical evidence gained from research with the P-F. Rosenzweig continues his theorizing in this vein (Rosenzweig and Adelman, 1977). In challenging Leary's (1957) five levels of communication, Klopfer (1968, p. 529) proposes his own three levels: "I, the trait as viewed by significant others; Level II, the trait as viewed by the individual himself; and Level III, the trait as judged from projective tests." This approach in many respects is a reflection of Rosenzweig's (1950) earlier ideas. L'Abate (1964) follows the approach of Rosenzweig, encouraging the study of personality through assessment procedures directed toward the study of genotypic, phenotypic, and historical behavior. He suggests that, in this way, differentiation and knowledge of levels of personality can best be dealt with in assessment.

Other researchers have focused on less broad issues of the levels hypothesis, directing their efforts more toward the symbolic nature of various projective materials such as the Rorschach (Meer and Singer, 1950; Rosen, 1951).

An innovative approach to the study of levels of personality is McCully's (1971) work. Because of the similarity of the Rorschach inkblots to paleolithic art (which he assumes was one of the earliest attempts of man to express his unconscious), McCully suggests that the Rorschach provides an excellent opportunity to study not only the unconscious of man but also his collective unconscious. McCully's approach seems to transcend the statement made by Rosen (1951, p. 244): "The Rorschach would thus appear to consist of stimuli which have a practical, but not total, symbolic communality for [subjects]."

Elaboration on Critical Points

The levels hypothesis is based on the following assumptions: (1) There are different levels of personality functioning. (2) There is an unconscious level that cannot be studied directly. (3) Conscious levels of personality function attempt to conceal the functioning of the personality at its unconscious level. (4) There is a gradient of awareness between the conscious and unconscious levels of functioning. (5) As observers, professionals understand the unconscious aspects of the subject more clearly than the subject himself does. (6) In their responses to unstructured test stimuli, subjects will express aspects of their unconscious without awareness that they are doing so. Although Coleman (1969) indicates that perhaps the levels hypothesis in its present form cannot be validated through research, some research does attempt to do this (Craddick and others, 1976). The present state of the research in general suggests that new approaches are needed in order to investigate the levels hypothesis and that the subject should be made an integral part of such investigation. Increased pressure on personality assessment and its relationship to invasion of privacy may indeed dictate that future research be conducted in a more open way.

Personal Views and Recommendations

Much more work needs to be done on the levels hypothesis through speculative thinking and generation of hypotheses and research. Subjects must be made a more integral part of the research to determine the personal relevance of test stimuli to them. Too often, in their zeal to study the meaning of test stimuli indirectly, investigators overlook their most important data—the subject's statements about the meaning of the stimuli. Perhaps by asking different subjects, whose personality adjustment ranges from normal to psychotic, which of the test stimuli best represent them and other important persons in their lives, professionals could more easily and accurately answer many questions relating to personality functioning. Fischer (1970, 1972), Dana and Leech (1974), Dana and Graham (1976), and Craddick (1972, 1975) have indicated the meaningfulness of involving subjects in their assessment and reporting of results.

The most recent and unique theorizing about assessment of the unconscious level of personality functioning has been offered by McCully (1971). A strength of his theory is his hypothesis that only with evidence that conscious processes are no longer operative will a response emerge that suggests some contact with the collective unconscious archetypal energy: "*Only* when the stimulus includes a means of bypassing conscious grasp does it have the power to activate collective sources" (p. 33). Should future research support McCully's hypothesis, much light will be cast on existing knowledge of the collective unconscious, as well as on the processes through which it is energized. Such research should also add to the knowledge of symbol formation from the stance of both conscious and unconscious processes. The Rorschach is a major test through which to investigate McCully's hypothesis. The Kahn Test of Symbol Arrangement (KTSA) (Craddick and L'Abate, 1972; Kahn, 1956, 1957; L'Abate and Craddick, 1965) may be another valuable test instrument. One major value of the KTSA is that it provides an opportunity to observe different aspects of behavior, ranging from conscious to unconscious, and permits the tracking of the manner in which the subjects deal with objects that they arranged in various ways, named, symbolized, and, finally, selected as best representing self, mother, father, spouse, and other important figures. Continuing research with this instrument holds much promise.

The levels hypothesis is directly related to many ethical issues in personality assessment, particularly as related to the invasion of privacy. It is important to ascertain the level of personality functioning that is being measured and that subjects be made aware of the possibility of their responding from levels below their conscious awareness and control. A major problem is the ascertaining beforehand of the levels of functioning that will be tapped, since not all persons may have the same accessibility to the various levels of their unconsciousness. Gaining approval of subjects to examine levels of their psychic functioning of which they may have no knowledge, including the eliciting of archetypal collective energy, will be problematic.

A second important ethical problem involves the reporting of the test findings. The issue is whether test results can be reported to subjects in a meaningful way when the results might include unconscious behavior of which the subject was unaware. Another problem is that, in reporting test results to individuals other than the subject, the examiner must be fully aware of the level of personality functioning that he is dealing with in each portion of the report, and he must be able to support his findings by means of the original test data. Klopfer (1968) warns against the use of shorthand clichés, noting that in using higher-order concepts one is naturally led to higher-order abstracting, and thus is several stages removed from the data representing the subject's response. This can be a very dangerous kind of abstraction and becomes an ethical issue because of the possibilities of misinterpretation.

One attempted resolution to the problem of levels has been to dispense entirely with the idea of an unconscious level of personality functioning and to use tests dealing only with observable behavior. Behavioral assessment (Wolff and Merrens, 1974) appears to be of value for the purposes for which it was developed, in the prediction of behavior and assessment of behavior changes. However, since so much personality theory is concerned with unconscious motivation of behavior, work involving the levels hypothesis must be given high priority by personologists and researchers in this area.

As a final comment, it is recommended that future research of the levels hypothesis address itself to the areas of developmental psychology (investigating the development of levels of personality in the infant to the aged), studying different vocational groups to determine different developmental levels of personality, and investigating the different levels of personality as reflected through physiological and psychological measures.

Application to Particular Variables

The levels hypothesis is of value in understanding personality dynamics. For example, psychotics with limited ego defenses will more readily express primary process material in relatively unstructured tests such as the Rorschach than will neurotics, whose defenses do not permit as direct a contact with their unconscious. The borderline personality may exhibit primary process materials when responding to the Rorschach but not when responding to more structured stimuli. Creative individuals who are able to exhibit regression in the service of the ego will produce responses reflecting their contact with and control of primitive processes. A major difference between the psychotic and the creative individual is that the former is overwhelmed by his unconscious processes whereas the latter is in control and uses them for his own purposes.

References

Blatt, S. J. "The Validity of Projective Techniques and Their Research and Clinical Contribution." *Journal of Personality Assessment,* 1975, *39,* 327-343.

Carr, A. C. "Intra-individual Consistency in Response to Tests of Varying Degrees of Ambiguity." *Journal of Consulting Psychology,* 1954, *18,* 251-258.

Carr, A. C. "The Relation of Certain Rorschach Variables to the Expression of Affects in the TAT and SCT." *Journal of Projective Techniques,* 1956, *20,* 137-142.

Carr, A. C. "The Psychodiagnostic Test Battery: Rationale and Methodology." In D. Brower and L. E. Abt (Eds.), *Progress in Clinical Psychology.* Vol. 2. New York: Grune and Stratton, 1958.

Coleman, J. C. "The Levels Hypothesis: A Re-examination and Re-orientation." *Journal of Projective Techniques and Personality Assessment,* 1969, *33,* 118-122.

Craddick, R. A. "Humanistic Assessment: A Reply to Brown." *Psychotherapy: Theory, Research and Practice,* 1972, *9,* 107-110.

Craddick, R. A. "Sharing Oneself in the Assessent Procedure." *Professional Psychology,* 1975, *6,* 279-282.

Craddick, R. A., and L'Abate, L. "The Kahn Test of Symbol Arrangement (KTSA): A Second Critical Review." *International Journal of Symbology,* 1972, *1,* 1-27.

Craddick, R. A., and others. "Further Investigation of Coleman's Levels Hypothesis." *Journal of Personality Assessment,* 1976, *40,* 569-572.

Dana, R. H., and Graham, E. D. "Feedback of Client-Relevant Information and Clinical Practice." *Journal of Personality Assessment,* 1976, *40,* 464-469.

Dana, R. H., and Leech, S. "Existential Assessment." *Journal of Personality Assessment,* 1974, *38,* 429-435.

Eysenck, H. J. "Levels of Personality, Constitutional Factors and Social Influence: An Experimental Study." *International Journal of Social Psychiatry,* 1960, *6,* 12-24.

Fischer, C. T. "The Testee as Co-Evaluator." *Journal of Counseling Psychology,* 1970, *17,* 70-76.

Fischer, C. T. "Paradigm Changes Which Allow Sharing of Results." *Professional Psychology,* 1972, *3,* 364-369.

Fisher, S., and Hinds, E. "The Organization of Hostility Controls in Various Personality Structures." *Genetic Psychological Monographs,* 1951, *44,* 3-68.

Frank, L. K. "Projective Methods for the Study of Personality." *Journal of Psychology,* 1939, *8,* 389-413.

Hanfmann, E. "Projective Techniques in the Assessment Program at the Office of Strategic Services." In *Exploring Individual Differences.* Washington, D.C.: American Counsel on Education, 1947.

Hanfmann, E., and Getzels, J. W. "Studies of the Sentence Completion Test." *Journal of Projective Techniques,* 1953, *17,* 280-294.

Jung, C. G. "The Association Method" [1910]. In L. D. Goodstein and R. Lanyon (Eds.), *Readings in Personality Assessment.* New York: Wiley, 1971.

Kahn, T. C. "Manual of Administration: Kahn Test of Symbol Arrangement." *Perceptual and Motor Skills,* 1956, *6* (4), 299-334.

Kahn, T. C. "Clinical Manual: Kahn Test of Symbol Arrangement." *Perceptual and Motor Skills Monograph,* 1957, *7* (1), 97-168.

Klopfer, W. "Integration of Projective Techniques in the Clinical Case Study." In A. J. Rabin (Ed.), *Projective Techniques in Personality Assessment.* New York: Springer, 1968.

L'Abate, L. *Principles of Clinical Psychology.* New York: Grune & Stratton, 1964.

L'Abate, L., and Craddick, R. A. "The Kahn Test of Symbol Arrangement (KTSA): A Critical Review." *Journal of Clinical Psychology Monograph,* 1965, 1-23.

Leary, T. *Interpersonal Diagnosis of Personality: A Functional Theory in Methodology for Personality Evaluation.* New York: Ronald Press, 1957.

McCully, R. S. *Rorschach Theory and Symbolism: A Jungian Approach to Clinical Material.* Baltimore: Williams and Wilkins, 1971.

Meer, B., and Singer, J. L. "A Note on the 'Father' and 'Mother' Cards in the Rorschach Inkblots." *Journal of Consulting Psychology,* 1950, *14,* 482-484.

Meltzoff, J. "The Effect of Mental Set and Item Structure upon Response to a Projective Test." *Journal of Abnormal and Social Psychology,* 1951, *46,* 177-189.

Murray, H. A. *Explorations in Personality.* New York: Oxford University Press, 1938.

Murstein, B. I. *Theory and Research in Projective Techniques.* New York: Wiley, 1963.

Murstein, B. I., and Wolf, S. R. "An Empirical Test of the 'Levels' Hypothesis with Five Projective Techniques." In *Proceedings of the VII International Congress of Rorschach Projective Techniques.* Glendale, Calif.: Society for Projective Techniques and Rorschach Institution, 1968.

Rapaport, D. "Principles Underlying Projective Techniques" [1942]. In M. M. Gill (Ed.), *The Collected Papers of David Rapaport.* New York: Basic Books, 1967.

Rosen, E. "Symbolic Meanings in Rorschach Cards: A Statistical Study." *Journal of Clinical Psychology,* 1951, *7,* 239-244.

Rosenzweig, S. "Levels of Behavior in Psychodiagnosis with Special Reference to the Picture-Frustration Study." *American Journal of Orthopsychiatry,* 1950, *20,* 63-72.

Rosenzweig, S., and Adelman, S. "Construct Validity of the Rosenzweig Picture-Frustration Study." *Journal of Personality Assessment,* 1977, *41,* 578-588.

Schafer, R. *Psychoanalytic Interpretations in Rorschach Testing.* New York: Grune and Stratton, 1954.

Shneidman, E. S. "Some Relationships Between Rorschach Technique and Other Psychodiagnostic Tests." In B. Klopfer and others (Eds.), *Developments in the Rorschach Technique.* Vol. 2. New York: Harcourt Brace Jovanovich, 1956.

Stone, H. K. "A Factorial Analysis of Hostility as Reflected in Certain Psychological Test Variables." Unpublished doctoral dissertation, Adelphi College, 1955.

Stone, H. K., and Dellis, N. P. "An Exploratory Investigation into the Levels Hypothesis." *Journal of Projective Techniques,* 1960, *24,* 334-340.

Theiner, E. C. "The Magnitude of Four Experimental Needs as Expressed by Two Projective Techniques." *Journal of Projective Techniques,* 1962, *26,* 354-365.

Thorne, F. C. "An Operational Approach to the Diagnosis of Levels of Personality Integration or Psychopathology." *Journal of Clinical Psychology,* 1959, *15,* 255-259.

Wolff, W. T., and Merrens, M. R. "Behavioral Assessment: A Review of Clinical Methods." *Journal of Personality Assessment,* 1974, *38,* 3-16.

73

James C. Crumbaugh

Graphoanalytic Cues

Graphoanalytic cues are based on a particular system of graphology or handwriting analysis, which in turn is a particular dimension of graphokinesics or expressive movements made graphically. Interpretation of all forms of graphokinesics for the purpose of assessing the personality and character of the subject is based on the fundamental concept in clinical psychiatry and psychology that personality is expressed by or "projected" into all of the individual's responses to the environment. The person may respond in either of two ways: (1) cortically, by perception or interpretation of an ambiguous stimulus (as in the case of the Rorschach inkblots); or (2) behaviorally, by a motor reaction (as in the case of such expressive movements as projective drawing or handwriting).

Projective techniques of the perceptual type include (1) the Rorschach, Holtzman, and other inkblot tests; (2) the Murray Thematic Apperception Test (TAT) (which requires the subject to interpret ambiguous pictures of persons and objects, containing more structure than inkblots but still open to very broad interpretation); (3) the Shneidman Make a Picture and Story Test (a variant of the TAT); (4) the Twitchell-Allen Three

Dimensional Apperception Test (which offers small objects for both visual and kines-thetic perception); and (5) the tautophone test (ambiguous recorded sounds which can be unstructured like inkblots or more definitive like the apperception tests)—to name but a few. Most projective methods have been of the perceptual type, and most of these have involved visual perception.

The chief expressive movement types of projectives are the various forms of pro-jective drawing or writing: (1) the Goodenough (1926) Draw-a-Person Test and the Buck (1948) House-Tree-Person Test (which require the subject to draw his or her own version of persons or objects); (2) the Mira (1940) Myokinetic Test (which requires a blindfolded subject to draw different types of lines free-hand in various planes with both hands alter-nately); and (3) handwriting analysis. Of these, the Goodenough and the Buck tests are the most widely used, although most clinicians "crystal ball" them and do little in the way of objective scoring. In spite of this and the additional fact that studies of validation have offered poor support for them, many practitioners believe that they are among the most revealing of all projective methods. The Mira Myokinetic Test is more objective in evaluation but is rather complicated in administration and has never been widely em-ployed. Handwriting analysis offers the advantage of being more easily measurable, while at the same time allowing the seasoned analyst to drop elaborate details of measurement and to make overall (global) interpretations based on a subjective fusing of the relation-ships between the data trends.

"Sign" interpretations (tying specific personality traits to exact details or signs in inkblots, drawings, or handwriting) have never validated well for any projective tech-niques, and it is often said that the validity is always in the clinician and not in his tools. Global validation has consistently been superior among these techniques, which means that what is actually valid is the experience of the clinician in putting together in a totally unanalyzable way the overall picture of personality yielded by the complex interaction of all of the signs. Since the meaning of a sign changes as it interacts with other signs, a sign cannot be interpreted in a constant manner from subject to subject. (Allergists experience the same problem; a patient may not be allergic to an apple as such but may respond severely to the combination of an apple and an orange.)

As mentioned, handwriting analysis permits the experienced clinician to make global interpretations and also offers the learner and less expert practitioner adequate quantification to depend on until "holistic" expertise is developed. (The Rorschach also offers this, but most projective methods are inadequate in this respect.) Handwriting analysis has some further advantages: (1) The sample of writing can be taken by a clerk without expenditure of professional time. (2) It can be taken without the subject's know-ing what it is for. (3) Samples can be obtained from most subjects over a span of many years (since most people have something which they have written by hand at most key periods of life), thus making possible a longitudinal study of personality. This usually cannot be done by other techniques of evaluation, since test data are usually not available from the earlier life stages.

Background and Current Status

The first organized attempt to analyze handwriting was probably that of Camillo Baldi, an Italian scholar and physician.* While a professor at the University of Bologna in 1622, he published a book, *Treatise on a Method to Recognize the Nature and Quality of*

---

*The historical material in this section is taken primarily from Lecture No. 3 of the general course of the International Graphoanalysis Society.

a Writer from His Letters. The next published work was by Johann Kasper Lavater (1741-1801), a Swiss scholar of personality at the University of Zurich. These early publications interested many intellectuals but had little following as a possible method of personality analysis. The reason for neglect was simple; very few people could read and write.

As education became more widespread in the nineteenth century, handwriting analysis rapidly gathered interest. It was practiced far more as an art than a science, but often with amazing intuitive skill, by such assorted figures of the history of this period as Goethe, Poe, the Brownings, Leibniz, Balzac, Dickens, and many others. It is said that Gainsborough achieved the lifelike quality of his portraits by having before him, while painting, a handwriting specimen of his subject. He felt that the handwriting enabled him to capture the essence of the subject's personality.

In France serious study of handwriting was undertaken by Abbé Louis J. H. Flandrin and the Archbishop of Cambrai. Their only real contribution, however, was the training of their assistant, Abbé Jean Hippolyte Michon, who published in Paris in 1875 the most scholarly work on handwriting up to that time. Entitled *The Practical System of Graphology,* Michon's work coined the generic term for handwriting analysis. He tirelessly studied hundreds of graphic signs which were supposed to indicate specific personality traits, and his system became known as "the school of fixed signs."

In the late nineteenth century, a disciple of Michon, Crépieux-Jamin, expanded his master's studies and modified to some degree the rigid one-to-one relationship that Michon assumed to exist between handwriting strokes and personality traits. But the basic theory of "isolated signs" remained dominant in French schools of handwriting analysis.

Near the turn of the century, Crépieux-Jamin interested the great French psychologist Alfred Binet (who originated the first intelligence tests) in handwriting analysis as a technique for testing personality. Binet's experiments indicated that handwriting experts could distinguish successful from unsuccessful persons by their writing with an accuracy of 61 to 92 percent. This was very remarkable in view of the crude methods of the day. Binet was also able to determine (to a considerable degree) the intelligence and honesty of writers, but not their age or sex. These findings have been verified in the graphoanalytic system of handwriting analysis.

In Germany there were also serious students of handwriting during the last half of the nineteenth century. William Preyer at the University of Berlin demonstrated an essential similarity between handwriting, foot writing, teeth writing, opposite-hand writing, and even crook-of-the-elbow writing; and he noted that "all writing is brain writing." Later, psychiatrist Georg Meyer showed important differences between spontaneous writing and drawn or copy writing.

The biggest name in German handwriting analysis became (and remained for some years) that of Ludwig Klages. He coined the term *expressive movement* to refer to all motor activities performed habitually and automatically without conscious thought: walking, talking, gesturing, facially responding, and especially handwriting. But while Klages' influence was strong for a time in Germany, it did not spread, because his system was esoteric and subjective, intuitive in the extreme, complex and mixed with an intricate personal philosophy that made it incomprehensible, and of dubious authenticity to serious scholars.

Although Klages' work was not followed widely by handwriting experts elsewhere, his name had gathered enough momentum in German circles (which were the top circles in science in those days) to cause many scholars to evaluate the validity of handwriting analysis on the basis of their appraisal of the validity of his system. When American psychology developed from the historical foundations of German psychology (which was the cornerstone of the scientific study of the mind), many early American psychologists did the same.

Graphoanalysis, founded by M. N. Bunker in 1929, has been called a protest against the atomistic one-to-one "sign" graphology that typified the French school, and also against the broad, sweeping, intuitive graphology of the German school. This middle-of-the-road compromise position drew heavily from the then new Gestalt school of psychology, which insisted that people must be studied as dynamic wholes and that these wholes are more than the sum of their atomistic parts. Bunker based his method of personality evaluation through handwriting on this fundamental Gestalt concept, thus considering how the interplay of related traits produces an overall effect that is different from that of any single trait; and this holistic or global personality pattern may be produced by a variety of single-trait combinations, all of which must be learned by experience.

Until his death in 1961, Bunker developed his school and continued to augment its teachings by empirical studies of the handwriting specimens of various personality types. Following Bunker's death, V. Peter Ferrara of Chicago assumed the leadership. Holding a master's degree in psychology, Ferrara emphasized sound validation research to support the concepts of graphoanalysis and to modify those that did not prove valid.

Graphoanalysis now has certified practitioners in all states of the union and in most countries of the world. It has a wide variety of practical applications. The chief areas of use are (1) in business and industry (Fullmer, 1971; Rast, 1966), where graphoanalysts assist personnel specialists in job applicant selection based on specific aptitudes, in job placement and promotion, and in the determination of character in credit risks; (2) in education (International Graphoanalysis Society, 1975), where graphoanalysts help vocational counselors determine areas of aptitude and help teachers determine the patterns of personality that cause either the student to have difficulty in school or the school to have trouble with the student; (3) in mental health clinics and hospitals (Root, 1966; Watanuki, 1963), where graphoanalysts help psychiatrists and psychologists understand the personality structure, traits, and psychodynamics of patients (it should be noted that graphoanalysts do *not* offer diagnoses of either mental or physical illnesses, and they do not do therapy); and (4) in forensic or questioned-document work, where graphoanalysts serve as expert witnesses in authenticating legal instruments (International Graphoanalysis Society, 1975).

Graphotherapy (training the subject to employ strokes in his or her writing that usually represent desirable traits and to eliminate strokes that usually imply undesirable traits) has been explored, but this is in a strictly experimental stage at present and is not taught in graphoanalysis or permitted by the code of graphoanalytic ethics except in collaboration with mental health specialists in a clinical setting. The validity of this type of therapy is questionable. Although favorable results can be demonstrated by it, they can also be explained as placebo effects. Further, the face validity of such therapy is poor; there is no logical reason why traits *reflected in* handwriting but *not caused by* handwriting should yield to a manipulation that is unrelated to their cause.

Critical Discussion

General Areas of Concern

The general procedure of graphoanalysis is based on the following steps: First, a *perspectograph*—an analysis of the first hundred *upstrokes* that appear in the sample of writing—is constructed. This sample, incidentally, is desirably a full page or more of spontaneous writing made with a ball-point pen or pencil on unruled paper without the subject's knowing that it is for analysis. The rules for determination and measurement of these upstrokes are rather complex. The result yields the percentage of each of seven different degrees of slant to be found in the writing, from far forward to markedly backward. Each upstroke is marked and measured by a specially constructed gauge, and each of the seven degree spans of the gauge indicates a degree of emotional responsiveness of the writer. In general, far-forward writing is found in extremely emotional persons, while backward writing indicates emotional constraint and blockage. This characteristic becomes important in determining the way in which many traits found in one's writing will affect one's behavior. The percentage of each slant span is plotted on a bar graph for reference as other traits are revealed. The interpretation of slant is demonstrated in Figure 1: 1a shows back slant and its meaning; 1b shows vertical slant and its significance; 1c represents forward slant and its interpretation.

Figure 1. Levels of Emotional Responsiveness

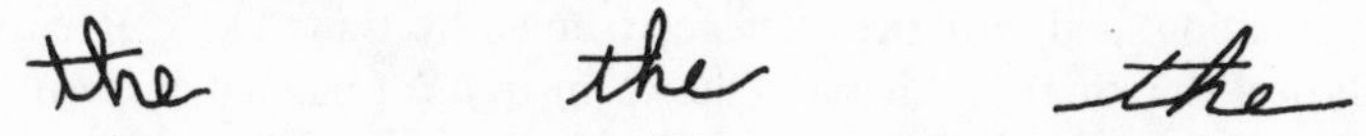

| (a) | (b) | (c) |
| Withdrawal | Objectiveness | Intense responsiveness |

The second general step in constructing a graphoanalysis is completion of a special worksheet listing around one hundred "primary" personality traits and some fifty "evaluated" traits. A primary trait is one that can be determined from a single-stroke formation. For example, temper is indicated by t-bars made to the right of the t-stem. An evaluated trait is one that must be inferred from two or more other traits. For example, timidity is a product of lack of self-confidence, shyness, self-consciousness, and clannishness. Both primary and evaluated traits are rated as to intensity in the sample on a three-point scale in which "X" is slight, "XX" is moderate, and "XXX" is strong.

The worksheet is divided into trait groups, which serve to delineate the personality. Among these groupings are:

1. Emotions, revealed by slant and depth of writing, as shown in Figure 2.

Figure 2. Mental Processes

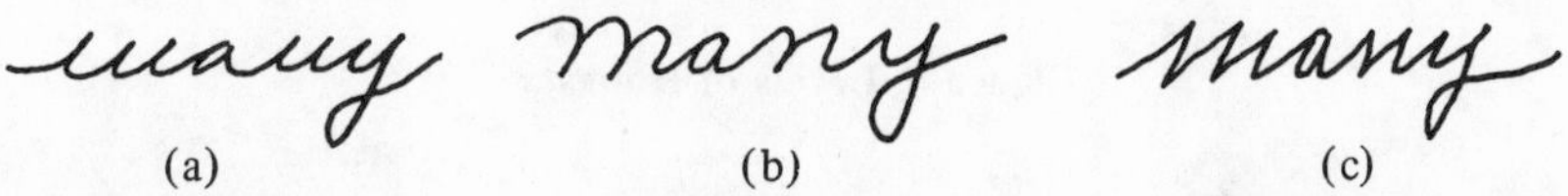

| (a) | (b) | (c) |
| Comprehensive thinking | Cumulative logical thinking | Exploratory or investigative thinking |

2. Mental processes, revealed by such traits as comprehensive, cumulative, and exploratory thinking, as demonstrated in Figure 2. The sharp points of *m* and *n* in 2a show comprehension; the rounded tops of the loops of the same letters in 2b show logical thinking; the wedges of *m* and *n* in 2c show investigative thinking. Mental processes are intensified by traits like conservatism, generosity, optimism, loyalty, positiveness, broad-mindedness, and tenacity; they are reduced by such traits as impulsiveness, pessimism, prejudice, and narrow-mindedness.
3. Social behavior (supported by such specific traits as diplomacy, frankness, humor,

optimism, poise, and self-reliance; negated by such traits as clannishness, selectivity, selfishness, and impatience), as illustrated in Figure 3. Note the tight loops of the *m* and *n* in 3a, which indicate repression, and the spread loops in 3b, which show the opposite.

Figure 3. Social Responsiveness

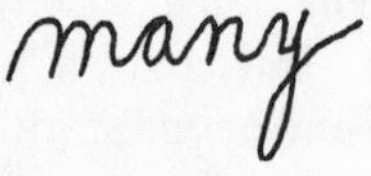

(a)
Repression

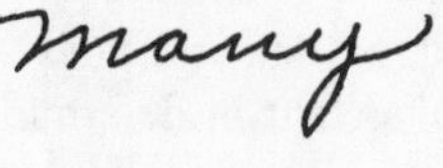

(b)
Uninhibition

Fears and defenses, and the degree and type of adjustment, are indicated by such traits as caution, bluff, dignity, decisiveness, pride, tenacity, and persistence. Special aptitudes are evaluated in the fields of business (indicated by such traits as diplomacy, decisiveness, determination, and initiative), science (shown by traits like creativity, imagination, and analytical thinking), mechanics (shown in traits of manual dexterity, precision, rhythm, and the like), and other areas. Further illustrations of stroke interpretations in the determination of personality traits are shown in Figures 4 through 10.*

Figure 4. Approach to Achievement

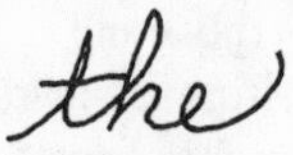

(a)
Lack of
self-confidence

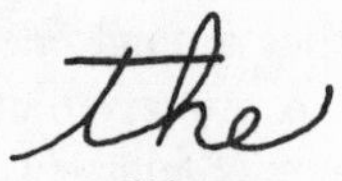

(b)
Strong
will power

Figure 5. Levels of Social Appeal

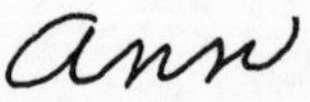

(a)
Simplicity,
modesty

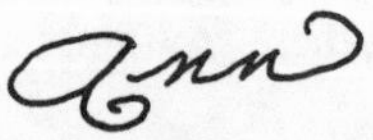

(b)
Ostentation

Figure 6. Levels of Honesty

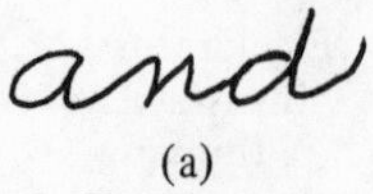

(a)
Frankness

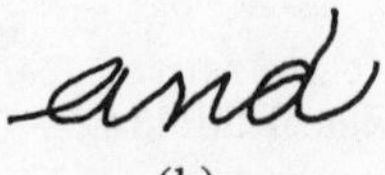

(b)
Self-deception or
rationalization

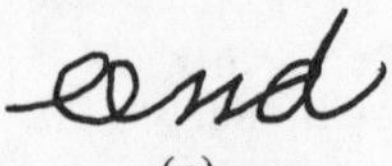

(c)
Intentional
deception

*Constructed by Teresa Croteau-Crumbaugh, MGA, Master Graphoanalyst.

Figure 7. Levels of Imagination

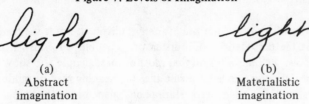

(a)
Abstract
imagination

(b)
Materialistic
imagination

Figure 8. Attitude Toward Life

(a)
Depression
Pessimism

(b)
Optimism

Figure 9. Levels of Determination

(a)
Strong
determination

(b)
Weak
determination

Figure 10. Levels of Attention

(a)
Close attention
to details

(b)
Inattention

   The low t-bar in Figure 4a reveals a lack of self-confidence, while the high t-bar of 4b indicates an opposite trait of strong will power. (Graphoanalytic definitions of traits are often different from the definitions most commonly employed among mental health disciplines, although personality theorists differ so much among themselves that few uniform definitions are possible.) Figure 5a shows simplicity or modesty in the small *a* of *Ann,* while 5b reveals ostentation in the large *a.* Figure 6a shows frankness in the closed *a* of *and;* 6b shows self-deception in the initial loop of *a;* and 6c shows purposive or intentional deceit in the double loop of *a.* Figure 7a demonstrates abstract imagination in the large upper loop of the letter *l,* while 7b reveals materialistic imagination in the large lower loop of the letter *g.* Figure 8a portrays depression or pessimism in the downward droop of the word *many,* while 8b indicates optimism in the upward trend of the word. Figure 9a shows strong determination in the bold downstroke of *y,* while 9b shows weak determination in the short light downstroke of this letter. Figure 10a reveals close attention to details in the closely dotted *i,* while 10b portrays inattention in the high and removed dot of the *i.*

These cues will not be "sure fire" for any individual, but if the reader will check a given cue against the personalities of a dozen or so people who show it in their writing and whom he knows well, he will find that most of these people also show the trait represented by the cue. Of course, in a given case the cue meaning may be modified by overriding counter cues, and the true interpretation on balance requires broad clinical experience.

When the worksheet has been completed, the true skill of the graphoanalyst is tested by his ability to put all these data together into a unified, meaningful Gestalt, or total pattern, which yields a valid picture of the personality of the writer. Graphoanalysis, like the Rorschach or any other good projective technique, thus becomes not a cut-and-dried mechanical process but, rather, a dynamic means of assessment which can be learned only through broadly based experience. The fundamentals and basic procedures can be taught in school, and the neophyte must depend on them until he or she gradually accumulates the experience necessary to make adequate clinical judgments based on intuitive feelings about the meaning of the various patterns of traits. Here again is verification of the adage that the validity of a projective technique is in the clinician and not in the instruments. The beginner can, upon mastery of the instrument of graphoanalysis, offer considerable helpful information about the writer's personality and style of dealing with life situations, but only years of practice will make him a master of the art.

The gross description of the graphoanalytic technique given previously is a "barebones" outline of the total procedure. The many variations of each handwriting stroke and the probable meaning of each variation is studied. After mastering these elements, the student is coached and given practice in putting together the tremendous mass of data into a personality picture that shows the trait interactions and the overall effect of these interactions in producing the individual's unique personal Gestalt.

Comparative Philosophies and Theories

The theory of handwriting analysis rests on solid ground as a projective technique of the expressive movement type, but it has historically been plagued by the label of a pseudoscience because the early psychologists reacted negatively to the intuitive and loose systems of early graphology. Psychologists have typically written in elementary textbooks that handwriting *should* logically reveal personality (that it has good "face validity"—it looks as if it should work) but that the systems just do not validate and that they must be classed with astrology, phrenology, and the like. In more recent years, many texts have reexamined the evidence, particularly that for graphoanalysis, and have concluded otherwise. Ruch (1967, p. 117), for example, says: "Although many psychologists feel [graphology] has no more value than palmistry or reading tea leaves, it has been studied scientifically in recent years by rigorously controlled methods. The general conclusion is that graphology may eventually prove to have value in predicting personality traits." Within the last ten years more validating research has appeared and will be presented in the next section.

Because of the poor early scientific start of handwriting analysis, the majority of psychologists turned to other projective techniques of expressive movement (like projective drawing). Projective drawings have long been a part of the armamentarium of every clinical psychologist, even though they have validated very poorly (Murstein, 1965). But with more and improved studies of validation of handwriting analysis, a number of psychiatrists (and other physicians) and psychologists have begun to take training in graphoanalysis.

Elaboration on Critical Points

The question of validation continues to be raised by critics, and these critics are primarily psychologists. While some have seen the advantages and have taken the training, the majority apparently feel that the assorted methods in which they already have been schooled are the only burdens they wish to assume. Perhaps this is understandable in view of the fact that the training required to become expert in handwriting analysis is at least as great as that required to master the Rorschach. (It should be noted that all this applies primarily to America; in Germany many universities have required training in graphology as a part of the work for a Ph.D. in psychology.)

Since validation continues as the critical issue, evidence should be available. The chief studies are cited and abstracted in a brochure published by and available from the International Graphoanalysis Society (1970). The studies listed in the section on references in the present chapter seem to be the most effective in demonstrating a scientific basis for the assumption that handwriting can be as valid in personality assessment as the other major projective techniques. As demonstrated in the studies of Eysenck (1945), Wolfson (1949), Weinberg, Fluckiger, and Tripp (1962), and Crumbaugh and Stockholm (1977), "global" or "holistic" validation has proved to be the most effective approach. As with the other projective techniques, "atomistic" or "molecular" or isolated "sign" validation has not worked out very well, which means, as noted earlier, that in all clinical assessment procedures the validity is primarily in the clinician rather than in the technique. Only experience blended with good intuitive judgment makes for valid assessment by any instrument. Further substantial validation evidence has been offered by Fluckiger, Tripp, and Weinberg (1961), Mann (1961), Naegler (1958), and Thomas (1964).

Personal Views and Recommendations

The present state of graphoanalytic art and science warrants its practical employment by well-trained graphoanalysts in a variety of working situations, though neither graphoanalysis nor any other single assessment technique should ever be used alone in making any important life decision. For example, neither handwriting nor any other psychological test of personality should determine whether one enters a certain occupation, gets credit, and so forth. Tests must be combined with clinical, educational, demographic, and all other reasonable sources of data. The validation of graphoanalysis is neither better nor worse than that of most other projective techniques. While all projectives leave something to be desired in adequate "hard-core" validation, no experienced clinician doubts that any one of them may constitute a useful tool in the hands of one who believes in it, studies it deeply, and gains broad experience in the relationships between the responses it elicits and various patterns of behavior and personality traits.

Application to Particular Variables

Even the infant shows personality tendencies in graphic movements, and these tendencies do not disappear in old age. While handwriting reflects the motor failure of advanced age, neither age nor sex can be assessed by handwriting. Education (beyond basic literacy) and socioeconomic status are not factors in analysis. Vocation is also not a factor, although vocational aptitudes and interests are reflected in handwriting. Ethnic and racial factors have no bearing on the ability of graphoanalysis to determine character and personality.

As has been noted, neither mental nor physical disease can be diagnosed by graphoanalysis, although handwriting does often give information that helps the physician make a better estimate of the cause of symptoms. IQ is never determined by the graphoanalyst, although one can estimate the level of intellectual efficiency. Graphoanalysts can help those professionals who are charged with responsibility for almost all types of disorders—though they do not in any case assume this professional responsibility themselves—by offering a picture of personality patterns that gives very helpful clues. These clues often can point up the presence of underlying organic factors in the etiology of psychiatric disorders.

References

Buck, J. N. "The House-Tree-Person Test." *Journal of Clinical Psychology,* 1948, *4,* 151-158.

Crumbaugh, J. C., and Stockholm, E. "Validation of Graphoanalysis by 'Global' or 'Holistic' Method." *Perceptual and Motor Skills,* 1977, *44,* 403-410.

Eysenck, H. J. "Graphological Analysis and Psychiatry: An Experimental Study." *British Journal of Psychology,* 1945, *35,* 70-81.

Fluckiger, F. A., Tripp, C. A., and Weinberg, G. H. "A Review of Experimental Research in Graphology, 1933-1960." *Perceptual and Motor Skills,* 1961, *12,* 67-90 (Monograph Supplement 1-V12).

Fullmer, T. P. "The Use of Graphoanalysis in Personnel Selection." *Best's Review,* 1971, *72* (2).

Goodenough, F. L. *Measurement of Intelligence by Drawings.* Yonkers, N.Y.: World Book, 1926.

International Graphoanalysis Society. *An Annotated Bibliography of Studies in Handwriting Analysis Research.* Catalogue No. G1059. Chicago: International Graphoanalysis Society, 1970.

International Graphoanalysis Society. *Field Reports from IGAS Students and Graduates: The Many Varied and Successful Uses of Graphoanalysis.* Catalogue No. G623 0475. Chicago: International Graphoanalysis Society, 1975.

Mann, W. R. "A Continuation of the Search for Objective Graphological Hypotheses." Unpublished doctoral dissertation, University of Ottawa, 1961.

Mira, E. "Myokinetic Psychodiagnosis: A New Technique for Exploring the Cognitive Trends of Personality." *Proceedings of the Royal Society of Medicine,* 1940, *33,* 173-194.

Murstein, B. I. (Ed.). *Handbook of Projective Techniques.* New York: Basic Books, 1965.

Naegler, R. C. *A Validation Study of Personality Assessment Through Graphoanalysis.* Catalogue No. 309. Chicago: International Graphoanalysis Society, 1958.

Rast, G. H. "The Value of Handwriting Analysis in Bank Work." *Burroughs Clearing House,* 1966, *50,* 40-41 ff.

Root, V. T. "Graphoanalysis—An Aid in Solving Human Relations Problems." *Hospital Topics Magazine,* July 1966.

Ruch, F. L. *Psychology and Life.* (7th ed.) Glenview, Ill.: Scott, Foresman, 1967.

Thomas, D. L. "Validity of Graphoanalysis in the Assessment of Personality Characteristics." Unpublished master's thesis, Colorado State University, 1964.

Watanuki, H. H. "Graphoanalysis: A Tested Tool in Clinical Counseling." *Journal of Graphoanalysis,* July 1963, *3* (12), 11, 13.

Weinberg, G. H., Fluckiger, F. A., and Tripp, C. A. "The Application of a New Matching Technique." *Journal of Projective Techniques,* 1962, *26,* 221-224.

Wolfson, R. *A Study in Handwriting Analysis.* Ann Arbor, Mich.: Edwards Brothers, 1949.

74

Peter W. Sheehan

Expectancy Behavior in Hypnosis

It is commonly believed that personal expectancies and need states influence perception and interpretation of reality. Specifically, expectations tend to encourage or facilitate the appearance of events that are consonant with those expectations and to inhibit the appearance of events that are not. In this chapter the term *expectancy response* describes a situation where the expectancies of hypnotic subjects distinctively influence or structure their behavior through motivated cognitive commitment (that is, an active cognitive involvement by the subject in building up, in a motivated fashion, the desired response as suggested by the hypnotist). The term should be distinguished from general conformity reactions to standard hypnotic suggestions, where there is no clear objective evidence of motivated cognitive commitment on the part of the hypnotized person. Consistent with the historical literature on the influence of motivation on perception, the term is chosen because it peculiarly indexes the influence of subjects' motivational state on their cognizing about what the hypnotist intends. The evidence indicates that a small sample of susceptible people will become personally involved with the hypnotist and his or her wishes to the extent that they will cognitively structure and work on the communications or suggestions they receive. This commitment to a positive reaction is a highly motivated one, and it depicts the hypnotic person as an active rather than a passive recipient of the communications that are received.

Hypnotized persons may respond to suggestions in many ways. They may report "This is what I heard," or they may incorporate instruction at a deeper level of involvement by stating "This is what I think." That is, some persons may simply acknowledge that something has occurred, whereas others will accept the event in question as true. Hypnosis produces substantial changes in the normal cognitive frame of reference of some deeply susceptible persons; the boundary blurs between that which belongs to the person and that which does not. When commitment to the intent and wishes of the hypnotist is especially strong, expectancy response may be expressed in terms of such an alteration in consciousness. Some subjects come to be deluded that what the hypnotist is suggesting is, in fact, true.

The presence of delusion is an important manifestation of expectancy response. The process of delusion implies that a person's belief is held in the face of contradictory evidence, and the concept of expectancy response is intended precisely to convey that fact. Persons will respond in expectancy fashion when the needs and motivations that define their cognitive commitment structure the response against the influence of determining factors that are known to ordinarily affect their behavior in other ways. One such constraint, for example, is the set of attitudes which the hypnotized person brings to the hypnotic setting and which can conflict with the intent or wishes of the hypnotist. In the face of this kind of conflict, the person who responds in expectancy fashion will respond according to the influence of the hypnotist and his communications given in the trance setting rather than to the influence of the set of attitudes that define the alternative response.

Background and Current Status

The processes that lie behind formulation of the concept of expectancy response date back to the very early days of hypnosis. The reactions of the nervous patients treated by Anton Mesmer offer perhaps the most colorful illustrations of the needs and motivations of the hypnotic subject and how they may operate to influence behavior. Some patients remained calm for Mesmer, while others became agitated, were tormented by convulsions, and moved about hysterically. There is little doubt that the personal relationship between Mesmer and his patients was an important determinant of their reactions. Clients' needs and expectations were probably as integral to understanding their reactions as any theory about the individual effects of hypnotic induction. History reveals, in fact, that there is a peculiarly inconstant character about hypnotic events (Sheehan and Perry, 1976). The effects induced by Mesmer, Marquis de Puysegur, Abbé di Faria, James Braid, and Jean Charcot indicate a remarkable assortment of hypnotic outcomes. This variability of reaction to hypnosis forces the conclusion that people's motivations differed greatly from one practitioner to the other in ways that the historical figures encouraged, either by the drama of their theories or the personal charisma of their presence.

With time, coherent theoretical frameworks were built around the personal needs of the hypnotized person, and these have been largely focused around the concepts of transference, archaic involvement (Shor, 1962), and psychic depth (Schilder, 1927), particularly as they are evidenced in the therapeutic setting. Here, the emphasis is placed on the intensity of personal rapport between hypnotherapist and subject or patient. When the interpersonal relationship between the subject and the hypnotist is intense, the hypnotized person has a special wish to please, and the hypnotist's demands and communications assume critical importance through the motivated involvement of the subject to do what is required. The clinical meaning of the word *expectancy* is most appropriately viewed in this context.

Recent research has validated the concept of expectancy and advocated it as a prime mediating variable in accounting for hypnotic behavior. For the most part, however, the concept has been stripped of its potential clinical significance and has been formulated as a functional variable of little clinical utility. For example, subjects are said to routinely bring expectancies about appropriate responses with them to the hypnotic setting, and much evidence exists to illustrate that influence. In the same way, the preconceptions of the hypnotist may actually determine the effects that are obtained. In fact, it is sometimes hard to know how much biases of both these kinds are responsible for the hypnotic effects that are observed. The notion of expectancy response advocated here, however, argues something different. It indexes specifically the commitment of the hypnotized person to pursue what the hypnotist wishes or intends. This is quite distinct from the influence of social attitudes or other sources of influence that exist outside the hypnotic setting and are brought with the subject to the trance session.

Distinctive behavioral effects that discriminate the performance of hypnotic and waking subjects index the concept of expectancy response and these have been isolated within the laboratory setting in a series of three studies. Each has separately looked at ways in which the expectancy of the hypnotized person actually overrides influences of other kinds when the subject is motivated especially to cooperate with the hypnotist. In the first of the three experiments (Sheehan, 1971), data showed that hypnotic, but not nonhypnotic (role-playing), subjects overcame the influence of a lecture demonstration on appropriate ways to respond hypnotically. Following induction, hypnotic subjects distinctively captured the intent of the hypnotist and behaved according to her wishes when the hypnotist indicated subtly that subjects should behave in an altogether different way. The other two studies (Sheehan and Dolby, 1975; Dolby and Sheehan, 1977) investigated the prediction that the influence of the hypnotist's communications is particularly significant in determining the nature of hypnotic response of very susceptible persons. Using Boring's ambiguous wife/mother-in-law figure and procedures developed in a nonhypnotic context by Epstein and Rock (1960), the investigators established unique conditions for subjects in the waking state under which the events seen just previously—and *not* what was expected—reliably influenced subsequent perception. Data showed that in hypnosis susceptible hypnotic subjects exclusively demonstrated stable expectancy response (as opposed to normal recency behavior). They consistently behaved in accordance with the communications of the hypnotist when there was strong constraint in the test situation to do otherwise. There was also strong evidence of delusory thinking among some subjects and clear indications of preferred modes of cognition operating in those who followed the hypnotist's suggestions.

The data from all three studies can be comfortably accommodated within a framework which appeals to the "motivated cognitive commitment" of subjects structuring the test situation as they perceived it so as to resolve the conflict existing for them about the true intent of the hypnotist. The studies just reviewed highlight the phenomenon of expectancy response, because they uniquely established perfectly legitimate reasons why—if subjects were not committed to cooperate with the intent of the hypnotist—they ought to have resolved the conflict that was present in another, more realistic, way.

In arguing for the relevance of motivated cognitive commitment on the part of subjects, one should emphasize the internal processes of the hypnotized person and the relationship among perceptions, affect, and motivation. Clinical evidence suggests that it is highly inappropriate to compartmentalize subjects' reactions to emphasize just one aspect of internal process functioning. Cognitions of subjects relate in an important way to motivational states, and the concept of expectancy response highlights the relevance of this interaction and brings the scientific study of the interpersonal rapport features of the hypnotist-subject relationship into methodological reach. In turn, the focus on internal processes puts the concept firmly within the framework of contemporary cognitive theorizing about hypnosis.

Recently, hypnosis theorizing has converged on internal processes. Contemporary theorizing has focused on the relevance, in particular, of imaginative involvement, dissociation, and delusion. Susceptible persons, for example, may accept the hypnotist's communications and translate them easily into imaginative events. The contemporary significance of the present concept, however, is that it argues further that some hypnotized subjects, because of the special persuasiveness of the hypnotist's intent, will work in a committed fashion to cognitively construct the behavior that they consider is most appropriate to what the hypnotist wants. The cognitive aspects of that translation clearly relate to current theorizing on the divided consciousness of hypnotic subjects (Hilgard, 1977) and to the importance of isolating the "cohesive cognitive organizations" (Rapaport, 1957, p. 184) that characterize our consciousness.

Critical Discussion

General Areas of Concern

The phenomenon of expectancy response in hypnosis raises three major concerns. The first is the uniqueness of the phenomenon (how typical is it for the hypnotic population?). The second is the extent to which the phenomenon focuses on the role cognitive processes play in explaining hypnotic behavior. Finally, insofar as expectancy response indicates that the hypnotized person is reacting in an unreal way, the phenomenon raises the question "To what extent does the behavior parallel the pathological reactions of those who are naturally disturbed?"

Every person has had a hallucination or delusory reaction at one time or another. Binet and Féré (1888) went so far as to suggest that in every act of imagination there is a germ of a hallucination. What a person imagines is happening—especially when that act of imagination derives its impetus from what he or she wants to happen—can often seem convincing enough that, for a moment at least, it really seems to be occurring. In that instant, normal behavior can be said to manifest some of the attributes of expectancy reaction. By no means, then, is irreality of cognition a phenomenon that is unique to hypnosis. On the contrary, hypnotic processes simply focus on and clarify processes that are evident in the normal waking state. Throughout the clinical literature on disorders in the content of thought, ample recognition is given to the fact that all persons develop or adopt elaborate beliefs or ways of thinking in an effort to satisfy inner needs. When that demand for satisfaction is insistent, reality can be disregarded and delusional reactions temporarily may result.

The second major implication of the expectancy response is that it focuses particularly on the cognitive activity of the hypnotized person. Clinically speaking, argument is made that altered experiences in consciousness consequent upon induction can best be understood in terms of how subjects interpret the communications that they receive and how their own processes of ideation and cognition accommodate them to the suggestions that are given. In hypnosis, it is not the text of the communication that matters, but the way that the communication is cognized, interpreted, modified cognitively, and ultimately acted on in ways that are consistent with how it is perceived. The distinction is somewhat analogous to that made between therapies that focus on behavior and those that emphasize the relevance of patients' cognitions. Just as attribution therapy and rational-emotive therapy target cognitions directly, so also expectancy responses in hypnosis index directly the distinctive cognitive states organized by subjects around the communications that they are given.

Finally, it is important to distinguish the salient features of hypnotic reaction from clinical phenomena occurring in patient populations. For example, delusional behavior among psychotically disturbed people reflects an essentially autistic perception of the environment. Patients actively preserve their preferred cognitive organization, just as hypnotized persons do; but the need states are much more dominant, primary process influence much stronger, and cognitions more resistant to influence from secondary process thinking and reality aspects of the total stimulus situation. Just as one may understand the hypnotized person's behavior, though, by acknowledging the motivations that are being expressed, so also does severely disturbed behavior become rational once the wishes and intents that underlie the behavior are acknowledged. One discriminates expectancy reactions and clinical manifestations of thought disorder in the same way; that is, by analyzing (1) the content of the thought, (2) the satisfactions that are being expressed, and (3) the attentional processes that are brought to bear upon their expression.

The claim has been made about the early studies of the interaction between needs and perceptions (for example, Bruner and Postman, 1948), that perceptions themselves are altered or modified by need states. The data are far more consistent, however, with the claim that attentional processes are affected by the drives in question. Incoming information is most likely coded to accord with subjects' prevailing needs and expectations; that is, "focused attention" substitutes for "selection of sensory information" as the dominant process involved. This analysis is exactly consistent with the data on expectancy response in hypnosis.

Constructivist theories of perception (Bruner, 1973; Neisser, 1967) emphasize the notion that people use hypotheses or plans of responding to direct their cognitions and processing of incoming information. A hypothesis may operate not only through anticipating the structure of a stimulus but also by anticipating the appropriate search requirements necessary to achieve its identity. The involvement of the hypnotized person in the intent and wishes of the hypnotist serves to make the hypnotist's communications especially salient in this sense. Given the strong expectancy state in which they are placed, hypnotic subjects will actively seek out the relevant features of a stimulus so that it fits with the message that the hypnotist is communicating. Some respond actively, so to speak, to cognitively "work up" the desired response in a way that is consistent with their individual interpretation of the suggestion in question. This view of the way in which needs and cognitions interact recognizes both the individual character of the hypnotized person's response and also the effortful way in which subjects may go about producing the desired response.

Clinically speaking, the hypnotized person is traditionally represented as the passive, inert responder who accepts and responds to the suggestions that he or she receives. Certainly some subjects do appear to react passively in this way and also show few signs of effort in performing the desired response, but others tend to individually interpret instructions and illustrate quite effortful, planful processing of suggestions. For these latter subjects, attentional processes appear to be important and it seems that needs and cognitions interact effectively through subjects selecting and actively processing those cues that are most compatible with their motivation.

The clinical literature on delusion and its manifestations illustrates the essential points of this analysis of expectancy response. For example, Heilbrun and Bronson (1975) talk of delusion in terms of heightened vigilance and selective attention to cues. Maher (1970) also discusses delusions in relation to normal processes of behavior (for example, misconceptions and attentional deficits). La Barre (1975) illustrates the concept further by linking it integrally with motivation and need states. Delusion, says La Barre, "varies along a vector of increasing psychological intensity, subjective needfulness, and relative incorrectability" (p. 9). The most consistent earmark of delusory states, however, is that they exist despite abundant evidence that the beliefs in question are patently false; their invalidity is clear, yet the beliefs are held tenaciously.

Expectancy response in hypnosis may take the form of delusory response in just these ways. In the studies that have been discussed (for example, Dolby and Sheehan, 1977), subjects selectively attended to cues that fitted best their expectancy and were mistaken in their conviction that what they saw was correct (even to the point where some of them mismatched the figure they had seen just previously). They remained impervious to the same factors that influenced other subjects to give an altogether different response—one that was quite out of line with what the hypnotist wanted. While the influence of "recent" perceptions pulled other subjects away from the suggested response, this sample of hypnotized subjects continued to report what they had seen in terms of what the hypnotist had led them to expect.

In the clinical setting, certain features of delusory reactions further relate meaningfully to the notion of expectancy response in hypnosis. For instance, Cameron (1959) talks of the active delusional reconstructions that occupy the thinking of clinical patients. Delusions, he says, are shaped to the patient's internal dynamics, pattern of drives, defenses, conflicts, and fantasies. Cognitions are clearly directed, and the need states provide the basis for the interpretation of environmental events that have particular meaning for the patient concerned. The cognitive processing posited by Cameron is active rather than passive.

Persons who are deluded in hypnosis may search through stimulus events in order to accommodate themselves to what is being suggested (but in quite unreal fashion to an external observer). Deluded patients may organize their environment in a similar planful and motivated fashion. As stated earlier, however, the degree to which cognitions are at the mercy of need states may well differ across the hypnotic and patient populations. Autistic thinking characterizes the cognitions of the psychotically deluded person in a way that is rarely evident in the thought processes of hypnotized persons who are observed in the standard hypnotic setting.

Just as the levels of acceptance of irreality, as well as the passivity that this acceptance may engender, vary among clinical populations, so too do they differ among members of the hypnotic population. Some hypnotized persons may actually be aware that their behavior is inconsistent with reality (and be unperturbed by that fact), while others may function in a more clear-cut dissociated fashion. For instance, hypnotic subjects may be aware that some part of them is participating actively in promoting amnesia, even though they do not feel as if they are providing the initiative (Hilgard, 1977). The response of those persons who passively receive suggestions—even ones involving radical alterations in perception—accords with the general picture of hypnosis that is painted in the clinical textbooks, but this picture represents the hypnotic population quite inadequately.

The differences between the separate modes of cognition that hypnotized persons may display raise important questions about the delusory thinking of the clinically disturbed. For example, to what extent are psychotic delusions accompanied by perceptual or cognitive processing of a distinctive kind? That is certainly a meaningful question to ask about hypnotic reaction, since some hypnotized persons who are deluded merely respond with conviction, while others take time and effort to reinforce their delusion by planful cognitive processing (Dolby and Sheehan, 1977). Another question that is relevant to ask is "How active are deluded subjects in assimilating themselves to the environment in which they are placed and in reconstructing it so that it fits with their current needs." It seems plausible to argue, for instance, that the needs of patients are tied to their cognitive activity and efforts in the same sense that is apparent for some hypnotized subjects. The clinical literature reveals that patients evaluate the messages that they receive selectively. Cues that do not fit with current needs are not simply blocked out; the processing of information in thought disorders is far more complicated than this. Although psychotically deluded persons frequently do not appear to behave rationally, they must organize the world around them in some way to shape it to their motivations, and the delusions they develop may well illustrate a degree of planfulness and construction that says a great deal about their potential alertness. Primary and secondary processes of thinking may adaptively coexist in clinically defined delusions, just as they do in hypnotically defined ones and in ways that have been insufficiently recognized to date.

Hypnotic delusion differs from naturally occurring (clinical) delusion, then, largely in terms of (1) the degree to which the persons who are experiencing the delusions will socially distance themselves from reality; and (2) the overriding and pervasive influence of the need states that are aroused. Cognitions change in hypnotized persons much more readily than they do among the severely disturbed; and delusions among psychotics are clearly resistant to modification in ways that hypnotic reactions are not. Realistic appraisal is far more difficult for the disturbed person. For example, the needs that are operating are internal in origin rather than drawing their influence from the communications of another person (as they do in hypnosis). The locus of control of needs is an especially important area of inquiry, then, for furthering psychologists' understanding of the primary differentiating features of the delusory manifestations of expectancy reaction.

Comparative Philosophies and Theories

Many theories that acknowledge the usefulness of the concept of altered state may be invoked to explain expectancy reactions. Hilgard's (1977) neodissociation theory and Gill and Brenman's (1961) concept of hypnotic behavior as "regression in the service of the ego" are two major examples. The concepts attached to these theories are both flexible and broad ranging in their explanatory power. For example, the process of dissociation is importantly linked with that of selective attention and inattention; dissociated persons can concentrate on one part of their sensory field with the same alacrity as they can exclude perception or cognition of others. The classic notion of dissociation implied that the hypnotized individual is simply in a state of temporary fragmentation, but the evidence supports the proposition that the hypnotic subject is altogether too discriminating to be regarded comfortably in this light. The notion of the automatic and passive responder is too inflexible to embrace the full variability of hypnotic reaction. Hilgard's concept of neodissociation, however, does refocus much needed attention on some of the complexities of divided consciousness that appear to characterize the hypnotized person's behavior. The concept of neodissociation also recognizes that cognitive reorganization, as in hypnosis, can be achieved in other states as well (states such as fugue, drug intoxication, and meditation). It does not, however (as does the notion of expectancy response) focus specifically on the interaction of need states and cognitions.

Theories other than state formulations of hypnosis also aim to account for the conviction of subjects about their hypnotic response. Spanos and Barber (1974), for example, view hypnosis in terms of "involvement in suggestion-related imaginings," and Sarbin and Coe (1972) talk of "believed-in imaginings." Such concepts blur the boundaries of state and nonstate theorizing, but the two accounts do vary in their underlying assumptions and philosophy; these differences are elaborated elsewhere (Sheehan, 1978).

Elaboration on Critical Points

The phenomenon of expectancy response among highly susceptible subjects raises two critical questions. First, what motivated cognitive components characterize susceptible subjects' reactions to suggestions? Second, what cognitive processing characterizes delusory thinking in hypnosis? Hypnotized persons do not simply accept uncritically what the hypnotist suggests to them, and close analysis needs to be conducted of the constructive processes that some hypnotic subjects bring to bear on their mistaken beliefs. The study of these processes is likely to be as relevant to our understanding of naturally occurring delusions as it is to our understanding of delusions that occur in hypnosis. Clinically speaking, there may be important differences in the implications for therapy of those persons whose delusions are accompanied by relatively little constructive processing, as opposed to those who actively reconstruct their cognitions in line with their personal expectancies and needs. In the former instance, because the delusions have less cognitive effort to support them, the convictions could be said to be more amenable to change. However, any active restructuring of cognitions by a therapist might actually work better with patients who are naturally predisposed to interpret events in a constructive way.

Severely disturbed persons, immersed in their delusions, interpret their environment in a mistaken fashion; all reality testing is preempted, and their interpretation of the environment is typically autistic. The psychotic identity is preserved in terms of the needs that exist, and the delusional organization is subservient to internalized processes of control. Sacks, Carpenter, and Strauss (1974) have formulated a phase of recovery from delusions that seems somewhat akin to the processes that appear to define the expectancy response in hypnosis, especially as it manifests itself in delusory thinking. These investigators refer to the initial phase of the recovery process as "double-awareness"; that is, reality intrudes into the delusional situation and creates a more flexible state of consciousness than existed before. In this phase the patient is no longer totally immersed in the delusions and becomes able to gain distance from them and to interact socially with others in a more responsive way. Although the patient is still delusional, he comes to recognize that the delusion is a symptom and is able to discriminate perceptions from ideas. Relationships with others actually provide support for the reality testing that is impaired; cognitions are no longer completely subservient to the needs that exist; and motives lose their pervasive influence. In this phase reality testing, delusional ideation, and the trust of the patient undergo a change in the patterning of their interrelationship and the patterning is such that cognitions are more amenable to restructuring.

The double-awareness phase of delusional thinking is analogous to hypnotic expectancy behavior in several major respects. For example, the hypnotized person who manifests this response is in touch with reality, but his thinking is nevertheless impaired. Further, needs are not completely dominant but are nevertheless still influential. The most obvious point of distinction, however, is that social relationship factors critically determine hypnotic response. The psychotically deluded person is unable to engage or participate adaptively in thinking that is socially responsive, and it is only in recovery from that stage that greater receptiveness to social influence can be assumed. In contrast, the hypnotically deluded person is always subject to the influence of the hypnotist. The delusion that results is part of the social interaction of subject and hypnotist, and the motivated cognitive commitment of the subject that characterizes his expectancy response stems directly from the interpersonal involvement of the subject in the ongoing social interaction. The autistic perception and poverty of cooperativeness characterizing primary psychotic delusions are replaced by the reality demands of a positive relationship in which the hypnotic subject takes an active, cooperative role.

Hypnotic expectancy reaction is not at all evident among persons who have no susceptibility for suggestible response, and it is thus possible that personality factors are basically responsible for the susceptible person's capacity to respond in an unreal way to suggestions that fit his needs, motives, and expectations. One of the important implications of the data, however, is that not all susceptible persons manifest the behavior in question. In the studies conducted, only a small sample of highly susceptible people demonstrated expectancy response and expressed their conviction in a way that was totally inconsistent with reality constraints (Dolby and Sheehan, 1977). Expectancy responders are routinely capable of experiencing radical alterations in perceptual functioning (for example, visual hallucinations and amnesia for the events of trance); but some people who experience these alterations do not respond in expectancy fashion. Hypnotic subjects clearly differ in the nature of their commitment to the hypnotist's communications. These distinct types of involvement are not sufficiently recognized in the clinical and experimental literature to date and need to be measured.

Personal Views and Recommendations

The notion of expectancy response reinforces the current emphasis in contemporary hypnosis theorizing on the processes of cognition and attention. The concept used to explain expectancy behavior—namely, motivated cognitive commitment—captures this focus and appeals as well to the special relevance of motivational processes to our understanding of hypnotic events. Specifically, this commitment has been defined in terms of the relationship factors adhering to the hypnotist-subject interaction and to the special sensitivity of the hypnotized subject to the hypnotist's intent. Also emphasized is the *active* nature of the cognitive involvement of subjects in their attempts to construct an appropriate response. The concept is entirely supportive of the individual character of hypnotized subjects' personal reactions to the suggestions that they receive.

Greater clinical and empirical analysis should be conducted of individuals' needs and expectancies and the way that they shape and modify cognitions in the active attempts by hypnotized persons to explore the meaning and character of what is suggested. It is disappointing that the modern literature in the field has virtually ignored the task of analyzing the hypnotized person in terms of interactive processes at work. It is expectancies and needs *in relation to* cognitions that will seemingly provide the key to understanding the full clinical significance of hypnotic phenomena, and far more adequate recognition should be given to the different types of commitment that hypnotic persons display. Sensitive awareness of the interactive aspects of functioning and recognition of the essential variability among hypnotic subjects in commitment to their tasks will also facilitate better rapprochement of clinical and laboratory workers in the field.

The clinician working in the therapeutic setting is predominantly concerned to assess hypnotic responsiveness in interviews. It is important, then, to recognize ways in which expectancy reactions can be indexed in such a setting and the commitment of subjects encouraged. To do this, the clinician should be sensitive to the appearance of "individuation" in clients' hypnotic response—a process defined elsewhere (Sheehan, McConkey, and Cross, 1978) as the clients' attempts to interpret the hypnotist's remarks in an idiosyncratic and personal way. The motivated nature of clients' commitment is likely to be manifest in the degree to which the suggestions of the hypnotherapist are accepted and acted on by the client in a cognitively idiosyncratic or individualized fashion. The clinician should also be alert to any particular desire on the client's part to please the therapist, or to the presence of some awareness that the hypnotherapist is someone who is personally important or meaningful. Commitment of this kind can be naturally encouraged in therapy when the client or patient has a special investment in cure and trusts the therapist to help him pursue that goal. Active encouragement of the client's involvement may occur through hypnotically suggested dreams and age regressions, for example, where the hypnotherapist has ample opportunity to reinforce the constructive fantasies of the subject and share in the client's attempts to personalize suggestions. It is motivated involvement by the subject that characterizes expectancy reactions, and the therapist ought to be able to foster a client's cognitive commitment by encouraging his personal initiative.

Application to Particular Variables

Expectancy response in hypnosis is a phenomenon that is distinctive to subjects who are highly susceptible to hypnosis. Therefore, it represents an idiosyncratic response among those persons who have the definite aptitude and capability to respond successfully to suggestions. There is no evidence at this stage, however, that age, sex, education, socioeconomic status, vocation, or ethnic/racial factors bear any relationship to the response in question, nor is the phenomenon specifically indicative of any disorder or disability, although it promotes radical shifts in thinking that are consistent with the nature of the suggestion given. In an objective sense, expectancy response is defined in terms of a reliable difference in the performance (and experience) of hypnotized and normal waking subjects. It may also, like hypnotic delusion, be described as a cognitive deficit response since it can imply some degree of aberration in thinking. Such a description would be misleading, however, for it inadequately represents the social thinking aspects of hypnotic response and the degree to which the hypnotized person may planfully construct a cognitive organization so as to reflect the personal intent of the hypnotist in a cooperative fashion.

Finally, since not all persons display expectancy reactions in hypnosis, population characteristics relevant to the phenomenon have yet to be determined. It is likely, however, that these will relate less to demographic characteristics than to inherent differences among susceptible subjects themselves in the nature of the interaction that exists between subjects' motivations and their preferred modes of cognition.

References

Binet, A., and Féré, C. *Animal Magnetism* [1886]. New York: Appleton-Century-Crofts, 1888.

Bruner, J. S. *Beyond the Information Given.* New York: Norton, 1973.

Bruner, J. S., and Postman, L. "Symbolic Value as an Organizing Factor in Perception." *Journal of Social Psychology,* 1948, *27,* 203-208.

Cameron, N. "Paranoid Conditions and Paranoia." In S. Arieti (Ed.), *American Handbook of Psychiatry.* Vol. 1. New York: Basic Books, 1959.

Dolby, R. M., and Sheehan, P. W. "Cognitive Processing and Expectancy Behavior in Hypnosis." *Journal of Abnormal Psychology,* 1977, *86,* 334-345.

Epstein, W., and Rock, I. "Perceptual Set as an Artifact of Recency." *American Journal of Psychology,* 1960, *73,* 214-228.

Gill, M. M., and Brenman, M. *Hypnosis and Related States.* New York: International Universities Press, 1961.

Heilbrun, A. B., and Bronson, N. "Fabrication of Delusional Thinking in Normals." *Journal of Abnormal Psychology,* 1975, *84,* 422-425.

Hilgard, E. R. *Divided Consciousness: Multiple Controls in Human Thought and Action.* New York: Wiley, 1977.

La Barre, W. "Anthropological Perspectives on Hallucination and Hallucinogens." In R. K. Siegel and L. J. West (Eds.), *Hallucinations: Behavior, Experience, and Theory.* New York: Wiley, 1975.

Maher, B. "Delusional Thinking and Cognitive Disorder." Paper presented at meeting of American Psychological Association, Miami, Sept. 1970.

Neisser, U. *Cognitive Psychology.* New York: Appleton-Century-Crofts, 1967.

Rapaport, D. "Cognitive Structure." In *Contemporary Approaches to Cognition: A Symposium Held at the University of Colorado.* Cambridge, Mass.: Harvard University Press, 1957.

Sacks, M. H., Carpenter, W. T., and Strauss, J. S. "Recovery from Delusions." *Archives of General Psychiatry,* 1974, *30,* 117-120.

Sarbin, T. R., and Coe, W. C. *Hypnosis: A Social Psychological Analysis of Influence Communication.* New York: Holt, Rinehart and Winston, 1972.

Schilder, P. *Hypnosis.* (S. Rothenberg, Trans.). New York: Nervous and Mental Disease Publishing Co., 1927.

Sheehan, P. W. "Countering Preconceptions About Hypnosis: An Objective Index of Involvement with the Hypnotist." *Journal of Abnormal Psychology,* 1971, *78,* 299-322.

Sheehan, P. W. "Hypnosis Considered as an Altered State of Consciousness." In G. Underwood (Ed.), *Aspects of Consciousness.* London: Academic Press, 1978.

Sheehan, P. W., and Dolby, R. M. "Hypnosis and the Influence of Most Recently Perceived Events." *Journal of Abnormal Psychology,* 1975, *84,* 331-345.

Sheehan, P. W., McConkey, K., and Cross, D. "Experiential Analysis of Hypnosis: Some New Observations on Hypnotic Phenomena." *Journal of Abnormal Psychology,* 1978, *87,* 570-573.

Sheehan, P. W., and Perry, C. W. *Methodologies of Hypnosis: A Critical Appraisal of Contemporary Paradigms of Hypnosis.* Hillsdale, N.J.: Lawrence Erlbaum Associates, 1976.

Shor, R. E. "Three Dimensions of Hypnotic Depth." *International Journal of Clinical and Experimental Hypnosis,* 1962, *10,* 23-28.

Spanos, N. P., and Barber, T. X. "Toward a Convergence in Hypnosis Research." *American Psychologist,* 1974, *29,* 500-511.

Wolberg, L. R. *Medical Hypnosis.* Vol. 1: *The Principles of Hypnotherapy.* New York: Grune & Stratton, 1948.

75

William C. Coe

Posthypnotic Amnesia

Posthypnotic amnesia is a failure to recall what has taken place during hypnosis. Amnesia is usually suggested by the hypnotherapist while the subject is hypnotized, although it may occur spontaneously without the therapist's suggestion. The suggestion for amnesia may be that the subject will not remember *anything* that happened during hypnosis or that the subject will forget specific events that occurred during hypnosis.

In the usual experimental setting, subjects are told that they will not remember anything that has happened while they were hypnotized, until they are later told that they can remember. After awakening, they are asked to tell everything that happened since they entered hypnosis. The events that they recall are recorded. After they recall no more, they are told: "Now you can remember everything." Anything else that they recall is then recorded.

The usual way to judge whether or not subjects "passed" posthypnotic amnesia is to employ an objective criterion; for example, if subjects recall fewer than four out of twelve items on the Stanford Hypnotic Susceptibility Scale, Forms A and B (Weitzenhoffer and Hilgard, 1959a), they are scored as passing posthypnotic amnesia. Such a measure is called "recall" amnesia. The additional number of items recalled after they are told that they can remember may also be used as a criterion for amnesia. This is called a measure of "reversibility." The combination of low recall and high reversibility is a more valid measure than either one by itself; that is, it assures the investigator that subjects have not simply forgotten.

In experimental settings, amnesia may also be suggested for specific isolated events during hypnosis (see Evans, 1972; Spanos and Ham, 1973). However, suggestions for selective amnesia are probably more common in clinical practice. Therapists may have special reasons for not wanting their clients to remember some specific material. For example, a therapist may think it unwise at an early point in therapy for the client to remember a traumatic event that came up during hypnotic age regression.

The amnesia suggestion may be given in a very specific and emphatic way, which is often the case in experiments, or it may be permissive and open-ended, which is often the case in clinical settings (Kline, 1966). An experimenter may say, "You will not remember *anything* until I tell you that you can remember," while a hypnotherapist may say, "You will remember only what you are ready to remember."

Spontaneous posthypnotic amnesia seems to occur more often in clinical settings, where clients fail to recall certain aspects of a session, than it does in experimental settings. Complete spontaneous amnesia is quite rare. In any event, it is difficult to determine whether amnesia is ever really "spontaneous," since the hypnotherapist might give subtle indications that act as suggestions for amnesia, or subjects may give themselves suggestions with the same effect. However, when spontaneous amnesia does seem to occur, the content of the forgotten material may help the clinician to understand the psychodynamics of the client.

Background and Current Status

Posthypnotic amnesia is believed to have first been recorded by Armand Chastenet, Marquis de Puysegur, in 1784.* The marquis was a lay mesmerist who practiced animal magnetism (the term used for hypnotic responsiveness before James Braid coined the term *hypnosis* in the mid 1800s). The marquis recognized a group of responses which he categorized as "artificial somnambulism," or artificial sleepwalking. Some mesmerized subjects appeared capable of speaking lucidly, of walking around with their eyes open, of responding to the mesmerist's wishes and commands, and, upon being aroused, of having no recollection of their experiences.

Throughout the history of hypnosis, posthypnotic amnesia has been considered a characteristic response of highly susceptible subjects. The early scales of hypnotic susceptibility, as well as those in current use, include posthypnotic amnesia as one of the more difficult items to pass (see Hilgard, 1965, or Sarbin and Coe, 1972, for a detailed history of hypnotic susceptibility scales). Thus, if subjects respond to posthypnotic amnesia, it is reasonable to predict that they will also respond to many other hypnotic suggestions.

Earlier investigators, mostly practitioners of the healing arts, were interested in

*The reader interested in a detailed history of hypnosis can refer to the following Binet and Féré, 1888; Bramwell, 1903; Ellenberger, 1970; Fromm and Shor, 1972; Gordon, 1967; Sarbin and Coe, 1972; Sheehan and Perry, 1976).

spontaneous amnesia following hypnosis. However, interest in spontaneous amnesia lessened as susceptibility scales became psychometrically sophisticated and as hypnosis was being studied more in the scientific laboratory, probably because the spontaneity of the amnesia could not be accurately determined. Currently, the most frequently employed standardized scales of hypnotic responsiveness measure only *suggested* posthypnotic amnesia (London, 1962; Shor and Orne, 1962; Weitzenhoffer and Hilgard, 1959a, 1959b, 1963). Clinicians, nevertheless, remain interested in spontaneous amnesia and the meaning it may have for their clients' psychodynamics.

The clinical uses of posthypnotic amnesia can be reported only in qualitative terms. By and large, only clinicians from psychodynamic orientations have been interested in posthypnotic amnesia and its uses in facilitating therapy (Fromm, 1965; Gill and Brenman, 1959; Haley, 1967; Kline, 1963; Kroger, 1977; Sacerdote, 1967; Schilder, 1956; Schneck, 1963; Wolberg, 1945). Some examples follow.

Spontaneously forgotten material may be investigated for its psychodynamic significance. When clients spontaneously forget parts of a session, it may be postulated that these parts are associated with symbolic material of an unconscious or regressive nature; in that sense, the amnesia may act similarly, if not identically, to repressive processes. Hypnotic sessions may stimulate more unconscious or regressive material compared to waking sessions; therefore, selective amnesia for hypnotic sessions may occur more often, perhaps with the effect of expediting therapy (Kline, 1966).

Suggested amnesia may be of assistance in the hypnotic exploration of threatening material at an early time in therapy. On the assumption that hypnosis facilitates the recall of dynamic material, repressed incidents could be uncovered; if considered wise at the time, the therapist would then suggest amnesia for it (Wright, 1966).

Inducing pseudomemories may be another facilitative maneuver. Memories for events that did not occur may be induced in clients who respond to posthypnotic amnesia. If the therapist decides that therapy would benefit by the client's believing that his past was different in some way, the client may be told to remember events that did not actually occur and to forget the real events of trance. Upon awakening, the client will recall the suggested events (Orne, 1966).

Laboratory research has led to the development of standardized, reliable measurements of suggested posthypnotic amnesia. These measures may be separated into two groups: (1) those that subjects can easily modify and (2) those that they cannot.

Most standard scales of hypnotic susceptibility use measures that depend solely on the subjects' reports and are, therefore, easily modified. Subjects are asked to recall everything that happened during hypnosis; the number of items recalled is used to judge the degree of amnesia (recall amnesia). After the amnesia suggestion is lifted, subjects are asked to recall anything else they remember (reversibility of amnesia). Only recall amnesia is used on most scales, reversibility being used more often in research studies. Other methods of recall have also been employed. The "forgotten" items may be presented to subjects for recognition. The degree of recognition recall in posthypnotic amnesia is usually higher than free recall, as it also is in studies of normal memory. The way in which subjects recall, judged by their nonverbal behavior (Do they appear puzzled? Are they trying?), may also be employed as a subjective estimate of the process of recall.

All the above measures could be easily simulated should subjects be so inclined; therefore, their validity as indicators of actual experience during recall is unknown. Because of this difficulty, measures that are not easily modified have been used in attempts to determine whether the temporarily forgotten material still affects subjects, even though they claim not to remember it.

Difficult-to-modify measures generally fall into two categories: (1) physiological responses and (2) subtle measures of recall. Physiological measures, like those used in lie detection, can be taken in order to determine whether the material which subjects claim not to remember is nevertheless affecting their physiological responses (responses which subjects presumably cannot control voluntarily). For example, galvanic skin response (GSR) may be monitored during recall. Subjects are given suggestions to forget certain "key" words while they are hypnotized. During recall, the key words are interspersed with neutral words, and subjects are asked which words they recognize. If subjects claim nonrecognition yet show different GSRs to the neutral and key words, the words probably are available at some level. The subtle ways of testing recall also are not easy to modify (see Coe, 1978, or Cooper, 1972, for more details). An example is the effect of retroactive inhibition. If subjects learn two lists of similar words, the efficiency of recalling the first list is decreased by their learning the second list. Subjects learn one list before they are hypnotized and one list while they are hypnotized. Posthypnotic amnesia is suggested for the second list. They are then asked to recall both lists. If subjects do not recall the second list (amnesia), that should not interfere with their recalling the first list (by comparison to subjects who are not amnesic). However, when amnesic subjects recall the first list no better than nonamnesic subjects do, the forgotten material apparently still actively affects recall on some level.

Research with difficult-to-modify measures has generally supported the notion that the amnesic material is still active. That is, subjects judged amnesic by easily modified measures do not appear amnesic on difficult-to-modify measures. Since the unreported and presumably forgotten material is clearly available at some level, rather than being temporarily ablated from memory, the question of accounting for these observations is raised.

Other studies have suggested a special sort of posthypnotic amnesia, source amnesia, which is claimed to be independent of suggested recall amnesia (Cooper, 1966; Evans, 1971; Evans and Thorn, 1966). Source amnesia is the ability to recall information but not where or when it was learned. Evans interprets his data as indicating that source amnesia is a characteristic of hypnosis and a state-dependent phenomenon. His approach is to teach subjects a little-known fact (for example, the mean diameter of the earth) while they are hypnotized; he then asks them to answer the question when they are awake. A small percentage give the correct answer but forget where they learned it; that is, they exhibit source amnesia. Evans did not suggest to his subjects that they would forget the source; the forgetting occurred spontaneously. However, Cooper tested both suggested and spontaneous source amnesia in his sample and found that it occurred more frequently when suggested. The status of the phenomenon is not clear at this point, but the research is relevant to the major issues currently surrounding posthypnotic amnesia.

Critical Discussion

General Areas of Concern

According to nearly all researchers, the material that is not reported and presumably forgotten during posthypnotic amnesia is still available to influence memory processes. Therefore, the major questions left to resolve are (1) What processes are involved in posthypnotic amnesia and (2) When has posthypnotic amnesia in fact been observed? There is an increasing interest in subjects' phenomenal experiences during amnesia as an indicator of the "reality" of its existence. Of necessity, what subjects report about their experience is the primary datum, a measure which is easily modified and difficult to evaluate in terms of veridicality. Investigators are attempting to prove or disprove the credibility of posthypnotic amnesia and to theorize about how to account for its occurrence. From the theoretical side, there is quite a bit of agreement. However, theorists differ in their emphasis on which variables they believe are the important ones to investigate and whether something is *happening* to subjects so that they cannot recall or whether subjects are *doing* something so that they do not recall.

The above issues are reflected in studies of two classes: (1) studies that examine the verbal report for validity and (2) studies aimed at showing that what is happening to subjects is mostly beyond their control and therefore that posthypnotic amnesia is a characteristic of a special state.

Regarding subjects' reports of their experience, research by Spanos and his colleagues has suggested that many subjects who are scored as amnesic purposely withhold information. In studies where the process of recall was being examined (more detail will be given in the next section), from 40 percent to 63 percent of subjects who appeared completely amnesic (total nonrecall) admitted postexperimentally that they had suppressed their reports during recall (see Spanos and Bodorick, 1977). In another study on selective amnesia for the number 4, only 10 percent of the "amnesic" subjects later rated themselves as completely amnesic.

The above findings suggest what is perhaps a major difficulty in assessing posthypnotic amnesia. That is, studies that rely on the usual objective criteria for scoring posthypnotic amnesia—the number of items recalled and/or reversibility—may grossly overestimate the percentage of subjects who have a convincing phenomenal experience of not being able to remember. Spanos and Bodorick call subjects who later admit suppressing their report "nonamnesic." If other investigators agree, then studies that have failed to obtain postexperimental reports about the subjects' experiences probably have included many subjects in their amnesia sample who are not amnesic.

Spanos and Bodorick also found that about half of the subjects who did not admit suppressing their reports said that they tried to forget, and about half said that they did not try to forget. Suppression appears to be a common method employed by subjects who try to forget; they said that they tried not to think of the material. Others said that they tried to distract themselves by thinking of other things. Subjects who said that they did not try to forget reported somewhat differently. Some said that they were unable to report the material even though they recalled it; for example, it was as if their throats or jaws were stuck. Others said that they lacked motivation; they were too relaxed to make the effort, although they believed they might have been able to recall had they done so. A few subjects reported that they felt they had no role in forgetting; they simply relaxed, and the material was gone. Again, these findings suggest that posthypnotic amnesia is not a simple, unidimensional phenomenon that can be easily assessed. At least from the subjects' reports of their experiences, there appears to be wide individual differences in the processes involved.

As for happenings and special states, research that has claimed support for special-state explanations of posthypnotic amnesia has tried to demonstrate that contextual factors do not affect amnesia or that there are special defects in the memory process of amnesic subjects.

One kind of study involves applying external pressure on amnesic subjects to tell more. Posthypnotic amnesia is said to be breached if amnesic subjects under such pressure report more than amnesic subjects not under pressure. If posthypnotic amnesia cannot be breached, support is obtained for theories postulating hypnosis as an altered state. That is, something is happening to these subjects, presumably their altered state, that causes them to be unable to remember. Contrarily, if subjects breach, there is evidence that they are in control of remembering and nonstatic positions are supported.

Bowers (1966) examined this issue by designing a study that deceived subjects into believing the experiment was completed when it was not. Half of his subjects were given a posthypnotic suggestion for amnesia, and half were told to pretend that they had been hypnotized when he read them the same suggestion. The subjects who pretended that they were hypnotized were told to act subsequently as they thought they would had they actually been hypnotized. A second waking session followed with another experimenter while the amnesia suggestion was in effect. Both groups of subjects responded to the tasks in this session in the same way. That is, both simulating and real subjects responded to the amnesia suggestion equally. However, after the waking session, subjects were asked to talk with another person who needed subjects for a pilot study. After they agreed, Bowers said, "And listen, since we're all finished here, *I want you to be completely honest with him, regardless of what I've said before*" (p. 45, italics his). The third experimenter then asked the subjects a series of questions, embedded in a matrix of other irrelevant questions, to determine whether they remembered doing what had been suggested and whether they felt that they had done it voluntarily or involuntarily. The amnesic suggestion, of course, had not been rescinded at this time. Bowers found that all the simulating subjects remembered doing what had been suggested, and all were rated as doing it voluntarily. However, only 43 percent of the hypnotized subjects remembered doing it, and only 14 percent of them were rated as doing it voluntarily. Bowers interpreted his findings as support for the position that a demand for honesty does not breach hypnotic amnesia.

Kihlstrom and others (1979; also reported in Kihlstrom, 1977) tested the breaching hypothesis in four samples of subjects who were administered the Harvard Group Scale of Hypnotic Susceptibility (Shor and Orne, 1962). Subjects were first allowed three minutes to write down everything they remembered since they had been hypnotized. Then each sample was given different instruction as follows: (1) *retest,* asked to recall again; (2) *cue,* asked to list the items in chronological order; (3) *challenge,* asked to overcome amnesia by exerting more effort to recall; and (4) *honesty,* cautioned not to fail to report what they had remembered. They were then allowed another recall period, after which posthypnotic amnesia was lifted and followed by a third recall (reversibility). The responses of subjects in each sample who were amnesic on recall 1 were compared on recalls 2 and 3. None of the groups differed on the number of items recalled on recalls 1, 2, or 3. Kihlstrom and Evans, using sample 1 (the retest instructions sample) as a control, interpreted the findings as evidence that contextual demands do not breach amnesia. However, their data also showed that approximately half of the initially amnesic subjects in all groups were breached; that is, they recalled significantly more items on recall 2.

Other studies (for example, the studies on source amnesia) have looked for peculiarities in recall or special amnesic phenomena which suggest that posthypnotic amnesia results from a changed state related to being hypnotized. The studies that follow have focused on the ways in which amnesic subjects recall. They show that the way such subjects recall is different from the ways in which nonamnesic subjects recall.

Temporal order of recall, recalling the items in order from first to last, has been investigated by Evans and Kihlstrom (1973). They report that susceptible subjects, who respond to the amnesia suggestion with partial recall, do not recall the items in temporal order, whereas unsusceptible subjects, who do not respond to the amnesia suggestion, do tend to recall items in temporal order. The interpretation of the data is that the recall process of hypnotized subjects is disrupted, presumably as a result of an altered state of consciousness that occurs in hypnotized subjects.

The degree of clustering, recalling two words from the same category together, in a free-recall paradigm has also been investigated to evaluate further the disrupted retrieval hypothesis. Coe and associates (1973), using a list of thirty-five words, found no differences between highly susceptible subjects and others in clustering. However, Spanos and Bodorick (1977), using an eight-word list learned to criterion, found that retrieval is disrupted in posthypnotic amnesia; that is, highly susceptible subjects showed less clustering.

Space does not permit a detailed critique of the studies on source amnesia, breaching amnesia, and disrupted retrieval. Suffice it to say that there are problems with each which make their interpretations open to criticism. The interested reader is referred to Coe (1978) for a detailed presentation of these criticisms.

Comparative Philosophies and Theories

Three theories of posthypnotic amnesia will be briefly reviewed. These theories reflect the differences noted earlier—differences in emphasis on certain variables and in their views of amnesia as a "happening" versus a "doing." Hilgard's neodissociation theory and Kihlstrom's "tip-of-the-tongue" analogy emphasize the importance of variables inside of subjects and view them as persons to whom things happen. Both suggest an altered state of consciousness as an explanation. Sarbin and Coe's model is more general in character. It views all aspects of the context as important and conceptualizes subjects as persons who are actively engaged in interacting with their surroundings. (Barber, Spanos, and Chaves, 1974, have presented a theory that is identical in most respects to that of Sarbin and Coe; only the terminology is different.)

Neodissociation Theory. Hilgard (1974, 1977a, 1977b) believes that the subjective experience of doing something but not being aware of it—or, as in posthypnotic amnesia, knowing something but not being aware of it—is an important characteristic of hypnosis. Such observations are labeled "dissociations." Hilgard has developed what he terms a "neodissociation theory" to help explain them. The theory emphasizes cognitive structures, cognitive subsystems, and cognitive barriers, which are postulated to account for subjects' experiences during dissociative episodes.

Hypnotic talent, a characteristic of the subject, is important in determining who will experience dissociative phenomena in hypnosis. An executive system, which presumably responds to the combination of the subjects' hypnotic talent and the induction instructions, determines the degree of shifts that occur in cognitive controls. A shift in executive controls is noted when a normally voluntary activity becomes inaccessible to voluntary control. These shifts can be minor or quite widespread, implying a change in total state.

Hilgard's cognitive barriers are characterized by permeability. A permeable barrier allows for an easy interchange between subsystems; an impermeable one essentially prevents exchanges between subsystems. In complete posthypnotic amnesia, for example, the barrier between subsystems—namely, the subsystem that is able to communicate with the outside environment and the subsystem that contains the material to be recalled—is impermeable. The subject, therefore, is not consciously aware of the material. However, the subsystem containing the material has permeable barriers along its contacts with other subsystems. The material may, therefore, affect other subsystems involved in memory (which explains the findings of the difficult-to-modify measures of posthypnotic amnesia) and still remain out of phenomenal awareness. Partial dissociations are also possible because the barriers may be partially permeable. Subjects who remember some material and are judged only partially amnesic may be explained in this way.

Tip-of-the-Tongue Analogy. Kihlstrom (1977, 1978) views posthypnotic amnesia as analogous to knowing you know something but not being able to remember it; he deems this the "tip-of-the-tongue" phenomenon. Thus, like other memory processes, posthypnotic amnesia is amenable to study with the same concepts as those used for information-processing theories of contemporary cognitive psychology.

Kihlstrom's model presents memory "as a network of 'locations' corresponding to events, concepts, and the like" (1977, p. 294). Memories are stored in locations that are associated with other locations, each having "tags" that hold information about the memory stored there—for example, information about when and where an event occurred. The process of remembering is seen metaphorically as the person searching for the proper tags and associations and then deciding what is the correct memory to recall. This search is facilitated by various organizational cues and strategies that help a person systematically sift through the large mass of possible associations. The more efficient these strategies, the more effective a person's recall.

Recognizing something that is to-be-remembered (TRB) is easier than trying to recall it without help because the process of searching for the memory is aided. Seeing an item TRB supplies cues about the possible locations where it may be stored. Only the tags in those locations need to be evaluated before a decision is made. Since recognition memory is much superior to simple recall memory in posthypnotic amnesia, Kihlstrom's model postulated a disruption in amnesic subjects' organized search-and-retrieval processes. Further, the findings that partially amnesic subjects do not recall the hypnotic events in the order in which they occurred as often as nonamnesic subjects do suggests that hypnosis disrupts the episodic relationships (order of occurrence in time) among the TRB hypnotic events. The amnesic subject's behavior can therefore be viewed as a selective disruption of certain access routes to memory.

The process or processes that account for the disruption in memory retrieval that Kihlstrom postulates remain to be discovered. Although cautious on this point, he suggests (1977) an altered state of consciousness as a viable candidate.

Recent research (Kihlstrom, 1978; St. Jean and Coe, 1979) demonstrates that the disrupted retrieval hypothesis is not viable. This hypothesis predicts that highly susceptible subjects gain more in remembering on recognition testing than on recall testing compared to the gain made by less susceptible subjects. Highly susceptible subjects presumably experience disrupted retrieval while low susceptibles do not. Therefore, highly susceptible subjects need extra help when they are shown TRB items at recognition testing because the need for the search function is essentially eliminated. However, recent research indicates that susceptible subjects in all ranges—high, medium, and low—all show equal gains on recognition testing compared to recall testing. Even so, Kihlstrom (1978, 1979) continues to support research aimed at evaluating normal memory functions and to maintain the theoretical position that the underlying process in posthypnotic amnesia is a special state that causes cognitive dissociations.

Contextual View. Sarbin and Coe (1972, in press; Coe, 1978) offer a broad-based theory that emphasizes the importance of the entire context in understanding hypnotic conduct. The emphasis is on the ongoing interactions among persons and their surroundings. It follows, then, that posthypnotic amnesia cannot be fully understood if one focuses solely on the internal (cognitive) workings of subjects, since there is wide variation across persons and since the effects of the setting can dramatically alter the occurrence and experience of posthypnotic amnesia. The contextual view focuses on questions such as these: "Which conditions or contexts encourage self-disclosure, and which do not?" "Under what conditions do we believe subjects' reports about not being able to remember?" "What leads subjects to believe their own statements?" Investigation moves into the domains of "secrets," "believing," and "self-persuasion." Contextual variables— such as the "plot" of the interaction, the relationship between hypnotist and subject, the contingencies of reinforcements in operation, the effects of ambiguity, the hypnotherapists' belief system, the subjects' involvement in their imaginings, the expectations in the context of being hypnotized, and the effects of truth telling in the context—are examined. The skills and abilities of the subjects are also important and interact with other contextual variables. Amnesic subjects are viewed as persons who do things. They employ cognitive skills (such as distraction, redirecting attention, or directed imagining) that assist in creating the experience of posthypnotic amnesia.

Elaboration on Critical Points

Future research will probably attempt to define the criteria for posthypnotic amnesia more precisely. For example, subjects, such as those in Spanos' studies, who admit that they purposely suppressed their reports will probably not be considered amnesic, nor will subjects who report that they did something to prevent remembering or that they made no attempt to remember. Therefore, researchers who support altered-state positions and view subjects as victims of happenings will of necessity turn toward examining a very small percentage of the population, perhaps 1 percent or less, who are, so to speak, hypnotic "virtuosos." These subjects are the ones who seem to present the most convincing evidence that something has happened to them which prevents them from remembering; that is, something inside them has changed significantly, so that their usual voluntary controls over remembering are removed. Their reports of not being able to remember seem credible. They are uttered convincingly along with nonverbal communications that make them more believable. It leads one to believe that they may have experienced an altered state which made them powerless to remember.

More research will also undoubtedly follow on disruptions in the usual processes of recall in subjects who are responsive to hypnosis. However, such studies face a major methodological problem because they are unable to examine the ways in which completely amnesic or almost completely amnesic subjects recall. These subjects do not report remembering anything or they recall so few items that they cannot be included in the calculations. The result is that the most amnesic subjects cannot be examined. However, St. Jean and Coe (1979) employed recognition testing in examining disorganization in the order of recall. Because of the greater number of items recognized than recalled, they were able to include many subjects in the computation who had shown amnesia on recall testing. The hypothesis (Evans and Kihlstrom, 1973) that episodic memory is disorganized received only minor confirmation. In fact, the results from the larger subject pool seriously questioned the validity of the disorganized recall hypothesis. Nevertheless, Spanos and his colleagues (Spanos and Bodorick, 1977, for example) continue to support disorganization in recall by the low level of clustering shown in amnesic subjects recalling lists of words.

A third line of future investigation will probably entail examining contextual variables in attempts to breach amnesia. The techniques employed by current studies in this area do not appear unduly persuasive, and methodological shortcomings (see Coe, 1978) have left the interpretation of their outcomes unclear. Methods employing lie detectors or large rewards (for example, twenty dollars per item recalled) should produce more convincing findings. Two recent studies (Howard and Coe, in press; Schuyler and Coe, 1978) using a lie detector condition for breaching show that about half of the amnesic subjects breach. However, subjects who had reported that they were in control of remembering (about 50 percent) were the ones who breached. Therefore, the studies show support for state theories in the subjects who did not breach and support for nonstable theories in those who did.

Personal Views and Recommendations

Approaches following from the contextual view are necessary if there are to be gains in useful understanding of posthypnotic amnesia—or, for that matter, any sort of social conduct. Attempting to study posthypnotic amnesia in the same way as memory processes are studied in the verbal-learning laboratory ignores the complexity of the hypnotic context. Altered-state theorists such as Hilgard, Orne (1977), and Kihlstrom tend to view contextual variables as "artifacts" that must be eliminated or controlled rather than studied and understood. Whatever is learned about posthypnotic amnesia under such conditions, however, is likely to be artificial. Trying to understand cognitive activities by themselves, without taking into account the interplay of other events in the context, does not seem to be fruitful. Current statistical procedures are unfortunately inadequate for studying the context in its entirety, and, regrettably, there are no known viable alternatives. It is hoped, nevertheless, that the complexity of evaluating the entire context will be recognized and that it will not impede further research efforts.

The recent evidence that many subjects are suppressing their reports is worthy of investigation. If we confine our efforts to searching out the very few subjects who appear to be actually unable to remember, we will miss a good opportunity to study the processes of influence communication. Interesting questions arise. For example, "What leads so many subjects to deceive us?" "How do they go about it?"

Another aspect of the research on posthypnotic amnesia leaves an uneasy feeling. As mentioned earlier (Coe, 1978), the studies on source amnesia, breaching amnesia, and disrupted retrieval are not very convincing. Yet, results of these studies have seemingly been greatly overstated and almost uncritically accepted. Researchers may be trying too hard to prove their theories at the expense of a more conservative, cautious evaluation of the data. Whether or not our favored theory is supported by the data, it has been useful simply by providing testable ideas; we must not be too inflexible in our attachment to certain theories.

Finally, I believe the search for a special state has reached the end of its usefulness. It served as an interesting metaphor for early investigators; as results have accumulated, however, it seems increasingly likely that hypnotic behavior can be accounted for without recourse to special concepts. To keep the state notion alive, state theorists must determine an arbitrary point on an apparent behavioral continuum and call this point a change in state. For example, Hilgard (1977a, pp. 55, 58) encourages inquiry "as to the degree of hypnotic involvement necessary for the performance under study and the basic hypnotic talent required. . . . When, however, the dissociations are more massive, as evidenced by the variety of responses yielded by the highly hypnotizable person when hypnotized and by his own self-reports, a description of the change according to hypnotic state or hypnotic trance is entirely appropriate." According to Hilgard, increasing hypnotic responsiveness means increasing dissociative activity. Yet, in defending the state position, he draws a line at some point along this continuous process, sets it apart as different, and labels it a state. It does not seem parsimonious or helpful to make such a distinction. If the focus is on continuous variables, their span should be examined and an effort made to understand what accounts for individual variation along them. It is of little use to say at some point that the issue is now one of dealing with a state. (See Coe, in press, for an elaboration on definitions of "state" in hypnosis.)

There are two primary ethical considerations when employing hypnosis and post-hypnotic amnesia. First, the client's permission should always be obtained before hypnosis is used. Second, since hypnosis is only an adjunct to the primary therapeutic process, therapists should be qualified in their specialty before they begin to learn techniques of hypnosis (Coe and Buckner, 1976). The American Psychological Association has a separate division (Division 30) for persons interested in hypnosis; and the medical, dental, and psychological professions have board qualifications for users of hypnosis. Since some states have laws restricting the use of hypnosis, persons interested in practicing hypnotherapy should familiarize themselves with local regulations.

Formal training programs in universities are rare. However, the Society for Clinical and Experimental Hypnosis (140 West End Ave., New York 10023) and the American Society of Clinical Hypnosis (800 Washington Ave. S.E., Minneapolis 55414) offer courses and workshops several times a year throughout the United States.

Application to Particular Variables

In general, there are no strict population criteria that restrict the use of hypnosis. As long as the person responds, it may be helpful. Hypnosis is not stressful in and of itself; however, the suggestions used may create stress. Children under 7 or 8 years of age are often not responsive, and responsiveness declines in old persons. Severely and profoundly retarded persons are also unlikely to be responsive, as are "chronic schizophrenics" with long histories of hospitalization. While many seemingly pass the criterion for posthypnotic amnesia, it is questionable whether they experience amnesia or simply do not learn the material in the first place. Some psychodynamically oriented therapists advise against using hypnosis with "borderline schizophrenics"; however, convincing documentation is lacking, both for the reliability of this diagnosis and for the dangers of hypnosis.

References

Barber, T. X., Spanos, N. P., and Chaves, J. F. *Hypnosis, Imagination, and Human Potentialities.* Elmsford, N.Y.: Pergamon Press, 1974.

Binet, A., and Féré, C. *Animal Magnetism.* New York: Appleton-Century-Crofts, 1901.

Bowers, K. S. "Hypnotic Behavior: The Differentiation of Trance and Demand Characteristics Variables." *Journal of Abnormal Psychology,* 1966, *71,* 42-51.

Bramwell, J. *Hypnotism, Its History, Practice and Theory.* London: Grant Richards, 1903.

Coe, W. C. "The Credibility of Posthypnotic Amnesia: A Contextualist's View." *International Journal of Clinical and Experimental Hypnosis,* 1978, *26* (4), 218-245.

Coe, W. C. "On Defining Altered States of Consciousness in Hypnosis." *Bulletin of the British Society for Experimental and Clinical Hypnosis,* in press.

Coe, W. C., and Buckner, L. G. "Expectation, Hypnosis, and Suggestion Methods." In F. Kanfer and A. Goldstein (Eds.), *Helping People Change.* Elmsford, N.Y.: Pergamon Press, 1976.

Coe, W. C., and others. "An Investigation of the Dissociation Hypothesis and Disorganized Retrieval in Posthypnotic Amnesia with Retroactive Inhibition in Free-

Recall Learning." In *Proceedings of the 81st Annual Convention*. Washington, D.C.: American Psychological Association, 1973.

Cooper, L. M. "Spontaneous and Suggested Posthypnotic Source Amnesia." *International Journal of Clinical and Experimental Hypnosis,* 1966, *14* (2), 180-193.

Cooper, L. M. "Hypnotic Amnesia." In E. Fromm and R. E. Shor (Eds.), *Hypnosis: Research, Developments, and Perspectives*. Chicago: Aldine, 1972.

Ellenberger, H. F. *The Discovery of the Unconscious: The History and Evolution of Dynamic Psychiatry*. New York: Basic Books, 1970.

Evans, F. J. "Contextual Forgetting: A Study of Source Amnesia." Paper presented at 42nd meeting of Eastern Psychological Association, New York, April 17, 1971.

Evans, F. J. "Posthypnotic Amnesia and the Temporary Disruption of Retrieval Processes." Paper presented at 80th annual meeting of American Psychological Association, Honolulu, Sept. 4, 1972.

Evans, F. J., and Kihlstrom, J. F. "Posthypnotic Amnesia as Disrupted Retrieval." *Journal of Abnormal Psychology,* 1973, *82,* 317-323.

Evans, F. J., and Thorn, W. A. "Two Types of Posthypnotic Amnesia: Recall Amnesia and Source Amnesia." *International Journal of Clinical and Experimental Hypnosis,* 1966, *14* (2), 162-179.

Fromm, E. "Hypnoanalysis: Theory and Two Case Excerpts." *Psychotherapy, Theory and Research,* 1965, *2,* 127-133.

Fromm, E., and Shor, R. E. (Eds.). *Hypnosis: Research, Developments, and Perspectives*. Chicago: Aldine, 1972.

Gill, M. M., and Brenman, M. *Hypnosis and Related States: Psychoanalytic Studies in Regression*. New York: International Universities Press, 1959.

Gordon, J. E. (Ed.). *Handbook of Clinical and Experimental Hypnosis*. New York: Macmillan, 1967.

Haley, J. (Ed.). *Advanced Techniques of Hypnotism and Therapy: Selected Papers of Milton H. Erickson, M.D.* New York: Grune and Stratton, 1967.

Hilgard, E. R. *Hypnotic Susceptibility*. New York: Harcourt Brace Jovanovich, 1965.

Hilgard, E. R. "Toward a Neodissociation Theory: Multiple Cognitive Controls in Human Functioning." *Perspectives in Biology and Medicine,* 1974, *17,* 301-316.

Hilgard, E. R. "The Problem of Divided Consciousness: A Neodissociation Interpretation." *Annals of the New York Academy of Sciences,* 1977a, *296,* 48-59.

Hilgard, E. R. *Divided Consciousness: Multiple Controls in Human Thought and Action*. New York: Wiley-Interscience, 1977b.

Howard, M. L., and Coe, W. C. "The Effects of Context and Subjects' Perceived Control in Breaching Posthypnotic Amnesia." *Journal of Personality*, in press.

Kihlstrom, J. F. "Models of Posthypnotic Amnesia." *Annals of the New York Academy of Sciences,* 1977, *296,* 284-301.

Kihlstrom, J. F. "Context and Cognition in Posthypnotic Amnesia." *International Journal of Clinical and Experimental Hypnosis,* 1978, *26* (4), 246-267.

Kihlstrom, J. F. "Organization of Recall in Episodic Memory and Posthypnotic Amnesia." Paper presented at meeting of American Psychological Association, New York, September 1979.

Kihlstrom, J. F., and others. "Attempting to Breach Posthypnotic Amnesia." Unpublished manuscript, Howard University, 1979.

Kline, M. V. (Ed.). *Clinical Correlations of Experimental Hypnosis*. Springfield, Ill.: Thomas, 1963.

Kline, M. V. "Hypnotic Amnesia in Psychotherapy." *International Journal of Clinical and Experimental Hypnosis,* 1966, *14* (2), 112-120.

Kroger, W. S. *Clinical and Experimental Hypnosis.* Philadelphia: Lippincott, 1977.

London, P. *Children's Hypnotic Susceptibility Scale.* Palo Alto, Calif.: Consulting Psychologists Press, 1962.

Orne, M. T. "On the Mechanisms of Posthypnotic Amnesia." *International Journal of Clinical and Experimental Hypnosis,* 1966, *14* (2), 121-134.

Orne, M. T. "The Construct of Hypnosis: Implications of the Definition for Research and Practice." *Annals of the New York Academy of Sciences,* 1977, *296,* 14-33.

Sacerdote, P. *Induced Dreams.* New York: Vantage Press, 1967.

St. Jean, R. F., and Coe, W. C. "Recognition and Recall in Posthypnotic Amnesia: Failure to Support the Disrupted Retrieval and Disorganization of Memory Hypotheses." Unpublished manuscript, 1979.

Sarbin, T. R., and Coe, W. C. *Hypnosis: A Social Psychological Analysis of Influence Communication.* New York: Holt, Rinehart and Winston, 1972.

Sarbin, T. R., and Coe, W. C. "Hypnosis and Psychopathology: On the Futility of Mental State Concepts." *Journal of Abnormal Psychology,* in press.

Schilder, P. F. *The Nature of Hypnosis.* New York: International Universities Press, 1956.

Schneck, J. M. *Hypnosis in Modern Medicine.* (3rd ed.) Springfield, Ill.: Thomas, 1963.

Schuyler, B. A., and Coe, W. C. "Physiological Correlates of Posthypnotic Amnesia." Paper presented at meeting of Western Psychological Association, San Diego, April 1978.

Sheehan, P. W., and Perry, C. *Methodologies of Hypnosis: A Critical Appraisal of Contemporary Paradigms of Hypnosis.* Hillsdale, N.J.: Lawrence Erlbaum Associates, 1976.

Shor, R. E., and Orne, E. C. *Harvard Group Scale of Hypnotic Susceptibility.* Palo Alto, Calif.: Consulting Psychologists Press, 1962.

Spanos, N. P., and Bodorick, H. L. "Suggest Amnesia and Disorganized Recall in Hypnotic and Task-Motivated Subjects." *Journal of Abnormal Psychology,* 1977, *86* (3), 295-305.

Spanos, N. P., and Ham, M. L. "Cognitive Activity in Response to Hypnotic Suggestion: Goal-Directed Fantasy and Selective Amnesia." *American Journal of Clinical Hypnosis,* 1973, *15* (3), 191-198.

Weitzenhoffer, A. M., and Hilgard, E. R. *Stanford Hypnotic Susceptibility Scale, Forms A and B.* Palo Alto, Calif.: Consulting Psychologists Press, 1959a.

Weitzenhoffer, A. M., and Hilgard, E. R. *Stanford Hypnotic Susceptibility Scale, Form C.* Palo Alto, Calif.: Consulting Psychologists Press, 1959b.

Weitzenhoffer, A. M., and Hilgard, E. R. *Stanford Profile Scales of Hypnotic Susceptibility, Forms I and II.* Palo Alto, Calif.: Consulting Psychologists Press, 1963.

Wolberg, L. R. *Hypnoanalysis.* New York: Grune and Stratton, 1945.

Wright, E. "Symposium on Posthypnotic Amnesia: Discussion." *International Journal of Clinical and Experimental Hypnosis,* 1966, *14* (2), 135-138.

76

Peter H. Waxer

Nonverbal Cues

Nonverbal cues in psychodiagnosis are bodily signs that provide information about an individual's psychological adjustment. Current research findings suggest that nonverbal cues not only signal when something is amiss with an individual but, in addition, convey information regarding the specific nature of a person's problem. Thus, when a person is anxious, a specific constellation of nonverbal cues associated with anxiety will signal the presence of this emotion.

The current rebirth of interest in nonverbal behavior reiterates two basic premises throughout the history of psychology's periodic attention to this area. First, there appears to be a form of *isomorphic* relation between how an individual feels and the specific nonverbal behavior displayed. For example, current research reflects the long-standing clinical observation that when people feel depressed and downcast, their appearance is likewise downcast. Moreover, this specific nonverbal display for depression is different from nonverbal cues associated with other emotional conditions. Second, it seems that nonverbal cues are somehow a more *direct* index of man's inner condition than judgments based on written or spoken materials.

Background and Current Status

Charles Darwin is most frequently cited as the first Western scientific thinker to devote major effort to the examination of nonverbal behavior. Although many writers through the ages, ranging from Theophrastus (Edmonds, 1929) to Spencer (1881), have commented on the nonverbal aspects of expression, Darwin ([1872] 1965), in *The Expression of the Emotions in Man and Animals,* articulated a number of theoretical concepts and scientific observations that continue to be echoed in current research. As such, Darwin's work can be viewed as the historical foundation for studies in this area. Relevant to the clinical focus herein, it should be noted that the mentally ill were an important source of information for Darwin in the writing of his treatise. Darwin believed that psychiatric patients should be closely examined "as they are liable to the strongest passions and give uncontrolled vent to them" ([1872] 1965, p. 13).

On the basis of material generated from the insane, children, cross-cultural comparisons, animals, and early photographic studies, Darwin formulated three major concepts that have relevance to the issue of psychodiagnostics under discussion here. First is the hypothesis that nonverbal behavior provides a more direct, less distorted or falsified channel to man's inner condition than verbal behavior does: "They reveal the thoughts and intentions of others more truly than do words, which may be falsified" (p. 304). This hypothesis finds contemporary reiteration in the "leakage hypothesis" of Ekman and Friesen (1969), which will be examined more closely in the following pages. Second, Darwin argued that many of our basic emotions (such as fear, sorrow, joy, and anger) are universal, generating nonverbal displays identical in form across races and cultures. This hypothesis of universality is currently receiving much attention in cross-cultural studies. Third, Darwin hypothesized the existence of unique patterns of nonverbal display for each emotion.

Chronologically, the next major theoretical statement pertinent to the examination of nonverbal behavior is the James-Lange theory of emotions (James, [1890] 1950; Lange and James, [1922] 1967). This theory gave rise to much debate over whether emotion is the result or the cause of bodily change. What nonverbal behavior owes to this theory is the fact that James employed much of Darwin's work in support of his arguments. In doing so, James brought Darwin's thinking more directly before the attention of the psychological community. Briefly, James suggested that distinct patterns of autonomic-somatic activity exist for each emotional state, many of these patterns generating nonverbal displays: "We feel sorry because we cry, afraid because we tremble" (James, [1890] 1950, p. 450).

Expression of emotions has continued to be an area of psychological research over the years. Reviews by Woodworth and Schlosberg (1954) and Bruner and Taguiri (1954) provide a good picture of directions and theoretical issues explored in the years preceding the current rebirth of experimental interest in this area.

Concurrent with empirical examination of nonverbal behavior, clinical commentary over the years indicates no lack of awareness of the important role that nonverbal behavior plays in the therapeutic context. For example, the writings of Sigmund Freud indicate that the founder of the psychoanalytic tradition was well aware of the diagnostic implications of nonverbal behavior: "He that has eyes to see and ears to hear may convince himself that no mortal can keep a secret. If his lips are silent, he chatters with his fingertips; betrayal oozes out of him at every pore" (Freud, [1905] 1933, p. 94).

Wilhelm Reich is another psychoanalytic thinker who spent time considering the diagnostic aspects of nonverbal behavior. In his *Character Analysis,* Reich (1945) argued that different pathological types can be identified by characteristic nonverbal displays. For example, he described the "phallic-narcissistic character" as "self-assured, sometimes arrogant, elastic, energetic, often impressive in his bearing" (p. 217).

In the area of current clinical theory and practice, Lowen (1975) has carried on

Reich's earlier efforts to define pathology in terms of specific body signs. For example, Lowen states: "The body doesn't lie. Even when a person tries to hide his true feelings by some artificial postural attitude, his body belies the pose in the state of tension that is created" (p. 100). Thus, a "masochistic" character structure produces physical features of a thick, short, muscular body with the pelvis pulled abnormally forward: "The skin of all masochistic characters tends to have a brownish hue owing to stagnation of energy" (p. 165).

Other clinical thinkers are utilizing nonverbal cues—such as the way that a person *breathes* (Proskauer, 1977), the way that he *walks* or *moves* (Pesso, 1973), or the specific configurations of body *musculature* and *fascia* (Schutz and Turner, 1977)—to make decisions regarding forms of psychopathology.

Collectively, these writers tend to articulate their premises within a psychoanalytic framework that does not readily lend itself to direct empirical demonstration. Their efforts, however, provide a rich source of theoretical material for development of the literature on nonverbal cues.

Experimental research literature discussing nonverbal aspects of psychodiagnostics can be divided into three general areas: studies attempting to demonstrate that pathology is evidenced by nonverbal cues; studies attempting to isolate and identify specific nonverbal cues associated with various forms of pathology or emotions; and studies attempting to demonstrate that nonverbal cues can be of use in tracking changes in psychological conditions.

In the 1970s a number of studies focused demonstrating that there is a significant difference between nonverbal behavior of normal and of pathological populations. Thus, Ellsworth and Ludwig (1972), in their overview of gaze behavior, observed that deviation from normal gaze patterns is a hallmark of severe pathology. One study demonstrating this observation is reported by Hutt and Ounsted (1966), who found that autistic children spent significantly less time in looking behavior than normals do. Similarly, Rutter and Stephenson (1972) report that patients diagnosed as schizophrenic and patients diagnosed as depressed had significantly shorter gaze duration patterns than normals did. Argyle (1967) reports that chronic schizophrenics engaged in significantly less eye contact than normals, frequently looking at an angle of 90 degrees from their conversational partner. These studies show that individuals given traditional diagnoses such as depressed or schizophrenic do manifest nonverbal behavior (for instance, gaze behavior) differing from that of normals.

Not all studies in this area have focused on the nonverbal behavior of eye movement. Ekman and Friesen (1974) report on the relationship between *manual* activity and diagnostic categorization. Utilizing clinicians' ratings on the Brief Psychiatric Rating Scale (Overall and Gorham, 1962), Ekman and Friesen found that manual gestures intentionally used to complement verbal output decreased for patients scoring high on scale areas of withdrawal and motor retardation. At the same time, nervous, jittery, manual activity increased in patients scoring high on items tapping anxiety and guilt feelings.

Other researchers have attempted to isolate nonverbal cues associated with specific forms of pathology. For example, Waxer (1974, 1976) attempted to establish an empirically based taxonomy for nonverbal cues associated with depression. He found that raters viewing silent videotapes of psychiatric patients were able to distinguish between depressed and nondepressed patients on the basis of nonverbal cues alone. Nonverbal cues identified as most salient for depression were the body areas of the eyes, mouth, head angle, and hands. Depressed patients showed poor eye contact, with eyes tending to gaze down and away from the therapist. In addition, depressed patients showed down-turned mouths, angled their heads down, and kept their hands quite still. Nondepressed patients looked at their therapist more often and for longer periods of time, smiled more frequently, and utilized manual gestures to embellish their speech.

In a similar study, Waxer (1977) asked raters to assess anxiety levels in psychiatric patients, indicating which nonverbal cues they associated with this emotion. The raters accurately evaluated patients' anxiety levels, achieving ratings that correlated significantly with the patients' actual anxiety levels, as determined by two independent anxiety scales. Nonverbal cues seen as signaling high anxiety to raters were the hands, eyes, mouth, and torso. Examination of hand activity for highly anxious patients showed a high frequency of jittery, twitching movements and a low frequency of purposeful signaling gestures. Highly anxious patients engaged in significantly less eye contact than low-anxious patients. Highly anxious patients showed significantly lower incidence of smiling and a rigid, less flexible torso posture compared to low-anxious patients. In discussing these results, Waxer (1977) suggests that the separate nonverbal constellations for anxiety and for depression support the Darwinian hypothesis of unique patterns of nonverbal cues for the different emotions and pathological states.

The third area of nonverbal research relevant to diagnostics considers the dynamic aspects of assessment. As therapists are well aware, diagnosis of a patient's condition changes over time. A few studies have empirically attempted to follow these changes. Hinchliffe, Lancashire, and Roberts (1971) report an empirical finding that supports a long-standing anecdotal observation by many therapists. This is the phenomenon of a client generating more social interaction and then becoming more socially engaging, both verbally and nonverbally, with recovery. Hinchliffe and her colleagues examined the amount of eye contact that depressed patients engaged in over the course of therapy. They found that recovery from depression led to an increase in both the frequency and the duration of eye contact.

Kiritz (1971) examined another body area for nonverbal cues to therapeutic progress. He hypothesized that gestures of the hand would systematically vary with therapeutic progress, and the results of his investigations suggest that such is the case. When the manual behavior of a group of psychotic depressives was analyzed, there was a significant increase in the frequency of purposeful, communicative gestures over the course of therapy.

A patient's condition varies not only from session to session but also within any given session. A number of studies have examined the relation between body movement and changes in patients' inner states during a therapy session. Dittman (1962) noted that anger on the patient's part was evidenced by an increase in head and leg movement, while depression produced the opposite effect. Freedman and Hoffman (1967), Mahl (1968), and Ekman and Friesen (1972) all noted an increase in nervous, jittery, manual activity with increased patient distress. Also, as a patient's discomfort increased, there was a parallel reduction in purposeful signaling manual gestures. Collectively, these studies provide some clues to how a given patient is responding to the course of therapy.

Critical Discussion

General Areas of Concern

The first area of concern in research approaches to nonverbal aspects of psychodiagnostics is in essence a "hardware" issue. Investigators in this area frequently note how embryonic and fragmented research efforts to date have been. Systematic empirical investigation of nonverbal cues has waited on the development of techniques and apparatus by which nonverbal behavior could be scientifically explored. The advent of relatively low-cost videotape recording equipment has now made this type of research more feasible and constitutes one of the major factors generating a renaissance of research into nonverbal behavior. Only with such "hardware" has it been possible to scrutinize nonverbal behavior closely enough to find data satisfying empirical rules of evidence. As Darwin ([1872] 1965, p. 12) noted long ago, "The study of Expression is difficult, owing to the movements being often extremely slight, and of fleeting nature." Video recording now permits the researcher to gain a permanent record of this "fleeting" phenomenon.

Although technical and apparatus problems appear to be issues that can be resolved with increased experience, other concerns will likely be independent of any level of technical wizardry. One of the major difficulties with this type of research is that the goals of therapy and the goals of research are often in conflict. Berger (1970) has noted that an enthusiastic therapist-in-training is more willing to sit in front of a video camera than a troubled patient is. Yet, specifically in the area of psychodiagnostics, it is an accurate record of a patient's nonverbal behavior that is sought. In his review of nonverbal aspects of psychotherapy, Gladstein (1974) emphasizes the need for greater exploration of patients' nonverbal behavior: "Although it is difficult, expensive, and time consuming to carry out naturalistic studies, they must be done if we are to identify practical applications" (p. 41). A cursory glance at current studies into nonverbal aspects of therapy supports the observations of both Berger and Gladstein. There are numerous studies on the nonverbal aspects of therapists' behavior, but relatively few empirical studies of the nonverbal behavior of patients.

A corollary to this discussion involves the ethical stance of the clinician as researcher. Videotaped material possesses a much greater potential for violation of an individual's civil liberties than, say, audiotapes. Extreme caution must be exercised in the use of such recordings, and the wisest approach seems to be one where videotaped patients have full knowledge of how material in which they appear is to be used. Experience suggests that patients' consent is more readily forthcoming when distribution and exposure of actual video materials are restricted. Berger (1970) has delineated a number of approaches to these ethical concerns surrounding use of videotaped material. This issue of knowledgeable consent is a compounded problem when one is dealing with a severely pathological patient. It is one thing to gain consent from an anxious neurotic who fully understands how material in which he appears will be employed. It is, of course, a much more complex ethical issue when a researcher wishes to investigate nonverbal behavior of an extremely repressed schizophrenic who lacks any meaningful reality orientation.

There exists, in essence, what amounts to a paradox when issues of nonverbal research and application of such research are contrasted. On the one hand, use in therapy of nonverbal research findings provides the clinician with a potential diagnostic device that is unobtrusive, nonreactive, and more rapid in generating a diagnosis than many conventional assessment procedures. All that is required of the practitioner is a studied observation of the patient for signs of specific nonverbal cues signaling various disorders. On the other hand, research procedures required to satisfy scientific standards as to the reliability of interpreting such nonverbal cues fall prey to the technical and ethical problems indicated above.

Even if researchers somehow resolve the aforementioned difficulties, there is still the issue of how best to introduce such research into the domain of the practitioner. Some form of training procedure seems in order. However, when one attempts such training, the embryonic state of knowledge in this area becomes apparent. To date, there is no body of literature on which to base an intelligent approach to clinical training in aspects of nonverbal behavior. Many systems of therapy training do, of course, give some attention to nonverbal behavior, but there does not appear to be any empirically grounded approach to this area of learning. One is left to fall back on traditional clinical guidelines, many of which are based on the theory of a given therapy system rather than on observation of repeated and demonstrable behavior.

The ambiguity in this area has been long noted. More than a quarter of a century ago, Reik (1948) expressed his concern that therapist-training systems were not providing sufficient attention to nonverbal aspects of psychotherapy. Admonishing clinicians to "listen with the third ear" (p. 144), Reik stated: "The greatest danger (and the one favored by our present way of training students) is that these seemingly insignificant signs will be missed, neglected, brushed aside" (p. 145). In addition, a comprehensive training approach to nonverbal behavior should entail more than psychodiagnostic aspects alone. To be of maximum benefit, training would have to address itself to other areas of psychotherapy as well. Issues such as nonverbal cues signaling patient resistance or transference or nonverbal cues of therapists which enhance or interfere with therapeutic progress have just as much relevance to therapist training as they do for psychodiagnosis. In spite of these provisos, there continues to be some interest in generating training techniques in this area. Ekman and Friesen's (1975) current work with their Facial Affect Scoring Technique (FAST) is one example of this approach. Although it is premature to render a final statement on efforts in such training, it does appear from work such as Ekman and Friesen's that individuals can be trained to accurately identify the constellations of nonverbal cues associated with various emotions. As such, it is not illogical to assume that similar training, utilizing nonverbal material reflecting emotions and pathological states commonly found in therapy, could be possible.

Comparative Philosophies and Theories

One issue that remains a concern to investigators in the area of nonverbal research is the absence of any comprehensive theory of nonverbal behavior. Although several theories of emotion (for example, Izard, 1971; Plutchik, 1962; Tomkins, 1962, 1963) devote varying amounts of attention to nonverbal behavior, there is no comprehensive empirically based theory for nonverbal behavior per se. As indicated, much of contemporary thinking harkens back to Darwin for its theoretical underpinnings. A clear example is Ekman and Friesen's (1968) "leakage" hypothesis. These investigators reiterate Darwin's perceptions when they suggest that nonverbal behavior "might function as a leakage channel of communication less susceptible to either conscious deception or unconscious masking" (p. 181). In spite of a number of methodological problems surrounding the experimental examination of nonverbal behavior, Ekman and Friesen continue to maintain that nonverbal behavior is one of the best avenues to a true picture of an individual's inner state. Problems such as response-set biases, construct validity, and faking (which require careful attention in the use of written or verbally based assessments) are considered to be less an issue when one examines the nonverbal output of an individual. It is this implied potential for nonverbal behavior as a more direct, reliable, and economical assessment index that attracts investigators to this area. In their efforts lies the opportunity for a new data-based theory of nonverbal behavior, founded on empirical findings. Various writers (for example, Marx, 1950) suggest that this is perhaps the most fruitful approach to theory building.

Elaboration on Critical Points

An overview of material discussed above indicates a number of substantive challenges to the ready utilization of nonverbal behavior in the therapy setting. Technical limitations and cost factors have hampered the collection of nonverbal data. Research goals have not always sat easily within the confines of therapy practice and ethics. Approaches to both training and theoretical paradigms in this area are still only in their beginning stages. Yet investigators continue to believe that much can be gained from a fuller understanding of nonverbal behavior in the clinical setting.

Over the years, various schools of thought have advanced their chosen techniques as the "royal road" to the understanding of man's pathology. Thus, early analytic thinkers stated that "free association" was the *ne plus ultra* in the understanding of the unconscious mind. Some of the more recent writers in the nonverbal area have similarly fallen prey to the making of exaggerated claims and oversimplifications for the clinical role of nonverbal behavior. For example, Lowen (1975) is now well known for his statement that "The body doesn't lie" (p. 100). The picture currently emerging from clinical research in this area tends to be more conservative and cautionary in nature. Discussion of two research areas should suffice to indicate that things are never quite as simple as early enthusiastic claims might suggest.

One research area that has direct implications for diagnostic use of nonverbal cues is the exploration of nonverbal faking. While research in the area of verbal and written behavior has clearly delineated a number of ways in which such actions may be willfully distorted, concomitant findings in the area of nonverbal behaviors are still forthcoming. We are only currently isolating those ways in which individuals might alter the nonverbal information they convey. Current findings (such as Ekman and Friesen, 1975) suggest that nonverbal behavior is, in general, a much less practiced skill area than writing or speech, in which all of us receive formal education. As such, it appears that individuals often experience more difficulty in controlling their nonverbal displays; thus the bases of Ekman and Friesen's (1968) "leakage hypothesis." At the same time, research has indicated that people can and do alter their expressions. Ekman and Friesen (1975) discuss what they call "facial management techniques," whereby individuals act to alter their facial expressions. For example, individuals may attempt to falsify emotional display by simulating a feeling when the feeling does not actually exist; neutralizing a strong emotional reaction by attempting to show no sign of feeling; or making one feeling with the display of another (often the converse). Those in therapeutic practice can likely find examples of all three of these faking techniques. Such actions obviously diminish the confidence with which diagnostic decisions based on nonverbal cues can be made. Much more research is in order to clearly identify the operation of such distorting activities.

A second area of nonverbal research having long-range implications for therapy practice concerns the interplay of verbal and nonverbal behavior. The practicing therapist is rarely exposed to nonverbal behavior in isolation. More common is the constant mixing of verbal and nonverbal components of communication. Much research (for example, Mehrabian and Wiener, 1967; Haase and Tepper, 1978) suggests that nonverbal cues provide, far and away, the greatest amount of information. Other studies (for example, Strahan and Zytowski, 1976), argue for the dominance of verbal over nonverbal channels. An additional complication arises when the interaction of verbal and nonverbal communication is examined. Once again, researchers have opposing beliefs. Some believe that verbal and nonverbal channels operate relatively independently of one another. For example, Burns and Beier (1973, p. 127) state that the impact of information encoded in one channel "is not paralleled to a significant extent in the other." In contrast, investigators such as Haase and Tepper (1978) report interaction effects between visual and vocal communication channels. Thus, these investigators state that positively keyed nonverbal displays (warmth, interest, friendliness, and so on) interact with verbal material to enhance ratings of this material while negative nonverbal displays (coolness, disinterest, remoteness) act to corrode such ratings.

For the issues of nonverbal faking and verbal-nonverbal interaction, research is far from over. Although nonverbal behavior in the clinical setting appears to hold the promise for a more direct and economical diagnostic approach, we need fuller understanding of nonverbal variables before we can with complete confidence base therapeutic practice on this type of behavior.

Personal Views and Recommendations

Additional efforts in research, theory, and practical application of findings clearly are in order for this infant topic of nonverbal behavior. At the same time, the current lack of a coherent body of knowledge in this area is not necessarily a discouraging state of affairs. As this investigator (Waxer, 1978, p. 18) has suggested elsewhere: "Given the relatively recent development of technology permitting scientific exploration of nonverbal behavior, we are, perhaps for the first time, in a position where our methodology and perceived applied requirements can be carefully consolidated before we tackle the exploration of nonverbal behavior. Coming late to the point where we are able to systematically explore this area, perhaps we will be able to avoid much of the *post hoc* nature of other earlier considered areas of therapy. The field is wide open, the tools are now available, and all efforts have an equal opportunity for contribution, given the absence of established doctrine."

Application to Particular Variables

No significant differences in the pattern of nonverbal cues associated with pathology have been shown to exist for populations differentiated on the basis of age, sex, income or status level, or racial or ethnic background. For example, Waxer (1974, 1977) examined nonverbal displays in psychiatric populations quite heterogeneous in age, sex, and ethnic background. Thus, Canadians, Americans, West Indians, Hungarians, Scots, Italians, and native North Americans ranging in age from the mid-teens to mature adults (50 years old) all manifested the same types of nonverbal cues for anxiety or depression. This phenomenon has obvious implications for assessment. It appears as if diagnosis based on nonverbal cues may cut across demographic factors without the complications arising from a culturally biased protocol or metrics inappropriate to a client's age or comprehension level. Once again, the potential for diagnosis based on nonverbal cues in terms of economy and ease of utilization is underlined. Many disorders are already identified through clinical observation of nonverbal cues. For example, assessment of mental retardation is often based on the physical appearance (nonverbal behavior) of the retardate. Organic disorders are likewise frequently identified by nonverbal means. Thus, the dramatic display of delerium tremens provides a nonverbal signature of advanced alcoholism. In a similar vein, research has now isolated and identified nonverbal cues for basic emotions (such as fear, anger, and joy) and for specific emotional states (depression and anxiety) relevant to the traditional categories of functional disorders. These areas constitute only a small fraction of pathological behavior possessing a nonverbal component. Additional research is needed to establish empirically whether diagnostic categorization based on clinical observation is accurate in its description of nonverbal cues.

References

Argyle, M. *The Psychology of Interpersonal Behaviour.* Middlesex, England: Penguin Books, 1967.

Berger, M. M. *Videotape Techniques in Psychiatric Training and Treatment.* New York: Brunner/Mazel, 1970.

Bruner, J. S., and Taguiri, R. "The Perception of People." In G. Lindsey (Ed.), *Handbook of Social Psychology.* Vol. 2. Reading, Mass.: Addison-Wesley, 1954.

Burns, K. L., and Beier, E. G. "Significance of Vocal and Visual Channels in the Decoding of Emotional Meaning." *Journal of Communication,* 1973, *23,* 118-130.

Darwin, C. *The Expression of the Emotions in Man and Animals* [1872]. New York: Philosophical Library, 1965.

Dittman, A. T. "The Relationship Between Body Movements and Moods in Interviews." *Journal of Consulting Psychology,* 1962, *26,* 480.

Edmonds, J. M. *Theophrastus, the Characters.* London: Heinemann, 1929.

Ekman, P., and Friesen, W. V. "Nonverbal Behavior in Psychotherapy Research." In J. Schlien (Ed.), *Research in Psychotherapy.* Vol. 3. Washington, D.C.: American Psychological Association, 1968.

Ekman, P., and Friesen, W. V. "Nonverbal Leakage and Clues to Deception." *Psychiatry,* 1969, *32,* 88-105.

Ekman, P., and Friesen, W. V. "Hand Movements." *Journal of Communication,* 1972, *22,* 353-374.

Ekman, P., and Friesen, W. V. "Nonverbal Behavior and Psychopathology." In R. J. Friedman and M. M. Katz (Eds.), *The Psychology of Depression: Contemporary Theory and Research.* Washington, D.C.: Winston and Sons, 1974.

Ekman, P., and Friesen, W. V. *Unmasking the Face.* Englewood Cliffs, N.J.: Prentice-Hall, 1975.

Ellsworth, P. C., and Ludwig, L. M. "Visual Behaviour in Social Interaction." *Journal of Communication,* 1972, *22,* 375-403.

Freedman, N., and Hoffman, S. P. "Kinetic Behavior in Altered Clinical States: Approach to Objective Analysis of Motor Behavior During Clinical Interviews." *Perceptual and Motor Skills,* 1967, *24,* 527-539.

Freud, S. *Fragment of an Analysis of a Case of Hysteria* [1905]. In *Collected Papers.* Vol. 3. London: Hogarth Press, 1933.

Gladstein, G. A. "Nonverbal Communication and Counseling/Psychotherapy: A Review." *Counseling Psychologist,* 1974, *4* (3), 34-52.

Haase, R. F., and Tepper, D. T. "Verbal and Nonverbal Communication of Facilitative Conditions." *Journal of Counseling Psychology,* 1978, *25* (1), 35-44.

Hinchliffe, M. K., Lancashire, M., and Roberts, F. B. "Study of Eye Contact in Depressed and Recovered Patients." *British Journal of Psychiatry,* 1971, *119,* 213-215.

Hutt, C., and Ounsted, C. "The Biological Significance of Gaze Aversion with Particular Reference to the Syndrome of Infantile Autism." *Behavioral Science,* 1966, *2,* 346-356.

Izard, C. E. *The Face of Emotion.* New York: Appleton-Century-Crofts, 1971.

James, W. *The Principles of Psychology* [1890]. New York: Dover, 1950.

Kiritz, S. A. "Hand Movements and Clinical Ratings at Admission and Discharge for Hospitalized Psychiatric Patients." Unpublished doctoral dissertation, University of California, 1971.

Lange, C. G., and James, W. *The Emotions* [1922]. New York: Hafner, 1967.

Lowen, A. *Bioenergetics.* New York: Penguin Books, 1975.

Mahl, G. F. "Gestures and Body Movements in Interviews." In J. Schlien (Ed.), *Research in Psychotherapy.* Vol. 3. Washington, D.C.: American Psychological Association, 1968.

Marx, M. H. "The General Nature of Theory Construction." In M. Marx (Ed.), *Psychological Theory*. New York: Macmillan, 1950.

Mehrabian, A., and Wiener, M. "Decoding of Inconsistent Communications." *Journal of Personality and Social Psychology,* 1967, *6,* 108-114.

Overall, J. E., and Gorham, D. R. "The Brief Psychiatric Rating Scale." *Psychological Reports,* 1962, *10,* 799-812.

Pesso, A. *Experience in Action: A Psychomotor Psychology.* New York: New York University Press, 1973.

Plutchik, R. *The Emotions.* New York: Random House, 1962.

Proskauer, M. "The Therapeutic Value of Certain Breathing Techniques." In C. A. Garfield (Ed.), *Rediscovery of the Body: A Psychosomatic View of Life and Death.* New York: Dell Books, 1977.

Reich, W. *Character Analysis.* New York: Orgone Institute Press, 1945.

Reik, T. *Listening with the Third Ear: The Inner Experience of a Psychoanalyst.* New York: Farrar, Straus, 1948.

Rutter, D. R., and Stephenson, G. M. "Visual Interaction in a Group of Schizophrenic and Depressed Patients." *British Journal of Social and Clinical Psychology,* 1972, *11,* 57-65.

Schutz, W., and Turner, E. "Bodymind." In C. A. Garfield (Ed.), *Rediscovery of the Body: A Psychosomatic View of Life and Death.* New York: Dell Books, 1977.

Spencer, H. *The Principles of Psychology.* (3rd ed.) London: Williams and Norgate, 1881.

Strahan, C., and Zytowski, D. G. "Impact of Visual, Vocal, and Lexical Cues on Judgments of Counselor Qualities." *Journal of Counseling Psychology,* 1976, *23* (4), 387-393.

Tomkins, S. S. *Affect, Imagery, Consciousness.* Vol. 1: *The Positive Affects.* New York: Springer, 1962.

Tomkins, S. S. *Affect, Imagery, Consciousness.* Vol. 2: *The Negative Affects.* New York: Springer, 1963.

Waxer, P. H. "Nonverbal Cues for Depression." *Journal of Abnormal Psychology,* 1974, *83,* 319-322.

Waxer, P. H. "Nonverbal Cues for Depth of Depression: Set Versus No Set." *Journal of Consulting and Clinical Psychology,* 1976, *44,* 493.

Waxer, P. H. "Nonverbal Cues for Anxiety: An Examination of Emotional Leakage." *Journal of Abnormal Psychology,* 1977, *86* (3), 306-314.

Waxer, P. H. *Nonverbal Aspects of Psychotherapy.* New York: Praeger, 1978.

Woodworth, R. S., and Schlosberg, H. *Experimental Psychology.* New York: Holt, Rinehart and Winston, 1954.

77

Larry C. Loesch

Nonverbalized Feelings

The nonverbal communication of affect is the expression of a person's affective or emotional state or "feelings" without the use of an oral linguistic modality. Thus, "nonverbalized feelings" may be defined as emotions or feelings which the individual is unable to put into words (for whatever reason) but which are being communicated nonetheless, even though the person may not be aware that they are being communicated. Relatedly, nonverbalized feelings may occur in the absence of or in conjunction with other feelings that are being linguistically communicated.

Nonverbalized feelings are typically evaluated in terms of three primary characteristics: (1) frequency of occurrence, (2) duration, and (3) intensity. However, comprehensive understanding of nonverbalized feelings also includes consideration of two additional factors. The first is the "specificity" of the nonverbalized feeling. For example, resentment is a more specific feeling than negativeness. The second is the "target" of the feeling. For example, is the nonverbalized feeling of, say, anger directed at another person, the self, the situation, or what?

Background and Current Status

Nonverbalized feelings predate language, since people were "communicating" even before formal language systems were developed. Consider, for example, ancient artifacts depicting people in various expressions or poses. Were these not at least in part intended to communicate the artifact maker's interpretation of the subject's affective state? Also, if human development in some ways recapitulates evolution, it is noteworthy to point out that infants less than 2 years of age can interpret many forms of nonverbal communication, particularly those involving affect (Knapp, 1972).

Even in the light of this long history, however, the study of nonverbalized feelings is a relatively recent phenomenon. Freud was among the first to call attention to discrepancies between verbal and nonverbal expressions of emotions (Birdwhistell, 1970). Shortly thereafter, social psychology and communications began to develop a distinct but related disciplines. As these disciplines developed their respective theories, the study of nonverbal communication in general and nonverbalized feelings in particular rose in prominence. At the same time, associated research methodologies improved, and both the theoretical and the empirical bases for the understanding of nonverbalized feelings increased as a result.

Prominent theorists and researchers typically have covered multiple components of nonverbal communication over the histories of their investigations. It is therefore difficult to make clear associations between particular nonverbal communication components and particular investigators. However, Birdwhistell's (1970) pioneering endeavors and later work on kinesics, Ekman's (1964) work on facial expressions and emotions, and Mehrabian's (1971) studies of the efficacy of nonverbal communication in interpersonal relationships are worthy of note in the current context.

Today the use of modern technology, particularly filming and videotaping, has made the study of nonverbalized feelings commonplace among a variety of professionals, such as psychotherapists, physicians, educators, media specialists, and business personnel. Moreover, the lay public has recently demonstrated an extensive interest in nonverbalized feelings. For example, consider the record sales of books such as *Body Language* (Fast, 1970), *Here Comes Everybody* (Schutz, 1972), and *How to Read a Person Like a Book* (Nierenberg and Calero, 1972). Nonverbalized feelings are apparently becoming more important to more people every day.

Critical Discussion

General Areas of Concern

The major concerns in the assessment of nonverbalized feelings focus on the advantages and disadvantages of the various available assessment techniques. The three methods currently in use are (1) naturalistic observation, (2) physiological response recording, and (3) self-report.

Naturalistic Observation. Naturalistic observation is the most common approach to the assessment of nonverbalized feelings. In this approach, one person (typically called an observer, evaluator, or rater) views the behaviors of another person (typically called the subject) and makes anecdotal records of what is observed. Originally, naturalistic observation included only the assessments made when the subject was in some "natural" circumstance. However, it has since been extended to encompass divergent situations such as the use of laboratory analogs, films, or videotapes. It should be noted that the observer may or may not be a participant in the situation where the subject's nonverbalized feelings are being assessed. Similarly, situations where multiple observers focus on one subject or where one observer assesses several subjects are common.

The primary consideration in naturalistic observation assessment of nonverbalized feelings is determination of which of the subject's behaviors will be observed (Jones, Reid, and Patterson, 1975). The various types of possible behaviors to observe, in fact, constitute some of the components of nonverbal communication. Each of these types of behaviors allows for a different mode of expression of nonverbalized feelings. Accordingly, each will be discussed separately. At any given time, however, any given nonverbalized feeling may be simultaneously expressed in more than one behavior.

Perhaps the most common target behavior in naturalistic observation is kinesic movement. Leathers (1976) defines kinesics as the study of meaningful movement in interpersonal communication. The essence of kinesics in the present context is the assumption that people express nonverbalized feelings through observable physical body movements. The study of kinesics has focused on three primary physical behaviors: (1) facial expressions, (2) gestures, and (3) postures. Each of these three kinesic behaviors has been a source of both fascination and frustration to social scientists. The fascination results from their universality within the human species. The frustration results from the difficulty of trying to achieve agreement on the interpretations of various movements. For example, a smile, an extended open hand, and a forward trunk lean are generally accepted as indicative of "positive" nonverbalized feelings. Similarly, a frown, arms crossed across the chest, and a backward trunk lean are generally accepted as indicative of "negative" nonverbalized feelings. However, when more specific body movements are considered, the problems of interpretation become more acute. What, for example, does a "smirk" mean? Does a clenched fist slammed on the table imply positive or negative nonverbalized feelings? What message is being sent by people who rock on their feet while listening to other people? Thus, the assessment of nonverbalized feelings through interpretation of kinesic movements is an extremely complex process. It seems reasonable to suggest that the validity (at least in terms of interpretation agreement) of the assessment of nonverbalized feelings through observation of kinesic movements decreases as the specificity of the movements being studied increases.

The second common target behavior in naturalistic observation assessment of nonverbalized behaviors is proxemic movement. Proxemics is the study of how people use physical space to communicate (Leathers, 1976). The study of proxemics is usually concerned with two situations. The first is the physical distance between people in situations where they are free to manipulate that distance. Generally, the closer a person moves to another, the more positive are the nonverbalized feelings being expressed. However, extremely close positions *may* be indicative of negativeness, as in the case of intimidation. The second behavior is the ways in which people organize their life spaces or immediate physical environments. That is, given the choice, how do people arrange the objects in their lives? For example, a counselor who continually sits behind a desk when conversing with clients *may* be sending a nonverbalized feeling message of restricted receptivity to the client's concerns. As with kinesics, the study of proxemics becomes more complex as the behaviors observed become more specific.

The use of artifacts to adjust or modify behavior is another target behavior that has been studied in regard to the expression of nonverbalized feelings (Knapp, 1972). In a colloquial sense, people dress the way they feel, and vice versa. In either case, the artifacts (such as clothing, cosmetics, or jewelry) that a person uses communicate the global affective state of the person at that time. Moreover, changes in the use of the artifacts are assumed to reflect changes in the person's affective state. Examples of this type of nonverbalized feeling expression are plentiful: kings or queens who wear crowns may be projecting feelings of omnipotence; popular music stars who use a multitude of different eyeglasses may be nonverbally communicating "I'm unique"; and so on. In general, the investigation of nonverbalized feelings through observation and interpretation of artifacts is simpler than with kinesics or proxemics because the behaviors are typically of much longer duration. However, the major difficulty with this approach is determining whether the artifacts represent the nonverbalized feelings the person has or would like to have.

The study of tactile communication is concerned with "touching" as a means of sending or receiving messages (Leathers, 1976). It is yet another important, though considerably less researched, target behavior relevant to the expression of nonverbalized feelings (Patterson and Sechrest, 1970). The interpretation of tactile behaviors is similar to those for the preceding target behaviors and in many ways equally perplexing. Some behaviors have generally agreed-on interpretations. For example, if one person puts an arm around another person's shoulder, this is generally accepted as indicating positive nonverbalized feelings (warmth, closeness, or support). Other behaviors are more ambiguous. A parent may hold a child's arm to indicate either love or anger, depending on the firmness of the grip. If this grip is viewed in isolation, it is extremely difficult to determine the nonverbalized feeling that the parent is expressing. The most definitive statement that can be made about tactile behaviors, as a means of inferring nonverbalized feelings, is that there is a need for considerably more research in this regard.

The last target behavior to be considered here is nonlinguistic vocalic communication, a method of vocally expressing affect without the use of words (Leathers, 1976). Vocalic communication is typically considered from two major perspectives. The first is concerned with the use of nonlinguistic sounds. For example, an "ooh" or an "aah" is usually indicative of "surprise." Unfortunately, the situation becomes much more complex when the second concern, intonation, is brought into play. For example, consider the many different nonverbalized feelings a person can convey just by saying "hmmm" in different ways. The voice qualities that should be considered for valid interpretation of the vocalic communication of nonverbalized feelings include such things as pitch, timbre, loudness, rate, duration, and regularity (Davitz and Davitz, 1961). The many possible combinations of these variables for a single utterance make the assessment process extremely complex. Moreover, the assessment process is further compounded by the physiological (voice and hearing) limitations of the subject and the observer. In sum, the assessment of nonverbalized feelings through the observation of nonlinguistic vocalic behaviors is extremely difficult, and the opportunity for misinterpretation is great.

Naturalistic observation, then, is a commonly used method for the assessment of nonverbalized feelings; but the approach is not without methodological limitations. The primary one is that focusing on any one particular target behavior excludes valuable information available from other behaviors. However, it is practically and psychometrically difficult to attempt simultaneous observation and recording of multiple target behaviors. These limitations have caused some researchers to look to other methods for the assessment of nonverbalized feelings.

Physiological Response Recording. The two most commonly used devices for recording human physiological responses in order to infer nonverbalized feelings are the galvanic skin response (GSR) recorder and the electroencephalogram (EEG). Each of these instruments, and others like them, are capable of recording even the smallest fluctuations in the body's physiological state. Moreover, numerous studies suggest that there are distinct physiological patterns indicative of various affective states (see Leathers, 1976).

The physiological response assessment method has several definite advantages. First, it helps to reduce the human subjectivity factor so obvious in naturalistic observations. Second, the sensitivity of these instruments allows them to record nonverbalized feeling occurrences or changes that might go unnoticed by human observers. Third, this approach provides more specific information about the durations and intensities of nonverbalized feelings. Fourth, this approach has the highly unique advantage of providing information about the rate of buildup or dissipation of nonverbalized feelings.

This approach is not, however, without its disadvantages. Since the necessary equipment is expensive, the approach is limited to individuals or organizations with extensive fiscal resources. The method also necessitates highly trained individuals to interpret the information garnered from the instruments. Further, the subject must be connected to the equipment, thereby eliminating other than laboratory-based assessments and also raising ethical concerns. Finally, this approach does not entirely eliminate problems of subjective judgments, since the interpretation of which pattern corresponds to which affective state (nonverbalized feeling) is still left to the investigator. Currently the disadvantages (particularly cost factors) of physiological response methods of assessment seem to outweigh the advantages.

Self-Report. Self-report approaches, based on the premise that the person best qualified to interpret and evaluate a subject's nonverbalized feelings is the subject, have been implemented in primarily two ways. The first is what may be called the post hoc (after-the-fact) approach. That is, the subject is asked to evaluate nonverbalized feelings some time after they actually occurred. The second is the in-process approach. Here the subject identifies nonverbalized feelings as they occur.

The post hoc approach typically involves filmed or videotaped interactions of the subject with another person or persons (see Kagan, Krathwohl, and Miller, 1963). Under optimal circumstances, subjects are unaware that they are being filmed or videotaped. Some time after the conclusion of the interaction, the subject is shown the film or videotape and asked to identify and evaluate various nonverbalized feelings that occurred during the interaction. Usually this procedure is repeated several times in order to allow subjects to be certain in their evaluations.

The post hoc assessment procedure has several advantages. First of all, since the subject determines the nonverbalized feeling being expressed, inferential error is reduced. In addition, the use of film or videotape allows for repeated viewing, which in turn reduces the need for "instantaneous" determination of which nonverbalized feeling is being expressed. Finally, the number of people (such as observers) that need to be involved in order to make valid assessments is greatly reduced. This approach also has its disadvantages. First and foremost, it is subject to error due to selective recall; that is, the subject may not be able to adequately recall a particular nonverbalized feeling. Second, the subject may not want to admit having had certain nonverbalized feelings and thus may withhold information or provide erroneous information. Third, there may be a problem with expense because of the necessity of film or videotape equipment.

In the in-process assessment approach, the subject is provided with some device or mechanism that enables him or her to identify, and often record, nonverbalized feelings as they occur during an interaction (see Loesch, 1975). Like the other methods described, this procedure has both advantages and disadvantages. On the positive side, the approach allows for (almost) instantaneous identification of the subject's nonverbalized feelings. Similar to the preceding approach, there is need for few if any observers. In addition, if the equipment is sophisticated enough, the subject may specify not only the frequencies but also the durations and intensities of nonverbalized feelings. On the negative side, this approach allows for only the identification of nonverbalized feelings which the subject is aware of having. Moreover, typically only a limited number of (usually general) nonverbalized feelings may be assessed at any one time. There is also the problem of whether the subject is willing to divulge all the nonverbalized feelings being experienced. Finally, the nature of the necessary equipment again raises cost concerns.

Comparative Philosophies and Theories

Major theorists and researchers generally agree about the nature of nonverbalized feelings and their assessment. Central to this agreement is the recognition that there are multiple components to the expression of nonverbalized feelings. Thus, while at any given time researchers may focus on particular components, each seems willing to acknowledge the limitations of singular investigations and the values of considering the parts played by other components.

Similar agreement and professional respect also exist in regard to the methods of assessing nonverbalized feelings. Here again the choice of a particular method seems more a matter of professional circumstance than of professional preference. Researchers will use the most sophisticated procedures available to them yet seldom fail to acknowledge the potential benefits of using alternative procedures for studying the same phenomena.

Elaboration on Critical Points

The assessment of nonverbalized feelings, like any other type of assessment, raises major issues in regard to reliability and validity; and given the nature of nonverbalized feelings, it is little wonder that these issues are extremely complex.

Turning first to reliability issues, consider that reliability may be roughly defined as an indicator of the consistency of assessment. The consistency of any assessment is due at least in part to the consistency of the phenomenon being assessed. Unfortunately, the consistency of expression of nonverbalized feelings is difficult to establish. For example, the nonverbalized feeling of anger may manifest itself in any of a wide variety of (nonverbal) behaviors, depending on the constellation of factors present at any given time. Thus, reliability of nonverbalized feeling assessment is, in part, contingent on phenomena with potentially inconsistent patterns of occurrence. Therefore, the reliabilities of nonverbalized feelings assessments are typically moderate at best.

Numerous traditional approaches have been used for the establishment of nonverbalized feeling assessment reliability. For example, when naturalistic observation is the method of assessment, the typical procedure is to establish intra- or interobserver reliability. Usually a sample film or videotape is repeatedly shown while observers are trained; they practice until they reach some predetermined level of reliability in recognizing various nonverbal signals of feelings. In more stringent methodologies, an intra- or interobserver agreement criterion level is also achieved. When physiological methods of assessment are used, two types of reliability must be established. The first is the reliability of the measuring device in producing a consistent pattern any time a given nonverbalized feeling is experienced. The second is the reliability of the interpretations of the response patterns produced by the measuring device. Again, repeated practice prior to actual assessments is typically used to achieve criterion levels. The self-report method of assessment has the most problems in establishing reliability. In essence, the question becomes "How consistently do people assess their own nonverbalized feelings?" Since most people are not "trained" in this type of assessment, the reliability of this procedure is commonly minimal at best. Moreover, practical considerations often preclude the establishment of reliabilities for self-report assessment procedures.

While problems in the reliability of nonverbalized feeling assessment may seem difficult, they are, to a large extent, overshadowed by validity problems. Validity may be roughly defined as the extent to which an assessment procedure measures what it is supposed to measure. Again, concerns in this regard focus more on the nature of nonverbalized feelings than they do on the actual assessment procedures. Researchers must contend with questions about the specificity, duration, subjectivity, and lack of universality of nonverbalized feelings.

Nonverbalized feelings have a wide range of specificity. Unfortunately, this wide range is inversely related to the ease and validity of nonverbalized feeling assessment. For example, it may be relatively easy to discern that person A feels "positive" toward person B. Beyond that, however, assessment becomes more difficult. Does person A merely enjoy being in person B's presence; does A feel gratitude toward B; does A "love" B? This situation seems to be true for naturalistic observation, physiological assessment, and self-reports. People generally have great difficulty in attempting to identify specifically their own nonverbalized feelings. Thus, the most valid assessments are those that concentrate on broad or general descriptors of nonverbalized feelings.

Nonverbalized feelings are also typically of very limited duration. These limited durations make observations and interpretation difficult, since it is easy to miss the "clues" to a nonverbalized feeling. The potential for invalid assessment due to inaccurate observation (even in the case of self-reports) is great. Obviously, physiological response assessment methods offer the best safeguard against overlooking all or part of the expression of a nonverbalized feeling. However, even with the use of this type of assessment, the nonverbalized feeling may be so fleeting that a distinctly identifiable pattern may not be produced. Hence, nonverbalized feelings durations significantly affect validity to the extent that they affect the opportunities for valid assessment.

By definition, nonverbalized feelings are highly subjective experiences and, therefore, raise issues about who is best able to assess and evaluate them. For example, if in a recall self-report situation the subject and an observer disagree about the interpretation of a nonverbalized feeling, who should be considered correct? It would be easy to suggest that the subject *must* be (considered) correct; yet there is ample research indicating that people have great difficulty in interpreting their own feelings. Further, are not observers typically *trained* to be able to identify nonverbalized feelings? Such a situation raises concerns about the universality of the expressions of nonverbalized feelings. The highly subjective nature of nonverbalized feelings suggests highly subjective (and, therefore, distinctly individualized) modes of expression. Again, this lack of expression consistency creates problems for validity similar to those for reliability. Nonverbalized feeling assessment validity is, thus, hindered by subjectivity factors that make both identification and interpretation difficult. In addition, subjectivity factors are interrelated with specificity factors in that broad or general nonverbalized feelings typically have the greatest degrees of generalizability or universality and, therefore, are usually more validly assessed.

Certain ethical considerations also must be addressed when nonverbalized feelings are evaluated. First, at what point in the process are individuals told that their nonverbalized feelings are being assessed? Naturalistic observations, for example, will be most effective when individuals are unaware that they are being observed; yet individuals have the right to be informed that they are being assessed. Does informing people immediately after assessments are completed satisfy all ethical obligations? Second, to what extent does the assessment of nonverbalized feelings interrupt or interfere with natural interactions? For example, does the use of physiological response or in-process recording equipment disrupt interactions so much that they can no longer be considered natural or normal? The final ethical consideration concerns the whole idea of assessing nonverbalized feelings. That is, nonverbalized feelings are, by definition, emotions that the individual does not wish to verbalize linguistically. From one perspective, it may be assumed that the individual does not want other people to know about those feelings. Does the assessment of nonverbalized feelings under this condition constitute an invasion of privacy? Like all ethical concerns, the ones cited here are subject to personal interpretations and methods of resolution. Unfortunately, it is impossible to specify universal recommendations for these ethical concerns other than to say that they should be identified and resolved *before* the assessment of nonverbalized feelings is begun.

It should be evident at this point that the assessment of nonverbalized feelings, like the assessment of any psychological dynamic, is and should be a sophisticated process. Consequently, it should be engaged in only by individuals who have had proper training. This training should include strong academic preparation, wide-based field experience, and supervised practice. Moreover, this training should probably focus on one type of assessment, yet include exposure to each of the other types. While any of a number of professionals could become competent in the assessment of nonverbalized feelings, this training would probably be most effective for persons concentrating on counseling, social or clinical psychology, social work, or communications because the "peripheral" training in these disciplines would supplement training in nonverbalized feeling assessment.

Personal Views and Recommendations

The reliability and validity concerns imply two primary recommendations for the assessment of nonverbalized feelings. First, such assessments should focus on broad or general nonverbalized feelings such as positiveness, negativeness, happiness, or sadness, as opposed to highly specific nonverbalized feelings such as insecurity, gratitude, or disappointment. This focus not only increases validity (and probably credibility) but also simplifies the assessment procedure. Second, combinations of procedures probably should be used to assess nonverbalized feelings. Each of the procedures described previously has both advantages and disadvantages. If two or more of these assessment procedures are employed concurrently, the multiplicative effect will improve the validity of the assessment. Each procedure serves as a validator of the other(s). Moreover, the limitations of any one approach are to some extent compensated for by the advantages of the other(s). In sum, the use of multiple assessment procedures enhances the probability of valid nonverbalized feeling assessment by capitalizing on the strengths of each method.

If a singular approach must be used, the self-report method of assessing nonverbalized feelings seems to offer the greatest opportunity to obtain valid data. If subjects willingly participate in the assessment process, then the information they provide must necessarily be accurate and valid, since external (observer) interpretation subjectivity is eliminated. However, again, it should be remembered that self-report assessments may not be possible in some circumstances, and in those cases either naturalistic or physiological response assessments may be most appropriate.

Application to Particular Variables

As alluded to earlier, nonverbalized feelings are present throughout all humans' lives. Accordingly, the assessment of nonverbalized feelings may be applied to any human being. A few human limitations, however, should be considered. First, patterns of behavioral expressions of nonverbalized feelings become more distinctive and diverse as age increases (Rosenfeld and Civikly, 1976). Preadolescents will typically have a smaller repertoire of nonverbal expressive behaviors than will adolescents or adults. Second, the modes of expression of nonverbalized feelings are to a certain extent culturally or sociologically bound. That is, individuals in particular cultural or sociological circumstances may use modes of expression that are deemed culturally or sociologically inappropriate in other circumstances (Rosenfeld and Civikly, 1976). For example, female modes of expression of nonverbalized feelings will often involve less physical body movement than those for males. Consider also the differences in vocalic (nonlinguistic) communication such as geographically identifiable "accents." There may also be distinct pattern differences between various subculture groups. People may establish their interpersonal affiliations on the basis of factors such as their vocational situations, racial or ethnic identifications, socioeconomic levels, or educational backgrounds, and they may develop modes of nonverbalized feeling expression which are unknown to other groups. For example, a wide variety of "hand signals" may be observed among the workers at a large building construction site yet the meanings of these signals are often unknown to casual observers. Thus, the assessment of nonverbalized feelings must necessarily take into account the life circumstances of the individual being assessed.

There are two situations where the assessment of nonverbalized feelings is seriously circumscribed. The first is where the individual being assessed has some physical limitation(s). In this situation the individual will be able to experience a full range of nonverbalized feelings, yet will be limited to physically possible modes of expression. Thus, assessment is difficult in that any one physical expression may be indicative of more than one nonverbalized feeling. The second severely limiting circumstance is where the individual has psychological disturbances that interfere with "normal" functioning. If the individual has difficulty in coping with "reality," any given nonverbal expression of emotion may or may not be indicative of the nonverbalized feeling that the individual actually is experiencing. Under these circumstances, it is extremely difficult to make valid assessments. It should be remembered, however, that neither of these situations entirely prohibits the assessment of nonverbalized feelings. What they do is create a circumstance where the assessment process is so complex that results can be considered only tentative at best.

In conclusion, nonverbalized feelings are an important component in human behavior not only because of the high frequency of their occurrence but also because they are the only reasonable alternative to vocal communication of emotions. Consequently, valid assessment of nonverbalized feelings is essential to a comprehensive understanding of human behavior. There are effective methods available for assessing and evaluating nonverbalized feelings; if used properly, these methods can help us to achieve that understanding.

References

Birdwhistell, R. L. *Kinesics and Context: Essays on Body Motion Communication.* New York: Ballantine Books, 1970.

Davitz, J. R., and Davitz, L. "Nonverbal Vocal Communication of Feeling." *Journal of Communication,* 1961, *11,* 81-86.

Ekman, P. "Body Position, Facial Expression, and Verbal Behavior During Interviews." *Journal of Abnormal and Social Psychology,* 1964, *68,* 295-301.

Fast, J. *Body Language.* Philadelphia: Lippincott, 1970.

Jones, R. R., Reid, J. B., and Patterson, G. R. "Naturalistic Observation in Clinical Assessment." In P. McReynolds (Ed.), *Advances in Psychological Assessment III.* San Francisco: Jossey-Bass, 1975.

Kagan, N., Krathwohl, D. R., and Miller, R. "Stimulated Recall in Therapy Using Videotape—A Case Study." *Journal of Counseling Psychology,* 1963, *10,* 237-243.

Knapp, M. L. *Nonverbal Communication in Human Interaction.* New York: Holt, Rinehart and Winston, 1972.

Leathers, D. G. *Nonverbal Communication Systems.* Boston: Allyn and Bacon, 1976.

Loesch, L. C. "Nonverbalized Feelings and Perceptions of the Counseling Relationship." *Counselor Education and Supervision,* 1975, *15,* 105-113.

Mehrabian, A. *Silent Messages.* Belmont, Calif.: Wadsworth, 1971.

Nierenberg, G. I., and Calero, H. H. *How to Read a Person Like a Book.* New York: Simon and Schuster, 1972.

Patterson, M. L., and Sechrest, L. B. "Interpersonal Distance and Impression Formation." *Journal of Personality,* 1970, *38,* 161-168.

Rosenfeld, L. B., and Civikly, J. M. *With Words Unspoken: The Nonverbal Experience.* New York: Holt, Rinehart and Winston, 1976.

Schutz, W. C. *Here Comes Everybody.* New York: Harper & Row, 1972.

78

Vernon L. Allen

Social Conformity

Social conformity is a term used to denote behavior that adheres to some social standard; that is, to a set of real or assumed expectations concerning appropriate and inappropriate behavior. Deviance, often considered the reciprocal of conformity, designates a lack of adherence to some particular set of societal standards, rules, or legal strictures. Most frequently employed by sociologists and criminologists, the term *deviance* has also been used by psychologists in connection with attitudes or opinions that are extremely discrepant from a group norm.

Care must be taken to distinguish between social conformity as defined here (that is, as behavior influenced by a social norm) and other instances of uniformity of behavior among persons. Conformity should not be equated with mere equivalence of behavior among a group of individuals. Persons often respond independently to the same stimulus situation in complete absence of any social norm or group pressure. For example, if several persons seek shelter in a building when it is raining, this uniformity in behavior should not be construed as social conformity. Likewise, speaking the same language as one's compatriots should not be defined as social conformity, even though uniformity of behavior is indisputably present. The latter example makes explicit the implied criterion that choice or intentionality must be involved in the definition of social conformity.

Background and Current Status

Social conformity has long been recognized by social philosophers and social scientists as one of the central concepts in the analysis of behavior of individuals in complex social settings. In his book *On Liberty,* John Stuart Mill denounced social conformity, or "the despotism of custom," as a hindrance "to human advancement" (Mill, [1859] 1947, p. 70). Other early social scientists (for example, Sumner, 1906) also recognized the importance of social conformity to both the individual and the state or social system, but they gave a more balanced assessment of consequences, stressing the positive role played by social conformity and custom in maintaining social control and political stability.

At a psychological level, several interrelated concepts became the object of intense armchair speculation, theorizing, and some empirical work around the turn of the twentieth century. Imitation, suggestion, contagion, and social influence are the most prominent of many concepts introduced to help explain the tendency of individuals to be affected by the behavior and expectations of their fellows. According to Cooley (1902), people conform simply because nonconformity is painful and inconvenient. Some early writers (for example, Tarde, 1890) attempted to formulate a few simple "laws" of imitation in order to account for social conformity. Contributing greatly to the development of concepts and theory was a body of writings (for instance, by Le Bon, 1895) dealing with the behavior of persons in crowds. This theoretical analysis focused attention on the homogeneity of behavior among persons in a crowd and offered suggestibility and imitation as central explanatory mechanisms.

Following the rather diffuse and uncritical speculations characteristic of the early discussions of social conformity, the concept has been subjected to increasingly more precise empirical and theoretical analyses during the last fifty years. Several notable developments can be identified as contributing to the differentiation, elaboration, and revision of this concept.

In an early series of experimental studies, Allport (1920) discovered that individuals express more extreme opinions when they are alone than when they are with other people. According to Allport, one assumes an attitude of conformity in the presence of other persons in order to avoid the appearance of being more extreme than the others. Additional research explored the relative effect of different sources of social influence, such as peers versus experts (Moore, 1921) or persons of high versus low prestige.

The study of social conformity was advanced greatly in the 1930s by the research and writings of Sherif (1936), which linked social conformity to the formation and change of social norms. Using the experimental paradigm of the autokinetic effect, Sherif investigated in the laboratory the process of formation of social norms by observing the interaction of individuals in an ambiguous situation. Complementary to Sherif's experimental approach was the more naturalistic work of Newcomb, who studied the influence of norms on political opinions in a small university community. Newcomb (1943) introduced the important idea of reference group to explain why some persons conform to the social norm and others do not. In the 1950s a series of studies by Asch (1951, 1956) provided a major impetus to the redefinition of conformity by demonstrating in a dramatic fashion the power of a social group. These studies used a very simple perceptual task (judging length of lines), and the group members were instructed to give erroneous answers that clearly contradicted physical reality. A substantial percentage of subjects did conform to the group, that is, they gave the same erroneous answers that the group had given. This series of experiments stimulated a great deal of further research. Other research conducted during this time showed that a group reacts negatively to a member who remains an attitudinal deviant by refusing to conform (Schachter, 1951).

Additional research, and also certain political events in the 1950s, contributed further to the developing conceptualization of social conformity. First, two popular books of the period—*The Lonely Crowd* (Riesman, Glazer, and Denny, 1950) and *The Organization Man* (Whyte, 1957)—made social conformity salient to scientists and laymen alike by emphasizing the centrality of conformity ("other directedness") as a character trait of Americans and by indicating the pervasiveness of conformity pressures in business organizations. Second, the social and political climate of the times, as exemplified by McCarthyism and the House Un-American Activities Committee, also influenced thinking about social conformity. It became readily apparent that extreme conformity pressures in a society are capable of producing significant and even tragic effects on individuals.

It might appear that there is little pressure for social conformity at the present period in history. A closer examination suggests, however, that conformity is still pervasive, although the content of some social norms has changed. The behavior of certain groups (for example, young people) may be different today as compared to ten or twenty years ago, but a range of appropriate and inappropriate behaviors is still clearly specified and understood, and the amount of conformity to norms probably does not differ from that of former times. The concept of social conformity remains relevant today and will probably always be essential for the effective functioning of a social system and for the satisfaction of personal relations between an individual and other members of the social group.

Critical Discussion

General Areas of Concern

Conformity has sometimes been contrasted with nonconformity or independence, terms that imply the failure of attempted social influence. To regard conformity as the opposite of nonconformity or independence assumes a continuum, with conformity at one end and its opposite, nonconformity or independence, at the other. Some analysts (Willis, 1963), however, argue that nonconformity consists of two conceptually distinct types of behavior. Nonconformity may reflect independence, or it may actually be an anticonformity response. Thus, three types of behavior—conformity, independence, and anticonformity—can be represented by two different dimensions, one ranging from conformity to anticonformity; the other ranging from independence to dependence.

The two-dimensional conception emphasizes that conformers and anticonformers are both strongly influenced by the social norm. The conformer changes in order to agree with the norm, and the anticonformer changes in order to disagree. The independent person differs from both the conformer and the anticonformer by evaluating the stimulus independently of the group norm; that is, the norm is not given any weight at all in the judgment of the truly independent person.

It is clear that conformity and nonconformity cannot be satisfactorily conceptualized if analysis is restricted to the phenotypic level; responses that are phenotypically identical may nevertheless reveal themselves, on closer examination, to be dramatically different. A person's public and private responses to a social norm (Allen, 1965) must therefore be clearly distinguished. A combination of these responses yields four different categories of behavior: (1) public conformity and a consistent private response; (2) public conformity and an inconsistent private response; (3) public nonconformity and a consistent private response; and (4) public nonconformity and an inconsistent private response. Thus, ostensibly identical public conformity responses may actually reflect very different psychological states. The same is true of public nonconformity. It is clear, then, that responses that seem to be identical on the surface are, in fact, extremely different in their meaning and in their consequences for future behavior. For example, the accuracy of a prediction about future behavior would depend on whether the observed public agreement with a norm reflects a true change in the person's private position as well.

To what extent is social conformity due to personality-dispositional factors as opposed to situational-environmental factors? This question has been one of the central concerns of research on conformity. Early research found a large number of personality characteristics that correlated significantly with conformity. In the Asch type of situation, high conformers were revealed as possessing personality traits such as low self-esteem, low intelligence, lack of confidence, low ego strength, conventional attitudes, and high need for approval (Crowne and Marlowe, 1964; Crutchfield, 1955), which seemed to indicate "neurotic" tendencies. In contrast, later studies failed to obtain significant correlations between high conformity and scales from the Minnesota Multiphasic Personality Inventory (MMPI) and the California Psychological Inventory (CPI) (Barocas and Gorlow, 1967; Barron, 1953). It seems fair to say that a firm and simple conclusion concerning the personality correlates of conformity is not possible in view of such conflicting and ambiguous research findings (Berg and Bass, 1961; Mann, 1959).

When an individual's conformity across situations is examined, only a limited degree of generality or consistency seems to exist (Vaughan, 1964). Some persons exhibit high or low conformity across different types of situations, but the behavior of most persons is relatively situation specific. Therefore, it would not be congruent with empirical knowledge to describe an individual as having a "conformist" or a "nonconformist" personality. More accurately, an individual can be designated as a high or low conformer in a given situation. Situational variables resulting in high conformity include such conditions as attractiveness and cohesiveness of the group, unanimity of the group members' responses, similarity between the individual and group members, competence of the individual, and ambiguity and difficulty of the task (Allen, 1965). In the presence of any one of these variables, some persons conform more than others, indicating that dispositional (personality) factors are important in accounting for individual differences in a particular situation. In sum, the most reasonable way to interpret social conformity is to view it as the joint outcome of personality and the situation: conformity depends on the interaction between personality and situational factors. This conception suggests that social conformity is a complex phenomenon in which both personality and the situation always play important causative roles, but not in a simple and invariant way.

Comparative Philosophies and Theories

Social conformity has been subjected to a variety of detailed theoretical analyses; these theories can be classified into four broad categories. First, cognitive theories emphasize the essentially rational and problem-solving nature of conforming behavior (Asch, 1952). Faced with a conflict between one's own perception or belief and the position espoused by a group, an individual attempts to resolve this conflict in the most reasonable way possible under the circumstances. From the vantage point of the individual exposed to group pressure, conformity may be perceived as a rational and intelligent solution to a cognitive dilemma. Objective methods do not exist for determining the "correctness" or "incorrectness" of subjective matters pertaining to behavior, opinions, and the like; consequently, the "correctness" of a response must be based on the behavior of other persons. Only by relying on cues in the form of the behavior of others can one ascertain the nature of "social reality" (Festinger, 1954).

Second, functional or instrumental theories have been proposed to explain conformity (Walker and Heyns, 1962). These theories view conformity as the means by which an individual tries to attain a desired goal. The nature of the goal being served by conforming behavior may be task related, interpersonal, or even intrapersonal. These theories, then, focus investigation on the functions of conforming behavior or the role of conformity in mediating other end states. Explanations of social conformity based on personality dynamics can also be seen as a special case of functional or instrumental theories. For instance, one psychodynamic theory of compulsive conformity posits that conformity serves as a defense mechanism (Hoffman, 1957).

A third set of theories employs terminology from learning theory (reinforcement and conditioning). When facing social pressure, a person receives positive social reinforcement for complying to the group's norm and negative reinforcement for not complying. Also, a person's current conformity can be explained by his childhood training; through the mechanisms of either classical or operant conditioning, conformity or nonconformity could have been learned during socialization.

Finally, social exchange theories have been applied to the problem of social conformity (Nord, 1969). Exchange theory derives from economics and utilizes concepts such as reward, cost, supply, and demand as determinants of behavioral outcomes. This framework is closely related, of course, to reinforcement theories. One advantage of social exchange theory lies in its dynamic conceptualization of the individual-group relationship, which requires an analysis of the cost-reward outcomes for both parties to the interaction. The theory is highly abstract, however, and a complex set of social behaviors cannot always be cast into the restrictive mold of economic man.

Elaboration on Critical Points

An individual faces social pressures to conform not just to a single norm but to many norms. The existence of multiple norms usually creates a condition of less than complete consistency or agreement among some of them; hence, an individual frequently is faced with conflicting pressures that are very difficult to resolve. Such pressures often take the form of conflict between one set of norms held by a face-to-face group and another set of norms held by a group whose members are not present. In such cases, nonconformity to the physically present group may actually represent conformity to the norms of the absent group—that is, the person is merely marching to a distant drummer.

Further complicating the social conformity situation is the fact that a person's perception of a norm may not be completely veridical. Inconsistency between the norm as sent by group members and as perceived by the individual may result, for example, in an individual believing that he is conforming to the norm whereas group members perceive the same behavior as nonconforming. Because of the ambiguity of many social situations, such erroneous perception of norms (pseudonorms) is not uncommon.

In considerations of social conformity, the temporal dimension is critical. Conformity or nonconformity is certainly not an ahistorical event; that is to say, any behavior has consequences for the individual and the group. Thus, attempts to make an individual conform are more successful if that person had earlier conformed to a group norm (Hollander, 1960). Along the same line, the style of one's behavior over time has important consequences. Thus, consistent and repeated disagreement by a minority can cause the group majority to change its responses toward the dissenters' position (Moscovici, 1976).

Discussions of social conformity frequently imply that it is a categorical, all-or-none, phenomenon—that one either conforms or does not conform to the social norm. The concepts of conformity and nonconformity may give the impression that the behaviors in question are distinct and qualitatively different and that behavior can only be in either complete agreement or disagreement with the norm. It is important to correct this misconception by emphasizing that conformity can almost always be expressed quantitatively in terms of the distance of a person's behavior from the position demanded by the group. In the event of a discrepancy between a norm and a person's own preferred behavior, the most frequent resolution of the conflict is to compromise—to move part of the total distance toward the group norm, but not the entire distance (Allen, 1965). Thus, it must be kept in mind that social conformity can and usually does vary in a quantitative manner.

Personal Views and Recommendations

In our society social conformity has acquired a negative connotation and is often contrasted unfavorably with more desirable and socially approved behaviors (such as independence or creativity). For many persons the term *social conformity* implies a slavish submission to other persons or an insincere expression of attitudes. It is true that many psychological studies have been designed in such a way that conformity is maladaptive, in the sense of being factually incorrect, dishonest, or detrimental to the group's attempt to achieve its goal. But a one-sided evaluation of the negative aspects of social conformity is a greatly oversimplified interpretation of a complex phenomenon. Conformity to social norms frequently improves the functioning of a group or social system in terms of both goal attainment and smoother interpersonal relations. Moreover, in factual or objective matters the consensus of several persons may be more truthful than the views of a single individual; and, in the social area, being overly individualistic and resistant to social norms is often inappropriate and maladaptive. In short, in certain situations conformity is an entirely constructive and appropriate response; yet in many other situations the obverse is true. Conformity or nonconformity must not be evaluated simply in a generally negative or positive way; any assessment should take into account the specific circumstances facing the individual at the time, and the likely consequences of the behavior for the individual, the social group, and the social system.

Although pressures to conform are often passive and indirect, ethical problems regarding control of another person's behavior are the same as in more direct and coercive control procedures (Milgram, 1956). Ethical issues involved in changing behavior by conformity pressure are particularly critical if the individual whose behavior is being affected is not aware that the process is taking place. Subtle conformity pressure from group members is often employed by professionals as a technique for influencing behavior in sensitivity groups (Back, 1972) and other group-oriented treatment programs. Even though social influence is diffused across all group members (rather than concentrated in the person of the professional in charge), serious ethical issues still exist when conformity pressure is intentionally mobilized to influence another person (Sampson and Marthas, 1977). Another ethical issue concerns the tendency to assess the adjustment of another person in terms of conformity to, or deviation from, one's own norms. Because norms may differ dramatically across various subgroups within society, one should proceed very cautiously in evaluating the normalcy or deviancy of another person's behavior.

In terms of needed research, more attention should be directed to two important themes: (1) the antecedents and consequences of nonconformity (see Allen, 1975) and (2) the influence of an individual on the group (see Moscovici, 1976).

Application to Particular Variables

Age. Research findings on the relation between conformity and age have not shown complete agreement. Some studies report a curvilinear relation, with conformity being higher in middle childhood than at younger and older ages (Hartup, 1970). Most available research indicates, however, that the level of conformity to unanimous peer groups and to adult norms decreases as age increases (Allen and Newtson, 1972). The small amount of available research with samples of elderly persons suggests a higher level of conformity in comparison with middle-aged persons, but there are serious methodological problems in these studies.

Sex. Most discussions of conformity claim that females conform more than males. The nature of the female sex role (with stress on submissiveness and docility) has been offered as an explanation. In contrast to this popular view, a recent literature survey reached a different conclusion (Eagly, 1978). A review of fifty-four conformity studies showed no sex differences in 62 percent of them; females conformed more than males in 35 percent; and males conformed more than females in 32 percent of the studies. Thus, a lack of difference between males and females is the most common finding. Furthermore, recent research has demonstrated that either males or females may exhibit higher conformity, depending on whether the task is more familiar and involving to members of one sex than the other (Sistrunk and McDavid, 1971).

Education. There has been little research dealing with the effect of education on conformity. Education does, of course, highly overlap with socioeconomic status and intelligence, on which more research has been conducted. Available findings suggest that more highly educated persons are less conforming (Tuddenham, 1959).

Socioeconomic Status. Few behavioral studies have examined the relation between socioeconomic status and conformity. On the basis of questionnaire data, it has been found consistently that persons of lower socioeconomic status strongly endorse values that reflect high conformity as opposed to individualistic behavior (Kohn, 1969). The available behavioral studies tend to show that persons of lower socioeconomic status are more conforming in general and that greater conformity is exhibited when social pressure emanates from persons of higher status (Lefkowitz, Blake, and Mouton, 1955; Tuddenham, 1959).

Vocation. Research relevant to this variable is not available, though the close relation between occupation and socioeconomic status would enable one to make fairly accurate predictions concerning expected level of conformity for various vocational categories.

Ethnic/Racial Factors. A few studies have addressed racial differences in social conformity, but ethnic differences have not been investigated. One study failed to find any general difference in level of conformity for blacks and whites, but differences did appear depending on the similarity between an individual's race and the race of the group (Schneider, 1970). With this factor as well as the others covered in this section, the composition of the social pressure group should always be taken into consideration. As mentioned in an earlier section, conformity cannot be understood satisfactorily without taking into account the characteristics of the person and of the group exerting the social pressure.

Mental and Physical Factors. Almost no information is available concerning the relation between physical disorders and conformity. The only relevant study compared the conformity of paraplegics and normals in response to group pressure from either a group of paraplegics or a group of normals (Linde and Patterson, 1964). Results showed higher conformity when the group was homogeneous (all disabled or all able-bodied) than when an individual differed from the pressure group. As for the relation between intelligence and conformity, several studies found that highly intelligent persons tend to show lower conformity than less intelligent persons do (Crutchfield, 1955; Tuddenham, 1959). It appears that schizophrenics (Spohn, 1956) and persons suffering from other psychiatric disorders are less susceptible to social norms (Levine and others, 1954). But these results might also be due to the inaccurate perception of the social norm by the subjects.

Collective/Interactional Factors. Direct data are not available for this category. Research on riots and crowd behavior indicates that social norms tend to emerge in collective situations, and it has been suggested that the homogeneity of behavior in a crowd may be due to adherence to these norms (Turner, 1964).

References

Allen, V. L. "Situational Factors in Conformity." In L. Berkowitz (Ed.), *Advances in Experimental Social Psychology*. Vol. 2. New York: Academic Press, 1965.

Allen, V. L. "Social Support for Nonconformity." In L. Berkowitz (Ed.), *Advances in Experimental Social Psychology*. Vol. 8. New York: Academic Press, 1975.

Allen, V. L., and Newtson, D. "Development of Conformity and Independence." *Journal of Personality and Social Psychology*, 1972, *22*, 18-30.

Allport, F. H. "The Influence of the Group upon Association and Thought." *Journal of Experimental Psychology*, 1920, *3*, 159-182.

Asch, S. E. "Effects of Group Pressure upon the Modification and Distortion of Judgment." In H. Guetzkow (Ed.), *Groups, Leadership, and Men*. Pittsburgh: Carnegie Press, 1951.

Asch, S. E. *Social Psychology*. Englewood Cliffs, N.J.: Prentice-Hall, 1952.

Asch, S. E. "Studies of Independence and Conformity. A Minority of One Against a Unanimous Majority." *Psychological Monographs*, 1956, *70*, No. 9 (Whole No. 416).

Back, K. W. *Beyond Words: The Story of Sensitivity Training and the Encounter Movement*. New York: Russell Sage Foundation, 1972.

Barocas, R., and Gorlow, R. "Self-Report Personality Measurement and Conformity Behavior." *Journal of Social Psychology*, 1967, *71*, 227-234.

Barron, F. "Some Personality Correlates of Independence of Judgment." *Journal of Personality*, 1953, *21*, 287-297.

Berg, I. A., and Bass, B. M. (Eds.). *Conformity and Deviation*. New York: Harper & Row, 1961.

Cooley, C. H. *Human Nature and the Social Order*. New York: Scribner's, 1902.

Crowne, D. R., and Marlowe, D. *The Approval Motive*. New York: Wiley, 1964.

Crutchfield, R. S. "Conformity and Character." *American Psychologist*, 1955, *10*, 191-198.

Eagly, A. H. "Sex Differences in Influenceability." *Psychological Bulletin*, 1978, *85*, 86-116.

Festinger, L. "A Theory of Social Comparison Processes." *Human Relations*, 1954, *7*, 117-140.

Hartup, W. W. "Peer Interaction and Social Organization." In P. H. Mussen (Ed.), *Carmichael's Manual of Child Psychology*. Vol. 2. New York: Wiley, 1970.

Hoffman, M. L. "Conformity as a Defense Mechanism and a Form of Resistance to Genuine Group Influence." *Journal of Personality*, 1957, *25*, 412-424.

Hollander, E. P. "Competence and Conformity in the Acceptance of Influence." *Journal of Abnormal and Social Psychology,* 1960, *61,* 361-365.

Kohn, M. L. *Class and Conformity.* Homewood, Ill.: Dorsey Press, 1969.

Le Bon, G. *Psychologie des Foules.* Paris: Oléon, 1895.

Lefkowitz, M., Blake, R. R., and Mouton, J. S. "Status Factors in Pedestrian Violation of Traffic Signals." *Journal of Abnormal and Social Psychology,* 1955, *51,* 704-706.

Levine, J., and others. "Conforming Behavior of Psychiatric and Medical Patients." *Journal of Abnormal and Social Psychology,* 1954, *49,* 251-255.

Linde, T. F., and Patterson, C. H. "Influence of Orthopedic Disability on Conforming Behavior." *Journal of Abnormal and Social Psychology,* 1964, *68,* 115-118.

Mann, R. D. "A Review of the Relationships Between Personality and Performance in Small Groups." *Psychological Bulletin,* 1959, *56,* 241-270.

Milgram, S. "Some Conditions of Obedience and Disobedience to Authority." *Human Relations,* 1956, *18,* 57-75.

Mill, J. S. *On Liberty* [1859]. New York: Appleton-Century-Crofts, 1947.

Moore, H. T. "The Comparative Influence of Majority and Expert Opinion." *American Journal of Psychology,* 1921, *32,* 16-20.

Moscovici, S. *Social Influence and Social Change.* New York: Academic Press, 1976.

Newcomb, T. M. *Personality and Social Change: Attitude Formation in a Student Community.* New York: Dryden, 1943.

Nord, W. R. "Social Exchange Theory: An Integrative Approach to Social Conformity." *Psychological Bulletin,* 1969, *71,* 174-208.

Riesman, D., Glazer, N., and Denny, R. *The Lonely Crowd: A Study of the Changing American Character.* New Haven, Conn.: Yale University Press, 1950.

Sampson, E. E., and Marthas, M. S. *Group Process for the Health Professions.* New York: Wiley, 1977.

Schachter, S. "Deviation, Rejection, and Communication." *Journal of Abnormal and Social Psychology,* 1951, *46,* 190-207.

Schneider, F. W. "Conforming Behavior of Black and White Children." *Journal of Personality and Social Psychology,* 1970, *16,* 466-471.

Sherif, M. *The Psychology of Social Norms.* New York: Harper & Row, 1936.

Sistrunk, F., and McDavid, J. W. "Sex Variable in Conforming Behavior." *Journal of Personality and Social Psychology,* 1971, *17,* 200-207.

Spohn, H. E. "The Effect of Group Norms upon Perception in Chronic Schizophrenic Patients." *American Psychologist,* 1956, *11,* 366. (Abstract.)

Sumner, W. G. *Folkways.* New York: Ginn, 1906.

Tarde, G. *The Laws of Imitation* [1890]. New York: Holt, Rinehart and Winston, 1903.

Tuddenham, R. D. "Correlates of Yielding to a Distorted Group Norm." *Journal of Personality,* 1959, *27,* 272-284.

Turner, R. H. "Collective Behavior." In R. E. L. Faris (Ed.), *Handbook of Modern Sociology.* Chicago: Rand McNally, 1964.

Vaughan, G. M. "The Trans-situational Aspect of Conformity Behavior." *Journal of Personality,* 1964, *32,* 335-354.

Walker, W. L., and Heyns, R. W. *An Anatomy for Conformity.* Englewood Cliffs, N.J.: Prentice-Hall, 1962.

Whyte, W. J., Jr. *The Organization Man.* New York: Simon and Schuster, 1957.

Willis, R. H. "Two Dimensions of Conformity-Nonconformity." *Sociometry,* 1963, *26,* 499-513.

79

Aprile M. Holland
John B. Miner

Leadership
Potentials

The effective functioning of any group appears to depend on the presence of leadership ability within the group. The assessment of leadership potential involves evaluating an individual's possible, latent, or perhaps undeveloped capabilities for leadership. To define leadership potential, it is necessary to first understand the concept of leadership. There is, however, no single universal definition. Stogdill (1974) has provided a broad overview of the various definitions and conceptions of the term as well as suggesting one of his own: "the process of influencing group activities toward goal setting and goal achievement" (Stogdill, 1948, p. 35). Fiedler and Chemers (1974, p. 4) have identified two common threads running through many of the proposed definitions: (1) "leadership is a relationship between people in which influence and power are unevenly distributed on a legitimate base" and (2) "There can be no leaders in isolation. . . . Followers must explicitly or implicitly consent to their part in this influence relationship." Vroom and Yetton (1973) have suggested that decision sharing is a manifestation of leadership and have developed a normative theory around this specific facet (Vroom, 1976).

Miner has recommended a reconceptualization of the concept of leadership through a broadly defined control concept. In his initial statements (Miner, 1975b) and subsequently, he suggests a classification of control or inducement systems as follows:

Administrative/Hierarchic—a system characterized by an assumed hierarchy or scale of authority, appropriate managerial style reflective of the concept of initiating structure, and motivation by the desire to manage (Miner, 1974b).

Professional/Ideological—A system relying on the values, norms, ethical precepts, codes, and so on of the professional reference group. The appropriate managerial style emphasizes the use of expert power, expertise, and professional accomplishment. The motivational base may vary somewhat depending on the nature of the profession; for example, Miner (1971b) found a motivational base of eliteness among professionals in a large consulting firm. However, acquiring knowledge, acting independently, accepting status, providing help, and being professionally committed are generally important.

Group—A system in which control is exercised through group pressure. The appropriate managerial style is highly reflective of consideration and emphasizes concern for people or employee-centered approaches. The primary motivational base is the need to conform and leads to increased responsiveness of any "leader" to the desires of the group.

Task—A system in which the pushes and pulls of sanctions are built into the task to be performed and thus into the work itself. The motivating force in this system appears to be that of achievement (McClelland and Winter, 1969). The entrepreneurial roles are apt examples of effective task control or task inducement systems.

This classification suggests that different types of leadership (managerial) styles or behaviors are appropriate and effective in the different inducement systems. Thus, the specific composition of leadership potential would differ across the four systems.

Campbell and associates (1970, p. 1) have indicated the importance of "effective direction of human efforts" within our industrial society. This idea seems to reflect many of the conceptions and thoughts as to what makes up leadership in any group setting. Drawing upon these various definitions we may conclude that the assessment of leadership potential involves an evaluation of an individual's capabilities in several key areas: (1) in the area of perception and adherence to a set of role behaviors or role prescriptions of the "leader" in a specific situation (see Miner, 1965, 1974b, 1977); (2) in the area of influencing and persuading others on certain critical issues relating to group functioning (see Stogdill, 1948); (3) in the area of selecting the appropriate degree of decision sharing and participation (see Vroom, 1976; Vroom and Yetton, 1973).

Historically and to a large extent currently, various theoretical bases for this evaluation process have been adopted. Most of these may be classified into two extreme schools of thought. The trait approach suggests the evaluation of individuals' personal characteristics as the basis for identification of leadership potential. Much of the research in this area deals with physical or constitutional factors, intelligence, or personality (Gibb, 1954). In addition, various attempts at observing and ultimately describing the behavioral characteristics of leaders have been made. In this view, the leader's behavior becomes essentially a personal characteristic. The other extreme, the situational approach, emphasizes the situation as determining any individual's ability to perform as a leader. Research in this area examines mainly the dimension of the situation and uses this information to describe the leadership process. The current state of knowledge concerning leadership characteristics and situational contexts is stated by Stogdill (1974, pp. 72, 82): "The view that leadership is entirely situational in origin and that no personal characteristics are predictive of leadership . . . seems to overemphasize the situational and underemphasize the personal nature of leadership. Strong evidence indicates that different leadership skills and traits are required in different situations. . . . The *trait approach* tended to treat personality variables in an atomistic fashion, suggesting that each trait acted singly to determine leadership effects. The *situationist approach,* on the other hand, denied the influences of individual differences, attributing all variance between persons to fortuitous demands of the environment." Many additional writers believe that the characteristics and overt behaviors of effective leaders vary across situations (Campbell and others, 1970; Fiedler and Chemers, 1974; Harrell, 1961; Piotrowski and Rock, 1963; Vroom, 1976; Vroom and Yetton, 1973). Accordingly, in one sense or another, all are espousing the viewpoint that contingency is a major factor in shaping leadership behavior.

Background and Current Status

The assessment of leadership potential, initially a primarily subjective process utilizing relatively simple and unvalidated devices, has evolved currently to a quite sophisticated state. The present evaluation of leadership potential involves the use of more objective information and more thoroughly validated devices. These devices tend to be much more sophisticated as they aim to evaluate the multidimensionality of individuals.

The identification of leadership potential within specific situational contexts has evolved from a very fragmented approach to the role of contingency to current methods using a limited-domain concept. The limited-domain approach involves an identification of leadership potential within an area or particular situation constrained by a number of boundary criteria. These criteria deal with such considerations as motivation, decision-making practices, communication networks, and power or influence relations which specify the domain within which the theory applies. Role prescriptions within each limited area or situation are converted to the dimensions of evaluation and are assessed through a variety of devices to identify the specifically desired leadership capabilities.

While the dimension under consideration may vary across situations, a number of measurement techniques are used in varying degree to identify leadership potential within the four domains. To aid in the review of the use of such instruments and techniques, a categorization of the commonly used devices has been developed. While this categorization allows for some overlap in the classification of techniques, the explanation of each category should clarify the basis for inclusion in each.

"Trait" measures include instruments or techniques used to describe specific personal characteristics of individuals, as well as their overt behavior. This category has been subdivided into two subclasses: (1) self-descriptions *by* the individual and (2) descriptions *of* the individual by others. *Measures of abilities, aptitudes, and interests* include instruments and techniques designed to assess the specific abilities, skills, predispositions, interests, and potential for learning of individuals. *Projective techniques* consist of loosely structured stimuli for which responses are interpreted to develop a descriptive analysis of the individual. *Measures of attitudes and values* include instruments to identify specific predispositions of individuals toward specific issues or objects. *Situational or simulated task techniques* are a more recently developed class of techniques and are included as a separate category due to their proven contribution to the identification and evaluation of important leadership dimensions (Hinrichs, 1969).

The use of the schema presented in Table 1 for the assessment of leadership potential has many contemporary implications. Managerial shortages have been discussed by a number of writers (Campbell and others, 1970; Miner, 1974b). The identification of

Table 1. Situational Contexts

Assessment Devices	Task	Group	Professional/ Ideological	Hierarchical/ Administrative
"Trait" measures				
(a) Self-Description	*	*	*	*
(b) Description of others		*		*
Measures of abilities, aptitudes,				
interests	*	*		*
Projective techniques	*	*		*
Measures of attitudes/values	*	*	*	*
Situational or simulated task exercises		*		*

*Denotes use of specific device in particular situations.

leadership potential and the development of such capabilities are of critical importance in all types of organizations (Mahoney, Jerdee, and Nash, 1960). Through classification of an organization or an organizational component into one of the four control or inducement systems, a simpler examination of the various techniques appropriate for use in the identification of leadership potential can be made. Equally important to organizations are the Equal Employment Opportunity (EEO) Guidelines affecting them. Using validated techniques in making selection and/or promotion decisions is often necessary for compliance with EEO regulations. Selection of appropriate assessment devices, validation studies, and the use of appropriate experimental designs hopefully can be facilitated through the categorization presented herein. The danger of using techniques in selection or promotion which lack job relatedness has been amply demonstrated in numerous court decisions. The aforementioned issues emphasize the need for adequate and valid assessment of leadership potential.

Critical Discussion

Comparative Philosophies and Theories

Since a situation or type of organization categorization has been suggested, it seems appropriate to review the use of psychological instruments and other assessment devices within each, utilizing the previously presented classification for assessment devices (Miner, 1975b and Table 1). This will allow a comparison of the uses of the various techniques in specific situational contexts. Since the greatest amount of research has been conducted in the hierarchic/administrative situation, this will be the major emphasis and point of departure.

Elaboration on Critical Points

Trait measures utilized in the hierarchic area are numerous and varied. One of the more traditional of the self-description measures is a structured interview, which is generally viewed with considerable suspicion and distrust by industrial psychologists (Ghiselli, 1966). The use of application blanks or biographical forms also provides background data for use in evaluation of potential. Owens (1976, p. 609) states: "The importance of background data as an aid to . . . prediction . . . is enormous."

Another well-known self-description trait measure is the Self-Description Inventory (SDI) developed by Ghiselli (1954). The SDI utilizes a forced-choice technique with personality descriptive adjectives and assesses thirteen traits (Ghiselli, 1971). Ghiselli

(1971, p. 108) has concluded that "the general properties of managerial talent are a restrained democratic leadership, a creative and effective intelligence, a faith in one's own self and a desire for achievement." Traits similar to these have been reported elsewhere (Bray, Campbell, and Grant, 1974; Ghiselli, 1963, 1968; Miner, 1976b). The Miner Sentence Completion Scale (MSCS) (Miner, 1974b) has been shown to be related to managerial performance in hierarchic organizations. The MSCS has been described as a projective measure (Miner, 1976b) but is included under the rubric of trait measures due to its assessment of an individual's motivation to manage through its seven subscales. Research support of the validity of the MSCS measures as indexes of managerial talent in large, hierarchic business organizations has been established with some consistency (Miner, 1965, 1977).

The F Scale (Adorno and others, 1950) has been utilized for many years as a measure of authoritarianism and has tended to establish itself as a prototype measure of this trait (Vroom, 1960). Gough's (1957) California Psychological Inventory is an untimed questionnaire regarding habits and specific attitudes, with scores being obtained for some thirteen scales. The use of the CPI as a personality trait measure is well documented (Gough, 1976). The Leadership Opinion Questionnaire (Fleishman, 1957b) is a self-descriptive questionnaire administered to leaders to obtain indications of how they think they should behave. An additional self-descriptive trait measure is the Least Preferred Co-worker (LPC) Scale developed by Fiedler (1967). The LPC appears to be at least in part an index of a motivational hierarchy, with the choice behaviors reflecting the hierarchic arrangement of goals. The LPC measure has been used extensively in research in hierarchic situations and particularly to test Fiedler's contingency theory of leadership effectiveness (Sample and Wilson, 1965; Fiedler, 1967, 1971a, 1971b, 1972; Hunt, 1967; Hill, 1969; Mitchell, 1970; Chemers and Skrzypek, 1972; Sashkin, 1972; Tumes, 1972).

Trait descriptions of individuals by others include a variety of types of devices. Peer nominations (Hollander, 1957; Prien and Liske, 1962; Nelson, 1964; Miner, 1974a) have been used a great deal, as have descriptions of individuals by superiors and subordinates. These types of ratings appear to provide a great deal of valuable information (Springer, 1953; Prien and Liske, 1962; Roadman, 1964; Miner, 1974a); so too does the Leader Behavior Description Questionnaire (LBDQ) (Fleishman, 1957a; Hemphill and Coons, 1957). Subordinates are given the LBDQ questionnaire and are asked to describe the behavior of their superior. This instrument, similar to the self-descriptive LOQ, yields scores on the dimensions of initiating structure and consideration.

Aptitude and ability measures utilized in the hierarchic situation have been thoroughly reviewed by Dunnette (1976) and are inclusive of the various paper-and-pencil intelligence and ability tests. Interest measures used include the Strong Vocational Interest Blank (Nash, 1965) and the Kuder Preference Record, as well as additional inventories. Relevant research in this area has been extensively reviewed by Holland (1976).

Projective techniques are "instruments to which responses are provided to an ambiguous or loosely defined stimulus" (Finkle, 1976, p. 863). Subsequently, interpretations are made to yield a descriptive analysis of the individual. The Rorschach technique has been adapted through the development of a perceptanalytic executive scale (Piotrowski and Rock, 1963) for use in the hierarchic area. A variety of projective techniques are used in assessment centers, and the contributions of these techniques to the assessment of management potential is reviewed by Bray, Grant, and Katkovsky (1967). The Thematic Apperception Test (TAT) has been used exclusively in McClelland's study of achievement and power motivation among managers (McClelland, 1961; McClelland and Winter, 1969).

Attitude/value measures utilized within a hierarchic setting include the Allport-Vernon-Lindzey Study of Values, Gordon's Survey of Interpersonal Values, and most recently the Personal Value Questionnaire (PVQ) (England, 1968, 1975). These value and attitude measures have formed the basis of a great deal of research (Guth and Tagiuri, 1965; England, 1968; England and Keaveny, 1969; Sikula, 1971; Lusk and Oliver, 1974). Additional attitudinal measures are presented by Robinson and Shaver (1973).

The use of situational or simulated task exercises has been brought to the forefront through their use in management assessment centers (Bray, Campbell, and Grant, 1974). This category includes the use of in-basket exercises and leaderless group situations (Bass, Klubeck, and Werster, 1953). Meyer (1970) has examined the validity of the in-basket approach, and Hinrichs (1969) has compared the situational exercises and other assessment center procedures to "real-life" assessments of managerial potential. Finkle (1976) has presented a thorough coverage of the managerial assessment centers and gives considerable attention to the use of the situational exercises. Wollowick and McNamara (1969) have examined the relationship of the various components utilized in assessment centers to management success. MacKinnon's (1975) overview of assessment centers provides a thorough coverage of all procedures and specific characteristics of the techniques.

In the professional/ideological category, research on and use of special measures is notably lacking. However, certain applications of some specific procedures can be cited. Buel, Albright, and Glennon (1966) have studied the use of the personal history as a means of identifying creative research scientists. Lacey (1974) has noted the discriminability of the MSCS among supervisory and nonsupervisory scientists and engineers. Miner (1970a, 1970b, 1971a) has examined the use of personality tests, psychological evaluations, and interviews as predictive of success in consulting organizations. The evidence has suggested that psychological evaluations and interviews often "contribute little toward predictive efficiency" (Miner, 1971a, p. 191). Miner (1976a) has also examined industrial relations managers with the MSCS and suggests that while that instrument is applicable to the identification of managerial potential in this area, a professional model or instrument oriented toward other motivational bases might be equally applicable. Tagiuri (1965) has reported the use of the Allport-Vernon-Lindzey Study of Values with research managers, executives, and industrial scientists; he has noted both similarities and differences among the three groups.

In the group category, the major concern is with situations involving cohesive groups with stable memberships and to a large extent the potential of an individual as an "emergent leader." Stogdill (1974) has covered the emergence of leadership in this context. He cites the use of a variety of observational techniques which may be likened to the category of situational exercises. These include the sociometric method for determining interpersonal preference structure among group members (yielding results similar in certain respects to those from the LBDQ), peer evaluations, specific ability and aptitude assessment, and a variety of personality assessment devices. Stogdill (1974) also notes the impact of norms and reference groups in emergent leadership and cites the use of a variety of attitudinal instruments. In summary, all categories of assessment devices have been utilized in the identification of emergent leader potential, but due to the wide variety of factors involved it would appear that all dimensions of the individual must be tapped for proper assessment; thus, the utilization of the entire spectrum of devices may be warranted.

The task categorization is most readily visible in the area of entrepreneurship. While the amount of research in this area has not been great historically, the importance of this sector has been realized, and numerous research efforts in this area are in progress.

The work of Collins, Moore, and Unwalla (1964) illustrates the use of several categories of assessment devices. They utilized projective techniques, the TAT, and in-depth interviews in their research, as well as specific attitude and value assessments of the entrepreneur. The results of this research, along with that of Smith (1967), Wainer and Rubin (1969), Hornaday and Bunker (1970), Hornaday and Aboud (1971), and Hines (1973), emphasize the critical difference between the entrepreneur and the "business hierarch." The use of the TAT and other projective techniques, along with interest inventories, interviews, and value questionnaires, reflects the application of a broad range of assessment devices, though situational exercises have not been used.

Personal Views and Recommendations

This review provides support for two strongly felt views. First, it is readily apparent that the dimensions of importance for leadership in one situational context are or can be vastly different from those important in another context. For this reason, it is recommended that a limited-domain approach be adopted for both research and practice within the area of assessment of leadership potential. Second, considerable research and relevant literature support the conclusion that no one single factor, be it trait or situation, can fully explain the leadership process. In addition, the widely differing role prescriptions for leaders in the various situational contexts, as well as the complexity of the leadership process in general, leads to the following recommendation: Individuals are multidimensional. It is therefore imperative that multiple assessment devices be utilized to adequately tap the relevant dimensions. Specific dimensions to be tapped, however, are a function of the situation and the position.

Implications for training and certification fall in essentially three areas. First, the matter of assessor training points up the need for intensive training programs for interviewers, assessment center assessors, and all personnel involved in an assessment procedure of any type. The formalization of such training on a broad scale could serve to improve the overall level of assessments of leadership potential. Second, training in interpretation can aid in the use of various devices. More emphasis on training in this area of interpretation, especially of projective techniques and situational exercises, as well as selection interviews, should be forthcoming. Third is the need for validation training. The necessity for validation of any and all assessment devices, as suggested by the American Psychological Association (1974), should provide the impetus for training in the design and execution of such studies. The execution of well-conducted validation studies could aid in identifying the relevant devices and yield better predictions of leadership potential in specific situational contexts. The end result of such improvements in predictive effectiveness would be the better functioning that is the primary goal of all groups.

Application to Particular Variables

It is of major concern in the evaluation of leadership potential to note the validity of techniques in various populations. The relationship of age to leadership appears to be rather complicated. Stogdill (1974, p. 76) notes that outstanding achievements of individuals in the professional and task categories occur at relatively early ages. Stogdill's review of corporate executives emphasizes the dependence on knowledge and proven ability that comes only through experience in that particular situational context.

With respect to sex, the assessment center technique, which incorporates sampling from all categories of assessment devices, has been shown to be equally valid for females and for males (Moses and Boehm, 1975). Moses and Boehm found the same dimensions important to managerial success in females as were found in males. Miner has examined various samples of women in conjunction with the testing of the MSCS and has found a somewhat lower motivation to manage among female college students. However, among school administrators and department store managers, males and females do not differ in overall score level, and validity coefficients against success criteria are at the same levels as well (Miner, 1974c, 1977).

Regarding education, Stogdill (1974) has reported some fourteen references indicating positive relationships between education and leadership. In view of the increased educational attainment in our society, it might eventually be more difficult to discriminate between leaders and followers on this basis. General intelligence, although not necessarily a reflection of educational level attained, does appear to be a factor in leadership effectiveness in the hierarchic context (Ghiselli, 1971; Bray, Campbell, and Grant, 1974). The research in the area of entrepreneurial activity, however, has indicated a lower attained educational level (Collins, Moore, and Unwalla, 1964). The assessment center technique has proven its ability to identify potential both among college and noncollege graduates (Bray, Campbell, and Grant, 1974).

As for socioeconomic factors, Stogdill (1974) notes that there are certain specific conclusions to be drawn with reference to socioeconomic background and its association with leadership. First, "high socioeconomic status is an advantage in attaining leadership status"; second, "the leaders who rise to high-level positions in industry tend to come from lower socioeconomic strata at present than they did a half a century ago" (p. 72). Harrell (1961) has acknowledged the variability in traits across specific vocations or occupations, as well as between various levels within an organization. Mintzberg (1973) has also indicated that the roles assumed by managers may vary from level to level. This suggests the need for an in-depth job analysis, so that important dimensions of a particular leadership position can be identified.

With the pressure from EEO regulations, it is important to note the validity of various of the techniques across racial or ethnic lines. Since the assessment center technique incorporates all different types of devices, it seems appropriate to recognize the documented evidence of validity of the technique with members of both black and white racial groups (Huck and Bray, 1976), as well as the need for establishing the job relatedness of the various devices employed.

While the idiosyncratic characteristics of various personality disorders are not relevant to the topic of this chapter, the concept of disorders in general is. Leadership disorders manifest themselves in hierarchic, professional, group, and task situations as ineffective performance. Miner (1975a) and Miner and Brewer (1976) have presented an extensive coverage of the literature on the management of ineffective performance. Miner has designed managerial role motivation training to teach methods of dealing with such problems. While organizations must be cognizant of the impact of disorders which contribute to reduced leadership effectiveness, they also must consider the variety of methods for dealing with them as well as avoiding them through the use of more efficient and appropriate leadership potential assessment.

References

Adorno, T., and others. *The Authoritarian Personality*. New York: Harper & Row, 1950.

American Psychological Association. *Standards for Educational and Psychological Tests.* Washington, D.C.: American Psychological Association, 1974.

Bass, B. M., Klubeck, S., and Werster, C. R. "Factors Influencing the Reliability and

Validity of Leaderless Group Discussion Assessment." *Journal of Applied Psychology*, 1953, *37*, 26-30.

Bray, D. W., Campbell, R. J., and Grant, D. L. *Formative Years in Business: A Long-Term AT&T Study of Managerial Lives.* New York: Wiley, 1974.

Bray, D. W., Grant, D. L., and Katkovsky, W. "Contributions of Projective Techniques to the Assessment of Management Potential." *Journal of Applied Psychology*, 1967, *51*, 226-232.

Buel, W. D., Albright, L. E., and Glennon, J. R. "A Note on the Generality and Cross-Validity of Personal History for Identifying Creative Research Scientists." *Journal of Applied Psychology*, 1966, *50*, 217-219.

Campbell, J. P., and others. *Managerial Behavior, Performance, and Effectiveness.* New York: McGraw-Hill, 1970.

Chemers, M. M., and Skrzypek, G. J. "An Experimental Test of the Contingency Model of Leadership Effectiveness." *Journal of Personality and Social Psychology*, 1972, *24*, 172-177.

Collins, O. F., Moore, D. G., and Unwalla, D. B. *The Enterprising Man.* East Lansing: Graduate School of Business, Michigan State University, 1964.

Dunnette, M. D. "Aptitudes, Abilities, and Skills." In M. D. Dunnette (Ed.), *Handbook of Industrial and Organizational Psychology.* Chicago: Rand McNally, 1976.

England, G. W. "Personal Value Systems of American Managers." *Academy of Management Journal*, 1968, *10* (1), 53-68.

England, G. W. *The Manager and His Values: An International Perspective.* Cambridge, Mass.: Ballinger, 1975.

England, G. W., and Keaveny, T. J. "The Relationship of Managerial Values and Administrative Behavior." *Manpower and Applied Psychology*, 1969, *3* (1,2), 63-75.

Fiedler, F. E. *A Theory of Leadership Effectiveness.* New York: McGraw-Hill, 1967.

Fiedler, F. E. *Leadership.* New York: General Learning Press, 1971a.

Fiedler, F. E. "Validation and Extension of the Contingency Model of Leadership Effectiveness: A Review of the Empirical Findings." *Psychological Bulletin*, 1971b, *76*, 128-148.

Fiedler, F. E. "Personality, Motivational Systems, and Behavior of High and Low LPC Persons." *Human Relations*, 1972, *25*, 391-412.

Fiedler, F. E., and Chemers, M. M. *Leadership and Effective Management.* Glenview, Ill.: Scott, Foresman, 1974.

Finkle, R. B. "Managerial Assessment Centers." In M. D. Dunnette (Ed.), *Handbook of Industrial and Organizational Psychology.* Chicago: Rand McNally, 1976.

Fleishman, E. A. "A Leader Behavior Description for Industry." In R. M. Stogdill and A. E. Coons (Eds.), *Leader Behavior: Its Description and Measurement.* Research Monograph No. 88. Columbus: Bureau of Business Research, Ohio State University, 1957a.

Fleishman, E. A. "The Leadership Opinion Questionnaire." In R. M. Stogdill and A. E. Coons (Eds.), *Leader Behavior: Its Description and Measurement.* Research Monograph No. 88. Columbus: Bureau of Business Research, Ohio State University, 1957b.

Ghiselli, E. E. "The Forced-Choice Technique in Self-Description." *Personnel Psychology*, 1954, *7*, 201-208.

Ghiselli, E. E. "The Validity of Managerial Traits in Relation to Occupational Levels." *Personnel Psychology*, 1963, *16*, 109-113.

Ghiselli, E. E. "The Validity of the Personnel Interview." *Personnel Psychology*, 1966, *19*, 389-395.

Ghiselli, E. E. "Interaction of Traits and Motivational Factors in the Determination of Success of Managers." *Journal of Applied Psychology*, 1968, *52*, 480-483.

Ghiselli, E. E. *Explorations in Managerial Talent.* Pacific Palisades, Calif.: Goodyear, 1971.

Gibb, C. A. "Leadership." In G. Lindzey (Ed.), *Handbook of Social Psychology.* Vol. 2. Reading, Mass.: Addison-Wesley, 1954.

Gough, H. G. *Manual for the California Psychological Inventory.* Palo Alto, Calif.: Consulting Psychologists Press, 1957.

Gough, H. "Personality and Personality Assessment." In M. D. Dunnette (Ed.), *Handbook of Industrial and Organizational Psychology.* Chicago: Rand McNally, 1976.

Guth, W., and Tagiuri, R. "Personal Values and Corporate Strategies." *Harvard Business Review*, 1965, *43* (5), 123-132.

Harrell, T. W. *Managers' Performance and Personality.* Cincinnati: South-Western, 1961.

Hemphill, J. K., and Coons, A. E. "Development of the Leader Behavior Description Questionnaire." In R. M. Stogdill and A. E. Coons (Eds.), *Leader Behavior: Its Description and Measurement.* Research Monograph No. 88. Columbus: Bureau of Business Research, Ohio State University, 1957.

Hill, W. "The Validation and Extension of Fiedler's Theory of Leadership Effectiveness." *Academy of Management Journal*, 1969, *12* (1), 33-47.

Hines, G. H. "Achievement Motivation, Occupation, and Labor Turnover in New Zealand." *Journal of Applied Psychology*, 1973, *58* (3), 313-317.

Hinrichs, J. R. "Comparison of 'Real Life' Assessments of Management Potential with Situation Exercises, Paper-and-Pencil Ability Tests, and Personality Inventories." *Journal of Applied Psychology*, 1969, *53*, 425-432.

Holland, J. L. "Vocational Preferences." In M. D. Dunnette (Ed.), *Handbook of Industrial and Organizational Psychology.* Chicago: Rand McNally, 1976.

Hollander, E. P. "The Reliability of Peer Nominations Under Various Conditions of Administration." *Journal of Applied Psychology*, 1957, *41* (2), 85-90.

Hornaday, J. A., and Aboud, J. "Characteristics of Entrepreneurs." *Personnel Psychology*, 1971, *24*, 141-153.

Hornaday, J. A., and Bunker, C. S. "The Nature of the Entrepreneur." *Personnel Psychology*, 1970, *23*, 47-54.

Huck, J. R., and Bray, D. W. "Management Assessment Center Evaluations and Subsequent Job Performance of White and Black Females." *Personnel Psychology*, 1976, *29*, 13-30.

Hunt, J. G. "Fiedler's Leadership Contingency Model: An Empirical Test in Three Organizations." *Organizational Behavior and Human Performance*, 1967, *2*, 290-308.

Lacey, L. A. "Discriminability of the Miner Sentence Completion Scale Among Supervisory and Nonsupervisory Scientists and Engineers." *Academy of Management Journal*, 1974, *17*, 354-358.

Lusk, E. J., and Oliver, B. L. "American Managers' Personal Value Systems Revisited." *Academy of Management Journal*, 1974, *17*, 549-554.

McClelland, D. C. *The Achieving Society.* New York: D. Van Nostrand, 1961.

McClelland, D. C., and Winter, D. G. *Motivating Economic Achievement.* New York: Free Press, 1969.

MacKinnon, D. W. *An Overview of Assessment Centers.* Greensboro, N.C.: Center for Creative Leadership, 1975.

Mahoney, T. A., Jerdee, T. H., and Nash, A. N. "Predicting Managerial Effectiveness." *Personnel Psychology*, 1960, *13*, 147-163.

Meyer, H. H. "The Validity of the In-Basket Test as a Measure of Managerial Performance." *Personnel Psychology,* 1970, *23,* 297-307.

Miner, J. B. *Studies in Management Education.* Atlanta: Organizational Measurement Systems Press, 1965.

Miner, J. B. "Psychological Evaluations as Predictors of Consulting Success." *Personnel Psychology,* 1970a, *23,* 393-405.

Miner, J. B. "Executive and Personnel Interviews of Predictors of Consulting Success." *Personnel Psychology,* 1970b, *23,* 521-538.

Miner, J. B. "Personality Tests as Predictors of Consulting Success." *Personnel Psychology,* 1971a, *24,* 191-204.

Miner, J. B. "Success in Management Consulting and the Concept of Eliteness Motivation." *Academy of Management Journal,* 1971b, *14,* 367-378.

Miner, J. B. "Management Appraisal: A Review of Procedures and Practices." In W. C. Hamner and F. L. Schmidt (Eds.), *Contemporary Problems in Personnel.* Chicago: St. Clair Press, 1974a.

Miner, J. B. *The Human Constraint: The Coming Shortage of Managerial Talent.* Washington, D.C.: BNA Books, 1974b.

Miner, J. B. "Motivation to Manage Among Women: Studies of Business Managers and Educational Administrators." *Journal of Vocational Behavior,* 1974c, *5,* 197-208.

Miner, J. B. *The Challenge of Managing.* Philadelphia: Saunders, 1975a.

Miner, J. B. "The Uncertain Future of the Leadership Concept: An Overview." In J. G. Hunt and L. L. Larson (Eds.), *Leadership Frontiers.* Kent, Ohio: Kent State University Press, 1975b.

Miner, J. B. "Levels of Motivation to Manage Among Personnel and Industrial Relations Managers." *Journal of Applied Psychology,* 1976a, *61,* 419-427.

Miner, J. B. "Relationships Among Measures of Managerial Personality Traits." *Journal of Personality Assessment,* 1976b, *40,* 383-397.

Miner, J. B. *Motivation to Manage: A Ten Year Update on the "Studies in Management Education" Research.* Atlanta: Organizational Measurement Systems Press, 1977.

Miner, J. B. "The Miner Sentence Completion Scale: A Reappraisal." *Academy of Management Journal,* 1978, *21,* 283-294.

Miner, J. B., and Brewer, J. F. "The Management of Ineffective Performance." In M. D. Dunnette (Ed.), *Handbook of Industrial and Organizational Psychology.* Chicago: Rand McNally, 1976.

Mintzberg, H. *The Nature of Managerial Work.* New York: Harper & Row, 1973.

Mitchell, T. R. "Cognitive Complexity and Leadership Style." *Journal of Personality and Social Psychology,* 1970, *16,* 166-173.

Moses, J. L., and Boehm, V. R. "Relationship of Assessment Center Performance to Management Progress of Women." *Journal of Applied Psychology,* 1975, *60,* 527-529.

Nash, A. N. "Vocational Interests of Effective Managers: A Review of the Literature." *Personnel Psychology,* 1965, *18,* 21-37.

Nelson, P. D. "Similarities and Differences Among Leaders and Followers." *Journal of Social Psychology,* 1964, *63,* 161-167.

Owens, W. A. "Background Data." In M. D. Dunnette (Ed.), *Handbook of Industrial and Organizational Psychology.* Chicago: Rand McNally, 1976.

Piotrowski, Z. A., and Rock, M. R. *The Perceptanalytic Executive Scale.* New York: Grune and Stratton, 1963.

Prien, E. P., and Liske, R. E. "Assessments of Higher Level Personnel. III: Rating Criteria: A Comparative Analysis of Supervisor Ratings and Incumbent Self-Ratings of Job Performance." *Personnel Psychology,* 1962, *15,* 187-194.

Roadman, H. E. "An Industrial Use of Peer Ratings." *Journal of Applied Psychology,* 1964, *48,* 211-214.

Robinson, J. P., and Shaver, P. R. *Measures of Social Psychological Attitudes.* Ann Arbor: Institute for Social Research, University of Michigan, 1973.

Sample, J. A., and Wilson, T. R. "Leader Behavior, Group Productivity, and Rating of Least Preferred Co-worker." *Journal of Personality and Social Psychology,* 1965, *13,* 266-270.

Sashkin, M. "Leadership Style and Group Decision Effectiveness: Correlational and Behavioral Tests of Fiedler's Contingency Model." *Organizational Behavior and Human Performance,* 1972, *8,* 347-362.

Sikula, A. F. "Values and Value Systems: Importance and Relationship to Managerial and Organizational Behavior." *Journal of Psychology,* 1971, *78,* 277-286.

Smith, N. R. *The Entrepreneur and His Firm: The Relationship Between Type of Man and Type of Company.* East Lansing: Graduate School of Business, Michigan State University, 1967.

Springer, D. "Ratings of Candidates for Promotion by Co-workers and Supervisors." *Journal of Applied Psychology,* 1953, *37,* 347-351.

Stogdill, R. M. "Personal Factors Associated with Leadership: A Survey of the Literature." *Journal of Psychology,* 1948, *25,* 35-71.

Stogdill, R. M. *Handbook of Leadership.* New York: Free Press, 1974.

Tagiuri, R. "Value Orientations and the Relationship of Managers and Scientists." *Administrative Science Quarterly,* 1965, *10,* 39-51.

Tumes, J. "The Contingency Theory of Leadership: A Behavioral Investigation." Paper presented at Eastern Academy of Management meetings, Boston, May 1972.

Vroom, V. H. *Some Personality Determinants of the Effects of Participation.* Englewood Cliffs, N.J.: Prentice-Hall, 1960.

Vroom, V. H. "Leadership." In M. D. Dunnette (Ed.), *Handbook of Industrial and Organizational Psychology.* Chicago: Rand McNally, 1976.

Vroom, V. H., and Yetton, P. W. *Leadership and Decision Making.* Pittsburgh: University of Pittsburgh Press, 1973.

Wainer, H. A., and Rubin, I. M. "Motivation of Research and Development Entrepreneurs: Determinants of Company Success." *Journal of Applied Psychology,* 1969, *53* (3), 178-184.

Wollowick, H. B., and McNamara, W. J. "Relationship of the Components of an Assessment Center to Management Success." *Journal of Applied Psychology,* 1969, *53,* 348-352.

80

Victor C. Joe

Conservatism and Resistance to Change

Social scientists have long been intrigued with the liberal-conservative dimension. The research in this area has progressed in two separate, yet related, directions. Researchers who have construed the dimension as a political variable have been particularly concerned with the prediction of voting behavior and responses to political-economic issues. Investigators who have interpreted the dimension as a psychological variable have been concerned with conceptualizing and assessing it as a personality syndrome that can influence a person's responses (including voting behavior and political opinions) to a wide range of social and physical stimuli. This chapter discusses the liberal-conservative dimension as a psychological variable.

Systematic study of psychological conservatism began with the publication of *The*

Authoritarian Personality (Adorno and others, 1950) and has continued for nearly three decades. In more recent years, G. D. Wilson and his colleagues have studied the concept extensively and have constructed a Conservatism Scale (Wilson and Patterson, 1968, 1970) which, in their view, measures the concept more satisfactorily than the Fascism Scale constructed by Adorno and his associates. Wilson (1973) defines the term *conservatism* as a tendency to exhibit resistance to change and to prefer traditional and conventional values, goals, and behaviors. Furthermore, he and his colleagues are concerned with a psychological (not a political) concept. For instance, an aging labor union person may be politically liberal (favoring the labor movement and government aid) but psychologically conservative (resistant to change and in favor of traditional values). The converse, of course, could occur in that a middle-class person (for instance, a university professor) may be politically conservative but psychologically liberal. Finally, Wilson contends that conservatism is a general factor underlying the entire field of social attitudes, similar to the notion of intelligence as a general factor that partly determines abilities in different areas.

In addition to describing the conservative individual as resistant to changes, moderate, cautious, and avoiding risks, Wilson and his colleagues also enumerate eight characteristics of the extremely conservative person: (1) religious fundamentalism; (2) pro-Establishment politics; (3) insistence on strict rules and punishments; (4) militarism; (5) preference for conventional art, clothing, institutions; (6) antihedonistic outlook; (7) intolerance of minority groups; and (8) superstitious resistance to science. Wilson (1973) believes that these conservative attitudes reflect a fear of uncertainty. According to his hypothesis, religious dogmatism, for example, arises from fears of death, supernatural forces, and the unknown—which are all forms of uncertainty. Similarly, the conservative's adherence to external authority, conventionality, rigid morality, and opposition to sexual freedom stems from the threat of complexity and loss of control of one's own feelings and desires. Table 1 illustrates the notion that a particular conservative attitude stems from a particular fear of uncertainty. In turn, this fear of uncertainty is thought to come from feelings of insecurity and inferiority—which are internalizations of the low evaluation of oneself held by significant others. According to Wilson (1973, p. 259), these feelings of insecurity and inferiority arise from (1) genetic factors, such as "anxiety proneness, stimulus aversion (sensitivity to strong stimuli), low intelligence, . . . old age"; and (2) environmental factors, such as "parental coldness, punitiveness, rigidity, and inconsistency." Hence, the conservative person is intolerant of change because any new change increases the complexity of his life. Figure 1 summarizes the hypothesized antecedents of the fear of uncertainty and conservative attitudes.

Background and Current Status

The Authoritarian Personality (Adorno and others, 1950) has been criticized by numerous investigators, many directing their criticisms to the conceptual and methodological weakness of the original work (see Brown, 1965; Kirscht and Dillehay, 1967). For instance, the F Scale has been criticized for being poorly phrased, measuring specific sets of attitudes rather than a general syndrome, being contaminated with acquiescence response set (the tendency for a subject to agree with any opinion or attitudinal statement, regardless of its meaning or content), and confusing authoritarianism with political right-wing ideology (although it was intended to identify authoritarianism regardless of specific political beliefs). Hence, there was a great need to develop a better measure of psychological conservatism.

Table 1. Fear of Uncertainty as the Hypothesized Basis of Conservative Attitudes

	Source of Threat	Attitudinal Manifestation	
	Supernatural forces	Superstition	
	Death	Religious dogmatism	
	The unknown and unpredictable		
	Ambiguity		
	Anarchy	Right-wing politics	
	Social disruption		
	Unfamiliar people	Ethnocentrism	
	Foreign influences	Militarism	
	Deviant behavior	Intolerance of minorities	
Fear of Uncertainty	Anomie	Authoritarianism	General Conservatism
	Disorganization	Punitiveness	
	Dissent	Rigid morality	
	Decisions	Antihedonism	
	Loss of control of own feelings and desires	Adherence to external authority	
	Complexity	Conventionality	
	Novelty	Conformity	
	Innovation		
	Technological change	Antiscience	
	Erosion of traditional ideas		

Source: Wilson (1973).

Wilson and his co-researchers became the successors to *The Authoritarian Personality*. They prefer the label of conservatism to that of authoritarianism or dogmatism because the former is "relatively free of derogatory value tone" (Wilson, 1973, p. 4). Wilson and Patterson (1968) also constructed a scale that appears to be free of the limitations of the F Scale. Since the 1968 introduction of the Wilson-Patterson Conservatism Scale (C Scale), there has been increasing evidence for the construct validity of this scale (Wilson, 1973). Recent investigations have demonstrated that the scale is related to (1) stimulus seeking, (2) art preference, (3) premarital sexual experiences, (4) birth control practices, (5) belief in the Protestant ethic, (6) the volunteering for certain psychological experiments that were assumed to require more openness, and (7) attitudes toward patient care and psychiatric treatment. These studies are discussed in subsequent sections.

Critical Discussion

General Areas of Concern

The F Scale and other related personality measurements employed to assess conservatism have a number of shortcomings. As mentioned previously, the F Scale has been criticized for being contaminated with acquiescence response set. In an attempt to deal with this problem, subsequent researchers constructed a parallel set of items matched in content but reversed or negatively worded, so that an endorsement of these items is

Figure 1. A Theory of the Psychological Antecedents of Conservatism

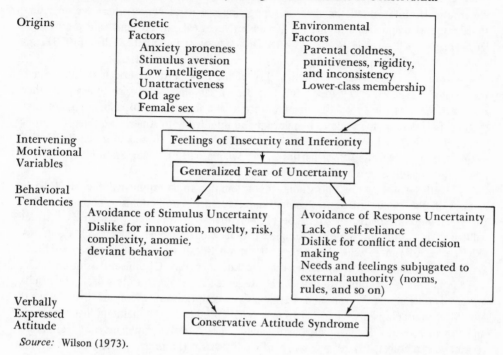

Source: Wilson (1973).

scored authoritarian. Wilson and Nias (1972), however, noted that these attempts to correct the acquiescence problem were unsuccessful because the correlation between the original F Scale and the reversed items was very low. These two researchers also pointed out that acquiescence to the F Scale items may be due to (1) item content ambiguity, (2) grammatical structuring of the sentences (particularly sentences with a double-negative or multinegative grammar), and (3) the directional nature of the items (the wording of the sentence strongly suggests a particular response by the respondent).

In response to the criticisms of the F Scale and other related scales, Wilson and Patterson (1968) developed the Conservatism Scale (C Scale), which contains fifty brief labels (one- and two-word items, such as "birth control," "suicide," "church authority," and "death penalty") to which respondents are instructed to respond with "yes," "?," or "no" according to the extent to which they favor or believe in these items. Because the items of this scale are not lengthy propositional statements, Wilson and Patterson expected that acquiesence response set would be minimized. Wilson (1973) reviewed the research on the C Scale and reported that the scale is internally consistent, free of acquiesence response set, and less susceptible to social desirability, and that it has high test-retest reliability.

Since Wilson and his colleagues (Bagley, Wilson, and Boshier, 1970; Wilson and Shutte, 1973) have hypothesized that religious, political, racial, moral, and sexual attitudes are to some degree intercorrelated and that conservatism is the general factor underlying this field of social attitudes, it was imperative that there be evidence to support the notion that the C Scale is predominantly unidimensional in content. Wilson (1970) performed a principal components analysis of the responses of two hundred British males to the C Scale. He reported that the first factor extracted accounted for 18.67 percent of the variance; and, more important, that many items representing different attitude areas (such as sex, race, religion, politics, and law) in the scale loaded substantially on this dimension. He interpreted the data as supporting a general conservatism factor. Additional support came from studies replicated in New Zealand, England, and the Netherlands (Bagley, Wilson, and Boshier, 1970). On the basis of these data, Wilson (1973) concluded that the C Scale adequately samples all areas of social attitudes.

A final concern was the applicability of the C Scale to American samples. Since the original C Scale was developed and tested on a sample of New Zealanders and other European samples, many of the items were relevant and unique to respondents of that culture. In order for the scale to be relevant and intelligible to American subjects, a number of items had to be changed. Bahr and Chadwick (1974) altered fourteen items. For example, they substituted "pot parties" for "pyjama parties," "segregation" for "apartheid," and "paddling in school" for "birching."

Until 1974 there were no studies that attempted to determine whether the C Scale assesses all the characteristics (religious fundamentalism, antihedonistic outlook, and so forth) of the conservative person. Joe (1974) further investigated the scale's construct validation by using an American sample. The Jackson Personality Research Form AA (PRF), the Adorno F Scale, the Crowne-Marlowe Social Desirability Scale, the Mirels-Garrett Protestant Ethic (PE) Scale, the Kluckhorn-Murray Optimism-Pessimism Scale, and the C Scale were administered to 416 students (201 males, 215 females). The results appeared to support Wilson and Patterson's description of a conservative. Subjects exhibiting conservatism seemed (1) to have a *high* need (PRF) to maintain high standards and to work toward distant goals (achievement), (2) to dislike ambiguity in information (cognitive structure), (3) to avoid risk of bodily harm (harm avoidance), (4) to dislike disorganization (order), (5) to be held in high esteem by acquaintances (social recognition), and (6) to seek the protection and reassurance of others (succorance). And they revealed (1) a *low* need to break away from restraints or restrictions of any kind (autonomy), (2) a dislike of change (change), (3) a low tendency to give vent readily to emotions and wishes (impulsivity), (4) a low preference for spending a good deal of time in amusement activities (play), (5) a nonhedonistic view of life (sentience), and (6) a low value for intellectual curiosity and the synthesis of logical thought (understanding).

High conservative subjects agreed more strongly with the F Scale; this supports the idea that the conservative person has an intolerance for minority groups, a superstitious resistance to science, a belief in religious fundamentalism, and so on. Similarly, the significant relationship obtained between the C Scale and PE Scale indicates that the conservative believes that hard work leads to success and that excellence and self-reliance are desirable virtues. Thus, the correlations obtained between the C Scale and the other scales provide evidence for the construct validity of these instruments.

During the years 1968 to 1971, research with the C Scale dealt predominantly with the psychometric properties (such as internal consistency, test-retest reliability, and unidimensionality) of the scale. Since then, however, most research has been concerned with the notion that conservative attitudes reflect a fear of uncertainty (see Table 1). For instance, several studies have tested the proposition that the high conservative avoids advanced sexual activities because of a fear of loss of control of personal feelings and desires.

Joe and Kostyla (1975) examined the relationship of conservatism to reports of sexual experiences and movie attendance. Sixty-six male and sixty-four female undergraduates were administered the C Scale and the Zuckerman Heterosexual Experience Scales. Twenty-nine of the males and twenty-four of the females were also given a scale related to movie experiences. High conservative males, when compared to low conservative males, reported a significantly lower number of experiences in (1) feeling covered breasts, (2) lying prone on female without penetration, (3) feeling nude breasts, (4) oral contact with the breast, (5) manipulation of the vagina, (6) female manipulation of the penis, (7) cunnilingus, (8) coitus with male in superior position, and (9) coitus with female in superior position. High conservative females reported a lower number of experiences in (1) having their covered breasts felt, (2) males lying prone on them without penetration, (3) male oral contact with breast, (4) male manipulation of the vagina, (5) coitus with male in superior position, (6) coitus in rear-entry position, (7) coitus in side position, and (8) coitus with female in superior position. Results of the movie attendance scale indicated that high conservative males had fewer experiences with R- and X-rated movies than did low conservative males. Meanwhile, high conservative females, when compared with low conservative females, had fewer experiences with X-rated movies only. There were no observed significant differences on G- and PG-rated movies for both males and females differing in conservatism.

Similarly, Thomas (1975) found significant negative relationships between conservatism and sexual experience (for example, petting and coitus) and favorable attitudes toward premarital sexual behavior. Using sixty-four male and fifty female introductory psychology students, Joe, Brown, and Jones (1976) studied the relationship of conservatism to reports of sexual experiences and reasons for nonparticipation. Consistent with the Joe and Kostyla study, conservatism was found to be inversely related to the frequency and variety of sexual behavior. Furthermore, high conservative subjects gave the reason "It is morally wrong" more often than any other reason for not engaging in coital activities and more intimate forms of petting. In another test of this proposition, Joe and associates (1979) examined the relationship between conservatism, birth control usage, and knowledge of birth control information. High conservative females who reported premarital coital activity were found to be significantly less knowledgeable of birth control information and used significantly fewer birth control techniques when compared to their low conservative peers. More specifically, high conservative females, in comparison with low conservative females, reported a lower usage of spermicides and the rhythm method, plus a lower tendency of their male partners to use a condom as a contraceptive technique.

The consistent and substantial relationships found between conservatism and sexual behaviors argue strongly for the notion that the attitudinal manifestations of antihedonism and rigid morality are determinants in the lower number and variety of sexual experiences and that the expression of these attitudes stems from the threat of loss of control of one's own impulses. By avoiding sexual intercourse, intimate forms of petting, and factual sexual information, high conservative subjects are able to control and to lessen their feelings of fear and guilt. This notion is strengthened by the finding that both high conservative males and females frequently believe that "it is morally wrong" to engage in the intimate forms of sexual behaviors.

Another proposition that has received research attention is that high conservative subjects cope with the threat of complexity and novelty by limiting the range of experiences to which they are open. Wilson, Ausman, and Mathews (1973) hypothesized that high conservatives would find complex and abstract art works aversive or threatening. An art expert selected twenty paintings that differed along a simplicity-complexity and an abstract-representational dimension, so that there were five paintings in each of four categories: simple representational, simple abstract, complex representational, and complex abstract. Simplicity-complexity was defined as "the number and concentration of different elements (lines, shapes, colors, objects, etc.) contained within the painting" (p.

286). The abstract-representational dimension was defined as the "extent to which elements were familiar and identifiable and the degree to which the whole picture showed isomorphism (correspondence) with visual reality" (p. 286). High conservative subjects preferred simple and representational paintings and showed a definite dislike of the complex representational and complex abstract paintings. In contrast, low conservative subjects preferred the complex and abstract works.

Joe, Jones, and Ryder (1977) performed two studies that examined the relationship between conservatism and openness to experiences. In the first study, the responses of sixty-four males and sixty females to the C Scale and the Coan (1972) Experience Inventory were correlated. For the total sample, conservatism was significantly related to the total score on the Experience Inventory plus six of the seven component scales. More specifically, high conservative subjects reported (1) a lower variety of aesthetic experiences; (2) fewer unusual ways of experiencing oneself, one's body, and one's physical environment; (3) a dislike of abstract ideas and intellectual puzzles; (4) less willingness to entertain ideas in such realms as astrology, extrasensory perception, and reincarnation; (5) an avoidance of daydreaming; and (6) a preference to think along orderly and realistic lines. The second study examined the relationship between conservatism and the expressed willingness to volunteer for certain psychological experiments that were assumed to require more openness. High conservative subjects, as compared to low conservative subjects, were less willing to volunteer for the three experiments (human sexual response, aesthetic interests, and fantasy production) that required more openness. However, high conservative subjects were just as likely as low conservative subjects to volunteer for two experiments (decision making and humor rating) that were assumed to require less openness.

These results—plus those of Kish, Netterberg, and Leahy (1973), who found a negative relationship between the C Scale and the Zuckerman Stimulus-Seeking Scales—support the notion that the conservative's adherence to external authority, conventionality, and simplicity stems from the threat of complexity and novelty. Both the Wilson, Ausman, and Mathews and the Joe, Jones, and Ryder studies are noteworthy because they tested the proposition in the context of stimulus uncertainty rather than at the response phase of behavior.

Wilson and his colleagues hypothesized that religion comes from fears of various kinds (for instance, the fear of death, ambiguity, supernatural forces, or the unpredictable and unknown). This idea has received partial support from Sales (1972), who studied the impact of economic crisis (such as the Great Depression) on conversion rates to authoritarian and nonauthoritarian churches. He studied the conversion rates of churches from 1920 to 1929 (which were years of economic prosperity) and compared them to the conversion rates from 1930 to 1939 (which were years of overwhelming depression). The data indicated that there were increased conversion rates to authoritarian churches during times of economic crisis, while during economic good times there were increased conversion rates to nonauthoritarian churches. Sales noted that there was a replication of this phenomenon in Seattle, Washington, during the 1960s. In times of economic crisis (which brings about conditions of ambiguity, the unknown, and the unpredictable), individuals—especially conservative ones—may turn to a certain religion because it is geared to provide the leadership, ethnocentricism (all members of the congregation are similar), and religious doctrine to make life bearable.

Comparative Philosophies and Theories

As mentioned previously, the F Scale has been criticized for (1) being poorly phrased; (2) being contaminated with acquiescence response set; and (3) measuring political, rather than general, authoritarianism. Consequently, there have been numerous attempts to develop a scale that eliminates these criticisms. Robinson and Shaver (1969) reveal that twenty-six scales (excluding the F Scale) have been developed to assess authoritarianism or psychological conservatism. Some scales—such as the Balanced F Scale (Athanasiou, 1968), which has an equal number of positively and negatively worded statements—were designed to eliminate the contamination of acquiesence response set. Other scales, such as the Intolerance of Ambiguity Scale (Budner, 1962), were constructed to tap specific dimensions or components of the authoritarian personality syndrome. Still other scales, such as the Dogmatism Scale (Rokeach, 1960), were developed to assess general authoritarianism instead of authoritarianism of the political right. The degree of success of these attempts is limited and in some cases questionable. One reason is that all the scales cited by Robinson and Shaver (1969) involve lengthy propositional statements, and that type of statement, according to Wilson and others, is a major source of acquiescence response set for such scales.

Elaboration on Critical Points

Despite Wilson's claim that his scale is unidimensional and less susceptible to social desirability, research has not consistently supported his claim. Robertson and Cochrane (1973) factor-analyzed the responses of 329 students to the C Scale. Their first factor accounted for only 12.9 percent of the variance and had a definite religious theme. They concluded that the C Scale is not unidimensional and hence does not measure a general dimension of conservatism. Similarly, Bahr and Chadwick (1974) found no general factor of conservatism for their Native American sample. In no factor analytic study of the C Scale has the first factor accounted for more than 20 percent of the variance. Even the data of studies used to support the idea of unidimensionality have not been very strong. For instance, Wilson (1970) reported that the first factor accounted for 18.67 percent of the variance, and Bagley, Wilson, and Boshier (1970) reported that the first factor accounted for 19 percent of the variance for an English sample, 14 percent for a New Zealand sample, and 15 percent for a Dutch sample.

In relation to social desirability, Schneider (1973) reported three brief studies indicating that the C Scale is not independent of social desirability. In one study Schneider (1973) found that "for 70 percent of the items, circling the conservative answers means giving a socially desirable response" (p. 90).

Personal Views and Recommendations

One shortcoming of the research on conservatism is the lack of research evidence for how environmental conditions and parents contribute to the development of insecure and defensive individuals who adhere to conservative attitudes. Research on the psychological antecedents of conservatism is seriously lacking. Correspondingly, there is virtually no evidence to support the notion that conservative attitudes stem from fears of uncertainty. Wilson (1973, chap. 17, table 3) lists only three separate studies (and one of these is an unpublished master's thesis) that are concerned with this relationship. A few more studies have been concerned with this notion in the last two or three years, but additional supportive research is needed.

Although some studies (for example, Joe and Kostyla, 1975) support the notion that fear of uncertainty is the basis of conservative attitudes, these studies are correlational and do not specify precisely the cause-and-effect sequences. Future investigations concerned with the causal directionality of these relationships will increase confidence in these findings.

Application to Particular Variables

The Wilson-Patterson C Scale has been standardized and tested on samples that have varied in age, sex, education, socioeconomic status, and vocation. For instance, Wilson and Patterson (1968) standardized the scale by using subjects whose ages ranged from the late teens to the middle 60s. Their subjects were drawn from both sexes and various occupational groups (such as students, businessmen, professionals, skilled and unskilled workers, and housewives). Subsequent studies concerned with these demographic variables have reported similar data (see Wilson, 1973). Hence, the C Scale appears to be applicable to a large segment of the population—largely because the scale's use of one- or two-word items minimizes the likelihood that responses will be influenced by intellectual and cognitive processes, verbal sophistication, concentration, and social desirability.

The Wilson-Patterson C Scale has been employed in several cross-cultural studies. These cross-cultural studies have used samples from the Netherlands, England, and New Zealand (Bagley, Wilson, and Boshier, 1970); Australia (Feather, 1975); the United States (Bahr and Chadwick, 1974; Hogan, 1977); South Africa (Wilson and Shutte, 1973); and West Germany (Schneider, 1973) to test the reliability and factor structure of the scale. In nearly all these studies, the data supported a cross-cultural similarity in responses to the C Scale. There was, however, one exception to the above findings. Bahr and Chadwick (1974) factor-analyzed the responses of 122 Native Americans and 304 whites to the C Scale. They found that the unrotated general factor accounted for 15 percent of the variance for both groups but that the general conservatism factor was considerably stronger for the whites than for the Native Americans. Hogan (1975) administered the C Scale along with several other personality assessments to 287 black and white subjects and noted a number of differences between the mean C-Scale scores of blacks and whites, with the whites being significantly less conservative on a number of comparisons. These studies suggest that the C Scale may also be applied to various racial groups.

Regarding the C Scale's applicability to subjects with psychological disorders, Caine and Leigh (1972) assessed the attitudes of eighty-five neurotic outpatients toward psychiatric treatment. The subjects were given the C Scale and a scale composed of items assessing their assumptions about the nature of their illness and the kind of treatment that they should receive. The more conservative patients tended to assume that their illness was physical or physiological rather than psychological. The investigators reasoned that the conservative patients, by assuming physical explanations for their illnesses, might have been avoiding personal responsibility for their psychiatric symptoms. Furthermore, the conservative patients showed more favorable attitudes to conventional, authoritarian therapy. This study suggests that the C Scale may be applied to patient samples; because of the paucity of research in this area, however, no definite statement can be made at this time.

References

Adorno, T. W., and others. *The Authoritarian Personality*. New York: Harper & Row, 1950.

Athanasiou, R. "Technique Without Mystique: A Study of Authoritarianism in Engineering Students." *Educational and Psychological Measurement*, 1968, *28*, 1181-1188.

Bagley, C., Wilson, G. D., and Boshier, R. W. "The Conservatism Scale: A Factor-Structure Comparison of English, Dutch, and New Zealand Samples." *Journal of Social Psychology*, 1970, *81*, 267-268.

Bahr, H. M., and Chadwick, B. A. "Conservatism, Racial Intolerance, and Attitudes Toward Racial Assimilation Among Whites and American Indians." *Journal of Social Psychology,* 1974, *94,* 45-56.

Brown, R. "The Authoritarian Personality." In *Social Psychology.* New York: Free Press, 1965.

Budner, S. "Intolerance of Ambiguity as a Personality Variable." *Journal of Personality,* 1962, *30,* 29-50.

Caine, T. M., and Leigh, R. "Conservatism in Relation to Psychiatric Treatment." *British Journal of Social and Clinical Psychology,* 1972, *11,* 52-56.

Coan, R. W. "Measurable Components of Openness to Experience." *Journal of Consulting and Clinical Psychology,* 1972, *39,* 346.

Feather, N. T. "Factor Structure of the Conservatism Scale." *Australian Psychologist,* 1975, *10,* 179-185.

Hogan, H. W. "Test of the Validity of the Wilson-Patterson Conservatism Scale." *Perceptual and Motor Skills,* 1975, *40,* 795-801.

Hogan, H. W. "Cross-Cultural Reliability and Factor Structure of the Wilson-Patterson Conservatism Scale." *Psychological Reports,* 1977, *41,* 453-454.

Joe, V. C. "Personality Correlates of Conservatism." *Journal of Social Psychology,* 1974, *93,* 309-310.

Joe, V. C., Brown, C. R., and Jones, R. N. "Conservatism as a Determinant of Sexual Experiences." *Journal of Personality Assessment,* 1976, *40,* 516-521.

Joe, V. C., Jones, R. N., and Ryder, S. "Conservatism, Openness to Experience and Sample Bias." *Journal of Personality Assessment,* 1977, *41,* 527-531.

Joe, V. C., and Kostyla, S. "Social Attitudes and Sexual Behaviors of College Students." *Journal of Consulting and Clinical Psychology,* 1975, *43,* 430.

Joe, V. C., and others. "Birth Control Practices and Conservatism." *Journal of Personality Assessment,* 1979, *43,* 536-540.

Kirscht, J. P., and Dillehay, R. C. *Dimensions of Authoritarianism: A Review of Research and Theory.* Lexington: University of Kentucky Press, 1967.

Kish, G. B., Netterberg, E. E., and Leahy, L. "Stimulus-Seeking and Conservatism." *Journal of Clinical Psychology,* 1973, *29,* 17-20.

Robertson, A., and Cochrane, R. "The Wilson-Patterson Conservatism Scale: A Reappraisal." *British Journal of Social and Clinical Psychology,* 1973, *12,* 428-430.

Robinson, J. P., and Shaver, P. R. "Authoritarianism, Dogmatism and Related Measures." In *Measures of Social Psychological Attitudes.* Ann Arbor: Survey Research Center, Institute for Social Research, University of Michigan, 1969.

Rokeach, M. *The Open and Closed Mind.* New York: Basic Books, 1960.

Sales, S. M. "Economic Threat as a Determinant of Conversion Rates in Authoritarian and Nonauthoritarian Churches." *Journal of Personality and Social Psychology,* 1972, *23,* 420-428.

Schneider, J. F. "The Conservatism Scale: Independent of SD?" *British Journal of Social and Clinical Psychology,* 1973, *12,* 90-91.

Thomas, D. R. "Conservatism and Premarital Sexual Experience." *British Journal of Social and Clinical Psychology,* 1975, *14,* 195-196.

Wilson, G. D. "Is There a General Factor in Social Attitudes? Evidence from a Factor Analysis of the Conservatism Scale." *British Journal of Social and Clinical Psychology,* 1970, *9,* 101-107.

Wilson, G. D. *The Psychology of Conservatism.* London: Academic Press, 1973.

Wilson, G. D., Ausman, J., and Mathews, T. R. "Conservatism and Art Preferences." *Journal of Personality and Social Psychology,* 1973, *25,* 286-288.

Wilson, G. D., and Nias, D. K. B. "Measurement of Social Attitudes: A New Approach." *Perceptual and Motor Skills*, 1972, *35*, 827-834.

Wilson, G. D., and Patterson, J. R. "A New Measure of Conservatism." *British Journal of Social and Clinical Psychology*, 1968, 7, 264-269.

Wilson, G. D., and Patterson, J. R. *Manual for the Conservatism Scale*. Windsor, England: National Foundation for Educational Research, 1970.

Wilson, G. D., and Shutte, P. "The Structure of Social Attitudes in South Africa." *Journal of Social Psychology*, 1973, *90*, 323-324.

81

Glen M. Vaught
Norman E. Whitten, Sr.

Authoritarianism

The authoritarian personality consists of a cluster of personality traits that, when taken together, predicts how an individual will behave toward others in a variety of contexts. It is a multidetermined personality structure that underlies an individual's opinions, attitudes, and values. It is acquired much the same as any other personality structure; that is, from early family experiences and childrearing practices. Basically, there are nine personality attributes that define authoritarianism. These same personality attributes are also the basic dimensions of the Fascism Scale (F Scale). The following enumeration and description of these nine personality dimensions are taken from Adorno and his associates (1950), Byrne (1974), and Sahakian (1974).

The first dimension, conventionalism (rigid adherence to conventional middle-class values), is simple enough to understand. Byrne (1974), however, has indicated that a distinction is needed to separate those persons who are highly conventional because of a well-developed superego from those whose conventionalism reflects weaker superego development. Conventional persons with a weak superego development are thought to rely more heavily on external standards as a basis for value judgments than conventional persons with a stronger superego.

The second dimension, authoritarian submission (uncritical attitude toward idealized moral authorities of the in-group), characterizes obedience to authority, whether it be leaders of state or authority figures in general.

The third dimension is authoritarian aggression (tendency to seek out, condemn, and punish those who violate conventional values). Conflict within the authoritarian individual arises from repressed obedience to authority figures and yielding to superficial cultural values. Conflict, frustration, and hostility are then displaced to those outside the in-group.

The fourth dimension is anti-intraception (opposition to the subjective, the tender-minded, and the imaginative). The authoritarian person responds to concrete and direct information and is quite literal in interpreting the surrounding world. Fear of losing control is thought to motivate this anti-imaginative mode of thinking.

Fifth, the authoritarian person is characterized by superstition and stereotypy (thinking in rigid categories and belief in mystical determinants of fate). In order to remain blameless for personal failings, this individual tends to attribute the cause of such failings to fate or some mystical force outside himself. Stereotypy refers to black-and-white reasoning, with simplistic reasons given for complex occurrences.

The sixth dimension is power and toughness (exaggerated assertion of power and toughness, preoccupation with strong-weak, dominance-submission, and identification with power figures). In order for the authoritarian to compensate for personal feelings of weakness, fear, and low self-esteem, exaggerated importance is attributed to the self, powerful others, and the in-group.

Seventh, the authoritarian manifests destructiveness and cynicism (generalized hostility and contempt for human nature). One way in which the authoritarian is able to cope with personal disturbances, conflicts, and hostilities is to generalize these feelings to others. By doing so, the person obtains some relief from personal misery through the delusional belief that all others possess the same misery.

The eighth dimension is projectivity (predisposition to believe that the world is dangerous and evil). Internal feelings (such as fear, sexual thoughts, and perceived weaknesses) are projected outward, so that one's most unacceptable impulses and thoughts regarding the self are to be seen in the world. Thus, the authoritarian is able to identify potential evil and to design elaborate safeguards against such sources of danger.

The final dimension is sex (exaggerated concern with sexuality). Authoritarians take a moralistic view of human sexuality and are quick to condemn those who do not conform to the norm. Sex is often confused with hostility and aggressive impulses.

Background and Current Status

Following the rise of Fascism in Italy and Nazism in Germany in the late 1930s, world attention was directed to the emergence of what seemed to be a kind of national character, the ingredients of which provided a rich and varied subject matter. Out of this matrix of social and political turmoil, there arose a renewed interest in prejudice and anti-Semitic ideology. A scholarly research program on authoritarianism was launched at the University of California at Berkeley in the late 1940s, culminating in a book entitled *The Authoritarian Personality* (Adorno and others, 1950). This seminal work furnished the motivation, theoretical structure, and research methodology that set the tone for most of the research that was to follow. In order to cast their assumptions regarding the nature of the link between culture and personality into a theoretical framework, the Berkeley group, as they came to be called, relied heavily on psychoanalytic and neoanalytic thinking. By using Freudian theory, they were able to speculate in terms of the origins of prejudice and antidemocratic attitudes; at the same time, they were able to attribute these personality expressions to (1) the development of the id, ego, and super-ego; and (2) the interplay of these basic personality structures. Research methodology included scale development, questionnaire techniques, and the use of both structured and unstructured interviews for data collection and for scale validation. The Berkeley group of the late 1940s had at their disposal sufficient raw materials from which to construct a viable research program, but it took a monumental effort to apply their approach to such a complex subject matter.

Authoritarianism seemingly emerged as a personality syndrome after the development of the Fascism Scale (F Scale). All the while, however, the Berkeley group believed that antidemocratic ideas, feelings, and overall tendencies are rooted in personality. With this in mind, they began to develop scales that would measure characteristics of individuals holding such attitudes. The Anti-Semitism Scale (A-S Scale) was the first scale developed; it purported to yield an index of an individual's willingness to oppose or favor anti-Semitic ideology. The Ethnocentrism Scale (E Scale) followed and was thought to measure the degree of preference for in-group versus out-group. It also provided a distinction between emphasis on culturally determined attitudes and those based on ethnic considerations. The Politico-Economic Conservatism Scale (PEC Scale) came next; it distinguished between those who held conservative and those who held liberal opinions and attitudes.

Using information gained from research with the other scales, Adorno and his colleagues developed the Fascism Scale (F Scale). The F Scale consists of nine personality dimensions that define the authoritarian personality. The investigators considered this scale to be less obvious in terms of what it was measuring than the other scales, and it had the added advantage of incorporating the other three scales. After a number of revisions, the Berkeley group constructed an instrument that included the nine basic personality characteristics of the authoritarian and could differentiate among those who were or were not accepting of antidemocratic information.

Although the authoritarian personality (authoritarianism) concept, viewed primarily from F-Scale measurement, has come under scrutiny from a variety of sources (see Bass, 1955; Christie and Jahoda, 1954; Rokeach, 1960; Wrightsman, 1973), it continues to influence current thinking and measurement of antidemocratic ideology. Christie and Cook (1958) summarized a number of concerns about the validity of the construct, scale construction, values inherent in the authoritarian that are not present in the United States, and so on. More contemporary concerns have been voiced by Rokeach (1960), whose work led to the development of the Dogmatism Scale. Rokeach's twofold view was that (1) people can be open-minded or closed-minded whether they are politically liberal or conservative and (2) the structure of beliefs is just as important as the content of beliefs. He also sought to separate from the concept of authoritarianism any reference to political ideology and, therefore, derived a measure that would encompass either end of extreme ideologies. Current literature reflects the wide use of Rokeach's Dogmatism Scale as a general measure of authoritarianism.

Others have argued that, since agreement with the items of the F Scale indicates authoritarianism, the scale possibly introduces confounding of authoritarianism with acquiescence response set. Acquiescence response set refers to the tendency of individuals to agree with each item of a scale in order to present themselves in a favorable light. This tendency is thought to be exacerbated when items of a scale are keyed so that agreement with the item always indicates authoritarianism. Some investigators (for example, Rorer,

1965; Samuelson and Yates, 1967) have argued that acquiescence response set is not an important issue, while others (Messick and Jackson, 1957) contend that it is a very important issue. Byrne (1974) has attempted to develop a balanced scale with acquiescence response set removed. He indicates that future research will have to determine whether his new scale represents a decided improvement over the basic F Scale.

One important manifestation of authoritarianism is obedience to authority. Milgram (1974, p. 207) has called it "the ideal regulatory mechanism of fascism." Obedience or overobedience describes the tendency of authoritarians to submit to authority and is one of the nine personality dimensions contained in the F Scale under the rubric "authoritarian submission." Milgram's (1974) study of obedience represents a classic effort to understand how the so-called average person, under certain conditions, is able to behave with blind obedience while others manage to disobey in the same circumstances. In his book entitled *Obedience to Authority,* Milgram discusses and answers many of the criticisms leveled at him concerning both methodological and ethical problems. While Milgram's findings are not to be taken as representative of all the characteristics underlying obedience to authority found in the confessions of Nazi war criminals, or even as synonymous with authoritarianism, his work does afford insight into a side of human nature that is difficult to understand and accept; it also indicates the wide range of the phenomena associated with authoritarianism.

Critical Discussion

General Areas of Concern

Many of the larger concerns over the importance and value of the authoritarianism concept have been discussed by Deutsch and Krauss (1965), Sahakian (1974), and Wrightsman (1973). These concerns have often been expressed as criticisms, and they run the gamut from the development of the concept to its measurement. Fortunately, much of the criticism has stimulated new theorizing, resulting in new research trends in the professional literature. Klein, Barr, and Wolitzky (1967) have summarized these trends in the following way: (1) There is a continuation of the original efforts to explore the relationship between authoritarianism and social attitudes. (2) There is some attempt to relate authoritarianism to personality. (3) Other attempts focus on the antecedents of authoritarianism. A few writers (for example, Byrne, 1974; Wrightsman, 1973) discuss increases and decreases in authoritarianism within individuals as a function of social and cultural change. According to these writers, increased levels of education should result in lower authoritarianism scores per se; however, as extremist groups increase, many people give up their civil liberties to authoritarians.

By and large, the F Scale continues to be the most popular means of measuring authoritarianism, in spite of the findings that these scores are sensitive to educational differences, acquiescence, socioeconomic differences, and a host of additional variables. Nevertheless, F-Scale scores have been shown to relate to a number of attitudes much the same as the Berkeley group had predicted. In a sample of urban adults, Martin and Westie (1959) found that authoritarianism correlated with antiblack attitudes independent of religious affiliation or occupational mobility. Others have shown that authoritarianism is related to sexual attitudes, prejudice, political and economic attitudes, and the assignment of blame and punishment (Byrne, 1974).

Attempts to relate authoritarianism to personality attributes or to view it within the personality structure have met with some success. Epstein (1965) was able to show that extremely authoritarian people were more likely to aggress toward low-status individuals, while the opposite was true for equalitarians. Mitchell and Byrne (1973) showed that authoritarians were less sure of assigning guilt to a person they liked but were more punitive in awarding punishment to a disliked person. Other studies have shown that authoritarians are more rigid and less resistant to change than equalitarians (Steiner and Johnson, 1963). Byrne (1974) found that authoritarianism is not directly related to maladjustment.

Renewed interest in the antecedents of authoritarianism accompanied the development of Levinson and Huffman's (1955) Traditional Family Ideology Scale (TFI). The TFI permits an examination of the degree to which family ideology is associated with the authoritarian-equalitarian personality dimension. Levinson and Huffman found evidence to support the assumption that autocratic family ideology underlies authoritarian personality development. Later studies have shown that child-parental interactions do contribute to the development of authoritarian tendencies; however, the interactions are complex and often subtle. Byrne's (1974) research is a good example of one attempt to understand the subtle nature of child-parent interactions thought to underlie authoritarianism. He concluded that authoritarian traits are more likely to develop when neither parent is low on authoritarianism and the same-sexed parent is extremely high on authoritarianism. Equalitarian children come from homes where at least one parent is low on authoritarianism and the same-sexed parent is even lower on authoritarianism.

Comparative Philosophies and Theories

Deutsch and Krauss (1965) make the point that the concept of authoritarianism evolved from concerns over the rise of Fascism and Nazism but not from concerns over Communism because it was "cloaked in humanistic ideas of Marxism" (p. 159). It seemed obvious to many that authoritarianism could and did exist at either end of the political spectrum. The concept of dogmatism was advanced by Rokeach (1960) to account for the occurrence of authoritarianism independent of ideology. As a result of this change in theory and measurement, the importance of examining belief structure was recognized, whereas attention previously had been focused on the content of beliefs. This shift in emphasis made it possible to view authoritarians as dogmatic or closed-minded persons apart from political leanings.

Harvey's four conceptual systems (belief systems) continued the trend toward viewing authoritarianism in terms of belief structure (Harvey, Hunt, and Schroder, 1961). Structure I represents an authoritarian world view reminiscent of the original conceptualizations of Adorno and colleagues. Here, emphasis is also on conventionalism, rigid thinking, belief in mystical determinants of fate, and a general extrinsic view of one's reward systems. To some extent, Harvey's Structure I is similar to Rotter's (1966) internal-external control variable, developed from social learning theory. Both constructs emphasize differences among those who feel that they have some control over their reward systems (internals) and those who feel that fate or things beyond their control determine their rewards (externals).

Milgram's (1974) work on obedience to authority called attention to the philosophical conflict between obeying for the good of society and disobeying for the good of individual conscience. Obedience to authority is a very important dimension of authoritarianism that has been empirically confirmed.

Elaboration on Critical Points

Application of authoritarianism to related concepts and to people requires that measurement techniques reflect reasonably concise theorizing and sound scaling practices. To date, research indicates that many of the earlier applications of this concept were too broad in scope and that expectancies often exceeded possibilities. There is little doubt that authoritarianism is a measurable quantity, but it is much more complex than was originally thought. Much like the development of personality theory, larger theories have given way to the so-called minitheories that attempt to deal with a more restricted range of phenomena. For example, expansive speculation about the antecedents of authoritarianism has been replaced by specific attempts to isolate singular sources of influence as they interact to form complex patterns. Sources of influence occur in a context; current theorizing and measurement attempt to deal with this newer consideration.

Relevant to measurement of authoritarianism, current thinking continues to change with the advancement of research. A good example of the way in which change has come about may be seen in the literature on dogmatism. Concern about the biases built into the F Scale motivated Rokeach to develop an instrument that would yield a valid measure of authoritarianism without ideological bias. Such a scale, however, would be useless unless it could be demonstrated that it was indeed a true measure of authoritarianism. To this end, Kerlinger and Rokeach (1966) factor-analyzed the combined items of the F Scale and the Dogmatism Scale and concluded that "the F and D Scales are factorially discriminable, even though both are measures of authoritarianism" (p. 398). At the same time, they concluded that "F and D are related phenomena with, probably, a common core of authoritarianism" (p. 397). This kind of refinement not only leads to improved measurement practices but also results in theory modification. Thus, dogmatic persons, regardless of political ideology, are expected to behave in an authoritarian way.

Personal Views and Recommendations

The concept of authoritarianism continues to influence theory construction, research directions, and social awareness. It has provided professionals with a language through which they may articulate, understand, and identify potential sources of social problems. It has provided a means for exploring the link between personality attributes, beliefs, and attitudes. It has highlighted the need to study beliefs and attitudes in terms of structure as well as content. Milgram's work on obedience further alerts professionals to the fact that they are dealing with differences among individuals in degree and not in kind. No doubt, future theorizing about authoritarianism will reflect attempts to relegate it to a position more in keeping with other personality attributes. The more recent studies clearly suggest that this trend is already in progress.

Application to Particular Variables

Critics have been concerned about educational biases inherent in the assessment and application of authoritarianism. People who are educated tend to be evaluated as possessing more liberal attitudes, beliefs, and traits. Simpson's (1972) research on the relationship between education and authoritarianism shows that years of education are accompanied by a reduction in authoritarianism in the United States but not in Mexico. Related factors, such as socioeconomic and vocational considerations, also contribute to assessment biases. For example, Gonzalez-Tamayo (1974) showed that students from higher socioeconomic classes are less dogmatic than those from lower socioeconomic classes in both the United States and Spain. In a similar way, Weller and Nadler (1975) found authoritarianism to be associated with job preference. Herman (1974) showed that vocational undecidedness, in contrast to decidedness, is related to dogmatic characteristics. Rouff (1975) reported a negative correlation between task complexity and dogmatism.

There is reason to believe that people who score high on measures of authoritarianism are also predisposed to view the less intelligent and the mentally ill with beliefs and attitudes that are largely negative. However, there is little evidence that authoritarianism itself is directly related to mental illness; liberalism does not guarantee the absence of psychopathology. Hood (1974) found that highly dogmatic persons tended to reject the mentally ill more often than less dogmatic persons did. Also, when confronted with information thought to reduce stereotypic cognitive rejection of the mentally ill, highly dogmatic persons became even more rejecting than before exposure to the information. Butts and Chotlos (1974) found that schizophrenics were more dogmatic than a sample of nonalcoholics, but they found no differences between alcoholics and schizophrenics. In terms of organic impairment, Kahn, Pollack, and Fink (1960) showed that convulsive shock increased authoritarianism in a group of patients. Further, increases in degree of brain dysfunction were associated with increases in authoritarianism. Organically impaired people are susceptible to authoritarianism labels, partly because organicity leads to rigid behavior patterns and stereotyped functioning in general.

Age and sex of persons are also related to authoritarianism and corresponding concepts. Whitten (1976) found that authoritarianism decreased in similar subjects between 1950 and 1973. Ondrack (1976) found a similar trend for dogmatism in subjects from 1958 to 1968. Heikkinen (1975) reported a tendency for older counseling students to be relatively more dogmatic than younger students. Everly (1975) reported a stronger correlation between dogmatism and externality for males than for females; however, in a sample of counselor trainees, Heikkinen (1975) found no sex differences in the relation of dogmatism to teaching experience, illness, and liberalism. Gonzalez-Tamayo (1974) found a tendency for boys to be less dogmatic than girls in both the United States and Spain.

Ethnic and racial considerations also influence assessment and application of authoritarianism to various populations. For example, Rubovits and Maehr (1973) found that authoritarian teachers were more encouraging of white school children than black children, and they tended to ignore statements of black children more frequently than statements of white children. Hassan and Sarkar (1975) found attitudes of Indian college students toward the caste system to be correlated with measures of authoritarianism. Heaven (1976) found significant intercorrelations among measures of authoritarianism and ethnocentrism in a sample of white Afrikaan-speaking students.

Use of the concept of authoritarianism carries some responsibility with it. Ethical considerations of human welfare, such as the feelings of ethnic groups, are often negated by use of stereotypes and labels. These should be avoided as harmful and too often inaccurate.

References

Adorno, T. W., and others. *The Authoritarian Personality*. New York: Harper & Row, 1950.

Bass, B. M. "Authoritarianism or Acquiescence." *Journal of Abnormal and Social Psychology,* 1955, *51,* 616-623.

Butts, S. V., and Chotlos, J. "Closed-Mindedness in Alcoholics." *Quarterly Journal of Studies on Alcoholism,* 1974, *35,* 906-910.

Byrne, D. *An Introduction to Personality*. Englewood Cliffs, N.J.: Prentice-Hall, 1974.

Christie, R., and Cook, P. "A Guide to the Published Literature Relating to the Authoritarian Personality Through 1956." *Journal of Psychology,* 1958, *45,* 171-199.

Christie, R., and Jahoda, M. (Eds.). *Studies in the Scope and Method of "The Authoritarian Personality."* New York: Free Press, 1954.

Deutsch, M., and Krauss, R. M. *Theories in Social Psychology.* New York: Basic Books, 1965.

Epstein, R. "Authoritarianism, Displaced Aggression, and Social Status of the Target." *Journal of Personality and Social Psychology,* 1965, *2,* 585-589.

Everly, G. S., II. "The Dogmatism/Externality Correlation for College Students." *Psychological Reports,* 1975, *37,* 190.

Gonzalez-Tamayo, E. "Dogmatism, Self-Acceptance, and Acceptance of Others Among Spanish and American Students." *Journal of Social Psychology,* 1974, *94,* 15-25.

Harvey, O. J., Hunt, D. E., and Schroder, H. M. *Conceptual Systems and Personality Organization.* New York: Wiley, 1961.

Hassan, M. K., and Sarkar, S. N. "Attitudes Toward Caste System as Related to Certain Personality and Sociological Factors." *Indian Journal of Psychology,* 1975, *50* (4), 313-319.

Heaven, P. C. L. "Authoritarianism and Ethnocentrism: A South African Sample." *Psychological Reports,* 1976, *39,* 656.

Heikkinen, C. A. "Another Look at Teaching Experience and Closed-Mindedness." *Journal of Counseling Psychology,* 1975, *22* (1), 79-83.

Herman, A. "The Relationship of Vocational Decidedness and Satisfaction with Dogmatism and Self-Esteem." *Journal of Vocational Behavior,* 1974, *5,* 95-102.

Hood, R. W., Jr. "Cognitive and Affective Rejection of Mentally Ill Persons as a Function of Dogmatism." *Psychological Reports,* 1974, *35,* 543-549.

Kahn, R. L., Pollack, M., and Fink, M. "Social Attitude (California F Scale) and Convulsive Therapy." *Journal of Nervous and Mental Disease,* 1960, *130,* 187-192.

Kerlinger, F., and Rokeach, M. "The Factorial Nature of the F and D Scales." *Journal of Personality and Social Psychology,* 1966, *4,* 391-399.

Klein, G. S., Barr, H., and Wolitzky, D. L. "Personality." In *Annual Review of Psychology.* Palo Alto, Calif.: Annual Reviews, Inc., 1967.

Levinson, D. J., and Huffman, P. E. "Traditional Family Ideology and Its Relation to Personality." *Journal of Personality,* 1955, *23,* 251-273.

Martin, J. G., and Westie, F. R. "The Tolerant Personality." *American Sociological Review,* 1959, *24,* 521-528.

Messick, S., and Jackson, D. N. "Authoritarianism or Acquiescence in Bass's Data." *Journal of Abnormal and Social Psychology,* 1957, *54,* 424-426.

Milgram, S. *Obedience to Authority.* New York: Harper & Row, 1974.

Mitchell, H. E., and Byrne, D. "The Defendant's Dilemma: Effects of Jurors' Attitudes and Authoritarianism on Judicial Decisions." *Journal of Personality and Social Psychology,* 1973, *25,* 123-129.

Ondrack, D. A. "Time-Series Analysis of Dogmatism Norms Among College Students." *Journal of Applied Social Psychology,* 1976, *6,* 134-144.

Rokeach, M. *The Open and Closed Mind.* New York: Basic Books, 1960.

Rorer, L. G. "The Great Response-Style Myth." *Psychological Bulletin,* 1965, *63,* 129-156.

Rotter, J. "Generalized Expectancies for Internal Versus External Control of Reinforcement." *Psychological Monographs,* 1966, *80* (Whole No. 609).

Rouff, L. L. "Openness, Creativity and Complexity." *Psychological Reports,* 1975, *37,* 1009-1010.

Rubovits, P. C., and Maehr, M. L. "Pygmalion Black and White." *Journal of Personality and Social Psychology,* 1973, *25* (2), 210-218.

Sahakian, W. S. *Systematic Social Psychology.* New York: Chandler, 1974.

Samuelson, F., and Yates, J. F. "Acquiescence and the F Scale: Old Assumptions and New Data." *Psychological Bulletin,* 1967, *68,* 91-103.

Simpson, M. "Authoritarianism and Education: A Comparative Approach." *Sociometry,* 1972, *35,* 223-234.

Steiner, I. D., and Johnson, H. H. "Authoritarianism and Tolerance of Trait Inconsistency." *Journal of Abnormal and Social Psychology,* 1963, *67,* 388-391.

Weller, L., and Nadler, A. "Authoritarianism and Job Preference." *Journal of Vocational Behavior,* 1975, *6* (1), 9-14.

West, S. G., and Gunn, S. P. "Some Issues of Ethics and Social Psychology." *American Psychologist,* 1978, *33,* 30-38.

Whitten, N. E. "Authoritarian Personalities, 1950-1973." *Journal of Personality Assessment,* 1976, *40,* 622-625.

Wrightsman, L. S. *Social Psychology in the Seventies.* Monterey, Calif.: Brooks/Cole, 1973.

82

Therese L. Baker

Nonauthoritarianism

The early historical development of nonauthoritarianism can be recognized only as a side show to the primary concern, authoritarianism. The major methodological concerns and developments have largely centered on authoritarianism. Although nonauthoritarianism scales (stemming from earlier authoritarianism scales) have broken away to become independent measures, they have not yet been subject to the rigorous critiques applied to scales such as the Fascism Scale (F Scale) (Adorno and others, 1950). Full-scale systematic and critical research focusing directly on nonauthoritarianism remains to be carried out.

As defined by Adorno and his associates, nonauthoritarianism is the converse of the following attributes: conventionalism, authoritarian submission and authoritarian aggression (indicators of moralistic standards and adherence to those who establish social roles), anti-intraception (opposition to the subjective and the imaginative), superstition and stereotypy (oversimplification of human events, rigid categorization), power and toughness (exaggerated strength, interpersonal relations dominated by power and submission to power), destructiveness and cynicism (impulsive aggressiveness, the belief that humans are naturally exploitative), projectivity (ascription of distorted attributes to outgroups), and exaggerated concern with sex (aggression toward sexual deviants).

These psychological dimensions are not easily reversed. Webster, Sanford, and Freedman's (1955) Social Maturity Scale was derived by inverting the scores of items showing a significant correlation with the F Scale (though shorn of items measuring power, toughness, superstition, and projected sexuality). Social maturity was said to represent the negative pole of authoritarianism. Its vagueness and generality reflect the indefiniteness with which the opposite pole of authoritarianism is conceived.

Rokeach's (1960) study of dogmatism attempted to free the concept of authoritarianism/nonauthoritarianism from any specific ideological content. Open-mindedness, measured by low scores on Rokeach's Dogmatism Scale, was conceived of as a belief system that (1) tolerates contradiction; (2) rejects primitive beliefs, and (3) is optimistic toward the future, grounded in the present, and realistic about the past. Once again, the conceptualization of open-mindedness was developed largely as the converse of closed-mindedness.

Background and Current Status

Authoritarianism/nonauthoritarianism are concepts that stem from German-Austrian origins—specifically, from the work of the Frankfurt Institute of Social Research, established in Weimar Germany in 1923 as an autonomous, privately funded research institute associated with the University of Frankfurt. The objective of the institute was to pursue the theoretical implications of Marxism through rigorous social research. With the takeover by the Nazis in 1933, the institute went into exile, first in Geneva and then at Columbia University. It was later connected with the University of California at Berkeley (whence came *The Authoritarian Personality*) and finally returned to Frankfurt in the postwar period. (For a stimulating historical analysis of this institute and its work, see Jay, 1973.)

Perhaps the primary achievement of the institute was in drawing together the theories of Marx and Freud. Its most prominent Freudian, Erich Fromm, was influenced by the work of another German psychoanalyst (not connected to the institute), Wilhelm Reich. Both Reich and Fromm investigated the role of personality in ideological movements. Both viewed socialization in the family as critical for developing the patterns of authority which form the basis of ideology and social behavior.

In *The Mass Psychology of Fascism,* Reich ([1933] 1971) explored the authoritarian ideology, which he regarded as characteristic, to varying degrees, of all families. The human condition, Reich argued, is a psychological struggle toward freedom. For most, the struggle is too difficult, and the individual escapes from freedom by accepting the narrow-minded platitudes and saviors of the day. Those who achieve "freedom"—that is, those who are nonauthoritarian—have overcome the restrictiveness of their families and cultures.

Fromm's contributions to the institute's first work on authoritarianism, *Studien über Autorität und Familie* (Horkheimer, 1936), likewise stressed the salience of familial childrearing. In *Escape from Freedom,* published after his break from the institute, Fromm (1941) conceptualized freedom (nonauthoritarianism) as the realization of the self—the spontaneous expression of the emotional and intellectual aspects of personality.

In the late 1940s, T. W. Adorno, a leading member of the institute, in collaboration with a team of social psychologists at Berkeley, undertook a set of studies on anti-Semitism and ethnocentrism that culminated in the highly influential work *The Authoritarian Personality,* published in 1950. The most widely disseminated aspect of this study was the California F Scale—a Likert scale developed primarily by Daniel J. Levinson.

With the development of Rokeach's Dogmatism Scale in the mid 1950s (*The Open and Closed Mind* was in fact not published until 1960), the psychoanalytic explanations of authoritarianism offered by the Adorno group were challenged by a theory giving an account of authoritarianism as a result of defective cognition. By the late 1960s, other theorists, using a phenomenological approach, turned their attention to the process by which authoritarian ideas are weakened and nonauthoritarianism is generated. The structure and validity of the F Scale also were subjected to criticism. Frenkel-Brunswik's psychoanalytic interviewing of low scorers in the original study (Adorno and others, 1950) had led to a typology of nonauthoritarian types: the rigid, the protesting, the impulsive, the easygoing, and the genuine liberal. Sanford (1956, p. 290) described the genuine liberal as the "psychoanalytic ideal, representing a balance of superego, ego, and id." Not repressed, the genuine liberal is independent, resistive of interference with personal convictions and beliefs, and not intrusive with others. Quite simply, low scorers on the F Scale could be conceived of as either liberals (Sanford, 1956) or left-wing authoritarians (Shils, 1954). While the Adorno group attempted to differentiate "rigid" low scorers from "genuine liberals," Shils (1954) sharply criticized their work as focusing essentially on authoritarianism of the right and neglecting to study the authoritarianism of the left. This, Shils argued, was largely a consequence of their relatively undifferentiated study of the low scorers. Frenkel-Brunswik's psychoanalytic interpretations of the low scorers in the original study were largely in terms of comparisons with high scorers. Shils extracted a subgroup of low scorers whose deeper dispositions he considered closer to the dispositions of the high scorers. If these deviant low scorers had been separately studied, Shils argued, their left-wing authoritarianism might have been noted.

In the decade following the publication of *The Authoritarian Personality,* a number of other scales measuring concepts closely related to authoritarianism were developed. In England Eysenck (1954) developed a Tough-Mindedness Scale, on which Communists and Fascists scored as tough-minded; conservatives and liberals, as tender-minded. The sharply critical evaluations of Eysenck's T Scale by Rokeach and Hanley (1956) and Christie (1956), despite Eysenck's responses (1956a, 1956b), served to discredit the pursuit of this dimension—at least in the United States.

Perlmutter (1954) developed a Xenophile Scale to measure a constellation of attributes characteristic of a certain type of antiauthoritarian; namely, an individual who is very unconventional, identifies with the weak, glorifies impulses, attributes goodness to foreigners, hates government or authority, and supports anarchism and radicalism in politics. Correlations with the F Scale indicated that those scoring high on the Xenophile Scale were higher on the F Scale than those scoring low.

Smith and Rosen (1958) reconceptualized nonauthoritarianism as closely allied to worldmindedness. Comparing the Worldmindedness Scale to the F Scale, Sampson and Smith (1957) argued that the two scales are virtually interchangeable except that the W Scale more explicitly taps national and international issues.

Rokeach (1960) developed the Dogmatism Scale to alleviate the right-wing political biases of the F Scale. His D Scale measures cognitive style rather than political ideology. This scale, to be discussed more fully in a later section, has proved to be the most serious alternative to the F Scale.

By the mid 1950s the F Scale items were already becoming anachronistic. Sanford, in conjunction with other social psychologists (Webster, Sanford, and Freedman, 1955), developed a new scale from items that correlated negatively with F-Scale items. This Social Maturity (SM) Scale was first tested at Vassar College (1961). Its items are less ideological and more personality centered than F-Scale items; thus, the investigators argued that the SM Scale is less subject to variation in political climate than the F Scale. The principal factor generated from a factor analysis of the SM scale became the basis for the shorter Autonomy Scale (AU) developed by Heist and Yonge (1968) for the Omnibus Personality Inventory. In both SM and AU, nonauthoritarianism is the positive loading factor. In research administering SM and AU as a part of personality inventories, numerous studies of college students have indicated that these two scales differentiate college seniors from freshman better than any other personality factor measured.

Nonauthoritarianism/authoritarianism has continued to be of interest in personality inventories and therapeutic situations. In the 1960s a new interest emerged in relating nonauthoritarianism both to the New Left and to changing positions and attitudes toward minority racial groups. There has been less interest in the development and refinement of authoritarianism/nonauthoritarianism scales in the 1970s.

Critical Discussion

General Areas of Concern

Structure of Authoritarian/Nonauthoritarian Scales. The Adorno group developed a set of nine personality traits (derived from both psychoanalytic theory and in-depth interviewing of prejudiced individuals) to serve as the components of the F Scale. Scale items were developed to measure these nine traits, so that theoretically the F Scale includes nine factors. The only analyses of the relationships among these factors carried out by the California group were item-to-item correlations, which were quite low (Adorno and others, 1950). Christie and Garcia (1951) intercorrelated the items for two samples and found markedly higher relationships. When sets of items considered by the Adorno team as making up factors were analyzed as clusters, the items from one cluster were highly related to items in other empirical clusters—possibly because, as Christie (1954, p. 137) later argued, "the original ascription of specific items under the heading of one hypothetical variable may have had a certain arbitrariness."

Camilleri's (1959) factor analysis of the F Scale generated seven factors consistent with seven of the nine theoretical variables, but the correlations between these factors were so inconsistent as to challenge the unidimensionality of the concept of authoritarianism. Lee and Warr's (1969) balanced form of the F Scale, in which half of the items were worded negatively (though not mere reversals of the original item), generated the ten following factors: (1) parental authority, (2) censorship, (3) institutional toughness, (4) authoritarian submission, (5) conventionalism, (6) authoritarian aggression, (7) authoritarian moralism, (8) religious belief, (9) national assertiveness, and (10) military ideology. Reister and Irvine (1974), however, compared responses to Lee and Warr's scale with the F Scale and found only weak relationships between the two instruments.

Rokeach and his associates developed the Dogmatism Scale (D Scale) as a measure of general (rather than right-wing) authoritarianism. In their view, dogmatism is not indicative of specific ideological bents but is characteristic of the cognitive structure. Dogmatism, as measured by the D Scale, is characterized by strongly held convictions (positive or negative, or both), pessimism, fear, concern with power, and belief in absolute authority. Various forms of factor analysis have been carried out on the Dogmatism Scale. Fruchter, Rokeach, and Novak (1958) extracted three factors from a factor analysis of the total scores of the D Scale with the total scores of the F Scale, the Anxiety Scale, the Gough-Sanford Rigidity Scale, and the Ethnocentrism Scale. They were anxiety, liberalism-conservatism, and rigidity-authoritarianism. Kerlinger and Rokeach (1966) combined F-Scale and D-Scale items and factor-analyzed the items together and separately. They found the two scales factorially discriminable despite high correlations between them. Thus, they concluded that while F and D are discriminable entities, they are based on a common underlying factor—namely, authoritarianism. Of the ten factors generated from the two scales, items from the F Scale tended to separate from those of the D Scale. Pedhazur's (1971) factor analysis of the D-Scale items produced five factors with low intercorrelations. He therefore challenged the unidimensionality of the scale because, he argued, total scores on the D Scale could reflect combinations of items that are largely unrelated. Thus, Pedhazur stressed the complexity of the structure of dogmatism. In a comparison of the F and D Scales (and the research generated from each), Thompson and Michel (1972) questioned the superiority of the D Scale over the F Scale as a measure of authoritarianism.

Validity of Authoritarian/Nonauthoritarian Scales: Acquiescence Response Set. One of the major concerns over the F Scale was the issue of whether positive responses (which in the F Scale were in every case scored as authoritarian) were stimulated by the need to acquiesce. In an early study of the F Scale, Bass (1955) found support for the hypothesis "that performance on the F Scale has less to do with the content validity of the items than with the response set to acquiesce to any generalization about social issues —authoritarian or equalitarian" (p. 616). Messick and Jackson (1957) found methodological error in Bass's data analysis but nevertheless upheld his hypothesis.

Gage, Leavitt, and Stone (1957) suggested that acquiescence set is itself a component of authoritarianism. This creates the obvious difficulty that, in a scale which scores positive responses to positively worded statements as authoritarian, it is impossible to isolate acquiescence from other components of authoritarianism. Pursuing the debate over acquiescence, Christie, Havel, and Seidenberg (1958) developed a version of the F Scale where half of the items were reversed in such a way that they measured the converse of the original items. This scale reduced the tendency for response set and discriminated positively between individuals scoring high and low on the original F Scale. Comparing positive and negative versions of the F, D, Anti-Semitism, and Conservatism Scales, Peabody (1961) found that agreement was largely a function of acquiescence set and that disagreement was a function of the actual attributes measured. Peabody thus challenged the usefulness of the argument that acquiescence is an aspect of authoritarianism and argued instead that the acquiescence of high authoritarian scorers indicated an absence of strongly held attitudes.

Ethical Considerations. Since authoritarianism is not a quality that most would, knowingly, be proud to exhibit, there is a need for investigators to clothe the measure of authoritarianism in some other dress. Furthermore, the response set problem prompts researchers to be cautious not to suggest to the subjects what should be a favorable response. Thus, subjects studied in research on authoritarianism/nonauthoritarianism are generally not informed prior to the testing or experimental procedure about the exact nature of the project. What this means is that data on authoritarianism are purchased at the price of some degree of deception of the subjects.

Yet most research subjects have been college students. Their general sophistication and their greater ability to differentiate psychological testing from therapy should preclude most of the ethical questions that might be raised. It could, however, be argued that it is ethically suspect, outside a therapeutic context, to ask subjects to respond to attitudinal items that might be disturbing.

Problems of Sampling and Spuriousness. The F Scale was attacked by Hyman and Sheatsley (1954) on the ground of its nonrandom sampling design. Those studied by the Adorno group were largely middle class, Caucasian, from the San Francisco area, better educated, and members of formal, voluntary organizations. These qualities served to bias the representativeness of the sample. Numerous researchers have found nonauthoritarianism as measured by the F Scale to be largely a function of higher educational attainment.

Significance of Early Family Childrearing. The investigators of *The Authoritarian Personality* were convinced that early childrearing practices and patterns of authority in the family were the key to the development of nonauthoritarianism in adults. Levinson and Huffman (1955) developed a Traditional Family Ideology (TFI) scale to identify the authoritarian family. The scale was constructed around five factors: (1) conventionalism, (2) authoritarian submission, (3) exaggerated masculinity and femininity, (4) extreme emphasis on discipline, and (5) moralistic rejection of impulse life. The TFI was shown to correlate strongly with the F Scale. Ernhart and Loevinger (1969) developed an Authoritarian Family Ideology Scale from an earlier family problems scale.

Hart (1957) found a correlation between a mother's degree of authoritarianism and the punitiveness of maternal responses to some specific behaviors of her children (but not including sex or dependency behaviors). In particular, Hart did not find low authoritarian mothers less punitive toward their children's sex or dependency behaviors. Dickens and Hobart (1959) tried to assess the influence of parental authoritarianism/nonauthoritarianism on a sample of college students and their mothers. Using the mothers' retrospective evaluations of how they raised their college-aged children (a questionably reliable indicator), the investigators found similarly high correlations between parental dominance and ethnocentrism of child ($r = .48$) and parental ignoring and ethnocentrism of child ($r = .51$).

Using the F Scale and the TFI Scale, Byrne (1965) found, in a sample of college students and their parents, that the parents correlated significantly with each other on the two scales; that fathers correlated positively with sons; and that mothers correlated positively with offspring of both sexes. Since the magnitude of the relationships by no means accounted for all the variance, Byrne questioned how far parental influence is crucial in determining authoritarian or nonauthoritarian attitudes of children. Greenberg and associates (1963) found no relationship between birth order and the F Scale. Wisdom and Walsh (1975) found first borns scoring highest on the Dogmatism Scale, followed by middle born and then youngest; these differences, however, were not statistically significant.

Relationship to Anomie and Alienation. In a randomly sampled study in Springfield, Massachusetts, Srole (1956) found positive relationships between authoritarianism (as measured by the F Scale); attitudes toward minorities (based on structured interview items); and a five-item scale of anomie, which measured (1) indifference of community leaders to self, (2) fickle and unpredictable social order, (3) retrogression from personal goals, (4) loss of internalized social norms, and (5) immediate personal relationships no longer predictable or supportive. McDill (1961) replicated Srole's study, factor-analyzed the correlations, and found one factor accounting for 45 percent of the total variance of the items comprising the three scales. This factor was characterized as a negative *Weltanschauung* (dim world view). In a subsequent study using various measures of anomie and alienation in relation to authoritarianism and discrimination, Knapp (1976) factor-analyzed these scales and extracted ten factors. He concluded that "authoritarianism and alienation are multidimensional constructs" and that "some of the scales designed to measure these constructs, such as the California F Scale, are themselves multidimensional" (p. 210). Thus, earlier evidence of high correlations between authoritarianism, anomie, and alienation may indicate only that parts of the two scales are measuring the same dimension.

Relationship to Anxiety. Kogan (1956) found evidence that, in an experimentally induced threat situation, students with higher F scores repressed the perception of threat more than students with lower F scores. Rokeach (1960) argued that dogmatism is a cognitive defense system against anxiety. On the basis of retrospective data from college students, Rokeach (1960) speculated that childhood experiences generative of anxiety will encourage dogmatism in adulthood. Hanson and Bush (1971) found that workers threatened by loss of jobs from a factory closing were higher in dogmatism scores than comparable workers at a plant that was not threatened with closing. Hanson and Clune (1973), using a modified form of the D Scale for children (Dommert, 1967), studied seventh and eighth graders and replicated Rokeach's findings that anxiety and dogmatism are associated.

Relationship to Rigidity. Brown (1953) found that the rigidity-authoritarian relationship occurs only in an ego-involving environment. When the ego is threatened, the authoritarian's ability to solve problems is weakened. In a relaxed environment, little difference appeared between the "rigidity" levels of those with or without authoritarian beliefs. Jackson, Messick, and Solley (1957) discovered that the "rigid" subjects were as likely to agree with F-Scale items as with reversed F-Scale items, thus supporting the conclusion that acquiescence and conformity are the commonalities between rigidity and authoritarianism.

In an early article, Rokeach (1948) argued that the inability to restructure a field (rigidity) can manifest itself for either social or nonsocial problems. As distinguished from dogmatic thinking, which involves "total cognitive configurating ideas and beliefs organized into a relatively closed system, rigidity . . . points to difficulties in overcoming single sets or beliefs encountered in attacking, solving, or learning specific tasks or problems" (Rokeach, 1960, p. 183). Parrott (1971) factor-analyzed the D Scale and the Gough-Sanford Rigidity Scale and found clear separations between the scales, supporting their theoretical distinctiveness.

Relationship to Ambiguity Tolerance. In an early study, O'Connor (1952) found ethnocentrism to be highly related to "intolerance of ambiguity." MacDonald (1970) developed an ambiguity tolerance scale to tap the general tendency to perceive ambiguous material or situations as threatening. His AT-20 Scale showed significant negative correlations with the D Scale, the F Scale, and the Gough-Sanford Rigidity Scale. Using MacDonald's scale, Chabassol and Thomas (1975) found negative correlations between dogmatism and ambiguity tolerance.

Relationship to Self-Awareness. In a study using a self-rating scale of the eleven dimensions of the F Scale, Wrightsman (1962) found that those high on the F Scale were aware of their prejudiced attitudes and authoritarian predispositions.

Comparative Philosophies and Theories

The Authoritarian Personality, as well as much of the subsequent work it generated, was psychoanalytic in its theoretical framework; that is, it regarded the human personality as subject to the driven desires of the id and the rationalizing forces of the superego. In this view, authoritarianism is inherent in the personality and is weakened only when the individual's ego is able to gain sufficient control. Thus, the groundwork for the nonauthoritarian personality is laid down in early childhood, and only deep psychoanalytic intervention will tap its foundations. Such a theory minimizes the potential importance of sociocultural factors or learning in altering authoritarianism.

With the work of Rokeach, the study of authoritarianism moved toward cognitive explanations. Such work had been foreshadowed by the strong associations consistently found between nonauthoritarianism and educational attainment, but the work of

Rokeach, first on mental rigidity and then on dogmatism, formulated a kind of cognitive authoritarianism as it applied to entire belief systems. Recognizing both the irrational model of personality characteristic of psychoanalysis and the rational model of the Gestalt theorists, Rokeach assumed that the human personality is subject to both the cognitive need to understand and the rationalizing need to reduce threat. Rokeach (1960, pp. 67-68) stated: "To the extent that the cognitive need to know is predominant and the need to ward off threat absent, open systems [nonauthoritarianism] should result. . . . As the need to ward off threat becomes stronger, the cognitive need to know should become weaker, resulting in more closed belief systems."

The relationship of education to nonauthoritarianism also raised the question of how higher education predisposes those who experience it to become less authoritarian. Finding that the less educated, the aged, the rural, members of disadvantaged minorities, the lower classes, members of dogmatic religious groups, the socially isolated and those raised in authoritarian families are more authoritarian, Stewart and Hoult (1959, p. 274) suggest that "the degree of so-called authoritarianism manifested by a particular individual is, on the average, negatively correlated with the number of social roles he has mastered." Limited opportunities for role playing narrow the range of reference groups to which the individual can relate, and thereby constrict perspectives on human behavior and society. These limited perspectives, in turn, further reduce the individual's ability to take on still newer roles. Kelman and Barclay (1963) assert that breadth of perspective is the result of both the opportunity for widening experiences through increased role taking and the capacity of individuals to shift contexts and accept differences. An incapacity to broaden one's perspective is the core of the authoritarian personality.

Gabennesch (1972) attempted to determine why a person who is aware of a wide variety of viewpoints (that is to say, a person with breadth of perspective) becomes tolerant of differences in ideology. The authoritarian with a narrow breadth of perspective, Gabannesch argues, reifies human action and institutions. Viewing the world in reified terms, such a person is incapable of recognizing social reality as the result of human actions: "Applied to a general outlook on the world . . . increased social awareness can cause social reality to be recognized more fully as human reality rather than as something superordinate to man and independent of his wishes and powers" (Gabbennesch, 1972, p. 868). Such a phenomenological theory of authoritarianism as reification is close to Piaget's (1965) conception of the moral realism of the child.

While a reified outlook may develop early in life, exposure to certain situations might make some conceptions less reified and thereby bring about nonauthoritarianism. Berger and Pullberg (1965) have suggested three such environments: (1) disintegration of social structures (as in major catastrophes), (2) environments that induce "culture shock," and (3) social marginality. In an empirical test of the theory that de-reification occurs as a result of culture shock, Baker (1976a, 1976b) found that, over the course of their first year in a predominantly white college, black freshmen exhibited a greater weakening of authoritarianism than did whites.

Elaboration on Critical Points

The original conceptualization of nonauthoritarianism, based on the analysis of low scorers on the F Scale, was ambiguous. Is "rigid" nonauthoritarianism not distinct from "liberal" nonauthoritarianism? Critics with political interests questioned whether left-wing adherents are not as authoritarian as right-wing adherents (Eysenck, 1954; Shils, 1954); others, such as Rokeach, argued that nonauthoritarianism can only be conceived once the concept of authoritarianism is stripped of its ideological bent.

If authoritarianism is a "proauthority" set of beliefs, is nonauthoritarianism an "antiauthority" or a "neutral-authority" set of beliefs? As long as the conceptualization of authoritarianism/nonauthoritarianism was grounded in psychoanalytic theory, the unchangeable quality of this factor (a product of early family life experiences) largely precluded interest in determining the conditions under which authoritarian beliefs are altered. The strong correlations between higher educational attainment and nonauthoritarianism indicated that authoritarianism is subject to weakening. How this process occurs has recently become the subject of increasing interest. Piaget (as well as psychoanalytic writers) postulated the essential authoritarianism of children. As children encounter more complex and differentiated experiences, and have increased contacts with others whose attitudes and life styles vary, they are forced to recognize that the views of other people often are different from their own.

During the years of maturation (simultaneous with the school years), authoritarianism is most subject to weakening. Two explanatory models can be offered to account for this phenomenon. According to the social-psychological "grow-up" model, certain social circumstances (for example, attending college) *broaden* one's opportunity to encounter new people, new ideas, and new information and therefore enable the individual to view multiple ways of playing similar roles and to explore a greater variety of roles. As a result, the individual achieves a greater understanding of and sympathy for the values and behaviors of strangers. Such a process would seemingly lead to greater open-mindedness. The phenomenological or "shake-up" model argues that unusual social environments (such as war or environments that create "culture shock" or a sense of "marginality") *alter* the individual's construction of social reality and thereby provide multiple viewpoints or perspectives. As a result, the individual is unable to conceive of society's institutions as something above and beyond human effort; that is to say, as reified. Rather, the fixedness of the social order is shaken, and the potential for social change is realized.

Personal Views and Recommendations

Although the social-psychological and phenomenological models have been presented as competing alternatives, they may be complementary. In some cases a phenomenological "shake-up" that ends the reification of social reality, presenting it in a new light as an open world offering a multiplicity of social roles and options, may be part of the process by which an individual takes advantage of the broadening opportunities of a social environment. Too much of a "shake-up," however, might have the opposite effect. It might stimulate the kind of stability-maintaining mechanisms that Feldman and Newcomb (1969) found among college students from lower-class or minority group backgrounds who were reacting to the cultural discontinuity of college life. These discontinuous college students were unable to "enter in" to the broadening context of the new social environment of college. Baker's study (1976a, 1976b) of the weakening of authoritarianism of black and white students at a predominantly white college found that lower-class black students, subject to "culture shock," were more likely to change on the antiauthoritarian factor of the Autonomy Scale (a derivation of the F Scale), less likely to change on the anticonventionalism factor, and least likely to change on the open-mindedness factor. On the contrary, middle-class white students, subject to social broadening, changed more in the direction of the open-mindedness factor.

Antiauthoritarianism, as represented by the factor analysis of the Autonomy Scale, suggests a perception of society as restrictive of individual autonomy and a questioning of authority. Society is seen as something over and against the individual; in other words, it is reified. The "givenness" of the traditional social order is no longer accepted.

But there is no clear indication that society is open to individual initiative in role defini-tion and fulfillment. Instead, there is a sense of alienation. Society is seen as an order not simply "given" but "imposed." The antiauthoritarian has negatively reified society.

The open-mindedness factor on the Autonomy Scale seems to suggest an opposite conception. It implies a perception of society as open to many possibilities and an atti-tude toward individual conduct within society as relatively free from social restraints. This open-minded vision of the social order suggests the least reified conception of soci-ety as a continuum of possibilities and choices. Anticonventionalism as a factor on the Autonomy Scale seems to fall between the negative renewal of reification of social reality implied in antiauthoritarianism and the positive de-reification implied in open-minded-ness. The individual questions the conventional social order but may not be capable of accepting or even seriously considering a new social order. Distrust of conventional wisdoms suggests that de-reification has occurred but not necessarily to the point where the individual is fully open-minded. A Guttman Scale analysis suggested that antiauthori-tarianism might be an earlier phase of nonauthoritarianism; anticonventionalism an inter-mediate phase; and open-mindedness a later phase, in which antiauthoritarian beliefs have been superseded by more relativistic beliefs (Baker, 1976a).

Application to Particular Variables

Age. MacKinnon and Centers (1956) found that authoritarian responses to an authoritarianism-equalitarianism scale generally increased among older people. Their Los Angeles data of age cohorts indicated that those in their 30s were the most equalitarian, exceeding those in their 20s and all older groups. The explanation for the high authoritar-ianism of those in their 20s was that they were not sufficiently independent from their family of origin. The investigators explained the relationship between young adulthood and equalitarianism as the result of the favorable socioeconomic and life-cycle position.

Sex. The Adorno group (1950) found means on the F Scale generally higher (more authoritarian) for men than for women, but this finding was largely accounted for by the larger proportion of lower-class and deviant (prisoner) men than women in their sample. Examining the theory that authoritarianism might be the result of restrictive up-bringing, to which girls are more subject, Anderson (1962) tested students from grades 8 through 12, using an abbreviated version of the D Scale. The relationship between sex and dogmatism was not significant, but the interaction of sex with intelligence indicated greater dogmatism for intelligent females than for intelligent males. In a more recent study, Gray-Little (1974) found no sex difference in Dogmatism scores for a sample of college students, but found that women were more disapproving than men of MMPI "con-flict with authority" items and that dogmatism significantly influenced these responses.

Education. The Authoritarian Personality was criticized for largely ignoring the educational attainment of those studied (Hyman and Sheatsley, 1954). Since that time, numerous studies attest to the weakening of authoritarianism as a function of educational attainment. In their compendium of the massive body of research generated in the 1950s and 1960s on the "effects of college," Feldman and Newcomb (1969, vol. 1, p. 31) found "seniors to be less authoritarian, less dogmatic, less ethnocentric, and less prejudiced than freshmen." Similar findings of the effects of college have been noted for university stu-dents in foreign countries (see, for example, Diab and Prothro, 1975).

In a cross-sectional design, Greenberg, Marvin, and Bivins (1959) found high school seniors planning to attend college less authoritarian than those not planning to attend, college freshmen less authoritarian than high school seniors, and college seniors less authoritarian than college freshmen. Comparing a group of high school seniors who went to college with a group who did not, Trent and Medsker (1968) found the college attenders less authoritarian, both initially and increasingly over time, while those who did not attend college maintained their high school levels of authoritarianism.

In a comparative analysis, Simpson (1972) showed that in the United States increasing education is inversely related to authoritarianism, whereas in Costa Rica only education beyond the eighth grade is related to nonauthoritarianism, and in Mexico the two factors are unrelated. According to Simpson, nonauthoritarianism comes about not merely as a result of more years of schooling but as a result of perfecting cognitive processes or interaction with nonauthoritarian teachers. Where education is largely rote learning, a weakening in authoritarianism is not one of its outcomes.

Intellectual Factors. The original Adorno study found only weak relationships between intelligence levels and the F Scale. This was true for a sample of psychiatric patients as well as for healthy samples. Only a sample of veterans indicated a strong negative correlation ($r = -.48$) between the F Scale and intelligence as measured by the Otis Higher Form Intelligence Test (Adorno and others, 1950). Using scores on the American Council on Education test (ACE) as rough measures of intelligence, Rokeach (1960) found virtually no relationship between dogmatism and intelligence ($r = -.02$).

Socioeconomic Status. The F Scale was early criticized by Shils (1954) as solely a measure of authoritarianism of the political right. That criticism stimulated examination of the authoritarianism of those more susceptible to the political left; namely, the working classes. Lipset (1963) found a ripe culture fostering authoritarian beliefs in the authoritarian familial atmosphere, low levels of education, low participation in voluntary organizations, insecure economic position, and religious orientations of the working classes. This multifactor explanation was challenged, however, by Lipsitz (1965), who showed that the relationship between class and authoritarianism is largely a function of education. When comparisons between noncollege-educated middle- and working-class men were made, workers were found to be less authoritarian on items measuring political attitudes. Studies on acquiescence (discussed earlier) indicate that the lower classes are consistently more susceptible to response bias. Using a situational scale on protest attitudes toward acquiescence, Hopple (1976) found little difference between union members and high school teachers.

Vocation. The incidence of nonauthoritarianism/authoritarianism among groups of people categorized by their vocation has been studied for a number of reasons. First, to improve the validity of the scales, subjects from various occupational sectors have been tested (Adorno and others, 1950). Second, the study of authoritarianism and vocations helps in understanding the nature of work environments. Third, nonauthoritarianism may be a desirable trait for those who hold certain types of occupations, in particular counselors and therapists. Vroom and Mann (1960) found that workers' satisfaction was related to the level of authoritarianism of their supervisors. In some work groups, authoritarian supervisors led to greater worker satisfaction; in others, nonauthoritarian supervisors had more satisfied workers. Size of work groups altered the relationship between authoritarian style of supervision and satisfaction of workers. Large groups were happier with authoritarian leaders.

In a study of organizational stress, Kahn and associates (1964) found that authoritarian workers were more committed to fulfilling responsibilities assigned by superiors. Conflict might occur if such workers were expected to do too much work. Because of their openness to multiple sources of influence, nonauthoritarian workers experienced greater conflict. Comparisons of the authoritarian levels of workers in organizational settings, and of professionals and clients, have been used to evaluate the climate of the work atmosphere. Gilbert and Levinson (1956), using a Custodial Mental Illness Scale (CMI), compared doctors, nurses, student nurses, and aides at four hospitals. They found that CMI scores (measuring either a custodial or a humanistic orientation to mental health) were strongly associated with F scores; the congruence between workers at various levels within a hospital suggested that recruitment, selective turnover, or socialization could explain this occurrence. Toobert, Scott, and Lewis (1962) discovered that methods of managing a large mental hospital (such as work detail and privilege cards for patients) varied with the authoritarianism of the employees.

Authoritarianism/nonauthoritarianism has been studied in relation to various aspects of the therapist-client relationship. In a study of patients and therapists in a psychiatric clinic and a counseling center, Vogel (1961) found authoritarianism (measured by the F Scale) was related to authoritarian attitudes towards therapy for both patient samples and the therapists in the counseling center. There was no clear evidence that equalitarian patients were able to form better therapeutic relations than authoritarian patients, neither was there support for the hypothesis that congruence between therapists and clients on authoritarianism or equalitarianism would facilitate their relationship.

In a study of counseling students and a noncounseling control group, Kemp (1962) found that while scores on the D Scale did not change significantly over time for the control group, a change towards an "open belief" system was significant for the experimental group. Kurtz, Kurtz, and Hoffnung (1970) discovered that psychiatric residents and social work students who were high on authoritarianism (F Scale) judged the histories of lower-class clients more negatively than those lower in authoritarianism. The difference was significant for the residents and close to significant for the social work students.

Baker and Schulberg (1967, 1969) determined that community health ideology, as measured by a scale they developed, was significantly negatively correlated to dogmatism for a sample of 140 members of a citizens mental health board. Khajavi, Hekmat, and Mehryar (1973) studied various types of mental health workers and found all of them lower in authoritarianism than a control group. Furthermore, those mental health workers with greater experience (staff psychiatrists) were lower in authoritarianism than psychiatric residents.

Using a Democratic Values Scale as a measure of nonauthoritarianism, Lerner (1973) found that, regardless of the level of impairment of the client, the more nonauthoritarian therapists had more positive effects on clients than authoritarian therapists did. In a study of the preferences for psychotherapy of mental health hospital patients, Canter (1971) found that patients with higher levels of authoritarianism (F Scale) preferred structured over less structured (group therapy) sessions. Using a different design, Fernbach (1973) studied the preferences of authoritarian and nonauthoritarian college students for directive or nondirective therapy. Exposing the subjects to films of Carl Rogers and Albert Ellis interviewing the same client, he discovered that the authoritarian students preferred the directive therapist, whereas the nonauthoritarian students preferred the nondirective therapist.

Resnick and Berk (1975) related the Whitehorn-Betz A-B Scale to authoritarianism (F Scale). Type A therapists, who disavow an interest in manual, technical, and mechanical activities, have been shown to be more effective with schizoid patients, while type B therapists, who do not deny an interest in these activities, are more effective with neurotics. These investigators found only minimal support for the hypothesis that type-A individuals are less authoritarian than type-B individuals. Finally, in a study of the effects of authoritarianism on telephone crisis center volunteer behaviors, Schoenfeld and Neal (1976) found that nonauthoritarian volunteers spoke more profusely and gave fewer referrals. They concluded that nonauthoritarianism is related to altruism.

Ethnic/Racial Factors. Studies of differences in authoritarianism/nonauthoritarianism as a result of ethnic and racial differences include (1) evidence on authoritarian levels of non-American samples, (2) comparisons of Americans and non-Americans, (3) intra-American comparisons of religious groups, and (4) intra-American comparisons of racial groups.

Nonauthoritarianism was found to be positively correlated with increasing levels of education for German nationals (Cohn and Carsch, 1954). In a study of South African nationals, Pettigrew (1958) found no clear relationship between levels of authoritarianism (F Scale) and prejudiced attitudes toward black Africans. Such attitudes may express cultural conditioning rather than psychological motivations. Siegman (1961) found, in an Israeli sample, an association between authoritarian and prejudiced attitudes toward Morrocan Jewish immigrants and Arabs.

Comparing American college students to Lebanese Moslem students, Melikian (1956) found the American students to be significantly more nonauthoritarian than the Middle Eastern. Thomas (1974) found that North Americans were more nonauthoritarian than Australians.

In a comparative, cross-sectional study of Jewish, Protestant, and Catholic freshmen and seniors at three American colleges, Brown and Bystryn (1956) found the Jewish students (especially those attending a small, nondenominational liberal arts college) to be most subject to change toward nonauthoritarianism. They offer a contextual explanation—the effects of minority status in a less traditional environment—as the cause of the change.

Steckler (1957) found that black college students who identified with white middle-class values (conservative, anti-Negro) and dissociated themselves from blacks were high on authoritarianism (F Scale). Comparing black and white college students, Smith and Prothro (1957) found whites to be more nonauthoritarian than blacks. Baker (1976b) examined black and white college students over the course of a year in a predominantly white college and found black students becoming more nonauthoritarian than white—though a factor analysis of the scale indicated that black students were more subject to change on the antiauthoritarian rather than the open-minded items of the nonauthoritarian Autonomy scale.

Physical Disorders. Hogan (1970) found deaf (black and white) adolescents high on authoritarianism (with the blacks scoring lower than whites).

Psychiatric Disorders. The authors of *The Authoritarian Personality* argued that psychologically disturbed individuals might be found within all ranges of authoritarianism and that the most disturbed individuals might well be found in the middle quartiles. Yet research that followed the study presumed that high scorers are mentally unhealthy. To clarify this concern, Freedman, Webster, and Sanford (1956) related authoritarianism to psychopathology as measured by the MMPI. They found extrapunitiveness and schizoid tendencies unrelated to authoritarianism, impunitiveness (measured by the Hysteria Scale) negatively related to authoritarianism, and intropunitiveness (guilt feelings and attitudes of inferiority) positively related to authoritarianism. To the degree that intropunitiveness as a measure of conscience would allow for realistic self-criticism, it should also be characteristic of low authoritarianism, but Freedman and his colleagues argued that, as a measure of early incorporated hostility against the self (due to punitive, restrictive upbringing), intropunitiveness is associated with high authoritarianism.

In a study of hospitalized drug addicts (classified from psychotic to neurotic), Lefcourt (1962) found that the psychotic group was the more dogmatic. Butts and Chotlos (1974) studied dogmatism in alcoholics and found a strong relationship. They concluded that therapists should "focus on helping [alcoholics] to socialize their need for power so that they [will] not feel isolated and helpless" (p. 909).

Ehrlich and Bauer (1966) found that patient Dogmatism scores were strong indicators of level of impairment, susceptibility to treatment, and outcome. High dogmatic patients were more often diagnosed as functionally psychotic, as suffering from thought disorders, and as having greater occupational and social impairment. Treatment also varied by level of dogmatism. High dogmatics were more often administered drugs and had longer stays in hospital. No evidence was noted for an association between dogmatism and anxiety or paranoia; nor was dogmatism associated with change from electroconvulsive therapy or final prognosis. The Dogmatism scores of the therapists were not clearly related to treatment of or judgments concerning the patients. Scheid and Gelso (1971) discovered, in a study of neuropsychiatric patients during and after hospitalization, that open-minded (D Scale) patients improved more during hospitalization than closed-minded patients, but this relationship did not hold up for posthospital adjustment.

In a study of reactions to the mentally ill, Hood (1974) found that highly dogmatic social psychology students held more stereotyped attitudes toward the mentally ill but were more subject than low dogmatic students to attitude change after a series of lectures. On semantic differential scales measuring affective attitudes toward the mentally ill, however, high dogmatic students increased their rejection as a result of the lectures.

Collective/Interactional Factors. The evidence for the applications of authoritarianism to individuals in group environments would suggest the following five general patterns:

First, authoritarians are more subject to group pressure than nonauthoritarians in a laboratory experiment in autokinesis (Canning and Baker, 1957).

Second, conformity by high F subjects is only temporary, whereas conformity by low F subjects is more lasting (in an experiment where conformity was first induced in a laboratory setting and was again measured in a private setting) (Steiner and Vannoy, 1966).

Third, low dogmatic individuals in a classroom group prefer essay examinations and are more spontaneous in discussion, concerned with psychological issues, less dependent on the leader, more willing to ignore minor regulations, less embarrassed by tardiness, more relaxed, more dissatisfied with social conditions, and better able to express annoyance than high dogmatics. In a small-group class on controversial materials, low dogmatics were more casual about selection of a group leader and easier about discussing controversial material than high dogmatics (Zagona and Zurcher, 1964).

Fourth, weak evidence of the relation of authoritarianism to group task effectiveness exists, particularly in groups that are highly organized, so that personality characteristics of specific members have little import (summarized by Heslin, 1964).

Fifth, a study of the effects of ten weeks of a prison environment on changes in authoritarianism of first-time inmates indicated only one significant change. The prisoners became less resistant to examining issues from a humanistic perspective—that is, they were less anti-intraceptive (Rosenfield and Linn, 1976). On the basis of this study, the degree to which nonauthoritarianism may result from punitive collective environments appears to be minimal.

References

Adorno, T. W., and others. *The Authoritarian Personality.* New York: Harper & Row, 1950.

Anderson, C. C. "A Developmental Study of Dogmatism During Adolescence with Reference to Sex Differences." *Journal of Abnormal and Social Psychology,* 1962, *65,* 132-135.

Baker, F., and Schulberg, H. "The Development of a Community Mental Health Ideology Scale." *Community Mental Health Journal,* 1967, *3,* 216-225.

Baker, F., and Schulberg, H. "Community Mental Health Ideology, Dogmatism, and Political-Economic Conservatism." *Community Mental Health Journal,* 1969, *5,* 433-436.

Baker, T. L. "The Dimensions of Nonauthoritarianism." *Journal of Personality Assessment,* 1976a, *40,* 626-634.

Baker, T. L. "The Weakening of Authoritarianism in Black and White College Students." *Sociology and Social Research,* 1976b, *60,* 440-460.

Bass, B. M. "Authoritarianism or Acquiescence?" *Journal of Abnormal and Social Psychology,* 1955, *51,* 616-623.

Berger, P., and Pullberg, S. "Reification and the Sociological Critique of Consciousness." *History and Theory,* 1965, *4,* 196-211.

Brown, D. R., and Bystryn, D. "College Environment, Personality, and Social Ideology of Three Ethnic Groups." *Journal of Social Psychology,* 1956, *44,* 279-288.

Brown, R. W. "A Determinant of the Relationship Between Rigidity and Authoritarianism." *Journal of Abnormal and Social Psychology,* 1953, *48,* 469-476.

Butts, S. V., and Chotlos, J. "Closed-Mindedness in Alcoholics." *Quarterly Journal of Studies on Alcoholism,* 1974, *35,* 906-910.

Byrne, D. "Parental Antecedents of Authoritarianism." *Journal of Personality and Social Psychology,* 1965, *1,* 269-373.

Camilleri, S. F. "A Factor Analysis of the F Scale." *Social Forces,* 1959, *37,* 316-323.

Canning, R. R., and Baker, J. M. "Effect of the Group on Authoritarian and Nonauthoritarian Persons." *American Journal of Sociology,* 1957, *62,* 579-581.

Canter, F. M. "Authoritarian Attitudes, Degree of Pathology and Preference for Structured Versus Unstructured Psychotherapy in Hospitalized Mental Patients." *Psychological Reports,* 1971, *28,* 231-234.

Chabassol, D. J., and Thomas, D. "Need for Structure, Tolerance of Ambiguity, and Dogmatism in Adolescents." *Psychological Reports,* 1975, *37,* 507-510.

Christie, R. "Authoritarianism Re-examined." In R. Christie and M. Jahoda (Eds.), *Studies in the Scope and Method of "The Authoritarian Personality."* New York: Free Press, 1954.

Christie, R. "Some Abuses of Psychology." *Psychological Bulletin,* 1956, *53,* 439-451.

Christie, R., and Garcia, J. "Subcultural Variation in Authoritarian Personality." *Journal of Abnormal and Social Psychology,* 1951, *46,* 457-469.

Christie, R., Havel, J., and Seidenberg, B. "Is the F Scale Irreversible?" *Journal of Abnormal and Social Psychology,* 1958, *56,* 143-159.

Cohn, T. S., and Carsch, H. "Administration of the F Scale to a Sample of Germans." *Journal of Abnormal and Social Psychology,* 1954, *49,* 471.

Diab, L. N., and Prothro, E. T. "Changes in Authoritarianism Associated with University Residence in the Arab Middle East." *Journal of Social Psychology,* 1975, *97,* 155-162.

Dickens, S. L., and Hobart, C. "Parental Dominance and Offspring Ethnocentrism." *Journal of Social Psychology,* 1959, *49,* 297-303.

Dommert, E. M. "An Adaptation of Rokeach's Dogmatism Scale for Use with Elementary School Children." Unpublished master's thesis, Texas Women's University, Denton, 1967.

Ehrlich, H. J., and Bauer, M. L. "The Correlates of Dogmatism and Flexibility in Psychiatric Hospitalization." *Journal of Consulting Psychology,* 1966, *30,* 253-259.

Ernhart, C. B., and Loevinger, J. "Authoritarian Family Ideology: A Measure, Its Correlates, and Its Robustness." In *Multivariate Behavioral Research Monographs.* Austin, Tex.: Society of Multivariate Experimental Psychology, 1969.

Eysenck, H. J. *The Psychology of Politics.* London: Routledge and Kegan Paul, 1954.

Eysenck, H. J. "The Psychology of Politics: A Reply." *Psychological Bulletin,* 1956a, *53,* 177-182.

Eysenck, H. J. "The Psychology of Politics and the Personality Similarities Between Fascists and Communists." *Psychological Bulletin,* 1956b, *53,* 431-438.

Feldman, K. A., and Newcomb, T. M. *The Impact of College on Students.* (2 vols.) San Francisco: Jossey-Bass, 1969.

Fernbach, R. "Authoritarianism: A Selection Variable for Psychotherapy." *Journal of Counseling Psychology,* 1973, *20,* 69-72.

Freedman, M., Webster, H., and Sanford, N. "A Study of Authoritarianism and Psychopathology." *Journal of Psychology,* 1956, *41,* 315-322.

Fromm, E. *Escape from Freedom.* New York: Holt, Rinehart and Winston, 1941.

Fruchter, B., Rokeach, M., and Novak, E. G. "A Factorial Study of Dogmatism, Opinionation, and Related Scales." *Psychological Reports,* 1958, *4,* 19-22.

Gabennesch, H. "Authoritarianism as World View." *American Journal of Sociology,* 1972, *77,* 857-875.

Gage, N. L., Leavitt, G. S., and Stone, G. C. "The Psychological Meaning of Acquiescence Set for Authoritarianism." *Journal of Abnormal and Social Psychology,* 1957, *55,* 98-103.

Gilbert, D. C., and Levinson, D. J. "Ideology, Personality, and Institutional Policy in the Mental Hospital." *Journal of Abnormal and Social Psychology,* 1956, *53,* 263-271.

Gray-Little, B. "Attitudes Toward Conflict with Authority as a Function of Sex, I-E, and Dogmatism." *Psychological Reports,* 1974, *34,* 375-381.

Greenberg, H., Marvin, C., and Bivins, B. "Authoritarianism as a Variable in Motivation to Attend College." *Journal of Social Psychology,* 1959, *49,* 81-85.

Greenberg, H., and others. "Order of Birth as a Determinant of Personality and Attitudinal Characteristics." *Journal of Social Psychology,* 1963, *60,* 221-230.

Hanson, D. J., and Bush, A. M. "Anxiety and Dogmatism." *Psychological Reports,* 1971, *29,* 366.

Hanson, D. J., and Clune, M. "Dogmatism and Anxiety in Relation to Childhood Experience." *Journal of Social Psychology,* 1973, *91,* 157-158.

Hart, I. "Maternal Child-Rearing Practices and Authoritarian Ideology." *Journal of Abnormal and Social Psychology,* 1957, *55,* 232-237.

Heist, P., and Yonge, G. *Omnibus Personality Inventory—Form F.* Berkeley: Center for the Study of Higher Education, University of California, 1968.

Heslin, R. "Predicting Group Task Effectiveness from Member Characteristics." *Psychological Bulletin,* 1964, *62,* 248-256.

Hogan, H. W. "Authoritarianism Among White and Black Deaf Adolescents: Two Measures Compared." *Perceptual and Motor Skills,* 1970, *31,* 195-200.

Hood, R. W., Jr. "Cognitive and Affective Rejection of Mentally Ill Persons as a Function of Dogmatism." *Psychological Reports,* 1974, *35,* 543-549.

Hopple, G. W. "Protect Attitudes and Social Class: Working Class Authoritarianism Revisited." *Sociology and Social Research,* 1976, *60,* 229-246.

Horkheimer, M. (Ed.). *Studien über Autorität und Familie.* Paris: Félix Alcan, 1936.

Hyman, H. H., and Sheatsley, P. B. " 'The Authoritarian Personality'–A Methodological Critique." In R. Christie and M. Jahoda (Eds.), *Studies in the Scope and Method of "The Authoritarian Personality."* New York: Free Press, 1954.

Jackson, D. N., Messick, S. J., and Solley, C. M. "How 'Rigid' Is the Authoritarian?" *Journal of Abnormal and Social Psychology,* 1957, *54,* 137-140.

Jay, M. *The Dialectical Imagination: A History of the Frankfurt School and the Institute of Social Research 1923-50.* Boston: Little, Brown, 1973.

Kahn, R., and others. *Organizational Stress: Studies in Role Conflict and Ambiguity.* New York: Wiley, 1964.

Kelman, H., and Barclay, J. "The F Scale as a Measure of Breadth of Perspective." *Journal of Abnormal and Social Psychology,* 1963, *67,* 608-615.

Kemp, C. G. "Influence of Dogmatism on the Training of Counselors." *Journal of Counseling Psychology,* 1962, *9,* 155-157.

Kerlinger, F., and Rokeach, M. "The Factorial Nature of the F and D Scales." *Journal of Personality and Social Psychology,* 1966, *4,* 391-399.

Khajavi, E., Hekmat, H., and Mehryar, A. "Patterns of Alienation and Authoritarianism Among Mental Health Professionals and Trainees." *Journal of Community Psychology,* 1973, *1,* 164-167.

Knapp, R. J. "Authoritarianism, Alienation, and Related Variables: A Correlational and Factor-Analytic Study." *Psychological Bulletin,* 1976, *83,* 194-212.

Kogan, N. "Authoritarianism and Repression." *Journal of Abnormal and Social Psychology,* 1956, *53,* 34-37.

Kurtz, N., Kurtz, R., and Hoffnung, R. "Attitudes Toward the Lower and Middle-Class Psychiatric Patient as a Function of Authoritarianism Among Mental Health Students." *Journal of Consulting and Clinical Psychology,* 1970, *35,* 338-341.

Lee, R. E., and Warr, P. B. "The Development and Standardization of a Balanced F Scale." *Journal of General Psychology,* 1969, *81,* 109-129.

Lefcourt, H. M. "Clinical Correlates of Dogmatism." *Journal of Clinical Psychology,* 1962, *18,* 327-328.

Lerner, B. "Democratic Values and Therapeutic Efficacy: A Construct Validity Study." *Journal of Abnormal Psychology,* 1973, *82,* 491-498.

Levinson, D. J., and Huffman, P. E. "Traditional Family Ideology and Its Relation to Personality." *Journal of Personality,* 1955, *23,* 251-273.

Lipset, S. M. *Political Man.* London: Mercury Books, 1963.

Lipsitz, L. "Working-Class Authoritarianism: A Re-evaluation." *American Sociological Review,* 1965, *30,* 103-109.

McDill, E. L. "Anomie, Authoritarianism, Prejudice, and Socioeconomic Status: An Attempt at Clarification." *Social Forces,* 1961, *39,* 239-245.

MacDonald, A. P., Jr. "Revised Scale for Ambiguity Tolerance: Reliability and Validity." *Psychological Reports,* 1970, *26,* 791-798.

MacKinnon, W. J., and Centers, R. "Authoritarianism and Urban Stratification." *American Journal of Sociology,* 1956, *61,* 610-620.

Melikian, L. H. "Some Correlates of Authoritarianism in Two Cultural Groups." *Journal of Psychology,* 1956, *42,* 237-248.

Messick, S., and Jackson, D. N. "Authoritarianism or Acquiescence in Bass's Data." *Journal of Abnormal and Social Psychology,* 1957, *54,* 424-426.

O'Connor, P. "Ethnocentrism, Intolerance of Ambiguity, and Abstract Reasoning Ability." *Journal of Abnormal and Social Psychology*, 1952, *47*, 526-530.

Parrott, G. "Dogmatism and Rigidity: A Factor Analysis." *Psychological Reports*, 1971, *29*, 135-140.

Peabody, D. "Attitude Content and Agreement Set in Scales of Authoritarianism, Dogmatism, Anti-Semitism, and Economic Conservatism." *Journal of Abnormal and Social Psychology*, 1961, *63*, 1-11.

Pedhazur, E. J. "Factor Structure of the Dogmatism Scale." *Psychological Reports*, 1971, *28*, 735-740.

Perlmutter, H. V. "Some Characteristics of the Xenophilic Personality." *Journal of Psychology*, 1954, *38*, 291-300.

Pettigrew, T. F. "Personality and Sociocultural Factors in Intergroup Attitudes: A Cross-National Comparison." *Journal of Conflict Resolution*, 1958, *2*, 29-42.

Piaget, J. *The Moral Judgment of the Child.* New York: Free Press, 1965.

Reich, W. *The Mass Psychology of Fascism* [1933]. New York: Farrar, Straus and Giroux, 1971.

Reister, R. W., and Irvine, L. F. "A Methodological Inquiry into the F Scale." *Journal of Social Psychology*, 1974, *94*, 287-288.

Resnick, J. H., and Berk, S. "A-B Type Therapists and the Authoritarian Personality." *Psychological Reports*, 1975, *36*, 167-170.

Rokeach, M. "Generalized Mental Rigidity as a Factor in Ethnocentrism." *Journal of Abnormal and Social Psychology*, 1948, *43*, 259-278.

Rokeach, M. *The Open and Closed Mind.* New York: Basic Books, 1960.

Rokeach, M., and Hanley, C. "Eysenck's Tender-Mindedness Dimension: A Critique." *Psychological Bulletin*, 1956, *53*, 169-186.

Rosenfield, J., and Linn, M. W. "Perceptions of Penal Environment and Attitude Change." *Journal of Clinical Psychology*, 1976, *32*, 548-553.

Sampson, D. L., and Smith, H. P. "A Scale to Measure World-Minded Attitudes." *Journal of Social Psychology*, 1957, *45*, 99-106.

Sanford, N. "The Approach of the Authoritarian Personality." In J. L. McNary (Ed.), *Psychology of Personality: Six Modern Approaches.* New York: Logos Press, 1956.

Scheid, A. B., and Gelso, C. J. "Dogmatism, Hospital Behavior, and Post-Hospitalization Adjustment." *Journal of Consulting and Clinical Psychology*, 1971, *37*, 164.

Schoenfeld, L. S., and Neal, P. D. "Altruism and Authoritarianism and Their Relationship to Number of Referrals Made by Crisis-Center Volunteers." *Psychological Reports*, 1976, *39*, 705-706.

Shils, E. "Authoritarianism: 'Right' and 'Left.'" In R. Christie and M. Jahoda (Eds.), *Studies in the Scope and Method of "The Authoritarian Personality."* New York: Free Press, 1954.

Siegman, A. W. "A Cross-Cultural Investigation of the Relationship Between Ethnic Prejudice, Authoritarian Ideology, and Personality." *Journal of Abnormal and Social Psychology*, 1961, *63*, 654-655.

Simpson, M. "Authoritarianism and Education: A Comparative Approach." *Sociometry*, 1972, *35*, 223-234.

Smith, C. V., and Prothro, J. W. "Ethnic Differences in Authoritarian Personality." *Social Forces*, 1957, *35*, 334-338.

Smith, H. P., and Rosen, E. W. "Some Psychological Correlates of Worldmindedness and Authoritarianism." *Journal of Personality*, 1958, *26*, 170-183.

Srole, L. R. "Social Integration and Certain Corollaries: An Exploratory Study." *American Sociological Review*, 1956, *21*, 709-716.

Steckler, G. A. "Authoritarian Ideology in Negro College Students." *Journal of Abnormal and Social Psychology*, 1957, *54*, 396-399.

Steiner, I. D., and Vannoy, J. S. "Personality Correlates of Two Types of Conformity Behavior." *Journal of Personality and Social Psychology*, 1966, *4*, 307-315.

Stewart, D., and Hoult, T. "A Socio-psychological Theory of the Authoritarian Personality." *American Journal of Sociology*, 1959, *65*, 274-279.

Thomas, D. R. "The Relationship Between Ethnocentricity and Conservatism in an 'Authoritarian' Culture." *Journal of Social Psychology*, 1974, *94*, 179-186.

Thompson, R. C., and Michel, J. B. "Measuring Authoritarianism: A Comparison of the F and D Scales." *Journal of Personality*, 1972, *40*, 180-190.

Toobert, S., Scott, F., and Lewis, J. "Relation of Various Indicators of Ward Management to Measures of Staff Attitudes in a Large Mental Hospital." *Journal of Health and Human Behavior*, 1962, *3*, 185-193.

Trent, J. W., and Medsker, L. L. *Beyond High School: A Psychosociological Study of 10,000 High School Graduates.* San Francisco: Jossey-Bass, 1968.

Vassar College, Mary Conover Mellon Foundation for the Advancement of Education. *Measurement and Evaluation of Change in College Women.* Poughkeepsie, N.Y.: Vassar College, 1961.

Vogel, J. L. "Authoritarianism in the Therapeutic Relationship." *Journal of Consulting Psychology*, 1961, *25*, 102-108.

Vroom, V. H., and Mann, F. C. "Leader Authoritarianism and Employee Attitude." *Personnel Psychology*, 1960, *13*, 125-140.

Webster, H., Sanford, R. N., and Freedman, M. "A New Instrument for Studying Authoritarianism in Personality." *Journal of Psychology*, 1955, *40*, 73-84.

Wisdom, G., and Walsh, R. P. "Dogmatism and Birth Order." *Journal of Individual Psychology*, 1975, *31*, 32-36.

Wrightsman, L. S., Jr. "Authoritarianism and Self-Awareness." *Journal of Social Psychology*, 1962, *56*, 179-185.

Zagona, S. V., and Zurcher, L. A., Jr. "Participation, Interaction, and Role Behavior in Groups Selected from the Extremes of the Open-Closed Cognitive Continuum." *Journal of Psychology*, 1964, *58*, 255-264.

83

Paul G. Schauble

Facilitative Dimensions in Communication

Facilitative dimensions in communication are those behaviors whereby a message is sent from one person (or speaker) to another person (or listener). Successful communication is facilitated by speakers through *owning of feelings* (identifying and disclosing their reactions to themselves and others), *commitment to change* (resolving to work at maintaining and improving communication), *differentiation of stimuli* (identifying and discriminating between various sources of affect and anxiety and the corresponding reactions they stimulate), and *internalization* (immediate awareness of their actions and feelings, with appropriate recognition of the effects and impact of their behaviors). Listeners facilitate communication through *empathic understanding* (responding clearly and directly to the speaker so as to demonstrate hearing and understanding of what the speaker is saying), *concreteness* (responding so as to aid speakers in identifying and discussing their most relevant concerns), *genuineness* (demonstrating spontaneous and congruent reactions in a constructive manner), *respect* (the communication of regard and caring for the speaker's worth as a person), *confrontation* (constructively confronting the speaker with inconsistencies or conflicts which the listener experiences in the interaction), and *immediacy* (the expression of an awareness of dynamics between speaker and listener at any point in the relationship).

To the extent that an individual has not developed skills in these behaviors, that person's interactions will suffer accordingly. Listeners in counseling, therapy, or other "helping" relationships employ these skills to assist speakers (clients or other "helpees") to identify and cope with their personal difficulties, which in turn results in improved and more healthy communication behaviors in the helpee. Communication behaviors thus operationalized are readily observable in interpersonal interaction, and are valuable for assessing an individual's overall coping skills.

Background and Current Status

One of the most important advances for the helping professions has been the delineation of the so-called "facilitating conditions." Rogers (1961) set the foundation with the three major postulates of the client-centered (nondirective) approach: empathy, congruence, and positive regard. According to this approach, if the helper manifests these qualities in the therapeutic session and effectively communicates them to the helpee, the therapeutic relationship will facilitate psychological growth for the helpee. From this rather simplistic beginning came a plenitude of scientific research (much of which was empirical and highly respectable in terms of research design).

Most of the early research and literature treating the facilitative dimensions examined the behaviors of the helping agent (counselor, therapist, teacher) as an influence on the progress of the client, student, or other target of the helping process under examination (for a summary of this literature, see Truax and Carkhuff, 1967). The dimensions identified as important for "facilitating" change were eventually dubbed "core conditions." Included in the core conditions were two categories of helper response: *responsive* or attending behaviors (empathic understanding, concreteness, genuineness, and respect) and *initiative* or action-oriented behaviors (confrontation and immediacy).

The presence or absence of these behaviors was initially measured by independent ratings of behavior samples of subjects in treatment—generally based on audiotape or videotape recordings. Such samples were submitted to independent judges who had been specially trained in the use of scales for measuring each of the dimensions. These scales presented a series of points on a continuum describing the particular dimension to be rated. The continuum was built on a semantic differential base, requiring a positive or negative judgment as to the presence or absence of the behavior being rated. Thus, for empathic behavior the rating scale might range from a low rating of 1.0 ("The responder is preoccupied with his own intellectual interpretations of speaker behavior and fails to recognize the speaker's most obvious feelings") to a high rating of 5.0 ("The responder demonstrates a sensitive understanding of the speaker's feelings, both in content and intensity"). Several such rating scales (ranging from three rating categories to twenty-seven categories) were designed by different researchers, but the most frequently used are those described by Carkhuff (1969), which employ five categories or levels. Research has consistently demonstrated that such scales can be reliably applied; that is, the correlations of judges' ratings with the scales on samples of a variety of therapeutic interactions generally demonstrate a high level of agreement. Many studies also suggest that the clients of helpers who provide high levels of these behaviors show improvement in treatment, whereas the clients of helpers who provide low levels of these behaviors do not change or even change for the worse (Carkhuff, 1969; Carkhuff and Berenson, 1967).

The value of speaker dimensions was slower to emerge, and much of the literature centered on the "degree of client self-exploration" or the clients' willingness to reveal and explore their feelings in the presence of the therapist. Later research operationalized the four speaker dimensions identified above (Schauble and Pierce, 1974), which seem to develop along a continuum of effective communication (Schauble, 1973). Thus, speakers at the lower levels of effectiveness (including clients and most "helpers") may have difficulty identifying and owning their feelings. The goal of a helping communication (psychotherapy or other treatment) at this point is to aid clients in developing the identifying or owning skill; and to determine the clients' commitment to change or maintainence of the behaviors that underlie their feelings. If a commitment to change is made, the focus of treatment is to assist clients in analyzing the sources of their behaviors; that is, in differentiating stimuli to which they have learned particular responses. As insight into the nature of their responses increases, clients learn to develop alternative coping strategies by internalizing the control of their behavior. At this point, the client is a competent communication agent (both as speaker and listener) and no longer is in need of the "helping" communication of treatment. The speaker dimensions were scaled similar to the listener dimensions, and applied to ratings of samples of clients in therapy. Research has demonstrated that (1) these behaviors can be defined and reliably assessed; (2) they can be deliberately taught; (3) they are influenced by helper functioning; and (4) they correlate with traditional "outcome" criteria (Pierce, Schauble, and Farkas, 1970; Pierce, Schauble, and Wilson, 1971; Schauble and Pierce, 1974).

The facilitative dimensions are especially useful in assessment when they are applied to interpersonal systems (such as the family), where communication conditions have a profound effect on the interaction as well as on each member of the system. For example, assessment of the functioning level of parents can be instrumental in predicting the types of behavior and conflict presented by children. The extent to which children are successful in learning communication and coping skills depends on modeling (especially as demonstrated by parents and siblings) and on the experience of being "listened to" or heard. Children with high-functioning parents and family contacts tend to develop satisfactory communication and functioning skills; children with parents functioning at low levels generally do not (Stover and Guerney, 1967). These dimensions are also useful in assessment for individual treatment, since they can help the diagnostician determine the individual's capacity to devise alternative strategies and to develop and use positive resources in the environment.

The most formal (and perhaps accurate) manner of assessing the functioning level for the facilitative conditions is through ratings of tapes of subject behavior. This method is a time-consuming and costly process, however, and is better suited to research evaluation than clinical assessment. Paper-and-pencil instruments (such as the Rotter locus of control or I-E scale) offer some promise, although they have not yet been adequately developed and refined for clinical application. The third and perhaps most practical approach is for the therapist to incorporate these dimensions into a clinical appraisal of the individual's level of functioning. One application of an early internalization scale used therapist assessment of new clients' internalizing behavior and found that these assessments correlated with "success" in treatment (Kirtner and Cartwright, 1958). A later study indicated that therapist assessment of client internalization behavior correlated more with independent judge ratings ($r = .80$) than did the Rotter I-E scale ($r = .57$) (Pierce, Schauble, and Farkas, 1970).

Therapists (or diagnosticians) can base assessments of individual functioning levels on a variety of behaviors. One source of data is the initial screening and assessment interview(s). Behavior in preliminary interaction with the therapist provides many direct cues to the client's capacity to formulate and own problems, feelings, and their sources. In fact, the presence (or absence) of such direct cues provides an indirect demonstration of commitment to the change (and treatment) process. The extent to which clients understand therapist communications is an excellent indication of their ability to establish and make use of support systems in their environment. The individual who avoids confronting immediate feelings in the clinical interview is often experiencing conflict with assertive behavior and dependency. Direct queries concerning the client's *self-assessment* of skill levels (for example, "To what extent do *you* feel that you are committed to change?") also provide cues for assessment, in both the content and manner in which the client responds. Clients' nonverbal behaviors in the course of treatment (for example, breaking appointments or failing to follow through on treatment "contracts") also provide valuable data. Another source of data is available through samples of client behavior in various nonclinical interactions. A boon to such behavioral observation has been the development of audiotape cassette recorders, through which evaluation of taped samples of clients' interactions with significant others in their living environment can be incorporated by the clinician into the data provided in interview interaction. In addition to aiding the clinician's diagnosis of client functioning level, such tapes can provide data to help the client understand the assessment and formulate treatment alternatives.

There is a general acceptance that clinicians in training need to learn to provide facilitative listening conditions in treatment, and most graduate programs provide some experiential (if not didactic) training in these dimensions. More recently, attention has been directed to a systematic consideration of the facilitative speaking (or client-behavior) dimensions and their application in assessment, treatment planning, and evaluation.

Critical Discussion

General Areas of Concern

The value of client behavior in the clinical interview setting has been questioned for use in measurement and assessment, since such interview behavior is influenced by the clinician's expectations and reinforcement. Thus, the empathic, supportive atmosphere of the clinical setting is likely to promote healthy, risk-taking behavior (such as owning and disclosing feelings) that may not carry over to the client's daily interactions outside the clinical setting. This argument highlights a crucial issue in assessment/treatment research: the identification of suitable and acceptable outcome criteria. Although assessment of client interview behavior on these dimensions may not assure a one-to-one correlation with noninterview behavior, the absence of such behavior in the clinical situation would indicate a similar absence in the nonclinical situation. In other words, it would be expected that clients would demonstrate their *highest* levels of facilitative communication in the clinical interview. Evidence of behavior change in treatment may not assure that the same degree of change is taking place outside treatment, but change outside treatment would almost certainly be reflected by similar change in the treatment situation. In fact, client behavior in treatment has been found to correlate with an independent measure for success in treatment (Schauble and Pierce, 1974). At the same time, there is an obvious advantage to using an additional data source for assessing clients' interpersonal functioning, as mentioned above: using cassette recordings of samples of their interactions outside the treatment situation for measurement.

Since the facilitative dimensions are defined in terms of the presence or absence of specific behaviors in communication, it is a fairly simple matter for an independent practitioner to become familiar enough with the dimensions to apply them in assessment. Many clinicians have been exposed to the dimensions in their formal training programs; others have come across the dimensions in the professional literature and research of the last decade. Perhaps the most efficient method of gaining proficiency in the use of the dimensions is through a formal instruction program. These programs are generally brief workshops (10-25 hours), in which participants are instructed in the use of rating scales for each dimension. Participants attempt to apply these scales to a series of taped excerpts of clinical interactions, after which the basis for assigning a particular rating is discussed among the group until consensus is reached (subsequent to training, it is common for interrater agreement to exceed $r = .80$). Such workshops are conducted by clinicians who themselves have undergone similar training and who use the dimensions in their own research and practice. In addition, in order to use the dimensions effectively in assessment, the clinicians' own communication behavior must meet at least a minimal functioning level as rated by the scales. The assumption is that clinicians who are not themselves functioning at healthy or "minimally facilitative" levels in the clinical situation are unable to make accurate discriminations when using their scales with their clients (Carkhuff and Berenson, 1967). While this requisite for minimal clinical competence seems appropriate for the application of *any* assessment procedure, it is especially important with the facilitative conditions because they are instruments based in total on the clinician's observation and judgment of the communication process (rather than on specific and discrete client responses that can be scored according to a prescribed standard).

Comparative Philosophies and Theories

The facilitative dimensions evolved out of a psychodynamic, "humanistic" theoretical orientation, initially stressing the importance of listener behaviors for the therapist. While proponents of different approaches might argue that the therapist's behavior is of minimal importance (as data) in formulating the assessment, it is obvious that a measure of *client behavior* is crucial in the assessment process. In other words, the capacity of a client to demonstrate an awareness or "owning" of discomfort, to identify and differentiate the sources of that discomfort, and to commit energy to attempting directed change would be as important to establishing a treatment plan for a "behavior therapist" as it would for a "Gestalt therapist." Similarly, the goals of increasing a client's range of behavioral alternatives and improving the quality of his or her interactions or communications are desirable regardless of theoretical orientation. Thus, the facilitative dimensions appear to be a relevant framework for assessing client behavior for any theoretical or philosophical approach.

Elaboration on Critical Points

The facilitative dimensions include speaking and listening behaviors that are critical to the clinician's understanding of a client's self-perception and capacity to function interpersonally. The dimensions define the progressive development of healthy communication, and thus provide the clinician with a framework that allows ongoing assessment of client function during (as well as before) the course of treatment. Assessments of client functioning can be based on behavior in the clinical interview or audiotaped samples of client behavior in the home environment. The latter also allows the therapist to form some objective perception of the interpersonal environment in which the client lives. While familiarity with the facilitative dimensions and some formal training in their application may be required for reliable assessment, the nature of the dimensions is such that they are relative as assessment criteria for any theoretical approach.

Personal Views and Recommendations

A major value of the facilitative dimensions is that they serve to operationalize concepts that most clinicians incorporate implicitly into their assessment and treatment behaviors. The role of the diagnostician is not simply to identify the presenting problem of the client, but to consider the manner in which the problem is presented. If client A clearly articulates a presenting problem, is able to identify specific feelings of discomfort relative to the problem, and expresses a clear commitment to engage in efforts to alleviate the problem, then client A presents a different base for assessment and treatment prescription than client B, who presents only vague feelings of anxiety and reluctance to explore these feelings and their source—despite the fact that both client A and client B may be assigned the same diagnostic classification (for example, clinical depression). The manner in which people relate to their interpersonal environment and develop supportive resources is a direct function of their skill in facilitative communication. Continued refinement of methods to measure the facilitative dimensions can lead to more practical, useful assessments of client coping capacity.

Application to Particular Variables

The facilitative dimensions measure an individual's capacity to communicate and cope in interpersonal interaction; thus, they are appropriate measures for any age, sex, or racial group. Of course, it is essential that the clinician understand the influences that an individual's maturational development, sexual identification, or racial/cultural background have on the form of expression through which that individual communicates. For example, familiarity with the vernacular of a particular racial minority group would be essential for application of the facilitative dimensions in assessment with a member of that group. Similarly, the dimensions are relevant to making a prognosis of behavior change for any designation of clinical disorder (physical, intellectual, or emotional).

References

Carkhuff, R. R. *Helping and Human Relations.* Vol. 2. New York: Holt, Rinehart and Winston, 1969.

Carkhuff, R. R., and Berenson, B. G. *Beyond Counseling and Therapy.* New York: Holt, Rinehart and Winston, 1967.

Kirtner, W. L., and Cartwright, D. S. "Success and Failure in Client Centered Therapy as a Function of Initial In-Therapy Behavior." *Journal of Consulting Psychology,* 1958, *22,* 329-333.

Pierce, R. M., Schauble, P. G., and Farkas, A. "Teaching Internalization Behavior to Clients." *Psychotherapy: Theory, Research, and Practice,* 1970, *7,* 217-220.

Pierce, R. M., Schauble, P. G., and Wilson, F. R. "Employing Systematic Human Relations Training for Teaching Constructive Helper and Helpee Behaviors in a Group Therapy Situation." *Journal of Research and Development in Education,* 1971, *4,* 97-110.

Rogers, C. R. *On Becoming a Person.* Boston: Houghton Mifflin, 1961.

Schauble, P. G. "Facilitating Conditions: Basic Dimensions for Psychological Growth and Effective Communications." In R. H. Woody and J. D. Woody (Eds.), *Sexual, Marital, and Familial Relations: Therapeutic Interventions for Professional Helping.* Springfield, Ill.: Thomas, 1973.

Schauble, P. G., and Pierce, R. M. "Client In-Therapy Behavior: A Therapist's Guide to Progress." *Psychotherapy: Theory, Research, and Practice,* 1974, *11,* 229-235.

Stover, L., and Guerney, B. G. "The Efficacy of Training Procedures for Mothers in Filial Therapy." *Psychotherapy: Theory, Research, and Practice,* 1967, *4,* 110-115.

Truax, C. B., and Carkhuff, R. R. *Toward Effective Counseling and Therapy: Training and Practice.* Chicago: Aldine, 1967.

84

Richard H. Dana

Receptivity to Clinical Interpretation

Receptivity to clinical interpretation describes the immediate and long-term impact on clients and referral sources of the communication of assessment findings. Receptivity pertains to audience readiness for understanding or incorporation of the contents of interpretation and any eventual utilization of that information. Clinical interpretation refers to the evaluation of assessment information, and is usually in the form of a written psychological report, though this report is often preceded or followed by oral communication of interpretations. The audience for the clinical interpretation may be the referral source(s), the client assessed, or both simultaneously.

Background and Current Status

The development of personality assessment instruments (word associations, Rorschach, Thematic Apperception Test, Minnesota Multiphasic Personality Inventory) over a forty-year period preceded their applications. Thus, it was not until approximately 1940 that clinical assessment became a widespread professional practice. From 1940 to the early 1970s, the prevailing model of assessment practice was a fourfold process: (1) assessor receives referral (written/oral) from referral source person; (2) patient is informed by referral source person that assessment is necessary; (3) assessor sees patient and administers tests; (4) assessor provides referral source person with a written report. The clinical interpretation, usually in written format, was provided to the referral source person exclusively, although there were a few notable exceptions to this model (see, for example, Baker, 1964; Comer, 1965).

The rise of humanistic values within the culture has led to the communication of assessment findings to patients/clients as well as referral sources (Dana and Graham, 1976). These new practices have been variously labeled as a "contextual approach" (Fischer, 1970, 1973), "existential assessment" (Dana and Leech, 1974), "joint feedback" (Erdberg, 1977), and "sharing oneself" (Craddick, 1975). This new model for assessment practice differs from the traditional model in several aspects: (1) assessor confers with referral source person in order to define problems and the assessor role during feedback or communication of findings; (2) assessment procedures and rationale for consultation are discussed with the client by the referral source person, with emphasis on the roles of all participants during feedback and the potential usages of findings; (3) assessor sees client, describes procedures, and administers tests; (4) assessor describes and discusses findings with client and referral source person simultaneously; (5) assessor provides copies of written report to referral source person and to client; (6) assessor and referral source person maintain communication in order to provide feedback for assessor regarding subsequent utilization of findings. Clinical interpretation thus potentially becomes the consultation procedure or the activity of sharing assessment results with referral source person(s) and assessee(s), in addition to the provision of a written report.

Both the traditional model and the humanistic model are being used at the present time. There are strong societal pressures for adoption of the humanistic model. These pressures are part of an increasing demand for accountability in the delivery of professional services. They may eventually include statutory requirements for information sharing with the consumers of assessment services. In addition, the necessity for service providers to clearly label and identify their skills for licensure dovetails with the widespread use of contracts with clients for specified services. Finally, and perhaps most important, clinical assessment is undergoing a transition from a routine, ancillary, and poorly esteemed professional activity to a recognized clinical psychological specialty that is no less respectable than psychotherapy.

Critical Discussion

General Areas of Concern

Surveys have periodically reported the frequencies with which specific assessment instruments are used (see Wade and others, 1978). Surveys have also sampled opinions regarding the usefulness of assessment findings for particular referral source populations, notably psychiatrists (Smyth and Reznikoff, 1971), psychoanalysts (Olive, 1972) and psychotherapists (Wiedemann and Mintz, 1974). Similarly, attitudes and opinions regarding the usefulness of reports have been reported for such settings as Veterans Administration hospitals (Tallent and Reiss, 1959) and child guidance (Lacey and Ross, 1964).

There has been dissatisfaction with the adequacy of communication contained in reports. While the "don'ts" of written communication have been labeled as Barnum (applicable to everybody), Aunt Fanny (nondifferentiating), trade-marked (assessor concerns), and prosecuting attorney (negative view) reports and concepts (Tallent, 1956), only the area of Barnum concepts has received systematic research attention. By early 1978 there were thirty-eight studies dealing with Barnum reports, or false feedback, and only two studies that provided honest feedback. This Barnum literature is clearly not helpful for providers and consumers of psychological reports.

A more relevant literature explores the contents of reports used in clinical settings. Prospective consumers do differ in their understanding of report contents (Grayson and Tolman, 1950), with as much as half of the contents having different meanings for the assessor and professional consumers (Cuadra and Albaugh, 1956). A significant negative relationship has been found between report content and the usefulness of reports for making decisions about treatment (Hartlage and others, 1968). However, reports can adequately communicate requested information or new information in addition to providing a relevant contribution to patient management (Affleck and Strider, 1971). Reports have also been useful in predicting the outcome of juvenile probation counseling when specific treatment recommendations are followed (Dana and others, 1963). Reports were valid predictors of adjustment to home care subsequent to psychiatric hospitalization whenever conformity to rules and social expectations was explicitly discussed (Ullmann, Berkman, and Hamister, 1958). Case study examples of helpful applications to psychotherapy continue to be reported (Aronow and Reznikoff, 1971; Bellak, Pasquarelli, and Braverman, 1949).

Several constructive approaches to writing reports have been used: (a) Reports on psychiatric clinic patients were rewritten on the basis of reactions by professional consumers (Garfield, Heine, and Leventhal, 1954); (b) Independently prepared student reports on the same data have been compiled into a composite report after evaluation by the client being assessed (Dana, 1975). The composite report was found to be considerably more acceptable to the client; (c) Bias or eisegesis in student reports can be reliably abstracted using a design that has several reports on the same client by different assessors as well as several reports on different clients by the same assessor (Dana, 1966a); (d) Errors in Rorschach scoring can be matched with scorer personality characteristics in an effort to confront assessors with potential sources of report inaccuracy (Voigt, 1966; Voigt and Dana, 1964); (e) Sharing an interpretation with a client has also been used for instructional purposes (Dana, 1975; Rader and Schill, 1973). Evaluation of the report by the client becomes the basis for revision of the report.

At one time prospective assessors were provided with prefabricated outlines of relevant report content (Lodge, 1953; Mayman, 1959; Taylor and Teicher, 1946; Thorne, 1956) and models of reports written for different purposes (Lyle, Gilchrist, and Groh, 1958; Sargent, 1951). Models of report writing are helpful in training student assessors, and report outlines have situational relevance. However, both models and outlines have limited utility because the contents of reports change over time. Consumers' interests in different kinds of assessment information also change. For example, referral requests for clinical diagnosis were reduced from 64 percent to 29 percent between 1956 and 1965 in one setting (Dollin and Reznikoff, 1966), while diagnostic issues and descriptive adjectives were replaced by process description, especially of assets and liabilities in ego functions, between 1950 and 1958 in another setting (Korner, 1962). When three report formats were compared during a six-month period in a setting using 1,000 reports per year, consumer preferences for an outline format were found (Lacks, Horton, and Owen, 1969).

While interest in the contents of reports has waned in most settings, several books do attempt to remedy the problems of content and style that contribute to consumer dissatisfaction (Huber, 1961; Klopfer, 1960; Tallent, 1976). There is now increased sensitization to the kind of language used in reports (Harty, 1978). An action language has been proposed that dispenses with psychoanalytic terms and diagnostic labels; it provides, instead, a set of rules for the equation of every psychological process or behavior with an action to be designated by an action verb and/or an adverb or adverbial statement of the action mode (Schafer, 1976). In addition, Erikson's "disciplined subjectivity," a sensing of what life is like for referral source person(s) and assessed clients alike, has been suggested as a rationale for presentation of reports that include both experiential and descriptive information (Shectman, 1978).

Comparative Philosophies and Theories

A general model of clinical inference provides four levels of clinical interpretation (Dana, 1966b; Sargent, 1953). Level I is composed of the best responses that have been elicited with whatever reliability is inherent in the assessment procedures themselves or in their application by assessors. For example, projective techniques have a subjective data base that is due to "the selectivity of observers and the unsteadiness of facts" (Wyatt, 1967) while observational data can be used directly to describe specific aversive or prosocial behaviors. Level II is a translation to descriptive adjectives by inference. This level is composed of concepts or short-hand descriptions of the original response data. Such concepts may differ greatly among themselves in operational validity. Level III provides a context for these concepts in order to describe personality dynamics, a description-explanation of how the person functions in different settings, at different times, and under conditions of stress and distress. It is a psychological portrait of the person that becomes an information resource for treatment planning or a source of treatment recommendations and the rationale for these suggestions. Finally, on the basis of these three previous levels as data a clinical diagnosis or Level IV statement may be made.

Elaboration on Critical Points

While there has been much debate over the legitimacy of clinical assessment data for use at each of these four levels (see Dana, 1970; Griswold and Dana, 1970; Lewinsohn and others, 1963; Powers and Hamlin, 1957), how the clinical interpretation is to be employed is clearly an elective procedure. The problem of determining at which level to provide the clinical interpretation is resolved by agreement or contract among the concerned participants: the assessor, the referral source person, and the client. Clinical interpretation can potentially provide behavioral description, adjectival description, a rendition of the experience or the psychodynamics, and a clinical diagnosis in the idiom of the current diagnostic and statistical manual. Clinical interpretation is thus independent of the philosophy, theory, or frame of reference used to account for personality, psychopathology, or well being. However, clinical interpretation can be used within any of these theories or frames of reference (for example, the medical model, the sociopsychologicalbehavioral approach, or the humanistic-existential model) depending on the level chosen for emphasis, the contents of the particular level, the kinds of assessment instruments used, and the style of communication.

Personal Views and Recommendations

Clinical interpretation of assessment findings is coming of age by recognizing that the interpretation process itself is a legitimate clinical activity. Clinical interpretation constitutes a consultative role in which the assessor has a professional obligation to provide the interpretation within a clinical context. The role of the assessor thus assumes an independent and equal status with that of the referral source person. The final clinical interpretation is a collaborative effort by assessor, referral source person, and client.

From the client's standpoint, hearing data about oneself that constitutes a description of personal experience can be a unique event, especially in a medical setting. Much of the assessment mystique is thereby removed and replaced by a realistic and appropriate knowledge. Clients have the right to full and honest disclosure of information regarding themselves, and there is no clinical or research evidence to suggest that harm may be done to clients in this manner. In fact, the accumulated experience of assessors and referral source persons suggests that clinical benefit accrues from the feedback experience. Respect for the client as a responsible human being is communicated by the assessment content as well as by a discussion that provides an experiential processing of the content. While clients are unlikely to learn new facts about themselves, they may share another perspective and a sense of communion in the clinical setting.

The use of clinical interpretation as a consultive procedure also potentially provides lessons for the assessors with regard to the utility of their instruments and clinical skills. Feedback to the assessor regarding the quality of clinical interpretation, either in training for assessment practice or within the relationship with clients and referral source persons, can be a catalyst for the sustained growth of clinical skills.

Application to Particular Variables

Age, intellectual level, and especially socioeconomic status are relevant to the client's receptivity to clinical interpretation. Very young children or mentally defective persons may not benefit markedly by being recipients of the contents or information derived from clinical interpretation. However, if the clinical interpretation is provided to the parents or other responsible persons in the presence of the child or the adult with limited intellectual abilities, some content may be understandable. A sense of being understood and considered worthy of receiving such information about oneself may also be experienced.

For persons who have less education and a less conceptual mode of dealing with their experiences, the process of hearing data about oneself may be altered somewhat. The language used by the assessor and the style of communication must be understandable to the client. Lower-class persons often prefer straight talk to complex explanation. They are less involved or cooperative in treatment planning and take less responsibility for the procedures involved in such treatment (Graham, 1957). While these social-class differences in participation with diagnosis and treatment may be due to an inability to share the professional person's scientific-deterministic ideology, middle-class professionals do often "cool out" clients or patients who are different from themselves.

Evidence concerning the information-giving process (Ley, 1966) indicates that initial visits by predominantly lower-class medical patients to an outpatient clinic result in very limited memory for information received. One third of the information was not re-called immediately after the visit. Less than 25 percent of the patients remembered all that they had been told. Patients did, however, remember diagnostic statements better than other informational statements, and intelligence was unrelated to memory. Ley's findings suggest that the context in which communication of assessment findings occurs and the manner in which this service is provided may be of even more consequence for lower-class clients than for middle-class persons.

The effectiveness of the services themselves thus are closely related to the inter-personal milieu in which the services are rendered. While the client's receptivity to clinical interpretation is affected by demographic considerations, the assessor is obliged to inform the client by making assessment findings available in a form that is relevant to treatment plans. How this is accomplished and the extent to which the client feels like a valued human being with dignity and the capacity for self-understanding has import for the entire treatment process.

References

Affleck, D. C., and Strider, F. D. "Contribution of Psychological Reports to Patient Man-agement." *Journal of Consulting and Clinical Psychology,* 1971, *37,* 177-179.

Aronow, E., and Reznikoff, M. "Applications of Projective Tests to Psychotherapy: A Case Study." *Journal of Personality Assessment,* 1971, *35,* 379-393.

Baker, G. A. "A Therapeutic Application of Psychodiagnostic Test Results." *Journal of Projective Techniques,* 1964, *28,* 3-8.

Bellak, L., Pasquarelli, B., and Braverman, S. "The Use of the Thematic Apperception Test in Psychotherapy." *Journal of Nervous and Mental Disease,* 1949, *110,* 51-65.

Comer, P. E. "Initially Structured Short-Term Psychotherapy in a College Student Coun-seling Center." Unpublished doctoral dissertation, West Virginia University, 1965.

Craddick, R. A. "Sharing Oneself in the Assessment Process." *Professional Psychology,* 1975, *6,* 279-283.

Cuadra, C. A., and Albaugh, W. P. "Sources of Ambiguity in Psychological Reports." *Journal of Clinical Psychology,* 1956, *12,* 108-115.

Dailey, C. A. "The Practical Utility of the Clinical Report." *Journal of Consulting Psychology,* 1953, *17,* 297-302.

Dana, R. H. *Foundations of Clinical Psychology.* New York: D. Von Nostrand, 1966a.

Dana, R. H. "Eisegesis and Assessment." *Journal of Projective Techniques and Personality Assessment,* 1966b, *30,* 215-222.

Dana, R. H. "A Hierarchal Model for Analysing Personality Data." *Journal of General Psychology,* 1970, *82,* 199-206.

Dana, R. H. "Ruminations on Teaching Projective Assessment: An Ideology, Specific Usages, Teaching Practices." *Journal of Personality Assessment,* 1975, *39,* 563-572.

Dana, R. H., and Graham, E. D. "Feedback of Client-Relevant Information and Clinical Practice." *Journal of Personality Assessment,* 1976, *40,* 464-469.

Dana, R. H., and Leech, S. "Existential Assessment." *Journal of Personality Assessment,* 1974, *38,* 428-435.

Dana, R. H., and others. "Psychological Reports and Juvenile Counseling." *Journal of Clinical Psychology,* 1963, *19,* 352-355.

Dollin, A., and Reznikoff, M. "Diagnostic Referral Questions in Psychological Testing: Changing Concepts." *Psychological Reports,* 1966, *19,* 610.

Erdberg, S. P. "Assessment in Private Practice: A Clinical Application." Paper presented at midwinter meeting of Society for Personality Assessment, San Diego, March 1977.

Fischer, C. T. "The Testee as Co-evaluator." *Journal of Counseling Psychology,* 1970, *17,* 70-76.

Fischer, C. T. "Contextual Approach to Assessment." *Community Mental Health Journal,* 1973, *9,* 38-45.

Garfield, S., Heine, R. W., and Leventhal, M. "An Evaluation of Psychological Reports in a Clinical Setting." *Journal of Consulting Psychology,* 1954, *18,* 281-286.

Graham, S. "Socioeconomic Status, Illness, and the Use of Medical Services." *Milbank Memorial Fund Quarterly,* 1957, *35,* 58-66.

Grayson, H. M., and Tolman, R. S. "A Semantic Study of Concepts of Clinical Psychologists and Psychiatrists." *Journal of Abnormal and Social Psychology,* 1950, *45,* 216-231.

Griswold, P. M., and Dana, R. H. "Feedback and Experience Effects on Psychological Reports and Predictions of Behavior." *Journal of Clinical Psychology,* 1970, *26,* 439-442.

Hartlage, L., and others. "Decisional Utility of Psychological Reports." *Journal of Clinical Psychology,* 1968, *24,* 481-483.

Harty, M. K. "Action Language in the Psychological Report." Paper presented at annual meeting of Society for Personality Assessment, Tampa, March 1978.

Huber, J. T. *Report Writing in Psychology and Psychiatry.* New York: Harper & Row, 1961.

Klopfer, W. G. *The Psychological Report.* New York: Grune and Stratton, 1960.

Korner, I. N. "Test Report Evaluation." *Journal of Clinical Psychology,* 1962, *18,* 194-197.

Lacey, H. M., and Ross, A. O. "Multidisciplinary Views on Psychological Reports in Child Guidance Clinics." *Journal of Clinical Psychology,* 1964, *20,* 522-526.

Lacks, P. B., Horton, M. M., and Owen, J. D. "A More Meaningful and Practical Approach to Psychological Reports." *Journal of Clinical Psychology,* 1969, *25,* 383-386.

Lewinsohn, P. M., and others. "The Reliability and Validity of Quantified Judgments from Psychological Tests." *Journal of Clinical Psychology,* 1963, *19,* 64-73.

Ley, P. "What the Patient Doesn't Remember." *Medical Opinion and Review,* 1966, *1* (7), 69-73.

Lodge, G. T. "How to Write a Psychological Report." *Journal of Clinical Psychology,* 1953, *9,* 400-402.

Lyle, J., Gilchrist, A., and Groh, L. "Three Blind Interpretations of a TAT Record." *Journal of Projective Techniques,* 1958, *22,* 82-96.

Mayman, M. "Style, Focus, Language, and Content of an Ideal Psychological Test Report." *Journal of Projective Techniques,* 1959, *23,* 453-458.

Olive, H. "Psychoanalysts' Opinions of Psychologists' Reports: 1952 and 1970." *Journal of Clinical Psychology,* 1972, *28,* 50-54.

Powers, W. T., and Hamlin, R. M. "The Validity, Bases, and Process of Clinical Judgment Using a Limited Amount of Projective Test Data." *Journal of Projective Techniques,* 1957, *21,* 286-293.

Rader, G., and Schill, T. "Blind Test Interpretation to Overcome Student Resistance to Projective Techniques Courses." *Journal of Personality Assessment,* 1973, *37,* 213-216.

Sargent, H. D. "Psychological Test Reporting: An Experiment in Communication." *Bulletin of the Menninger Clinic,* 1951, *15,* 175-185.

Sargent, H. D. *The Insight Test.* New York: Grune and Stratton, 1953.

Schafer, R. *A New Language for Psychoanalysis.* New Haven, Conn.: Yale University Press, 1976.

Shectman, F. "Problems Around Communicating Assessment Findings: Why Won't They Listen to Me?" Paper presented at annual meeting of Society for Personality Assessment, Tampa, March 1978.

Smyth, R., and Reznikoff, M. "Attitudes of Psychiatrists Toward the Usefulness of Psychodiagnostic Reports." *Professional Psychology,* 1971, *2,* 283-288.

Tallent, N. "An Approach to the Improvement of Clinical Psychological Reports." *Journal of Clinical Psychology,* 1956, *12,* 103-109.

Tallent, N. *Psychological Report Writing.* Englewood Cliffs, N.J.: Prentice-Hall, 1976.

Tallent, N., and Reiss, W. J. "Multidisciplinary Views on the Preparation of Written Clinical Psychological Reports. III: The Trouble with Psychological Reports." *Journal of Clinical Psychology,* 1959, *15,* 444-446.

Taylor, J. L., and Teicher, A. "A Clinical Aporoach to Reporting Psychological Test Data." *Journal of Clinical Psychology,* 1946, *2,* 323-332.

Thorne, F. C. "A New Outline for Psychological Report Writing." *Journal of Clinical Psychology,* 1956, *12,* 115-122.

Ullmann, L. P., Berkman, V. C., and Hamister, R. C. "Psychological Reports Related to Behavior and Benefit of Placement in Home Care." *Journal of Clinical Psychology,* 1958, *14,* 254-459.

Voigt, W. "Personality Variables in Rorschach Scoring." *Journal of Projective Techniques and Personality Assessment,* 1966, *30,* 153-157.

Voigt, W., and Dana, R. H. "Inter- and Intra-scorer Rorschach Reliability." *Journal of Projective Techniques and Personality Assessment,* 1964, *28,* 92-95.

Wade, T., and others. "The Status of Psychological Testing in Clinical Psychology: Relationships Between Test Use and Professional Activities and Orientations." *Journal of Personality Assessment,* 1978, *42,* 3-11.

Wiedemann, C., and Mintz, J. "Student Therapists' Assessment of Diagnostic Testing." *Journal of Personality Assessment,* 1974, *38,* 203-214.

Wyatt, F. "How Objective is Objectivity?" *Journal of Projective Techniques and Personality Assessment,* 1967, *31,* 3-20.

85

R. William English

Stigma

Stigma is a universal phenomenon. It applies not only to all persons with clinical conditions but to all persons who vary substantially from established societal norms or conventions (Lemert, 1967). Because stigma refers to an undesirable differentness, stigmatized individuals are perceived as abnormal and sometimes as nonhuman "deviants." As an inverted behavior, stigma is a construct that is culturally defined and culture bound. Moreover, because of the inherent subjectivity and cultural relativism of what is "normal," perspectives of stigma are capricious and highly subject to change.

Key terms that contribute to the understanding of stigma are stigmatization, deviant, deviant social role, ambiguity, and stigma management.

Stigmatization is a devaluing process that sets persons with perceived differences apart from normal peers. Stigmatization occurs when others decide that a person is dangerous, untrustworthy, or repugnant (Lemert, 1967). The process begins with the application of one or more labels that are symbols or signs of the moral inferiority of the stigmatized person.

Stigma terms or labels, according to Goffman (1963), are routinely applied to numerous *deviants,* who may be classified as belonging to one of three broad groups: (1) individuals with physical disabilities and deformities, such as blindness, cerebral palsy, epilepsy, facial disfigurement, or paraplegia; (2) individuals with character blemishes—for example, the mentally retarded, the mentally ill, or the substance abuser; and (3) tribal (racial, national, or religious) outsiders. Semantic labels that symbolize the stigmatization of each of these types of deviants are easily recognized. They include such terms as spastics, crips, retards, psychos, junkies, cons, boozers, niggers, nips, and yids. While these are colloquial terms, there are professional acronyms, commonly used as shorthand jargon to speed up communications, that are just as stigmatizing—for example, MRs, MIs, CPs, paras, and quads (English, 1971a).

Beginning with the application of stigma terms, deviant persons are continually devaluated and set apart from normal individuals. Their status becomes that of a minority, as characterized by (1) underprivileged social status, (2) group stereotypes, and (3) overlapping roles (Barker, 1948).

Stigmatized persons are more socially isolated and have more limited vocational opportunities than nonstigmatized persons. Their status mobility and that of their families is—if not actually downward—at least restricted (Malone, 1969).

Group stereotypes, applied to all those who carry stigmatized labels, are often so strong that they represent a type of "master status," where the stigmatized are considered to be generally—versus specifically—deviant (Becker, 1963). The unfortunate consequence of such salient group stereotypes is that the stigmatized person adopts a *deviant social role*; that is, deviants are almost certain to give in to reaffirming stigmatizing expectations (Parsons, 1958; Yamamoto, 1971). Why not be more limited than you really are if almost everyone expects this of you? Alcoholics, for example, are often expected to be dependent, passive-aggressive, and irresponsible; or retarded persons are stereotyped as docile, forgetful, distractible, perseverating, and childlike. Such strong stigmatizing stereotypes can represent irreversible life scripts that isolate the different, deprive them of their rights and uniqueness, and guarantee the circular maintenance of the stereotype itself. Convicted criminals may be barred from employment after imprisonment, and reformed alcoholics may continue to be regarded as irresponsible long after their last drink.

The third minority group characteristic mentioned above, that of "overlapping roles," pertains to the *ambiguity* involved in interpersonal encounters between so-called normal persons and stigmatized deviants. Normals are uncertain whether to interact according to the stigmatized stereotype (or "virtual social identity") or whether to risk seeking out the real (or "actual") social identity of the deviant (Goffman, 1963). Consequently, so-called normal persons are likely to act indecisively and ungenuinely for fear of making a social error that may result in embarrassment to themselves or injury to the stigmatized deviant. In turn, the stigmatized are faced with considerable unknowns, especially when concerned with risking exposure of their actual identities in dealing with the inappropriate behaviors of nondeviants. Because the proportional weight of ambiguity is so great in interpersonal encounters between normal and deviant persons, both parties frequently feel a diminished amount of self-control and increased tension (Davis, 1961).

The process of coping with and reducing stigmatization is referred to as *stigma management*. Efforts to contain and overcome the effects of stigma can be undertaken at an individual and a social systems level. In Western cultures, in fact, there is virtually a mandatory expectation that social deviants will make some conscientious effort to manage their stigma (Lemert, 1967; Mercer, 1977). For example, convicted felons are expected to serve prison terms, epileptics are expected to take medication, and psychiatrically disturbed persons are generally expected to participate in psychotherapy. (Four aspects of stigma management are presented in the "Personal Views and Recommendations" section of this chapter.)

Background and Current Status

The ancient Greek word for *stigma* referred to bodily signs connoting something unusual and bad about a person's moral status. The Greeks went so far as to cut or burn the stigmatizing symbol into the person's body. These body signs were forms of direct advertisement that publicly communicated the identity of blemished persons (such as slaves, criminals, and traitors) who were to be avoided (Goffman, 1963).

In Christian times the term *stigma* was extended to have religious significance (Goffman, 1963). In some instances, eruptions of the skin were assumed to represent bodily signs of holy grace, while certain physical disorders were interpreted as a basis for inferring celestial disgrace. Consequently, religion has been a major influence effecting much of the cultural relativism that surrounds stigma. It provides a rationale for understanding why ancient Sparta had disabled babies hurtled to their deaths from cliffs and why some persons who are epileptic or abusers of hallucinogenic opiates are deified in some African countries and in Brazil (Safilios-Rothschild, 1968).

In twentieth-century America, *stigma* has lost most, if not all, of its association with religion and is now applied to all forms of culturally defined deviance. In all instances, however, the consequences of the stigma are the same—whether the person be known because of epilepsy, Down's syndrome, drug abuse, schizophrenia, sexual deviance, or whatever. Regardless, the person is labeled, devalued, and deprived of rights and opportunities.

The impact of stigma extends beyond a labeled deviant to conjugal families, extended families, neighborhoods, and communities. This is well illustrated by nine negative consequences noted by Malone (1969) through interviews conducted with twenty-five persons representing the families of twenty persons with aphasia. He reported that the nonhandicapped immediate relatives of aphasics often said they experienced: (1) role changes—more dependency by the aphasics as well as more fragmentation and isolation by the nonaphasic family members, (2) greater irritability, (3) more guilt, (4) restricted social life, (5) increased financial problems, (6) increased health problems, (7) neglect of job responsibilities, (8) overprotection of the aphasic, and (9) rejection of the aphasic. Although such negative outcomes are related to the effect of aphasia as a severely disabling medical condition and not just to stigma as a socially handicapping concomitant, such consequences undoubtedly reflect both phenomena—physical disability and social handicap.

Critical Discussion

General Areas of Concern

The major concern relevant to stigma resides in its potential to affect stigmatized persons very negatively. The preceding list of problems associated with aphasia is generally representative and also illustrative of the fact that stigma is attached to deviance in virtually all life context areas: medical, personal, social, economic, and vocational. Ironically, the debilitating secondary effects of stigma are often more severe obstacles to be overcome than the immediate behavioral consequences of one's being labeled as a stigmatized deviant. Because stigma is such a debilitating reality, the general concerns in this area are: to understand the dynamic processes that contribute to it; to explore the unique meaning of stigma to particular individuals; and to examine the various mechanisms for coping with stigma.

In the following analysis of the concerns surrounding stigma, specific attention is focused on two issues: (1) the affective dimension of stigma and (2) seven critical situational components of stigma.

The affective/emotional dimension of stigma refers to the fact that stigma is an emotionally charged and often illogical phenomenon. A wheelchair-bound quadraplegic, for example, not only must intellectually comprehend architectural barriers and restricted employment opportunities; he must also emotionally/affectively understand and accept the fact that some persons regard persons in wheelchairs as ugly, reprehensible, and even contagious. In the area of physical disability, for instance, there is often a pervasive tone of chronic sorrow resulting from stigmatization that remains long after medical restoration and physical adaption (Cohen, 1977).

The seven *critical situational components of stigma* include (1) observability, (2) frustration and tension, (3) ambiguity, (4) prejudice by invitation, (5) socioeconomic conditions, (6) vicarious victimization, (7) self-perception and projection.

Unquestionably, stigmatization is conditionally related to *observability*. Becker (1963) has noted that a behavior or act will lead to stigmatization only if it is observable and can be given a discreditable label because of the potential negative consequences for others. In many instances, however, a person's differentness will go unnoticed (as in the cases of a darkened movie theater where obese or facially disfigured persons will not attract attention to themselves) or where it is not sufficiently disruptive to merit a discreditable label (for example, where a young boy can be seen urinating in the woods near a picnic grounds).

Frustration and tension, which are virtually synonymous, frequently lead to aggression toward discredited groups (Berkowitz, 1969; Bettelheim and Janowitz, 1964). *Ambiguity,* or uncertainty about expectations and appropriateness of role, frequently contributes to disruptive interactions between normal and different persons. New and unfamiliar situational encounters particularly contribute to ambiguity (English, 1971a).

In some instances, stigmatized persons deliberately or inadvertently invite prejudice from others (Wright, 1960). Pronounced overcompensation, dependency, or begging are examples of such *prejudice by invitation.* Another form of invited prejudice occurs when the cause of a person's stigma was disreputable and contributed to personal injury or was destructive to others. A person who becomes paraplegic as a consequence of an attempted suicide is unquestionably inviting prejudice and will experience a deeper form of stigmatization than a person whose paraplegia occurred as a consequence of a heroic act.

Some evidence indicates that the amount and intensity of stigma vary with general *socioeconomic conditions.* Essentially there appears to be more altruism and less stigmatization when times are good and more stigmatization when times are bad. Specifically, Hanks and Hanks (1948) suggest that there are fewer expressions of stigma when there is greater economic productivity, when competitive achievement is minimized, and when achievement criteria are less formal. In related research Bettelheim and Janowitz (1964) found that stigma decreases with increased urbanization and with growth in middle-income occupations and areas of professionalization.

Vicarious victimization occurs when persons who associate with stigmatized deviants are also stigmatized. In such instances, the message in the depreciating communication is that the deviant's associate—usually a family member, friend, or professional helper—is a less valuable and potent person for affiliating with the stigmatized. The clear inference is that "There must be something wrong with you or else you wouldn't be associated with that [stigmatized] person." Persons who share another person's stigma are quite logically one of the greatest sources of emotional support for the stigmatized. At

Encyclopedia of Clinical Assessment

the same time, normal confederates must accept the fact that theirs is a "courtesy stigma," which gives them associative entry to a deviant group but almost never gives them all the in-group privileges and statuses of the stigmatized, for example, feeling part of a very unique group and being able to use the secondary gain associated with this unique disability. In this sense, so-called normal persons who associate closely with the stigmatized may occasionally find that they are excluded and devalued by both a normal group and a deviant group (Goffman, 1963).

Self-perception and projection refers to the fact that much of the psychological meaning of stigma has to be considered as uniquely reflective of the self-perceptions of the perceiver (Wright, 1960). Two persons may share similar background characteristics and the same disability—for instance, amputation—but have radically different perceptions about the potential consequences of the disability. Likewise, two normal persons of similar backgrounds may have radically different perceptions upon encountering the amputee. One may find it aesthetically disgusting and pity the amputee, while another person may give only nominal attention to the disability but focus on other aspects of the person.

These observations are borne out by the author's own experiences in teaching curriculum on psychosocial aspects of disability, where students have been asked to write down the disability label they would personally find most difficult to accept. In each instance a wide variety of disabilities have been identified, but rarely has one disability been chosen much more than another. Moreover, persons with disabilities do not cite their own condition as the most unacceptable to them. All this suggests that much of any person's response to a notable human difference is a psychological projection and can only be understood and explained by the subjective meaning that the difference holds for each individual.

Comparative Philosophies and Theories

Theoretical contributions in the area of somatopsychology of stigma are sorely lacking. Little material has been produced, and that which is available is highly speculative (English, 1971c). Psychoanalytic theorists (Bettelheim and Janowitz, 1964) underscore the likelihood that stigmatizing attitudes are solidified at an early age, probably before the start of formal schooling. Adlerian-related theorists have brought out the importance of the self-concept, while other neo-Freudians have focused attention on the importance of body image and body anxiety as sources of stigmatizing attitudes. Social role theory, however, has probably offered the most insightful propositions to date, in positing that there is a set of complementary expectations for social interactions between normal and disabled persons predicated on the sick or socially deviant role stereotype. Examples of complementary roles for normal and disabled persons are independent-dependent, active-passive, healthy caretakers and sick patient, and superior-inferior.

Elaboration on Critical Points

A substantial majority of writings on the topic of stigma are descriptive and theoretical. At the same time, some technology does exist to assess stigma, either through relatively objective standardized measures or by means of rather subjective nonstandardized measures. Two basic references that contain descriptions of such measures are the *Handbook of Research Design and Social Measurement* (Miller, 1977) and *Measures of Social Psychological Attitudes* (Robinson and Shaver, 1973). Following is a brief description of the major types of objective and subjective techniques that can be used for the measurement of different aspects of stigma. These descriptions are representative of a range of usable instruments and techniques but are not inclusive. At the present time, no single instrument can be cited as the best index of stigma.

Four types of standardized social-psychological instruments lend themselves to the measurement of stigma: (1) group structure and dynamics scales; (2) social participation indexes; (3) scales of attitudes, values, and norms; and (4) personality measures. Examples of some of the more meaningful instruments follow, abstracted from the basic resource by Miller (1977). Characteristically, most standardized measures contain continuous scaling systems and yield one or more scores, which can be normed on various reference groups.

Group structure and group dynamics scales suited to the measurement of stigma include Bales' Interaction Process Analysis, the sociometry scales of spontaneous choice, and the Bogardus Social Distance Scale. The Bales measure can be used to observe and evaluate the characteristics of personal interaction of individuals involved in problem-solving groups. Sociometry scales are useful indicators of the interpersonal attraction of members in groups and can be used repeatedly to assess the morale and productivity of different configurations of group members. The Bogardus Scale is useful for estimating the amount of potential or real conflict between members of any specialized group—in vocational, residential, or other life phases—and a dominant majority group. Bogardus' measure has great flexibility and probably has had the greatest amount of influence on the development of related social-psychological instruments.

Two social participation indexes that might be useful for the measurement of stigma are Chapin's Social Participation Scale and the Leisure Participation and Enjoyment Scale. Both instruments can provide an estimate of the extent to which stigmatized deviants are engaging in social and recreational activities with other persons.

Among the various scales of attitudes, values, and norms, the most promising for the measurement of stigma are Neal and Seeman's Powerlessness Scale, Srole's Anomie Scale, and Dean's Alienation Scale. In contrast to social participation indices, these measures lend themselves to assessing the extent to which stigmatized deviants perceive themselves, and are perceived by others, as isolated and alienated from the mainstream of society.

The fourth major type of standardized instrument that lends itself to the assessment of stigma is the personality measure. Two premier instruments in this area are the Authoritarian Personality (F) Scale and the Semantic Differential Scales. The F Scale is valuable in the measurement of stigma, as is Budner's Intolerance of Ambiguity Scale, because high authoritarianism and low tolerance of ambiguity are associated with engaging in stigmatization. The Semantic Differential Scales have great breadth of utility and allow for stigma, and other attitudes, to be examined according to three dimensions: evaluation, potency, and activity. Bi-polar adjectives have been developed to illustrate each dimension of attitude. "Good-bad" reflects an evaluation attitudinal continuum, "strong-weak" shows potency, and "fast-slow" illustrates activity.

In addition to the above-mentioned scales, which are quite general in focus, certain standardized instruments examine attitudes toward specific groups of stigmatized deviants. Examples include the Attitudes Towards Disabled Persons Scale, the Attitude Towards Old Persons Scale, and the Racial Stereotype Index. Information about these types of measures can be best retrieved through special-interest organizations and resources such as the most recent edition of the *Mental Measurements Yearbook*.

Besides both general and specific standardized measures, stigma can be assessed in more experiential and subjective terms. While subjective measures have more limited generalizability than standardized instruments, they may have more personal value to the individual's own development through education and training. Examples of subjective techniques for evaluating stigma include biographical/autobiographical narratives, additive observations of interpersonal behaviors in relationships between persons (use of personal pronouns and open/closed forms of body posturing), and role-playing exercises.

Personal Views and Recommendations

Five issues merit personal comment. *First, it is believed that all discredited persons serve a functional purpose for any given society.* The stigmatized help maintain a system of social stratification, they contribute to the economy (largely by staying out of the labor force or performing entry-level jobs), they provide jobs for professional caretakers, and they help make the nonstigmatized feel psychologically superior. While all these functional purposes help explain why stigma continues, they are not vital functions to a society's survival, and they do not negate the fact that stigma is dehumanizing for all persons in a society. Consequently, it seems obvious that the practical price of maintaining stigma is too high.

Second, what persons read into stigma is largely a personal projection. The roots of a society's problems are imbedded in all members of that society.

Third, much of the key to unlocking stigma's door lies in bringing appropriate structure to situations of high ambiguity. In addition, persons can be taught skills that will give them more tolerance for ambiguity. Skills reflecting structure that will reduce high ambiguity include the use of questions, sharing of behavioral observations ("You're walking with a limb"), self-disclosures ("I can see faces but can't read words"), and a sense of humor.

Fourth, the single greatest need of the stigmatized is for survival skill training in areas of social interaction. More often than not, the chronic failure repeatedly experienced by stigmatized persons occurs because they lack such basic interpersonal skills as sufficient assertiveness to ask a question or state that they are confused and need direction in order to proceed. Human service workers have simply not devoted enough time and energy to anticipating and preparing the stigmatized to cope with incidents that have a high potential for failure. Rather than skirting potential failure, professionals need to encourage their clients to simulate threatening experiences and risk failing while they are still receiving direct care.

Fifth, stigma is not something to just feel bad about. It can be coped with and combatted by adopting a multifaceted approach involving individuals, professionals, environmental modifications, and community education. Brief mention of some suggestions are made here, and readers are referred to another source for more details (English, 1971b).

Individual coping strategies can be devised to assist stigmatized persons. Stigmatized persons themselves are probably in the best possible position to cope with stigma, since they are the ones who directly experience it and can deal with it immediately. Professional assistance to stigmatized individuals should involve combinations of counseling (individual or group), teaching, and advocacy. In all instances, efforts should be directed at helping the stigmatized to manage both tension and information in interactions with so-called normals (Goffman, 1963).

Humor and relaxation are often the best techniques for managing tension. In the area of information management, stigmatized persons need to be able to accept realistic information about their unique disability, while rejecting information that will be socially or vocationally handicapping. Four excellent suggestions for achieving this objective are described by Wright (1960): (1) enlarge the scope of values to include more than the disability; (2) subordinate the importance of lost function as a consequence of disablement; (3) contain negative disability effects; and (4) uphold asset versus comparative values.

In addition to managing tension and information, many stigmatized individuals need to be taught adequate social skills, so that they can survive in community living and work environments. Moreover, they need to be encouraged, and sometimes assisted, to organize themselves politically and to be a vocal force for constructive change in matters pertaining to the stigmatized.

Professionals can help to reduce stigma through education and modeling. Individually, professionals need to examine their own attitudes toward the particular clinical population with whom they are currently working. This can be accomplished through introspection, study, simulation, and peer encounter. Of great importance, professionals need to examine whether they are giving clients and families maximum opportunities for expression and responsibility or are in fact stifling initiative and self-sufficiency by being overactive and controlling (Gellman, 1959; Kutner, 1969). In addition, professionals can reduce stigma by providing social skill training to so-called deviant persons and their family members. Role playing and group simulation techniques, by professionals and previously treated disabled peers, will be helpful intervention techniques, as will videotape feedback, for shaping and reinforcing behavioral change.

Modifications in interpersonal relationships, between professionals and stigmatized deviants, and in working environments will also reduce stigma. Professionals need to attempt to increase the amount of meaningful contact between themselves and the stigmatized served, and to advocate humanistic changes in their own organizational work environments. Are contacts strictly business, or is there also some sense of an egalitarian social exchange to break down the traditional helper/helpee or superior/inferior treatment relationship? Several investigators (Gellman, 1959; Kutner, 1969; Stubbins, 1977) have argued that many service organizations reinforce the passive, dependent, childlike social deviant role of their clients by closely adhering to a formal authoritarian organizational model. They suggest that the elimination of constraining environmental status barriers—like hospital garb, separate dining and recreational facilities, and separate social affairs—would help considerably to reduce "we" versus "they" polarization and give stigmatized persons a stronger source of internal control and sense of self-directiveness.

Stigma can also be reduced through community education. It is critical to attempt to persuade the mass media, especially television, to present disability and disabled persons realistically. Disabled persons need to be cast as more than villains or patients. Furthermore, individuals must continue to lobby for legislation that will repeal dysfunctional statutes and adopt contemporary reform measures aimed at improving client service delivery.

Overall, in managing stigma it is important to offer one expansion on the preceding comments. That is, research evidence now substantiates that attempts to change negative attitudes toward physically and mentally disabled persons are generally effective only when they increase the amount of meaningful contact between deviant and nondeviant persons and disseminate accurate information about stigma (Anthony, 1972). The two approaches together are quantitatively more potent and richer as well, because they combine experiential/practical learning with didactic/abstract learning.

Application to Particular Variables

Numerous studies have examined the association between specific background characteristics and stigma (English, 1971a; Shontz, 1970; Yuker, Block, and Campbell, 1966). While these studies have usually focused on one or more groups of physically disabled persons, the findings probably have broad applicability to most stigmatized groups, in that negative attitudes toward traditional racial and religious minorities have been consistently similar, correlating about $r = .40$, to attitudes toward the physically disabled (English, 1971a).

Demographic factors that bear a significant relationship to stigma are sex, socio-economic status, and education. Females have been consistently found to be less stigmatizing than males, as are persons with more years of formal education. The socioeconomic status (SES) variable is more complex, in that higher-status groups are more accepting of the physically disabled, but lower-status groups are more accepting of the mentally and intellectually impaired (English, 1971a; Yuker, Block, and Campbell, 1966).

In the realm of personality, five factors have consistently been reported as related to stigma toward the physically disabled: (1) high authoritarianism, (2) high anxiety, (3) low social desirability or need to please other persons, (4) low tolerance of ambiguity, and (5) low self-concept (English, 1971a; Yuker, Block, and Campbell, 1966).

The anatomy of prejudice toward discredited persons is also revealed by variables that have been consistently shown not to bear a significant relationship to stigma. Unrelated variables include (1) age, (2) religion, (3) marital status, (4) nationality, (5) race, (6) intelligence, and (7) type of disability. Of all these findings, the last is the most interesting because it has been studied repeatedly over many years and shows that stigma is not uniquely related to disability type, severity of disability, etiology (hereditary versus acquired), or age of disablement (English, 1971a; Shontz, 1970).

References

Anthony, W. A. "Societal Rehabilitation: Changing Society's Attitudes Toward the Physically and Mentally Disabled." *Rehabilitation Psychology,* 1972, *19* (3), 117-126.

Barker, R. C. "The Social Psychology of Physical Disability." *Journal of Social Issues,* 1948, *4,* 29-28.

Becker, H. S. *Outsiders: Studies in the Sociology of Deviance.* New York: Free Press, 1963.

Berkowitz, L. *Roots of Aggression.* New York: Atherton, 1969.

Bettelheim, B., and Janowitz, M. *Social Change and Prejudice.* New York: Free Press, 1964.

Cohen, S. *Special People: A Brighter Future for Everyone with Physical, Mental, and Emotional Disabilities.* Englewood Cliffs, N.J.: Prentice-Hall, 1977.

Davis, F. "Deviance Disavowal: The Management of Strained Interaction by the Visibly Handicapped." *Social Problems,* 1961, *9* (2), 121-132.

English, R. W. "Correlates of Stigma Towards Physically Disabled Persons." *Rehabilitation Research and Practice Review,* 1971a, *2* (4), 1-17.

English, R. W. "Combatting Stigma Towards Physically Disabled Persons." *Rehabilitation Research and Practice Review,* 1971b, *2* (4), 18-27.

English, R. W. "The Application of Personality Theory to Explain Psychological Reactions to Physical Disability." *Rehabilitation Research and Practice Review,* 1971c, *3* (1), 35-41, 47.

Gellman, W. "Roots of Prejudice Against the Handicapped." *Journal of Rehabilitation,* 1959, *25* (1), 4-6.

Goffman, E. *Stigma: Notes on the Management of Spoiled Identity.* Englewood Cliffs, N.J.: Prentice-Hall, 1963.

Hanks, J. R., and Hanks, L. M. "The Physically Handicapped in Certain Non-Occidental Societies." *Journal of Social Issues,* 1948, *4* (4), 11-20.

Kutner, B. "Professional Antitherapy." *Journal of Rehabilitation,* 1969, *35* (6), 16-18.

Lemert, E. M. *Human Deviance, Social Problems, and Social Control.* Englewood Cliffs, N.J.: Prentice-Hall, 1967.

Malone, R. L. "Expressed Attitudes of Families of Aphasics." *Journal of Speech and Hearing Disorders,* 1969, *34,* 146-151.

Mercer, J. R. "Labeling the Mentally Retarded." In E. Rubington and M. S. Weinberg (Eds.), *Deviance: The Interactionist Perspective.* New York: Macmillan, 1977.

Miller, D. C. *Handbook of Research Design and Social Measurement.* New York: McKay, 1977.

Parsons, T. "Definitions of Health and Illness in the Light of American Values and Social Structure." In E. G. Jaco (Ed.), *Patients, Physicians, and Illness.* New York: Free Press, 1958.

Robinson, J. P., and Shaver, P. P. *Measures of Social Psychological Attitudes.* Ann Arbor: Institute of Social Research, University of Michigan, 1973.

Safilios-Rothschild, C. S. "Prejudice Against the Disabled and Some Means to Combat it." *International Rehabilitation Review,* 1968, *19* (4), 8-10, 15.

Shontz, F. C. "Physical Disability and Personality: Theory and Recent Research." *Psychological Aspects of Disability,* 1970, *17* (2), 51-69.

Stubbins, J. (Ed.). *Social and Psychological Aspects of Disability.* Baltimore: University Park Press, 1977.

Wright, B. A. *Physical Disability: A Psychological Approach.* New York: Harper & Row, 1960.

Yamamoto, K. "To Be Different." *Rehabilitation Counseling Bulletin,* 1971, *14* (3), 180-189.

Yuker, H. E., Block, J. R., and Campbell, W. J. *The Measurement of Attitudes Toward Disabled Persons.* Albertson, N.Y.: Human Resources Foundation, 1966.

86

Alfred J. Butler
Kenneth R. Thomas

Disability
Acceptance

More than two decades ago, Dembo, Leviton, and Wright (1956) wrote what is still considered the most definitive presentation on the dimensions of disability acceptance. They conceptualized disability acceptance, or "acceptance of loss," as a process involving changes in the value system of the disabled person. Such changes would, in their view, help the individual overcome such effects of disability as all-inclusive suffering, mourning, devaluation produced by damage to appearance, and devaluation produced by the negative reactions of others.

The two major areas of value changes considered crucial to acceptance were (1) enlargement of scope of values and (2) changes from comparative values to asset values. The term *enlargement of scope of values* refers to the eventual realization by the disabled person that the values "lost" through disability are but part of the person's total value system and that life can be meaningful in spite of disability-related difficulties. The term *changes from comparative values to asset values* refers to the development of a personal rather than a social frame of reference in evaluating performance. Disabled persons also need to realize that they do have certain abilities and that, in any case, abilities as such do not determine personal worth.

The assessment instrument that most comprehensively reflects Dembo, Leviton, and Wright's value changes approach to acceptance is Linkowski's (1971) Acceptance of Disability Scale. This fifty-item, six-point Likert scale was constructed on the premise that the process of acceptance involves value changes in four areas: (1) enlargement of scope of values, (2) subordination of physique, (3) containment of disability effects, and (4) transformation from comparative to asset values.

Alternative approaches to disability acceptance include the semantic differential technique (Osgood, Suci, and Tannenbaum, 1957) and the body image and self-concept theory (English, 1971; McDaniel, 1969; Parsons, 1958; Safilios-Rothschild, 1970). Most of the assessment techniques stemming from these approaches provide measures from which acceptance of disability must be indirectly inferred.

Background and Current Status

Formal use of the term *acceptance of disability* began with the presentation of Dembo, Leviton, and Wright (1956). It is difficult to trace earlier usage of the term in either theory or clinical practice. Psychological explorations of adjustment to disability (that is, the inability to satisfy individual desires, particularly in the formative years of development) may be traced back through modern psychology to the psychoanalytic theory of Freud. Physical disability per se, however, was not the prime concern of the early psychoanalysts. In Adler's (1927) individual psychology, striving for superiority is posited as an innate drive. Concepts such as compensation for the organic deficit or organ inferiority probably should be viewed as alternative attempts to understand psychological adjustment to disability rather than precursors of the term *disability acceptance*. Body image theory, developed by Schilder (1950), has a closer theoretical relationship; that is, attitudes toward the self are seen as determined in large part by perceptions of physique. There is substantial disagreement concerning the synonymity of self-concept and body image, with body image theorists viewing the two as nonequivalent. From an eclectic standpoint, however, acceptance of disability may be inferred from the quality of the body image itself.

Disability acceptance is most closely related to the interpersonal or somato-psychological school of thought, represented by the writings of Barker, Wright, and Gonich (1946); Dembo, Leviton, and Wright (1956); Myerson (1955); and Wright (1960). In addition to disability acceptance, these investigators have elaborated on related explanatory concepts, such as spread (generalizing negative value of disability to total self-concept), value loss (devaluation of self due to loss of function or attractiveness), expectancy discrepancy (depreciation of expected achievement), new and overlapping situations (ambiguous situations in which either normal or disabled role may be appropriate) or as-if behavior (pretending disability does not exist). Despite the theoretical appeal of these descriptors, they have not been used extensively in research or clinical assessment.

Disability acceptance has been approached directly in research assessment through Linkowski's (1971) Acceptance of Disability Scale, briefly described above, and through the semantic differential technique (see Thomas, Weisner, and Davis, 1978). Less direct methods of assessing acceptance of disability include the Attitudes Towards Disabled Persons Scale (ATDP) (Yuker, Block, and Younng, 1970), the Handicap Problems Inventory

(Wright and Remmers, 1960), the Human Service Scale (Reagles and Butler, 1976), and the Tennessee Self-Concept Scale (Fitts, 1964-5). These instruments provide measures from which acceptance may be inferred to a limited extent and in global terms (but not in terms of the specific dynamics tapped by the Linkowski Scale). If use of the concept may be measured by frequency of references in the psychological literature, it may be of interest to note that acceptance of disability has been explicitly cited in the *Psychological Abstracts* fewer than ten times in the last ten years, as opposed to thousands of explicit references to self-concept. The significance of the concept within a theoretical framework for understanding the dynamics of disability has been explored in only a few scattered studies (for example, Thomas, Davis, and Hochman, 1976) on the correlates of the Linkowski Scale and somewhat more extensively in research with the ATDP Scale, represented by the thorough review by Yuker, Block, and Younng (1970). While psychologists, counselors, and other rehabilitation workers may be attending to acceptance of disability by their clients, there is no evidence of a systematic approach to formal assessment in rehabilitation practice to date.

Critical Discussion

General Areas of Concern

In the context of assessment, concerns about the concept of disability acceptance focus on two general and interrelated considerations: (1) the reliability and validity of the instruments used to measure the construct and (2) the usefulness of the construct in the delivery of diagnostic and treatment services.

The history of the disability acceptance concept in psychological assessment has been too short and too dispersed to permit a systematic comparison of the reliability, validity, and other psychometric attributes of instruments. If the meaning of *acceptance* were limited primarily to enlargement of scope of values and shift from comparative values to asset values, then there would be a restriction to use only the single instrument, the Linkowski Scale, that provides direct measures of these concepts. If acceptance were viewed in terms of the relative value placed on physique, disability, handicap, or selected attributes, the construct could be assessed by the semantic differential technique. If disability acceptance is equated with the integrity of the body image, a number of instruments (both projective and objective) might be used. Or acceptance may be inferred from a measure of a disabled person's attitudes toward the disabled (for example, the ATDP Scale). It may also be inferred, although more remotely, from self-concept measures (such as the Tennessee Self-Concept Scale), from measures of the level of satisfaction of needs (the Human Service Scale), or from measures of perceived problems stemming from the disability (the Handicap Problems Inventory).

A summary appraisal of the psychometric attributes of these varied approaches can be given only in general terms. The Linkowski Scale provides a direct measure of four dimensions: (1) enlargement of scope of values, (2) subordination of physique, (3) containment of disability effects, and (4) transformation from comparative values to asset values. The split-half reliability of the fifty-item scale was reported to be $r = .86$, with a full-scale reliability (estimated by the Spearman-Brown Prophecy formula) of $r = .96$. According to Linkowski (1971), the factor analysis of the fifty items indicated that 48 to 69 percent of the common variance, depending on the sample tested, could be attributed to the principal factor. Both analyses indicate that the instrument is measuring one major dimension. Linkowski also reported a correlation of $r = .81$ between the scale and the ATDP Scale (fifty-item Form B). This shared variance of approximately 66 percent indicates the need for more extensive study of the interrelationship of the two measures. The potentially high similarity between the relatively new and untried Linkowski Scale and the ATDP Scale (which has been extensively analyzed) raises some questions about the uniqueness of the former. Psychometric attributes of the ATDP Scale have been reported in minute detail by Yuker, Block, and Younng (1970), with sufficient evidence of reliability, content, and construct- and criterion-related validity to provide an adequate basis for acceptance or rejection by the clinician.

Use of the semantic differential technique in assessing disability acceptance has been limited to research with insufficient evidence of reliability and validity to warrant clinical use. With so many potential approaches to body image and the scattered nature of the research, no convincing data have emerged to warrant a recommendation concerning the clinical application of the semantic differential technique.

As to the other instruments from which disability acceptance might be inferred, some (particularly the Tennessee Self-Concept Scale) have had extensive psychometric evaluation. Indices of reliability and validity pertain to the concepts which they were designed to measure, not to disability acceptance per se.

Comparative Philosophies and Theories

Perceived importance of disability acceptance in psychological adjustment is a function, understandably, of the theoretical approach to understanding this adjustment. According to the somatopsychological approach of Wright (1960), acceptance, defined in terms of the four dimensions underlying the Linkowski Scale, is of central importance. If one subscribes to this viewpoint, disability acceptance logically becomes a focus for assessment and treatment. In almost all other theories of adjustment to disability, acceptance is either a peripheral concept or its importance must be inferred. For the body image theorist, who equates acceptance with body image, the concept is of major importance, but it is explained, measured, and acted on in other terms. For most self theorists, disability acceptance would be seen as only one dimension of self-esteem and would also be explained, measured, and acted on in other terms. It is likely, then, that only the researcher or clinician with a somatopsychological viewpoint would see great merit in the concept of acceptance for assessment purposes.

Elaboration on Critical Points

There seems to be little value in serious consideration of the term *disability acceptance* as a basis for client assessment unless one is a proponent of, or at least receptive to, the somatopsychological view of adjustment to disability. If one subscribes to other theories, acceptance of disability is not a focal point for either assessment or treatment. Consequently, only the measurement approaches represented by the Linkowski Scale, the ATDP Scale, and the semantic differential technique seem justifiable, and these have serious limitations. The Linkowski Scale was designed for and well fits the somatopsychological model. However, considerable psychometric research is required before it can be applied clinically. Since four aspects of acceptance presumably are being tapped by the measure, which theoretically could be more independent than factor analysis of the fifty-item scale would suggest, construct validity of the scale needs further scrutiny. Also, the potentially close relationship to the ATDP Scale is bothersome. A common criticism of the ATDP Scale is its susceptibility to social desirability. It is possible that the Linkowski Scale has the same weakness. The extensive study of the ATDP Scale, with reasonably satisfactory indices of reliability and validity, points to its usefulness—the social desirability criticism being set aside. Since this scale purports to measure only the extent to which the disabled are seen as different, less desirable conceptually, it may be recommended only as one means of assessing the validity of a Linkowski type of scale (which is theoretically more tenable). Use of the semantic differential technique is recommended only for research and in those situations where a subtle and indirect approach is indicated.

Personal Views and Recommendations

Use of disability acceptance in assessment should be limited to (1) those professionals who understand and are committed to the somatopsychological viewpoint and (2) those settings where the treatment process encompasses the value changes integral to acceptance, as seen under that theoretical framework. Any enthusiasm for its use should be based on the theoretical potential of the concept, not on the basis of the limited research and evidence of its clinical use as reported in the literature. Finally, a number of limitations relative to its use with specific populations (discussed in the next section) should be noted.

Application to Particular Variables

In assessing disability acceptance in older adults and very young children, clinicians must be especially certain that the subjects clearly understand what is expected of them in the testing situation and that they are capable of responding appropriately to the particular instrument employed. Although DeWolfe, Barrell, and Cummings (1966) found that older patients with more severe illness expressed less discomfort than younger patients with milder disabilities, no significant relationship was found between age and acceptance of disability in a recent study by Thomas, Davis, and Hochman (1976), which employed amputees ranging in age from 17 to 74. Also, although several prominent authorities (Super, 1957; Wright, 1960) have hypothesized that persons with adventitious disabilities have a more difficult time with acceptance and adjustment than congenitally disabled individuals, no empirical evidence is available to support this hypothesis.

The research literature indicates that, except where the disability severely affects physical appearance, females are more accepting of a disability than males are (see Thomas, Davis, and Hochman, 1976; Thomas and Britton, 1973). In addition, studies have rather consistently shown that women have more favorable attitudes toward persons with a disability than men do (Chesler, 1965; Siller, 1963; Yuker, Block, and Younng, 1970). In a cosmetically disabled population of adolescents, however, Smits (1965) found that mildly disabled females and severely disabled males were more accepting than severely disabled females were.

Patterns of disability acceptance on the basis of sex appear to be very closely related to culturally defined sex-role expectations. Specifically, males tend to be less accepting when disability affects their ability to be seen as virile and self-sufficient, and females tend to be less accepting when disability interferes with their ability to fulfill traditional womanly roles. As culturally defined differences in sex-role expectations diminish in our society, these tendencies toward sex-related differences in acceptance may diminish.

Level of education, as hypothesized by Safilios-Rothschild (1970), appears to have a significant impact on one's ability to accept the functional limitations imposed by a disability. This hypothesis was supported directly in the study by Thomas, Davis, and Hochman (1976), previously cited. Also, studies have consistently shown that educational level is a significantly positive correlate of rehabilitation success (Ayer, Thoreson, and Butler, 1966; DeMann, 1963; Ehrle, 1961; Lesser and Darling, 1953; McPhee, Griffiths, and Magleby, 1963; Schletzer and others, 1957).

Safilios-Rothschild (1970) has hypothesized that the more "resources" a person has available, the less threatened he or she will be by the functional limitations imposed by a disability. Moreover, research has indicated that higher-income persons are more accepting of individuals with intellectual and emotional deficiencies than are lower-income persons (Farber, 1968; Jabin, 1966). However, in the study by Thomas, Davis, and Hochman (1976), neither premorbid nor current annual income was found significantly related to acceptance. Probably the most accurate statement that can be made concerning the relationship between socioeconomic status and acceptance is that acceptance will be most difficult when the disability adversely affects the person's ability to initiate or continue to do things that are personally valued or considered important by significant others. Such activities are more likely to require intellectual or social competence in the case of higher-income persons and physical competence in the case of lower-income persons.

While it has been hypothesized that occupation is a factor in disability acceptance (Safilios-Rothschild, 1970), the importance of personal adjustment in determining one's ability to obtain and maintain employment has been recently downplayed by several authorities in the field of rehabilitation (Walls and Tseng, 1976). Thomas, Davis, and Hochman (1976) identified differences in acceptance among amputees working in seven different occupational categories. Specifically, clerical and sales workers were found most accepting, and those engaged in processing occupations were found least accepting. In this same study, however, amputees without work experience tended to be more accepting than those with work experience, and no significant relationships were found between acceptance and current employment status, premorbid annual income, or current annual income. Apparently, then, the socioeconomic aspects of one's occupation are less critical than whether a change in occupational or vocational plans has been necessitated by the disability.

No research evidence is available to indicate that either race or ethnic identification is a factor in acceptance. However, a rather substantial body of research evidence suggests that religious preference is a factor. Several of these studies have dealt with the attitudes of parents and others toward the mentally retarded (Farber, 1968; Robinson and Robinson, 1965; Stubblefield, 1965; Zuk, 1959-60). In general, these studies indicate that Catholics are more accepting of retarded offspring than either Protestants or Jews are. Similarly, Thomas, Davis, and Hochman (1976) found Catholic amputees to be more accepting of their disabilities than either Protestants or persons expressing no religious preference. On the basis of results from their study, Thomas and his associates suggest that a religiosity factor is involved in acceptance; that is, they speculate that the intensity of one's religious beliefs may be more important to acceptance than the specific religion itself.

Disability acceptance has been applied almost exclusively to the physically disabled. The somatopsychological and body image approach to the concept would be inapplicable to other disabilities. Social-role theory does provide a feasible avenue through examination of attitudes to mental retardation or mental illness, but no instrumentation is readily available for that purpose. The semantic differential technique could also be used. Feasibility of this instrument for the retarded has been tested by Rybold (1967) and may be assumed to be appropriate for use with most psychiatric populations. Again, well-researched instrumentation is unavailable. The substantial research and instrumentation relating to the self-concepts of psychiatric populations are limited by validity prob lems, so that disability acceptance cannot be inferred from these measures.

Within the physically disabled populations, limitations to measurement are frequently encountered as a result of specific sensory and motor deficits. For example, oral or Braille presentation is required for the blind and visual presentation for the deaf. Generally, no serious difficulties would be encountered with the Linkowski Scale, the ATDP Scale, the semantic differential technique, or most instruments relevant to body image and self-concept. With some disabilities, certain measurement approaches to assess body image (for example, the Draw-a-Person Test) are obviously inappropriate.

References

Adler, A. *The Practice and Theory of Individual Psychology.* New York: Harcourt Brace Jovanovich, 1927.

Ayer, J., Thoreson, R., and Butler, A. "Predicting Rehabilitation Success with the MMPI and Demographic Data." *Personnel and Guidance Journal,* 1966, *44,* 631-637.

Barker, R., Wright, B., and Gonick, M. *Adjustment to Physical Handicaps and Illness: A Survey of the Social Psychology of Physique and Disability.* New York: Social Science Research Council, 1946.

Chesler, M. "Ethnocentrism and Attitudes Toward the Physically Disabled." *Journal of Personality and Social Psychology,* 1965, *2,* 877-882.

DeMann, M. "A Predictive Study of Rehabilitation Counseling Outcomes." *Journal of Counseling Psychology,* 1963, *10,* 340-343.

Dembo, T., Leviton, G., and Wright, B. "Adjustment to Misfortune—A Problem of Social Psychological Rehabilitation." *Artificial Limbs,* 1956, *3,* 4-62.

DeWolfe, A., Barrell, R., and Cummings, J. "Patient Variables in Emotional Response to Hospitalization for Physical Illness." *Journal of Consulting Psychology,* 1966, *30,* 68-72.

Ehrle, R. "The Predictive Value of Biographical Data in Vocational Rehabilitation." Unpublished doctoral dissertation, University of Missouri, Columbia, 1961.

English, R. W. "The Application of Personality Theory to Explain Psychological Reactions to Physical Disability." *Rehabilitation Research and Practice Review,* 1971, *3* (1), 35-41, 47.

Farber, B. *Mental Retardation: Its Social Context and Social Consequences.* Boston: Houghton Mifflin, 1968.

Fitts, W. *Tennessee Self-Concept Scale.* Nashville: Counselor Recordings and Tests, 1964-5.

Jabin, N. "Attitudes Toward the Physically Disabled as Related to Selected Personality Variables." Unpublished doctoral dissertation, New York University, 1966.

Lesser, M., and Darling, R. "Factors Prognostic for Vocational Rehabilitation Among the Physically Handicapped." *Archives of Physical Medicine and Rehabilitation,* 1953, *34,* 73-81.

Linkowski, D. "A Scale to Measure Acceptance of Disability." *Rehabilitation Counseling Bulletin,* 1971, *14,* 236-244.

McDaniel, J. W. *Physical Disability and Human Behavior.* Elmsford, N.Y.: Pergamon Press, 1969.

McPhee, W., Griffiths, K., and Magleby, F. *Adjustment of Vocational Rehabilitation Clients.* Washington, D.C.: Vocational Rehabilitation Administration, U.S. Department of Health, Education and Welfare, 1963.

Myerson, L. "Somatopsychology of Physical Disability." In W. M. Cruickshank (Ed.), *Psychology of Exceptional Children and Youth.* Englewood Cliffs, N.J.: Prentice-Hall, 1955.

Osgood, C., Suci, G., and Tannenbaum, P. *The Measurement of Meaning.* Urbana: University of Illinois Press, 1957.

Parsons, T. "Definitions of Health and Illness in the Light of American Values and Social Structure." In E. G. Jaco (Ed.), *Patients, Physicians, and Illness.* New York: Free Press, 1958.

Reagles, K., and Butler, A. "The Human Service Scale: A New Measure for Evaluation." *Journal of Rehabilitation,* 1976, *42* (3), 34-38.

Robinson, H., and Robinson, N. *The Mentally Retarded Child: A Psychological Approach.* New York: McGraw-Hill, 1965.

Rybold, G. "Use of the Semantic Differential with the Mentally Retarded." Unpublished doctoral dissertation, University of Missouri, Columbia, 1967.

Safilios-Rothschild, C. *The Sociology and Social Psychology of Disability and Rehabilitation.* New York: Random House, 1970.

Schilder, P. *The Image and Appearance of the Human Body.* New York: Wiley, 1950.

Schletzer, V., and others. "Factors Related to Employment Success." In *Minnesota Studies in Vocational Rehabilitation.* Vol. 7. Minneapolis: University of Minnesota Industrial Relations Center, 1957.

Siller, J. "Reactions to Physical Disability." *Rehabilitation Counseling Bulletin,* 1963, *7,* 12-16.

Smits, S. "The Reactions of Self and Others to the Obviousness and Severity of Physical Disability." *Rehabilitation Counseling Bulletin,* 1965, *9,* 41-46.

Stubblefield, H. "Religion, Parents, and Mental Retardation." *Mental Retardation,* 1965, *3,* 8-11.

Super, D. *The Psychology of Careers.* New York: Harper & Row, 1957.

Thomas, K., and Britton, J. "Perceptions of Family Dependence by the Physically Disabled." *Rehabilitation Counseling Bulletin,* 1973, *16,* 156-161.

Thomas, K., Davis, R., and Hochman, M. "Correlates of Disability Acceptance in Amputees." *Rehabilitation Counseling Bulletin,* 1976, *19,* 509-511.

Thomas, K., Weisner, S., and Davis, R. "Semantic Differential Ratings as Indices of Disability Acceptance." Unpublished manuscript, University of Wisconsin-Madison, 1978.

Walls, R., and Tseng, M. "Measurement of Client Outcomes in Rehabilitation." In B. Bolton (Ed.), *Handbook of Measurement and Evaluation in Rehabilitation.* Baltimore: University Park Press, 1976.

Wright, B. *Physical Disability: A Psychological Approach.* New York: Harper & Row, 1960.

Wright, G., and Remmers, H. *Manual for the Handicap Problems Inventory.* Lafayette, Ind.: Purdue University Research Foundation, 1960.

Yuker, H., Block, J., and Younng, J. *The Measurement of Attitudes toward Disabled Persons.* Albertson, N.Y.: Human Resources Center, 1970.

Zuk, G. "The Religious Factor and the Role of Guilt in Parental Acceptance of the Retarded Child." *American Journal of Mental Deficiency,* 1959-60, *64,* 139-147.

87

Brian F. Bolton

Rehabilitation Needs

Individual deficiencies or problem areas that can be ameliorated through the provision of rehabilitation services are here referred to as rehabilitation needs. While it is a truism that disabled persons have the same basic needs as the nondisabled, their specific life circumstances are usually aggravated by difficulties that result from an impairment, disability, or handicap. Since rehabilitation services exist to address the special needs of disabled persons, the term *rehabilitation needs* includes, by implication, the concept of service needs.

Because rehabilitation services and the concept of disability are inextricably related to the term *rehabilitation needs,* it will be helpful to introduce some standard definitions at this point. The Comprehensive Service Needs Study (Urban Institute, 1975) developed the following vocabulary: (1) an *impairment* refers to the residual limitation resulting from a congenital defect, disease, or injury; (2) a *disability* exists when the impairment results in an inability to perform some key life functions; and (3) a *handicap* results when the disability interacts with the environment to impose impediments to the individual's goals. Thus, rehabilitation needs can have their genesis in the individual's impairment, disability, or handicap. This distinction is not a trivial one. It is a well-documented axiom of rehabilitation psychology that individuals react differently to impairment (Roessler and Bolton, 1978). Thus, similar impairments may result in disabling or handicapping conditions of a different nature or degree of severity. The critical implication for the assessment of rehabilitation needs is that the effects of impairment, and the difficulties and service needs that ensue, usually require a unique configuration of rehabilitation treatments.

In view of the foregoing, it should be recognized that (1) rehabilitation needs are deficiencies or problems that are presumed to be the direct result of the occurrence of impairment; (2) these needs can be assessed by means of a variety of appropriate techniques; and (3) rehabilitation services can be provided to alleviate the deficiencies or problems.

The terms *need, drive,* and *motive* are often used interchangeably. Yet there are important distinctions among these concepts. English and English (1958, p. 338) recommend that *need* be used to indicate "the lack of something which, if present, would tend to further the welfare of the organism or of the species, or to facilitate its usual behavior." In other words, a need is a deficiency that interferes with, or prevents, normal human functioning. Furthermore, when need (as defined above) is equated with *motive,* it is implied that the need or deficit directly evokes action.

The definition of the term *rehabilitation needs* adopted in this chapter is clearly consistent with English and English's recommended usage. But this primary emphasis on needs as deficiencies is not intended to exclude the motivational interpretation. Rehabilitation needs can also initiate action; in fact, client motivation has been a prominent topic in the rehabilitation literature (for reviews see Barry and Malinovsky, 1965; Lane and Barry, 1970).

Kravetz (1973) has isolated six aspects of the need construct that provide a useful framework for the derivation of measurement indices:

1. *Preference.* Needs may be inferred from the individual's preferences for certain categories of objects, situations, or activities.
2. *Trans-situational generality.* Objects, situations, and activities that appear different from one another often lead to the satisfaction of the same need and, therefore, are sometimes interchangeable.
3. *Reinforcement value.* A reward system can help to ensure the recurrence of many of an organism's activities that are potential ways to satisfy needs.
4. *Deprivation.* Organisms that are deprived of the conditions for need satisfaction are stunted physiologically and psychologically and, when given the opportunity, tend to search out these satisfactions.
5. *Gratification.* The process of need satisfaction may account for much of the change that occurs in human behavior.
6. *Awareness.* Although individuals may often be unaware of their basic needs, suitable assessment techniques can bring them into consciousness.

The need theories and associated instruments that are discussed in this chapter focus on a few selected characteristics, while neglecting other aspects of the need construct. For example, the Minnesota Theory of Work Adjustment is a reinforcement theory in which vocational needs are measured by a series of preferences among activities and situations. In contrast, the Human Service Scale is based on a formulation that stresses "the trans-situational generality of needs and the manner in which the results of need deprivation and gratification interact to relate sets of needs to each other" (Kravetz, 1973, p. 58).

Background and Current Status

The concepts of needs, drives, instincts, motives, or any other propensities to action are essential to any comprehensive explanation of human behavior. Most of the classical philosophers, as well as prominent political philosophers who lived from the sixteenth to the nineteenth century, addressed the issue of human motives or drives, usually in terms of observable elements of human nature, such as hunger, thirst, fear, sex, pain avoidance, and desire for recognition (Murphy, 1949). The most basic and all-encompassing motive, adopted by Machiavelli, Thomas Hobbes, Jeremy Bentham, James Mill, and others, is that of self-interest or self-enhancement. Not surprisingly, this primary need has continued to be a popular explanatory mechanism in modern personality and motivational theories.

A comprehensive review of the term *need* in twentieth-century psychology is simply beyond the scope of this chapter; furthermore, such a chronology is not necessary to the major concern of this chapter—the assessment of rehabilitation needs. However, a few individuals deserve mention because of the central role of the need construct in their theorizing.

According to Madsen (1973), Edward Tolman was the first learning theorist to introduce needs (or drives) into the psychology of learning. Clark Hull's behavior theory includes the key mechanism of "need reduction," which later become "drive reduction." His definition of need and its effects appears to be the source of English and English's definition, quoted previously: "When a condition arises for which action on the part of the organism is a prerequisite to optimum probability of survival of either the individual or the species, a state of need is said to exist. . . . The need is often said to motivate or drive the associated activity" (Hull, 1943, p. 57). Other learning theorists for whom the need construct assumed a major role were O. H. Mowrer, Gregory Razran, and Kurt Lewin.

Lewin occupies a special place in rehabilitation psychology, because his field theory provided the foundation for the somatopsychological school, represented in the writings of Barker and associates (1953); Dembo, Leviton, and Wright (1956); and Wright (1960). Madsen (1973, p. 680) states that Lewin's theory is "the only theory of motivation which is in any way connected with classical, experimental psychology." His early (1920s) conceptual analysis of "determining tendencies" of behavior, which were subsequently called needs, provided the basis for the motivational variable of psychological force in his later (1930s) topological system. Ironically, despite the widespread recognition of Lewin's theory as a useful conceptual model for understanding adjustment to disability, it has not generated any formal assessment techniques.

Numerous contemporary personality theories also rely on the concept of need. For example, Gestalt theory postulates that needs are the organizers of behavior. The essential human need is homeostasis and includes such specific requirements as self-awareness, self-integration, and self-fulfillment. Coven (1977) has summarized the applications of Gestalt techniques to rehabilitation problems. Another example is Rogers' (1951) popular theory, which holds that "behavior is basically the goal-directed attempt of the organism to satisfy its needs" (p. 491).

In the remainder of this chapter, attention will be restricted to those theories or approaches that have provided the foundation for one or more need assessment techniques that have been applied in rehabilitation settings. These orientations, which are outlined in the following sections, include: (1) Abraham Maslow's motivational theory; (2) the Minnesota Theory of Work Adjustment; (3) an empirical measurement approach that has resulted in instruments for assessing problems related to disablement, ability to perform the activities of daily living, and degree of functional independence; (4) Henry Murray's motivational theory of personality; and (5) Raymond Cattell's quantitative theory of motivation.

Critical Discussion

General Areas of Concern

The five conceptual approaches to the organization and assessment of rehabilitation clients' needs can be analyzed by asking four questions. First, are needs innate or learned, physiologically determined or socially derived? Second, do needs operate or influence behavior at the conscious level, or are individuals unaware of them? Third, are needs organized in a hierarchy of importance, or is the order of satisfaction an individual matter? And fourth, are need categories broadly defined, or are specific needs described in detail?

The first three concerns are less important from the assessment perspective, while the fourth is critical. Although all theorists have recognized that multiple needs exist, they have chosen to focus on the need construct at different levels of abstraction or degrees of specificity. At the two extremes are Rogers' emphasis on the single, global need for self-actualization (which, incidentally, can be quantified, by means of the Q-sort technique, as the discrepancy between ideal self and real self) and Murray's detailed descriptions of forty needs. The degree of specificity is an important consideration in the assessment of rehabilitation clients' needs because the provision of services is predicated on the relatively precise diagnosis of the individual client's needs or problem areas. However, broader measures of need satisfaction are often more useful in assessing the benefits that result from rehabilitation services, especially when the client's perspective is deemed important.

A more detailed analysis of the five orientations follows. However, fine distinctions within the need construct—derived need, manifest need, effect need, and many others—are not considered. Only those distinctions or refinements that have potential implications for the use of need assessment techniques are included here. Interested readers are referred to Madsen (1973) for a comprehensive review of all motivational concepts.

Comparative Philosophies and Theories

Maslow's (1954) theory of human motivation postulates a hierarchical arrangement of basic needs, in which a fundamental distinction is made between higher and lower needs. The lower needs represent deprivation motivation, or the biological requirements for physical survival, and must be satisfied before the higher needs, which are characterized as growth motivation and reflect human potentialities that serve to enrich life, can be addressed. In other words, the lower a need is in the hierarchy, the greater is its prepotency. Maddi and Costa (1972) analyzed Maslow's numerous writings on the subject and concluded that he intended six categories of human needs, which are listed in ascending order of their prepotency: (1) physiological, (2) safety, (3) belongingness and love, (4) esteem, (5) self-actualization, and (6) cognitive understanding. In Maslow's theory, needs are organismic requirements that direct behavior toward gratification; moreover, needs organize and structure external reality. This all-pervasive influence of needs derives from their "instinctoid" status; that is, they are similar to instincts and, as such, have their sources in the individual's temperament and physical constitution. Furthermore, every need is present in every member of the human species, although the form of expression varies for different persons.

The Human Service Scale (Kravetz, 1973) was designed to assess clients' needs, in order that appropriate services can be rendered, and to measure (via retest) the extent to which the services were successful in satisfying the needs. Thus, it is both a diagnostic tool and a program evaluation instrument. Eighty items that require either biographical information or self-ratings are scored on seven-factor analytically derived subscales that have parallels to five of Maslow's need categories: (1) physiological, (2) emotional security, (3) economic security, (4) family, (5) social, (6) economic self-esteem, and (7) vocational self-actualization. Preliminary analyses of the subscale intercorrelations did not support Maslow's hierarchical ordering of needs (Kravetz, 1973). Reagles and Butler (1976) have summarized the possible uses of the Human Service Scale in assessing rehabilitation clients' service needs.

The Minnesota Theory of Work Adjustment originated in a program of research on the vocational placement of rehabilitation clients that began in the late 1950s at the University of Minnesota (Dawis, 1976). The two major constructs in the theory are needs and reinforcers. Specifically, the vocational needs, which are learned through previous reinforcing experiences, are defined as classes of preferences for reinforcers. Individuals differ in their need patterns, and work environments vary in terms of the reinforcers that they provide. The Minnesota theory postulates that work satisfaction is enhanced when the correspondence between an individual's needs and the reinforcers available in the work environment is maximized (Dawis, Lofquist, and Weiss, 1968). Twenty dimensions of vocational need were formulated: (1) ability utilization, (2) achievement, (3) activity, (4) advancement, (5) authority, (6) company policies, (7) compensation, (8) co-workers, (9) creativity, (10) independence, (11) moral values, (12) recognition, (13) responsibility, (14) security, (15) social service, (16) social status, (17) supervision—human relations, (18) supervision—technical, (19) variety, and (20) working conditions.

The Minnesota Importance Questionnaire is a 210-item pair comparison instrument that generates a highly reliable profile of a person's vocational needs (Gay and others, 1971). The need reinforcer patterns for 148 diverse occupations, which represent twelve occupational groups, have been published in two manuals (Borgen and others, 1968; Rosen and others, 1972). Thus, the correspondence between an individual's profile of vocational needs and the occupational reinforcer patterns of 148 occupations can be quantified via an index of similarity. An excellent manual that describes the uses of the Minnesota Importance Questionnaire in rehabilitation counseling is available from the Chicago Jewish Vocational Service (1975).

The empirical approach to the measurement of rehabilitation clients' service needs has its genesis in a pragmatic psychometric tradition. Numerous personality questionnaires, including the MMPI, the Strong and Kuder inventories, and many others, have eschewed a theoretical foundation in favor of a direct approach. Empirical assessment techniques designed for use in rehabilitation may be either self-report or, more commonly, observer rating instruments. The Handicap Problems Inventory (Wright and Remmers, 1960) illustrates the self-report technique. It is a checklist of 280 items that constitute a comprehensive sample of problems related to physical disablement. The Handicap Problems Inventory is scored on four scales: (1) vocational, (2) social, (3) family, and (4) personal. An excellent example of an observer rating instrument is the Programmed Summary of Functional Status (PSFS) (Granger, 1974), which is basically a taxonomy of functional abilities in the activities of daily living. It requires professional ratings of the client's degree of independence in the following ten areas: (1) active motion of limbs, (2) self-care, (3) mobility, (4) communication, (5) visual ability, (6) intellectual and emotional adaptability, (7) support from family, (8) ability in home, (9) financial ability, and (10) educational and vocational ability. Another instrument, the PULSES Profile (Moskowitz and McCann, 1957), provides a briefer assessment of the client's ability to function independently in six broad areas. The PULSES Profile, as modified by Granger (1974), and the PSFS are especially easy to use because each of the rating categories is behaviorally defined. An application of the modified PULSES Profile to the assessment of severely handicapped clients is described in the report of the Comprehensive Service Needs Study (Urban Institute, 1975), while Granger (1974) gives an example of the clinical use of the PSFS.

Murray (1938) developed a motivational theory of personality that integrates learning principles with psychoanalytic theory. He assembled a refined taxonomy of some forty specific needs, including thirteen viscerogenic and more than twenty psychogenic needs, that have provided a handy list of traits for the developers of personality questionnaires. For example, the Edwards Personal Preference Schedule (Edwards, 1953) and the Personality Research Form (Jackson, 1967) were designed to measure, respectively, fifteen and twenty of Murray's needs. Murray (1938, p. 123) defined need as follows: "A need is a construct . . . which stands for a force . . . in the brain region, a force which organizes perception, apperception, intellection, conation, and action in such a way as to transform in a certain direction an existing, unsatisfying situation." He hypothesized that an "environmental press," or perceived situational pressure, is necessary for a need to become a determinant of behavior. Furthermore, Murray subscribed to the concept of a hierarchy of prepotency and believed that learned needs develop out of unlearned needs. Instruments based on Murray's needs have been used in a variety of rehabilitation settings. For example, see Bolduc (1960) and Schwartz, Dennerll, and Yi-Guang (1968).

Cattell (1957; Cattell and Child, 1975) adopted concepts from McDougall, Freud, and others and integrated them with the results of numerous factor analytic studies into a quantitative theory of motivation. Ergs, or needs, are the basic variables in Cattell's theory. He defined ergs as follows: "It seems that we are so constructed that our final satisfactions have to be instinctive ones, or *ergic* ones. The term *erg* . . . is used in the dynamic calculus for a structure which . . . is the energy source behind behavior" (Cattell, 1965, pp. 185-186). While ergs are innately determined, they can be modified by experience. They are channeled into behavior through learned structures called sentiments and attitudes. The Motivation Analysis Test (Cattell and others, 1964), a battery of four objective tests, measures five ergs and five sentiments. Sweney (1969) has written a manual for users of the Motivation Analysis Test.

Elaboration on Critical Points

The theoretical formulations underlying the needs assessment techniques share a common characteristic: the empirical support for them has not been strong. For example, Wahba and Bridwell (1976) carefully reviewed the research evaluating the validity of various aspects of Maslow's theory in the work situation and found little support for his main propositions. Unfortunately, almost all the research on Cattell's theory and the Minnesota Theory of Work Adjustment has been carried out by the people who developed the theory and instrumentation. Because Murray's needs have usually been studied selectively, as exemplified by the research of David McClelland and John W. Atkinson, it would be difficult to reach a global evaluation of his theory of needs. Finally, the empirical approach to needs assessment can be evaluated only on the basis of the utility of a given instrument for a specific purpose in a particular setting.

In general, there is a vast chasm between the comprehensiveness and refinement of the various theoretical need formulations and the instruments that have been constructed to operationalize their major concepts. While the theories have provided an orientation and an initial organizing scheme for need assessment techniques, the instruments ultimately must be judged on their psychometric qualities and practical usefulness in the assessment of rehabilitation clients' service needs.

Personal Views and Recommendations

The three theoretically based instruments for the assessment of clients' needs—the Human Service Scale, the Minnesota Importance Questionnaire, and the Motivation Analysis Test—have excellent psychometric foundations. The inventory with the widest bandwidth, the Human Service Scale, is limited by the absence of an ongoing program of validation research. The Minnesota Importance Questionnaire, although restricted to the measurement of vocational needs, has the greatest potential as a counseling tool because of the associated occupational reinforcer patterns. And the Motivation Analysis Test, which is based on a quarter of a century of developmental research, is unique in that it uses objective tests to measure needs. All things considered, however, the various instruments that have been constructed following the empirical approach possess the greatest practical value, owing to the unlimited flexibility of the approach and its adaptability to virtually any situation that requires the assessment of service needs.

In summary, any of the currently available instruments for the assessment of clients' needs may be useful for some purpose. Psychologists and counselors should be familiar with the technical characteristics of the instruments before making a selection.

Application to Particular Variables

With few exceptions, the assessment techniques discussed above are appropriate for use with all persons aged 16 or older, regardless of sex, socioeconomic status, vocation, race, and nature of disabling condition. The exceptions pertain to minimal reading level (usually sixth grade) for the inventories and, if the disorder is psychiatric, the severity of the condition. Of course, the judgment of the psychologist will always have to be relied on in making decisions regarding the applicability of particular instruments.

One additional issue requires mention, and that concerns the implications of assessed deficiencies: Are there minimally acceptable levels of need satisfaction? While this question cannot be dealt with here, our humanitarian social service philosophy is premised on the notion that all disabled persons are entitled to rehabilitation services that will satisfy their needs and, ultimately, lead to happiness and a meaningful, productive life.

References

Barker, R. G., and others. *Adjustment to Physical Handicap and Illness: A Survey of the Social Psychology of Physique and Disability.* (Rev. ed.) New York: Social Science Research Council, 1953.

Barry, J. R., and Malinovsky, M. R. *Client Motivation for Rehabilitation: A Review.* Gainesville: Rehabilitation Research Institute, University of Florida, 1965.

Bolduc, T. E. "Social Value-Need Patterns in Mental Retardates." *Journal of Consulting Psychology,* 1960, *24,* 472-479.

Borgen, F. H., and others. *Occupational Reinforcer Patterns.* Vol. 1. Monograph 24. Minneapolis: University of Minnesota Industrial Relations Center, 1968.

Cattell, R. B. *Personality and Motivation Structure and Measurement.* New York: World, 1957.

Cattell, R. B. *The Scientific Analysis of Personality.* New York: Penguin Books, 1965.

Cattell, R. B., and Child, D. *Motivation and Dynamic Structure.* New York: Halstead, 1975.

Cattell, R. B., and others. *Handbook for the Motivation Analysis Test.* Champaign, Ill.: Institute for Personality and Ability Testing, 1964.

Chicago Jewish Vocational Service. *The Minnesota Importance Questionnaire and the Meaning of Work for Rehabilitation Clients.* Chicago: Jewish Vocational Service, 1975.

Coven, A. "The Gestalt Approach to Rehabilitation Counseling." *Rehabilitation Counseling Bulletin,* 1977, *20,* 167-174.

Dawis, R. V. "The Minnesota Theory of Work Adjustment." In B. Bolton (Ed.), *Handbook of Measurement and Evaluation in Rehabilitation.* Baltimore: University Park Press, 1976.

Dawis, R. V., Lofquist, L. H., and Weiss, D. J. *A Theory of Work Adjustment: A Revision.* Monograph 23. Minneapolis: University of Minnesota Industrial Relations Center, 1968.

Dembo, T., Leviton, G. L., and Wright, B. A. "Adjustment to Misfortune—A Problem of Social Psychological Rehabilitation." *Artificial Limbs,* 1956, *3* (2), 4-62.

Edwards, A. L. *Manual for the Edwards Personal Preference Schedule.* New York: Psychological Corporation, 1953.

English, H. B., and English, A. C. *A Comprehensive Dictionary of Psychological and Psychoanalytical Terms.* New York: McKay, 1958.

Gay, E. G., and others. *Manual for the Minnesota Importance Questionnaire.* Monograph 28. Minneapolis: University of Minnesota Industrial Relations Center, 1971.

Granger, C. V. *A Monograph on Medical Rehabilitation.* II: *Programming Care and Measuring Outcomes.* Boston: Tufts New England Medical Center, 1974.

Hull, C. L. *Principles of Behavior.* New York: Appleton-Century-Crofts, 1943.

Jackson, D. N. *Personality Research Form Manual.* Goshen, N.Y.: Research Psychologists Press, 1967.

Kravetz, S. "Rehabilitation Need and Status: Substance, Structure, and Process." Unpublished doctoral dissertation, University of Wisconsin, 1973.

Lane, J. M., and Barry, J. R. "Recent Research on Client Motivation." *Rehabilitation Research and Practice Review,* 1970, *1* (4), 5-25.

Maddi, S. R., and Costa, P. T. *Humanism in Personology: Allport, Maslow, and Murray.* Chicago: Aldine, 1972.

Madsen, K. B. "Theories of Motivation." In B. Wolman (Ed.), *Handbook of General Psychology.* Englewood Cliffs, N.J.: Prentice-Hall, 1973.

Maslow, A. H. *Motivation and Personality.* New York: Harper & Row, 1954.

Moskowitz, E., and McCann, C. "Classification of Disability in Chronically Ill and Aging." *Journal of Chronic Disease,* 1957, *5,* 342-346.

Murphy, G. *Historical Introduction to Modern Psychology.* (Rev. ed.) New York: Harcourt Brace Jovanovich, 1949.

Murray, H. *Explorations in Personality.* New York: Oxford University Press, 1938.

Reagles, K. W., and Butler, A. J. "The Human Service Scale: A New Measure for Evaluation." *Journal of Rehabilitation,* 1976, *42,* 34-38.

Roessler, R., and Bolton, B. *Psychosocial Adjustment to Disability.* Baltimore: University Park Press, 1978.

Rogers, C. R. *Client-Centered Therapy.* Boston: Houghton Mifflin, 1951.

Rosen, S. D., and others. *Occupational Reinforcer Patterns.* Vol. 2. Monograph 29. Minneapolis: University of Minnesota Industrial Relations Center, 1972.

Schwartz, M. L., Dennerll, R. D., and Yi-Guang, L. "Neuropsychological and Psychosocial Predictors of Employment in Epilepsy." *Journal of Clinical Psychology,* 1968, *24,* 174-177.

Sweney, A. B. *A Preliminary Descriptive Manual for Individual Assessment with the Motivation Analysis Test.* Champaign, Ill.: Institute for Personality and Ability Testing, 1969.

Urban Institute. *Report of the Comprehensive Service Needs Study.* Washington, D.C.: Urban Institute, 1975.

Wahba, M. A., and Bridwell, L. G. "Maslow Reconsidered: A Review of Research on the Need Hierarchy Theory." *Organizational Behavior and Human Performance,* 1976, *15,* 212-240.

Wright, B. A. *Physical Disability: A Psychological Approach.* New York: Harper & Row, 1960.

Wright, G. N., and Remmers, H. H. *Manual for the Handicap Problems Inventory.* Lafayette, Ind.: Purdue University Research Foundation, 1960.

88

Stephen M. Auerbach

Surgery-Induced Stress

The term *surgery* as used here refers to any operative procedure involving incision into the skin which aims to preserve or restore injured or diseased body parts. Surgery is considered a stressor in that it elicits high levels of anxiety and other dysphoric mood states in most people who are confronted with it. In this connection, a distinction has been made between state anxiety (often equated with fear), which is transitory and fluctuates in response to environmental demands; and trait anxiety, which tends to be stable over time and across situations. In some individuals emotional problems existing prior to surgery are exacerbated, and adjustment and recovery during the postsurgical convalescence period may be impeded.

Behavioral scientists have been interested in the surgical situation for two broad reasons. First, it has provided a convenient vehicle for the evaluation of emotional response to a naturalistic physical danger situation. Research investigations of this type have focused on theoretical questions and placed little emphasis on the clinical aspects of the surgery experience. Second, from a clinical standpoint there has been interest in the assessment of the relationship between preoperative emotional status and recovery or adjustment after surgery. Following Janis's (1958) initial inquiry and attempts to follow up on his findings, clinical investigators have focused on the development of preoperative preparatory procedures designed to facilitate postoperative adjustment and recovery.

Background and Current Status

The relationship between psychopathology and surgery has long been a major area of interest within the medical community, especially among psychoanalytically oriented surgeons and psychiatrists. It has been noted that some patients, rather than exhibiting normal levels of fear prior to surgery, actually actively and compulsively seek it out, sometimes pressuring surgeons with requests that are questionable from a medical standpoint (see Menninger, 1934). Attempts to explain such behavior have centered around symbolic drives such as the desire for castration, the need for attention from a symbolic father figure with sadistic characteristics (the surgeon), and the desire for a child by surgical means. Theoretical speculation about the symbolic threats posed by surgery for extremely fearful individuals (see Deutsch, 1942; Titchener and Levine, 1960) has also been couched in psychoanalytic terminology and is difficult to translate into testable terms. Because of this difficulty, these psychodynamically based conceptualizations have not generated a great deal of research. Contemporary psychological research has rather emphasized (1) the assessment of the emotional impact of surgery and the development of objective measures that may predict what types of individuals will experience unusual levels of anxiety when confronted with the prospect of surgery; and (2) the development of psychotherapeutic intervention techniques, usually administered prior to (but sometimes after) surgery, which are designed to enhance adjustment and speed and ease recovery during the postsurgical convalescence period.

As noted, many theorists and clinicians (for example, Drellich, Bieber, and Sutherland, 1956; Elman, 1951) have observed highly variable preoperative anxiety levels in surgical patients and have emphasized its significance as a factor in recovery. Some have assumed that presurgical anxiety always impedes the patient's adjustment and have advocated techniques for its minimization (Bernstein and Small, 1951; Dumas, 1963). Perhaps the starting point for the empirical investigation of the effects of surgery-induced stress on the emotional reactions and subsequent adjustment of patients was Janis's (1958) pioneering clinical study. Janis attempted to establish a relationship between preoperative fear level and postoperative personality adjustment. He interviewed in depth twenty-two patients (twelve males and ten females) on two occasions: (1) one or two days before each patient was scheduled for routine surgery and (2) about one week after the operation. On the basis of the preoperative interview data and independent confirmatory evidence in the form of behavioral records made by staff physicians and nurses, Janis divided his patients into three groups: "extremely low preoperative fear," "moderate preoperative fear," and "extremely high preoperative fear." His major finding was that patients with moderate preoperative fear showed better adjustment in the postoperative convalescence period than did those with either low or high preoperative fear (adjustment was assessed on the basis of postoperative interview data and confirmatory behavioral records). Patients in the moderate preoperative fear group accepted the uncomfortable procedures of the postoperative period with compliance and cooperation. In contrast, most of the patients rated as having low preoperative fear exhibited anger, resentment, and general lack of cooperation in the convalescence period; and patients in the high preoperative fear group had more hypochondriacal concerns and excessive timidity about their treatments during the postoperative period.

Janis's study has served as a model and source of hypotheses for much of the subsequent work in the area of emotional reactions to surgery. While his findings have not been unequivocally validated, it is clear that an individual's emotional status prior to a surgical procedure is an important factor in determining ease of adjustment to the discomforts of the postoperative period and speed of recovery.

Contemporary interest in emotional reactions to surgery falls into two categories. As noted above, some investigators are interested in studying surgery primarily because it is a naturally occurring physical danger situation that allows one to obtain various measures of psychological functioning both before and after the impact of the stressor (see Auerbach, 1973; Sime, 1976; Vernon and Bigelow, 1974). More clinically oriented studies treat surgery as a crisis situation involving sudden disruption of customary life style, physical discomfort, and the threat of death; and they focus on assessment of the efficacy of various intervention techniques designed to minimize emotional dysphoria and enhance adjustment and recovery (see Auerbach and Kilmann, 1977). A summary of the literature in both of these areas follows.

Critical Discussion

General Areas of Concern

Research studies in the area of emotional reactions to surgery have yielded (1) data attempting to validate Janis's (1958) findings; (2) data on the effects of surgery-induced stress on state and trait anxiety; (3) data on the effectiveness of trait anxiety and other measures as predictors of level of state anxiety experienced in the surgical situation; and (4) data on the efficacy of various patient preparatory procedures designed to ease the various stresses associated with surgery. Research in the first two areas will be discussed here, and findings pertaining to the latter two areas will be evaluated in subsequent sections.

Studies bearing directly on Janis's (1958) findings have produced equivocal results. Auerbach (1973), using the state anxiety scale of Spielberger, Gorsuch, and Lushene's (1970) State-Trait Anxiety Inventory, measured preoperative fear levels in fifty-six male general surgery patients. Subjects were divided into low, moderate, and high preoperative state anxiety groups, and adjustment during the postoperative convalescence period was evaluated with a three-part self-report measure (the Pleasure-Displeasure Quotient; DeWolfe, Barrell, and Cummings, 1966). When preoperative fear was defined in terms of absolute level of state anxiety prior to surgery, the findings indicated that patients who tended to worry more about hospital-related matters postoperatively were those who were highest in state anxiety prior to surgery and who were more prone to worry in general. (Similar findings were obtained by Chapman and Cox, 1977, who found that some patients who seemed to enter surgery already anxious and depressed were likely to show the greatest levels of pain and anxiety postoperatively.) However, when preoperative fear level was defined in terms of degree of elevation of preoperative state anxiety level over postoperative (baseline) state anxiety level, a curvilinear relationship was obtained between this variable and adjustment as measured by the Patient's Opinion Form, which asks the patient to express his or her feelings about various factors relating to hospitalization. This finding indicated that intermediate levels of preoperative fear facilitate postoperative adjustment and thus was consistent with Janis's (1958) observations. The findings of three other studies (Andrew, 1970; Cohen and Lazarus, 1973; De Long, 1970), when taken together, provided some support for Janis's contention that preoperative intervention techniques should be geared toward generating realistic appraisal of the impending surgery (intermediate levels of state anxiety) in order to avert unduly elevated fear levels or unrealistic denial responses (see Auerbach and Kilmann, 1977). However, in two studies with general surgery patients (Sime, 1976; Vernon and Bigelow, 1974), the data obtained generally failed to support Janis's findings.

The relationship between preoperative emotional status and adjustment and recovery following surgery is clearly a complex one which is dependent on many factors, such as the amount of pain experienced by the patient (Chapman and Cox, 1977; Martinez-Urrutia, 1975) and the specific manner in which preoperative emotional status and postoperative adjustment or recovery are operationally defined. Assessing adjustment and recovery is a particular problem, since a wide range of measures have been used to define these variables across investigations. Adjustment has been defined by various patient self-report mood state measures and nurses' or physicians' ratings of critical behaviors (such as response to painful stimuli, response to anesthesia, uncooperative behavior, nervousness, and ability to cope with stress). Recovery has been defined in terms of such variables as postoperative days until discharge, pain relievers and sedations requested postoperatively, operative urinary retention, and speed of return to oral intake (see Wolfer, 1973, for detailed discussion of this area). The type of measure one is able to use meaningfully is often a function of the type of surgery undergone by the patient. For example, in a sample of high-risk open heart surgery patients undergoing extracorporeal circulation by pump oxygenation perfusion, Kilpatrick and associates (1975)—using a preoperative battery including intellectual, personality, and neuropsychological assessment procedures as well as ratings of cardiac impairment—were able to predict, in 86 to 100 percent of the cases, whether or not the patient would survive.

Studies evaluating the effects of surgery-induced stress on state and trait measures of personality functioning have used objective self-report measures and, to a lesser degree, projective tests. Several investigations (Auerbach, 1973; Auerbach and others, 1976; Martinez-Urrutia, 1975; Spielberger and others, 1973) have shown that major or minor general surgery is a transitory stressor for most patients. That is, high levels of state anxiety are elicited prior to surgery; but, barring complications, the anxiety tends to decline fairly rapidly and returns to a "normal" level after surgery. In three of these studies (Auerbach, 1973; Martinez-Urrutia, 1975; Spielberger and others, 1973), in which the trait anxiety scale of the State-Trait Anxiety Inventory was administered prior and subsequent to surgery, no changes were found on this measure, thus validating the stability of the scale and suggesting that the experience of surgery tends not to produce dispositional or longer-term changes in anxiety level. Spielberger and associates (1973) also administered the Mini-Mult, a short-form version of the Minnesota Multiphasic Personality Inventory (MMPI), before and after surgery and found no changes in any of the clinical scale scores. This finding was interpreted as indicating that the Mini-Mult (as well as the full MMPI) measures relatively stable personality characteristics.

In two studies the effects of surgery-induced stress on projective inkblot measures of personality were evaluated. Heenan (1953) administered the Rorschach to male patients one day prior to their first major surgical operation and again postsurgically, after the patients were assured by their physicians that they were recovering without complications. On both occasions the patients' pulse rate and degree of apprehensiveness were evaluated. Higher ratings of apprehensiveness and faster pulse rates indicated that the patients were more anxious before than after surgery. Rorschach performance changed significantly from presurgery to postsurgery on six variables. The sum of weighted color responses, the number of responses involving shading, and shading percent decreased; and percentage of pure form responses, the number of destroyed objects, and the total number of responses increased. The findings for the shading variables and total number of responses were consistent with those of other studies utilizing experimentally induced and naturally occurring stresses in which systematic changes in these Rorschach variables were associated with changes in state anxiety (Auerbach and Spielberger, 1972). Auerbach and Edinger (1977) evaluated the effects of surgery-induced stress on anxiety as measured by the Holtzman Inkblot Technique (HIT), which was developed to remedy some of the psychometric deficiencies of the Rorschach. Form A of the HIT was administered just prior to general surgery, and Form B was administered after surgery while the patients were convalescing. Patients also responded to the state anxiety and trait anxiety scales of the State-Trait Anxiety Inventory on both occasions. Barrier (Br), which reflects perception of protective coverings that might be symbolically related to body image, seemed to be the best single measure of trait anxiety. Br scores remained stable from pre- to postsurgery; and, as expected, high Br scores tended to be associated with low trait anxiety scores. No single HIT variable emerged as an acceptable measure of state anxiety. In a multiple regression format, the HIT variables of Location, Balance, Form Appropriateness, Animal, Movement, and Anxiety produced an R of .53, thus accounting for 27.3 percent of the variance in trait anxiety; Movement, Human, and Location produced an R of .43 for state anxiety, thus accounting for 18.3 percent of the variance in this variable. The high number of rejected cards obtained in this study suggested that a shorter test requiring less total responses might be more appropriate for personality assessment via projective inkblot tests, especially under conditions of high situational stress (such as impending surgery) or with individuals of diminished concentration ability and attention span.

A continuing problem in personality assessment has been the degree to which broadly conceived personality trait measures can effectively predict behavior in specific situations. Of particular interest here is the construct of trait anxiety, conceptualized as reflecting "differences in the disposition to perceive a wide range of stimulus situations as dangerous or threatening. . . . Persons who are high in A-Trait tend to perceive a larger number of situations as dangerous or threatening than persons who are low in A-Trait, and to respond to threatening situations with A-State elevations of greater intensity" (Spielberger, 1972, p. 39). Empirical evidence has indicated that trait anxiety measures account for variance in the predicted fashion primarily in situations involving ego threats or threats to self-esteem but not in stress situations such as surgery, where the primary stressor is apparently threat of physical danger. In four studies with general surgery patients (Auerbach, 1973; De Long, 1970; Martinez-Urrutia, 1975; Spielberger and others, 1973), subjects high in trait anxiety were higher in state anxiety than subjects low in trait anxiety both before and after surgery, but there was no difference in degree of decline in state anxiety from pre- to postsurgery for the two groups. Endler and Okada (1975) have proposed that perhaps threat of physical danger is a viable unitary component of trait anxiety. However, it seems questionable whether a single generalized measure of physical danger anxiety can predict state anxiety difference across the whole range of physical threat situations, many of which could well contain a component of self-esteem threat for given individuals (for example, fear of being viewed as cowardly if one should show fear in the dentist's chair, fear of having one's exposed body viewed as unattractive in surgery). To date, with few known exceptions, only highly situation-specific measures of physical harm anxiety have successfully predicted state anxiety changes in physical threat situations. These have included (1) the Dental Anxiety Questionnaire (Corah, 1969), a four-item self-report scale which successfully predicted elevations in state anxiety in oral surgery patients from a low-stress period (on the average 24.4 days prior to surgery) to the day of surgery (Auerbach and others, 1976); and (2) the Fear of Surgery Scale

(Martinez-Urrutia, 1975), a single-item questionnaire which successfully predicted decrements in state anxiety in general surgery patients from a high-stress period the day before surgery to a follow-up period approximately ten days after surgery. In one study (Auerbach, 1973; see also Auerbach, 1971) a generalized measure of physical harm anxiety (the Harmavoidance Scale of the Personality Research Form) was unsuccessful in predicting state anxiety differences in response to impending general surgery. In another study (Kendall, 1975) a generalized measure of physical harm anxiety (the Physical Danger Scale of the S-R Inventory of General Trait Anxiousness; Endler and Okada, 1975) did successfully predict differential state anxiety reactions; but the stressor was a vicarious physical threat with no apparent ego-threat component.

The studies reviewed above, and associated investigations involving other physical threats, demonstrate the superiority of specific versus general trait measures in predicting state anxiety responsiveness to impending surgery. Thus, they support the current trend toward situation specificity in personality assessment. In addition, this research has resulted in new measures (the Dental Anxiety Questionnaire, the Fear of Surgery Scale) that may be useful in identifying potential problem patients well before surgery and thus in adjusting patient management procedures to minimize anxiety.

Comparative Philosophies and Theories

Psychoanalytic theory has raised a number of questions regarding various symbolic aspects of surgery and the surgeon which might induce disproportionate anxiety in some patients but might magnetically draw other patients to the experience. State-trait anxiety theory, as developed by Spielberger (1972), has generated a number of recent studies (reviewed earlier), and as a result there has been a considerable increment in knowledge regarding the impact of the surgical experience on emotional states and personality trait functioning and in terms of identifying the types of individuals who seem to find surgery particularly threatening.

The major construct in Janis's (1958) influential model is the "work of worrying." He hypothesized that patients with low preoperative fear who subsequently exhibit excessive anger and resentment postoperatively did not adequately prepare themselves through the normal worry process, whereas high preoperative fear patients who are highly anxious postoperatively were overvigilant and engaged in the worry process to an unrealistic degree preoperatively. The patient who is moderately fearful preoperatively discriminates carefully between signs of danger and reassurance, recognizes his vulnerability, and plans how to minimize his distress while facing the danger directly. Through the work of worrying, the patient rehearses the upcoming event, fills gaps in his understanding of the danger, develops self-delivered reassurances, and cooperates after surgery. As noted above, the findings of studies bearing on Janis's hypothesized curvilinear relationship between preoperative fear and postoperative adjustment are conflicting. However, his model has served as the jumping-off point for current approaches (for example, Andrew, 1970; Auerbach and others, 1976; Cohen and Lazarus, 1973; De Long, 1970; Parrish, 1976), in which preferred defensive style and other individual differences are objectively evaluated and an attempt is made to standardize and control the type of information received by the patient prior to surgery.

Elaboration on Critical Points

Impending surgery has been conceptualized as a crisis situation; that is, it typically involves individuals who ordinarily function adequately, and it sometimes evokes disabling levels of anxiety to the point where emotional equilibrium is disrupted and normal coping behaviors are rendered ineffective (Auerbach and Kilmann, 1977). Research investigations have moved away from concern with assessment of the impact of surgery per se on emotionality and have increasingly focused on assessment of the efficacy of various treatment packages in alleviating the deleterious effects of surgery-induced stress. In contrast to other crisis situations, surgery lends itself quite readily to the institution of such preventive procedures, since the stressor eliciting the crisis response is focalized and predictable to some degree and there is time to institute programmed treatment packages at crucial stress impact periods.

Auerbach and Kilmann (1977) identified thirteen studies, nine of them published since 1973, that employed crisis intervention techniques with surgical patients. Nine of these studies employed specific information designed to engender accurate expectations about the impending surgery as one of the treatment procedures. For example, Auerbach and associates (1976) presented one group of patients about to undergo dental extraction with detailed information (via a seven-minute videotape) regarding the manner in which teeth become dysfunctional, the specific procedures the dentist would use to numb and loosen and finally remove the tooth, and the instructions they would be given postoperatively to help minimize pain and swelling; a control group was provided general, marginally relevant information about the dental clinic in which the surgery was being performed. The use of such an information package permitted standardization of intervention across patients.

A few investigators used more traditional psychotherapeutic procedures, which are, by definition, individualized and not standardized. For example, in Gruen's (1975) study, myocardial infarction patients were given psychotherapy pre- and postoperatively for an average of a half hour for five to six days per week until release from the hospital. Therapy centered around ten therapeutic components geared to facilitate coping and unearth psychological resources and hidden strengths. Matched control subjects apparently received no psychological treatment of any kind.

Methodological problems with many of the studies in this area make the literature difficult to evaluate. A major weakness of several of the studies was the fact that treatment consisted of multiple components, making it impossible to isolate the salient aspects of the treatment package. In other studies treatment groups were compared with marginal-contact groups—a procedure that did not adequately control for nonspecific effects of attention and expectancy, thus making it impossible to attribute group differences in patient adjustment or recovery to the treatment procedures employed. The most definitive conclusion that may be made at this time is that when standardized treatment packages are employed, it seems important to utilize intervention procedures most appropriate for individuals differing in their typical manner of dealing with stress (Auerbach and Kilmann, 1977).

Personal Views and Recommendations

Some well-designed studies have recently been published on both the assessment of the emotional impact of surgery-induced stress and on the effectiveness of procedures designed to minimize the negative aspects of the surgical experience. Most of these studies have dealt with elective general surgery patients, who can reasonably expect full recovery and return to normal functioning shortly after completion of the surgical procedure. However, operative procedures such as radical mastectomy, radical head and neck surgery for cancer, surgery involving amputation of a limb, cosmetic surgery, and surgical treatment for problems of sexual identification likely produce a broad range of emotional and behavioral changes and generate psychological problems much different from those engendered by general surgery. For example, the cardiac surgery patient may have to adjust to the role of responsible, productive citizen after a lifetime of passive dependence; therefore, to meaningfully evaluate the effects of surgery, one would need to measure long-term social, economic, and community adjustment rather than simply immediate postoperative adjustment. Parrish's (1976) findings in a study with patients undergoing major head and neck or rectal-colon surgery associated with cancer demonstrate that data obtained with general surgery patients may fail to generalize to patient groups who are facing a psychologically different situation. These patients, for whom the stress of surgery was not elective and transient but necessary for survival and leading to disfigurement or permanent loss, showed no changes in state emotionality (anxiety, hostility, depression) from presurgery to just prior to discharge from the hospital, and stress-relevant information given prior to surgery had no effect on recovery. Cosmetic or aesthetic surgery for the purpose of enhancing physical attractiveness also is psychologically different from general surgery. Though a number of descriptive and clinical case studies have been published in this area, there are few objective data on the long-term effects of such procedures as augmentation mammaplasty and rhinoplasty on such variables as self-esteem and social, marital, and sexual adjustment.

From a clinical standpoint, researchers must be constantly aware that the surgical patient is in an extremely vulnerable position psychologically. The main ethical considerations in this situation involve assuring that there is no coercion involved in getting patients to participate in research projects, protecting the confidentiality of any information obtained from patients, and interacting with patients in a manner that will not precipitate emotional problems or exacerbate existing difficulties. Regarding potential coercion, it has been observed that once a researcher is presented as a member of the hospital staff, he or she is perceived as a "danger-control authority" figure (Janis, 1958), and most patients readily comply with any procedure that appears reasonable. It is important for the researcher to inform the patient at the outset of the exact procedures to be employed, the implications of the study, and any possible negative aspects; an assessment study should not be represented as aimed at providing direct benefits to the patient. The patient must be clearly given the option of withdrawing at any time. Data sheets should be coded and names discarded as soon as possible. Before approaching a patient, the researcher should ascertain that that patient has already been informed by the surgeon of the impending surgery and when it is to take place. The researcher should not attempt to give any medical advice or information but should take responsibility for assuring that the patient's emotional needs are cared for from the point of contact until the time that the patient leaves the hospital.

Application to Particular Variables

Regarding age, Auerbach (1973), in a study with general surgery patients ranging from 20 to 65 years, found no relationship between age and degree of decline in state anxiety from pre- to postsurgery. However, Volicer, Isenberg, and Burns (1977) obtained a significant negative correlation between age and perceived stress in a sample of 535 medical and surgical patients. Comparatively few studies have evaluated the effects of surgery-induced stress on children; this area has recently been reviewed by Melamed (1977).

Most investigators use single-sex samples to control for possible sex differences. However, Auerbach and Kendall (1978) found that females responded to an informational tape received prior to dental surgery with increased anxiety and showed poorer adjustment in surgery than males, and Volicer and Burns (1977) found that female surgical patients reported more stress than males.

Regarding severity of disorder, Janis (1958) found no relationship between preoperative fear and medical diagnosis or duration of preoperative illness in general surgery patients, and Auerbach (1973) found that patients recovering from major surgery showed no greater decline in state anxiety from presurgical levels than those recovering from minor surgery. Chapman and Cox (1977) compared patterns of state anxiety arousal in renal donors, renal recipients, and general surgery patients; they concluded that state anxiety response trends in surgical patients are in part a function of the meaning of the operative procedure for the patient. According to Volicer, Isenberg, and Burns (1977), the patient's cognitive appraisal of the situation may be more important in this regard than actual physical condition. These investigators found no relationship between seriousness of illness and perceived stress, but they found a strong relationship between perceived stress and unfamiliarity of surroundings, loss of independence, and threat of severe illness.

References

Andrew, J. M. "Recovery from Surgery with and Without Preparatory Instruction, for Three Coping Styles." *Journal of Personality and Social Psychology,* 1970, *15,* 223-226.

Auerbach, S. M. "The Effects of Surgery-Induced Stress on State and Trait Anxiety." Unpublished doctoral dissertation, Florida State University, 1971.

Auerbach, S. M. "Trait-State Anxiety and Adjustment to Surgery." *Journal of Consulting and Clinical Psychology,* 1973, *40,* 264-271.

Auerbach, S. M., and Edinger, J. D. "The Effects of Surgery-Induced Stress on Anxiety as Measured by the Holtzman Inkblot Technique (HIT)." *Journal of Personality Assessment,* 1977, *41,* 19-24.

Auerbach, S. M., and Kendall, P. C. "Sex Differences in Anxiety Response and Adjustment to Dental Surgery: Effects of General vs. Specific Preoperative Information." *Journal of Clinical Psychology,* 1978, *34,* 309-313.

Auerbach, S. M., and Kilmann, P. R. "Crisis Intervention: A Review of Outcome Research." *Psychological Bulletin,* 1977, *84,* 1189-1217.

Auerbach, S. M., and others. "Anxiety, Locus of Control, Type of Preparatory Information, and Adjustment to Dental Surgery." *Journal of Consulting and Clinical Psychology,* 1976, *44,* 809-818.

Auerbach, S. M., and Spielberger, C. D. "The Assessment of State and Trait Anxiety with the Rorschach Test." *Journal of Personality Assessment,* 1972, *36,* 314-335.

Bernstein, S., and Small, S. "Psychodynamic Factors in Surgery." *Journal of Mount Sinai Hospital,* 1951, *17,* 938-958.

Chapman, C. R., and Cox, G. B. "Determinants of Anxiety in Elective Surgery Patients." In C. D. Spielberger and I. W. Sarason (Eds.), *Stress and Anxiety.* Vol. 4. Washington, D.C.: Hemisphere, 1977.

Cohen, F., and Lazarus, R. S. "Active Coping Processes, Coping Dispositions, and Recovery from Surgery." *Psychosomatic Medicine,* 1973, *35,* 375-389.

Corah, N. L. "Development of a Dental Anxiety Scale." *Journal of Dental Research,* 1969, *48,* 396.

De Long, R. D. "Individual Differences in Patterns of Anxiety Arousal, Stress Relevant Information, and Recovery from Surgery." Unpublished doctoral dissertation, University of California, Los Angeles, 1970.

Deutsch, H. "Some Psychoanalytic Observations in Surgery." *Psychosomatic Medicine,* 1942, *4,* 105-115.

DeWolfe, A. S., Barrell, R. P., and Cummings, J. W. "Patient Variables in Emotional Response to Hospitalization for Physical Illness." *Journal of Consulting Psychology,* 1966, *30,* 68-72.

Drellich, M. G., Bieber, I., and Sutherland, A. M. "The Psychological Impact of Cancer and Cancer Surgery. VI: Adaptation to Hysterectomy." *Cancer,* 1956, *9,* 1120-1126.

Dumas, R. G. "Psychological Preparation for Surgery." *American Journal of Nursing,* 1963, *63,* 52-55.

Elman, R. *Surgical Care: A Practical Physiological Guide.* New York: Appleton-Century-Crofts, 1951.

Endler, N. S., and Okada, M. "A Multidimensional Measure of Trait Anxiety: The S-R Inventory of General Trait Anxiousness." *Journal of Consulting and Clinical Psychology,* 1975, *43,* 319-329.

Gruen, W. "Effects of Brief Psychotherapy During the Hospitalization Period on the Recovery Process in Heart Attacks." *Journal of Consulting and Clinical Psychology,* 1975, *43,* 223-232.

Heenan, J. E. "An Investigation of Certain Indices of Anxiety in Presurgery and Post-surgery Patients." Unpublished doctoral dissertation, University of Nebraska, 1953.

Howells, J. G. (Ed.). *Modern Perspectives in the Psychiatric Aspects of Surgery.* New York: Brunner/Mazel, 1976.

Janis, I. L. *Psychological Stress.* New York: Wiley, 1958.

Kendall, P. C. "Differential State Anxiety Reactions for Subjects Differing in Measures of Trait Anxiety." Unpublished doctoral dissertation, Virginia Commonwealth University, 1975.

Kilpatrick, D. G., and others. "The Use of Psychological Test Data to Predict Open-Heart Surgery Outcome: A Prospective Study." *Psychosomatic Medicine,* 1975, *37,* 62-73.

Martinez-Urrutia, A. "Anxiety and Pain in Surgical Patients." *Journal of Consulting and Clinical Psychology,* 1975, *43,* 437-442.

Melamed, B. G. "Psychological Preparation for Hospitalization." In S. Rachman (Ed.), *Contributions to Medical Psychology.* Vol. 1. Elmsford, N.Y.: Pergamon Press, 1977.

Menninger, K. "Polysurgery and Polysurgical Addiction." *Psychoanalytic Quarterly,* 1934, *3,* 173.

Parrish, J. M. "Individual Coping Styles, Level of State Anxiety, Stress Relevant Information, and Recovery from Surgery Associated with Cancer." Unpublished master's thesis, Virginia Commonwealth University, 1976.

Sime, A. M. "Relationship of Preoperative Fear, Type of Coping, and Information Received About Surgery to Recovery from Surgery." *Journal of Personality and Social Psychology,* 1976, *34,* 716-724.

Spielberger, C. D. "Anxiety as an Emotional State." In C. D. Spielberger (Ed.), *Anxiety: Current Trends in Theory and Research.* New York: Academic Press, 1972.

Spielberger, C. D., Gorsuch, R. L., and Lushene, R. E. *Manual for the State-Trait Anxiety Inventory.* Palo Alto, Calif.: Consulting Psychologists Press, 1970.

Spielberger, C. D., and others. "Emotional Reactions to Surgery." *Journal of Consulting and Clinical Psychology,* 1973, *40,* 33-38.

Titchener, J. L., and Levine, M. *Surgery as a Human Experience: The Psychodynamics of Surgical Practice.* New York: Oxford University Press, 1960.

Vernon, D. T. A., and Bigelow, D. A. "Effect on Information About a Potentially Stressful Situation on Responses to Stress Impact." *Journal of Personality and Social Psychology,* 1974, *29,* 50-59.

Volicer, B. J., and Burns, M. W. "Preexisting Correlates of Hospital Stress." *Nursing Research,* 1977, *26,* 408-415.

Volicer, B. J., Isenberg, M. A., and Burns, M. W. "Medical-Surgical Differences in Hospital Stress Factors." *Journal of Human Stress,* 1977, *3,* 3-13.

Wolfer, J. A. "Definition and Assessment of Surgical Patients' Welfare and Recovery." *Nursing Research,* 1973, *22,* 394-401.

89

Everett Moitoza
Oliva M. Espin

Pain

The human pain experience, a universal yet complex phenomenon, has for centuries intrigued and eluded those who have attempted to understand and control it. Merskey and Spear (1967, p. 21) provide a succinct operational definition of pain: "An unpleasant experience which we primarily associate with tissue damage or describe in terms of tissue damage or both." This short definition refers to three dimensions of the pain experience which lend themselves to assessment or measurement: (1) What is the nature of the painful stimulus? (2) How does the person experience the painful stimulus? (3) How does the person report his perception of the painful stimulus? Although overlap may occur, understanding each of these three areas is vital in understanding the dimensions of pain assessment and treatment.

Regarding the first dimension, the nature of the painful stimulus, one must assess whether the pain is acute or chronic; how severe the pain is; whether it is of known or unknown origin; and what psychological components exist with the pain experience. In short, the objective is to know where the pain comes from and what physical and psychological components might be responsible. Second, the individual's subjective pain experience is often greatly affected by psychological, cultural, cognitive, and situational factors that may enhance or dampen the individual's perception of pain. Third, pain is reported during the assessment process through verbal content and delivery style, as well as the affective and motivational themes of the individual's presentation.

In order to provide a clear and mutual understanding of the terms used in pain assessment, the following definitions are offered:

Acute pain: usually of identifiable etiology; short duration or easily relieved.
Chronic pain: of long duration, usually constant, with variable intensity; not always of identifiable etiology or easily reduced.
Psychogenic pain: physical pain that has no apparent organic basis and can be described best in psychological terms.
Somatogenic pain: physical pain that has an identifiable organic origin.
Threshold: the lowest stimulus level at which a person notes pain.
Tolerance: the degree to which a person can bear or endure painful stimuli.

Background and Current Status

Derived from the Greek word *poinē*, meaning *penalty,* pain once was viewed as a punishment, a fine imposed for some wrongdoing. Consequently, praying to higher beings for the relief of pain seemed the most probable way of seeking its reduction. Religion and religious approaches, then, played an early and important role in providing individuals with a psychological means of dealing with their pain expectations and tolerance levels.

Beginning with Descartes's ([1644] 1970) concept of the physical pain pathway and continuing through the writings of theorists in the nineteenth and twentieth centuries, physical pain has been considered less and less frequently to be in the domain of the psychological therapies. As science and technology have become more sophisticated through the centuries, people have come to see pain as a valuable signal that something is wrong with their bodies. Thus, the fields of physiology and clinical medicine have become the main disciplines for conceptualizing and ameliorating human pain. Indeed, the most common reason for seeking medical help today is pain. However, during the past two decades, and particularly the last ten years, there has been a tremendous increase in research on and usage of both the psychological components of pain and treatments available for individuals in physical pain. Traditionally, the helping professions have been divided into those concerned with physical pain and those concerned with psychological pain. The two divisions rarely coincided except for those instances where pain was of the psychogenic type; that is, of unknown physical origin. Now, however, health professionals are becoming increasingly aware of the psychological components of pain perception, as well as individuals' idiosyncratic reactions to physical pain (Beecher, 1956; Bond and Pearson, 1969; Ramsay, 1977; Sternbach, 1974; Szasz, 1957).

Perhaps most responsible for the increased interest in pain research was the development of the gate control theory of pain by Melzack and Wall (1965). This theory and its modifications (Melzack, 1973; Melzack and Wall, 1970) have generated much laboratory and clinical research in both the physiological and psychological sciences. A tide of interest in pain study has been building for the last decade with the appearance of many books, articles, reviews, and conferences on the subject (Bonica and Albe-Fessard, 1976; Espin and Ganikos, 1975; Liebeskind and Paul, 1977; Weisenberg and Tursky, 1976). In 1973, at an international symposium on pain (Bonica, 1974b), the International Association for the Study of Pain (IASP) was formed. Beginning in 1975 this organization began publication of a quarterly journal entitled *Pain,* which has become one of the most comprehensive and scholarly forums for the study of pain.

Today numerous psychological techniques are being studied and applied in the assessment and management of acute and chronic pain. The relevant techniques include hypnosis, operant conditioning, meditation (TM), yoga, imagery, desensitization, relaxation, autogenic training, biofeedback, and counseling. All these procedures have played useful roles in pain control (Espin and Ganikos, 1975). Recent assessment techniques and instruments for determining an individual's pain perception, tolerance level, and affective involvement have shown promising results in both clinical and experimental settings (Melzack, 1975a; Sternbach, 1974; Sternbach and others, 1974). Psychological therapies and assessment techniques are also playing an important role in treatment at pain clinics throughout the country (Bonica, 1974a; Clark, Gosnell, and Shapiro, 1977). The Oriental technique of acupuncture has been the subject of increased interest and study in the field of pain control (Dubner, 1976; Toomey and others, 1977). Practitioners of this controversial technique claim that acupuncture involves psychological as well as physiological mechanisms in its mode of action.

Chronic pain patients who suffer from migraine headaches, neuralgias, terminal cancer pain, muscle and joint pain, causalgia (an intense, burning pain that occurs frequently after a gunshot wound or other such trauma), or phantom limb pain (occurring after some amputations and paraplegia) may be partially assisted in controlling their pain with psychological treatment techniques. Acute pain may also show good response to these psychologically based interventions. Acute pain conditions include dental pain, pain associated with childbirth, headache, and post-surgical pain (Dick-Read, 1959; Egbert and others, 1964; Mackenzie, 1968; Mitchell and White, 1977).

Critical Discussion

General Areas of Concern

The phenomenon of pain cannot be explained solely in physical terms (Beecher, 1956; Bond and Pilowski, 1966; Parkes, 1973; Sternbach, 1976; Wolff and Langley, 1968). The role of psychologists as consultants to professionals (physicians, dentists, nurses, aides, and others) can be invaluable. Both traditional forms of counseling and newer psychological techniques are being implemented in the training of health professionals (Weisenberg, 1976b). The consultant role of counselors and psychologists to these professionals should include help in understanding differences in cultural backgrounds, personality traits, personal problems, individual history, and cognitive and other factors, all of which affect the patient's reaction to pain. Psychological needs that may be satisfied by physical pain (Engel, 1959; Pilling, Brannick, and Swenson, 1967; Szasz, 1968) may be more easily understood and, therefore, more effectively handled by the physician with the help of the psychologist (Sternbach, 1974).

Psychological research on the experience of pain, however, is hampered on many fronts. The difficulty begins with the complex variables that are inherent in human reports of pain (Hilgard, 1973). A person's pain experience and subsequent report are not determined simply by the level of the noxious stimuli experienced in one-to-one, experience-to-report ratio (Melzack, 1973). Rather, pain perception (be it threshold, tolerance, or magnitude) is a tremendously complex psychophysiological puzzle. Pain perception seems to be mediated by such factors as one's unique early life experiences, the meaning one gives to the pain situation because of one's culture, and one's state of mind at the time of the pain report. In addition, a person's perception of pain in an experimental pain setting may differ from his perception in a real-life pain situation (Szasz, 1957). Finally, ethical concerns in investigating pain produced in the laboratory with animal and human subjects limit the experimental techniques that can be used in pain research.

Currently available assessment techniques are designed to obtain useful, reliable, and objective indices of the pain experienced and reported by the pain patient. For example, the submaximum tourniquet technique (Smith and others, 1966; modified by Sternbach and others, 1974) provides a reliable and valid means of describing the intensity (magnitude) of a patient's clinical pain and compares that to the maximum he identifies as tolerable. The technique also provides an indication of the individual's tendency to exaggerate or accurately describe the intensity of pain experiences.

The words used by patients to describe their pain have also been of interest to researchers. Verbal reports are by far the most available and most frequently used method for understanding, diagnosing, and treating pain patients. The McGill Pain Questionnaire, developed by Melzack (1975a), is used to specify the subjective experience of pain in the sensory, affective, and evaluative areas of the pain experience. Good reliability and validity are reported with this questionnaire; it has also been documented as a sensitive instrument for detecting and describing differences in treatments and methods used to relieve pain (Melzack, 1975a).

Sternbach (1974) has used the Minnesota Multiphasic Personality Inventory (MMPI) to depict certain personality characteristics of pain patients. Although Sternbach warns against premature prediction and generalizability of results, they are nevertheless worth noting. He has identified four different and specific MMPI profiles for pain patients and individuals with chronic diseases. Hypochondriacal, reactive depressive, somatization reaction, and manipulative reaction profiles are seen as having poor treatment prognoses.

Important in any psychological assessment procedure is the clinical interview. Sternbach (1974) approaches the interview with specific attention to the chronic pain patient's interpersonal style. The possible payoffs and consequences of the pain, as well as the patient's past history of overdependence or abuse of medications, are important psychological indicators in the assessment process. The task of the interview is not to identify the causes of the pain or the sources of increased pain but, rather, the factors or situations that reinforce the pain. The interviewer must also be careful to note the presence of depression, which allegedly decreases pain tolerance levels (Sternbach, 1970). Other interviewers (Engel, 1959; McCraine, 1973) assess an individual's tendency toward a masochistic life style, an interpersonal style that may provoke others to attack, exploit, or humiliate them. These patients may present a life history of pain complaints, which may be interpreted as a penance for wrongdoings they feel they have committed.

Push-button treatments for the pain patient are not available presently through either the medical or the behavioral sciences. Psychological techniques, as well as most other methods, are usually unable to abolish pain completely. Moreover, these techniques take time and effort on the part of the patient and the clinician. In fact, it has been suggested that the patient-clinician relationship is one of the most powerful factors in the effectiveness of physiological and psychological techniques of pain control (Caterinicchio, 1976; Egbert and others, 1964).

Placebo effects (Beecher, 1959) are important components in pain control with hypnosis (McGlashan, Evans, and Orne, 1969), acupuncture (Gaw, Chang, and Shaw, 1975), and drugs (Beecher, 1959). Placebo effects do not imply that the person is not in real pain but, rather, demonstrate the powerful effects of suggestion on pain perception and its control. Other cognitive psychological treatments in pain control are those that manipulate a person's attention away from the pain (Melzack, 1973); this is one possible and partial explanation for the effectiveness of such techniques as meditation, imagery, yoga, and hypnosis. Hill and associates (1952a, 1952b) have shown that subjects reported the same noxious stimulus as less painful under conditions of low anxiety than under conditions of high anxiety. Therefore, the use of relaxation techniques to reduce anxiety may ultimately assist pain control.

Hypnosis remains the most widely used psychological technique for the control of pain. Hilgard (1973) has suggested that under hypnosis cognitive systems are altered and in turn alter the perception of the pain experience. This, he believes, explains the analgesic capabilities of hypnosis. Although the actual mode of action of hypnosis remains unknown, it has proved to be an extremely effective pain control device in the medical and dental fields (Barber and Mayer, 1977; Hilgard, 1975). Variations of the hypnotic state include the use of visual imagery and systematic desensitization (Klepac, 1975; Wittmer, 1973) to control pain. These techniques, used in both medical and dental settings, perhaps affect sensory transmission of pain cognitively through changes in the patient's anxiety and attention and through suggestion (Melzack, 1973). Other techniques using these cognitive control mechanisms are progressive relaxation methods (French and Tupin, 1974), yoga, and meditation (Green, Green, and Walter, 1970). These methods have been applied in different ways, in different settings, and to varying degrees; however, they do seem to provide some degree of pain reduction for many patients and even large reduction of pain for a few individuals.

Biofeedback—a technique that provides a person with information about his ongoing physiological processes—is one of the newest techniques used in acute and chronic pain control (Danskin and Walter, 1973; Gannon and Sternbach, 1971; Hendler and others, 1977; Reading and Mohr, 1976). When first introduced, biofeedback techniques and training were widely publicized and considered a cure-all for the problems of patients with acute and chronic pain. The hardware and techniques are, nevertheless, still being developed; there is a need for further study and research before such claims can be accepted as substantiated (Melzack, 1975b). The electroencephalogram (EEG) and the electromyogram (EMG), which measure brain activity and muscle activity, respectively, are the most frequently used instruments for biofeedback pain control. From the information provided by these instruments, it is assumed that the person will be able to control such things as degree of muscle tension, which may be causing tension headaches, or to maintain an alpha brain-wave state, which generally seems incompatible with severe pain. Biofeedback techniques have also been shown to produce relaxation (Green, Green, and Walter, 1969) and altered states of consciousness (Kamiya, 1969), as well as control of autonomic functions (Luce and Gattozzi, 1971).

Autogenic training (Schultz and Luthe, 1969), like biofeedback, allows patients to control their visceral reactions. Autogenic-training exercises teach the patient to develop images of heaviness and warmth, cooling, and cardiac and respiration rate changes, which thereby facilitate and mobilize brain-directed processes of self-normalization (Luthe, 1973). Autogenic training has frequently been combined with biofeedback techniques (Green and others, 1975) to provide immediate feedback regarding the results of the visualization process.

Operant conditioning has become another increasingly effective technique for the treatment of chronic pain patients (Fordyce and others, 1968). When this method is used, pain behavior is analyzed (desirable and undesirable behaviors); reinforcers are identified; and the patient's environment is programmed so that positive reinforcement becomes contingent on the occurrence of desirable behavior, and, conversely, positive reinforcers are withdrawn from behaviors to be decreased (Fordyce, 1976). Operant conditioning is often used in hospitalized chronic pain patients with other techniques of pain control drawn from both the psychological and medical realms (Swanson and others, 1976).

Comparative Philosophies and Theories

Various medically based pain theories have existed for centuries, often falling from favor with the discovery of new scientific facts. One such theory of pain, first articulated by Descartes ([1644] 1970) and later expanded upon in 1895 by Frey, a physician, is known as the "specificity theory." Simply, this theory posited a fixed direct-line pain system, which carries messages from pain receptors in the skin to a pain center in the brain. Further, the theory proposed that pain receptors in the skin are differentiated or specialized in order to receive and transmit particular types of stimuli. The theory failed psychologically in that it implied a one-to-one relationship between the psychological and the physical pain experience (Melzack and Wall, 1962, 1965). It also partially failed in terms of physiology, as shown in the clinical pain states associated with phantom limb pain, neuralgia, and causalgia, where pain exists despite the absence of either nerve endings or stimuli of any type.

Throughout this century, many theories of pain have evolved. Pattern theory (Goldscheider, 1894), central summation theory (Livingston, 1943), and sensory-interaction theory (Noordenbos, 1959) have added valuable contributions to the understanding of pain. Unfortunately, most theories have been concerned with physiological mechanisms and directed to the sensory factors involved in the experience of pain. At the turn of the century, Marshall (1894), a psychologist and philosopher, was instrumental in developing the concept of the presence of affect in the pain experience. He stated that pain has a strong negative affective quality, which individuals try to stop by motivation and emotion. Unfortunately, this distinction and the writings of Marshall and other psychologists (Sherrington, 1900; Titchener, 1909) on the affective and sensory qualities of pain were relegated to a position of secondary importance, behind sensory research. To describe these motivational and cognitive processes as merely reactions to pain, of secondary importance in the pain experience, was a mistake. It is in this area that pain research loses its connection with treatments. It is a point which forgets that man is more than a mechanistic physiologic system; that the human being is a "thinking reed," motivated, passionate, and possessed of some degree of freedom of will (Melzack, 1973; Melzack and Casey, 1968).

Although not universally accepted, the gate control theory of pain (Melzack and Wall, 1965) seems to be the first that consistently and comprehensively integrates the sensory and affective components of the pain experience, as well as providing sound theoretical formulation within each of the respective disciplines of physiology and psychology. Melzack (1973, p. 153) describes the theory as follows:

> A neural mechanism in the dorsal horns of the spinal cord acts like a gate which can increase or decrease the flow of nerve impulses from peripheral fibers to the central nervous system (brain). Somatic input is therefore subjected to the modulating influence of the gate before it evokes pain perception and response. The degree to which the gate increases or decreases sensory transmission is determined by the relative activity in large-diameter (A-beta) and small-diameter (A-delta and C) fibers and by the descending influences from the brain. When the amount of information that passes through the gate exceeds a critical level, it activates the neural areas responsible for pain experience and response.

This is a twofold theory. The gate can be modulated upward from the activity of the large- and small-diameter nerve fibers; or it can be modulated downward by a central biasing mechanism consisting of descending nerve fibers in the brain stem which can close the hypothetical gate. Moreover, Melzack and Wall (1965) propose that other parts of the brain—which relate emotions, memory of past experiences, suggestion, and attention—may also operate downward to open and close the gate.

Medical and physical pain control techniques are technically out of the realm of the psychological interventions. However, because of their widespread use and relative efficacy, they will be considered here as techniques that can be used in combination with psychologically based techniques. Medical treatment for the pain patient has been based historically on specificity theory. As a result, medical treatments have concerned themselves with severing the so-called pain pathway to the brain, usually through surgery. The techniques have been used primarily with chronic pain patients suffering from such maladies as phantom limb pain, causalgia, or neuralgia. Although surgery has been performed at every possible level of the peripheral and central nervous system and is often initially helpful, the pain returns in most cases and may be more severe than before the surgery (White and Sweet, 1972). Surgery is now reserved for some later-stage cancer pain patients and other situations that are not responsive to any other pain control treatment.

Pharmacological treatment of pain has been the primary medical tool in pain control. The effectiveness of drugs in controlling acute pain is well known; however, their ability to affect chronic pain over long periods of time remains fair at best. As more potent analgesics are necessary and as tolerance for these drugs develops, the side effects of the medications produce grogginess and there is often a need for increased dosage, thereby addicting the patient. However, recent advances in the psychopharmalogical treatment of chronic pain patients have shown some good results (Trick, 1976). For example, the effective combination of antidepressant and antipsychotic medication has proved effective in several instances (Merskey and Hester, 1972; Taub and Collins, 1974).

Physical methods of pain relief have included the injection of anesthetic blocking agents (such as novocaine) into tender skin areas, peripheral nerves, or sympathetic ganglia. This method has been used mainly for phantom limb pain and causalgia and has provided hours of pain relief, with occasional permanent relief occurring even though the anesthesia itself wears off in several hours (Kibler and Nathan, 1960; Livingston, 1943).

Electrical stimulation techniques and devices are perhaps the most frequently used physical methods of treating phantom limb pain, neuralgias, and back pain. Generally, two types are available. First, the dorsal-column stimulator consists of fine wire electrodes implanted in the spinal cord above the level of pain. The patient uses a small control box to apply the stimulation and obtain pain relief. Although reported results of this technique vary, effective relief has been noted frequently (Nashold and Friedman, 1972; Shealy, Mortimer, and Hagfors, 1970). Second, the transcutaneous stimulator consists of electrodes that are taped to the skin over the area of pain. An electrical current is then turned on, stimulating the surface of the skin. Effective for chronic pain patients in varying degrees, it has proved to be an effective noninvasive procedure (Long and Carolan, 1974; Wall and Sweet, 1967).

Acupuncture's reported effectiveness in pain control varies from good (Mann and others, 1973) to fair or questionable (Day and others, 1975). Psychological, cultural, and physiological factors appear responsible for its mode of action (Dubner, 1976), although the precise action of acupuncture is as yet unclear. At any rate, the use of acupuncture in acute and chronic pain states appears to be growing. Treatments focus most frequently on headache, postsurgical pain, childbirth, dental work, low back pain, phantom limb pain, causalgia, neuralgia, and cancer pain.

Elaboration on Critical Points

Acute and chronic pain patients present quite different situations and needs with respect to pain control. Acute pain is usually short-lived—though not necessarily less painful than chronic pain—and is exemplified by tension headaches, dental procedures, childbirth, and postsurgical pain. Assessment and treatment techniques for this group of patients are rather clear; and, although their pain is certainly expressed and mediated through complex cognitive and affective mechanisms, the source of acute pain is usually identifiable. With this understanding and identification of the source of their pain, along with an appropriate psychological and/or medical pain control technique, patients often experience a subsequent reduction in their reported pain.

Treating the chronic pain patient is more difficult, and both psychological and physical analyses are necessary. Patients in chronic pain experience constant discomfort, which increases and decreases in intensity but rarely disappears entirely. They have generally been suffering for several months or more with their pain. Their chronic pain condition may have been precipitated by an acute pain situation, a chronic physiological disorder, or by no physiologically understood cause (the latter, therefore, is labeled psychogenic pain). These patients are commonly seen as neurotically depressed and hypochondriacal (Merskey and Spear, 1967; Sternbach, 1974) as a consequence of enduring their chronic pain (whether somatogenic or psychogenic), and they become quite preoccupied with their pain state. Often the task is to help the patient live with the pain in a more productive and comfortable manner and to understand how that pain is experienced.

The terms *psychogenic pain* and *somatogenic pain* are often used to describe chronic pain patients. Unfortunately, these words seem to suggest that psychogenic pain (unlike somatogenic pain) is imagined or fake and that the patient feels no actual pain. This distinction is untrue and a poor one, as suggested by Sternbach (1968), Szasz (1957), and Merskey and Spear (1967). Psychogenic pain patients do not hurt less than somatogenic pain patients do, nor is their pain different. Indeed, so-called psychogenic chronic pain patients look the same psychologically as so-called somatogenic chronic pain patients (Sternbach and others, 1973; Woodforde and Merskey, 1972). In Sternbach's (1974) view, the term *psychogenic* should be used to describe pain that is better understood in psychological than in physical language; and, conversely, the term *somatogenic* should be used to describe pain that is better understood in physical than in psychological language.

As Merskey and Spear (1967) have reported, there is strong support for the notion that psychogenic or somatogenic chronic pain patients look the same psychologically. Both groups of patients are typically neurotically depressed and hypochondriacal. Psychogenic pain patients become neurotic due to early childhood settings, where attention to pain and suffering was associated with and substituted for normal affection by parents. In later life these people experience episodes of pain precipitated by loss or by self-directed anger for aggressive, sexual, or dependent feelings or for unwanted success in their lives. In contrast, somatogenic chronic pain patients become depressed and hypochondriacal following their long pain experience, with subsequent despair and hopelessness. They become overinvolved with their physical condition and begin to withdraw from those around them. The distinction to be made in assessing chronic pain is not whether the patient's pain is of physical or psychological origin but, rather, how the person experiences his pain; what cognitive, emotional, cultural, and social factors are operating; and to what degree these factors influence the pain experience. Such assessment can be facilitated by use of the McGill Pain Questionnaire (Melzack, 1975a); a patient's pain estimate figures, used in conjunction with the submaximum tourniquet pain score (Sternbach, 1974); or a clinical interview, designed not to ascertain what makes the pain better or worse but, rather, to gauge its effects on the patient's interactions with significant others (in health systems and in family, financial, and work situations).

Sternbach (1974) notes some characteristics of chronic pain patients who tend to do well in treatment. These patients (1) are married or living with someone; (2) have a good sexual adjustment before onset of pain; (3) remain at their work or begin to retrain themselves in a less demanding job; and (4) have tried prescribed analgesics, found little benefit, and stopped taking them. Those who do poorly in treatment, according to Sternbach, (1) have poor marital adjustment, (2) support themselves for extended time periods with disability or welfare monies, and (3) abuse drugs or alcohol.

The treatment of chronic pain patients has included the application of psychologically based techniques in conjunction with medical treatments. Results vary, but pain control often is provided to some appreciable degree. Particular effectiveness has been noted with the use of behavioral operant conditioning techniques (Cairns and others, 1976; Fordyce, 1976) in pain clinics and in general hospitals, both with and without other medical and psychological treatments.

Personal Views and Recommendations

Psychological assessment and treatment techniques for pain control now represent one of the most challenging and complex frontiers in the behavioral sciences. With the techniques now available, professionals are beginning to understand more and more about the psychological, cultural, social, and cognitive factors in pain perception. Current measures are, nevertheless, still quite crude, and explorations have touched only the "tip of the iceberg." Research must continue in both physical and psychological laboratories before there can be effective translation to clinical situations. The natural meeting place for research, applications, and continued evolution of both acute and chronic pain control methods appears to be in the relatively new multidisciplinary pain clinics located in the United States. Although usually devoted to chronic pain problems, these clinical settings could serve as effective locations for the study of acute pain as well.

The professional goal is to provide pain patients with effective, comprehensive, and appropriate pain control services. Sternbach (1974, p. 117) cautions all those dealing with pain assessment and control to "first do no harm." It is logical that any action should be preceded by a provision of a means for pain control, be it psychologically or medically based; thus, the professional must first be aware of where the pain is coming from as well as who is experiencing the pain.

The professional is obliged to represent skills, techniques, and treatments as they are, explaining both their advantages and disadvantages to patients. Eagerness to provide a viable service must not raise expectations beyond actual abilities or limits. Because of recent overstated claims and media publicity on the use of psychological techniques for pain control, the potential for abuse of misrepresentation by professionals is dangerously high. Professionals must resist the temptation to be all things to all people for all pain conditions.

The physical and psychological sciences are truly complementary with respect to the research, assessment, and treatment of people in pain. The dualism that has kept these two disciplines divided in many health care areas now finds unification in pain control research, an area heretofore believed to be most within the realm of physiological science. There is a need to provide each discipline with basic psychological training in pain assessment and treatments. Preferably this task would be assigned to graduate training centers in both disciplines. Specialized postdoctoral study in research, assessment, and treatment of pain patients will be necessary to advance the field. At present, the training of psychologists and counselors at the doctoral level does not provide adequate preparation in the area of assessment and treatment of pain. Further exposure, both didactically and clinically, to the psychological, physiological, cultural, and sociological aspects of pain is needed. Pain-related training would be best accomplished in a multidisciplinary setting. Pain clinics would be especially suitable sites for such a training sequence. Training might well be presented within a one- or two-semester course with a clinical practice laboratory portion.

At this time certification for psychologists who participate in the field as pain control specialists seems premature and unwarranted. What seems important now is that professionals begin to become familiar with the available specialized information, tools, and expertise. Psychological procedures should be used judiciously and in collaboration with other health care givers.

Most important, however, is the need to disseminate currently available skills and information to those psychologists, physicians, counselors, and dentists who are in clinical positions where pain control techniques could be useful. To advance the field of psychological pain assessment and control should be, at this time, the uppermost goal of professionals in the field.

Application to Particular Variables

Little conclusive research exists to relate any variable of age to pain perception. Research by Harkins and Chapman (1976, 1977) supports the supposition that changes in pain perception with age are complex and that, although pain threshold appears to increase with age, the elderly may simply have deficits in their ability to discriminate between noxious stimuli, or they may have biases for or against labeling noxious events as painful.

Men have been noted to tolerate more pain than women (Woodrow and others, 1972). However, this observation may be secondary to many social, cultural, and situational factors that are operating in the pain situation. No particular assessment concerns differentiating between male and female pain patients are apparent at this time.

The amount of education an individual has does not seem to influence the words that he uses to describe personal pain (Melzack, 1973). Adding to the complexity of the education factor is that education is often synonymous with socioeconomic, cultural, and racial considerations in the assessment situation. Where one factor begins and the other ends is difficult to ascertain. Education, however, may be an influential factor in the overall approach to treatment and in interpersonal relationships with pain patients. Caution should be taken during the assessment of highly educated individuals to assure that their tendencies to intellectualize and rationalize their pain condition do not create compelling distractions for the clinician.

Socioeconomic status exerts a varied and complex effect on a person's perception of pain (Wolff and Langley, 1968; Zborowski, 1969). This effect is, however, modified and influenced by other psychosocial and ethnocultural factors in the individual. Wolff (1977) has found that socioeconomic status decreases in importance as a variable as the individual's socioeconomic status increases.

Vocational factors can be important in the assessment of the chronic pain patient. Certain types of people—for instance, people who are dissatisfied with their vocational choice; people who, perhaps because of age, are unable or unwilling to continue a physically demanding job; people who have sustained an injury or developed an actual physical malady and who were premorbidly dissatisfied with their employment; and people who simply use their pain to foster litigation claims, welfare support, unemployment benefits, and disability claims—may demonstrate work-related pain complaints derived from their past, present, or future work situations. Usually they present themselves as wanting to return to their work and assert that people, especially the physician, are keeping them from working. These patients resist retraining for other less demanding employment, even if it is physically indicated (Sternbach, 1974). Most frequently identified in this group are patients with chronic low back pain.

Cultural background and attitude also have a powerful effect on an individual's pain perception (Fabrega and Tyma, 1976; Lambert, Libman, and Poser, 1960; Weisenberg, 1976a; Zborowski, 1969). It is presumed that pain perception differences exist in the areas of pain tolerance (a learned aspect) and pain threshold (the lowest stimulus level at which a person reports pain) (Hardy, Wolff, and Goodell, 1952). Tolerance differences have been demonstrated by Zborowski (1952), who found that Native Americans have an accepting, matter-of-fact attitude about pain. When in intense pain, they did not express their pain in front of others, whereas Jews and Italians displayed their pain in public in an effort to gain support and comfort. Generally, pain tolerance levels of the Northern European cultures tended to be higher than those of the Mediterranean cultures. Other research on Negro, Oriental, and Puerto Rican pain tolerance placed their tolerance levels below those of whites (Weisenberg and others, 1975; Woodrow and others, 1972), in that order.

There is no evidence that pain perception is affected by level of intelligence. However, as in any other clinical assessment situation, patients who are either extremely intelligent or extremely dull necessitate different interpersonal approaches during the assessment process. The assessor's vocabulary and level of abstraction used during the interview should be equal to the comprehension level of the individual.

The incidence of pain reported by psychiatric patients has been shown to be quite high (Merskey, 1965a, 1965b). Pinsky (1975) identifies four primary psychiatric diagnostic categories which frequently include pain as a prominent symptom. First, neurotic or psychotic depression is often masked by the presence of pain. These individuals are difficult to assess; since depression is often a result of chronic pain as well as a cause, it is hard to determine which conditions came first; moreover, when their depression lifts, their pain complaints often cease (Bradley, 1963; Sternbach and Timmermans, 1975). Second, hypochondriacal (see Pilowsky, 1967) and obsessional individuals often include pain complaints in their clinical pictures. Third, hysterical neurosis with pain is often seen in individuals who have demonstrated hysterical behavior (either conversion or characterlogical or both) in the past. Their symptoms have, previously, come and gone dramatically, and there has often been an actual past physical illness which produced similar symptomatology. There is usually no physical evidence to sufficiently explain the strength or nature of the pain. Finally, schizophrenic patients usually present their pain condition in a paranoid context (for example, hallucination or delusion). Frequently they report the pain as something that is persecuting them. Along with the particular expression, they show other typical signs and symptoms associated with paranoid schizophrenia.

References

Barber, J., and Mayer, D. "Evaluation of the Efficacy and Neural Mechanism of a Hypnotic Analgesia Procedure in Experimental and Clinical Dental Pain." *Pain,* 1977, *4,* 41-48.

Beecher, H. K. "Relationship of the Significance of Wound to Pain Experienced." *Journal of the American Medical Association,* 1956, *161,* 1609-1613.

Beecher, H. K. *Measurement of Subjective Responses.* New York: Oxford University Press, 1959.

Bond, M. R., and Pearson, I. B. "Psychological Aspects of Pain in Women with Advanced Cancer of the Cervix." *Journal of Psychosomatic Research,* 1969, *13,* 13-19.

Bond, M. R., and Pilowski, I. "Subjective Assessment of Pain and Its Relationship to the Administration of Analgesics in Patients with Advanced Cancer." *Journal of Psychosomatic Research,* 1966, *10,* 203-208.

Bonica, J. J. "Organization and Function of a Pain Clinic." In J. J. Bonica (Ed.), *Advances in Neurology.* Vol. 4. New York: Raven Press, 1974a.

Bonica, J. J. (Ed.). *Advances in Neurology.* Vol. 4. New York: Raven, 1974b.

Bonica, J. J., and Albe-Fessard, D. (Eds.). *Recent Advances in Pain Research and Therapy: Proceedings of the First World Congress on Pain.* New York: Raven Press, 1976.

Bradley, J. J. "Severe Localized Pain Associated with the Depressive Syndrome." *British Journal of Psychiatry,* 1963, *109,* 741-745.

Cairns, D., and others. "A Comprehensive Treatment Approach to Chronic Low Back Pain." *Pain,* 1976, *2,* 301-308.

Caterinicchio, R. P. "Interpersonal Trust in the Physician, and the Tolerance of Treatment Induced Pain: A Multivariate Analysis in a Natural Clinical Setting." *Dissertation Abstracts International,* 1976, *36* (6072).

Clark, M., Gosnell, M., and Shapiro, D. "The New War on Pain." *Newsweek,* April 25, 1977, pp. 48-50, 55-56, 58.

Danskin, D. C., and Walter, E. D. "Biofeedback and Voluntary Self-Regulation: Counseling and Education." *Personnel and Guidance Journal,* 1973, *51* (9), 633-638.

Day, R. L., and others. "Evaluation of Acupuncture Anesthesia: A Psychophysical Study." *Anesthesiology,* 1975, *43,* 507-517.

Descartes, R. *L'homme* [1644]. In M. Foster (Ed.), *Lectures on the History of Physiology During the 16th, 17th, and 18th Centuries.* New York: Dover Books, 1970.

Dick-Read, G. *Childbirth Without Fear.* New York: Harper & Row, 1959.

Dubner, R. "Efficacy and Possible Mechanisms of Action of Acupuncture Anesthesia: Observations Based on a Visit to the People's Republic of China." *Journal of the American Dental Association,* 1976, *92,* 419-427.

Egbert, L. D., and others. "Reduction of Postoperative Pain by Encouragement and Instruction to Patients: A Study of Doctor-Patient Rapport." *New England Journal of Medicine,* 1964, *270,* 825-827.

Engel, G. L. " 'Psychogenic' Pain and the Pain-Prone Patient." *American Journal of Medicine,* 1959, *26,* 899-918.

Espin, O. M., and Ganikos, M. L. "Counseling for Pain Control." *Counselor Education and Supervision,* 1975, *15,* 55-61.

Fabrega, H., and Tyma, S. "Language and Cultural Influences in the Description of Pain." *British Journal of Medical Psychology,* 1976, *49,* 349-371.

Fordyce, W. E. "Behavioral Concepts in Chronic Pain and Illness." In P. O. Davidson (Ed.), *The Behavioral Management of Anxiety, Depression, and Pain.* New York: Brunner/Mazel, 1976.

Fordyce, W. E., and others. "Some Implications of Learning in Problems of Chronic Pain." *Journal of Chronic Diseases,* 1968, *21,* 179-190.

French, A., and Tupin, J. P. "Therapeutic Application of a Simple Relaxation Method." *American Journal of Psychotherapy,* 1974, *28,* 282-287.

Gannon, L., and Sternbach, R. A. "Alpha Enhancement as a Treatment for Pain: A

Case Study." *Journal of Behavior Therapy and Experimental Psychiatry*, 1971, *2*, 209-213.

Gaw, A. C., Chang, L. W., and Shaw, L. C. "Efficacy of Acupuncture on Osteoarthritic Pain." *New England Journal of Medicine*, 1975, *293*, 375-378.

Goldscheider, A. *Über den Schmerz in Physiologischer und Klinischer Hinsicht*. Munich: Hirschwald, 1894.

Green, E. E., Green, A. M., and Walter, E. D. "Self Regulation of Internal States." In *Proceedings of the International Congress of Cybernetics*. London: Gordon and Breach, 1969.

Green, E. E., Green, A. M., and Walter, E. D. "Voluntary Control of Internal States: Psychological and Physiological." *Journal of Transpersonal Psychology*, 1970, *1* (1), 1-26.

Green, E. E., and others. "Autogenic Feedback Training." *Psychotherapy and Psychosomatics*, 1975, *25*, 400-410.

Hardy, J. D., Wolff, H. G., and Goodell, H. *Pain Sensations and Reactions*. New York: Williams and Wilkins, 1952.

Harkins, S. W., and Chapman, C. R. "Detection and Decision Factors in Pain Perception in Young and Elderly Men." *Pain*, 1976, *2*, 319-324.

Harkins, S. W., and Chapman, C. R. "The Perception of Induced Dental Pain in Young and Elderly Women." *Journal of Gerontology*, 1977, *32*, 428-435.

Hendler, N., and others. "EMG Biofeedback in Patients with Chronic Pain." *Diseases of the Nervous System*, 1977, *38*, 505-509.

Hilgard, E. R. "A Neodissociation Interpretation of Pain Reduction in Hypnosis." *Psychological Review*, 1973, *80*, 396-411.

Hilgard, E. R. "The Alleviation of Pain by Hypnosis." *Pain*, 1975, *1*, 213-231.

Hill, H. E., and others. "Effects of Anxiety and Morphine on Discrimination of Intensities of Painful Stimuli." *Journal of Clinical Investigation*, 1952a, *31*, 473-480.

Hill, H. E., and others. "Studies of Anxiety Associated with Anticipation of Pain. 1: Effects of Morphine." *Archives of Neurology and Psychiatry*, 1952b, *67*, 612-619.

Kamiya, J. "Operant Control of the EEG Alpha-Rhythm and Some of Its Reported Effects on Consciousness." In J. Tart (Ed.), *Altered States of Consciousness*. New York: Wiley, 1969.

Kibler, R. F., and Nathan, P. W. "Relief of Pain and Paraesthesiae by Nerve Block Distal to a Lesion." *Journal of Neurology, Neurosurgery, and Psychiatry*, 1960, *23*, 91-98.

Klepac, R. "Systematic Desensitization to Raise Pain Tolerance." *Journal of Behavior Therapy and Experimental Psychiatry*, 1975, *6*, 307-310.

Lambert, W. E., Libman, E., and Poser, E. G. "The Effect of Increased Salience of a Membership Group on Pain Tolerance." *Journal of Personality*, 1960, *28*, 350-357.

Liebeskind, J. C., and Paul, L. A. "Psychological and Physiological Mechanisms of Pain." In *Annual Review of Psychology*. Palo Alto, Calif.: Annual Reviews, 1977.

Livingston, W. K. *Pain Mechanisms*. New York: Macmillan, 1943.

Long, D. M., and Carolan, M. T. "Cutaneous Afferent Stimulation in the Treatment of Chronic Pain." In J. J. Bonica (Ed.), *Advances in Neurology*. Vol. 4. New York: Raven Press, 1974.

Luce, G., and Gattozzi, A. "The Use of Biofeedback Training in Enabling Patients to Control Autonomic Functions." In H. Siegal (Ed.), *Mental Health Program Reports*. No. 5. Rockville, Md.: National Institute of Mental Health, 1971.

Luthe, W. *Autogenic Therapy*. New York: Grune and Stratton, 1973.

McCraine, E. J. "Conversion Pain." *Psychiatric Quarterly*, 1973, *47*, 246-257.

McGlashan, T. H., Evans, F. J., and Orne, M. T. "The Nature of Hypnotic Analgesia and Placebo Response to Experimental Pain." *Psychosomatic Medicine,* 1969, *31,* 227-246.

Mackenzie, R. S. "Psychodynamics of Pain." *Journal of Oral Medicine,* 1968, *23,* 75-84.

Mann, F., and others. "Treatment of Intractable Pain by Acupuncture." *Lancet,* 1973, *13* (1), 94-99.

Marshall, H. R. *Pain, Pleasure, and Aesthetics.* New York: Macmillan, 1894.

Melzack, R. *The Puzzle of Pain.* New York: Basic Books, 1973.

Melzack, R. "The McGill Pain Questionnaire: Major Properties and Scoring Methods." *Pain,* 1975a, *1,* 277-299.

Melzack, R. "The Promise of Biofeedback: Don't Hold the Party Yet." *Psychology Today,* July 1975b, pp. 18-22, 80-81.

Melzack, R., and Casey, K. L. "Sensory Motivational, and Central Control Determinants of Pain: A New Conceptual Model." In D. Kenshalo (Ed.), *The Skin Senses.* Springfield, Ill.: Thomas, 1968.

Melzack, R., and Wall, P. D. "On the Nature of Cutaneous Sensory Mechanisms." *Brain,* 1962, *85,* 331-356.

Melzack, R., and Wall, P. D. "Pain Mechanisms: A New Theory." *Science,* 1965, *150,* 971-979.

Melzack, R., and Wall, P. D. "Psychophysiology of Pain." *International Anesthesiology Clinics,* 1970, *8,* 3-34.

Merskey, H. "The Characteristics of Persistent Pain in Psychological Illness." *Journal of Psychosomatic Research,* 1965a, *9,* 291-298.

Merskey, H. "Psychiatric Patients with Persistent Pain." *Journal of Psychosomatic Research,* 1965b, *9,* 299-309.

Merskey, H., and Hester, R. N. "The Treatment of Chronic Pain with Psychotropic Drugs." *Postgraduate Medical Journal,* 1972, *48,* 594-598.

Merskey, H., and Spear, F. G. *Pain: Psychological and Psychiatric Aspects.* London: Baillière Tindall, 1967.

Mitchell, K. R., and White, R. G. "Behavioral Self-Management: An Application to the Problem of Migraine Headaches." *Behavior Therapy,* 1977, *8,* 213-221.

Nashold, B. S., and Friedman, H. "Dorsal Column Stimulation for Pain: A Preliminary Report on 30 Patients." *Journal of Neurosurgery,* 1972, *36,* 590-597.

Noordenbos, W. *Pain.* Amsterdam: Elsevier, 1959.

Parkes, C. M. "Factors Determining the Persistence of Phantom Pain in the Amputee." *Journal of Psychosomatic Research,* 1973, *17,* 97-108.

Pilling, L. F., Brannick, T. L., and Swenson, W. M. "Psychologic Characteristics of Psychiatric Patients Having Pain as a Presenting Symptom." *Canadian Medical Association Journal,* 1967, *97,* 387-394.

Pilowsky, I. "Dimensions of Hypochondriasis." *British Journal of Psychiatry,* 1967, *113,* 89-93.

Pinsky, J. J. "Psychodynamics and Psychotherapy in the Treatment of Patients with Chronic Intractable Pain." In B. L. Crue, Jr. (Ed.), *Pain: Research and Treatment.* New York: Academic Press, 1975.

Ramsay, R. A. "Psychiatric Considerations in Chronic Pain States." In E. D. Wittkower and H. Warnes (Eds.), *Psychosomatic Medicine: Its Clinical Applications.* New York: Harper & Row, 1977.

Reading, C., and Mohr, P. D. "Biofeedback Control of Migraine: A Pilot Study." *British Journal of Social and Clinical Psychology,* 1976, *15,* 429-433.

Schultz, J. H., and Luthe, W. *Autogenic Therapy.* Vol. 1. New York: Grune and Stratton, 1969.

Shealy, C. N., Mortimer, J. T., and Hagfors, N. R. "Dorsal Column Electroanalgesia." *Journal of Neurosurgery,* 1970, *32,* 560-564.

Sherrington, C. S. "Cutaneous Sensations." In E. A. Schafer (Ed.), *Textbook of Physiology.* London: Pentland, 1900.

Smith, G. M., and others. "An Experimental Pain Method Sensitive to Morphine in Man: The Sub-maximum Effort Tourniquet Technique." *Journal of Pharmacology and Experimental Therapeutics,* 1966, *154,* 324-332.

Sternbach, R. A. *Pain: A Psychophysiological Analysis.* New York: Academic Press, 1968.

Sternbach, R. A. "Strategies and Tactics in the Treatment of Patients with Pain." In B. L. Crue, Jr. (Ed.), *Pain and Suffering: Selected Aspects.* Springfield, Ill.: Thomas, 1970.

Sternbach, R. A. *Pain Patients: Traits and Treatments.* New York: Academic Press, 1974.

Sternbach, R. A. "Psychological Factors in Pain." In J. J. Bonica and D. Albe-Fessard (Eds.), *Recent Advances in Pain Research and Therapy: Proceedings of the First World Congress on Pain.* New York: Raven Press, 1976.

Sternbach, R. A., and Timmermans, G. "Personality Changes Associated with Reduction of Pain." *Pain,* 1975, *1,* 177-181.

Sternbach, R. A., and others. "Traits of Pain Patients: The Low-Back 'Loser.' " *Psychosomatics,* 1973, *14,* 226-229.

Sternbach, R. A., and others. "Measuring the Severity of Clinical Pain." In J. J. Bonica (Ed.), *Advances in Neurology.* Vol. 4: *Pain.* New York: Raven Press, 1974.

Swanson, D. W., and others. "Program for Managing Chronic Pain: Program Description and Characteristics." *Mayo Clinic Proceedings,* 1976, *51,* 401-408.

Szasz, T. S. *Pain and Pleasure: A Study of Bodily Feelings.* New York: Basic Books, 1957.

Szasz, T. S. "The Psychology of Persistent Pain: A Portrait of 'L'homme Douloureux.' " In A. Soulairac (Ed.), *Pain.* London: Academic Press, 1968.

Taub, A., and Collins, W. F., Jr. "Observation on the Treatment of Denervation Dysesthesia with Psychotropic Agents. Postherpetic Neuralgia, Anesthesia Dolorosa, Peripheral Neuropathy." In J. J. Bonica (Ed.), *Advances in Neurology.* Vol. 4: *Pain.* New York: Raven Press, 1974.

Titchener, E. B. *A Textbook of Psychology.* New York: Macmillan, 1909.

Toomey, T. C., and others. "Acupuncture and Chronic Pain Mechanisms: The Moderating Effects of Affect, Personality, and Stress on Response to Treatment." *Pain,* 1977, *3,* 137-145.

Trick, K. L. "The Use of Psychotropic Drugs in a Pain Clinic." *Journal of International Medical Research,* 1976, *4,* 68-72.

Wall, P. D., and Sweet, W. H. "Temporary Abolition of Pain in Man." *Science,* 1967, *155,* 108-109.

Weisenberg, M. (Ed.). *Pain: Clinical and Experimental Perspectives.* St. Louis: Mosby, 1975.

Weisenberg, M. "Cultural and Racial Reactions to Pain." In M. Weisenberg (Ed.), *The Control of Pain.* New York: Psychological Dimensions, 1976a.

Weisenberg, M. "Teaching Behavioral Pain Control to Health Professionals." In M. Weisenberg and B. Tursky (Eds.), *Pain: New Perspectives in Therapy and Research.* New York: Plenum, 1976b.

Weisenberg, M., and Tursky, B. (Eds.). *Pain: New Perspectives in Therapy and Research.* New York: Plenum, 1976.

Weisenberg, M., and others. "Pain: Anxiety and Attitudes in Black, White, and Puerto Rican Patients." *Psychosomatic Medicine,* 1975, *37,* 123-135.

White, J. C., and Sweet, W. H. *Pain and the Neurosurgeon.* Springfield, Ill.: Thomas, 1972.

Wittmer, J. "The Use of Imagery in the Helping Professions." *Hypnosis Quarterly,* 1973, *27* (1), 5-9.

Wolff, B. B. "Psychosocial Aspects of the Patient with Chronic Pain." In P. L. Leroy (Ed.), *Current Concepts in the Management of Chronic Pain.* New York: Symposia Specialists, 1977.

Wolff, B. B., and Langley, S. "Cultural Factors and the Response to Pain." *American Anthropologist,* 1968, *70,* 494-501.

Woodforde, J. M., and Merskey, H. "Personality Traits of Patients with Chronic Pain." *Journal of Psychosomatic Research,* 1972, *16,* 167-172.

Woodrow, K. M., and others. "Pain Tolerance: Differences According to Age, Sex, and Race." *Psychosomatic Medicine,* 1972, *34,* 548-556.

Zborowski, M. "Cultural Components in Responses to Pain." *Journal of Social Issues,* 1952, *8,* 16-30.

Zborowski, M. *People in Pain.* San Francisco: Jossey-Bass, 1969.

90

Herman A. Walters

Dangerousness

For the welfare of society, the protection of the victim, and the protection of the violent person as an individual, it is crucial that means be found to predict violence; that is, to identify dangerousness. For this purpose, psychologists, psychiatrists, and certain other mental health professionals have been charged by society with applying and improving techniques for making these predictions. In the individual case, such a prediction sets in motion legal proceedings aimed at taking responsible action, so that the anticipated violence is intercepted and avoided. While on the surface this seems a humane and enlightened way to proceed, there are in fact severe problems and contradictions inherent in the laws and in the procedures that purport to implement the intentions of these laws. The terms *dangerous* and *violent* are rarely defined; and when they are, the definitions are not universally accepted. The imminence of violent behavior, predicted by the label "dangerous," is typically unspecified: the "dangerousness" exists now, but only rarely do the predictors attempt to say when, in the future, the violence will occur. An additional problem is the assumption that mental illness, particularly psychosis, is closely associated with violence and that psychotic people are, therefore, more dangerous than other citizens. It is further assumed that mental health professionals are better able to predict violence than are other people. Mental health professionals are generally guilty of complicity in preserving this belief, in spite of a lack of empirical evidence to support a contention of such predictive abilities.

Because of past abuses, active counterforces are attempting to alter this state of affairs. More stringent laws are creating greater protection for those who heretofore may have been labeled "dangerous." Within the mental health professions, there is a growing recognition of a lack of sound predictive techniques and a realization that many "experts" are not expert at all. Research and theoretical efforts are rapidly developing, but so far with only modest results (Sundberg, Snowden, and Reynolds, 1978). To compound the dilemma of the clinician, at the same time that greater protection is being afforded to the potentially violent offender, there is also a growing emphasis on the right of society to expect the professional person to provide warning against the impending actions of "dangerous" persons. Thus, there may be liability for hasty or ill-considered hospitalization of someone seen as potentially violent; but there is also liability for failing to recognize and take responsible action to protect the community against the violent behavior of one's patients. Throughout all this, the plight of potential victims, past and future, is of implicit concern but does not figure prominently in current legal or clinical examinations of the issue. The crux of the problem is to (1) find conceptual clarity and agreement in defining those behaviors that are so disruptive and threatening that they cannot be tolerated; (2) determine the balance point, acceptable to society, between the rights of individuals and the rights and protection of society; and (3) determine what combinations of procedures or disciplines may most accurately predict violent behavior. In few areas does one encounter a more perplexing entanglement of value judgments and empirical questions.

Background and Current Status

Since the earliest days of American history, this country has recognized the right of society to contain and control those citizens who were so deranged that they could not be tolerated by the community (Robitscher, 1974). Early laws allowed "dangerous" persons to be restrained or incarcerated, even though they had committed no violence or legal offense (Deutsch, 1949).

As society evolved, decisions such as the M'Naughten case established precedents that relieved the severely mentally ill from responsibility for criminal acts. Accompanying these precedents, however, was a particularly pernicious assumption that linked mental illness to an expectation of violence. "Dangerous to oneself and others" figured largely in early civil commitment laws and continues to do so. Although evidence on the point is equivocal (Frederick, 1976; Mesnikoff and Lauterbach, 1975), a general belief persists that mentally ill people are more likely than other individuals to commit crimes of violence. As a consequence of this belief, mentally ill individuals have been incarcerated without having committed any illegal act and have often been detained for prolonged periods on the ground that they are "dangerous." Also, although incarceration may be justified on the basis that the patient is "ill," treatment has often been unavailable. Because of such abuses, current legal opinion is beginning to weigh against such assumptions and practices (Bernard, 1977; *O'Connor* v. *Donaldson,* 1975).

At the present time, increasing emphasis is being placed on (1) requiring closer attention to due process for those who are considered for civil commitment; (2) improving, through strenuous challenge, the quality of assessments and the carefulness with which predictive statements are made by mental health professionals who examine these clients; (3) providing for periodic review of the status of hospitalized patients, to ensure that they are not kept any longer than necessary; (4) insisting that individuals committed for treatment must, in fact, receive appropriate treatment; and (5) encouraging an increase in the amount and quality of research aimed at understanding the nature and circumstances of violence, and a corresponding emphasis on examining the validity of procedures for predicting violence.

Critical Discussion

General Areas of Concern

Violence that is expressed under socially approved circumstances or in socially approved ways (sports or entertainment, for example) is typically of little concern to courts or clinics, despite some suggestions that in many subtle ways violence is societally taught, glamorized, and encouraged (Gerbner, 1972; Hartnagel, Teevan, and McIntyre, 1975; Liebert, Neale, and Davidson, 1973). However, when violence is directed at an individual, in such a way as to threaten immediate safety and welfare, society is required to take protective steps. In attempting to predict who will behave violently, society makes assessments of "dangerousness." As the term is used clinically and legally, *dangerous* does not refer to behavior that has already occurred; rather, it concerns behavior that might occur at some unspecified future time.

The first problem to be met concerns a definition of "violence." A wide variety of behaviors can be (and at times have been) included; these may range from physical assault, to verbal threats of harm, to merely an ominous and threatening air. Most current writing (Kozol, 1975; Tupin, 1975) restricts "violence" to those instances where serious bodily harm will result and where the danger is imminent.

A related but often unstated concern has to do with the degree of certainty with which the "expert" makes this prediction. It is no longer enough to hold the opinion that someone "may" do violence at some unspecified time or to view someone as vaguely "likely" to do violence. Instead, the prediction must include quantitative statements about the likelihood that is attached to the predicted behavior, and estimates must be made of when and to whom the violence will be done.

These requirements lead directly to one of the core problems in this area: the prediction of infrequent events (Meehl and Rosen, 1955; Rosen, 1954). Violence is an infrequent behavior, even on the part of those considered to be the most violent. They are not violent all the time; in fact, they are not violent most of the time. When a prediction of violence is made, therefore, the "violent" individuals probably will be deprived of their liberty in the interest of protecting society—when, in the vast majority of instances, these persons will not, in fact, be violent.

In addition, the notion of dangerousness has become deeply entangled with societal expectations of mentally ill persons. Merely finding that someone is disruptive, troublesome, or incomprehensible may be sufficient to label him insane (Fox, 1975), whether there is actual evidence for psychosis or not. The assumption is then made that "insane" persons are dangerous, even though empirical evidence does not substantiate the degree of correspondence between violence and mental illness that is admitted in the laws and procedures of many states.

The statistical and theoretical problems noted above are compounded by the generally conservative prediction strategies of many clinicians (Laves, 1975). The general decision rule in the medical tradition is "When in doubt, suspect disease." Translated into the present context, this means a strong emphasis on minimizing false negatives; that is, persons who are "insane" or "dangerous" but who may escape detection by assessment procedures.

The sum of all this is a general tendency to overpredict violence, and thus to label as dangerous many people who in fact are not. Part of this tendency is humanitarian. Since the patient may directly or indirectly be one of the victims of the violence, it seems clearly in the patient's best interest if the clinician is conservative; that is, it is better to hospitalize unnecessarily than to allow an assault or suicide attempt. However, this strategy fails to take adequate account of the social and personal consequences inherent in depriving people of their liberty on such questionable evidence.

Comparative Philosophies and Theories

Numerous theories exist regarding the etiology of violence. Causal or contributing forces that have been implicated include biological dysfunctions, sociocultural factors, intrapsychic conflicts, as well as transient states such as extreme provocation and lowered controls due to chemical agents.

An interesting typology suggested by Megargee (1966) posits two categories of individuals who may be particularly prone to violent acts. The *undercontrolled* person is described as violent, often from an early age. Such a person is easily provoked and is likely to seek confrontation. The *overcontrolled* individual, in contrast, tolerates severe frustration far beyond the limits of most people. This person is overtly cooperative and conforming, but rage and resentment build covertly. The explosion, when it finally comes, is violent and sometimes bizarre. Megargee's formulation is instructive, and the postulated antecedents provide a rich source of hypotheses. However, at present there is little information about the form, targets, or timing of the anticipated violence.

Some information relevant to the study of violence is available in a recent study on the development of criminal behavior (Mednick and Christiansen, 1977). This study attempts to weigh and integrate the multiplicity of physical and social factors associated with criminal behavior. It is instructive in its breadth and comprehensiveness but limited in its application to the study of violence, since only some criminal behavior is violent, and only some criminal behavior stems from emotional disturbance.

A general overview of available research literature suggests that a variety of factors are predisposing to violence: (1) sociocultural factors, such as poverty, family instability, and rejection; (2) role models, particularly physically abusive parents, who emphasized violence; (3) psychological disorders, including paranoia, easily threatened self-image, lack of ego controls, and depression; (4) biological contributors such as those mentioned earlier; and (5) lowered controls in the form of alcohol or drug abuse.

Because of the multiplicity of factors that appear to influence the likelihood of violent behavior, appreciable disagreement exists as to the feasibility of even attempting to make predictions of violence. Some investigators (Kozol, 1975; Lion, Madden, and Christopher, 1976; Tupin, 1975) report at least some progress in developing predictive measures or batteries for this population. Others (Gardner, 1976; Klein, 1976; Megargee, 1976; Monahan, 1975) are not nearly so optimistic. But despite this wide range of views regarding the accuracy of these predictions, the fact remains that they are made, and will no doubt continue to be made. This is, in fact, one of the most active interfaces between psychology and law, and there seems no alternative but to continue to seek ways to improve these judgments. With this in mind, it is instructive to look at some of the various techniques that have been used in this connection.

Elaboration on Critical Points

Given the tremendous breadth and variety of behavior encompassed in the study of violence, clinical purposes justify limiting the focus herein severely. Specifically, consideration will be given only to those acts, occurring in a spontaneous and unplanned manner, that produce severe harm to the victim. In addition, concern will be focused only on predicting such behavior as an immediately expected event.

In this vein, several efforts have been made to develop adequate predictors. Projective measures such as the Rorschach, the Holtzman Inkblot Technique, and the Thematic Apperception Test have been concerned with responses indicative of hostility (Exner, 1974; Hill, 1972). A relatively new procedure, the Hand Test (Wagner, 1962), has shown some promise in predicting acting-out behavior in a variety of populations, but, again, validity studies are mixed (Higdon and Brodsky, 1973). In addition to providing some direct indicators of hostile tendencies or preoccupations with violence, projective measures lend themselves to an analysis of ego controls, adaptive potential, and flexibility in meeting stress or provocation. Although an individual may show great preoccupation with violence, the likelihood of overt actions would be moderated by these and other variables. This point deserves careful consideration. The mere presence (assumed) of a behavior tendency, such as aggressiveness or dependency, is not in and of itself predictive of overt manifestations of that tendency. The likelihood of overt behavior is the criterion of interest. Moreover, the perennial questions of reliability and validity continue to pose problems for these as well as other projective techniques (Klopfer and Taulbee, 1976).

In contrast, various objective personality inventories include scores that, at least theoretically, appear to relate to violence. In particular, the MMPI Psychopathic Deviate-Hysteria (4-3) code profile has been postulated as predictive of acting out of impulses (Davis and Sines, 1971; Persons and Marks, 1971). However, this formulation has not received consistent support (Gynther, Altman, and Warbin, 1973). An additional problem with such approaches is that the form the hypothesized violence will take is typically not specified, nor is the imminence of the violence.

Various combinations of WAIS subscale scores have been used to try to predict violence (Kahn, 1959; Kunce, Ryan, and Eckelman, 1976). Once again, attempts to replicate these findings have not been successful (Shawver and Jew, 1978). The WAIS has also been used in combination with other instruments, such as the Bender Gestalt and the Memory-for-Designs Test (Graham and Kendall, 1946), to attempt to detect subtle brain dysfunction. The general theory posits that minimal brain dysfunction is at least predisposing to poor impulse control, which would then be predictive of a higher-than-average incidence of violence. While some studies (Maletsky, 1973; Mark and Ervin, 1970) suggest the presence of an episodic dyscontrol syndrome, others (Blumer, 1976) argue that the relationships between organic impairments and violence are not nearly so clear or linear as had been thought.

An examination of the broad lines of evidence available at present leads to the conclusion that an actual history of overt, violent behavior provides the single best predictor of future violence (Petersilia, Greenwood, and Lavin, 1977; PROMIS Research Project, 1977; Shah, 1978). While this index overpredicts violence in general (Rubin, 1972), it is important to note that a small proportion of multiple offenders account for an extremely high proportion of violent acts (Wolfgang, Figlio, and Sellin, 1972; Shinnar and Shinnar, 1975). Thus, those individuals with a history of more than a single violent act may be viewed as likely to commit future acts of the same nature.

What is left, then, is a recognition that each case must be approached in a comprehensive, individualized manner, with attention to a multiplicity of biological, social, and interpersonal factors. The situation has not changed materially from that described by Kozol (1975, p. 7): "There is no single test or combination of tests that can predict dangerous acting out." Violence may be the result of an extremely wide range of individual characteristics, interacting with an infinite variety of situational factors, mediated by unpredictable provocations. As a consequence, prediction of dangerousness continues to be one of the most perplexing tasks faced by clinicians and the society they serve.

Personal Views and Recommendations

Predicting dangerousness is, and must continue to be, a central concern of society. But such predictions are complicated by some of the most difficult and crucial questions in all of clinical practice (Monahan, 1975). The consequences of error may be of literally life-and-death significance to potential victims. The consequences for the impulsively uncontrolled violent offenders are hardly less severe. If no intervention occurs, both victim and offender suffer. Thus, these predictions must be made. However, mental health professionals tend to overpredict dangerousness. As a result, suspect individuals may be involuntarily incarcerated, or refused discharge or parole, solely on the basis of faulty and highly questionable predictive techniques (Klein, 1976; Laves, 1975; Monahan and Cummings, 1975). To minimize this problem, clinicians should be trained as thoroughly as possible in this specialty area, if only to arm them with a clear understanding of their limits. In addition, the public in general and the field of law in particular should understand the limitations of clinicians in predicting violence. Finally, other elements of the larger community should share the responsibilities of clinicians in assessing dangerousness. The last point merits particular consideration. It seems unreasonable and overambitious for the clinical specialties to assume major responsibility for making predictions of violence. Law, sociology, and some specialized branches of medicine could provide representatives to multidisciplinary teams, which could as a group represent the interests of the community in attempting to manage this complex and critical issue.

Recent concern about overprediction of dangerousness and overuse of involuntary commitment procedures has led to much-needed reevaluations of laws and procedures. However, these reassessments should not be so sweeping as to denigrate the fact that both victims and violent offenders need and have a right to expect whatever measures of protection the clinical specialties, operating in concert with other informed and knowledgable segments of society, can provide.

Application to Particular Variables

Statistical compilations of demographic data consistently indicate that the criminally violent individual is most likely young (under 25), male, of minority background and low socioeconomic status, and lives in the inner-city area of a large urban center. Such a description is accurate from a statistical point of view, but it does not contribute directly to the prediction of any single case of violence. Also, such an analysis strongly emphasizes violence as a behavior tendency that resides in the individual as an enduring trait; it fails to consider momentary environmental factors (such as great personal stress, lowering of inhibition through drug or alcohol abuse, or momentary provocations of great intensity).

Factors such as age, sex, education, socioeconomic status, vocation (or lack thereof), ethnic/racial background, and type of physical disorder may all play a role in predisposing individuals to violence. However, the relationships are extremely complex and poorly understood, and even attempts to employ sophisticated multiple regression techniques to combinations of these factors still yield little help in predicting individual cases (Mesnikoff and Lauterbach, 1975).

References

Bernard, J. L. "The Significance for Psychology of O'Connor v. Donaldson." *American Psychologist,* 1977, *32* (12), 1085-1088.

Blumer, D. "Epilepsy and Violence." In D. J. Madden and J. R. Lion (Eds.), *Rage, Hate, Assault, and Other Forms of Violence.* New York: Spectrum, 1976.

Davis, K., and Sines, J. "An Antisocial Behavioral Pattern Associated with a Specific MMPI Profile." *Journal of Consulting and Clinical Psychology,* 1971, *36,* 229-234.

Deutsch, A. "The Mentally Ill in America." Unpublished doctoral dissertation, Columbia University, 1949.

Exner, J. E. *The Rorschach: A Comprehensive System.* New York: Wiley, 1974.

Fox, R. W. "Madness in Urban America." *Dissertation Abstracts International,* 1975, *36* (No. 75-25527).

Frederick, C. J. "Determining Dangerousness in Regards to Civil Commitment." In V. Bradley (Ed.), *Paper Victories and Hard Realities.* Washington, D.C.: Health Policy Center, Georgetown University, 1976.

Gardner, M. R. "The Myth of the Impartial Psychiatric Expert: Some Comments Concerning Criminal Responsibility and the Decline of the Age of Therapy." *Law and Psychology Review,* 1976, *2,* 99-118.

Gerbner, G. "Violence in Television Drama: Trends and Symbolic Functions." In G. A. Comstock and E. A. Rubinstein (Eds.), *Television and Social Behavior.* Vol. 1: *Media Content and Control.* Washington, D.C.: U.S. Government Printing Office, 1972.

Graham, F. K., and Kendall, B. S. "Performance of Brain-Damaged Cases on a Memory-for-Designs Test." *Journal of Abnormal and Social Psychology,* 1946, *41,* 303-314.

Gynther, M., Altman, H., and Warbin, R. "A New Actuarial-Empirical Automated MMPI Interpretive Program: The 4-3/3-4 Code Type." *Journal of Clinical Psychology,* 1973, *29,* 229-231.

Hartnagel, T. F., Teevan, J. J., and McIntyre, J. J. "Television Violence and Violent Behavior." *Social Forces,* 1975, *54* (2), 341-351.

Higdon, J. F., and Brodsky, S. L. "Validity of the Hand Test Acting Out Ratio for Overt and Experimentally Induced Aggression." *Journal of Personality Assessment,* 1973, *37* (4), 363-368.

Hill, E. F. *The Holtzman Inkblot Technique.* San Francisco: Jossey-Bass, 1972.

Kahn, M. W. "A Comparison of Personality, Intelligence, and Social History of Two Criminal Groups." *Journal of Social Psychology,* 1959, *49,* 33-40.

Klein, J. F. "The Dangerousness of Dangerous Offender Legislation: Forensic Folklore Revisited." *Canadian Journal of Criminology and Corrections,* 1976, *18* (2), 109-122.

Klopfer, W. G., and Taulbee, E. S. "Projective Tests." In M. R. Rosenzweig and L. W. Porter (Eds.), *Annual Review of Psychology.* Palo Alto, Calif.: Annual Reviews, 1976.

Kozol, K. "The Diagnosis of Dangerousness." In S. A. Pasternach (Ed.), *Violence and Victims.* New York: Spectrum, 1975.

Kunce, J. T., Ryan, J. J., and Eckelman, C. C. "Violent Behavior and Differential WAIS Characteristics." *Journal of Consulting and Clinical Psychology,* 1976, *44,* 42-45.

Laves, G. "The Prediction of Dangerousness as a Criterion for Involuntary Civil Commitment: Constitutional Considerations." *Journal of Psychiatry and Law,* 1975, *3* (3), 291-326.

Liebert, R. M., Neale, J. M., and Davidson, E. S. *The Early Window: Effects of Television on Children and Youth.* Elmsford, N.Y.: Pergamon Press, 1973.

Lion, J. R., Madden, D. J., and Christopher, R. L. "A Violence Clinic: Three Years' Experience." *American Journal of Psychiatry,* 1976, *133* (4), 423-435.

Maletsky, B. M. "The Episodic Dyscontrol Syndrome." *Diseases of the Nervous System,* 1973, *34,* 178-185.

Mark, V. H., and Ervin, F. R. *Violence and the Brain.* New York: Harper & Row, 1970.

Mednick, S., and Christiansen, K. O. *Biosocial Bases of Criminal Behavior.* New York: Gardner Press, 1977.

Meehl, R. E., and Rosen, A. "Antecedent Probability and the Efficiency of Psychometric Signs, Patterns, or Cutting Scores." *Psychological Bulletin,* 1955, *52,* 194-216.

Megargee, E. I. "Undercontrolled and Overcontrolled Personality Types in Extreme Antisocial Aggression." *Psychological Monographs,* 1966, *80* (3), 1-29.

Megargee, E. I. "The Prediction of Dangerous Behavior." *Criminal Justice and Behavior,* 1976, *3* (1), 3-22.

Mesnikoff, A. M., and Lauterbach, C. G. "The Association of Violent Dangerous Behavior with Psychiatric Disorder: A Review of the Research Literature." *Journal of Psychiatry and Law,* 1975, *3,* 415-445.

Monahan, J. (Ed.). *Community Mental Health and the Criminal Justice System.* Elmsford, N.Y.: Pergamon Press, 1975.

Monahan, J., and Cummings, L. "Social Policy Implications of the Inability to Predict Violence." *Journal of Social Issues,* 1975, *31* (2), 153-164.

O'Connor v. *Donaldson,* 420 U.S. 563 (1975).

Persons, R., and Marks, P. "The Violent 4-3 MMPI Personality Type." *Journal of Consulting and Clinical Psychology,* 1971, *36,* 189-196.

Petersilia, J., Greenwood, P. W., and Lavin, M. *Criminal Careers of Habitual Felons.* Santa Monica, Calif.: Rand, 1977.

PROMIS Research Project. *Highlights of Interim Findings and Implications.* Washington, D.C.: Institute for Law and Social Research, 1977.

Robitscher, J. "Legal Standards and Their Implications Regarding Civil Commitment Procedures." In *Symposium on Dangerousness and Mentally Disturbed Persons.* Rockville, Md.: National Institute of Mental Health, 1974.

Rosen, A. "Detection of Suicidal Patients: An Example of Some Limitations in the Prediction of Infrequent Events." *Journal of Consulting Psychology,* 1954, *18,* 397-403.

Rubin, B. "Prediction of Dangerousness in Mentally Ill Criminals." *Archives of General Psychiatry,* 1972, *27,* 297-407.

Shah, S. A. "Dangerousness: A Paradigm for Exploring Some Issues in Law and Psychology." *American Psychologist,* 1978, *33* (3), 224-238.

Shawver, L., and Jew, C. "Predicting Violent Behavior from WAIS Characteristics: A Replication Failure." *Journal of Consulting and Clinical Psychology,* 1978, *46* (1), 206.

Shinnar, R., and Shinnar, S. "The Effects of the Criminal Justice System on the Control of Crime: A Quantitative Approach." *Law and Society Review,* 1975, *9,* 581-611.

Sundberg, N. D., Snowden, L. R., and Reynolds, W. M. "Toward Assessment of Personal Competence and Incompetence in Life Situations." In M. R. Rosenzweig and L. W. Porter (Eds.), *Annual Review of Psychology.* Palo Alto, Calif.: Annual Reviews, 1978.

Tupin, J. P. "Management of Violent Patients." In R. K. Shader (Ed.), *Manual of Psychiatric Therapeutics.* Boston: Little, Brown, 1975.

Wagner, E. E. *Hand Test: Manual for Administration, Scoring, and Interpretation.* Springfield, Ill.: Thomas, 1962.

Wolfgang, M. E., Figlio, R. M., and Sellin, T. *Delinquency in a Birth Cohort.* Chicago: University of Chicago Press, 1972.

91

Sylvan J. Schaffer
Melvin A. Gravitz

Forensic Conditions

Increasingly, applied behavioral scientists, particularly psychologists and psychiatrists, are being called on to participate in the legal system. Their roles in the courts, which are essentially adversary arenas, are varied, ambiguously defined, and often controversial. In general, the psychologist is asked to assess the mental status (past, present, and even future) of individuals involved or accused in criminal and civil proceedings. This assessment is often crucial to the court's decision in cases ranging from murder to child custody. In such cases, there is a complex interaction of a host of legal, ethical, professional, and emotional considerations, all of which are subsumed under the rubric of forensic psychology.

Background and Current Status

Ebbinghaus (1970) has said that "psychology has a long past but only a short history" (p. 1341). That statement also refers to the study of forensic conditions and the field of forensic psychology. Long ago, the legal implications of insanity were dealt with in Jewish Talmudic law, which did not hold the insane responsible for damage that they might have done and which did not recognize the contracts made by the mentally incompetent.

In general, however, western society did not deal with insanity or its legal implications in any systematic way. Often, insanity was treated as a spiritual question for clerics to assess. This assessment often determined the validity of confessions before the ecclesiastical courts, as well as whether the insanity was actually witchraft. In the sixteenth and seventeenth centuries, physicians were occasionally consulted on these issues (Bromberg, 1965).

In 1843 a landmark decision on forensic conditions was made by the so-called "M'Naughten Formula," which has remained the basis for determining criminal responsibility in instances of alleged insanity in most American and Canadian courts. The psychologist's role in this determination has undergone a significant change over the years. As long ago as 1906, Sigmund Freud spoke to a group of judges on the relevance of psychology to the law, while in a 1907 issue of Law Notes, "Advocate Moore writes that he would rather see Sherlock Holmes in court than a psychologist" (Gordon, 1976, p. 1). Still, when the United States Supreme Court heard the landmark *Brown* v. *Board of Education* (1954) case on school segregation, psychological expert testimony on the effects of segregation figured prominently in the decision. In that same year, the U.S. Court of Appeals for the District of Columbia developed the "Durham Formula," which is a variation on M'Naughten. In the 1962 *United States* v. *Jenkins* case, another landmark decision, psychologists were recognized as capable of rendering expert testimony on mental disorders. By the 1970s they were not only interpreting psychological test data but were also serving as primary witnesses in competency hearings. At the same time, the courts have become increasingly involved in the administration of mental hospitals and related institutions. For example, Judge Johnson in the noted *Wyatt* v. *Stickney* case (1972) determined that the court could intervene in the administration of Alabama's state mental hospital system and set minimum standards for patient care, including staff-patient ratios (Stone, 1974); and in 1975 the U.S. Supreme Court handed down the *O'Connor* v. *Donaldson* decision concerning involuntary confinement of nondangerous individuals in mental hospitals. It was approximately at the same time that Gormally and Brodsky (1973) held that psychologists had reversed the 40 year trend of that profession's relative noninvolvement in the justice system.

Forensic conditions appear to gain the most attention in cases where criminal responsibility is at issue, especially when the assessment involves noted defendants such as Patricia Hearst or Sirhan Sirhan. This attention is frequently heightened by the conflicting nature of the expert testimony. Such cases, however, comprise but a very small fraction of forensic conditions. There are about 50,000 civil commitments a year (Rubin, 1972), but these represent only a small number of the commitment procedures, since many of them result in release of the individual concerned. Forensic conditions presently play a role in many other areas, such as family law (including child custody and divorce), contractual capacity (including wills and contracts), and the legally mandated placement of mentally retarded and learning-disabled children in appropriate educational situations. Most major law schools have begun introductory courses in psychology and mental health, and the literature on forensic conditions is increasing. There is no division of forensic psychology as yet within the framework of the American Psychological Association, but the American Psychology-Law Society is flourishing. The latter organization has established a certification system, called the American Board of Forensic Psychology, which in August 1978 began to accept applications for its diploma.

Critical Discussion

General Areas of Concern

The role that forensic psychology plays in the definition, assessment, and reporting of forensic conditions is often ambiguous and controversial. Although the court ultimately determines whether someone is legally competent and responsible for his own behavior, the psychologist and psychiatrist must provide the court with the considered information required for such a decision. This information is based on the assessment process, and the validity of the assessment techniques employed by most psychologists and psychiatrists has come under repeated attack by members of the legal and the mental health professions. This alleged invalidity is of particular importance in the assessment of dangerousness, since the evaluative measures are required to predict future behavior. This problem is compounded by the ambiguity of the concept and definitions of dangerousness, the ethical considerations of involuntary confinement, and the acceptability of certain testing techniques in the courtroom.

One must also ask whom the psychologist represents in the courtroom, if indeed anyone. For example, should the psychologist consider the best interest of the patient-client in a decision that pits personal freedom against involuntary treatment or commitment? What is the role of informed consent in the assessment interview of an acknowledged psychotic or mentally retarded person (Stone, 1977)? Should the psychologist issue a warning prior to the evaluation; that is, a statement informing the individual that what he says may be used against him in a court of law (*Miranda* v. *State of Arizona*, 1966)?

Perhaps the most difficult problem one has in dealing with forensic psychology is that, as the name suggests, it is a combination of at least two complex, infinitely variable, and constantly changing fields. Since there are municipal, state, and federal court systems, each with different legal codes, which in turn may be interpreted differently by judges in the same jurisdiction, it is almost impossible to state a specific definition of criminal responsibility or dangerousness that would require, entail, or indicate commitment. The fields of psychology and psychiatry are equally varied and dynamic, each separately and in common possessing a variety of theories, diagnostic and therapeutic methods, and interpretive principles. As illustration, it would be difficult to compare the current statutes and psychological-psychiatric attitudes about homosexuality with those of only a decade ago.

Assessment. While it is not the intent of this chapter to analyze measurement validity and reliability, it is necessary to note that the quality of psychological assessment and reporting has been a major source of criticism by certain members of the legal profession. Judge David Bazelon, who handed down the "Durham Rule," has stated: "Psychiatry, I suppose, is the ultimate wizardry. My experience has shown that in no case is it more difficult to elicit productive and reliable expert testimony than in cases that call on the knowledge and practice of psychiatry" (Bazelon, 1974, p. 18). The criticism is based mainly on the types of assessment employed; that is, the clinical interview and a standard battery of intelligence tests and projectives such as the Rorschach and the Thematic Apperception Test. The validity, reliability, and objectivity of these tests have been questioned. Ziskin (1970) in his relevant book presents two full chapters that report limited validity of such measures. Although other studies may support their validity, one cannot say that they are accurate "beyond a reasonable doubt," as required by a court of law (Poythress, 1977). Gardner (1976) has raised the possibility of biases creeping into subjective assessments such as interviews and projectives, especially in cases where there may be ethical and moral issues such as knowledge of right and wrong. If these measures are not reliable indicators of the present status of the subject, how can they be used to assess past behavior or future behavior such as dangerousness? Indeed, Livermore, Malmquist, and Meehl (1968) have suggested that an actuarial approach would be superior to the clinical method of prediction. According to Gough (1962), actuarial prediction is superior to the clinical method, and sociologists are better predictors of the outcome of parole than psychiatrists are (see also Meehl, 1954).

There is also a problem of how the results of tests are presented to the court, in addition to the problems inherent in the measures themselves. Nash (1974) notes that the expert witness will frequently seek to justify a conclusion simply by referring to "clinical experience or feeling" without reference to data to support such assertions or conclusions. Bazelon (1974) alludes to the same problem. Such testimony might be viewed as less objective, impartial, and accurate than that of other expert witnesses, such as ballistics specialists.

Other assessment methods warrant mention at this point. The use of so-called lie detectors and truth drugs, which may help the examiner verify the subject's report, are of limited acceptability in a court, and the subject may in fact decline such methods. Electroencephalography and skull X rays may be useful in detecting head injuries and brain damage from other sources. In recent years, there has been some interest in XYY chromosomes and their reported effect on violent behavior (Jacobs, Brunton, and Melville, 1965; Montagu, 1968), because a disproportionate number of violent criminals allegedly have this chromosomal abnormality; however, no conclusive evidence supports such a contention.

Criminal Responsibility and Competency. According to Davidson (1965), responsibility indicates a duty or immunity, whereas competency refers to a right or privilege, such as making a contract. It is the duty of the court to determine whether the defendant has the mental capacity to stand trial or make a contract, or whether he should be held accountable for a criminal act that occurred in the past during a period when his mental condition was such that he was not "responsible" for his actions.

In general, most definitions of criminal responsibility are based on the 1843 M'Naughten Rule, which was developed in England: "To escape responsibility, the defendant must show that he was laboring under such defect of reason from disease of the mind as not to know the nature and quality of the act; or, if he did know it, that he did not know that he was doing what was wrong" (Davidson, 1965, p. 1). According to M'Naughten, the psychological or psychiatric examiner must investigate four basic factors. First, he must diagnose the defendant's mental condition at the time the act was committed. In most instances the only diagnosis acceptable under M'Naughten would be that of psychosis, since most neuroses would not negate responsibility in a legal sense. Second, it must be determined whether the defendant knew the physical quality of the act; for example, did he know that a knife can cut the skin? Third, the defendant's knowledge of the implications of the act in question must be evaluated; did he know, for example, that cutting someone's skin might be harmful? Fourth, the assessment focuses on the defendant's knowledge that the act was wrong—not, as Davidson (1965) notes, in the philosophical sense of good versus evil, but in the concrete legal sense. For example, Robin Hood may have philosophically justified his stealing from the wealthy in order to give to the poor, but he knew that stealing is legally wrong, as shown by his actions in flight from the authorities. This information is reported to the court, and it is the court and not the psychologist who then determines responsibility. A person diagnosed as psychotic, for example, might be held responsible by the court and accountable for the act. Or the court might find the defendant only partially responsible: for instance, lacking the capacity required for the intent and premeditation required for some crimes but capable of knowing the nature, quality, and wrongfulness of the act. In the state of California, this form of partial responsibility is known as diminished capacity (*People* v. *Gorshen,* 1959; *People* v. *Wells,* 1949). Such a doctrine allows for factors other than insanity to be presented to the court to demonstrate that the defendant did not have specific intent at the time of the crime. Such a defense would include an otherwise sane person who was intoxicated when he killed someone (*People* v. *Mosher,* 1969).

In 1954 a decision of the U.S. Court of Appeals for the District of Columbia resulted in the "Durham Formula," which held that a person is not responsible if his illegal act was the result of a mental disease or defect. According to this formula, less emphasis is placed on past history or the nature of the defendant's understanding. This formula, however, has not received as widespread acceptance by courts as the M'Naughten Rule.

The concept of competency to stand trial was studied by a National Institute of Mental Health committee in 1973. In its report the committee defined competence to stand trial as "the capacity to adequately defend [oneself] against . . . accusers in a court of law. The criteria for this capacity include an understanding of the nature of the legal process, a recognition of the consequences that could follow from the accusation, and the ability to assist legal counsel in one's own defense" (National Institute of Mental Health, 1973, p. 1; see also *Dusky* v. *United States,* 1960). While the NIMH research was done primarily in Massachusetts, the results may be worth considering in the context of other jurisdictions.

Briefly stated, some of the committee's observations were critical of the process for evaluating competency to stand trial. For instance, both the courts and mental health experts often do not understand the distinction between criminal responsibility and competency to stand trial. Unlike the general principle of criminal law that one is innocent unless and until proven guilty, in cases of competency there seems to be an underlying assumption of incompetency until proven otherwise. Legally, however, there should be a presumption of competence (*Lotman* v. *Security Mutual Life Insurance Company,* 1973). The study also found that the issue of competency is raised too frequently for the mentally disordered and too infrequently for the mentally retarded. As part of the project, two measurement instruments were developed to evaluate competency: the Competency Screening Test and the Competency Assessment Instrument (National Institute of Mental Health, 1973).

Competency is required in other important areas, such as marriage, divorce, contracts, and wills. As illustration, the marriage of a person who lacks the capacity to understand the requirements of marriage (for instance, someone who was intoxicated or psychotic at the time of the marriage) can be annuled on the grounds of lack of capacity at the time of marriage. In some cases, the incompetence of a spouse may prevent a divorce action, although the New York Domestic Relations Law (S-140) does allow for the annulment of a marriage on the ground of incurable insanity for five years (Zussman and Carnahan, 1974). Competency in making a will would require that the person know (1) that he is making a will; (2) the nature and extent of his property; and (3) those to whom he would naturally leave his property—that is, family and close friends. He does not have to leave anything at all to such persons, but he should at least know who they are. Lack of competency in contracts must be due to mental disorder and not simply to lack of technical knowledge.

Involuntary commitment is one of the most controversial aspects of forensic psychology, since the individual is being hospitalized against his will, ostensibly for treatment of a disorder. The state's commitment power is based on the principle of *parens patriae,* which is the power that citizens invest in the state to protect them. In the past, the free exercise of this power, with little review or due process, may have led to some abuse of the system. At one time, a woman could be committed by her husband without evidence of insanity (Slovenko, 1977). In 1975 the United States Supreme Court ruled that "the State cannot constitutionally confine without more [reason] a nondangerous individual who is capable of surviving safely in freedom by himself or with the help of willing and responsible family members and friends" (*O'Connor* v. *Donaldson,* 1975, p. 576). This decision raises three important issues: (1) the definition of the "dangerousness" required for commitment; (2) the concept of the "right to treatment"; and (3) the "least restrictive alternative" for treatment.

The general definition of dangerousness has been "dangerous to self and/or others" (Stone, 1977, p. 276); however, this definition is vague and in some cases has been interpreted so loosely as to mean even the writing of bad checks (*Overholser* v. *Russell,* 1960; *United States* v. *Charnizon,* 1967). The courts have sought to narrow the definition of dangerousness, and while such definitions vary widely, they generally reflect the likelihood of harm to self or others. This raises for the forensic psychologist the question of the prediction of such behavior. Shah (1975) cites a number of studies indicating that no current measures accurately predict dangerousness. In fact, several of these studies indicate that the incidence of violence among the general population is higher than that of the mentally disordered. As mentioned, there are those who feel that psychologists and psychiatrists are not as accurate as actuarial prediction and perhaps should not be involved, therefore, in such procedures. Rosen (1954) notes that there is very little likelihood of accuracy in predicting low-frequency occurrences, such as suicide, and that there may be from 50 to 99 false positives for each correct identification. To date, no adequate method of predicting dangerousness has been developed, and the problem remains.

The committed person's right to treatment is a concept and court ruling with far-reaching consequences. As Judge Frank Johnson has said: "To deprive any citizen of his or her liberty upon the altruistic theory that the confinement is for human and therapeutic reasons, and then fail to provide adequate treatment, violates the very fundamentals of due process" (*Wyatt* v. *Stickney,* 1972, p. 377). This same judge was responsible for the court's takeover of Alabama's mental hospitals in order to provide the opportunity for better treatment. While few would dispute the concept of the right to treatment, some do question what constitutes this right; that is, what is proper treatment? Stone (1974, 1977) has raised other questions about the right to treatment. For example, since the court decision does nothing to change existing resources, who will pay for and provide improved conditions in hospitals? Second, this mandate may have led to what is termed in some circles the "revolving door" for chronic patients who are not permitted to remain in long-term facilities, since the care available there is considered inadequate, and who therefore receive little or no care.

Recent mental health codes have specified that treatment should be done in the least restrictive settings. This has contributed to the movement toward community psychology, emphasizing outpatient treatment and involvement of members of the patient's family and community.

Comparative Philosophies and Theories

The various and often conflicting philosophies and techniques which are applicable to psychological theory and assessment in general (for example, psychodynamic versus behavioral and subjective tests versus objective) are also applicable and equally controversial in forensic assessment and therefore do not warrant separate comment. However, there is a particular philosophical schism to which forensic assessment is heir. Psychologists and lawyers often are working at cross-purposes because they differ on how to best serve the patient or defendant. This dichotomy is illustrated by the controversy over dangerousness. Shah (1975) notes that the lawyer's maxim would be "When in doubt, acquit." If it cannot be proved beyond a reasonable doubt that the individual is dangerous to self or others, then there should be no commitment to an institution and no involuntary treatment. The psychologist, however, would probably follow the maxim "When in doubt, treat," in order to be on the safe side. The lawyer seeks to avoid a Type I error (to predict violence erroneously), and the psychologist seeks to avoid a Type II error (the failure to anticipate a dangerous act).

Another controversy involves the application of the adversary system to psychiatric-medical issues. Some hold that the courtroom provides the necessary controls to protect the rights of the individual (Costopoulos, 1972; Thibaut and Walker, 1975). Others question whether the courtroom is designed for decisions of this nature (Redmount, 1971; Stone, 1977). Stone (p. 278) concludes: "I have presented a view of mental health litigation that many litigating attorneys would violently protest. . . . The legal solutions secured in the courtrooms have established the impressive edifice of due process, but beyond that legal structure, human suffering continues unabated and its relief is more difficult to achieve."

Elaboration on Critical Points

In his book designed to enable lawyers to deal with psychological testimony, Ziskin (1970) provides an important critique of psychological assessment. The data that lawyers can use to challenge the validity and reliability of the assessment measures, and hence the credibility and relevance of the expert testimony, are derived from the literature of psychology itself. Accordingly, lawyers can, in a sense, hoist the psychologists on their own petards by citing the published scientific data of the psychologists' own colleagues. Ziskin questions the validity and reliability of psychological tests and of the numerous diagnoses formulated by psychiatrists and psychologists. He cites numerous studies and reviews, such as those appearing in the *Sixth Mental Measurements Yearbook* (Buros, 1965) and others, which repudiate the predictive and concurrent validity of projective "techniques": "The Rorschach was found to have little or no predictive or concurrent validity when checked against such criteria as psychiatric diagnosis [and] response to therapy (Anastasi, 1961, p. 572). Plaut and Cromwell (1955) found that expert psychologists could only correctly identify 56.7 percent of drawings between what could be two clearly distinguishable groups, deteriorated schizophrenics versus normals. Goldberg (1959) found that staff psychologists using the Bender Gestalt Test were only able to distinguish records of patients with brain damage from those of nonorganic psychiatric origin with a 65 percent accuracy. Walker and Lyndon (1967) found that experienced psychologists were only able to perform at a rate of 49 percent correct in interpreting Sentence Completion Tests" (Ziskin, 1970, p. 142). Even the objective Minnesota Multiphasic Personality Inventory predicted final clinical diagnosis of new psychiatric admissions in only 60 percent of cases (Buros, 1965).

In his discussion of the reliability of mental diagnosis, Ziskin cites a number of studies reporting an agreement on diagnosis of 60 percent between two psychiatrists (Ash, 1949; Spitzer and others, 1967; Zubin, 1967) and 45 percent when there were three psychiatrists (Ash, 1949).

While Ziskin emphasizes the research reporting low validity and reliability, and gives little attention to the many other studies describing positive results, the skillful use of the negative data by a lawyer may effectively challenge and negate the testimony of many a competent expert witness.

Personal Views and Recommendations

Interdisciplinary skills are required if one is to function as a professional specialist in the field of forensic conditions. This would be true for psychologists, attorneys, and especially for judges. While most law schools have at least an introductory course dealing with psychology and psychiatry, relatively few clinical psychology training programs have a parallel course on forensics. Even so, the basic course available in the typical law school is not truly adequate, and both psychology and the law would benefit from cross-fertilization. In mid 1978 joint psychology-law degree programs were available at schools such as Johns Hopkins University and the University of Maryland; and this type of curriculum, which awards both degrees, will likely increase as the demand for forensic specialists increases. In the absence of such joint degree programs, consideration might be given to postgraduate courses attended by members of both professions and taught by experts from both fields. Not only would such courses expose both professions to common academic material but each group would be enabled to gain an insight to the other. This method might also foster increased sensitivity between the specialties, leading to enhanced cooperation in the courtroom.

Application to Particular Variables

Age. Forensic conditions affect people of virtually every age category. However, the legal rights of one group in particular—namely, children—have lagged behind those of the rest of the population. It is only within the past decade that (1) children were granted the right to legal representation in criminal cases, (2) girls were permitted to have abortions without their parents' consent, and (3) students were allowed a hearing when faced with disciplinary suspension from school. Parents were given almost total freedom in matters regarding the commitment and treatment of their children, and such freedom often led to abuse. In 1978 the U.S. Supreme Court heard the case of a young woman whose parents had requested that she be sterilized at the age of 15. The parents' request was not supported by any reported psychological or medical reports nor any mention of their daughter's I.Q. In fact, the parents admitted that she was in the appropriate grade in public school for children her age. The daughter was not told about the nature of the request and there is no evidence that the judge even met the girl before granting the order the very same day it was requested. The girl was taken to the hospital and told she would have her appendix removed. Instead, a tubal ligation was performed and she was sterilized. The Supreme Court ruled that despite the lack of formality in the court order, the judge was absolutely immune from damages liability (*Stump* v. *Sparkman,* 1978). The rights of minor children are expanding, however, and precommitment hearings have been mandated in some states (Goldstein, Freud, and Solnit, 1973).

Sex. Forensic conditions apply to both genders. The homosexual population provides an illustration of the changing nature of forensic matters. In the not too distant past, homosexuality was considered a distinct diagnostic category of mental disorder. Subsequently, the American Psychiatric Association declared that it is no longer a psychiatric diagnosis. There has also been a movement toward decriminalization and mandated equal rights in many jurisdictions, but this trend has recently encountered vocal opposition from some circles.

In addition, the United States Congress has passed the Equal Rights Amendment to the constitution, which would provide equality for women in all areas. If the required number of states ratify this amendment, it may have a significant effect on employment and on traditional family gender-based roles.

Education. The courts have become involved in the implementation of the mandate that every child must receive an appropriate education in the proper setting. That is, children diagnosed as learning disabled or otherwise handicapped are legally entitled to special classes, as are the mentally retarded (*Mills* v. *Board of Education of District of Columbia,* 1972; Education for All Handicapped Children Act, 1975). The validity of the diagnosis and the appropriateness of the placement may, of course, be contested by the child's parents. In addition, there has been an increase in the number of lawsuits by students and their parents to receive compensation for what they consider an inadequate education (*Pennsylvania Association for Retarded Children* v. *Commonwealth of Pennsylvania,* 1971).

Ethnic-Racial Factors. Forensic conditions apply to all racial and ethnic groups. Some minorities have recently brought the issue of psychological testing to court, alleging that the tests—especially intelligence tests—as constructed lead to discrimination. A Federal District Court in California recently ruled on this question saying that the use of these intelligence tests resulted in a grossly disproportionate number of black children in classes for the "educably mentally retarded" and, therefore, violates Title VI of the 1964 Civil Rights Act, the 1973 Rehabilitation Act, and the 1975 Education for All Handicapped Children Act. California was enjoined from using any standardized intelligence tests for placement of black children in "educably mentally retarded" classes without prior permission of the court. In addition, New York State has passed a law (effective January, 1980) requiring testing agencies which administer the standardized placement examinations (such as the SAT, LSAT, and GRE) to make available copies of the examination as well as scored test results (New York Education Law, 1979). Similar federal legislation has already been proposed. Both of these decisions will have a major impact on the design, use, and regulation of psychological tests.

References

Anastasi, A. *Psychological Testing.* (2nd ed.) New York: Macmillan, 1961.

Ash, P. "The Reliability of Psychiatric Diagnosis." *Journal of Abnormal and Social Psychology,* 1949, *44,* 272-276.

Bazelon, D. L. "Psychiatrists and the Adversary Process." *Scientific American,* 1974, *230,* 18-23.

Bromberg, W. *Crime and the Mind.* New York: Macmillan, 1965.

Brown v. *Board of Education,* 349 U.S. 294 (1954).

Buros, O. *Sixth Mental Measurements Yearbook.* Highland Park, N.J.: Gryphon Press, 1965.

Costopoulos, W. C. "Persuasion in the Courtroom." *Duquesne Law Review,* 1972, *10,* 384-409.

Davidson, H. A. *Forensic Psychiatry.* (2nd ed.) New York: Ronald Press, 1965.

Durham v. *United States,* 214 F2d 862 (1954).

Dusky v. *United States,* 362 U.S. 402 (1960).

Ebbinghaus, H. In *Encyclopedia Judaica.* Vol. 13. Jerusalem: Keter, 1970.

Education for All Handicapped Children Act, Public Law 94-142 (1975).

Freud, S. "Psychoanalysis and the Ascertaining of Truth in Courts of Law" [1906]. In *Collected Papers.* Vol. 2. New York: Basic Books, 1959.

Gardner, M. R. "The Myth of the Impartial Psychiatric Expert: Some Comments Concerning Responsibility and the Decline of the Age of Therapy." *Law and Psychology Review,* 1976, *2,* 99-118.

Goldberg, L. R. "The Effectiveness of Clinicians' Judgment." *Journal of Consulting Psychology,* 1959, *23,* 25-33.

Goldstein, J., Freud, A., and Solnit, A. J. *Beyond the Best Interests of the Child.* New York: Free Press, 1973.

Gordon, R. I. "The Application of Psychology to the Law." *Law and Psychology Review,* 1976, *2,* 1-8.

Gormally, J., and Brodsky, S. L. "Utilization and Training of Psychologists in the Criminal System." *American Psychologist,* 1973, *28,* 926-928.

Gough, H. "Clinical Versus Statistical Prediction." In L. J. Postman (Ed.), *Psychology in the Making.* New York: Knopf, 1962.

Jacobs, P. A., Brunton, M., and Melville, M. M. "Aggressive Behavior, Mental Subnormality, and the XYY Male." *Nature,* 1965, *208,* 1351-1352.

Larry P. v. *Riles,* 343 F. Supp. 1306 (1972); update, USDC N Calif Oct. 16, 1979.

Livermore, J. M., Malmquist, C. P., and Meehl, P. E. "On the Justification of Civil Commitment." *University of Pennsylvania Law Review,* 1968, *117,* 75-96.

Lotman v. *Security Mutual Life Insurance Company,* 478 F2d 868 (3rd Cir. 1973).

M'Naughten's Case, 8 Eng Rep 718 (1843).

Meehl, P. E. *Clinical Versus Statistical Prediction.* Minneapolis: University of Minnesota Press, 1954.

Mills v. *Board of Education of District of Columbia,* CA No. 1939-71 (1972).

Miranda v. *State of Arizona,* 384 U.S. 436 (1966).

Montagu, A. "Chromosomes and Crime." *Psychology Today,* 1968, *2,* 42-49.

Nash, M. M. "Parameters and Distinctiveness of Psychological Testimony." *Professional Psychology,* 1974, *5,* 239-243.

National Institute of Mental Health. *Competency to Stand Trial and Mental Illness.* Washington, D.C.: U.S. Government Printing Office, 1973.

New York Education Law. Standardized testing. Article 7-A, Section 340 (1979).

O'Connor v. *Donaldson,* 422 U.S. 563 (1975).

Overholser v. *Russell,* 283 F2d 195 (1960).

Pennsylvania Association for Retarded Children v. *Commonwealth of Pennsylvania,* 334 F. Supp. 1257 (E.D. Pa. 1971).

People v. *Gorshen,* 51 Cal 2d 716 (1959).

People v. *Mosher,* 1 Cal 3d 379 (1969).

People v. *Wells,* 33 Cal 2d 330 (1949).

Plaut, E., and Cromwell, B. "The Ability of the Clinical Psychologist to Discriminate Between Drawings by Schizophrenics and Normal Subjects." *Psychological Reports,* 1955, *1,* 153-158.

Poythress, N. G., Jr. "Mental Health Expert Testimony: Current Problems." *Journal of Law and Psychiatry,* 1977, *5,* 201-227.

Redmount, R. S. "Persuasion, Rules of Evidence, and the Process of Trial." *Loyola University Law Review,* 1971, *4,* 253-278.

Rosen, A. "Detection of Suicidal Patients: An Example of Some Limitations in the Prediction of Infrequent Events." *Journal of Consulting Psychology,* 1954, *18,* 397-403.

Rubin, B. "Prediction of Dangerousness in Mentally Ill Criminals." *Archives of General Psychiatry,* 1972, *27,* 397-407.

Shah, S. A. "Dangerousness and Civil Commitment of the Mentally Ill: Some Public Policy Considerations." *American Journal of Psychiatry,* 1975, *132,* 501-505.

Slovenko, R. "Criminal Justice Procedures in Civil Commitment." *Hospital and Community Psychiatry,* 1977, *28,* 817-826.

Spitzer, R. L., and others. "Quantification of Agreement in Psychiatric Diagnosis." *Archives of General Psychiatry,* 1967, *17,* 83-87.

Stone, A. "The Right to Treatment and the Psychiatric Establishment." *Psychiatric Annals,* 1974, *4,* 21-42.

Stone, A. "Recent Mental Health Litigation: A Critical Perspective." *American Journal of Psychiatry,* 1977, *134,* 273-279.

Stump v. *Sparkman,* 98 S. Ct. 1099 (1978).

Thibaut, J., and Walker, L. *Procedural Justice: A Psychological Analysis.* Hillsdale, N.J.: Erlbaum, 1975.

United States v. *Charnizon,* 232 A2d 586, 588 (1967).

United States v. *Jenkins,* 307 F2d 637 (D.C. Cir. 1962).

Walker, R. C., and Lyndon, J. "Varying Degrees of Psychological Sophistication in the Interpretation of Sentence Completion Data." *Journal of Clinical Psychology,* 1967, *23,* 229-231.

Wyatt v. *Stickney,* 344 F. Supp. 373 (M.D. Alabama 1972).

Ziskin, J. *Coping with Psychiatric Testimony.* Beverly Hills, Calif.: Law and Psychiatry Press, 1970.

Zubin, J. "Classification of the Behavior Disorders." In *Annual Review of Psychology.* Palo Alto, Calif.: Annual Reviews, 1967.

Zussman, J., and Carnahan, W. A. "Psychiatry and the Law: Changing the System Through Changing the Training." *American Journal of Psychiatry,* 1974, *131,* 915-918.

Name Index

A

Abel, G. G., 315, 317, 675, 681, 685, 687, 691
Abidin, R., 95, 98
Abikoff, H., 270, 279
Aboud, J., 990, 993
Abraham, K., 640, 654
Abrams, S., 129, 146, 500, 506
Abramson, L., 597, 598
Abramson, P. R., 603, 607, 608, 609, 610, 612
Abroms, G. M., 812, 816
Abse, D. W., 188
Abt, L. E., 98, 101
Abudabbeh, N. N., 436
Ach, N., 891
Achenbach, T. M., 113-127
Acker, M., 469-470, 472, 812, 818
Ackerman, M. W., 75, 79, 85
Ackerman, P. T., 269, 273, 276, 277, 279, 514-515, 519
Adams, G. R., 17n, 35, 43

Adams, R. L., 436, 702, 710
Adelman, H. S., 797, 799
Adelman, S., 912-913, 914, 918
Adler, A., 52, 58, 65, 66, 130, 131, 482, 484, 488, 603, 836, 846, 1061, 1066
Adler, D., 491, 493, 494, 495
Adler, F., 32, 39
Adorno, T. W., 464, 470, 483, 485, 488, 988, 991, 997, 1000, 1004, 1007, 1008, 1009, 1011, 1013, 1016, 1017, 1018, 1019, 1020, 1025, 1026, 1028, 1030
Affleck, D. C., 1044, 1047
Agle, D. P., 152, 162
Ahammer, I. M., 33, 39
Akutagawa, D. A., 565, 569
Albano, R. F., 231, 232, 239, 243
Albaugh, W. P., 1044, 1047
Albe-Fessard, D., 1089, 1099
Albert, R. S., 729-743
Albright, L. E., 989, 992
Alexander, F., 151, 162, 310, 317

Alexander, S., 565, 571
Algren, A., 769, 775
Alker, H. A., 432, 436
Alkire, A., 84, 85
Allan, K. H., 436
Allan, T. K., 436
Allan, W., 310, 317
Allegra, D., 154, 162
Allen, D. T., 852, 857
Allen, R., 266, 283
Allen, T., 289, 293
Allen, V. L., 975-983
Alley, G. R., 277, 279
Allinsmith, W., 368, 369, 372
Allison, J., 354, 358, 532, 536
Allon, N., 323, 328
Allport, F. H., 976, 982
Allport, G. W., 395, 399, 483, 488
Almquist, C., 465, 466, 469, 472
Alpern, G. D., 123, 125
Alpert, M., 814, 816
Alpert, R., 364, 374
Alschuler, A. S., 768, 774
Alstalt, L., 475-476, 480

Dennerll, R. D., 1073, 1076
Denney, D., 153, 163
Dennis, M., 815, 817
Denny, N. W., 24, 40
Denny, R., 977, 983
Densen, M., 354, 357, 359
Denzin, N. K., 89, 99, 212, 219
DePalma, D. J., 365, 372
Depue, R. A., 588, 592, 599
Deren, S., 703, 712
DeRenzi, E., 227, 228
Derlaga, V. J., 446, 450, 452
Derogatis, L. R., 466, 471
Descartes, R., 351, 1089, 1093, 1099
De Soto, C., 856, 858
Dessen, W., 800
Deubner, D. C., 316, 317
Deutsch, A., 1105, 1110
Deutsch, C. P., 96, 99
Deutsch, F., 33, 41
Deutsch, H., 89, 99, 685, 688, 690, 692, 1078, 1086
Deutsch, M., 1010, 1011, 1014
De Vos, G., 58, 499, 504, 505, 506
Dewey, J., 376
DeWolfe, A. S., 1064, 1066, 1079, 1086
Dey, G. R., 485, 489
Dhillon, P. K., 61, 71
Diab, L. N., 1025, 1030
Diamond, M. C., 814, 819
Diamond, S., 402, 408
Dick, A. O., 881, 887
Dick, R., 904, 909
Dick-Read, G., 1090, 1099
Dickens, C., 921
Dickens, S. L., 1021, 1030
Dicks, H. V., 65, 71
Dickson, C. R., 565, 570
Dickstein, E., 384, 388
Diers, E., 97, 98
Dillehay, R. C., 997, 1005
Dilling, C. A., 357, 359
Dillon, H. J., 706, 711
Dimond, S. J., 813, 816
Di Nardo, P. A., 144, 145
Dittman, A. T., 958, 963
di Vesta, F. J., 435, 440
Dix, D. L., 201
Doane, B., 456, 461
Docherty, J. P., 314-315, 318
Dodd, B. E., 237, 240
Dodds, J. B., 123, 126
Dodson, L. S., 393, 399
Dohrenwend, B. P., 57, 58, 144, 145
Dohrenwend, B. S., 57, 58, 144, 145
Doktor, R., 815, 817
Dolby, R. M., 932, 935, 936, 938, 940
Dole, V., 236, 240
Doleys, D. M., 290, 291, 293
Doll, E. A., 118, 126, 780, 788

Dollard, J., 130, 132, 483, 488, 552, 557, 560, 570
Dollin, A., 1045, 1047
Dommert, E. M., 1022, 1031
Donaldson, G., 705, 711
Doris, J., 716, 728
Doster, J. A., 447, 448, 450, 452
Douglas, V. I., 119, 126, 267, 269, 274, 278, 280, 284, 354, 357, 359
Doyle, A. C., 233
Doyle, K. O., Jr., 698, 711
Drachman, R. H., 160, 162
Draguns, J., xxxv, xxxix, 467-468, 469, 471, 499, 500, 505, 507
Drellich, M. G., 1078, 1086
Dresen, S., 97, 99
Drevdahl, J. E., 747, 753
Driessen, O., 303, 305
Drolette, M., 541, 545, 548
Drye, R. C., 343, 348, 624, 628
Dubeck, J. A., 609, 610
Dubey, D. R., 278, 280
Dubner, R., 1090, 1094, 1099
DuBois, P. H., 698, 711
Dudek, S. Z., 503, 505, 506, 520-539, 873, 875
Duff, F. L., 557
Duffy, E. L., 235, 243
Duke, M. P., 864, 865, 867
Duker, J., 214, 217, 355, 359
du Laurens, G., 685
Dumas, R. G., 1078, 1086
Dunbar, H. F., 245, 254, 310, 317
Dunham, H., 57, 58
Dunham, H. W., 211, 217
Dunham, R. M., 79, 85
Dunn, J. A., 568, 570
Dunn, L. M., 716, 727, 782, 788, 794, 800
Dunne, E. E., 66, 71
Dunnette, M. D., 988, 992
Durbin, E. F. N., 552, 557
Duvall, E. R., 79, 85
Dworkin, G., 9, 14
Dwyer, J., 322, 328
Dyer, W. W., 17, 40-41
Dykman, R. A., 267, 269, 273, 276, 277, 279, 280, 514-515, 519
Dymond, R., 445, 454

E

Eagle, C. J., 499, 500, 506-507, 531, 537
Eagly, A. H., 981, 982
Earhart, J., 267, 283
Earle, K. M., 302, 305-306
Earnest, M. P., 302, 306
Easton, W., 17n
Eaton, M. T., 199n, 212, 217
Ebaugh, F. G., 266, 280
Ebbinghaus, H., 891, 900, 1112, 1120
Eber, H. W., 342, 348, 482, 483, 486, 487, 488, 594, 599

Eckelman, C. C., 1108, 1110
Edelbrock, C. S., 114, 120, 121, 124, 125
Edelman, M. W., 436, 438
Edinger, J. D., 1081, 1085
Edmonds, J. M., 956, 963
Edmunds, G., 355, 359, 551-558
Edwards, A. L., 482, 483, 488, 1073, 1075
Edwards, P., 391, 399
Edwards, W., 429, 431, 438
Egbert, L. D., 1090, 1091, 1099
Egeth, H., 880, 887
Ehrenkrantz, J., 546, 548
Ehrenwald, J., 624, 628
Ehrhardt, A. A., 659, 670, 709, 710-711
Ehrle, R., 1064, 1066
Ehrlich, D., 466, 471
Ehrlich, H. J., 1029, 1031
Eichlseder, W., 278, 284
Eiduson, B. T., 733, 741
Eisdorfer, C., 21, 23, 25, 41, 45
Eisenberg, L., 265, 282
Eisenberg-Berg, N., 365, 374
Eisler, R., 566, 570
Eissler, K. R., 842, 847
Ekehammar, B., 584
Ekman, P., 956, 957, 958, 960, 961, 963, 966, 973
Eland, F. A., 449, 450, 452
Eldridge, R., 709, 711
Elias, J. W., 18, 28, 29, 41
Elias, M. F., 18, 28, 29, 41
Elias, P. K., 18, 28, 29, 41
Elizur, A., 499, 505, 507
Elizur, E., 287, 288, 294
Elkind, A. H., 310, 317
Elkins, J., 801
Ellenberg, J. H., 302, 306
Ellenberger, H. F., 130, 146, 211, 218, 943n, 953
Ellingson, R. J., 543, 548
Elliott, L. L., 806, 817
Ellis, A., 63, 130, 145, 396, 399, 412, 413, 419, 579, 584, 618, 620, 1027
Ellis, H. H., 685, 692, 732, 741
Ellis, M. J., 273, 280
Ellison, D. L., 155, 163
Ellsworth, P. C., 957, 963
Elman, R., 1078, 1086
Elrod, J. T., 270, 271, 272, 284, 285
Elzey, E. F., 718, 726
Emerson, P. E., 625, 628
Endicott, J., 346, 348, 588, 600
Endicott, N. A., 346, 348
Endler, N. S., 90, 99, 557, 562, 563, 564, 570-571, 1081, 1082, 1086
Endman, M. W., 273, 279
Enelow, A., 158, 163
Engel, B. T., 289, 290, 293
Engel, G., 48, 58

Heidegger, M., 411, 419, 445
Heider, F., 415, 419, 767
Heikkinen, C. A., 1013, 1014
Heilbrun, A. B., 4, 14, 467-468,
470, 471-472, 486, 488, 662,
663, 664, 670, 935, 940
Heilizer, F., 435, 439
Heilman, K. M., 297-298, 306
Heine, R. W., 1044, 1048
Heinrich, P., 582, 585
Heinroth, J. C. A., 151
Heist, P., 1019, 1031
Hekmat, H., 1027, 1032
Held, J. M., 495
Helfer, R. E., 95, 99, 101
Hellebusch, S., 870, 872, 873, 876
Heller, K., 449, 453
Heller, P. L., 80, 86
Helmholtz, H. von, 351
Helmreich, R., 660, 661, 663, 667,
668, 671
Hemphill, J. K., 988, 993
Henderson, D., 487, 488
Henderson, L., 880, 888
Henderson, P. B., 7, 16
Hendler, N., 1092, 1100
Hendrick, I., 502, 508
Henker, B., 267, 275, 285
Henry, G. W., 219
Herbert, M. E., 173, 188
Hergenhahn, B. R., 432, 440
Herman, A., 1012, 1014
Herman, K. D., 144, 146
Hermelin, B., 899, 901
Heron, W., 456, 461
Herr, E. L., 103-112
Herrick, C. J., 48, 58
Herrick, J. W., 151, 161, 164
Herriot, P., 892, 894, 897, 898,
899, 900
Herron, W. G., 345, 348
Hersch, C., 747, 753, 842, 848
Hersen, M., 562, 564, 565, 569,
571, 722, 727
Hertzman, M., 826, 832
Herzog, E., 90, 99
Heshka, S., 863, 867
Heslin, R., 1029, 1031
Hess, R. D., 91, 92, 94, 96, 99
Hessellund, H., 690, 693
Hester, R. N., 1094, 1101
Hetherington, E. M., 34, 41, 84, 86,
91, 94-95, 100
Hewlett, J. H. G., 492, 496, 812,
819
Heyman, D. S., 608, 611
Heyns, R. W., 979, 983
Hickey, J., 387, 388
Hicks, M. W., 60, 61, 62, 71
Hiers, J. M., 861, 867
Higbee, K. L., 430, 431, 435, 439
Higdon, J. F., 1108, 1110
Hildreth, G., 734, 741
Hiler, E., 583, 585
Hilf, F., 470, 472
Hilgard, E. R., 152, 164, 933, 936-

937, 940, 942-943, 944, 948,
951, 953, 954, 1090, 1092,
1100
Hilgard, J. R., 235, 241
Hill, D., 192, 198, 541, 543, 549
Hill, E. F., 1108, 1110
Hill, H. E., 235, 241, 1091, 1100
Hill, W., 988, 993
Hilliard, L., 756, 763
Himelstein, P., 449, 452, 453
Himes, B. S., 46-59
Himmelsbach, C. K., 235, 241
Hinchliffe, M. K., 958, 963
Hindmarsh, J. R., 289, 294
Hinds, E., 912, 917
Hines, G. H., 990, 993
Hinesley, R. K., 238, 240
Hinrichs, J. R., 986, 989, 993
Hinton, J. W., 546, 549, 550
Hinzie, L. E., 199-200, 217
Hippocrates, 200, 296, 319-320,
400-401, 589
Hiroto, D. S., 258-259, 263
Hirsch, S. J., 162, 164
Hirsch, S. R., 97, 100
Hirt, M. L., xxxii, xxxix, 512-519,
885, 889
Hitzig, E., 221
Hoagland, H., 354, 356, 360
Hobart, C., 1021, 1030
Hobbes, T., 474, 1070
Hobbs, N., 1, 6, 14, 719, 721, 727
Hoch, P. H., 685, 693
Hochman, M., 1062, 1064, 1065,
1067
Hodges, F. J., 302, 305
Hodgsson, R., 566, 573
Hoepfner, R., 871, 872, 873, 874,
875
Hoffman, L. W., 34, 42, 903, 909
Hoffman, M. L., 364, 369, 373,
383, 387, 903, 909, 979, 982
Hoffman, S. P., 277, 281, 958, 963
Hoffmann, H., 266, 281
Hoffmeister, J. K., 95, 101
Hoffnung, R., 1027, 1032
Hogan, H. W., 1004, 1005, 1028,
1031
Hogan, K. A., 685, 686, 688, 689,
692
Hogan, R., 237, 241, 383-384,
387-388, 856, 858
Hogarty, G. E., 213, 217
Hokanson, J. E., 544, 545, 548,
549
Holland, A. M., 984-995
Holland, J. L., 355, 357, 360
747, 753, 754, 769, 774, 988,
993
Holland, T., 839, 849
Hollander, E. P., 979, 983, 988
993
Hollender, M. H., 162, 164, 690,
693
Holley, J., 63, 71
Hollingshead, A. B., 144, 146

Hollingsworth, L. S., 731, 734,
735, 741, 742
Holmes, T. H., 95, 100, 152, 154,
156, 165, 166
Holstein, C. B., 337, 339, 368, 373
Holt, R. R., 497, 498, 499, 500-
501, 502, 503, 504, 505, 508-
509, 521, 523, 524, 525, 529,
530-531, 532, 533, 534, 536,
537-538
Holtzman, W. H., 354, 356, 357,
360, 582, 585, 835-836, 844,
848
Homme, L. E., 412, 419, 767, 774
Honigfeld, G., 213, 217
Hood, R. W., Jr., 1013, 1014,
1029, 1031
Hoon, E. F., 677, 678, 682, 683
Hooper, F. H., 23, 24, 42, 45
Hope, K., 553, 554, 557
Hoppe, S. K., 65, 71
Hoppener, R., 303, 305
Hopple, G. W., 1026, 1032
Hoppock, R., 104, 111
Horkheimer, M., 1017, 1032
Horn, J. L., 20, 21, 24, 42, 705,
711
Hornaday, J. A., 990, 993
Hornblum, J. N., 24, 42
Horne, D., 757, 763
Horne, W. C., 430, 439
Horney, K. H., 75, 81, 86, 130,
131, 603, 640, 654, 657, 670,
685, 693
Horosz, W., 416, 417, 419
Horowitz, I. A., 476, 480
Horowitz, M. J., 812, 814, 817
Horton, M. M., 1045, 1048
Hoult, T., 1023, 1034
House, J. S., 250, 254
Houser, D., 855, 858
Howard, H. E., 860
Howard, J. W., 62, 71
Howard, M. L., 951, 953
Howard, R., 860, 864-865, 866,
867
Howarth, C. I., 435, 441
Howarth, E., 355, 360
Howe, L. W., 365, 374
Howell, R. J., 436, 441
Howells, J. G., 1086
Howland, A., 295-307
Hoyer, W. J., 23, 42
Hoyt, K. B., 105, 111
Hsu, F., 49, 58
Huang, L., 432, 438
Huard, M., 531, 538
Huba, G. J., 630-638
Huber, J. T., 1045, 1048
Hubner, J., 854, 858
Huck, J. R., 991, 993
Hudson, L., 734, 736, 741, 841,
848
Huesmann, L. R., 588, 597, 599
Huffman, P. E., 1011, 1014, 1021,
1032

Spanos, N. P., 937, 941, 943, 946, 948, 950, 952, 954
Spark, G., 76, 85
Sparling, S., 619, 621
Spear, F. G., 1088, 1095, 1101
Spearman, C., 698, 703
Spence, J. T., 578, 586, 660, 661, 663, 665, 666, 667, 668, 671
Spence, K. W., 560, 562, 563, 568, 573-574, 578, 586
Spencer, H., 956, 964
Spencer, J., 436, 442
Spencer, R. F., 691, 695
Spencer, T. J., 885, 889
Sperling, G., 885, 889
Sperling, M., 624, 627, 629
Spielberger, C. D., 132, 213, 219, 559, 561, 562-563, 564, 565, 568, 571, 574, 583, 584, 587, 1079, 1080, 1081, 1082, 1085, 1086
Spies, E., 436, 441
Spiker, S. P., 212, 219
Spinetta, J. J., 92, 101
Spinoza, B., 351
Spitz, R. A., 89, 101, 596, 598, 600, 710, 824, 833
Spitzer, R. L., 191, 198, 588, 600, 1118, 1122
Spivack, G., 122, 127, 354, 356, 361
Spoehr, K. T., 881, 882, 889
Spohn, H. E., 982, 983
Spotts, J., 122, 127
Sprague, R. L., 268, 270, 275, 278, 284, 285
Spreen, O., 162, 167, 354, 356, 357, 361
Sprigle, H., 354, 356, 361
Spring, B., 219
Spring, C., 270, 277, 278, 279, 284
Springer, D., 988, 995
Springer, K. J., 845, 850
Spuck, D. W., 769, 775
Spuhler, J. N., 708, 712
Srole, L. R., 1021, 1034, 1055
Sroufe, L. A., 272, 284
Staats, A. W., 619, 621, 757, 764
Stachowiak, J. G., 79-80, 84, 87
Stagner, R., 482, 484, 489
Stainton, M. C., 92, 97, 101
Stamler, J., 252, 255
Stancer, H. C., 588, 600
Stanley, J. C., 731, 738, 743
Stanton, G., 854, 858
Stapp, J., 660, 661, 663, 671
Stare, F. J., 247, 253, 255
Starker, S., 632, 633, 635, 636, 638
Staub, E., 478-479, 480
Stearns, A. W., 170, 189
Steckler, G. A., 1028, 1034
Steele, B. F., 92, 101
Stefansson, J. G., 154, 167
Steger, J. C., 677, 678, 682

Stegner, W., 18, 45
Stein, K. B., 345, 349
Stein, M. I., 738, 743, 846, 850
Stein, P. J., 33, 45
Stein, Z., 286, 287, 294
Steiner, I., 423
Steiner, I. D., 1011, 1015, 1029, 1034
Steiner, J., 434, 436, 442
Steinfeld, J. J., 846, 848
Steinglass, P., 70, 73
Stenner, A. J., 273, 282
Stephens, B., 386, 388
Stephens, R., 239, 243
Stephens, T. M., 755-765
Stephens, W. B., 371, 374
Stephenson, G. M., 957, 964
Stephenson, W., 839, 850
Stern, G. G., 767, 769, 774
Stern, J. A., 271, 285
Stern, M. E., 354, 358, 361
Stern, W., 699, 837, 850
Sternbach, R. A., 152, 161, 167, 547, 549, 1089, 1090, 1091, 1092, 1095, 1096, 1098, 1099-1100, 1102
Sternberg, R. J., 887, 889
Sternberg, S., 517, 519, 880, 881, 885, 886, 889
Stevens, D. A., 269, 284
Stevens, K. N., 806, 817
Stevens, Q. J., 435, 438
Stevens, S. S., 219, 402, 409
Stevens-Long, J., 275, 277, 284
Stevenson, I., 158, 167
Stewart, D., 1023, 1034
Stewart, M. A., 265, 266, 272, 274, 278, 282, 284, 290, 294
Stierlin, H., 76, 87, 625, 629
Still, G. F., 266, 284
Stillman, S. M., 431, 443
Stinnett, N., 90, 92-93, 96, 97, 102
Stockholm, E., 927, 928
Stogdill, R. M., 984, 985-986, 989, 990, 991, 995
Stoller, R. J., 623, 624, 627, 629
Stolorow, R. D., 685, 686, 694, 695
Stone, A. A., 219, 1113, 1114, 1117, 1118, 1122
Stone, G. C., 766, 774, 1020, 1031
Stone, H. K., 912, 913, 914, 918
Stone, M. H., 808, 820
Stoner, J. A., 429, 442
Storandt, M., 23, 26, 40, 41
Storck, P., 24, 45
Stores, G., 304, 307
Storment, C. T., 499, 505, 510
Storr, A., 554, 558
Stouwie, R., 84, 86
Stover, L., 1037, 1041
Stoyva, J., 315, 318
Strachey, J., 552, 558
Strahan, C., 961, 964

Strahan, R. F., 667, 671
Strassberg, D. S., 447, 454
Strauss, A., 852, 858
Strauss, A. A., 266, 284, 801
Strauss, J. S., 937, 940
Straw, M. K., 723, 727
Streissguth, A. P., 687, 691, 695
Strelitz, Z., 88, 93, 94, 97, 101
Stricker, G., 156, 164
Stricker, S., 695
Strickland, B. R., 447, 452
Strider, F. D., 199-219, 1044, 1047
Strodtbeck, F. L., 81, 87
Stroebe, W., 430, 442
Stromberg, C. D., 219
Strother, C. R., 22, 45
Stroud, J., 337, 339
Struening, E. L., 59, 156, 166
Strumpfer, D., 583, 586
Stuart, I. R., 98, 101
Stuart, R. B., 323, 327, 330
Stubbins, J., 1057, 1059
Stubblefield, H., 1065, 1067
Stukalin, J. J., 435, 442
Stunkard, A. J., 321, 323, 327, 329, 330
Suchman, D. I., 444, 446, 447, 448, 450, 452, 454
Suci, G., 1061, 1066
Sudia, C., 90, 99
Sugarman, D., 685, 695
Suinn, R. M., 116, 127, 245, 249, 250, 252, 255-256, 565, 574
Sullivan, C., 333, 340
Sullivan, C. T., 808, 820
Sullivan, H. S., 75, 87, 130, 131, 185, 189, 202, 333, 340, 445, 454, 807, 820, 904, 910
Sullivan, J. S., 505, 510
Sulzbacher, S. I., 275, 284
Sumner, G., 779
Sumner, W. G., 976, 983
Sumption, M., 756, 765
Sundberg, N. D., xxxi, xxxii, xxxix, 3, 10, 16, 88, 96, 101, 705, 712, 723, 728, 1105, 1111
Sundstrom, E., 863, 868
Super, D. E., 56, 59, 104, 108, 111-112, 1064, 1067
Surma, M. E., 397, 399
Susser, M., 286, 287, 294
Sutell, B. J., 342, 348
Sutherland, A. M., 1078, 1086
Sutker, P. B., 235, 243
Sutton-Smith, B., 689, 696
Suziedelis, A., 667-668, 671
Svigos, J. M., 289, 294
Sviland, M. A. P., 243
Swallow, S. C., 3, 14
Swanson, D. W., 152, 167, 1092, 1102
Swartz, J., 687, 696
Swartz, J. D., 354, 356, 357, 360, 582, 585

Yuker, H. E., 1057, 1058, 1059,
   1061, 1062, 1063, 1064, 1067

Z

Zacker, J., 469, 472
Zagona, S. V., 1029, 1034
Zaidel, E., 815, 820
Zaks, M. S., 554, 558
Zaleski, A., 287, 294
Zborowski, M., 161, 168, 1097,
   1098, 1103
Zegiob, L. E., 95, 96, 102
Zentall, S. S., 271, 285

Zentall, T. R., 271, 285
Zetzel, E. R., 823, 833
Ziegler, D. K., 312, 318
Zilboorg, G., 219
Zillmann, D., 545, 550
Zimet, C. N., 354, 358, 503, 506,
   511, 532, 539
Zimmerman, J., 431, 443, 679,
   683
Zimmerman, W. S., 400, 405, 407,
   409, 488, 635
Zisfein, L., 436, 443
Ziskin, J., 1114, 1118, 1122
Zubek, J. P., 532, 539

Zubin, J., 2, 4, 16, 116, 127, 141,
   142, 147, 219, 1118, 1122
Zucker, K. B., 851-858
Zuckerman, H., 735, 739, 743
Zuckerman, M., 155, 168, 192,
   198, 258, 261, 264, 354, 355,
   361, 564, 565, 574, 677, 683,
   1000, 1002
Zuk, G., 1065, 1067
Zung, W. W. K., 588, 590, 595, 601
Zurcher, L. A., Jr., 1029, 1034
Zussman, J., 1116, 1122
Zytowski, D. G., 961, 964
Zyzanski, S. J., 245, 247, 255, 256

Subject Index

and perceptual-motoric behavior, 903, 907
and psychopathology, 907
recommendations on, 907-908
and reliability, 906
and selective attention, 904
theories of, 904-905
and treatment, 908
and validity, 906
and variables, 908
and vigilance, 904
and vulnerability to stress, 903, 904
Adience-Abience Scale, 905-907
Adjective Check List (ACL), 482, 485, 662, 663, 664, 668
Adjustable Body Distorting Mirror, 839
Adjustment
defined, 47
marital, 60-73
and normality, 51
Adjustment Scale, 213
Adolescence
developmental tasks during, 54-55
learning disabilities in, 12
psychosexual development in, 645-646
See also Behavior disorders of children and adolescents; Child and adolescent development
Adult development
age change versus age difference issue in, 19-20
analysis of, 17-45
areas in, 19-34
and auditory perception, 28
background of, 18-19
biological theories of, 37
crisis period in, 31-32, 38-39
critical points on, 37-38
cross-sectional study of, 20-21
cross-sequential study of, 22
discussion of, 19-39
and functional age, 20
and intervention procedures, 23, 24-25, 38
and learning, 25-26
longitudinal study of, 21-22
and memory, 26-28
methodological issues in, 19-20
models of, 19
and personality, 29-32
and psychometric assessment of cognition, 20-23, 38
and psychophysiology, 28-29
recommendations on, 38-39
social/psychological theories on, 34-37
and social roles, 32-34
theories on, 34-37

and variables, 39
and visual perception, 28
Adulthood
developmental tasks in, 55
periods in, 18, 36-37
psychosexual development in, 646-647, 651
Affect
and schizophrenia, 204
Affect Adjective Check List, Today (AACL-T), 564, 565
Affective disorders
issues of, 206-207
and variables, 215, 216
Affective guilt states
analysis of, 614-621
background of, 615-616
critical points on, 618-619
defined, 614
discussion of, 616-620
issues of, 616-618
measurement of, 616-617, 618-619
and other aspects of guilt, 617
recommendations on, 619-620
role of, 619
theories on, 618
and validity, 616-617
and variables, 620
See also Guilt
Affective personality
See Cyclothermic personality
Africa
risk taking in, 436
stigma in, 1052
Age
and aggression (physiological), 547
and altruism, 478-479
and ambiguity tolerance, 469
and antisocial personality, 196
and anxiety, 567
and associative elaboration, 874-875
and authoritarianism, 1013
and behavior disorders, 123
and career development, 110
and child and adolescent development, 10-11
and classroom motivation, 772
and clinical interpretation, 1046
and creative thinking, 751
and daydreaming, 635
and depression, 598
and developmental anxiety, 581-584
and disability acceptance, 1064
and dominance, 486
and ego delay, 357
and enuresis and encopresis, 292

and epilepsy, 301, 304, 305
and forensic psychology, 1119
and genius, 739
and headache, 316
and helplessness, learned, 262
and hyperactivity, 276-277
and integration theory, 815
and intelligence, 705
and interpersonal distance preference, 866
and leadership potentials, 990
and learning problems, 762
and marital adjustment, 67
and mental retardation, 725
and mnemonic organization, 898, 899
and moral development, 370
and moral reasoning, 386
and need systems, 398
and neurotic cues, 143-144
and nonauthoritarianism, 1024, 1025
and nonverbalized feelings, 972-973
and normality, 54-55
and obesity, 327
and organic brain syndromes, 227
and others-concept, 857
and pain, 1097
and personal responsibility, 418
and posthypnotic amnesia, 952
and primary process ideation, 531
and primitive drive-dominated thinking, 504
and psychosis/schizophrenia, 215
and psychosomatic disorders, 159-160
and risk taking, 435
and self-disclosure, 451
and sexual dysfunction, 681
and sexual fantasy, 689-690
and social conformity, 981
and surgery-induced stress, 1084
and symbiosis, 627
and temperament, 406-407
and Type A/B behavior, 252
and visual search ability, 887
Aged persons
psychosexual development of, 647
Agentic orientation
and masculinity, 657
Aggression
in authoritarianism, 1008
dominance related to, 481, 483, 485
and hyperactivity, 274
and object relations, 823-824

psychogenic, 314
psychosocial variables of, 311-312
recommendations on, 315-316
severity of, 313-314
and sex differences, 316
theories of, 314
and tonic muscle activity, 315-316
and variables, 316-317
Health Locus of Control, 156
Healthy personality
defined, 47
Hearing impairment
defined, 778
Hebephrenia
concept of, 201
Helpee Self-Exploration Scale, 448
Helplessness, learned
and age, 262
analysis of, 257-264
background of, 258-259
critical points on, 261
defined, 258
and depression, 589-590, 597
discussion of, 259-262
and educational/intellectual level, 262
issues of, 259-260
and physical disorders, 263
physiological concomitants of, 259-260
and psychiatric disorders, 263
and race, 262-263
recommendations on, 261-262
theories of, 260-261
and variables, 262-263
Henmon-Nelson test, 703
Heredity
and antisocial personality, 193
and cyclothermic personality, 175
and depression, 593, 596
and enuresis and encopresis, 288
and epilepsy, 301
and headache, 310
and mental retardation, 720
and normality, 48
and obesity, 322
and psychosis, 209
and schizoid personality, 177
and temperament, 403
Heroin
abuse of, 232, 235, 236, 237, 239
Heschl's Gyrus
and epilepsy, 300
Heterosexual Experience Scales, 1000
Hirschsprung's disease
and encopresis, 288
Histrionic personality
See Hysterical personality
Hobson v. Hansen, 717, 727

Holistic medicine
and psychosomatic disorders, 152
Holtzman Inkblot Technique (HIT), 235, 356, 842, 919, 1081, 1108
Homosexuality
and sex-role orientation, 664-665
Hopelessness Scale, 155
Hormic psychology
concept of, 392
Hospital for Incurables, 779
Hostility
and physiological aggression, 541, 547
and psychological aggression, 551
House-Person-Tree Test, 920
Human figure drawings (HFDs)
and developmental anxiety, 582-583
Human Movement (M), 842-843, 844
Human Service Scale, 1062, 1069, 1071-1072, 1074
Hyperactivity, childhood
and age, 276-277
analysis of, 265-268
background of, 266-268
critical points of, 272-276
defined, 265-266, 267, 268
discussion of, 268-276
drug treatment for, 267, 270, 273, 274, 275, 276
and education, 277
identification of, 268-272
incidence of, 268
and intelligence, 278
issues of, 268-272
observation of, 270-271, 272
and organic pathology, 278
parent interview and, 268, 272
and physical disorders, 278
primary and secondary symptoms of, 274- 277
and psychological stress, 278
and racial/ethnic factors, 278
rating scales for, 269-270
recommendations on, 276
and sex differences, 277
situational, 273
and socioeconomic status, 277
subgroups in, 273
as syndrome or symptom, 273-274
tests of, 269
theories of, 272
and variables, 276-278
and vocation, 277-278
Hyperkinetic/minimal brain dysfunction (HK/MBD)
See Hyperactivity, childhood
Hyperphasia
and obesity, 322

Hypersensitivity
and paranoid personality, 173
Hypertrophy
and obesity, 322
Hypnosis
See Expectancy behavior in hypnosis; Posthypnotic amnesia
Hypochondriacal syndrome
and neurotic cues, 137, 138
Hypochondriasis
as psychosomatic, 150, 151, 155, 157, 158
Hypomanic
and cyclothymic personality, 175
Hypothyroidism
and depression, 590
Hypsarhythmia
and epilepsy, 304, 305
Hysteria
concept of, 200
and neurotic cues, 135, 136-137, 138
as psychosomatic, 150, 151, 154, 155, 160, 161, 162
Hysteria Scale, 1028
Hysterical neurosis
hysterical personality distinct from, 181
Hysterical personality
analysis of, 181-184
defined, 181
healthy versus sick characteristics of, 182-183
incidence of, 181
issues of, 181-182
recommendations on, 183-184
theories of, 183
Hysterical psychosis
and hysterical personality, 183

I

Ideation
See Primary process ideation
Identification
and object relations, 824
Identity
in adolescence, 54-55
career, 103
Idiosyncratic considerations, 975-1034
Idiots Act of 1886, 716
Illinois Test of Psycholinguistic Abilities (ITPA), 118, 757
Illness behavior
and psychosomatic disorders, 149-150, 152, 157
Imaginal Processes Inventory (IPI), 632-633, 634, 635-636, 686
Impairment
defined, 1068

District of Columbia, 717, 728, 1120, 1121
Miner Sentence Completion Scale (MSCS), 988, 989, 991
Minimal brain damage
and information-processing deficit, 513, 517
Minimal brain dysfunction (MBD)
See Hyperactivity, childhood
Minnesota Child Development Inventory, 123
Minnesota Importance Questionnaire, 1072, 1074
Minnesota Multiphasic Personality Inventory (MMPI)
and adult development, 29
and aggression, psychological, 553
and antisocial personality, 192
and anxiety, 563
and behavior disorders, 118, 124
and creative thinking, 747
and dangerousness, 1108
and depression, 589, 594
and ego delay, 355, 357, 358
and ego strength, 342, 345 347
and forensic psychology, 1118
and guilt, 609
and integration theory, 812
and marital adjustment, 66
and moral reasoning, 386
and neurotic cues, 135
and nonauthoritarianism, 1025, 1028
and normality, 49-50
and organic brain syndrome, 224
and pain, 1091
and personal responsibility, 413
and personality disorders, 174
and psychosis, 213, 214
and psychosomatic disorders, 155, 160
and rehabilitation needs, 1072
and sexual fantasy, 691
and social conformity, 978
and substance abuse, 234, 235, 236, 239
and surgery-induced stress, 1080
and temperament, 403, 405, 406
Minnesota Tests of Creative Thinking, 872, 874, 875
Minnesota Theory of Work Adjustment, 1069, 1070, 1072, 1073
Miranda v. *State of Arizona,* 1114, 1121
Mirels-Garrett Protestant Ethic Scale, 1000
Mnemonic organization
and age, 898, 899

analysis of, 890-901
background of, 891-894
and cerebral disease, 899
clustering method of, 891-892
cognitive theories of, 891-894
critical points on, 898
cuing method of, 892
defined, 890-891
discussion of, 895-899
and education, 898
and encoding specificity or variability, 893-894
and episodic and semantic memory, 894
and free recall method, 890, 891
and functional disorders, 899-900
hierarchical, 893
and intelligence, 899
interference theory of, 891
issues of, 895-897
level-of-processing theory of, 894
measurement for, 895-896
and production deficiencies, 897
and racial factors, 898
recommendations on, 899
registration of, 896-897
and rehearsal, 894
and retrieval processes, 893
and sex differences, 898
and socioeconomic status, 898
sorting-and-recall method of, 892, 896, 899
and storage processes, 893-894
subjective, 892
theories on, 897-898
two-process theory of, 893
and variables, 898, 899-900
Monoamine oxidase inhibitors (MAOI)
and depression, 596
Moral development
and age, 370
and altruism, 362, 364, 365, 367, 369
analysis of, 362-374
background of, 363-366
and behavior, 362, 367, 368, 370
and cognition, 362, 363, 365
cognitive-developmental theory of, 369-370
consistency of dimensions of, 367-368
critical points on, 370
defined, 362-363
discussion of, 366-370
and education, 371
education in, goals for, 368-369
and emotions, 362, 367, 370
and ethical issues, 369
and functional disorders, 372

and guilt, 362, 363, 366, 368, 370, 371
and induction, 364, 369
and intellectual factors, 371
issues of, 366-369
measurement of, 366-367
and organic dysfunctions, 371-372
and physical disorders, 371
and punishment, 364, 369, 370
recommendations on, 370
and resistance to temptation, 362, 363-364, 367, 368, 370
and sex differences, 370-371
and shame, 362
social learning theory of, 369
and socioeconomic status, 371
theories on, 369-370
and variables, 370-372
Moral insanity
concept of, 191
Moral judgment
and adult development, 30
See also Moral reasoning
Moral reasoning
and age, 386
analysis of, 375-389
background of, 376-379
and collective/interactional disorders, 386
critical points on, 384-385
and culture, 386
defined, 375-376
discussion of, 379-386
and education, 386
facilitation of, 380-381
and intelligence, 386
issues of, 379-382
measures of, 379-380
and moral behavior, 385
and physical disorders, 386
recommendations on, 385-386
and role taking, 376, 378-379, 381, 382
and sex differences, 386
and socioeconomic status, 386
stage theories of, 376-379, 384-385
theories on, 382-384
and therapy, 381-382
and training, 385-386
and variables, 386-387
and vocation, 386
Morphine
abuse of, 232
Morphology
and psychosis, 209
Mother
employment of, 97
parenting role of, 88, 89, 91, 92, 93, 95, 97
and psychosexual development, 641-642, 643, 644

Motivated cognitive commitment
  See Expectancy behavior in
  hypnosis
Motivation
  for altruism, 475
  classroom, 766-775
  and risk taking, 431-432, 433
Motivation Analysis Test, 1073,
  1074
Motives
  See Need systems, personal
Motor behavior
  and schizophrenia, 204
Multifocal diseases
  and epilepsy, 300
Multimodal Assessment, 136
Multiple Affect Adjective Check
  List (MAACL), 155, 564
Munchausen Syndrome
  as psychosomatic, 150, 154
Mutuality of Autonomy Scale,
  830-831
Myers-Briggs Type Indicator, 747
Myokinetic Test, 920

N

Narcissism
  and object relations, 823, 825-
  826
Narcolepsy
  epilepsy distinct from, 299
National Association of State Di-
  rectors of Special Education,
  783, 788
National Association to Aid Fat
  Americans (NAAFA), 323,
  326
National Committee for Mental
  Hygiene, 115
National Conference for Planning
  for Moral/Citizenship Edu-
  cation, 368
National Council on Family Rela-
  tions, 90, 100
National Institute for Deaf-Mutes,
  779
National Institute of Mental
  Health (NIMH), 199*n*, 354,
  356, 361, 497*n*, 1116, 1121
National Institute on Drug Abuse
  (NIDA), 234, 630*n*
National Merit Scholarship Exam-
  ination, 698
National Science Foundation,
  630*n*
National Vocational Guidance
  Association, 104
Neal and Seaman's Powerlessness
  Scale, 1055
Need
  aspects of, 1069
  defined, 1069, 1073
  vocational, dimensions of, 1072
Need systems, personal
  and age, 398

analysis of, 390-399
background of, 391-393
and cognitive theory, 396
critical points on, 396-397
defined, 390-391
discussion of, 393-398
and ethics, 398
hierarchical relationships in,
  397
issues of, 393-395
and levels of consciousness,
  394, 398
and measuring motivations,
  393-394, 396-397, 398
and need elements, 396, 397-
  398
recommendations on, 397-398
and sex differences, 399
and systems perspective, 392,
  394-395
theories of, 395-396
and trait theory, 396
and variables, 398-399
Needs. *See* Rehabilitation needs
Negative Attitudes Toward Masturbation, 603, 609, 610
Neodissociation theory
  and expectancy behavior,
  936-937
  and posthypnotic amnesia,
  948-949
Neoplasms
  and epilepsy, 300
Netherlands
  conservatism in, 1000, 1003,
  1004
Neurasthenic neurosis
  asthenic personality distinct
  from, 184-185
Neurasthenic syndrome
  and neurotic cues, 137, 138
Neurological defects
  and psychosis, 209
  and psychosomatic disorders,
  161-162
Neuropsychology
  and organic brain syndrome,
  222, 226
Neurosis
  classifications of, 132-134
  concept of, 128, 129-131
  differentiations of term,
  129
  outcome of, 142
  and personal responsibility,
  412
  prevalence of, 143
  process of, 142-143
Neurotic cues
  and age, 143-144
  analysis of, 128-147
  background of, 129-134
  cognitive/behavioral theory of,
  138-139, 140
  critical points on, 140-142
  and cultural variables, 144

diagnostic interview for, 135-
  136
discussion of, 134-143
etiology of, 129
issues in, 134-138
models of, 141-142
and personality patterns, 137-
  138
phenomenological/humanistic
  theory of, 139, 140
psychodynamic/intrapsychic
  theory of, 139, 140
racial differences in, 144-145
recommendations on, 142-143
sample, sign, and symbol for,
  140-141
and sex differences, 144
and socioeconomic status, 144
theories of, 138-140
trait/type theory of, 139-140
and variables, 143-145
Neuroticism
  temperament of, 400, 401, 402,
  404-406
New Mexico
  marijuana legislation in, 233
New York Education Law, 1120,
  1121
New York Longitudinal Study
  (NYLS), 402, 404, 406
New Zealand
  conservatism in, 1000, 1003,
  1004
Nonauthoritarianism
  and age, 1024, 1025
  analysis of, 1016-1034
  background of, 1017-1019
  and collective/interactional
  factors, 1029
  critical points on, 1023-1024
  defined, 1016
  discussion of, 1019-1025
  and education, 1023, 1025-
  1026
  ethical issues of, 1020
  and ethnic/racial factors, 1028
  and family childrearing, 1021
  and intelligence, 1026
  issues of, 1019-1022
  and physical disorders, 1028
  and psychiatric disorders,
  1028-1029
  recommendations on, 1024-
  1025
  and sampling problems, 1020-
  1021
  and sex differences, 1025
  and socioeconomic status,
  1026
  and structure of scales, 1019-
  1020
  theories on, 1022-1023
  and validity, 1020
  and variables, 1025-1029
  and vocation, 1026-1028
  See also Authoritarianism

Organic brain syndromes
  and age, 227
  analysis of, 220-230
  background of, 220-222
  defined, 220
  discussion of, 222-227
  and education, 227
  equipotential theory of, 221,
    224-225
  examination for, purpose of,
    222
  and functional factors, 228
  individual versus standardized
    testing for, 222-223
  and intelligence, 228
  issues of, 207-209, 222-224
  localization theory of, 221,
    225
  measurement for, 225-226
  and personality assessment,
    224
  and physical disorders, 227-228
  quantitative versus qualitative
    procedures and, 223
  recommendations on, 226-227
  and single tests versus test bat-
    teries, 223-224
  theories of, 224-225
  and variables, 215, 216, 227-
    228
Organic delusional syndrome
  concept of, 208-209
Organic disorders
  and authoritarianism, 1013
  and child and adolescent de-
    velopment, 12-13
  and hyperactivity, 278
  and integration theory, 815-
    816
  and intelligence, 709-710
  and moral development, 371-
    372
  and primitive drive-dominated
    thinking, 505
  and risk taking, 436
Organization
  See Mnemonic organization
Others-concept
  and age, 857
  analysis of, 851-858
  background of, 852
  critical points on, 855-856
  defined, 851
  discussion of, 852-857
  and intelligence, 857
  issues of, 852-854
  methodological problems of,
    856
  recommendations on, 856
  and sex differences, 856, 857
  significance of, 855
  and socioeconomic status, 857
  theories on, 854-855
  and variables, 857
Otis Higher Form Intelligence
  Test, 1026

Otto Family Strength Survey, 80
Outer-Directedness
  and personal responsibility,
    414
Overeaters Anonymous, 324
Overholser v. Russell, 1117, 1121
Overweight
  obesity distinct from, 319

P

Pain
  and acupuncture, 1090, 1091,
    1094
  acute, 1095
  affect in, 1093
  and age, 1097
  analysis of, 1088-1103
  background of, 1089-1090
  chronic, 1095-1096
  clinics for, 1096
  control and treatment of,
    1090, 1091-1092, 1094,
    1096
  critical points on, 1095-1096
  and culture, 1098
  defined, 1088-1089
  discussion of, 1090-1097
  and education, 1097
  and ethical issues, 1090
  gate control theory of, 1089,
    1093-1094
  and intelligence, 1098
  issues of, 1090-1092
  measurement of, 1091
  and psychiatric disorders, 1098
  psychogenic or somatogenic,
    1095
  recommendations on, 1096-
    1097
  reports of, 1090-1091
  and sex differences, 1097
  and socioeconomic status,
    1097
  sources of, and psychosomatic
    disorders, 154
  specificity theory of, 1093
  theories of, 1093-1094
  training for, 1096-1097
  and variables, 1097-1098
  and vocation, 1097-1098
Pain Questionnaire, 1091, 1096
Paired Anxiety and Depression
  Scale, 155
Paired Hands Test (PHT), 851-857
Palo Alto Destructive Content
  Scale, 499, 505
Paradoxical calm
  and hysterical personality, 184
Paranoia
  concept of, 206
  paranoid personality distinct
    from, 173
Paranoid disorders
  issues of, 205-206
  shared, 206

  and variables, 215, 216
Paranoid disposition
  temperament of, 401
Paranoid personality
  analysis of, 172-175
  behavior theory of, 174
  defined, 172-173
  issues of, 172-173
  measurement of, 174
  psychodynamic theory of,
    173-174
  recommendations on, 174-175
  stages of, 174
  theories of, 173-174
Paranoid schizophrenia
  paraniod personality related
    to, 173
Paranoid state
  concept of, 206
  paranoid personality distinct
    from, 173
Paranoid subtype
  of schizophrenia, 204-205
Parent Behavior Form (PBF), 665,
    666
Parenting
  and abuse, 92, 95
  analysis of, 88-102
  and antisocial personality, 194,
    196
  areas of, 90-93
  and attitude data, 91
  background of, 89-90
  competence in, 88-89, 92, 96
  critical points on, 94-96
  defined, 88-89
  and developmental stages, 93
  discussion of, 90-96
  factors in, 89
  and marital satisfaction, 97
  and maternal employment, 97
  measurement for, 94-95
  and moral development, 364
  and object relations develop-
    ment, 822-831
  and pathology and illness, 97
  recommendations on, 96
  and social modeling, 91
  and socioeconomic status, 96-
    97
  theories of, 93-94
  and variables, 96-98
Parents Questionnaire, 122
Passive-aggressive personality
  and alcohol abuse, 185
  analysis of, 185-187
  defined, 185
  inadequate personality dis-
    tinct from, 187
  incidence of, 185
  issues of, 185-186
  prognosis of, 186
  theories on, 186-187
  types of, 186
Patient's Opinion Form,
    1079

Self-aware stage
    of ego development, 336, 337,
        338
Self-awareness
    and nonauthoritarianism, 1022
Self-concept
    and adult development, 30
    defined, 854
    and marital adjustment, 64
Self-Description Inventory (SDI),
    987-988
Self-disclosure
    and affect, 447-448
    and age, 451
    amount of, 446-447
    analysis of, 444-454
    background of, 445-446
    critical points on, 450
    defined, 444-445
    dimensions of, 445, 446-449
    discussion of, 446-451
    duration of, 447
    and ethics, 450
    factors affecting, 449
    and flexibility, 448-449, 450
    intimacy of, 447
    issues of, 446-449
    and measurement perspective,
        449
    and psychological disorders,
        451
    and race, 451
    recommendations on, 450
    theories of, 450
    by therapist, 445
    and variables, 451
Self-Disclosure Coding System, 450
Self-Disclosure Questionnaire, 80-
    81
Self-Disclosure Sentence Blank,
    448
Self-esteem
    and dominance, 481, 483, 484,
        485, 487-488
Self-Esteem Inventory, 64
Self-protective stage
    of ego development, 335, 337,
        338
Self Rating Depression Scale, 595
Self-reports
    and developmental anxiety,
        583-584
    for psychosomatic disorders,
        157
Semantic Differential Scales,
    1055
Sensorimotor intelligence stage
    stage of, 648-649
Sentence Completion Test
    (SCT), 213, 214, 912,
        913-914, 1118
Separation-individuation
    and symbiosis, 622-629
Serotonin
    and depression, 593, 595-596
    headache related to, 311

Sex differences
    and aggression (physiological),
        547-548
    and aggression (psychological),
        556
    and altruism, 479
    and ambiguity tolerance, 469
    and antisocial personality, 197
    and anxiety, 568
    and associative elaboration,
        875
    and authoritarianism, 1013
    and behavior disorders, 124
    and body image creativity, 845
    and career development, 110
    and child and adolescent de-
        velopment, 11
    and classroom motivation, 772
    and creative thinking, 751-752
    and daydreaming, 635
    and depression, 598
    and developmental anxiety,
        582-583, 584
    and disability acceptance,
        1064
    and dominance, 486
    and ego delay, 357
    and enuresis and encopresis,
        292
    and epilepsy, 304
    and forensic psychology,
        1119-1120
    and genius, 739
    and headache, 316
    and hyperactivity, 277
    and information-processing,
        518
    and integration theory, 815
    and intelligence, 705-706
    and interpersonal distance
        preference, 866
    and leadership potentials, 990-
        991
    and marital adjustment, 67-68
    and mental retardation, 725
    and mnemonic organization,
        898
    and moral development, 370-
        371
    and moral reasoning, 386
    and need systems, 399
    and neurotic cues, 144
    and nonauthoritarianism, 1025
    and nonverbalized feelings, 973
    and normality, 55-56
    and obesity, 327
    and others-concept, 856, 857
    and pain, 1097
    and primitive drive-dominated
        thinking, 504
    and psychosomatic disorders,
        160
    and risk taking, 435
    and sexual dysfunction, 680-
        681
    and sexual fantasy, 690

    and social conformity, 981
    and stigma, 1058
    and substance abuse, 238
    and surgery-induced stress,
        1084-1085
    and symbiosis, 627
    and temperament, 407
    and Type A/B behavior, 252-
        253
Sex Inventory, 609
Sex-role orientation
    analysis of, 656-672
    background of, 656-658
    biological basis of, 659
    classification of, 666-667
    critical points on, 660-666
    defined, 656
    dimensions of, 667-668
    discussion of, 658-669
    issues of, 658
    learning of, 665-666
    measures of, 660-662
    and personality, 659, 668-669
    recommendations on, 666-669
    and socialization, 659-660
    theories of, 659-660
    and variables, 669
Sex-Role Stereotype Question-
    naire, 661
Sexual Arousal Inventory (SAI),
    677-678
Sexual dysfunction
    and age, 681
    analysis of, 673-683
    background of, 673-675
    critical points on, 676-680
    defined, 673, 674
    discussion of, 675-680
    experiences checklists for, 677
    incidence of, 680-681
    interviews for, 676
    measures of, 675, 676-680
    patient diary for, 678-680
    recommendations on, 680
    sex differences in, 680-681
    subjective reaction measures
        of, 677-678
    theories on, 675
    unidimensional scales of, 676
    and variables, 680-681
Sexual fantasy
    and age, 689-690
    analysis of, 684-696
    background of, 685-686
    critical points on, 688-689
    defined, 684-685
    discussion of, 686-689
    and ethnic/racial factors, 690-
        691
    as functional or dysfunctional,
        686-687
    issues of, 686-688
    and physical disorders, 691
    and psychiatric disorders, 691
    recommendations on, 689
    and sex differences, 690

theories on, 688
and variables, 689-691
Sexual Interaction Inventory
(SII), 677, 678
Sexual Interest Measure (SIN), 677
Sexual Performance Evaluation,
676
Sexual preference
sex-role orientation distinct
from, 656
Sexuality, 639-696
and authoritarianism, 1008
development of, 640
of infants, 640-641, 651
Shame
guilt related to, 606
Sickness Impact Profile, 157
Significance
criteria of, 77-78
Sixteen Personality Factors (16PF)
Questionnaire, 213, 342, 406,
482, 483, 589, 594-595
Slow-to-Warm-Up (STWU)
temperament of, 404
Snake and Spider Questionnaires,
565
Sociability
temperament of, 400, 401,
402, 403, 404, 406
Social Avoidance of Distress
Scale, 565
Social Competence Scale, 122
Social Competency Scale, 718,
719
Social conformity
and age, 981
analysis of, 975-983
background of, 976-977
categories of, 977-978
and collective/interactional
factors, 982
critical points on, 979
defined, 975
discussion of, 977-981
and education, 981
and ethical issues, 980
and ethnic/racial factors, 981
exchange theory of, 979
functional theory of, 979
independence and anticon-
formity related to, 977
and intelligence, 982
issues of, 977-978
and personality-dispositional
factors, 978
and physical disorders, 981-
982
problem-solving theory of,
978-979
recommendations on, 980
reinforcement theory of, 979
and sex differences, 981
situation specificity of, 978
and socioeconomic status, 981
theories of, 978-979
and variables, 981-982

and vocation, 981
Social Desirability Scale, 64, 1000
Social Distance Scale, 1055
Social involvement, 821-974
Social learning
and cyclothymic personality,
176
Social maturity
as nonauthoritarianism, 1016-
1017, 1018-1019
Social Maturity Scale, 1016-1017,
1018-1019
Social Participation Scale, 1055
Social penetration
and self-disclosure, 444, 445
Social Readjustment Rating Scale,
156
Social Responsibility Scale, 29
Social roles
and adult development, 32-34
Society for Clinical and Experimental Hypnosis, 952
Society for Mental Hygiene, 201
Socioeconomic status
and aggression (physiological),
548
and aggression (psychological),
556
and antisocial personality, 197
and anxiety, 568
and associative elaboration, 875
and authoritarianism, 1012
and behavior disorders, 124
and career development, 110-
111
and child and adolescent development, 11
and clinical interpretation,
1046-1047
and creative thinking, 752
and daydreaming, 635
and developmental anxiety,
582, 583, 584
and disability acceptance,
1065
and dominance, 487
and ego delay, 357
and enuresis and encopresis,
292
and epilepsy, 304
and genius, 739
and hyperactivity, 277
and integration theory, 815
and intelligence, 706-707
and leadership potentials, 991
and marital adjustment, 68-69
and mental retardation, 725
and mnemonic organization,
898
and moral development, 371
and moral reasoning, 386
and neurotic cues, 144
and nonauthoritarianism, 1026
and normality, 57
and obesity, 327
and others-concept, 857

and pain, 1097
and parenting, 96-97
and primitive drive-dominated
thinking, 504-505
and psychosexual development,
652
and psychosis/schizophrenia,
211, 216
and psychosomatic disorders,
160-161
and risk taking, 435
and social conformity, 981
and stigma, 1053, 1058
and temperament, 407
and Type A/B behavior, 253
Sociopathic personality
concept of, 191
Somatopsychology
and disability acceptance, 1061,
1063, 1064, 1065
and rehabilitation needs, 1070
South Africa
authoritarianism in, 1013,
1028
conservatism in, 1004
Spain
authoritarianism in, 1012,
1013
Special education
analysis of, 776-789
background of, 779-780
classifications in, 777-779
critical points on, 783
defined, 776
and diagnosis, 781-783, 787
discussion of, 780-787
and individualized education
program, 783, 786, 788
issues of, 780-781
and labeling, 780-781
and learner characteristics,
783-787
recommendations on, 783-787
theories on, 781-783
and variables, 787-788
S-R Inventory of Anxiousness,
562, 563
S-R Inventory of General Trait
Anxiousness (S-R GTA),
563, 1082
Stability
and marital adjustment, 64-65
Stanford Binet Intelligence Scale,
11, 18, 21, 118, 504, 700,
701, 702, 780, 841
Stanford Hypnotic Susceptibility
Scale, 942
State-Trait Anxiety Inventory
(STAI), 213, 564, 565, 1079,
1080, 1081
Status
and marital adjustment, 65
Stereotypy
in authoritarianism, 1008
Stern Activities Index,
393

and child development, 11
and creative thinking, 747
and dangerousness, 1108
and daydreaming, 631, 635
and depression, 589, 594
and dominance, 482
and ego delay, 354, 357
and ego strength, 343
and family functioning, 81
and graphoanalysis, 919
and guilt, 604
and leadership potentials, 988,
  990
and need systems, 393, 397,
  398
and normality, 50
and object relations, 827
and primary process ideation,
  531
and primitive drive-dominated
  thinking, 499, 504
and psychosis, 213, 214
and self-disclosure, 448
and sex-role orientation, 662
and sexual fantasy, 686
Therapist
  See Clinicians
Thinking
  convergent and divergent, 734,
    736
  creative, 744-754
  disturbed, 490-496
  primary and secondary pro-
    cess, defined, 497-498
  primitive drive-dominated,
    497-511
Thorne Sex Inventory, 609
Thought, content and form of
  and schizophrenia, 203
Thought withdrawal
  and schizophrenia, 202
Thoughtfulness
  temperament of, 405
Three Dimensional Apperception
  Test, 919-920
Time
  estimation of, and ego delay,
    355-356, 357-358
Tobacco
  abuse of, 234, 238
Todd's Paralysis
  and epilepsy, 297
Tolerance for ambiguity, mental
  health implications of
  analysis of, 455-462
  background of, 456-457
  critical points on, 460
  defined, 455-456
  discussion of, 457-460
  and individual diffferences,
    458-459
  issues of, 457-459
  and psychotherapy, 460
  recommendations on, 460
  theories on, 459-460
  and variables, 460-461

See also Ambiguity tolerance
Tolerance-Intolerance of Ambiguity Scale, 465
Torrance Tests of Creative Thinking (TTCT), 531, 532, 747,
  872, 873, 875
Tough-Mindedness (T) Scale, 1018
Toxic disturbances
  and epilepsy, 301
Traditional Family Ideology (TFI),
  Scale, 1011, 1021
Training of practitioners
  and academic learning prob-
    lems, 762-763
  and antisocial personality, 196
  and behavior disorders, 125
  and child and adolescent de-
    velopment, 10
  and classroom motivation, 772
  and dangerousness, 1109
  and disturbed thinking, 494
  and dominance, 485-486
  and facilitative dimensions in
    communication, 1039
  and forensic psychology, 1119
  and leadership potentials, 990
  and learned helplessness, 262
  and learning ability/achieve-
    ment discrepancy, 799
  and mnemonic organization,
    899
  and moral reasoning, 385-386
  and nonverbal cues, 959-960
  and nonverbalized feelings,
    972
  and obesity, 327
  and organic brain syndromes,
    226-227
  and pain, 1096-1097
  and posthypnotic amnesia,
    952
  and risk taking, 434-435
Trait theory
  and personal need systems, 396
Transactional systems
  and normality, 52
Transcendence Index, 871, 873
Transient ischemic attack (TIA)
  epilepsy distinct from, 298-299
Trauma
  and epilepsy, 301
Tricyclic antidepressants, 595,
  596
Trust
  and mistrust, 642
  and paranoid personality, 174
Twitchell-Allen Three Dimensional Apperception Test, 919-
  920
Type A/B behavior
  and age, 252
  and alcoholism, 253
  analysis of, 244-256
  background of, 245-246
  characteristics of, 244-245
  as coping behavior, 251

coronary disease relationship
  of, 251-252
development of, 249, 252
discussion of, 246-252
and disorders, 253
and education, 253
and ethnic/racial factors, 253
issues of, 246-249
modifying, 249
pathophysical theory of, 249-
  250
and psychosomatic disorders,
  152, 156, 161
recommendations on, 252
and sex differences, 252-253
and socioeconomic status, 253
and stress, 250-251, 252
structured interview for, 247-
  248
theories on, 249-251
and variables, 252-253
and vocation, 253
and voice characteristics, 248

U

Undifferentiated subtype
  of schizophrenia, 205
Union of Soviet Socialist Republics
  childrearing in, 652
  integration theory in, 811-812
  intelligence testing in, 709
  learning ability/achievement
    discrepancy in, 795-796
United Kingdom
  aggression in, psychological,
    556
  competency evaluation in, 7
  conservatism in, 999-1000,
    1003, 1004
  forensic psychology in, 1115
  mental retardation in, 715-716
  and nonauthoritarianism, 1018
  substance abuse in, 232
United States
  academic learning problems
    in, 757, 758, 793
  adult demographics in, 17-18,
    33
  authoritarianism in, 1012,
    1013, 1021, 1025
  cardiovascular disease in, 252
  conservatism in, 1000, 1002,
    1003, 1004
  dangerousness in, 1105
  forensic psychology in, 1113,
    1116, 1117, 1119-1120
  hyperactivity in, 268
  intelligence testing in, 700,
    708, 709
  mental retardation in, 716
  moral reasoning in, 381
  neurotic cues in, 144
  nonauthoritarianism in, 1026,
    1028
  obesity in, 321